2ND EDITION ANN A. ABBOTT, EDITOR

ALCOHOL
TOBACCO
AND OTHER DRUGS

CHALLENGING MYTHS, ASSESSING THEORIES, INDIVIDUALIZING INTERVENTIONS

NASW PRESS

National Association of Social Workers
Washington, DC

James J. Kelly, PhD, ACSW, LCSW, *President*
Elizabeth J. Clark, PhD, ACSW, MPH, *Executive Director*

Cheryl Y. Bradley, *Publisher*
Lisa M. O'Hearn, *Managing Editor*
Sarah Lowman, *Project Manager*
Dac Nelson, *Copyeditor*
Juanita Ruffin Doswell, *Proofreader*
Bernice Eisen, *Indexer*

Cover by Metadog Design Group
Interior design by Electronic Quill Publishing Services
Printed and bound by Port City Press

Library of Congress Cataloging-in-Publication Data

Alcohol, tobacco, and other drugs : challenging myths, assessing theories, individualizing interventions / Ann A. Abbott, editor. — 2nd ed.
    p. cm.
  Includes bibliographical references and index.
  ISBN 978-0-87101-393-4
  1. Social work with alcoholics. 2. Social work with drug addicts. 3. Substance abuse—Prevention. I. Abbott, Ann Augustine, 1943– II. National Association of Social Workers.
  HV5275.A548 2009
  362.29—dc22

                  2009039799

Printed in the United States of America

Contents

List of Tables, Figures, and Case Examples

Tables

Figures

Case Examples

Preface

This second edition of *Alcohol, Tobacco, and Other Drugs: Challenging Myths, Assessing Theories, Individualizing Interventions* is dedicated to the pioneers who helped make the first edition so successful: Christine Boyle, Sondra Burman, Irene Bush, Patricia C. Dunn, and Katherine M. Wood. A special note of recognition is directed to Eileen Corrigan, who served as principal investigator for a Rutgers University five-year (1990–1995) Faculty Development Grant from the Public Health Service, Substance Abuse and Mental Health Services Administration, U.S. Department of Health and Human Services, which served as a stimulus for faculty interest in the study of substance dependence and abuse. The sign of a good teacher such as Eileen is the far-reaching influence of her or his knowledge. Although Eileen died shortly after publication of the first edition, the majority of authors contributing to this second edition were influenced by her knowledge and enthusiasm for the topic, either as her colleagues or her students.

Special thanks are given to everyone who in a variety of ways contributed to this volume. Not only did the authors from the first edition and the current authors contribute to this volume, but numerous students, clients and consumers, and colleagues also added significantly to the depth and breadth of the discussion by raising questions, debating issues, analyzing theories, suggesting alternatives, and, perhaps most important, stimulating the authors to move forward with their work.

As editor, I offer my personal thanks and appreciation to my colleagues who gave their valuable time and wisdom to making this volume come to life. To Laura Blankertz, Raymond Bolden Jr., Steven Granich, Langdon Holloway, Lloyd L. Lyter, Sharon C. Lyter, Gwenelle Styles O'Neal, Michael D. Paulus, and David I. Siegel, you're the best.

To my husband, Arthur C. Huntley, MD, who served as self-acclaimed assistant editor, chief critic, and major source of support, an A+.

I greatly appreciated being selected for sabbatical leave during fall 2008 by West Chester University of Pennsylvania to devote more time to the completion of this second edition. Without the extra time, this volume would have been an insurmountable challenge. Many thanks also go to the staff of NASW Press, in particular, Sarah Lowman, senior editor, for their patience, expertise, and support. None of your efforts went unnoticed.

Greatest thanks and admiration go to the many individuals who struggle daily with the challenges posed by alcohol, tobacco, and other drugs. They are the heroes and driving force behind this book. I truly hope the work presented here does justice to their daily struggles and unique needs.

Ann A. Abbott, PhD, LCSW (NJ), LCSW (PA)
—*Editor*

Prologue

Preparing Workers for a Response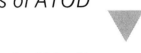
to the Challenges of ATOD

Ann A. Abbott

Most, if not all, social workers will encounter some forms of evidence of the effects of alcohol, tobacco, and other drugs (ATOD; whether illegal, prescribed, or over the counter). The evidence will take many forms, ranging from drug dependence, to alcohol abuse, to problematic use, to intentional or unintentional misuse, to secondary impact on innocent family members, to neighborhood fear, to crime, to child abuse or neglect, to domestic violence, and the list goes on.

The demographics presented in this volume support the fact that the effects of ATOD collectively compose one of the major social problems confronting society today (National Association of Social Workers [NASW], 2009). NASW has recognized the magnitude of the problem in a public social policy statement indicating to the professional community and policymakers the severity of the role that ATOD plays in the lives of society and, more specifically, social work clients.

It is one thing to recognize a problem; the more important issue is developing avenues for addressing the problem. NASW, in addition to the public social policy statement, has developed a specialty practice section (SPS) designed to facilitate communication and skill development among social workers dealing with clients and their families, all of whom are experiencing firsthand the ravages of substance abuse. The ATOD SPS produces frequent newsletters designed to exchange ideas and introduce best practices among section members. Members of NASW have also developed a set of standards to serve as performance expectations for those members working in the area of substance abuse treatment (NASW, 2005).

▼
▼
▼

The Council on Social Work Education (CSWE) recently increased its emphasis on the importance of accredited social work education programs teaching content relevant to ATOD, including assessment, intervention, practice evaluation, advocacy, program development, and policy analysis (CSWE, 2008).

This second edition was written in response to growing demand for social workers to address problems stemming from ATOD. The demand is driven by an increase in client use of ATOD, increased recognition of clients who present with co-occurring disorders (a substance-related problem coupled with a mental health problem), and professional emphasis on best practices and evidence-based practice. This volume was written to increase knowledge for beginning professionals and update best practices for seasoned professionals.

The ongoing debate about the preferred use of the terms "substance abuse" and "substance misuse" continues. For purposes of this second edition, "misuse" will be used to denote problematic or inappropriate use of a substance, for example, use of OxyContin for recreational purposes and not for pain relief as originally prescribed, or increased use beyond dosage recommended by the prescribing physician. "Abuse" will be used to denote "the use of a drug in such a manner or in such amounts or in situations such that the drug use causes problems or greatly increases the chances of problems occurring" (Ksir, Hart, & Ray, 2008, p. G5), for example, drinking alcohol on a daily basis to the point of inebriation or interference with daily responsibilities or obligations. The authors have chosen to use the terms abuse and dependence as defined in the *Diagnostic and Statistical Manual of Mental Disorders* (4th ed., text revision) (American Psychiatric Association, 2000). Throughout the book, the acronym ATOD is used both as a noun, for example, the impact of ATOD use, and as an adjective, for example, ATOD misuse or abuse.

The purpose of the book is to provide the reader with an overview of the problems associated with ATOD and an understanding of the effects of ATOD use, abuse, or misuse, not only on client performance and behavior, but also on families and significant others. The authors also examine a variety of models or strategies to address ATOD abuse and the problems accompanying it. The book builds on a systems or ecological perspective incorporating a bio-psycho-social-cultural-spiritual approach to guide both assessment and intervention. It expands on information included in the first edition by addressing more recent demographic data, greater emphasis on the importance of cultural competence and understanding the role of culture in both dynamics and treatment, and current evidence-based and best practices. New developments, since the first edition, include not only much greater recognition of evidence-based practices, but also new understanding in the areas of tobacco and in the recognition and treatment of co-occurring disorders. Content on best practices is interspersed throughout the book; content on tobacco and co-occurring disorders, although mentioned throughout, is highlighted primarily in two distinct chapters. More is now known about the important role of prevention and, thus, more emphasis is directed to recognizing its importance.

The growth and influence of the Internet has exploded since the first edition. As a result, much information, including sources of demographic data, governmental reports, assessment instruments, program protocols, and research findings, is now available at the touch of a key. Use of the Internet as a major tool is evident in the references and noted resources.

As noted in the Preface, the first edition grew out of a five-year (1990–1995) faculty development grant sponsored by the U.S. Department of Health and Human Services, in particular the Public Health Service and the Substance Abuse and Mental Health Services Administration. The grant provided funding for five social work educators to participate in concentrated study, clinical experience, and curriculum development in the area of ATOD. Three of the original five educators developed material for the first edition, and all served as mentors for the majority of authors participating in the second edition. It is safe to state that the intent of the grant has been achieved, with the editor being one of the original five and eight out of the nine other authors having been influenced by one or more of the original grantees.

The original grant contained a research component that clearly illustrated that, given appropriate knowledge and opportunity, social workers can learn to be more effective in helping clients, agencies, and service providers address substance-related problems and treatment issues. This volume is intended to continue the expansion of knowledge and positive outcomes in addressing ATOD issues.

This second edition reflects the professional experience and knowledge of 10 social workers who collaborated on developing a vehicle for helping other professionals gain a better understanding of the dynamics and complexities associated with ATOD.

Chapter 1 presents an overview of the context of ATOD practice—its challenges, existing myths, partial truths, exaggerations, and quagmires confronting workers in the field. Chapter 2 presents criteria for assessing the theories proposed for guiding practice related to ATOD issues. In addition, it focuses on a systems perspective and problem solving as important guides for successful practice.

Chapter 3 emphasizes the importance of recognizing values in working with clients struggling with substance-related issues and identifying ethical dilemmas that surface in working with a variety of professionals in addressing ATOD issues. This chapter also presents several formats for analyzing and addressing ethical dilemmas.

Chapter 4 delineates the dynamics of alcohol and other drug use. It contains information about the range and impact of various substances. Chapter 5 does the same for tobacco-related substances. This enhanced emphasis on tobacco is new to the second edition and is consistent with the increased recognition of the problems that use of tobacco poses for members of society.

Also new to the second edition, is the content of Chapter 6, which focuses on the dynamics and challenges of co-occurring disorders. This chapter addresses not only the complexity of identification and treatment issues, but also the role of stigma and the challenges of reshaping existing mental health and substance abuse treatment systems to accommodate the new focus on integrated treatment.

Chapter 7 addresses the journey of planned change, focusing on the challenges of how one proceeds from denial to embracing change. Chapter 8 provides guidance for facilitating planned change by assessing client needs, including useful instrumentation for supplementing the content gained from interviews with clients and their significant others, often including family.

Chapters 9, 10, and 11 focus on specific strategies to facilitate planned change. Chapter 9 introduces the reader to new strategies of intervention primarily used with individuals. Chapter 10 focuses on group strategies of intervention, which include self-help groups and professionally led interventions. Chapter 11 informs the reader of best practice with both family members who are using substances and those who are affected by the use of substances by other family members.

Chapter 12 focuses on the important role of prevention. It highlights the positive impact of a number of programs that have been helpful in reducing the use of substances or the severity of use.

The epilogue summarizes the content of the volume, but more important, identifies the wave of the future. The field of ATOD is a vibrant, vital one that is definitely not static. New ideas are surfacing daily and new trends are being born as this book goes to press. The wave of the future seeks the input of everyone involved in the field—consumer and client, family member, practitioner, researcher, policymaker, agency administrator, educator, and government official. Together, we must commit to greater understanding of the dynamics associated with ATOD use, abuse, and misuse; the role of drug treatment; law enforcement; international drug trade; and the importance of education and prevention. The scope of the emotional and financial impact is tremendous. It is the hope of the authors that this volume will be a start in preparing readers to enter the debate and to become better prepared practitioners, better researchers, and informed contributors to enhance programs, interventions, and solutions to a major social problem.

References

American Psychiatric Association. (2000). *Diagnostic and statistical manual of mental disorders* (4th ed., text rev.). Washington, DC: Author.

Council on Social Work Education. (2008). *Educational policy and accreditation standards.* Alexandria, VA: Author.

Ksir, C., Hart, C., & Ray, O. (2008). *Drugs, society, and human behavior* (12th ed.). Boston: WGB/McGraw-Hill.

National Association of Social Workers. (2005). *NASW standards for social work practice with clients with substance use disorders.* Washington, DC: Author.

National Association of Social Workers. (2009). Alcohol, tobacco, and other substance abuse. In *Social work speaks: NASW policy statements, 2009–2012* (8th ed., pp. 29–37). Washington, DC: NASW Press.

Context of Practice

Myths, Realities, and Quagmires Related to Alcohol, Tobacco, and Other Drugs

Ann A. Abbott

Alcohol, tobacco, and other drugs (ATOD) are so much a part of daily life in our society that few individuals remain untouched by their impact (Fisher, 2008; NASW, 2006). That influence spans the gamut from womb to tomb. Professional literature and mass media reports are replete with evidence supporting the effects of ATOD use by pregnant mothers on their fetuses; the negative influence of such substance use on the care and development of their older offspring; the impact of use by workers on their performance and safety; and the results of alcohol and other drug use on driving safety, on family relationships, on overall individual performance, on school performance, on health, and on general community safety (Cook, Peterson, & Moore, 1990; Dutra et al., 2008; Grant et al., 2004; Jacobson, 1997; Larkby & Day, 1997; Lasser et al., 2000; National Institute on Alcohol Abuse and Alcoholism [NIAAA], 2000; National Institute on Drug Abuse, 2008; Redman, 2008; Serdula et al., 1991; Substance Abuse and Mental Health Services Administration [SAMHSA], 2008; Welsh, 1996; Wolfgang, 1997). Evidence not only emphasizes the negative effects of so-called "street drugs" or illegal drugs, but also informs us of the dangers of misusing prescription drugs, mixing prescription drugs with alcohol or illicit drugs or using prescription drugs in combinations not prescribed (Fisher, 2008; SAMHSA, 2008).

All one has to do is turn on the radio or television, scan the Internet, or open the morning newspaper to learn of the ill effects of ATOD: Death, crime, neglect, violence, and abuse are the events making the headlines. These reports reflect but a tip of the iceberg with many other individuals beneath the spectacular surface struggling to overcome depression, poverty, unemployment, fear, stress, pain, and other overwhelming challenges. All share the common thread of using ATOD for relief from physical or psychological suffering, a range of disappointments, or the sense of ennui or meaninglessness that seems so pervasive throughout contemporary society.

In one's capacity as social worker, if one does not work directly with clients whose ATOD use is impinging on their performance, one will certainly be confronted by those who bear the scars of others' involvement with these substances. The scope of the problem is broad. A number of years ago, Daley and Raskin (1991) suggested that each user affects or seriously influences four to six other people. This continues to ring true today. Although challenges inherent in poverty and discrimination may increase vulnerability to substance use, use of such substances knows no geographic, economic, or cultural boundaries. Its use spans the broad historical spectrum, knowing no time limits. The past is filled with stories reflecting the impact of substance misuse, the present is ridden with evidence reflecting the same, and the future purports to hold additional challenges for those working in the field (van Wormer, 1995). Although only 2 percent of members of the National Association of Social Workers (NASW) indicated ATOD problems were representing their major area of practice, the magnitude of the problem was sufficient to serve as a driving force behind the NASW social policy statement on ATOD abuse endorsed by the 2005 Delegate Assembly of the organization (NASW, 2009). ATOD issues are encountered in every aspect of social work. The breadth of the problem is pervasive: child welfare, health care, criminal justice, schools, the workplace, community centers, mental health clinics, senior centers, and day care, to name a few (NASW, 2009).

To be effective in meeting those challenges, social workers, and others working in the field of addictions, need to understand the realities of working with clients presenting with problems stemming from the use of ATOD. They need to be able to decipher myth from reality, to understand the complexity of life's challenges that contribute to the murky quagmires that confound the field, to be knowledgeable about various treatment options, to be skillful in selecting and using relevant intervention strategies, to understand the full impact of providing service in a managed care environment, and to appreciate and commit to a systems approach in addressing the complex nature of ATOD. They need to be able to recognize the value of evidence-based practice, contribute to sound research, and support practice based on well-documented research findings.

The Scope of the Problem

Because of the illegal nature of many drugs, it is not possible to accurately report the extent of their use; however, we do know that each year the federal government spends billions of dollars on the control of substances and the treatment of their ill effects (NIAAA, 2000; SAMHSA, 2008). More than half the inmates in federal prisons are there because of drug law violations; over one-fifth of workers in the United States are working under the influence of drugs, costing employers and the general public billions of dollars; over two-thirds of young people under the age of 25 have experimented with various substances (Goldberg, 1998; Hart, Ksir, & Ray, 2009; SAMHSA, 2008); between 40 percent and 60 percent of people in long-term psychiatric facilities are classified as patients suffering from co-occurring disorders, with one diagnosis being a substance-related disorder and the other a mental health disorder (American Psychiatric Association, 2000; Coffey et al., 2008; Orlin & Davis, 1993; SAMSHA, 2008; Woody, 1996).

Cost of the Problem

The cost of addictions currently exceeds $500 billion annually (Potenza, 2007). The most recent report issued to Congress by NIAAA (Harwood, Fountain, & Livermore, 1998, as cited in NIAAA, 2000) estimated the economic cost of alcohol abuse was $148 billion in 1992. Costs for 1995 were $166.6 billion, and for 1998, $184.6 billion (Harwood, 2000, as cited in NIAAA, 2000). If history continues on its current trajectory, projected costs for 2010 could well exceed $260 billion.

Harwood and colleagues (1998), in analyzing 1998 projections for alcohol abuse costs, attribute more than 70 percent ($134.2 billion) of estimated costs to lost productivity (consisting of 87.6 billion or 65.3 percent for lost work and productivity, 36.5 billion or 27.2 percent for lost future earnings because of premature death, and 10.1 billion or 7.5 percent for lost productivity because of alcohol-related crime). Of the remainder, 26.3 billion or 14.3 percent of the total was spent on health care costs related to alcohol abuse, 15.7 billion or 8.5 percent on property damage or administrative costs related to alcohol-related motor vehicle accidents, and 6.36 billion or 3.4 percent on criminal justice system costs stemming from alcohol-related crime, with the remainder or approximately 2 billion related to fire destruction and social welfare administration (Harwood, 2000; Harwood et al., 1998).

Comparable costs related to other drug abuse for 1992 were $98 billion. Costs for 1995 approximated $110 billion and for 1998 $120 billion. Given the above rates and using the Harwood (2000) method of projection, costs for 2010 could well exceed $170 billion.

It is anticipated that 2010 expenditures could be much greater given that drug use is increasing at a greater rate than alcohol abuse, which is reported as showing minimal growth (National Institutes of Health [NIH], 1998).

Data for the mid-1990s collected by NIH estimated that of the total amount spent addressing alcohol and other drug abuse-related issues, 60 percent was spent on alcohol-related activities, with the remaining 40 percent used for other drug abuse and dependence (NIH, 1998). The above figures are more than 40 percent higher for alcohol and 50 percent higher for other drugs than those reported for 1985. Adjusting for inflation and population growth, the costs of alcohol are comparable to the average cost estimates for the previous 20 years; the costs of other drug abuse have shown a steady increase over that time period (NIH, 1998). Information from NIH (1998) revealed that more than two-thirds of the costs spent on alcohol abuse were related to lost productivity because of alcohol-related illness or death. For other drug abuse, almost 60 percent of the costs were because of drug-related crime—including lost productivity by victims and incarceration of perpetrators (20.4 percent), lost productivity by users (19.7 percent), and such costs as property damage, drug traffic control, and police, legal, and corrections services (18.4 percent). Of the remainder, it is estimated that only 10.2 percent was spent on related health care.

Expanse of Alcohol Abuse

Former Secretary of the U.S. Department Health and Human Services (HHS), Donna Shalala, in the forward to the *10th Special Report to the U.S. Congress on Alcohol and Health* stated that:

> alcohol problems, both those of individuals and those that affect society at large, continue to impose a staggering burden on our Nation. Domestic violence, child abuse, fires and other accidents, falls, rape, and other crimes against individuals such as robbery and assault—all are linked to alcohol misuse. Alcohol misuse also is implicated in diseases such as cancer, liver disease, and heart disease. Although often not aware of it, everyone shares a portion of this burden. For example, an estimated 20 to 40 percent of patients in large urban hospitals are there because of illnesses that have been caused or made worse by their drinking. This means that out of every 100 patients in such hospitals, *almost half* may be there because of their alcohol use. Each of us shares the price of these illnesses through rising health care costs. Because one in four children under the age of 18 lives in a household with one or more family members who are alcohol dependent or who abuse alcohol, our Nation will continue to be robbed of its future. As these children grow up, they too will be at risk for continuing the cycle of alcohol abuse and dependence that has plagued too many of our citizens for too long. (NIAAA, 2000, p. ix)

In the *Ninth Special Report to the U.S. Congress on Alcohol and Health* (NIAAA, 1997), former Secretary Shalala noted that approximately 14 million Americans, or almost 10 percent of adults, met diagnostic criteria for alcohol abuse and alcoholism. The report, which highlighted new knowledge uncovered since the *Eighth Special Report to the U.S. Congress on Alcohol and Health* (NIAAA, 1994) showed that although prevalence rates remained steady over time, some positive changes occurred: Abstention from use of alcohol increased, heavy drinking decreased, per capita consumption decreased, legal and social sanctions especially related to drinking and driving increased, and people were becoming more health conscious and less tolerant of substance abuse. Although the per capita rate of consumption fell, the decline was not uniform across age and gender: Men continued to have more alcohol-related problems than did women; consumption by women did not decrease as much as that of men; alcohol use and abuse were becoming more prevalent among young adults; alcohol-related traffic accidents remained a major cause of death, especially among young people; a growing elderly population contributed to an increase in problems among that group; and heavy drinking continued to contribute to overall poor health (Brennan & Moos, 1996; NIAAA, 1997; Parker, 1998; Wolfgang, 1997). Alcohol-related morbidity and mortality continued to be major challenges in American society.

The *10th Special Report to the U.S. Congress on Alcohol and Health* (NIAAA, 2000) indicated new knowledge in the areas of genetics, neural circuitry, fetal development, prevention, education, and therapies. Perhaps the single most important finding during the three-year period covered was the discovery that 50 percent to 60 percent of the risk for developing alcoholism was related to genetics.

Expanse of Other Drug Abuse

Although problems related to alcohol consumption continue to plague society and challenge those working in the field, the use of other drugs continues to put additional stress on the system. Results from the 2007 National Survey on Drug Use and Health [SAMHSA, 2008]; known as NSDUH since 2002, when it replaced the National Household Survey on Drug Abuse [NHSDA]) indicate that almost 20 million Americans age 12 or older had used an illicit drug in the month prior to the survey. This figure represents 8 percent of the population age 12 or older. Illicit drugs include marijuana or hashish, cocaine (including crack), heroin, hallucinogens, inhalants, or prescription-type psychotherapeutics used for nonmedical purposes. Slightly more than 50 percent (126.8 million) of Americans age 12 years or older reported being current drinkers of alcohol. Almost 71 million Americans age 12 or older indicated they were users of tobacco (SAMHSA, 2008, p. 10).

According to findings presented in the 2007 NSDUH (based on inquiry about past-month usage), marijuana was identified as the most commonly used illicit drug among 5.8 percent of people age 12 and older (14.4 million users in the month preceding the survey) (SAMHSA, 2008). It was followed in descending order by prescription-type psychotherapeutic drugs (2.8 percent or 6.9 million users), cocaine (0.8 percent or 2.1 million users), hallucinogens (0.4 percent or 1 million users), and methamphetamines (0.2 percent or 0.5 million users). The survey also revealed that among youths ages 12 to 17, illicit drug use remained stable between 2006 (9.8 percent) and 2007 (9.5 percent); however, between 2002 and 2007, illicit drug usage in that age group declined by 2 percent. However, it is important to note that among baby boomers ages 50 to 54, illicit drug usage increased more than 2 percent during the same time period from 2002 (3.4 percent) to 2007 (5.7 percent). Among unemployed adults age 18 and older in 2007, 18.3 percent reported being current users of illicit drugs, with full-time employed workers reporting 8.4 percent usage rates, and part-time employed workers reporting 10.1 percent. Of the current 17.4 million drug users age 18 and older in 2007, 75.3 percent were employed either part-time or full-time (SAMHSA, 2008).

In terms of reported alcohol use, in 2007 more than half (51.1 percent) of Americans age 12 and older (126.8 million) reported being current users of alcohol. More than one-fifth of this group reported participating in binge drinking (having five or more drinks on at least one day during the prior 30 days). This figure (57.8 million) approximates that reported in 2006. Rates of youth drinking reported in the 2007 survey were comparable to those reported in the 2006 survey findings (SAMHSA, 2008).

In terms of cultural differences, among users age 12 years and older reporting past-month alcohol use in the 2007 survey, the usage rates were 56.1 percent for whites, 47.5 percent for individuals reporting two or more races, 44.7 percent for American Indians or Alaskan Natives, 42.1 percent for Hispanics, 39.3 percent for blacks, and 35.2 percent for Asians (SAMHSA, 2008). In 2007, almost 13 percent of respondents indicated that they had driven while under the influence of alcohol during the previous year. On a more positive note, the reported figure is slightly less than that reported in 2002 (14.2%).

Expanse of Tobacco Use

The 71 million Americans age 12 years and older who reported being current users of tobacco represent almost 29 percent of the population, with 24.2 percent of the population reporting cigarette smoking, 5.4 percent cigars, 3.2 percent smokeless tobacco, and 0.2 percent pipes. Reported use of any tobacco product decreased by one percent between 2006 and 2007, and between 2002 and 2007 by approximately

2 percent. Usage rates among youths between 2002 and 2007 declined by more than 3 percent. This may be a misleading figure because reported use among this age group increased between 2006 and 2007 (SAMHSA, 2008).

On the basis of the above figures, the fact remains that no segment of the population is immune from the effects of substance abuse. Over 15 million Americans experience serious alcohol-related problems; almost 4 million experience serious drug-related problems, and more than 3 million meet the criteria for both drug and alcohol (NASW, 2009). Many others experience the fallout or indirect effects of ATOD use.

The Tip of the Iceberg

Although the surveys cited above seek broad representation, the numbers may not reflect the true breadth of the problem. Unfortunately, many individuals who are experiencing the problems, or fallout resulting from problematic use by others, may not be identified in surveys or may not come to the attention of treatment providers and, therefore, may not be reflected in actual figures provided. Many users seek treatment on their own through self-help groups such as Alcoholics Anonymous (AA) or Narcotics Anonymous (NA; both for users) or Al-Anon or Nar-Anon (for family and friends) and never surface in treatment statistics or through substance abuse surveys. Others rely on self-change efforts to deal with their problematic use (Klingemann & Sobell, 2007). This latter group is particularly difficult to quantify.

Many individuals experiencing substance-related problems are diverted into the criminal justice system, rarely receiving appropriate ATOD services during or after their incarceration (Anderson, 2003; U.S. Department of Justice, Office of Justice Programs, Bureau of Justice Statistics [BJS], 2008). In 2002, an estimated 1.5 million individuals were arrested for drug law violations, 1.5 million for driving under the influence (DUI), more than a half million for drunkenness, and almost two-thirds of a million for liquor law violations (Dorsey, Zawitz, & Middleton, 2003; NASW, 2009). The 1990s experienced more than a 60 percent increase in individuals incarcerated because of drug offenses (BJS, 2008). In 2002, 20 percent of incarcerated men and 30 percent of incarcerated women were serving time for drug offenses (BJS, 2008).

The Impact of International Drug Trade

As challenges in the global economy have increased, many developing countries have found significant financial success in providing illicit drugs to users in developed countries. Several examples include the opiate and heroin brought to the United States from Asia and Africa, or cocaine brought to the United States from Latin America. As the influx of drugs has increased, federal, state, and local governments have tended to spend more resources on drug control (law enforcement and interdiction) than on treatment initiatives. Although some efforts may have been successful in decreasing the supply of illicit substances or providing greater control of legal substances, many times these efforts have been accompanied by increased violence, with negative fallout for neighborhoods and their residents. On the one hand, increased availability itself can lead to increased crime and usage; on the other hand, more limited availability of substances has contributed to competition, crime, and related violence (Hammersley & Reid, 2002). The question remains as to where limited resources should be allocated to make the greatest impact on the serious problems surrounding the use of ATOD.

The above statistics and accompanying concerns contribute to the major challenge confronting social workers today, that being how best to address the full range of problems related to substance use and the complications associated with it. There are no absolutely correct answers. The best, or most informed, approach lies with policymakers and clinicians, working together, guided by wisdom founded on well-executed research.

Separating Myth from Reality

Despite increasing emphasis on evidence-based practice, grounded on sophisticated research, a number of myths continue to proliferate within the field (Brown, 2003). These myths are frequently compounded by the quagmire-like challenges surrounding the very nature of addiction or inappropriate use of substances. To perform effectively in addressing problems stemming from ATOD, social workers should not only be aware of these myths, but also must know reality and challenges the myths seek to mask. Prior to addressing popular myths related to ATOD, one must understand the nature of myths and accompanying quagmires. According to *Webster's Deluxe Unabridged Dictionary* (2nd ed.), a *myth* is defined as follows:

1. a traditional story of unknown authorship, ostensibly with a historical basis, but serving usually to explain some phenomenon of nature, the origin of man, or the customs, institutions, religions, rites, etc. of a people: myths usually involve the exploits of gods and heroes.
2. such stories collectively; mythology.
3. any fictitious story.
4. any imaginary person or thing, spoken of as though existing. Synonym: fable, fiction, legend, falsehood. (Dorset & Baber, 1983, p. 1190)

Joseph Campbell (1988), the 20th century master of myth, stressed the importance of the first and second definitions—stories that guide civilization and frequently transcend culture. Historically, social work has placed significant emphasis on the cultural heritage and the relevance of myth, which contributes to understanding and appreciation of client diversity. However, in social work practice with clients involved in problems stemming from ATOD, social work must go beyond, dispelling fictitious stories, beliefs, or falsehoods that impinge on the understanding and treatment. In this latter case, the definition cited by Brown (1993) has more relevance:

1. a traditional story, either wholly or partially fictitious, providing an explanation for or embodying a popular idea concerning some natural or social phenomenon or some religious belief or ritual; specifically one involving supernatural persons, actions, or events; a similar newly created story.
2. a widely held (especially untrue or discredited popular) story or belief; a misconception; a misrepresentation of the truth; an exaggerated or idealized conception of a person, institution, etc.; a person, institution, etc., widely idealized or misrepresented.
3. myths collectively or as a genre; the technique or habits of creating myths. (p. 1874)

It is the second definition that is probably the most pernicious because it often contains an element of truth. The skillful social worker must learn the underlying facts and how to separate fact from fiction, especially as it influences the effectiveness of social work practice. So much about the field of ATOD falls into the "gray" area of being neither fact nor fiction. Thus, frequently, it takes great skill and ongoing surveillance on the part of the social worker to separate reality from the predominating myth. At times an even greater challenge is posed by myths that primarily are exaggerations of the truth.

In addition to understanding the nature of myths, one must understand what makes myths so powerful, and so strongly and persistently believed. Myths are so powerful because they both reflect and direct our behavior and typically are accepted as unchallengeable fact. They provide "a clear, if impractical, answer to drug problems" (Hammersley & Reid, 2002, p. 12). They tell us how to live, how to proceed (Campbell, 1988). Humans seek a guiding force, a prescription, a set of beliefs (myths) to guide behavior (Hillman, 1995). And because of that need, they buy into the legitimacy and veracity of myths. In other words, myths persist because they are "functional" (Hammersley & Reid). However, myths do not always reflect complete reality. As we will see, there are many such myths, falsehoods, or partial truths operating in the field of ATOD today. They are based on inaccuracies of perceived influences of culture, gender, and nature of substance. It is hard to counter a myth. Any truth behind a myth gives it credence. Any challenge to the myth typically generates a rebuttal geared to supporting its continued merit.

Avoiding Quagmires Stemming from Mythical Thinking

Unless myths are untangled and clarified they can lead the social worker and his or her client onto a "slippery slope" or into a very complicated situation, similar to a quagmire from which it is very difficult to extricate oneself and more forward. For sake of clarification, *Webster's Deluxe Unabridged Dictionary* (2nd ed.) defines a *quagmire* as:

1.   soft, wet, miry ground that shakes or yields under the feet;
2.   a difficult position, as if one is sinking or stuck … synonymous with a swamp, marsh, morass, bog or slough. (Dorset & Baber, 1983, p. 1473)

It is the second definition that more accurately describes the challenges of attempting to operate on beliefs that are not firmly grounded. It is difficult enough to address the frequent ambivalence and stigma associated with clients struggling with the ATOD. But to work under false assumptions or partial truths makes it even more difficult.

The focus here is not only to challenge some well-known myths, partial truths, or exaggerations in the field of ATOD, but also to replace them with a questioning mind—one geared toward seeking new data, resulting in more accurate understanding and appraisal of human behavior, especially as it relates to ATOD use, and the avoidance of quagmirelike minefields.

General Myths Related to Substance Abuse

A number of general myths related to substance abuse are prevalent in the field. One major one that affects both assessment (including surveys) and treatment is based on the belief that people answer questions honestly when asked about their ATOD use. In reality, they frequently will reveal what information they want to be known (Davies, 1992). In some cases, it may entail minimizing or denying use; in other cases, it may emphasize maximizing use.

A number of theorists (Davies, 1992; Hammersley & Reid, 2002) challenge the idea that people are compelled to use substances because of the pharmacological impact of the substance. Davies (1992) suggested "that people take drugs because they want to and because it makes sense for them to do so given the choices available" (p. x). He contended that we are geared to believe that the behavior of drug users is beyond their control—that self-control is lost to the power of the drug or the earlier myth that once addicted, the individual is sentenced to a life of addiction (Gibson, Acquah, & Robinson, 2004; Hammersley & Reid, 2002). He noted that much of this belief is based on users' self-reports; he questions whether the self-reports are true or whether they are primarily self-serving.

Davies (1992) based his beliefs on attribution theory that focuses on the ways in which people explain why things happen. Attribution theory offers insights into the ways in which people explain their actions and those of others. The processes of attribution theory shed light on the difference between causal explanations and scientific statements. The former are based on the state of the explainer, and the latter on the state of confirmed knowledge. Davies contended that a lot has to do with locus of control. If people have a greater sense of internal control, they will have more control over substance use and will be more aware of their ability to affect use.

Ten years later, Hammersley and Reid (2002) questioned "why the pervasive addiction myth is still believed" (p. 7). They suggested that this myth persists because it is functional—the drug use took over the user's free will. They suggested that "abdicating control is often confused with losing it" (p. 22). If locus of control or degree of ability to control is important and an understanding of the role of control is put into the equation for each individual, the veracity of this myth varies for each individual.

If lack of control is verified, one is NOT responsible for one's actions, one's addiction, or one's crimes or abuse related to that addiction (Hammersley & Reid, 2002). Apparent loss of control is challenged repeatedly by users who give up drugs or alcohol on their own or with minimal support (Gibson, Acquah, & Robinson, 2004).

Allamani (2007) suggested that a primary myth surrounds the idea of free choice and control over the power of drugs. He charged contemporary marketing ideology with advancing the idea that anyone can achieve whatever she or he wishes, that individuals are endowed with free choice when confronted with options. Once ATOD abuse entered the realm of medicine in the *Diagnostic and Statistical Manual of Mental Disorders* (American Psychiatric Association [APA], 2000), however, substance abuse was removed from being a vice or defect in personal character or a lack of personal control to being a disease requiring appropriate outside intervention. At this point, if one accepts the disease model, the role of control becomes minimized in the equation.

Bailey (2005) believed it is not that simple; these myths or beliefs need further study. She suggested examining popular discourse on addiction to understand society's influence on the popular views on addiction. She suggested that society in general helps to maintain such beliefs as one being helpless in the grips of addiction, or the alternative, that a person can simply give up use if she or he wants to.

For the social worker, what this suggests is the need to undertake a comprehensive assessment, one focusing on assessment of control, primary substance being used, and client sense of hopelessness and helplessness. It also involves an assessment of strengths, supports, and a history of previous attempts at change. Specific details pertaining to assessment, the process of change, the power or impact of various drugs, and intervention will be addressed in subsequent chapters.

Examples of Myths Related to Culture

"The similarities among people affected by addiction and among those trying to help them are striking, but so are the cultural differences" (Straussner, 2008, p. 1). In dealing with substance abuse with clients from different cultures, it is important to understand the nuances and cultural differences (Cox & Ephross, 1998; Straussner, 2001). It also is critical to recognize the influence of myths that abound about the drinking patterns of different cultural groups. Many of these myths may, in fact, reflect an exaggeration of ongoing cultural observations. For example, many practitioners believe that the Irish are more likely to have a higher proportion of heavy and problem drinkers than individuals of Jewish background. Although the media may reinforce these myths, and one may note that predominately Irish communities have more pubs per capita than do Jewish communities, it does not follow that being Irish equates with problematic drinking or that being Jewish equates with minimal or nonproblematic drinking. If one buys into these myths, one is likely to step into a quagmire. The myth will likely influence one's assessment of both Irish and Jewish clients, the type of treatment provided to them, and the level of optimism surrounding change or the expectations for change—the result being the first step into the quagmire, or the route toward getting stuck and being diverted from the task at hand.

Another culturally based myth involves the use of alcohol by Native Americans. Leland (1976) pointed out that many individuals believe in the myth of the "drunken Indian," that Native Americans have an excessive craving for alcohol and are more susceptible to its influences. Navajo people themselves believe in the physiological susceptibility of American Indians (May & Smith, 1988). Although the myth is widely accepted, many components are questionable (SAMHSA, 2008); Native Americans do not suffer a major deficit in the rate of alcohol metabolism, and research has not supported a physiological predisposition to alcohol abuse among this group (Leland, 1976; May & Smith, 1988; Moran & May, 1997; SAMHSA, 2008).

As leaders in the Native American community have become more aware of rates of alcohol and other drug use within their communities, they have made major efforts toward elimination of substance abuse as a problem (Gilder, Lau, Corey, & Ehlers, 2008; Westermeyer, 2008). To a large extent they have been successful as illustrated by high-level remission rates. Twenty-five years ago remission rates of 0 percent to 21 percent were common; current rates triple those reported earlier (Gilder et al., 2008; Tan et al., 2008; Westermeyer & Peake, 1983; Westermeyer, 2008).

To counter the influence of such mythical thinking, one needs to assess each individual with an open mind, anticipating a full range of assessment outcomes, and offering a full range of treatment options. If one buys into the above myths, one might anticipate greater substance abuse, for example, drinking on the part of an Irish client or American Indian, and poorer prognoses given the so-called (mythical) propensity to alcohol abuse. In a similar vein, one may minimize the drinking of a Jewish client, be more optimistic about treatment outcomes, or entirely negate or deny the need for treatment.

Equally misleading myths relate to other cultures. For example, one might harbor the belief (myth) that to be Russian is to be addicted to vodka. Yes, vodka is readily available in Russia; yes, many Russians drink it regularly; no, not all Russians, or people of Russian heritage, are addicted to vodka (Abbott, 1996). Other examples of mythical thinking concern Italians typically drinking wine with their main meals and the French (Abbott, 2001) who are well known for their appreciation of fine wine. Because wine is considered a staple or key component of each meal, akin to food, it poses minimal risk of addiction or problematic use. If appreciating wine is expected of the culture, it must be a positive attribute with little inherent danger. In the earlier mentioned cases, these myths must be unraveled and examined in light of individual behavior, individual use, or addiction. Assessment, treatment strategies, and prognoses must be based on individual evaluation, not on general expectations or beliefs concerning specific cultural groups.

Examples of Myths Related to Gender

Numerous examples of gender-related myths, or exaggerations, have surfaced (Welsh, 1994b). For example, if women are viewed as inferior to men, it is anticipated that they will do less well in treatment. The effects of such thinking may be evident in a variety of ways, such as the fact that staff expectations of treatment outcome may reflect this inferior perspective and may contribute to a self-fulfilling prophecy. Data actually suggest that women and men have comparable success with treatment, if the treatment is geared to their specific individual needs (Abbott, 1995) or if men and women reflect comparable sociodemographic characteristics—such as marital status, economic level, employment status, and social stability—and similar levels of problem severity (Institute of Medicine, 1990). For the most part, women and men pose different treatment needs; however, once those needs are accommodated, treatment can proceed with equal chances for behavioral change and successful outcome. For example, women frequently leave inpatient treatment programs early because they fear that their children will be taken from them in their absence. If sufficient child care is provided, these women are more likely to remain in treatment.

Alcohol or other drug use by women, especially mothers, is frequently overlooked or minimized because of the belief (myth) that good women (good mothers) do not use such substances to excess. In addition, citations indicate that a smaller percentage of women than men experience ATOD-related problems. As a result, doctors, mental health professionals, clergy, family members, and even substance abuse counselors frequently overlook problems stemming from alcohol and other drugs and resist the accompanying need for treatment. Primary care physicians, for example, have been known to dismiss evidence of substance misuse in light of other, more acceptable, diagnoses for women. Because of this bias, both on the part of professionals and family members, women frequently enter treatment later, and at a more serious point in their addiction.

A third example of a myth related to gender is that men can "hold" their liquor better than women. In situations in which it appears that they cannot, they are perceived as being "on the town" or "just having fun with the boys," a more benign interpretation than that typically assigned to their female counterparts: "easy mark" for sexual advances or "scum," "second- or third-class citizens." Thus, negative repercussions run higher for women. In addition to being subjected to more castigation, women under the influence of alcohol and other drugs are frequently the targets of sexual harassment, sexual exploitation, and increased violence, including rape. This myth not only affects assessment and treatment, it also serves to perpetuate the denigration of women, or the historical sexual hierarchy that has existed in society.

The latter scenario can best be understood as social stereotypes or societal views of acceptable or unacceptable gender-specific behavior. A double standard prevails not only for the behavioral expectations but, as previously noted, for expectations for treatment or treatment outcomes. In reality, a smaller number of women use substances, and, as a result, such dependence is not systematically addressed.

In terms of the former scenario regarding the ability to "hold" alcohol, given comparable size and body fat, men and women should have similar capacity to metabolize alcohol. However, physiological differences exist that put women at greater risk. Because the body fat–water ratio of women typically differs from that of men, alcohol enters their systems at a less diluted rate, resulting in a higher blood alcohol level (BAL) and more potent impact (Abbott, 1994; Blume, 1992; Corrigan, 1985). So yes, men appear to "hold" their liquor better; however, it is not based on superiority of will and self-control but, rather, on physiological attributes. Clients and practitioners need to be aware of these physiological differences. In addition to differences in alcohol impact, physiological differences contribute to additional health-related problems among women who drink. These difficulties may be partly because of the more limited ability of women to metabolize alcohol, resulting in a greater amount of alcohol being directly absorbed through the stomach's protective barrier (Abbott, 1994; Blume, 1992; Van Den Bergh, 1991; Wilsnack, Wilsnack, & Hiller-Sturmhofel, 1994).

An additional gender-related myth that has been repeatedly challenged in recent years is one involving HIV/AIDS as being primarily contracted and spread through sexual activity of gay males. Such a myth misrepresents reality and negates the dangers of unprotected heterosexual activity and minimizes the dangers of needle sharing among injection drug users. The perpetuation of this myth has tremendous implications for prevention and early intervention. Such myths cause efforts to be turned from much-needed intervention and, in turn, contribute to the spread of HIV and the neglect of women.

Examples of Myths Related to Age

A number of myths exist related to age. Crome and Crome (2005) highlighted a few of them. One concerns older adults not misusing substances, when, in fact, a large number do—intentionally or unintentionally. Many older adults have received prescribed medications for a variety of ailments. Frequently they do not share their medication history with their full contingent of medical personnel. As a result, physicians may be prescribing medications that counteract, interfere with, or potentiate in other harmful combinations with other prescribed medications. Crome and Crome (2005) reported that 10 percent of older adults are receiving a drug that is "potentially inappropriate" (Gottlieb, as cited in Crome & Crome, 2005). Many older adults are also given low-dose opioid analgesics sufficient for developing dependence (Edwards & Salib, as cited in Crome & Crome, 2005). In addition, some older adults do not realize or do not appreciate the fact that medications should not be taken in combination with alcohol.

Many older adults do not seek treatment and, therefore, their addictions are not identified. When they are seen, medical personnel tend to overlook the possibility of misuse of both legal and illegal substances (Crome & Crome, 2005).

A myth that serves to compound misuse is one that suggests the outcome for older adult users is poor (Crome & Crome, 2005). Most large studies do not include older adults, many times because of ageism. When older adults do engage in treatment, the outcome is frequently very positive. As might be expected, better success is gained by treatment protocols that are geared to the specific needs of the older adult user (Brennen, Nichol, & Moos, 2003).

It is interesting that when older adults do engage in treatment they are more likely to have abstinence as a goal. Providers report that, once engaged, older adults tend to stick with the program to a great degree (Crome & Crome, 2005).

An additional risk that is frequently overlooked is that older adults may metabolize various substances at a slower rate than their younger counterparts. Thus, providers must modify doses to accommodate these differences. Family members, social workers, or friends should be more diligent in monitoring change related to substance use, including medications, by older adults, and report such changes to medical providers.

Myths about Drug and Alcohol Users in General

A widespread myth supports the idea that drug users, in general, are a different class from alcohol users, that people who use illegal drugs (or drugs that have criminal penalties associated with their use) are of lower caliber than those who are physically or psychologically dependent on alcohol. An additional, somewhat-related myth, which adds support, is that because alcohol is legal, it is a less dangerous drug to use than heroin, for example.

Challenging these myths, it is important to note that any one—regardless of socioeconomic status, gender, or cultural background—can become dependent on any one or any combination of the full range of substances. Psychological and physical dependence know no boundaries. Yes, certain drugs are illegal and their possession could prompt criminal penalties; no, illegal drugs are not more dangerous than legal drugs. All one has to do is examine the research related to the use of two legal drugs—tobacco and alcohol—to recognize their negative impact on health and quality of life (Hart et al., 2009).

Classifying drugs along a danger or risk scale or assigning a risk quotient may support the belief that marijuana is less harmful than other drugs and, thus, is all right or preferable to use. Although the immediate dangers may be less, marijuana is viewed as a "gateway drug" or one that frequently leads to or opens the door to more dangerous drugs. Research shows that over 75 percent of young people who reported using marijuana on a regular basis (200 times or more) go on to experiment with more dangerous drugs, such as cocaine (Hart et al., 2009; HHS, 1991). Tobacco is viewed as a "gateway" to alcohol and marijuana. However, a word of caution is in order. By assigning the gateway label, the myth could surface that cigarettes are less dangerous than other drug use that may follow. It is important to recall that all substances pose risks: risk to life, risk to health, risk to performance, and risk to opportunity. The challenge to avoid is minimizing the gateway and the resulting opportunities it may introduce. Another related myth is based on the idea that the use of any gateway drug will automatically lead to the use of other drugs. In reality, there is no proof that use of gateway drugs is synonymous with and directly contributes to the use of more dangerous drugs. What research has shown is that only 1 percent of adolescents begin their substance use with marijuana or another illegal drug; the vast majority started their use with cigarettes. And the majority who report using hard drugs used marijuana before their use of hard drugs began (Hart et al., 2009).

An additional myth related to dangers of using various drugs concerns beer. It is a common misperception that beer is okay to drink, that it is neither potent nor offers the same potential for dependency as does hard liquor. In fact, many believe that alcohol can be divided along a danger hierarchy with beer being the least dangerous, followed by wine, and then hard liquor or spirits. All three substances hold similar potential for dependence; all three hold similar potential for drunkenness. Typically, they are served in different-sized glasses, the result being one glass of each contributing to comparable ends. More specifically, 12 ounces of beer (at 4.2 percent alcohol), four ounces of wine (at 12 percent alcohol), and one ounce (at 100 proof or 50 percent alcohol) of hard liquor or spirits produce similar effect (Corrigan, 1979; Hart et al., 2009).

Another popular myth is that because vodka has no odor, its use cannot be detected. Therefore, it should be the beverage of choice. The fact is that vodka contains an amount of alcohol similar to other hard liquors or spirits and, as a result, will produce similar effects. It may not produce the characteristic smell of alcohol, but using vodka will produce similar physiological and behavioral responses as do equal amounts of other hard liquors.

Many people support the myth that if one does not drink multiple drinks in one hour, one will not achieve a 0.10 BAL. In reality, because of the cumulative effect, consumption of a relatively few drinks over several hours will also produce a BAL of that magnitude. The fact is that alcohol can only be processed or metabolized at a rate of about 0.25 or 0.3 ounces per hour. Whenever intake is greater than output, or the amount of alcohol ingested is more than the amount being metabolized, alcohol builds up in the system or accumulates, contributing to a rise in BAL (Hart et al., 2009; Ray & Ksir, 1999).

Another general myth is that it is okay to drink more alcohol when eating, that food neutralizes or offsets the impact of alcohol. Like many myths, this one contains elements of truth and may cause one to challenge use of the term "myth." However, one is reminded that the concept—"myth" according to Brown (1993)—does recognize partially fictitious stories. In this case, yes, presence of food does slow absorption rate of the alcohol, but it does not negate its impact completely. The absorption rate depends on the concentration of alcohol. If the alcohol is mixed with food or water, the concentration level in the stomach will be reduced and, thus, the effects will be tempered (Hart et al., 2009).

Additional beliefs involve the impact of drugs on sexual performance. For example, one such belief contends that cocaine enhances sexual desire, especially among women; another supports the use of heroin as an aphrodisiac; still another endorses quaaludes as sexual stimulants. Research has shown that alcohol and other drugs affect sexual sensation; however, the price of using typically outweighs the benefits. These myths definitely increase interest in using drugs and, for many, provide justification for using. The component that these myths disguise, or fail to disclose, is the fallout or repercussions of using (Covington, 1997; Hart et al., 2009; Roman, 1988).

Another myth grows out of the more recent emphasis on research findings about the influence of heredity on dependence. Because of the emphasis on these findings in the popular literature, many individuals buy into the myth that if one does not have a family history of alcohol or other drug dependence, one should use and not worry about becoming dependent. Yes, research does indicate that vulnerability or susceptibility to dependency on alcohol and other drugs may be inherited (Hart et al., 2009; NIAAA, 2000; SAMHSA, 2008); however, as previously noted in this chapter, no segment of the population is immune, and ATOD dependence knows no boundaries.

An additional myth advanced by the media is that smoking is an indication of sophistication, especially for women. It makes one appear youthful and glamorous. Needless to say, the current emphasis on the dangers of smoking has greatly challenged that myth; but the sale of cigarettes and their use by young people continue at a relatively high level (Hart et al., 2009; SAMHSA, 2008).

A similar message is offered by many beer commercials (Parker, 1998). If one drinks a certain brand of beer, one will win a beautiful mate or live the beautiful life; if one drinks another brand, one will not gain weight based on advertised low level carbohydrates (University of California–Berkeley, 2004). Parker (1998), in her study of alcohol advertisements, found a number of suggested myths appearing in commercials: beer as reward for hard play or work, beer as key element in rites of passage or initiation, beer as a way of gaining social acceptance, beer as a vehicle for male bonding, and beer as the beverage of athletes. And the list goes on. These myths are advertised as positives, and the implications of use are totally overlooked or hidden.

Some Myths Regarding Treatment

One myth perpetuated in the field is that "one size fits all," or one treatment program is suitable for all clients. This frequently has been the case advanced by many substance abuse programs. For example, typically substance abuse has been identified as a male problem and treatment has been developed with this bias in mind. Historically, the vast majority of treatment programs were designed by men, for men and, as a result, most research was based on male subjects and their experiences (Abbott, 1994; Van Den Bergh, 1991). Even the most popular self-help effort, AA, was developed by two white men. Treatment options based on feminist principles and expanding on the traditional biopsychosocial approach have begun to recognize the diversity present in the substance-abusing population and have begun to develop treatment programs and strategies that are more effective in responding to those individual needs (Abbott, 1994). Even AA has recognized the importance of addressing the needs of women by supporting women-only AA meetings. A variation on the treatment myth centers around the belief that intense 24-hour inpatient treatment—the traditional being of 14- to 28-day duration—is more effective than day hospital or outpatient treatment. Yes, intensive inpatient treatment is more effective for some clients; however, many clients benefit more or equally from a full range of outpatient services. Many benefit from the ability to continue to reside within the family structure; to work on a daily, although frequently reduced, basis; and to confront daily struggles with added support and encouragement (Anderson, 1992; Kaufman, 1992; L'Abate, 1992).

A myth permeates the field that recovered counselors are much more effective in treating recovering clients than are counselors who personally have not experienced dependency. This view is being challenged every day; however, for those who believe it, whichever side of treatment they represent—provider or client—the impact can be severe. In reality, counselors who have not used substances or personally experienced the challenges of misuse can provide effective treatment. Much depends on the fit between the worker and the consumer.

Some believe the myth that change can only be facilitated by professionally trained ATOD counselors, and suggest that the ideal of quitting "cold turkey" is highly impossible. In reality, many users respond best to self-help groups or self-change efforts. Although it is unknown how many individuals achieve sobriety or controlled use on their own or with the help of their peers, it is anticipated the rate is quite high (Klingemann & Sobell, 2007). Examples of individuals who quit on their own include the many patients who are prescribed high doses of opiates for pain and stop suddenly without major difficulty; the same holds true for many heroin users (Fitzpatrick, 2003). This latter group defies the myth that links success only to engagement in professionally guided treatment. It also defies the myth that addiction is instantaneous (Coomber & Sutton, 2006) and irreversible (Gibson et al., 2004).

Brewer (2003) challenged what he refers to as Fitzpatrick's myth supporting a "pull-your-socks-up" attitude describing the ease with which heroin addicts can give up their drug of choice "cold turkey." He does not dispute the fact that it may be possible for individuals to break bad habits on their own, but reminds us that fewer than half the individuals who engage in inpatient detoxification successfully complete the process (Gossling, Gunkel, Schneider, & Melles, as cited in Brewer).

Part of Brewer's challenge is based on the fact that frequently alcohol abusers experience delirium tremens or convulsions during withdrawal. He also noted the "demoralizing" abstinence syndrome experienced by many in opiate withdrawal, frequently sufficient to trigger relapse (Brewer, 2003). Brewer recognized that many heroin users age out of their addiction and give up the drug on their own. (This has been confirmed by the author in conversations with former users of a broad spectrum of substances.)

Another myth surrounds the belief that naltrexone leads to dysphoria by blocking the flow of endorphins. On the basis of this myth, many do not wish to use naltrexone in their treatment. The above is a medical myth or an opinion that is not substantiated by research (Miotto et al., 2002); however, it may come up in consultation with a client or for the social worker as member of a treatment team.

As noted previously, myths typically contain an element of truth. Fitzpatrick's (2003) beliefs may accurately reflect *his* experiences. Brewer challenged Fitzpatrick's beliefs, noting that withdrawal differs for different individuals and for different substances. Cave and Hallam (2003) bluntly stated that "the withdrawal syndrome is not a myth" (p. 1240). At least withdrawal is not as simplistic as Fitzpatrick and others suggest (Cave & Hallam, 2003).

Recently the criminal justice system has attempted to divert individuals with substance problems to drug courts that are designed to sentence individuals to appropriate treatment options (Anderson, 2003; Crunkilton & Robinson, 2008). An existing myth involves the belief that drug court efforts solve the myriad of substance abuse problems brought to the attention of the criminal justice system. Many hold to the belief that drug courts do work miracles. However, Anderson

(2003) purported that the very idea of drug courts being an answer to many related problems is a myth that has more to do with "reducing prison roles than liberation from addiction" (p. 260). One reason it appears that drug courts are so successful is that many individuals choose to participate to avoid the alternative of incarceration. Unfortunately, the courts frequently focus on one outcome measure—recidivism. Given this measure, it appears that the courts focus on treatment failures rather than successes.

An additional treatment-related myth surrounds the idea that incarceration in the criminal justice system will help address a pre-existing ATOD problem. Data support the fact that more than half the individuals contained in the criminal justice system are there because of substance-related activities; however, there is little supporting evidence that individuals receive appropriate treatment; some may even increase their use through subversive means while incarcerated, and some may have no real opportunities to address the underlying determinant of their addiction.

More recently, the newer approaches in drug courts have been designed to shift the focus to one of therapeutic jurisprudence, similar to the approach being used by mental health law, one based on justice and due process. McGuire (as cited in Anderson, 2003) noted that criminal sanctions alone are related to increased recidivism, whereas skill-oriented therapeutic programs can reduce recidivism by 25 percent to 30 percent. In this case, the half-truth associated with the myth is that the success of drug court depends on the humanistic, therapeutic support provided. As in other cases, success may also depend on the readiness and motivation of the participating consumer.

The impact of this relatively new concept within the criminal justice system is yet to be sufficiently tested (Anderson, 2003; Belenko, 1998; Redman, 2008). With the establishment of a number of drug courts, individuals who could be incarcerated for drug-related offenses are being court ordered to treatment. The jury is still out on the effectiveness of these efforts. The challenge posed to the social worker—to avoid that dangerous step into the quagmire—is to know the therapeutic dynamics of drug court and specific intervention strategies, to know the personal dynamics of each consumer, and to seek plans involving the most appropriate course of action.

Another challenge for both identification (diagnosis) and treatment is related to the fact that many ATOD users also have mental health issues, or other co-occurring disabilities (Coffey et al., 2008). These individuals frequently come under the veil of dual or triple stigmatization. If they are fortunate enough to connect with treatment, it may not be sufficiently integrated to meet the demands of their multiple problems and challenges. In addition to mental health and substance abuse problems, many individuals may suffer from such medical challenges as spinal cord injuries, traumatic brain injury, or a range of related medical conditions such as multiple sclerosis.

Some other issues that pose additional challenges to treatment include the fact that ATOD problems are not treated as medical conditions for various entitlement programs. ATOD alone is not sufficient to qualify for Supplemental Security Income, Social Security Disability Insurance, or various public assistance programs such as food stamps, housing, student loans, or Temporary Assistance for Needy Families. As a result, ATOD-using individuals have more limited access to treatment options and financial support as they attempt to successfully move away from a problematic life based on ATOD-related activities (NASW, 2009).

A number of so-called myths or fallacies may be presented by users themselves (Kowalksi, 2001). Consumers may state: "I can keep a clear head when drinking," denying the fact that alcohol interferes with normal brain functions such as judgment and motor skills, or "I can hold my liquor," denying the fact that people who drink heavily are unable to judge the effect liquor is having on them. "Alcohol will make me popular," but in reality, it could seriously interfere with good social relationships. "Everybody's drinking" (therefore, it cannot be that bad), is not supported by existing research.

Thinking that there is one underlying factor contributing to the dependency problem—and that sobriety or abstinence depends on discovering what that factor is—is another myth operating in the field. Multiple factors contribute to the problem. The key is not to seek one definitive underlying factor, but to discover effective ways to control behavior and to control the use of substances.

Carpenito-Moyet (2003), working as a nurse practitioner in a community health center serving predominately Hispanic men, identified three reasons why the center's consumers entered drug rehabilitation: family pressure, legal mandates, or being tired of a life on drugs. The ones who were most successful in achieving their goal were those who were tired of life on drugs. However, once they make the choice to leave that life, they must grapple with the multiple factors that contributed to the problem in the first place, for example, poverty, abuse, family problems, unemployment, and discrimination. Quitting or changing one's use sounds easy; in practice it is not free from difficulty.

The idea that abstinence must be the goal for all is another challenging myth. Although many professionals in the field believe that abstinence is essential to overcome dependency, others advocate a harm-reduction model that emphasizes controlled drinking or controlled using. The underlying philosophy is that this approach is less offensive to some clients and may facilitate their route to ultimate control or sobriety—and if it does not lead to that end, it will help to minimize the harm generated by the using of various substances (Duncan et al., 1994; Mancini, Linhorst, Broderick, & Bayliff, 2008; Marlatt, Larimer, Baer, & Quigley, 1993).

Two competing myths surrounding recovery or treatment are pervasive in the field (Mattaini, 1998). First is that of the "moral" model; second is that of the "disease" model. The first suggests that *all* it takes for a person to overcome his or her dependence on substances is an "act of will"; the second suggests that *all* it takes is sufficient treatment. Professionals in the field find that both are partially correct, that each extreme works for a small number of individuals, but that for the majority both segments are essential. The person needs to want to change, and frequently, he or she can do so if sufficient help, support, and treatment are available.

Some adhere to the "myth of labeling," believing that referring to someone as an addict or substance abuser will help to identify those in need of services, and, in turn, will facilitate their connection to appropriate treatment. On the one hand, it may lead to a treatment connection; on the other hand, labeling may lead to increased stigmatization, and doors to treatment may be blocked before an appropriate connection is made.

A number of professionals believe that identification of a co-occurring disorder will provide the necessary link to ATOD treatment. In reality, the presence of a co-occurring mental health diagnosis may result in additional stigmatization, closing the doors to treatment for both diagnoses. This is not to suggest that one should avoid diagnosing. What it does suggest is that the worker should examine the diagnoses and think carefully about a strategy to connect the consumer with treatment that is most likely to address both problems.

An additional challenge frequently surfaces when working with clients presenting with co-occurring disorders (APA, 2000). If a client accepts the value of abstinence, he or she may refuse to continue taking prescribed antipsychotic medications. The resulting confusion or psychological change may result in increased dependence on other substances such as illicit drugs or alcohol, many of which were taken in the past to combat the discomfort associated with psychiatric disorder.

Some additional myths involve the idea that illegal drug use occurs for very different reasons than does legal drug use. Many factors contribute to the use of ATOD, but choice of substance does not depend on or flow from particular factors or reasons. For some, it is availability of drugs, for others it is introduction to a specific drug or drugs, the sense of camaraderie created among users, or the relief or response offered. The reasons are as diverse and plentiful as the number of users.

The idea that "my doctor prescribed it, therefore, it cannot be bad" is another example of mythical thinking. The development of psychotherapeutic drugs has had a liberating effect on those suffering from mental illness. Phenothiazines, neuroleptics, and other antipsychotic drugs, for example, have virtually freed many psychiatric patients from the confines of institutions. If these patients take medications as prescribed, and not in combination with other mind-altering substances, the effects can be extremely positive. In some instances in which patients do not disclose their complete medication record to their physicians, the physicians do not closely monitor the full regimen of drugs they themselves are prescribing, or patients intentionally seek treatment from a number of different physicians who are unaware of the full extent of medications being prescribed, the results can be devastating. The same impact can befall nonpsychiatric patients taking multiple medications. This is of special concern among elderly patients who may be seeking treatment for a range of disorders. Not only must the physician be vigilant, but the clients, their families, and other professionals working with them around substance abuse must be also. In many instances, the social worker must help the clients and their support system become informed consumers.

Some believe that addictive drugs lead to instant addiction. In some instances this may be the case; however, in most other situations, it takes longer-term use before addiction occurs (Coomber & Sutton, 2006; Hammersley & Reid, 2002). Hammersley and Reid highlight another myth: Drugs force addicts to stoop to any crime and depravity to finance their addiction.

Hammersley and Reid (2002) and Davies (1992) believed that if one buys into the myths mentioned in the preceding paragraph, users do not have to take responsibility for their actions. Users argue that they cannot be held responsible for their behavior because of their addictions.

One myth related to death by drugs is that users of heroin frequently die from overdose. Yes, some die from heroin, but the greater reality is the ones who do die from polydrug use and related toxicity (Darke, 2003).

Many other myths are not really challenged in the research literature but raise examples of biased, myth-like, or fallacious thinking. A few examples include the following: Addicts are responsible for their sorry condition; one cannot believe a word that addicts say; every addict makes for five more addicts. The challenge for the professional is to recognize the absurdity of these examples and interact with the client with an open, inquisitive mind.

Connection to Content that Follows in Subsequent Chapters

The first step to prevent sinking into myth-supported quagmires is to recognize myths, appreciate the partial truths they represent, and maintain an open mind ready to assess the readiness, commitment, and characteristics of the consumers and substances involved. In some instances it may also involve the education of family members and significant others about myths and potential quagmires associated with ATOD problems.

Myths, partial truths, and exaggerations must be challenged. It is one thing if they permeate the views held by society at large; it is another if professionals buy into these inaccuracies as guides for practice. In many cases, if professionals do, they most likely would not ask the right questions, seek appropriate information, arrive at an accurate assessment, develop appropriate treatment options, formulate adequate prevention strategies, or facilitate the development of relevant social policy. Buying into myths and faulty thinking would definitely bias the vision and influence behavior, possibly leading to a giant step into a so-called quagmire, or at least a path filled with greater obstacles to successful outcomes.

Although the list contains several dozen myths, many more exist. The worker must learn to challenge strongly stated preferences or beliefs, seeking to validate or negate them based on current research and practice experience. Unfortunately, research in the field of ATOD has been quite uneven, especially in relation to gender, culture, and even drug of choice. Alcohol research has a much longer history and, therefore, is more plentiful than other drug research; however, noted gaps do exist. For example, the bulk of the research on women tends to be limited to their child-bearing years. One could question whether this is the direct result of the value assigned to women in their role in procreation (Abbott, 1994, 1995). More recently, greater research emphasis has been placed on understanding dependency of women across the life cycle (Welsh, 1994b, 1996) and on developing and assessing relevant treatment options (Welsh, 1994a). The same holds true for research pertaining to culture and the understanding and development of culturally relevant treatment variations (Straussner, 2001).

To date, the research on tobacco has been limited. Litigation ruling against the tobacco industry, and resulting in special support funding, has prompted increased interest in initiatives designed to better understand tobacco dependency and to guide the development of appropriate initiatives and treatment protocols. Greater emphasis has been placed on understanding the smoking patterns of young adolescents and the role cigarettes play as gateway drugs to other substances.

Much has been done to challenge existing myths, partial truths, or inaccuracies. The work is certainly not complete. As a result, the professional, working with clients struggling with ATOD abuse, must be constantly vigilant of the influence of myths and must strive to enhance an accurate understanding of reality. This is not a task to be accomplished on one's own. It requires continued learning, collaboration and consultation with other professionals in the field, participation in and support of research, and a strong commitment to truth and knowledge. Social work has a long and positive history in the field of addictions. Social workers appreciate the importance of a positive attitude toward change, a sincere appreciation of consumers and the challenges they confront, and the belief in their ability to tackle the tasks at hand. They also recognize the importance of research in supporting both policy and practice. With these convictions in mind, more myths will be uncovered, more quagmires will be avoided, and more positive treatment outcomes will be shared with clients.

References

Abbott, A. A. (1994). A feminist approach to substance abuse treatment and service delivery. *Social Work in Health Care, 19*(3–4), 67–83.

Abbott, A. A. (1995). Substance abuse and the feminist perspective. In N. Van Den Bergh (Ed.), *Feminist practice in the 21st century* (pp. 258–277). Washington, DC: NASW Press.

Abbott, A. A. (1996). Alcohol treatment in Russia: New solutions for old problems. *Issues of Substance, 1*(3), 13–14.

Abbott, A. A. (2001). Substance abuse treatment with clients of French background. In L. A. Straussner (Ed.), *Enthocultural factors in substance abuse treatment* (pp. 180–198). New York: Guilford Press.

Allamani, A. (2007). Addiction, risk, and resources. *Substance Use & Misuse, 42,* 421–439.

American Psychiatric Association. (2000). *Diagnostic and statistical manual of mental disorders* (4th ed., text rev.). Washington, DC: Author.

Anderson, J. F. (2003). Drug courts: Societal adaptation or demonic parody of an authentic myth? *Addiction Research & Theory, 11*(4), 257–262.

Anderson, L. P. (1992). Differential treatment effects. In L. L'Abate, J. E. Farrar, & D. A. Serritella (Eds.), *Handbook of differential treatments for addictions* (pp. 23–41). Boston: Allyn & Bacon.

Bailey, L. (2005). Control and desire: The issue of identity in popular discourses of addiction. *Addiction Research and Theory, 13*(6), 535–543.

Belenko, S. (1998). Research on drug courts: A critical review. *National Court Institute Review, 1*(1), 1–43.

Blume, S. B. (1992). Alcohol and other drug problems in women. In J. H. Lowinson, P. Ruiz, R. B. Millman (Eds.), & J. G. Langrod (Assoc. Ed.), *Substance abuse* (2nd ed., pp. 861–867). Baltimore: Williams & Wilkins.

Brennan, P. L., & Moos, R. H. (1996). Late-life drinking behavior: The influence of personal characteristics, life context, and treatment. *Alcohol Health and Research World, 20*(3), 197–204.

Brennan, P. L., Nichol, A. C., & Moos, R. H. (2003). Older and younger patients with substance use disorders: Outpatient mental health service use and functioning over a 12-month interval. *Psychology of Addictive Behaviors 17,* 42–48.

Brewer, C. (2003). Addiction myths? [Response to M. Fitzpatrick]. *Lancet, 362,* 1240.

Brown, G. (2003). Drug abuse and addiction. *Minority Nurse Newsletter, 10*(3), 4.

Brown, L. (Ed.). (1993). *The new shorter Oxford English dictionary on historical principles* (Vols. 1–2). New York: Oxford University Press.

Campbell, J. (1988). *The power of myth*. New York: Doubleday.

Carpenito-Moyet, L. J. (2003). The myths of drug addiction. *Nursing Forum, 38*(1), 3.

Cave, M., & Hallam, C. (2003). Addiction myths? [Response to M. Fitzpatrick]. *Lancet, 362,* 1240–1241.

Coffey, R. M., Buck, J. A., Kassed, C. A., Dilonardo, J., Forhan, C., Marder, W. D., & Vandivort-Warren, R. (2008). Transforming mental health and substance abuse data Systems in the United States. *Psychiatric Services, 59*(11), 1257–1263.

Cook, P. S., Peterson, R. C., & Moore, D. T. (1990). *Alcohol, tobacco, and other drugs may harm the unborn*. Rockville, MD: U.S. Department of Health and Human Services.

Coomber, R., & Sutton, C. (2006). How quick to heroin dependence? *Drug and Alcohol Review, 25,* 463–471.

Corrigan, E. M. (1979). Alcohol knowledge and practice issues. *Health & Social Work, 4,* 10–40.

Corrigan, E. M. (1985). Gender differences in alcohol and other drug use. *Addictive Behaviors, 10,* 313–317.

Covington, S. S. (1997). Women, addiction, and sexuality. In S.L.A. Straussner & E. Zelvin (Eds.), *Gender and addictions: Men and women in treatment* (pp. 71–95). New York: Jason Aronson.

Cox, C. B., & Ephross, P. H. (1998). *Ethnicity and social work practice*. New York: Oxford University Press.

Crunkilton, D. D., & Robinson, M. M. (2008). Cracking the "black box": Journey mapping's tracking system in a drug court program evaluation. *Journal of Social Work Practice in the Addictions, 8,* 511–529.

Crome, I., & Crome, P. (2005). "At your age, what does it matter?"—Myths and realities about older people who use substances. *Drugs: Education, Prevention and Policy, 12*(5), 343–347.

Daley, D. C., & Raskin, M. S. (1991). Preface. In D. C. Daley & M. S. Raskin (Eds.), *Treating the chemically dependent and their families* (pp. ix–xi). Newbury Park, CA: Sage Publications.

Darke, S. (2003). Polydrug use and overdose: Overthrowing old myths. *Addiction, 98,* 711.

Davies, J. B. (1992). *The myth of addiction: An application of psychological theory of attribution to illicit drug use*. Victoria, Australia: Harwood Academic.

Dorset and Baber. (1983). *Webster's deluxe unabridged dictionary* (2nd ed.). Cleveland: Author.

Dorsey, T. L., Zawitz, M. W., & Middleton, P. (2003). *Drugs and crime facts*. Washington, DC: U.S. Department of Justice, Bureau of Justice Statistics.

Duncan, D. F., Nicholson, T., Clifford, P., Hawkins, W., & Petosa, R. (1994). Harm reduction: An emerging new paradigm for drug education. *Journal of Drug Education, 24,* 281–290.

Dutra, L., Stathopoulou, G., Basden, S. L., Leyro, T. M., Powers, M. B., & Otto, M. W. (2008). A meta-analytic review of psychosocial interventions for substance use disorders. *American Journal of Psychiatry, 165,* 179–187.

Fisher, M. S. (2008). From the Chair. *NASW Alcohol, Tobacco & Other Drugs: Section Connection, 1,* 2–3.

Fitzpatrick, M. (2003). Addiction myths. *Lancet, 362,* 412.

Gibson, B., Acquah, S., & Robinson, P. G. (2004). Entangled identities and psychotropic substance use. *Sociology of Health & Illness, 26,* 597–616.

Gilder, D. A., Lau, R., Corey, L., & Ehlers, C. L. (2008). Factors associated with remission from alcohol dependence in an American Indian community groups. *American Journal of Psychiatry, 165,* 1172–1178.

Goldberg, R. (1998). Taking sides: Clashing views on controversial issues in drugs and society. New York: Duskin–McGraw-Hill.

Grant, B. F., Hasin, D. S., Chou, S. P., Stinson, F. S., & Dawson, D. A. (2004). Nicotine dependence and psychiatric disorders in the United States: Results from the National Epidemiologic Survey on alcohol and related conditions. *Archives of General Psychiatry, 61,* 1107–1115.

Hammersley, R., & Reid, M. (2002). Why the pervasive addiction myth is still believed. *Addiction Research & Theory, 10*(1), 7–30.

Hart, C. L., Ksir, C. J., & Ray, O. S. (2009). *Drugs, society, and human behavior* (13th ed.). New York: McGraw-Hall.

Harwood, H. (2000). *Updating estimates of the economic costs of alcohol abuse in the United States: Estimates, update methods and data* (Report prepared by the Lewin Group for NIAAA). Retrieved from http://www.niaaa.nih.gov/publications/economic-2000/

Harwood, H., Fountain, D., & Livermore, G. (1998). *The economic costs of alcohol and drug abuse in the United States, 1992* (NIH Pub. No. 98–4327). Rockville, MD: National Institute on Drug Abuse.

Hillman, J. (1995). *Kinds of power: A guide to its intelligent uses.* New York: Currency Doubleday.

Institute of Medicine (1990). *Broadening the base of treatment for alcohol problems.* Washington, DC: Academic Press.

Jacobson, S. W. (1997). Assessing the impact of maternal drinking during and after pregnancy. *Alcohol Health and Research World 21*(3), 199–203.

Kaufman, E. (1992). Family therapy: A treatment approach with substance abusers. In J. H. Lowinson, P. Ruiz, & R. B. Millman (Eds.), with J. G. Langrod (Assoc. Ed.), *Substance abuse: A comprehensive text* (2nd ed., pp. 520–532). Baltimore: Williams and Wilkins.

Klingemann, H., & Sobell, L. C. (2007). *Promoting self-change from addictive behaviors: Practical implications for policy, prevention, and treatment.* New York: Springer.

Kowalksi, K. M. (2001). Debunking myths about alcohol. *Current Health 27*(8), 6–11.

L'Abate, L. (1992). Guidelines for treatment. In L. L'Abate, J. E. Farrar, & D. A. Serritella (Eds.), *Handbook of differential treatments for addictions* (pp. 42–60). Boston: Allyn and Bacon.

Larkby, C., & Day, N. (1997). The effects of prenatal alcohol exposure. *Alcohol Health and Research World, 21*(3), 192–198.

Lasser, K., Boyd, J. W., Woolhandler, S., Himmelstein, D. U., McCormick, D., & Boh, D. H. (2000). Smoking and mental illness: A population-based prevalence study. *JAMA, 284,* 2606–2010.

Leland, J. C. (1976). *Firewater myths: North American Indian drinking and alcohol addiction.* New Brunswick, NJ: Rutgers Center of Alcohol Studies.

Marlatt, G. A., Larimer, M. E., Baer, J. S., & Quigley, L. A. (1993). Harm reduction for alcohol problems: Moving beyond the controlled drinking controversy. *Behavior Today, 24,* 461–504.

Mancini, M. A., Linhorst, D., Broderick, F., & Bayliff, S. (2008) Challenges to implementing the harm reduction approach. *Journal of Social Work Practice in the Addictions, 8,* 380–408.

Mattaini, M. A. (1998). Practice with individuals. In M. A. Mattaini, C. T. Lowery, & C. H. Meyer (Eds.), *The foundations of social work practice* (2nd ed., pp. 138–164). Washington, DC: NASW Press.

May, P. A., & Smith, M. B. (1988). Some Navajo Indian opinions about alcohol abuse and prohibition: A survey and recommendations for policy. *Journal of Studies on Alcohol, 49,* 324–334.

Miotto, K., McCann, M., Basch, J., Rawson, R., & Ling, W. (2002). Naltrexone or dysphoria: Fact or myth? *American Journal of Addictions 11,* 151–160.

Moran, J. R., & May, P. A. (1997). American Indians. In J. Philleo & F. L. Brisbane (Eds.), *Cultural competence in substance abuse prevention* (pp. 1–31). Washington, DC: NASW Press.

National Association of Social Workers. (2009). Alcohol, tobacco, and other drugs. In *Social work speaks: NASW policy statements 2009–2012* (8th ed., pp. 29–37). Washington, DC: NASW Press.

National Institute on Alcohol Abuse and Alcoholism (NIAAA). (1994). *Eighth special report to the U.S. Congress on alcohol and health.* Washington, DC: U.S. Superintendent of Government Documents.

National Institute on Alcohol Abuse and Alcoholism. (1997). *Ninth special report to the U.S. Congress on alcohol and health.* Washington, DC: U.S. Superintendent of Government Documents.

National Institute on Alcohol Abuse and Alcoholism. (2000). *Tenth special report to the U.S. Congress on alcohol and health.* Washington, DC: U.S. Superintendent of Government Documents.

National Institute on Drug Abuse. (2008). Teen substance abuse continues to decline. *NIDA Notes 21*(5), 15.

National Institutes of Health. (1998). *Economic costs of alcohol and drug abuse estimated at $246 billion in the United States* [News release—May 13]. Bethesda, MD: Author.

Orlin, L., & Davis, J. (1993). Assessment and intervention with drug and alcohol abusers in psychiatric settings. In S.L.A. Straussner (Ed.), *Clinical work with substance abusing clients* (pp. 50–68). New York: Guilford Press.

Parker, B. J. (1998). Exploring life themes and myths in alcohol advertisements through a meaning-based model of advertising experiences. *Journal of Advertising, 27*(1), 97–112.

Potenza, M. (2007). To do or not to do? The complexities of addiction, motivation, self-control, and impulsivity. *American Journal of Psychiatry, 164,* 4–6.

Ray, O., & Ksir, C. (1999). *Drugs, society, and human behavior* (8th ed.). Boston: WGB–McGraw-Hill.

Redman, D. (2008). Coping-related substance use motives and stressful life experiences among people with a history of incarceration. *Journal of Social Work Practice in the Addictions, 8,* 490–510.

Roman, P. M. (1988). *Women and alcohol use: A review of the research literature.* Rockville, MD: U.S. Department of Health and Human Services.

Serdula, M., Williamson, D. F., Kendrick, J. S., Anda, R. F., & Byers, T. (1991). Trends in alcohol consumption by pregnant women: 1985 through 1988. *JAMA, 265,* 876–879.

Straussner, L. A. (2001). *Ethnocultural factors in substance abuse treatment.* New York: Guilford Press.

Straussner, L. A. (2008). From the editor. *Journal of Social Work Practice in the Addictions, 8,* 1–2.

Substance Abuse and Mental Health Services Administration (SAMHSA). (2008). *Results from the 2007 National Survey on Drug Use and Health: National findings* (NSDUH Series H-34, DHHS Publication No. SMA 08–4343). Rockville, MD: SAMHSA, Office of Applied Statistics.

Tan, M. C., Westermeyer, J., Thompson, J., Thuras, P., & Cavine, J. (2008). Sustained remission from substance use disorder among American Indian veterans. *Addictive Disorders, Therapy & Treatment 7,* 53–63.

University of California–Berkeley. (2004). Alcohol and the low-carb myth. *Wellness Letter: Newsletter of Nutrition, Fitness, and Self-Care, 20*(11), 1.

U.S. Department of Health and Human Services (HHS). (1991). *Drug abuse and drug abuse research: The third triennial report to Congress from the Secretary, Department of Health and Human Services.* Rockville, MD: Author.

U.S. Department of Justice, Office of Justice Programs, Bureau of Justice Statistics (BJS). (2008). *Prisoners in 2007.* Retrieved September 6, 2009, from http://www.ojp.usdoj. gov/bjs/abstract/p07.htm

Van Den Bergh, N. (1991). Having bitten the apple: A feminist perspective on addictions. In N. Van Den Bergh (Ed.), *Feminist perspectives on addictions* (pp. 3–30). New York: Springer.

van Wormer, K. (1995). Chapter two: Historical context. In *Alcoholism treatment: A social work perspective* (pp. 20–37). Chicago: Nelson-Hall.

Welsh, D. M. (Ed.). (1994a). Advances in alcoholism treatment [Special issue]. *Alcohol Health & Research World, 18*(4).

Welsh, D. M. (Ed.). (1994b). Women and alcohol [Special issue]. *Alcohol Health & Research World 18*(3).

Welsh, D. M. (Ed.). (1996). Drinking over the life span [Special issue]. *Alcohol Health & Research World, 20*(3).

Westermeyer, J. (2008). A sea change in the treatment of alcoholism, *American Journal of Psychiatry, 165,* 1093–1095.

Westermeyer, J., & Peake, E. (1983). A ten-year follow-up of alcoholic Native Americans in Minnesota. *American Journal of Psychiatry, 140,* 189–194.

Wilsnack, S. C., Wilsnack, R. W., & Hiller-Sturmhofel, S. (1994). How women drink: Epidemiology of women's drinking and problem drinking. *Alcohol Health & Research World, 18*(3), 173–184.

Wolfgang, L. A. (1997). Charting recent progress: Advances in alcohol research. *Alcohol Health & Research World, 21*(4), 277–286.

Woody, G. (1996). The challenge of dual diagnosis. *Alcohol Health & Research World, 20*(2), 76–80.

2

Selecting Perspectives and Theories for ATOD Practice

Gwenelle S. O'Neal

Introduction

In this chapter, I briefly review social work's mission, the concepts that help to operationalize that mission, the ecological perspective, and the problem-solving and planning processes that are used as a framework to guide the social work practitioner in working with and on behalf of people affected by alcohol, tobacco and other drug (ATOD) problems. This work is guided by several factors.

The special mission of the social work profession involves the perspective of the interrelatedness of people and their environment. Engagement; appropriate selection of theories, methods, and practice principles; and systematic problem solving are components in the practice system and service delivery process. The current focus on evidence-based practice (EBP) is also embraced. "The term 'evidence-based' was coined by a medical group at McMaster University in Canada. Originating in medicine, evidence based practice (EBP) refers to the conscientious, explicit, and judicious use of current best evidence in making decisions about the care of individual patients" (Gibbs, 2003, p. 1).

Social work practice values, knowledge, and skills are delivered in a systematic manner related to the client systems involved. There are hundreds of theories, approaches, models, and methods that constitute a framework to guide the practitioner's steps in delivering services. The service delivery system in which clients are served also influences the intervention approaches. Social work practice operates under the aegis or confines of various organizational settings in which it is applied.

Treatment approaches are connected to administrative regulations and organizational culture dynamics. This chapter offers guidelines and criteria for the responsible practitioner to use when selecting among the array of theories, methods, and practice principles that exist in the field of ATOD.

Social Work's Mission

The mission of social work, like other professions, has a special function in society, a set of activities it performs to meet human needs. Social work is the professional activity of helping individuals, groups, families, and communities enhance or restore their capacity for social functioning. The professional also contributes to the establishment of societal conditions favorable to this goal. The profession's purpose implies that social work's job is to simultaneously focus on people, their environments, and the interactions between people and their environments to improve the quality of life for everyone. Social workers become involved in such interactions by using interventions that aim to influence factors creating, exacerbating, or perpetuating the problem. The social worker may focus on helping people to grow and change, linking people with resources and opportunities, changing the environment of people, or all, or any combination of these necessary for resolving problems.

According to Carol Meyer (1976), this avowed emphasis on people in transaction with their environments, the "easement of the adaptations between client and environment at their interface" (p. 40), makes social work the only profession with such an announced purpose. This is what differentiates social work from other professions. No other profession has defined its focus as mediating the interactions between people and their environments, where the environment itself is viewed as a variable to be worked with (Meyer, 1983). Harriett Bartlett (1970), writing about social work's purpose, emphasized the importance social work places on what goes on between people and the environment: "This dual focus ties them together. Thus person and situation, people and environment are encompassed in a single concept, which requires that they be constantly reviewed together." (p. 116)

1. Meyer (1983) observed that there is as much consensus within the profession about the major purposes of social work as we can possibly get, whether it is called: "person and environment or eco-system, the different terms all suggest the same idea, that social workers uniquely address cases … individuals, families, groups; social policies, planning, organizing, programming, and research with [the] same construct of people in their environments." (p. 4)

2. The profession's emphasis on social functioning and dual focus on per-son-in-situation interactions have profound implications for the develop-ment and selection of perspectives, frameworks, theories, principles, and methods for practice. The social work discipline focus, which is to work with clients by exploring the person in the environment, helps to improve individual, family, and community functioning, and helps gain access to resources. Recent attention to the roles social workers play includes con-sideration of the direct practice, systems, and research responsibilities social workers have (Hepworth et al., 2006).

Values and attitudes about substance users may vary with workers given their backgrounds and perspectives. As with all things, social workers demonstrate a range of feelings, beliefs, and opinions about people who drink alcohol and use drugs. The National Association of Social Workers (2000) *Code of Ethics* provides a value-based foundation as a guideline for working with other professionals, work-ing with the client systems we serve, and considering the society at large in devel-oping our approaches and interventions. Simultaneously, there are two perspec-tives that inform the social work discipline and practice: the ecological perspective and the strengths perspective.

Perspectives

The science of ecology, the study of interactions between living organisms and their environments, provided the concepts that evolved into social work's most promi-nent practice paradigm—"the ecological perspective." This perspective offers a view of evaluating the presence and absence or networks and resources to accom-modate healthy living (Hepworth et al., 2006). The ecological perspective provides a way for social workers to consider the complex interplay of biological, psycho-logical, social, economic, cultural, economic, and spiritual forces in client systems and incorporate micro- and macro-level interventions (Pardeck, 1996).

The Council for Training in Evidence-Based Behavioral Practice (2008) reported that,

the goal is to create a healthy community environment that provides health-promoting information and social support to enable people to live healthier lifestyles. This approach is based on ecological models that are increasingly viewed as having substantial potential to improve health. [It has] been applied to a variety of health issues including tobacco, obesity, and cancer screening.

▼
▼
▼

The "strengths perspective" drives the discipline's approach to viewing the people we serve. In concert with the ecological view, the strengths perspective, using an orientation that looks for positive qualities and undeveloped potential, seeks to raise the point of departure from weakness to abilities. Given the myths associated with people who struggle with addiction, identifying their strengths and resources is sometimes a challenge for practitioners. Nevertheless, when operating with recognition of resilience and tenacity, regardless of obstacles, a more contextualized view of the client system becomes available (Kemp, Whittaker, & Tracy, 1997). This expanded vision enhances the practitioner's ability to "acknowledge, build on, replenish, and enhance naturally occurring strengths, potentialities, and resources" (p. 63). Extending from these perspectives are the two foundation models that drive the provision of social work services: problem solving and planning for change.

A third model has emerged to also consider in developing the context of service delivery. This model, contextual fluidity, "places environment as integral to all interactions between persons giving help and persons seeking help" (Nelson & McPherson, 2004, p. 204). This model focuses on strengths. It is an alternative model that provides an indigenous viewpoint. Helping is perceived as the central concept rather than "planned changes directed toward remediation and solutions of identified problems" (p. 200). This model accepts self-help and self-change and provides a framework that is also useful in sharing culturally affirming resources. It supports prevention programming and expanding the range of resources offered in intake scenarios.

The Problem-Solving Process

A generic problem-solving process that can be used as a guide in almost every context is at the heart of professional helping (Bloom, 1990; Johnson, 1995). In her seminal work, *Social Casework: A Problem-Solving Process*, Helen Harris Perlman (1957) conceptualized what social workers do in practice as problem solving. Problem solving is a creative cognitive process that alerts the responsible practitioner to think carefully before acting and provides guidelines as to how to think carefully to develop understanding of the client in the situation. The problem-solving process is carried out in interaction with clients and people with the capacity to affect a client's situation in an important way.

Problem solving consists of a number of common activities that cut across all levels of practice (individual, family, group, community, and societal). These activities vary in number and can be approached in many ways. They are divided into sequential phases, each phase characterized by some broad goal that should be completed before moving into the next phase. However, in some cases the phases may be recurring. When problems are solved competently, as contrasted with trial and error, certain essential steps are followed. In general, authors writing about the problem-solving process state that practitioners must be successfully involved in recognition or definition of the problem, assessment, development of options, putting options into action, evaluation of results, termination when appropriate, and integration of systems and ecosystems principles (Bloom, 1990; Compton, Galaway, & Cournoyer, 2006; Johnson, 1995). Although, this process is an orderly one with specified phases, it does not progress in a clear-cut manner. The practitioner and the client are often working on more than one phase at a time. The problem-solving process is a means of proceeding over time through phases in a spiral manner. Compton and Galaway (1999) in describing the process stated that "problem solving is a squirming, wriggling, living process that embraces the social [transactions] between you [the worker], the client, and all the systems of which you [the worker] and the client are a part" (p. 90).

The "problem-solving process" has no assumptions about problems built into it; it does not suggest which theories, models, or practice concepts a practitioner should use. The phases of problem solving provide a broad framework for deciding what to do and doing it. These phases include the following:

1. The Engagement Phase—establishing a relationship, using multicultural resources in clarifying the problem as the client sees it, early exploration and data collection, preliminary goal setting, and contracting
2. The Assessment Phase—collection of data about strengths and needs of the client system; identification of environmental factors contributing to the problem, identification of available resources
3. The Goal Setting Phase—establishment of goals with the client based on assessment of results; considering theories and procedures that would provide a framework for potential intervention, formulating a plan of action, and establishing baseline and sequential measures
4. The Intervention Phase—providing ongoing collaboration and support to client during the action phase; collecting data
5. The Termination Phase—determining when the agreed-on goals have been accomplished (maintenance of gains) or have not been addressed
6. The Evaluation Phase—evaluating the results at each phase and evaluating status of how well gains have been maintained (Wood & Dunn, 2000).
7. The Follow-Up Phase—contacting client three to six months after termination for additional data regarding status, maintenance of goal achievement, and motivational support.

CASE EXAMPLE 2.1: The Case of Wilma

This case is an example of problem solving, planned change, and contextual fluidity. Wilma is a 19-year-old who started drinking in high school when her mother died in a car accident. She attends a community college and works part-time in a local grocery store. She lives with her dad and her younger sister. She wants to become a nurse but is having trouble in her classes. She was stopped at a traffic stop during the holidays and has had her license suspended. She spoke with a social worker who was involved in the Driving Under the Influence classes required to get her license returned. Because this was a single session the worker incorporated the problem-solving paradigm in a preliminary engagement episode.

The worker discussed the problem-solving method as a way to help Wilma evaluate where she is. She solicited Wilma's views of what this situation meant and asked her to list what needs to happen (using this framework) to move forward toward her goals. The worker encouraged her to consider further treatment for her drinking.

The Planned-Change Process

Even as the course of solving problems with clients begins, so does the process of planned change. These two paths of action are connected to the practitioner preparing to deliver service, the organizational structure for the service delivery, and the motivation of the client or client system. The planned change model is considered a model of intentional change (Prochaska, Norcross, & DiClemente, 1994). Also called the transtheoretical model, the model provides a foundation for considering the approach to be pursued for treatment. The stages are:

1. Pre-contemplation—thinking about pursuing change
2. Contemplation—defining the steps to be involved
3. Preparation—gathering materials, speaking with relevant stakeholders in this anticipated process; assessing insurance coverage
4. Action—implementing steps
5. Maintenance—considering the stages of service likely to occur following the basic structure of service delivery.

Although planning for change generally focuses on the stages mentioned in the preceding paragraph, the process must also incorporate contemporary concepts of recovery, wellness, and relapse. The terms "recovery" and "wellness" address the perceived value and stigma of people recovering from addiction, as well as contextual issues that may contribute to the ability to maintain gains and wellness.

Finally, relapse and possible termination must also be planned for. In developing plans with the consumer, consideration of the environmental situations, ongoing stressors, and potential adjustments must occur to accommodate these influences on goal maintenance.

Using this model, Wilma would likely begin to consider her need for professional intervention after her talk with the DUI course worker ("pre-contemplation").

Assuming she followed through and found a social worker or an ATOD health service she would be in the "contemplation" phase as she initiated a service relationship. Stages 3 through 5 ("preparation," "action," and "maintenance") would constitute the development and implementation of the service process.

The Contextual Fluidity Model

The contextual fluidity model would support self-help, mutual-aid groups, and personal and family strategies to terminate or modify the use of alcohol or unhealthy substances. In this scenario, Wilma might attend an AA meeting or ask a friend or family member to attend with her. She might talk with her minister or other people in her community and get support for her grief about her mother and gather other ideas about how to get beyond the DUI and begin to manage her life better. She would gather information herself about alcohol and addiction and self-improvement. She might identify other community self-help groups and enhance her support network. She could begin with visiting the American Self-Help Group Clearinghouse (http://www.selfhelpgroups.org) or the National Mental Health Consumer Clearinghouse (http://www.mhselfhelp.org). Wilma would be using a modified form of the planned change model as she increased the discipline regarding her drinking.

These three models (problem solving, planned change, and contextual fluidity), and the related dynamics of recovery, wellness, and relapse, offer a framework for discussing ATOD services with consumers and their families and in selecting appropriate theories by which to structure service interventions. The organizational setting, client system, and practitioner education and focus are variables in service delivery. Selected theories can provide a foundation and guide the practice intervention.

▼
▼
▼

The Need for Theory as a Guide for Practice

Hepworth and colleagues (2006) informed us that knowledge of numerous practice theories and techniques is necessary to make judicious choices to implement interventions. The need for a theory is connected to the professional goal to provide systematic and organized service provision. The term "theory" has often been used, very loosely, to include models of intervention strategies and approaches; modalities of intervention such as with individuals, families, or groups; unorganized conceptualizations of client problems or of practice; sets of practice principles; practice wisdom; philosophies of practice; and applications with reference to diverse populations. Technically, the term "theory" has a narrower and more exacting definition that requires the construction of a set of precisely stated, testable, and interconnected propositions. For purposes of this discussion, the looser definition will be used because it is generally used in this less precise way by practitioners and by many writers of professional books and articles.

Theories are viewed as conceptual boxes into which we attempt to stuff the reality our senses experience, to understand and explain that reality. Humans are natural theorizers and conceptual box builders, as the child psychologist Piaget recognized (Piaget, 1963; Piaget & Inhelder, 1958). One has only to observe a baby busily eyeing, listening to, fingering, and mouthing everything around him or her: One can almost see the gears whizzing around inside the little brain as the baby struggles to discover patterns, or conceptual boxes, such as "good-to-eat" or "doesn't-taste-good," or "sharp-hurts" or "soft-nice." The baby is using his or her developing intelligence, even before speaking, to begin to sort out conceptually the "booming, buzzing confusion" of his or her world.

A theory is necessary to structure and organize our thinking. The kinds of theoretical boxes we construct are influenced, usually outside our conscious awareness, by our underlying philosophical paradigm—our basic beliefs, values, and assumptions. Theories can be freeing, mind expanding, and essential to dealing with our world. Descriptive theories about the nature and causation of ATOD problems, and prescriptive theories about what to do to help a client with such problems, might present valuable cognitive maps for the practitioner in understanding the person and the problem he or she is dealing with, and as guidelines for intervention.

The Institute of Medicine, National Academy of Sciences (1990), reviewing theories concerning alcohol abuse, observed:

> theories have the advantage not only of making disparate facts meaningful but of transcending them by leaping from the particular to the universal.

Whether such a leap is justified, however, is problematic and, in view of the diversity of individuals and problems in the treatment of alcohol problems, universal approaches can only be viewed with some skepticism. (p. 293)

However, theories can also constrict and warp the way we perceive and relate to our world. Using a theory that is just plain wrong in its assertions about the nature of ATOD abuse or how to help such clients, is, of course, a sure formula for poor outcome and is likely also to result in iatrogenic (that is, caused by the service provider) damage to the client. Using a theoretical orientation that may apply to some ATOD clients, but is inappropriate for *this* client, may also result in failure. (Many ATOD descriptive and prescriptive theories, for example, were developed out of experience with white men; as such, they may not apply to women, to people from diverse cultural groups, or to adolescents.)

The practitioner may be forced to use theories with propositions that have not yet been subjected to careful controlled research testing. This issue is addressed by the contemporary focus on EBP. Being aware of all the research may be difficult and time consuming. There are outcome studies, meta-analyses, and program evaluations that should be available in the process of becoming informed practitioners serving the ATOD populations (Evidence-based practice online resources: See References for Web site). The practitioner is ethically responsible to remain aware that a particular theory's assertions that have not yet been substantiated should be used only with caution and awareness that the practitioner is using something that is actually still in the form of unvalidated hypotheses.

"Practice wisdom"—the accumulated experience of many practitioners with the same kinds of cases—is a kind of pre-theory, in that it has not been organized and translated into the testable propositions of a real theory. Many of the books and articles written about various aspects of practice are actually not "theories" per se, but, rather, collections of the particular author's practice wisdom based on his or her own practice experience. Practitioners who have borrowed a good supervisor's practice wisdom can attest that it can indeed be valuable, and the kind of practice wisdom found in much of the practice literature can also have value for the practitioner. But the same caveat applies. The supervisor or teacher or writer may have "tested" his or her claims in his or her own practice; however, because it typically has been such a loose kind of testing, and subject to so much bias, the claims cannot be said to have been supported as valid. Intervention techniques that work for one practitioner may be so tied to that practitioner's personal style that they may not be usable by other practitioners. To be really valuable for practitioners, practice wisdom needs to be organized and translated into testable propositions that are

CASE EXAMPLE 2.2: The Case of John

John presents to the local addictions services center, which is affiliated with a regional mental health center. He was discharged from the Marines about two years ago after serving two, two-year tours in Iraq. During his break between the tours he was married to his longtime girlfriend who lived in Pennsylvania with their three-year-old son. John has been having nightmares since returning, has had difficulty finding steady employment, and has exhibited occasional episodes of aggression at home. His drinking has increased in the past several months and his wife encouraged him to seek some help. The social worker who will be working with John and his family is aware there is little understanding of how military-related trauma may lead to aggressive behavior (Taft et al., 2007). However, strategies helpful to returning military service personnel and their families and posttraumatic stress disorder are developing and will be emphasized in serving this family.

subjected to unbiased, objective, and controlled testing. Contemporary social work practice urges ongoing rigorous evaluation for EBP.

The concept of addiction includes perceptions of disease, self-discipline, morality, and other elements. This range of considerations must be addressed in developing a theoretical formulation. Early notions about misuse of substances were tied to morality and views of personal discipline. Subsequent ideas link misuse, especially of alcohol, to biology and genetic predisposition. As the increased use and misuse of more substances has occurred, recognition of several diverse elements has emerged. Misuse of drugs (illegal and legal), liquid, pills, powder, tobacco, and food has expanded the elements to be examined to understand the dynamics that may develop and impede one's health. One's exposure to substances in prenatal conditions, home and school settings, and workplace environments are added to the factors that may affect one's level of misuse and opportunities for recovery.

Theory as Master or Theory as Tool

It is humanly understandable that many practitioners seek to find the one overarching theory that they can apply to all cases (for example, "I'm psychodynamically oriented," "I believe a 12-step approach is best for all ATOD clients," or "Group work is best for all client problems"). Practice is intellectually, emotionally, and physically demanding. Managed care and financial constraints on many agencies have meant increased caseloads, with a decrease in time for the practitioner to reflect, to critique—just to think. The plethora of theories in the ATOD practice field can make the practitioner feel confused and unsure of himself or herself, yet it is important that he or she brings to the transactions with the client a level of confidence in her or his ability to understand and to help.

Given this practice environment, it is intellectually much easier to adopt uncritically a particular theory or approach; it does away immediately with confusion and lack of sureness and creates an emotionally comfortable sense of closure. But there are real dangers, for both practitioner and client, in allowing theory to become one's master—in effect, to let some book run the case. It means, literally, that the practitioner has shut down his or her mind and has substituted something in the book (or a supervisor's or agency's preferred approach) for the practitioner's own intelligence, reasoning abilities, and critical judgment. Most dangerously, it means that the practitioner is not listening to and thinking about "the data of the case"—what the client is trying to tell the worker about herself, her ATOD problem, and her family and life situation. The practitioner is instead listening to the voice of the theory inside his or her own head. Information the client may offer that does not fit neatly into the narrow conceptual box of the theory may be discarded, or just not heard. If the client's problem does not improve, the theory-dedicated practitioner tends not to wonder whether this was because there was something amiss with the theoretical approach he or she used, or that perhaps there was something about this case that made the theoretical perspective inapplicable for this client. Denial and rationalization are usually the escape hatches (not only ATOD clients use these defense mechanisms!)—for example, the client was "unmotivated" or "not ready to use help," that is, the case failure was the client's fault, not the fault of the practitioner or the preferred theory.

Practitioners, however, cannot approach every case as if their heads were blank slates, as if they did not remember any other ATOD cases they have dealt with, as if they have never read anything about ATOD, or discussed any cases with colleagues. All of this is, indeed, inside every practitioner's head, tucked into more or less neatly arranged conceptual boxes. It can and should be called on, as a cognitive map to bring to the case, and as suggested interventive activities the practitioner might undertake. One's own previous practice experience, and the experience and insights of others that we are here lumping together as "theory," are tools for understanding and intervening. The practitioner picks and chooses from among the conceptual boxes stored in his or her mind those pieces that seem to help him or her to understand the client and the problem, and that seem to offer some fruitful ideas about how to go about intervening.

The more the propositions of a particular theory have received support from controlled research, the more confidence the practitioner can place in them. Much less confidence can be placed in unvalidated propositions, although the practitioner may be forced to use them for lack of anything better, albeit with caution. The caution also applies to the slippery slope that awaits the practitioner. The untested propositions of a theory are actually hypotheses: "what-if" statements of conjecture or speculation. These hypotheses have a way of sliding over in one's mind into assumptions; the practitioner tends to forget that they are merely speculative and untested and begins to assume that they are so. In the final slide, the practitioner begins to view them, and to use them, as if they were facts.

Sometimes the slide down this slippery slope is escalated by the popularization of particular theories or their propositions or hypotheses. Every so often some theory or theoretical ideas become very fashionable in the mental health community, or within an area of practice such as ATOD. They may achieve enthusiastic trendiness because their proponents are on to something that is really valuable that no one thought of before, or they may become fashionable just because people want to get on the bandwagon that everyone else is on. A cautionary example is the proposition, in the early years of the family therapy movement, that certain pathological family dynamics "caused" schizophrenia in one family member and that, therefore, family therapy, aimed at exorcising whatever family dynamics demons there were, was the appropriate treatment for the mental illness of the individual member (Wood & Geismar, 1989). Not only did this kind of family therapy not improve the illness of the member suffering from schizophrenia, but it also inflicted great iatrogenic damage on the families who clearly heard the message that they were to blame for their family member's terrible illness—despite the practitioner's assurances that he or she wanted only to help and not to blame. It is now clear to most practitioners that schizophrenia is an organic brain disease; and most modern family therapists have moved far away from this earlier therapy and now practice a psychoeducational therapy with such families, focused on education and support.

Another example, particularly relevant to ATOD practice, occurred in the 1940s and 1950s when psychoanalytic–psychodynamic theory was considered the dominant theory of psychotherapy. It was observed that the wife of an alcohol abuser was frequently very angry at her husband for what his alcohol abuse was doing to the family. Therapists concluded, according to the prism of their theory, that this behavior of the wife meant that she needed her husband to continue drinking, based on her unconscious need to castrate him, to keep him dependent, and that this was the real cause of his alcohol abuse. Treatment was then focused on the wife, on the assumption that if she could be cured of these pathological needs, then her husband would automatically stop drinking. The guilt and confusion created in the wife by the treatment approach inflicted damage—and, of course, the husband's continued drinking. Then sociologist Joan Jackson (1954) (who, because she was not a psychotherapist, was not locked in to the therapists' theory-derived way of viewing the data of the case) conducted a participant-observation study in which she listened to wives in Al-Anon groups describing their experiences. She drew a different conclusion about the meaning of the women's behavior and emotional upset: Jackson saw these as a reaction (or a result rather than a cause) to the stress and disruption their husbands' drinking was creating. This one article, which is now considered a classic, had a great impact in terms of expanding the theory-locked view of alcohol treatment therapists. (Parenthetically, however, the early assumption of the wife's pathology continues to exist under the label of "codependency.")

These are examples of the logical fallacy of teleology, or confusing effect with cause. They are also cautionary examples of how untested speculative hypotheses about the causation of schizophrenia or alcohol abuse slid, in the minds of practitioners, to acceptance of the hypotheses as assumptions, and then to belief that they were actual established facts. Because many other professionals were on the same slippery slope, it was easier for practitioners to be seduced onto the slope with them. The practitioners involved are ethically responsible for the damage that was inflicted on clients—not because they set out to hurt their clients, but because they were not sufficiently intellectually responsible. They had an ethical and professional responsibility to ask for the solid evidence to support these hypotheses, from research and not just from the claims of a theory.

Validation of ATOD Theories

The question of whether research evidence exists to support the propositions of various prescriptive theories concerning ATOD treatment approaches is presented in chapters 9, 10, and 11 concerning the effectiveness of various ATOD interventions with individuals, with formed groups, and with families.

Descriptive theories seek to define and explain the nature of ATOD abuse. Explanations of the nature and causation of ATOD abuse and dependence have varied greatly over the years, and even today the treatment field is characterized by conflicting views of the problem. Rogers and McMillin (1988) estimated that there were over 100 definitions of "alcoholism" alone. For this discussion, the most widely used of these theories are grouped into some general categories: the moral model, the disease model, the psychodynamic model, and the social learning model.

How the practitioner defines the client's problem determines—even controls—the intervention goals that will be set, and the actual intervention approach and activities. For example, if the practitioner defines ATOD abuse as moral or spiritual deficit (as in 12-step programs), then intervention will be oriented toward offering the client help with his or her spiritual development. If the practitioner accepts the disease model, then total abstinence will be set as the goal, and treatment activities will be directed toward this. A psychodynamically oriented practitioner will define the problem as a symptomatic expression of underlying psychological conflict or evidence of a pathological "addictive personality," leading to the choice of insight-oriented treatment, including exploration of past trauma. Yet another practitioner, who finds the social learning model to be more cogent, may gear treatment toward "unlearning" the use of ATOD as an adaptive response, and new learning of more constructive adaptive behaviors. Choice of a descriptive theory of ATOD abuse therefore is not of merely academic interest; it has very practical consequences for both practitioner and client.

One difficulty encountered in attempting to establish the empirical evidence for these "theories" is that some are really just perspectives, or philosophical viewpoints about ATOD. In this case, they cannot be empirically validated. A further difficulty is that some of these core notions apply to everyone, not just people with ATOD problems. For example, everyone could use further spiritual development, and everyone has some psychological conflict or some of the traits claimed to characterize addictive personalities. (Mark Keller ([1972], for example, one of the founders of the alcoholism treatment field, once caustically proposed "Keller's Law": The investigation of any trait in alcoholics will show that they have either more or less of it.) Because these "underlying" or "causal" problems can be found in all ATOD clients (and everyone else) does not mean they actually have a direct causal relationship to development of an ATOD problem. They may, or they may not, but that cannot be definitively established.

The proof of the pudding of these descriptive perspectives comes more from research into the effectiveness of the prescriptive theories, or intervention approaches, that are based on them. The disease model, for example, holds that alcohol abusers, based on their physiological characteristics, lack the ability to control their drinking once they have started and that it is this inability to moderate their drinking behavior that distinguishes them from nonproblematic social drinkers. The analogy is often made to people with diabetes who, because of their physiological characteristics, cannot properly metabolize certain foods. Like severe diabetes, ATOD abuse is considered a permanent, lifelong condition—that is, the person is still an "addict" or an "alcoholic" even though he or she may not have used ATOD for many years.

The client who has achieved sobriety is therefore always "in recovery" but never "recovered." The disease model may well apply to the relatively small group of problem drinkers who go on to develop severe alcohol "dependence" (as that term is used in the DSM IV-TR [American Psychiatric Association, 2000]) and for whom total abstinence is necessary, but research indicates that it does not seem to apply to the larger group of alcohol "abusers," most of whom do not progress to severe dependence (Institute of Medicine, National Academy of Sciences, 1990), and many of whom do succeed in controlling their use of alcohol rather than abstaining from it altogether (Hester & Miller, 1989). The disease model may also be applicable to users of other drugs, or tobacco, because those substances are known to have highly addictive properties. In general, however, the ATOD field is moving away from use of the term "disease," because there is no consensus on its conceptual definition: It means different things to different people. If a term cannot be conceptually defined unambiguously, then, of course, it cannot be operationally defined and, thus, cannot be tested for its validity. It can be noted here that it is unfortunately paradoxical that at present the field is eschewing use of the term "disease" to refer to individuals with ATOD problems, and also using the term to refer to ATOD abuse as a "family disease." What is being referred to is the psychological impact on family members of the abuser's ATOD problem, the disruption of family system roles and performances, and the unintentionally unhelpful "enabling" behaviors in which family members often become trapped. But it is only by unwarranted conceptual stretching (that is, use of the term "disease" in the sense only of a metaphor) that these phenomena can be called diseases in the same way as, for example, diabetes or schizophrenia. This results in fuzzy conceptualizing (Wood & Geismar, 1989). It also risks the practitioner's engaging in the logical fallacy of teleology or confusing effects with causes, and the fallacy of reification or treating a conceptual and linguistic invention as if it were a real thing. In this vein, use of the term "codependency" to refer to spouses or adult children of ATOD abusers may also be considered not the best way of conceptualizing the impact of ATOD abuse on these family members, or even choice of language because the term obfuscates rather than clarifies. The Institute of Medicine, National Academy of Sciences (1990) noted that "the treatment of children of alcoholics and other codependents is an area where definitions are unclear and research pertaining to etiology or outcome is lacking" (p. 392). They also observed that the same methods used to treat the person with alcohol problems are being used to treat codependents. Yet the appropriateness of these methods has not been justified, nor has the differential (marginal) effectiveness of these specialty approaches been evaluated in a series of clinical trials. (p. 392)

Family members of ATOD abusers do suffer and are being hurt by the abuse, they need attention and help from the practitioner, and they also may be an important resource in the abuser's struggle for recovery. Indeed, in her review of family-involved ATOD treatment research, McCrady (1988) concluded that treatment that involved the family in carefully planned interventions that emphasized, not the family members' assumed personality pathology or codependency disease, but, rather, teaching constructive interactions with the abuser and support for his or her recovery efforts, had better outcomes in terms of the abuser's sobriety than treatment approaches that did not involve salient family members. In the context of this discussion of descriptive theories, there is a risk—for clients and practitioners—in using theories or perspectives whose claims, because they are so metaphorically or otherwise fuzzily conceptualized, are not only unvalidated, but also unable to be validated.

According to the Institute of Medicine, National Academy of Sciences (1990), psychoanalytically oriented treatment has failed to achieve successful outcomes with ATOD problems. This may be because of one or several factors. The tendency in such treatment to focus on historical developmental issues, rather than on the ATOD abuse and the life problems it is currently creating, may be one such factor. Or it may be that the underlying descriptive theory of psychoanalytic and psychodynamic approaches is wrong, or is not applicable to ATOD problems. However, recent efforts to evaluate this view suggest that modified psychoanalytic treatment has reconsidered the role of psychotherapy, moved away from orthodox procedures, supports combinations of approaches, and concludes that successful outcomes do occur (Gottdiener, 2008; Yalisove, 1989).

Various behavioral and cognitive treatment approaches, based on social learning theory, have demonstrated a good success rate in terms of outcomes for ATOD problems. This might be because of any of several factors. It may indeed be that the social learning view that ATOD abuse is a learned response that can be unlearned and substituted for by more adaptive behaviors, is correct in terms of being the most valid explanation for a person's developing the problem. The better success of behavioral and cognitive approaches may be because they tend to be highly focused on the ATOD behavior and are less likely than approaches based on other descriptive theories to get sidetracked into some fascinating but dead-end therapeutic blind alley. It could also be that behavioral and cognitive practitioners tend to be more research oriented than practitioners who espouse other descriptive perspectives, and, thus, have been more responsible about doing practice research and integrating its findings into their practice.

The emphasis on EBP urges the social work profession to further "clarify and codify its methods" (Hall, 2008, p. 394). Hall suggested that the perception of social work as a legitimate profession is linked to the ability to substantiate generalist practice with various populations to measurable procedures and outcomes. According to a study conducted by Haug and colleagues (2008) people with current licenses or certification in addictions tended to report use of EBPs. In their sample, $N = 119$, 83 percent reported using some EBPs in the past year and 75 percent reported current use. Most practitioners reported the need for further training in the use of EBPs in addiction treatment.

With respect to evidence-based treatment, the validation of ATOD theories and best practices remains an area for continued research and replication, using induction and deduction, moving from individualized data about the client and the problem situation up to theory and back down to the data of the case again. The EBPs should not be assumed to "automatically result in superior outcomes" (Kelly, 2008).

Inductive and Deductive Reasoning in Practice

Use of theory in a given case is deductive thinking: Thinking from the generalized propositions of a theory downward to the particulars of a specific case—for example, "Can the propositions of descriptive theory A about ATOD help me to understand better this client's ATOD problem?" and "Does it seem as if the interventive techniques in prescriptive theory B would be helpful to this client?"—helps practitioners deduce. Inductive thinking, however, helps push reasons upward from the particulars of the case to a generalized inference or conclusion; for example, "Given what this client has told me about her relationship with her husband, does it seem as if he will be a resource or a hindrance in her struggle for recovery?"

Neither induction nor deduction is better or worse than the other; both have advantages and disadvantages, but both are needed for what Schon (1983) has called the "reflection in action" that is characteristic of truly skilled practitioners of whatever profession. The disadvantage of deduction, used alone, is that it locks the practitioner into a set of generalized theoretical principles. The disadvantage of induction is that different conclusions, or inferences, might be drawn from the same particularized data of the case, and one cannot know which conclusion is the correct one. The point is that, despite these inherent weaknesses of the way the human mind works, this is the way our minds reason—it's not only the best we have, but also all we have. Both induction and deduction are necessary for the practitioner's thinking about all aspects of the case. The practitioner is constantly moving between them, thinking about what the data of the case mean, thinking about whether and how the generalized propositions of various theories might apply. The practitioner is using theory, but not blindly or slavishly, or at the cost of ignoring data of the case that do not fit a preferred theory or that perhaps actually contradict it. The practitioner is exercising confidence in his or her own reasoning powers.

The preceding discussion focuses on the intellectual integration of ideas. The values, attitudes, and feelings that the practitioner brings to work with ATOD clients is connected to the service-delivery process. Compassion and a sincere desire to help are not enough for effective practice—the practitioner must be able to think. The practitioner must be able to use theory as one of the tools available, not as a master.

A Pluralistic and Transtheoretical Knowledge Base for Practice

Although many of the descriptive and prescriptive theories current in the ATOD field portray themselves as the only or the best understanding and approach, in ATOD as in other arenas of the mental health field generally there does not exist one grand overarching theory that succeeds in satisfactorily explaining people's problems or that offers the one best way for the practitioner to help. Some theories score better than others on the criteria for a good theory that we offer later. The practitioner should certainly place more reliance on these. People with ATOD problems have different degrees of severity of the problem, with different causes for their problem, in different life circumstances. Different ATOD clients respond differently to various interventive approaches. The skilled ATOD practitioner needs to have in-depth knowledge of a range of theories and approaches to ATOD clients.

Transtheoretical knowledge calls for non-judgmental acceptance of "where the client is" in terms of the client's accepting, rationalizing, or denying substance abuse and other behaviors that could be medically hazardous or self-destructive (Hsu, 2004). Research on the constructs of the transtheoretical model has been conducted with various populations—smokers, adoptive parents, eaters—to examine the presence of improved behaviors, and several samples of positive results exist. However, Callaghan (2005) has suggested that closer examination in some areas may be needed. Issues regarding sample size, retention, and attrition present areas for further research. Miller and Manuel (2008) also identify the need for multidimensional, empirical evidence that incorporates clinical judgments that may differ from the statistical significance of variables used in clinical trials.

Continuing research by the government agency, SAMHSA (Substance Abuse and Mental Health Services Administration) has identified several resources. "The National Registry of Evidence-based Programs and Practices (NREPP) is an online registry of mental health and substance abuse interventions that have been reviewed and rated by independent reviewers. The purpose of the registry is to assist the public in identifying approaches to preventing and treating mental and/or substance use disorders that have been scientifically tested and can be readily disseminated to the field. The product of a comprehensive, expansion and revision process, the new NREPP is one way SAMHSA is working to improve access to information on tested interventions and speed the transfer of scientific knowledge to the field" (SAMHSA, 2008).

Prochaska and colleagues (see DiClemente & Prochaska, 1988; Prochaska & DiClemente, 1982, 1984, 1986, 1992; Prochaska & Norcross, 1994; and Prochaska, Norcross, & DiClemente, 1994) have done great service not only to the field of ATOD practice, but also to the mental health field generally, by their transtheoretical analysis of five groupings of theories. This grouping of psychotherapy theories—psychoanalytic, humanistic or existential, gestalt or experiential, cognitive, and behavioral—has assisted in identifying the processes of change the client experiences in any of these therapeutic approaches. This group of colleagues matched these client change processes with specific practitioner techniques or activities, synthesized from the various theories, that are appropriate to where a client may be in a particular stage of the change process. Table 2.1 illustrates the work of Prochaska and colleagues (1994) and provides an excellent example of the extraction and synthesis of theoretical principles and intervention strategies as related to the processes of changes. Stages and processes of change are addressed in greater detail in chapter 7.

The ATOD practitioner cannot realistically be expected to be highly expert in the techniques of the several individual therapies, in family therapy, and in group therapy. Knowing when to refer the case to a more knowledgeable colleague, or to arrange for an additional simultaneous helping approach, is a skill in itself. But the practitioner, of whatever modality, needs to be "transtheoretical" in the sense this term is used by Prochaska and colleagues, using understandings and techniques

TABLE 2.1: Summary of the Principal Theories of Psychotherapy

Theory Representative Techniques	Notable Figures		Primary Process of Change
Psychoanalytic	Sigmund Freud Carl Jung	Consciousness-raising Emotional arousal	Analysis of resistance Free association Dream interpretation
Humanistic/ Existential	Carl Rogers Rollo May	Social liberation Commitment Helping relationships	Clarification and reflection Empathy and warmth Free experiencing
Gestalt/ Experiential	Fritz Perls Arthur Janov	Self-revaluation Emotional arousal	Choosing and feedback Confrontation Focusing
Cognitive	Albert Ellis Aaron Beck	Countering Self-reevaluation	Education Identifying dysfunctional thoughts Cognitive restructuring
Behavioral	B. F. Skinner Joseph Wolpe	Environment Control Reward Countering	Assertion Relaxation training Managing reinforcements Self-control training

Source: Prochaska, J. O., Norcross, J. C., & DiClemente, C. C. (1994). *Changing for good.* New York: William Morrow.

from a variety of theories, rather than being narrowly dedicated to one theory or set of techniques.

Using this transtheoretical perspective involves being pluralistic—knowing a good deal about each of the five major groupings of psychotherapy theories and their techniques. Just knowing about a theory is not enough; the knowledge acquired must also include a critical assessment of how good each theory is, as a theory—that is, the amount of reliance the practitioner can place in its claims.

In addition to being aware of several psychotherapy theories, there is also the need to conceptualize the factors that contribute to the variety of clients the theories must address. Emerging concepts and theories encourage consideration of a macro level of knowledge and related intervention strategies. The characteristics that may be contemplated in the process of theory selection include, but are not limited to, age, gender, biology or genetics, abilities or personality, cultural dynamics, religious or spiritual connections, household composition, developmental phase, family composition and family life-cycle stage, economic resources, and trauma experiences.

Criteria for Good Theory

There is no such thing as a perfect theory: No theory in use in the ATOD field, in mental health generally, in the social sciences (or, for that matter, in the physical sciences) earns a perfect score on each of the criteria for a good theory that have been developed by scholars of theory development methodology. Overall, a theory may be assessed in terms of its balance regarding health, flexibility, and diversity. Simultaneously, a theory should come close to meeting the following criteria:

- Operationalizability–testability
- Clarity of concepts employed
- Quality of logic employed
- Reasonableness and value-acceptability of underlying assumptions
- Explanatory power of the theory
- Level of abstraction
- Scope of the theory
- Parsimony
- Heuristic potential

(Wood & Dunn, 2000)

Operationalizability–Testability

Many writers on the philosophy of science have stressed the importance of remembering that a theory should not be "regarded as a description of real unobserved underlying processes, but rather as but a convenient summarizer and predictor" (Cook & Campbell, 1979, p. 21). A theory is not a fact, not a reality; it is only the conceptual invention of a human mind. The criterion of operationalizability has to do with whether the concepts of the theory can be translated into phenomena observable by the senses (perhaps assisted by mechanical devices such as audiotape recorders, video cameras, or microscopes). The abstract concepts have then been operationalized.

This criterion is closely related to the theory's testability; if the conceptual abstractions cannot be operationalized, then whether or not they actually correspond to reality cannot be observed and thus cannot be tested. Psychoanalytic theory, for example, has been criticized for the non-operationalizability of such concepts as the id. Similarly, the family therapy concept of homeostasis in the family system has been criticized by family therapists themselves as being so abstract and unoperationalizable that one cannot be sure that the resistance the therapist is seeing is indeed homeostasis and not something else. According to one family theorist, this "has led to quirky clinical formulations and a great deal of fuzzy theorizing" (Dell, 1982, p. 2).

Clarity of Concepts

The less clearly understandable a theory's concepts are, the less operationalizable they probably are, and therefore difficult or impossible to test whether they correspond to reality. It may be that the theorist is describing such a complex concept that it is really difficult for readers to understand. Alternatively, the problem may not be the reader's inability to comprehend but rather the theorist's inability to express the concepts in clearly comprehensible language. In the mental health field generally, more writers currently tend to use metaphors to express their ideas. A metaphor cannot be operationalized or tested.

Quality of Logic and Avoidance of Logical Fallacies

A theory writer in attempting to persuade his or her audience is presenting a logical argument for the views and propositions expressed. This criterion has to do with how logical that argument is. Does one portion of the argument flow smoothly into the next, or are there leaps in logic? The reader needs also to be alert to logical fallacies in the theory. Logicians have identified a number of these, but some of the most common in mental health theories are reification, tautology, and teleology. *Reification* is treating an abstract concept as if it materially existed in the real world; this is especially pernicious when the abstraction is a metaphor for a concept, not even the concept itself. *Tautology* is circular reasoning ("why is Mary so smart?—because she has a high IQ," and "why does John drink so much—because he is an alcoholic"). *Teleology* is confusing effects with causes; this was a fallacy committed in our earlier examples concerning families of people with schizophrenia and wives of alcohol abusers.

Reasonableness and Value: Acceptability of Assumptions

If the reader does not "buy" the underlying value and other assumptions of a theory, then the theory can, and probably should be, disregarded. One example might be a writer proposing certain interventive techniques for ATOD clients; careful reading might reveal that the writer assumes such clients to be childlike people who need a stern authoritarian parent to get them into line. Theory writers, however, rarely spell out clearly the assumptions they are starting from, sometimes because they are not fully aware of these themselves. The critical reader needs to search these out, by consciously asking what the underlying assumptions might be, and by "reading between the lines" for evidence of them.

Explanatory Power

The purpose of theory is to explain or account for phenomena. The issue in this criterion is how well the theory explains the phenomenon of interest. But the apparent explanatory power of a theory can be tricky. Psychodynamic theory seemed to explain the behavior and emotional state of families of schizophrenic members, and of wives of alcohol abusers, before alternative explanations were considered. Philosopher of science Karl Popper (1965) described the illusion that a theory's great explanatory power can create. As a young man, he became interested in the theories of Marx, Freud, and Adler:

> I found that those of my friends who were admirers of Marx, Freud and Adler were impressed . . . especially by their apparent explanatory power. These theories appeared to be able to explain practically everything that happened within the fields to which they referred. The study of any of them seemed to have the effect of an intellectual conversion or revelation, opening your eyes to a new truth hidden from those not yet initiated. Once your eyes were opened you saw confirming instances everywhere: the world was full of verifications of the theory. Whatever happened always confirmed it. . . .

> It was precisely this fact—that they always fitted, that they were always confirmed—which in the eyes of their admirers constituted the strongest argument in favor of these theories. It began to dawn on me that this apparent strength was in fact their weakness. . . .

> In some of its earlier formulations . . . the predictions [of the Marxist view of history] were testable, and in fact falsified. Yet instead of accepting the refutations the followers of Marx re-interpreted both the theory and the evidence in order to make them agree. In this way they rescued the theory from refutation; but they did so at the price of adopting a device which made it irrefutable. . . .

> The two psychoanalytic theories were in a different class. They were simply non-testable, irrefutable. There was no conceivable human behavior which could contradict them. (pp. 34–37)

The practitioner–consumer of theory needs to be cautious about a theory that claims to explain everything about ATOD abuse and ATOD clients. It is possible that someone may yet develop such an all-encompassing and validated theory—but is improbable because ATOD problems are so multivariate, and ATOD clients are so varied.

Scope of the Theory

A theory can attempt to cover too much, be too broad in scope, with the result that the theorizer is forced to such high-level abstractions that it becomes difficult to relate the theory to the real world, and to operationalize and test it. Family therapy can be criticized for, in its attempt to develop a grand theory that applies to all families, constructing too-abstract and ambitious overgeneralizations (Wood & Geismar, 1989). However, if a theory is too narrow in that it applies only to rarely encountered clients or client problems, it will have limited utility for practice. Many years ago, the sociologist Robert Merton (1957) called on social scientists to develop more "theories of the middle range" of scope. Theories like this in ATOD, are emerging, for example, concerning women clients, clients of certain cultural groups, adolescents, and theories that address environmental context and self change rather than only treatment. More middle-range theories are needed by the field.

Level of Abstraction

This criterion is related to the one about scope, although the two are different. A theory that attempts too wide a scope is almost forced to too-abstract conceptualizations. But the author of a more middle-range theory may also engage in an unnecessarily high level of abstraction. The current overuse of metaphors to express concepts is part of this problem. Perhaps a theorist's need to invent a new language for his or her theory to distinguish it from other theories on the subject leads to neologisms that only confuse the consumer and render the theory not only difficult to operationalize and test, but also difficult to apply to actual cases. However, the theorist may use concepts of such a low level of abstraction that the theory fails to be sufficiently generalizable.

As with scope, a theory earns good "scores" on these criteria to the extent that it achieves a balance in abstraction and in scope that fits the practice phenomenon of interest, and permits operationalizability both for testing and for use by practitioners.

Parsimony

Writing about diagnostic assessment in family practice, William Reid (1985) recommended that assessment be centered in the data of the case:

in terms of specific identifiable behaviors, beliefs, interactions, and the like. Following the rule of parsimony, these data are organized and analyzed with a minimum of assumptions. Simple, 'obvious' explanations are favored over complex interpretations based on notions of hidden processes. (p. 84)

Furthermore, as Hepworth and colleagues (2006) defined *assessment* as "a complex working hypothesis based on the most current data available" (p. 180), they are simultaneously referring to a process that occurs among the practitioner, the client in the environment, and the setting. Aiming for simplicity and parsimony is good advice for practice and for theory development. *Parsimony* of a theory is defined by Chafetz (1978) as "the smallest number of variables and propositions necessary to explain the dependent variable" (p. 81), the phenomenon of interest such as the nature or causes of ATOD abuse, or the effectiveness of suggested interventive strategies. Many of the theories used in the mental health field lack clearly expressed and operationalizable propositions. Complexity of a theory may be its weakness rather than strength.

Heuristic Value

The heuristic value of a theory is its potential for generating fruitful leads for further theory development or research. For example, one of the major values of psychoanalytic theory has been the preponderance of research and theory generated from its early inception. Psychodynamic theory is one example of theoretical development flowing from psychoanalytic roots. Cognitive theory and social learning theory have recently emerged as the foundation to best practices demonstrated through clinical research. These theories are tied to effective practice and the potential of preventive interventions.

Summary of Criteria

Of all the criteria, the most important is that of testability. Practitioners (let alone their clients!) cannot afford to believe that it is impolite to ask the proponent of a theory what evidence of controlled testing exists to support his or her claims. Practitioners are expected to be ethically responsible, and to conduct themselves in a professionally responsible manner. Practitioners must also be intellectually responsible, for the quality of the critical analysis and judgment that they apply to their use of theory for practice. Agencies that employ practitioners need to develop a learning culture within the organization that requires the professional staff to keep up with the research literature, and facilitate more practice research.

Conclusion

Service-oriented professions like social work should select theories based on the criteria presented and on their efficacy in helping to provide quality, effective, accountable service in a manner compatible with the mission and values of the profession. The theory selection process by which service interventions can be shaped must recognize the need to understand the complexity of factors associated with recovery. This process of theory selection must take into consideration the nature of the person-in-environment interaction, recognition that differences do not mean deficiencies, the importance of variations in the development of individuals and the societal context, and the potential of consumers to learn for themselves steps and procedures for enhancing the quality of their lives.

Note

The author wishes to thank and recognize Katherine M. Wood and Patricia C. Dunn for their contributions to an earlier version of this chapter, major portions of which are included here and appear in the first edition of *Alcohol, Tobacco, and Other Drugs.*

References

American Psychiatric Association. (2000). *Diagnostic and statistical manual of mental disorders* (4th ed., text rev.). Washington, DC: Author.

Bartlett, H. M. (1970). *The common base of social work practice.* Washington, DC: National Association of Social Workers.

Bloom, M. (1990). *Introduction to the drama of social work.* Itasca, IL: F. E. Peacock.

Callaghan, R. C. (2005). A closer look at the work of Brogan, Prochaska, and Prochaska (1999). *Psychotherapy: Theory, Research, Practice, Training, 42,*(2), 244–246.

Chafetz, J. S. (1978). *A primer on the construction and testing of theories in sociology.* Itasca, IL: Peacock.

Compton, B. R., & Galaway, B. (1999). *Social work processes* (6th ed.). Pacific Grove, CA: Brooks/Cole.

Compton, B. R., Galaway, B., & Cournoyer, B. (2006). *Social work processes.* (7th ed.). Pacific Grove, CA: Brooks/Cole.

Cook, T., & Campbell, D. (1979). *Quasi-experimentation.* Boston: Houghton Mifflin.

Council for Training in Evidence-Based Behavioral Practice. (2008). Retrieved January 19, 2009, from http://www.ebbp.org/competencies.html

Council for Training in Evidence-Based Behavioral Practice. (2008). *Definitions and competencies for evidence based behavioral practice (EBBP),* p. 3. Retrieved January 19, 2009, from http://www.columbia.edu/cu/musher/Website/Website/EBP_OnlineTraining_Mod3.htm

Dell, P. F. (1982). Beyond homeostasis: Toward a concept of coherence. *Family Process, 21,* 21–41.

DiClemente, C. C., & Prochaska, J. O. (1988). Toward a comprehensive, transtheoretical model of change. In W. Miller & N. Heather (Eds.), *Treating addictive behaviors* (pp. 3–24). New York: Plenum Press.

Gibbs, L. (2003). *Evidence-based practice for the helping professions: A practical guide with integrated multimedia* (Evidence Based Practice overview, Module 1 Handout, p. 1). New York: Columbia University Press. Retrieved January 19, 2009, from http://www.ebbp.org/resources.htm/

Gottdiener, W. H. (2008). Introduction to symposium on psychoanalytic research on substance use disorders. *Psychoanalytic Psychology, 25*(3), 458–460.

Hall, R. (2008). The evolution of social work practice: implications for the generalist approach. *International Journal of Social Welfare, 17*(4), 390–395.

Haug, N., Shropshire, M., Tajima, B., Gruber, V., & Guydish, J. (2008). Adoption of evidence-based practices among substance abuse treatment providers. *Journal of Drug Education, 38*(2), 181–192.

Hepworth, D., Rooney, R., Rooney, G. D., Strom-Gottfried, K., & Larsen, J. A. (2006). *Direct social work practice: Theory and skills.* Pacific Grove, CA: Brooks/Cole.

Hester, R. K., & Miller, W. R. (Eds.). (1989). *Handbook of alcoholism treatment approaches: Effective alternatives.* New York: Pergamon Press.

Hsu, J. (2004). Substance abuse and HIV. In G. J. Treisman & A. F. Angelino (Eds.), *The psychiatry of AIDS: A guide to diagnosis and treatment* (pp. 101–122). Baltimore: Johns Hopkins University Press.

Institute of Medicine, National Academy of Sciences. (1990). *Broadening the base of treatment for alcohol problems.* Washington, DC: National Academy Press.

Jackson, J. K. (1954). The adjustment of the family to the crisis of alcoholism. *Quarterly Journal of Studies on Alcoholism, 15,* 562–586. (Available as a reprint from Center of Alcohol Studies, Rutgers University, P.O. Box 969, Piscataway NJ 08855.)

Johnson, L. C. (1995). *Social work practice: A generalist approach* (5th ed.). Needham Heights, MA: Allyn & Bacon.

Keller, M. (1972). The oddities of alcoholics. *Quarterly Journal of Studies on Alcohol, 33,* 1147–1148.

Kelly, J. F. (2008). Accounting for practice-based evidence in evidence-based practice. *Brown University Digest of Addiction Theory and Application, 27*(10), 8.

Kemp, S, Whittaker, J., & Tracy, E. (1997). *Person-environment practice: The social ecology of interpersonal helping.* New York: Aldine De Gruyter.

McCrady, B. S. (1988). *Executive summary: Criteria and issues to consider when deciding to intervene at the marital/family level, the individual level, or both.* Washington, DC: Institute of Medicine.

Merton, R. K. (1957). *Social theory and social structure* (2nd ed.). New York: Glencoe.

Meyer, C. (1976). *Social work practice.* New York: Free Press.

Meyer, C. (1983, Winter–Spring). *CUSSW Student Day, November 8, 1982. Alumni Newsletter,* p. 4.

Miller, W. R., & Manuel, J. K. (2008). How large must a treatment effect be before it matters to practitioners? An estimation method and demonstration. *Drug and Alcohol Review, 27*, 524–528.

National Association of Social Workers. (2000). *Code of ethics.* Washington, DC: Author.

Nelson, C., & McPherson, D. (2004). Contextual fluidity: An emerging practice model for helping. *Rural Social Work, 9*, 199–208.

Pardeck, J. T. (1996). *Social work practice: An ecological approach.* Westport, CT: Greenwood Press.

Perlman, H. (1957). *Social casework: A problem-solving process.* Chicago: University of Chicago.

Piaget, J. (1963). *The origin of intelligence in children.* New York: W. W. Norton.

Piaget, J., & Inhelder, B. (1958). *The growth of logical thinking from childhood to adolescence.* New York: Basic Books.

Popper, K. R. (1965). *Conjectures and refutations: The growth of scientific knowledge.* New York: Harper & Row.

Prochaska, J. O., & DiClemente, C. C. (1982). Transtheoretical therapy: Toward a more integrative model of change. *Psychotherapy, 20*, 161–173.

Prochaska, J. O., & DiClemente, C. C. (1984). *The transtheoretical approach: Crossing traditional boundaries of therapy.* Melbourne, FL: Krieger.

Prochaska, J. O., & DiClemente, C. C. (1986). Toward a comprehensive model of change. In R. Miller & N. Heather (Eds.), *Treating addictive behaviors: Processes of change* (pp. 3–27). New York: Plenum Press.

Prochaska, J. O., & DiClemente, C. C. (1992). The trans-theoretical approach. In J. C. Norcross & M. R. Goldfried (Eds.), *Handbook of psychotherapy integration* (pp. 147–171). New York: Basic Books.

Prochaska, J. O., & Norcross, J. C. (1994). *Systems of psychotherapy: A transtheoretical analysis* (3rd ed.). Pacific Grove, CA: Brooks/Cole.

Prochaska, J. O., Norcross, J. C., & DiClemente, C. C. (1994). *Changing for good: The revolutionary program that explains the six stages of change and teaches you how to free yourself from bad habits.* New York: William Morrow.

Reid, W. J. (1985). *Family problem solving.* New York: Columbia University Press.

Rogers, R. L., & McMillin, C. S. (1988). *Don't help: A guide to working with the alcoholic.* Seattle: Madrona.

Schon, D. A. (1983). *The reflective practitioner: How professionals think in action.* New York: Basic Books.

Substance Abuse and Mental Health Services Administration. (2008). *National registry of evidence-based programs and practices.* Retrieved January 19, 2009, from http://nrepp.samhsa.gov

Taft, C. T., Kaloupek, D. G., Schumm, J. A., Marshall, A. D., Panuzio, J., King, D. W., & Keane, T. M. (2007). Posttraumatic stress disorder symptoms, physiological reactivity, alcohol problems, and aggression among military veterans. *Journal of Abnormal Psychology, 116*, 498–507.

Wood, K. M., & Dunn, P. C. (2000). Criteria for selecting theories and models for ATOD practice. In A. Abbott (Ed.), *Alcohol, tobacco, and other drugs: Challenging myths, assessing theories, individualizing interventions* (pp. 20–43). Washington, DC: NASW Press.

Wood, K. M., & Geismar, L. L. (1989). *Families at risk: Treating the multiproblem family.* New York: Human Sciences Press.

Yalisove, D. L. (1989). Psychoanalytic approaches to alcoholism and addiction: Treatment and research. *Psychology of Addictive Behaviors, 3*(3), 107–113.

3

Values, Ethics, and Ethical Dilemmas in ATOD Practice

Ann A. Abbott

Overview

Many social workers frequently encounter clients whose presenting problems concern substance abuse (Abbott, 2002). Although some workers have pursued specialized training for providing services directed at substance use disorders, others more likely have focused on other areas of practice, taking only one or no courses designed to address problems related to alcohol, tobacco, and other drugs (ATOD). In many cases, social workers just entering the field are inadequately prepared to address problems related to substance use disorders (Hall, Amodeo, Shaffer, & Vander Bilt, as cited in Bina et al., 2008).

The field of substance abuse poses unique challenges to social workers (Abbott, 2003b), including the constant need to reaffirm the social work value base, the importance of shaping service delivery to incorporate social work values, and the task of recruiting and educating others in the critical importance of ethical decision making (Burke & Clapp, 1997). Social workers have a clearly defined code of ethics (NASW, 2008) to guide professional conduct. The code emphasizes such critical concerns as client self-determination, confidentiality, dual relationships, and worker competence. Social workers have been taught to incorporate ethical decision making into all areas of their professional practice. In spite of this targeted focus, even the most ethically responsible workers have experienced or witnessed lapses in ethical practice.

▼
▼
▼

In the field of substance abuse, the dangers of ethical misconduct or misman-agement appear to be even more challenging. Ethical vulnerability increases with the heterogeneous pool of workers, many of whom are not privy to a shared value system, do not belong to a professional organization, and are not subject to any spe-cific code of ethics. Like social workers, most certified addiction counselors partici-pate in training pertaining to ethics; unlike social workers, they are certified but not licensed, and therefore not subject to the same sanctions stemming from ethical misconduct. Additional challenges surface from quick turnover in the workforce, and the fact that a number of workers are former service recipients turned provid-ers. As in other areas of health care, substance abuse treatment has experienced the impact of managed care in which nonprofessionals and business people are play-ing an increasing role in determining policy and procedures affecting the scope of practice, frequently focusing more on the bottom financial line than the outcome of an ethical audit.

The responsibility for ethical practice not only rests with the direct practitio-ner, but also with those workers whose major focus includes program planning, policy development, and administration. In many instances, the direct practitioner must not only monitor his or her own professional practice, but also advocate for the development and implementation of an overall agency ethical framework and push the administrative forces to act in an ethically responsible fashion. Reamer (2001a) strongly suggests that all practicing social work practitioners, whether they are involved in direct practice or administration, should engage in ongoing exami-nation of their own practice and their agency's "ethics-related practices, policies and procedures" (p. 3; see also Levy, 1982).

This chapter will provide a format for identifying social work values and addressing ethical challenges, emphasizing those challenges surrounding ATOD-use issues. Special attention will be given to the dilemmas emerging around patient–treatment matching, confidentiality, drug testing in the workplace, nee-dle-exchange programs, harm reduction, moderation versus abstinence, and the ethics of advertising, especially in relation to alcohol and tobacco products and prescription drugs. Additional attention will be devoted to challenges surrounding restriction of care, including managed care and cost containment. Unique ethical challenges arise from the myriad of dual relationships inherent in the substance abuse field, for example, recovering workers attending Alcoholics Anonymous (AA) meetings with clients or with their supervisors, or the changing role of some former clients to service providers within the very programs in which they recently received treatment.

Understanding the Social Work Value Base and Ethical Framework

Since its inception, social work has been concerned with values and ethics as keys to defining overall professional mission and behavior (Reamer, 1995). The intent of values is to define what is preferable or desirable; professional values tend to reflect how a profession perceives itself and envisions the scope of its activities. Ethics are concerned with what is right or correct, grow out of the value base, and aim to delineate the difference between right and wrong; ethics attempt to inform the course of activity. Neither values nor ethics guarantee moral behavior; however, ethics do set the stage for professional reprimand (Abbott, 1988, 2008). According to Reamer (2006a), codes of ethics are designed to address "problems of moral hazard," "issues of professional courtesy," and "issues that concern professionals' duty to serve the public interest" (p. 1). Banks (1995) equated "ethics" with rules of conduct delineating right or wrong, good or bad. She uses "values" to refer to principles, beliefs, or attitudes, all of which define the professional context of social work practice.

Throughout history, social work has focused on human rights and equity, social justice, social responsibility, and reform (Abbott, 1988; Reamer, 1990, 2006a, 2006b). Early on, greater emphasis was placed on client morality; over time that focus shifted to worker behavior, commitment, and responsibility. The values that have emerged as paramount are "dignity, uniqueness, and worth of the person, self-determination, autonomy, respect, justice, equality, and individuation" (Reamer, 2006b, p. 6). More recently, the focus has been broadened to include social responsibility and social action, including a return to the profession's earlier roots based on social change (Abbott, 1992).

The organized examination of values and ethics did not fully surface until the development of the first code of ethics by the NASW in 1960, and was fueled by the definitive work by Levy (1976), which focused on ethical principles and the underlying values from which they emerged. Much of this interest was spurred by an increase in patients' or clients' rights, malpractice and risk management, and overall professional accountability, all of which coincide with the maturation of the social work profession (Dolgoff, Loewenberg, & Harrington, 2009).

Although this chapter focuses primarily on the NASW *Code of Ethics* (NASW, 2008) and social work practice in the United States, it is important to recognize that the commitment to ethical practice is far-reaching. Despite the fact that specific countries may differ on some issues, the major international social work organizations have revised and endorsed a global set of ethical principles based on national statements and codes of ethics around the world (International Federation of Social Workers & the International Association of Schools of Social Work, 2004). This endorsement reflects major approval by the many international members of the two organizations.

A number of contemporary authors summarize the values inherent in social work. Reamer (2006b) provides a composite listing gleaned from over three dozen sources:

> individual worth and dignity, respect of persons, valuing individuals' capacity for change, client self-determination, providing individuals with opportunity to realize their potential, seeking to meet individuals' common human needs, seeking to provide individuals with adequate resources and services to meet their basic needs, client empowerment, equal opportunity, nondiscrimination, respect for diversity, commitment to social change and social justice, confidentiality and privacy, and willingness to transmit professional knowledge and skills to others. (p. 22)

Levy (1973, 1976) summarized values as falling into three primary categories: conceptions of people, conceptions of outcomes of work with people, and preferred ways of dealing or intervening with people. Later on, Levy (1984) reframed his classification of values based on the source of the values: societal, organizational or institutional, professional, and actual practice values. Loewenberg and Dolgoff (1996) expanded Levy's classification to include personal values, societal values, and professional values. They recognize that prior to active ethical decision making, the worker must be aware of the influence and interrelatedness of each of the three value sources.

More important than the listing of values is the goal that all social workers recognize and buy into a common professional value base. Thus, values (and ethical decision making) have been considered core educational content for accredited social work curriculums (Council on Social Work Education [CSWE] Commission on Accreditation, 1994); however, a noted lack in sufficient training (Black, Hartley, Whelley, & Kirk-Sharp, 1989; Reamer, 1997, 2001a) has raised cause for concern and prompted increased emphasis on required content on ethics in accredited social work curriculums (CSWE Commission on Accreditation, 2008) and as a continuing education requirement for social work licensure in many states. At present 31 state licensing boards require continuing education in ethics as a condition for licensure (personal communication with Donna DeAngelis, executive director, American Social Work Boards [ASWB], Culpeper, VA, January 30, 2009).

The most recent Educational Policy and Accreditation Standards (EPAS), developed and approved by the CSWE require that curriculums of social work educational programs seeking accreditation demonstrate educational content and outcome competencies illustrating that graduates identify as professional social workers and conduct themselves accordingly (CSWE Commission on Accreditation, 2008, Educational Policy 2.1.1), understand social work ethical principles, and apply them throughout their professional practice (Educational Policy 2.1.2). What this means is social work graduates should be able to fully understand and commit to the values and ethical principles detailed in the NASW *Code of Ethics* (NASW, 2008). This is defined more specifically in the EPAS as:

> social workers . . . recognize and manage personal values in a way that allows professional values to guide practice; make ethical decisions by applying standards of the National Association of Social Workers Code of Ethics and, as applicable, of the International Federation of Social Workers/International Association of Schools of Social Work Ethics in Social Work, Statement of Principles; tolerate ambiguity in resolving ethical conflicts; and apply strategies of ethical reasoning to arrive at principled decisions. (CSWE Commission on Accreditation, 2008, p. 4.)

As previously noted, ethics and ethical principles flow from the underlying value base of the profession. Values refer to what is preferred; ethics grow out of values that have been operationalized into what is right or wrong. In professions, the translation of underlying values to ethics is typically spelled out in the codes of ethics, or, less frequently, in standards of practice. For example, an underlying value of social work is respect for individuals' rights. This basic value is translated into ethical principles pertaining to confidentiality as delineated in the most recent NASW *Code of Ethics* (2008). Several specific examples from section 1.07 Privacy and Confidentiality include:

> 1.07 (a) Social workers should respect clients' right to privacy. Social workers should not solicit private information from clients unless it is essential to providing services or conducting social work evaluation or research. Once private information is shared, standards of confidentiality apply. (NASW, 2008, p. 10)

> 1.07 (h) Social workers should not disclose confidential information to third-party payers unless clients have authorized such disclosure. (NASW, 2008, p. 11)

Ethical Guidelines for Dealing with Ethical Dilemmas

In many cases, behavior is clearly wrong or right, clearly ethical or unethical. For example, the NASW *Code of Ethics* explicitly forbids sexual contact between worker and client. Because of its clear-cut nature, no ethical conflict should arise. In many other situations, however, the division between right and wrong is less evident. In fact, frequently core ethical values are in competition or conflict, the result being an "ethical dilemma" demanding a choice between "two equally unwelcome alternatives." Typically the outcome represents a "no-win" situation. The challenge for the social worker is to select the most beneficial or least offensive or unwelcome alternative. As Banks (1995) so aptly noted, in dealing with ethical dilemmas "there are not welcome outcomes, only less unwelcome ones" (p. 23). It is important to note that solutions to ethical dilemmas may vary from one situation to another. As a result, the worker must be prepared to evaluate each situation on its own unique merits.

Addressing ethical dilemmas becomes a lifelong challenge for any professional. One must commit to ethical practice and the accompanying actions in carrying out that commitment. Corey, Corey, and Callanan (2007) expressed that responsibility succinctly to professionals:

> The various . . . professions have developed codes of ethics that are binding on their members. As a professional, you are expected to know the ethical code of your specialty and be aware of the consequences of practicing in ways that are not sanctioned by your professional organization. In addition, responsible practice requires that you use informed, sound, and responsible judgment. It is essential that you demonstrate a willingness to consult with colleagues, to keep yourself up to date through reading and continuing education, and to continually attend to your behavior. (p. 3)

Corey and colleagues (2007) pointed out that a limited guiding framework exists in the form of laws and professional codes, both of which provide guidelines, yet neither of which provide specific answers. The two—law and professional codes—serve as "mandatory" standards. Corey and colleagues remind us that, in addition, as professionals, we also have "aspirational" standards that go well beyond the minimum, mandatory level. A major challenge surrounds the fact that both laws and codes of ethics cannot be applied in a rote manner, nor do they provide specific answers for the majority of situations. Final interpretation and action rests with the individual worker and depends very much on his or her personal experience, biases, and exposure to the ethical decision-making process.

Reamer (2006b) traced the ever-increasing development of new challenges inherent in social work practice and the accompanying increased emphasis on ethically responsible behavior. The history delineating the rise in emphasis on ethical behavior within social work parallels that of other diverse professions such as journalism, accounting, and the broad spectrum of health care professions. The result is the emergence of practical ethics with its applied and professional foci. In terms of the social work profession, all one has to do is peruse the professional literature to realize the exponential growth in focus on ethics since the 1970s and 1980s.

The increase in NASW standards for practice, of which there are 12 separate categories including a set for social work clients with substance use disorders (NASW, 2005), and a set of indicators for cultural competence in social work practice, delineate expected professional behaviors; the most recent NASW *Code of Ethics* (2008) clearly illustrates increased professional expectations and guidance in determining ethically responsible behavior.

Although the code, standards, and indicators indicate expectations for professional behavior and provide broad parameters for action, the final course of action in dealing with ethical dilemmas rests with the worker and his or her ability to act in an ethically responsible fashion.

Reamer (2006a) reinforced both the purpose of the NASW *Code of Ethics* and the fact that final "interpretation and action" rest with the worker:

> *The Code identifies core values on which social work's mission is based . . .* [It] *summarizes broad ethical principles that reflect the profession's core values and establishes a set of ethical standards that should be used to guide social work practice . . .* [and it] *is designed to help social workers identify relevant considerations when professional obligations conflict or ethical uncertainties arise.* (p. 9)

The NASW *Code of Ethics* (2008) is a tool to help workers deal with difficult ethical decisions; however, it does not provide the answer—The worker is responsible for arriving at that. In preparation for ethical practice, social workers should be familiar with models of ethical decision making. Several examples include those espoused by Dolgoff and colleagues (2009) and Reamer (2006b). Reamer (2006b) insisted that there is no precise format for solving ethical dilemmas; rather, there are general steps that, if followed, can facilitate successful resolution. He suggested the following format:

I. Identify the ethical issues, including the social work values and duties that conflict.

II. Identify the individuals, groups, and organizations who are likely to be affected by the ethical decision.

III. Tentatively identify all possible courses of action and the participants involved in each, along with the possible benefits and risks for each.

IV. Thoroughly examine the reasons in favor of and opposed to each possible course of action considering relevant codes of ethics and legal principles; ethical theories, principles, and guidelines; . . . social work practice theory and principles; personal values, . . . particularly those that conflict with one's own.

V. Consult with colleagues and appropriate experts . . . (such as agency staff; supervisors, administrators; attorneys; and ethics scholars).

VI. Make the decision and document the decision-making process.

VII. Monitor, evaluate, and document the decision. (pp. 74–86)

Dolgoff and colleagues (2009) advocate a general decision-making model, filtered by an ethical assessment screen, an ethical rules screen, and an ethical principles screen (pp. 59–68). Their "general decision-making model" includes the following elements:

Step 1. Identify the problem and the persons, institutions, clients, professionals, support systems, victims, and others that are involved in this problem.

Step 2. Determine who should be involved in the decision making.

Step 3. Identify the relevant values held by those identified in step 1, including the client and worker.

Step 4. Identify the goals and objectives whose attainment you believe may resolve (or reduce) the problem.

Step 5. Identify alternate intervention strategies and targets, and assess the effectiveness and efficiency of each alternative in terms of the identified goals.

Step 6. Select and implement the most appropriate strategy.

Step 7. Monitor the implementation, paying particular attention to unanticipated consequences; evaluate the results and identify additional problems, opportunities, and options. (p. 60)

Their general decision-making model applies to many different situations. To enhance its usefulness in helping with ethical challenges of practice, Dolgoff and colleagues (2009) highlight the importance of filtering decisions through an ethical assessment screen, followed by an ethical rules screen. The ethical assessment screen introduces the following dimensions:

1. Identify the relevant professional values and ethics, your own relevant values, and any societal values relevant to the ethical decision to be made in relation to this ethical dilemma.
2. What can you do to minimize conflicts between personal, societal, and professional values?
3. Identify alternative ethical options that you may take.
4. Which of the alternative ethical actions will minimize conflicts between your client's, others', and society's rights and protect to the greatest extent your client's and others' rights and welfare, and society's rights and interests?
5. Which alternative action will be most efficient, effective, and ethical, as well as result in your doing the "least harm" possible?
6. Have you considered and weighed both short- and long-term ethical consequences?
7. Final check: Is the planned action impartial, generalizable, and justifiable? (p. 61)

The ethical rules screen reminds the worker to examine the code of ethics for guidance and reminds the worker that ethical rules take precedence over personal preferences. In cases in which one or more items apply, the worker is reminded to follow the code; in cases in which competing or conflicting items are identified, or ethical guidance is lacking, Dolgoff and colleagues (2009) refer the worker to the ethical principles screen for a hierarchical ranking that proceeds as follows:

Ethical Principle 1. Principle of the protection of life

Ethical Principle 2. Principle of equality and inequality

Ethical Principle 3. Principle of autonomy and freedom

Ethical Principle 4. Principle of least harm

Ethical Principle 5. Principle of quality of life

Ethical Principle 6. Principle of privacy and confidentiality

Ethical Principle 7. Principle of truthfulness and full disclosure. (p. 66)

In a more practical vein, Blanchard and Peale (1988) suggested three key questions for guiding action: (1) Is it legal? (The term "legal" is loosely defined to go beyond the law to include the code of ethics and agency policy.); (2) Is it balanced (meaning, Is the decision fair as opposed to lopsided or weighing heavily in favor of one side?). They noted that lopsided situations typically end up in lose–lose outcomes, and more balanced decisions tend to produce more satisfying or ethically responsible results; (3) How will it make me (the worker) feel (focusing on the full range of standards including organizational, professional, and personal)?

Wells (1986) also recommended a series of questions to guide practice. In addition to those questions advanced by Blanchard and Peale (1988), Wells included a question about the client's point of view and preferred outcome.

Hill, Glaser, and Harden (1995) advanced a feminist model for ethical decision making. True to feminist principles, they ask us to pay closer attention to the importance of one's personal experiences, involvement, and reactions. They recognize that typically outcomes or decisions are influenced by the participants' views and priorities. For example, a person's experiences with oppression, discrimination, and control are bound to control his or her opinions and support of policies that serve to trigger or support similar feelings. In delineating a format for ethical decision making, they add a key component following the choosing of a solution, which serves to force the decision maker to evaluate how his or her values and personal biases might be influencing the process. Coupled with this review is the question of how "universalizable" the decision might be (Haas & Malouf, 1989). Is it equitable and does it apply to the wide range of situations?

Congress (1999) provided an easy-to-remember acronym, ETHIC, to help social workers and other helping professionals make quick, efficient ethically based decisions. Her approach provides guidelines that help avert capricious or impulsive decisions.

The "E" instructs the worker to "Examine relevant personal, societal, agency, client and professional values" (Congress, 1999, p. 31). It reminds the worker that his or her values are not paramount; rather, other values including those of the client, the agency, society, and the profession contribute to the context of the situation and the solution.

The "T" reminds the worker to "Think about what ethical standard of the NASW *Code of Ethics* applies to the situation, as well as about relevant laws and case decisions" (Congress, 1999, p. 31). The NASW *Code of Ethics* consists of more than 150 standards contained under six general categories: responsibilities to clients, to colleagues, in practice settings, as professionals, to the profession as a whole, and to the broader society. The worker is instructed to determine the categories most relevant to the situation, for example, responsibilities to clients, and seek guidance under that category. The worker is then expected to review relevant laws and related case decisions. Frequently a worker has greater knowledge of laws and case decisions related to his or her primary area of practice. For example, someone working in the field of ATOD should quickly become familiar with laws pertaining to such areas as substance possession, driving while under the influence, age at which minors can seek treatment, confidentiality pertaining to drug testing, and related case decisions.

The "H" asks the worker to "Hypothesize about the possible consequences of different decisions" (Congress, 1999, p. 32). If action A is taken, what are the potential consequences? If action B is taken, what other consequences are likely?

The "I" requests that the worker "Identify who will benefit and who will be harmed in view of social work's commitment to the most vulnerable" (Congress, 1999, p. 32). The NASW *Code of Ethics* recognizes the profession's commitment to the most vulnerable; workers are expected to act in ways that nurture strengths and opportunities to all individuals, especially those who are oppressed or disadvantaged. This step reminds workers to take this professional commitment very seriously in their deliberations.

The "C" asks the worker to "Consult with supervisor and colleagues about the most ethical choice" (Congress, 1999, p. 33). Talking to others and seeking guidance and alternative wisdom is viewed as a strength. Typically the supervisor is the first person approached; however, colleagues with strong commitment to ethical practice as advanced by the NASW *Code of Ethics* are another resource for informal consultation. Frequently ethical dilemmas can become content for case meetings or discussion, especially if the situation allows time for careful deliberation.

As social workers become more pressed for time and both agencies and workers become more aware of the importance of ethical practice, the need for a straightforward, easy-to-remember format for ethical decision making increases. Strom-Gottfried (2007), in *Straight Talk about Professional Ethics*, provides the answer, using "who?" "what?" "when?" "where?" "why?" and "how?" as guidelines. The questions are fleshed out in the following way:

Who will be helpful?

What are my choices?

When have I faced a similar dilemma?

Where do ethical and clinical guidelines lead me?

Why am I selecting a particular course of action?

How should I enact my decision?

(p. 27)

▼
▼
▼

The questions are not necessarily addressed in the stated order. They are presented in the above fashion to facilitate remembering; however, they may be addressed in different order, based on the circumstances. They all should be considered, but may be addressed in different order with different weightings.

How does Strom-Gottfried (2007) conceive of the action related to a specific question?

The "who" asks for the identification of those professionals or colleagues who will be most helpful in unraveling the key components of the dilemma, in helping to provide insight, to generate possible solutions, and to identify possible outcomes of various actions.

The "what" refers to getting all viable choices on the table, determining their feasibility, and assessing what each will mean to the individuals involved. This may be done in consultation with others such as those identified under "who" and also may be generated by existing literature and case decisions.

The "when" asks the worker to examine previous experience with similar situations. Although Strom-Gottfried (2007) did not specify consultation with others in relation to this specific question, it would seem logical that the worker may also seek consultation with other professionals about their experiences with similar situations.

The "where" asks the worker to identify where his or her knowledge of ethical and clinical guidelines leads him or her in terms of making a decision about the identified dilemma. The worker is expected to draw on a number of key resources: values, standards, principles of practice, knowledge of the social work profession and underlying value base and philosophy, knowledge of human behavior, knowledge of laws, regulations and policies, evidence-based practice, and personal experience.

The "why" asks the worker to check on his or her own motivations and preferences for selecting a particular action. Is his or her thinking clear? Does it reflect personal needs, biases, or faulty judgment? Does it truly reflect the values and philosophy espoused by the social work profession?

The "how" seeks to understand the fashion by which the worker plans to carry out the identified decision. This question is designed to address a broad spectrum of professional skills: cultural competence, consideration of the unique needs and strengths of the client, the goals and supports of the agency, the underlying values and philosophy of the profession, and the skills of the worker.

The above guidelines for ethical practice are important; however, they are only useful to the ATOD practitioner if they can be applied to ethical dilemmas and challenges evolving in that area of practice.

Ethical Challenges in ATOD Practice

Ethical dilemmas emerging from ATOD service delivery and policy development can be divided into several categories ranging from public and social policy to prevention and treatment efforts. Major policy issues confronting social workers today include, but are not limited to, the following: the legal status of drugs; issues surrounding drug testing by employers; the acceptance of needle-exchange programs as a harm-reduction effort to reduce the spread of HIV; the acceptance of controlled substance use or moderation management; the legal treatment or prosecution of pregnant drug users; and the control of advertising of legal drugs, including alcohol, tobacco, and prescription drugs. Additional issues surround the ethical status of tobacco-free environments.

The area of drug testing becomes an individual client treatment issue when one considers how to safeguard or control confidential testing information. Noncompliance of HIV-infected needle users in needle-exchange programs raises ethical issues incorporating the rights of sexually active injection drug users versus others who are at risk. Similar concerns surround the risks posed by pregnant drug users.

Given their very nature, ethical dilemmas do not harbor a correct answer. Rather, their challenges are multifaceted with a range of less than ideal options or alternatives. The challenge for the social worker is the evaluation and selection of choices that are least offensive and most beneficial overall. Throughout ethical decision making runs the thread of harm reduction, the intent of which hinges on selecting the alternative that is the least harmful to the greatest number of individuals (Inciardi & Harrison, 2000; Marlatt, 1998). The question that is paramount concerns what choices can serve to minimize harm without infringing on the legal rights of individuals or inflicting additional harm.

Drug Legalization

An ongoing debate surrounds the question of whether drugs and drug use should be legalized or decriminalized (Goldberg, 2008). For social work professionals the overall driving force behind the debate is very much tied in with the perspective of harm reduction. The overarching question concerns what action will serve to reduce drug abuse and its negative impact on human well-being. True to definition, an ethical dilemma, in this case, drug legalization, offers no answer that appears to be clearly the best or clearly the worst alternative. The ultimate choice rests on the interpretation and decision making of the individuals involved.

Many individuals argue that money spent on reducing drug availability and drug use would be more effectively spent on prevention and treatment-related programs. Others believe that money spent on interdiction and drug control is creating a positive impact and they, in turn, advocate for increased spending in this area. Some individuals believe that the criminalization of drug use and strong attempts to legally control drugs have driven prices up and drug quality down, and have significantly contributed to violence and crime in the enterprising drug underground. A turn away from the criminalization would free up a tremendous amount of money for treatment, education, and prevention. Goldberg (1998) contended that:

> people who favor legalizing drugs feel that legalization would give the government more control over the purity and potency of drugs and that it would allow the international drug trade to be regulated more effectively. Legalization, they argue, would also take the emphasis off of law enforcement policies and allow more effort to be put toward education, prevention, and treatment. Decriminalization advocates assert that most of the negative implications of drug prohibition would disappear. (p. 3)

Proponents of drug decriminalization argue "that strict enforcement of current drugs laws … drives people to violence and crime and that drug laws have a racist element associated with them. People arrested for drug offenses overburden the court system, thus rendering it ineffective" (Goldberg, 2008, p. 3). Opponents, however, contend that legalization and decriminalization of drugs is not the solution. They believe that such changes would fuel drug use. At present they recognize that the criminal justice system is overflowing with people who have violated drug laws, or who have been involved in other offenses directly stemming from drug activity, and still there is an abundance of drugs available and high rates of use. Reduced restrictions would only add to an already desperate situation.

Nadelmann and Wenner (1994) and Gorman (2006) strongly argued in favor of policies regarding the legalization of drugs. The suggestions flow from a strong commitment to harm reduction. For example, they believe that small amounts of marijuana should be available by prescription for medical purposes, and individuals using heroin should be switched to methadone. In a similar vein, they believe that needle-exchange programs serve as an excellent vehicle for harm reduction, especially as related to the spread of HIV. They contend that all of the preceding suggestions would reduce harm, including crime and the spread of HIV. By legalizing drugs, millions of dollars would be moved from the black market into the taxable economy. It also would free up significant amounts of money currently spent on law enforcement activities. They counter the argument that legalizing drugs would contribute to an increase in drug use with the argument that good prevention and education should serve to counter the effects of greater drug availability. Proponents of legalization argue that most polls show that people would not try drugs even if they were legal. Gorman, a retired law enforcement officer, makes a stronger case. He believes that the edicts of the War on Drugs have produced destructive, restrictive, and discriminatory laws that have converted law enforcement officers and drug users into antagonists in an uncontrollable violent war. He believes that the war itself is more detrimental than the effects of drug or alcohol abuse.

Inciardi and Saum (1996), however, provide strong arguments in opposition to drug legalization. They predict legalization would contribute to an increase in both drug use and in the number of users, coupled with an increase in crime and accompanying violence.

Kleber and Califano (1995) strongly supported the status quo—that most drugs remain illegal. They view legislation as seriously affecting the well-being of children, contributing to increased drug use in the workplace, adding significant cost to our already overburdened health care system, and impairing the ability of many individuals to develop skills and talents necessary for producing meaningful lives. With current legislation, drugs are not available to all; with legalization they would become available to all. They could become available everywhere. Kleber and Califano contend that legalization of drugs would not save money; legalization of alcohol certainly did not reduce the cost of law enforcement or health care or social services necessary to combat or minimize its impact. Legalization of drugs may increase the incidence of HIV/AIDS and other health-related challenges. In terms of decreasing violence and crime, Kleber and Califano remind us that much violence is driven by individuals under the influence of alcohol and other drugs.

More recently, King (2009) advocated a middle position, suggesting decriminalization or legalization of some drugs, which would minimize incarceration of nonviolent individuals, thus leaving more resources for taking action against those individuals who are identified as being more violent:

> According to a report on Philadelphia's prison system conducted by Temple University researchers and released in 2006, drug offenses accounted for a quarter of all city detainees awaiting trial, 38 percent of those held on probation or parole violations, and 37 percent of those serving sentences . . . people held on drug charges made up the largest group of offenders in the city prison population "by far." (p. A11)

All three points of view are based on speculation and clearly illustrate the diverse and justifiable solutions that can grow out of controversial situations or issues creating a dilemma. The extremes are based on the authors' analyses of the pros and cons of aspects of drug legalization and their views of resulting harm reduction. They recognize a serious problem and struggle with finding the best or least detrimental solution.

Applying Decision-Making Strategies to the Legality of Drugs and Drug Use

Using the format for general decision making, we can:

[**Step 1**] *Identify the problem* (increased drug use and the resulting harm, availability of drugs, individual drug problems, current legislation, strength of the black market economy) *and the persons, institutions, clients, professionals, support systems, victims, and others that are involved in the problem* (individual drug users, potential users, their families and friends, drug dealers and black market profiteers, politicians, supporters of interdiction, criminal justice system, treatment providers, current government policy regarding distribution of available tax dollars for treatment, prevention, and law enforcement);

[**Step 2**] *Determine who should be involved in the decision making* (to make major changes happen, a broad base must be involved in decision making, such as a national, or state vote. Policymakers need to formulate the arguments in support of the various options and solicit support from all constituencies involved [politicians, service providers, clients, their families, educators, medical specialists, law enforcement officials, researchers]);

[**Step 3**] *Identify the relevant values held by those identified in step 1, including the client and the worker* (those supporting legalization of drugs, antilegalization proponents, harm-reduction advocates, opponents to harm-reduction philosophy, those who believe that criminalization and corresponding incarceration are the only effective means of drug control, those who believe that money should be steered from the criminal justice system and directed to education, prevention, and treatment);

[**Step 4**] *Identify the goals and objectives whose attainment you believe may resolve (or reduce) the problem* (reduce the availability of drugs, reduce interest in using drugs, and reduce criminal activities related to drugs and drug distribution; standardize drug quality);

[**Step 5**] *Identify alternate intervention strategies and targets* (legalization of drugs, stepping up or decreasing efforts at control and interdiction [Goldberg, 1998], modification of prevention and treatment), *and assess the effectiveness and efficacy of each alternative in terms of identified goals* (we already know that the criminalization and fear of legal implications has not stopped the use of drugs, we know that education can lead to the reduction of use, e.g., stopping smoking campaign, we know that interdiction efforts have not interrupted or significantly reduced the availability of drugs, we do not know what legalization of drugs will do [one can only speculate that it would lead to greater quality control and a shifting of money from the black market to the main stream]);

[**Step 6**] *Select and implement the most appropriate strategy* (selecting the best alternative to advance and then educating the politicians and the public about its relevance. If one were to select legalization of drugs as the most appropriate strategy for harm reduction, one course of action would be followed; if increased law enforcement would be identified as the best alternative, another course would take priority. Once the course of action is selected, proceed with developing an implementation plan and carrying it out);

[**Step 7**] *Monitor the implementation, playing particular attention to unanticipated consequences* (as the plan is carried out, monitor the outcomes [both planned and unexpected] as well as the actual process itself); evaluate the results and identify additional problems, opportunities, and options (although ongoing assessment is essential in all planned change efforts, specific evaluation of end results is a given. Both serve to assess the quality of solutions and the relevance of goals and objectives. In this case, if legalization of drugs were selected as the strategy that would contribute the most to harm reduction, the impact of legalization efforts would be evaluated in the ongoing assessment of such outcomes as reduction in drug use, reduction of crime related to drug activity, and reduction of suffering among family members). (Dolgoff et al., 2009)

As Dolgoff and colleagues (2009) highlight, it is important to filter the decision-making process through an ethical assessment screen. Their first suggestion for the decision maker is to identify the relevant professional values and ethics, your own relevant values, and any societal values relevant to the ethical decision to be made in relation to this ethical dilemma. In this case, the worker might identify that he or she has strong personal feelings based on the negative drug history of a sibling or spouse as well as ongoing exposure to an alcoholic, tobacco-using parent. The worker may also believe that drug usage is a behavior that can be self-regulated, or that all ATOD users deserve the outcomes of their drug-related activities, that only innocent bystanders need to be protected. The worker may also believe that the problem is so pervasive that any action is a waste of time, money, and effort. However, the worker may feel very strongly that the legalization of drugs will contribute greatly to harm reduction. The most important component is being aware of one's personal view and how it influences decisions and actions.

The identification of societal values relevant to the decision may reveal that some members of society feel very strongly about the legal control of drugs and support any increased efforts in that direction; other factions may believe that legalization of drugs will lead to a significant reduction in harm. Still others may believe that harm reduction itself is an unacceptable goal, only abstinence will suffice.

The identification of relevant professional values and ethics as revealed in the NASW *Code of Ethics* (2008) states that:

> Social workers' primary responsibility is to promote the well-being of clients. In general, clients' interests are primary. However, social workers' responsibility to the larger society or specific legal obligations may on limited occasions supersede the loyalty owed to clients, and clients should be so advised. (Section 1.01, p. 7)

A myriad of questions surface concerning the legalization of drugs: Should the worker think primarily of clients' needs, should the worker think of significant others' needs, should the worker attempt to take action that he or she thinks will protect the safety of the client? In that vein would increased control of drugs, or reduced control of drugs, lead to greater safety for the client? The NASW *Code of Ethics* (2008) also speaks to client self-determination:

> Social workers respect and promote the right of clients to self-determination and assist clients in their efforts to identify and clarify their goals. Social workers may limit clients' rights to self-determination when, in the social workers' professional judgment, clients' actions or potential actions pose a serious, foreseeable, and imminent risk to themselves or others. (Section 1.02, p. 7)

Does controlling availability of drugs limit clients' self-determination? Should social workers intervene and, by doing so, protect clients from the dangers of drug use?

The second responsibility, from above, concerns "What can you do to minimize conflicts between personal, societal, and professional values?" This involves not only knowing the values of all players, but also identifying shared values and avenues for collaboration.

The preceding scenario allows the worker to move to the third challenge—"Identify alternative ethical options that you may take." Should the worker take action that attempts to limit the availability of illegal drugs or should the worker take action that would increase availability yet reduce the crime that accompanies illegal drug activity? Should the worker pay greater attention to restricting the availability of drugs or toward educating nonusers about the dangers of treating those already using? The fourth question that must be answered by the worker is "Which alternative ethical actions will minimize conflicts between your client's, others', and society's rights and protect to the greatest extent your client's and *others'* rights and welfare, and society's rights and interests?"

Dolgoff and colleagues (2009) then emphasize the need to, fifth, determine "which alternative action will be most efficient, effective, and ethical, as well as result in your doing the 'least harm' possible." Once an action is selected, the sixth task involves the review and selection of strategies relevant for carrying out the selected course of action, followed by the actual implementation of the selected course. The final, or seventh course of action, focuses on keeping a close eye on the actual implementation of the selected alternative coupled with detailed evaluation of both process and product. It should include identification of unexpected outcomes and, if appropriate, possible plans for future actions or modifications to the selected course.

By suggesting an ethical rules screen and the ethical principles screen, Dolgoff and colleagues (2009) force the worker to examine and adjust his or her personal preferences in light of the priority status of professional ethics, the details of which are contained in the NASW *Code of Ethics* (2008) and the hierarchical ranking of the various ethical principles. The worker must ask himself or herself what alternative will contribute to the greatest good, inflict the least harm, offer greatest protection to life and recognition of human rights, and well-being.

Using the preceding parameters to assess alternatives and to guide selected actions should help the worker confront many of the ethical challenges surrounding drug use and drug policy, as in the earlier scenario involving the legal status of drugs. Although the format exists for facilitating ethical decision making, it does not guarantee that the best or most successful alternative will be selected; it merely guarantees that careful analysis and deliberation, based on ethical principles, will be afforded by the worker.

Drug Testing by Employers

Drug testing is another area that stretches the ethical decision-making skills of the worker. Some individuals contend that employers and companies have the right to test their workers, for the purpose of protecting the safety of other workers and the effectiveness of the users themselves (Judge, 1993). More recently, others contended that students should be tested to reduce drug use and resulting negative behaviors and to improve the learning environment (Office of National Drug Control Policy [ONDCP], 2006). An additional argument is contained in the high costs associated with job-related accidents, many of which are the direct result of alcohol and other drug use (Harwood, 2000; Harwood, Fountain, & Livermore, 1998; Substance Abuse and Mental Health Services Administration, 2008), and for the student, the negative educational outcomes that ensue (ONDCP). Other individuals contended that the accuracy and effectiveness of drug testing and the limited control of confidential information are not sufficient to infringe on the workers' right to privacy (Goldberg, 1998, 2008).

Despite opposition, currently the U.S. government has a random drug testing policy as do many major corporations (Goldberg, 1998). The U.S. Supreme Court in a 2002 five-to-four decision ruled in favor of random drug testing for all middle and high school students participating in extracurricular activities (Goldberg, 2008). Some individuals argue that drug testing violates the Fourth Amendment; others argue that not doing so is being irresponsible and neglecting the rights of others who are harmed by work-related accidents and poor performance, resulting in higher costs. Judge (1993) contended that drug testing in the workplace takes precedence over individuals' right to privacy; the ONDCP (2006) believes that it leads to reduction in drug use and better learning outcomes for students. DeCew (1994) argued that drug testing does not necessarily prove that someone is under the influence of drugs in the workplace; rather, tests could reveal traces of drugs that had been used during non-work time and are not currently affecting performance. Some school officials (Kern et al., 2006) present a number of reasons why random drug testing of students is not a sound policy; it does not necessarily deter drug use, it's expensive, it can be legally risky (exposing schools to expensive law suits), it may drive some students from participation in extracurricular activities, and it can result in false positives and the accompanying punishment of innocent students. They suggest focusing on educational and extracurricular activities that will facilitate trust and positive relationships and communication between students and adults in the school system, which, in turn, may help students decide not to use drugs.

The ethical challenges of drug testing confronting social workers today should be subjected to a similar general decision-making model and filtered using an appropriate version of the ethical assessment screen, the ethical rules screen, and the ethical principles screen before they can arrive at an opinion or an appropriate course of action. One could use the three-question, more practical model suggested by Blanchard and Peale (1988), above: (1) Is it legal? (The social worker must determine if the Fourth Amendment designed to protect citizens from unreasonable searches takes priority over protecting the rights of individuals from direct harm by individuals using alcohol or other drugs.); (2) Is it balanced? (The social work must determine if it is a fair decision, which takes into account the rights of all parties involved.); (3) How will it make me feel? (Will the worker feel comfortable that the full range of ethical issues, professional standards, organizational policies, legal issues, and personal beliefs have been explored. Given his or her most educated and professional consideration, has a thorough, well conceived, ethical alternative been identified?)

If drug testing is operative, additional challenges surface surrounding treatment of individuals who test positive. Should they be fired, or mandated for treatment? How will test results be documented? How does one deal with the possibility of false positives? How will confidentiality be defined and maintained? If a decision is made not to use drug testing as a means of harm reduction, how can the rights and safety of others be protected?

Similar to the issues surrounding the legalization of drugs, the choices are not clear-cut. What is evident is the need for the worker as policymaker and service provider to weigh the alternative options carefully, selecting the ones that lead to the greatest harm reduction or well-being of the masses without infringing inappropriately on the rights of the individual users.

Tobacco-Free Environments

There have been many recent changes in emphasis on the danger that smoking poses to self and others. Some individuals strongly agree that tobacco is a product dangerous not only to smokers, but also to nonsmokers subjected to secondhand smoke (U.S. Department of Health and Human Services [HHS], Office of Public Health and Science, 2006). Others strongly believe that secondhand smoke is not that dangerous to others (Copas & Shi, 2000). Others contend that because smoking is not illegal, smokers should have the right to smoke whenever and wherever they wish. Limitations on smoking have increased in many communities, employment sites, and treatment settings. More recently, some college campuses, hospitals, and even restaurants have become smoke-free entities.

Although smoking in and of itself may not be considered an ethical issue, its uninvited impact on others can be. In examining the NASW *Code of Ethics* (2008), Section 1.02 notes that "social workers may limit clients' rights to self-determination when, in the social workers' professional judgment, clients' actions or potential actions pose a serious, foreseeable, and imminent risk to themselves or others" (p. 7).

One may argue that this refers primarily to the threat of murder; others contend that secondary smoke poses considerable threat and discomfort, sufficient to warrant a policy that limits the rights of the individual smokers. One could also argue that the presence of alcohol and other drugs in public areas also infringes on the rights of others and, in considering the commitment to the common good or general well-being, should be banned from public spots, or at least restricted to designated areas.

Advocates of drug-free environments in many instances have been very successful in curtailing smoking. They also have been successful in limiting the use of alcohol and other drugs in public spots. Some of their interests have been converted into laws; others have become part of ongoing policy. In some cases, the interest in preserving the rights of the nonuser has prevailed. In other situations the rights of the nonusers have been usurped by those of the users. How many children and other family members have been forced to endure the effects of secondhand smoke?

It is important to note that the use of tobacco and alcohol has not been outlawed, only its presence in certain public areas. The illegal status of some drugs has helped to control their use in public spots. Frequently, the activity under scrutiny has been relegated to a confined spot. For example, smoking has been banned from public lounges in some public and private psychiatric facilities; in some it has been totally banned by both staff and consumers. In consideration of smokers' rights, some facilities, including corporations and colleges or universities, have made designated smoking areas available. Others have totally banned smoking on the premises.

Citizens in some neighborhoods challenge the effectiveness of limiting use of certain drugs. Individuals in some neighborhoods disregard legal or illegal status of many substances. Neighborhoods have become active drug markets complete with unsupervised shooting or using sites (Siegel, Green, Abbott, & Mogul, 2007). The rights of citizens are completely overpowered by users, resulting in increased danger for all involved.

Using the ethical principles screen of Dolgoff and colleagues (2009), the preceding line of reasoning has followed their hierarchical ordering of ethical principles. The smoke-free policy in public areas has taken into account the primary principle in the hierarchy—the protection of life. The second principle relating to equality and inequality can be seen as being manifested in the development of covered smoking areas available 24 hours per day. Other principles in the hierarchy are considered, with priority given to the listing in descending order.

Needle-Exchange Programs

The major cause of death among young people in the United States is shifting from accidents to AIDS—and the second-leading cause of HIV has been identified as illegal-drug injection. Many people have contracted HIV in that fashion, to say nothing of the many individuals who have been infected because of unprotected sexual activity with injection drug users (Goldberg, 1998).

Two major challenges emerge: How can the use of injection drugs be reduced? And how can the risk of spreading HIV be reduced or controlled? Needle-exchange programs have been touted by many individuals as a viable solution to both questions. They believe that ongoing contact with the needle-exchange site will provide opportunities for education and treatment. In addition, availability of clean needles will minimize or reduce risk to others (Inciardi & Harrison, 2000; Mancini, Linhorst, Broderick, & Bayliff, 2008; Scheck, 2009). Some supporters of harm reduction even advocate for legally sanctioned injecting sites located near illicit-drug markets where users can inject prepurchased drugs under supervision (Hall & Kimber, 2005). In some such facilities, workers are on-site to respond to potential overdoses (Scheck, 2009). Although many users are saved from overdose when injecting in supervised injecting sites, one negative outcome recently identified in such programs is the unexpected use and overdose of workers or drug counselors associated with the sites (Scheck, 2009).

Opponents of needle-exchange programs contend that availability of needles will only increase use, making drug use seem more acceptable, and that only the already conscientious clean needle user will avail himself or herself of the clean needles provided (ONDCP, 1992). The data pertaining to drug use and overdose of workers at needle-exchange and supervised-injecting sites lend some support to the concerns of opponents of such facilities (Scheck, 2009).

Some opponents argue that the sharing of needles is a key part of the drug-taking ritual that cannot be easily altered. They believe that needle-exchange programs are only band-aid measures, which do not get at the root of the addiction, such as discrimination, low-level employment or unemployment, and other faltering, inadequate social supports.

Proponents believe that even though needle-exchange programs do not address the actual addiction, they do provide clean needles to many who could otherwise not afford them, thus lowering the risk of transmitting HIV and other related infections.

The ethical considerations have posed a myriad of challenges for social workers and others involved in policy development growing out of the harm-reduction model. Without a doubt, the issue of needle exchange is ridden with conflict—so much so that it demanded considerable debate in the 1997–1998 U.S. Congress, resulting in a lack of support for such activity. Another challenge for needle exchange may have hinged on that fact that President George W. Bush in 2000, shortly before assuming the presidency, stated:

> I do not favor needle-exchange programs and other so-called "harm reduction" strategies to combat drug use. I support a comprehensive mix of prevention, education, treatment, law enforcement, and supply interdiction to curb drug use and promote a healthy, drug-free America, not misguided efforts to weaken drug laws. . . . America needs a President who will aim not just for risk reduction, but for risk elimination that offers people hope and recovery, not a dead-end approach that offers despair and addiction. (as cited in Kleinig, 2008)

Although the U.S. Congress ruled in one direction, the ethical challenge continues as a professional issue. Using the ethical principles screen (Dolgoff et al., 2009), one can attempt to subject the concept of needle exchange to ethical scrutiny. In their hierarchical ranking, the primary principle is the protection of life. Does needle exchange provide an important vehicle that serves to protect the lives of those who are at risk? Or does it increase risk by encouraging drug use through increasing availability of drug paraphernalia? Would other alternatives provide additional protection for those at risk, in this case those at risk of contracting HIV? Where have President Bush's proposed risk reduction and elimination gotten us? Would increased emphasis on harm-reduction strategies have been more effective?

As with any ethical dilemma, a final answer is not apparent. The worker must look for research and practice evidence and arrive at the best educated alternative based on ethical analysis and guidance. In the case of needle exchange, evidence shows that programs in Europe have been very effective (Englesman, 1989; Inciardi & Harrison, 2000). However, trial programs in the United States have not been found to be as successful, primarily because of community fear and opposition, not user reluctance.

Prosecution of Pregnant Drug Users

Another controversial area encompasses the prosecution and treatment of pregnant drug users (Andrews & Patterson, 1995; Fullilove & Dieudonne, 1996; Goldberg, 1998, 2008; Marcellus, 2004). The question surfaces over primary rights—the mother or her unborn infant. Using the guidelines developed by Strom-Gottfried (2007), "who" can provide guidance pertaining to the answer. Medical researchers (Fullilove & Dieudonne, 1996) have raised some key concerns about the risks for fetal harm based on minimal use of a number of substances (alcohol, tobacco, marijuana, heroin, methadone, cocaine, prescription drugs, and so forth) and some legal experts believe it is the government's responsibility to protect fetal development from the impact of harmful substances (Logli, 1990). They emphasize the importance of intervention and prevention. Society at large tends to have both compassionate views and negative ones about pregnant women who use substances. Their views, plus those of some policymakers, are frequently compounded by other demographic biases associated with poverty, race, and marital status. Some of these negative views may be countered by the promise of potential long-term health care cost reductions, if prevention and early intervention are effective.

Social workers have multiple views on intervention. The NASW *Code of Ethics* (2008) clearly states that it is social workers' responsibility to protect the rights of the vulnerable (see Section 1.01 & 1.02 previously quoted). If the social worker's interpretation is to protect the unborn, a second challenge is posed by the questions "What are the choices?" and "How shall they be enacted?" Some social workers contend that pregnant drug users should be incarcerated, removed from drug use, and given proper prenatal care throughout the pregnancy (Logli, 1990). Others believe that, unless prosecuted and forced into treatment, drug users will avoid treatment because they fear being caught or penalized because of their drug use. Some also believe that fear of prosecution may force some women to modify their drug use prior to and during pregnancy. Others, such as Carter (2002) and Mahan (1996), advocate for increased outreach, education, and treatment for pregnant drug users, all of which would be directed toward more responsible prenatal care and ultimately toward the rehabilitation of the women involved. Carter contends that pregnant women avoid seeking prenatal treatment out of fear of legal prosecution, which, in turn, may result in greater harm to their babies.

The social worker should ask "Have I faced similar challenges in the past?" An example might be one involving the rights of smokers versus the rights of non-smokers being subjected to secondhand smoke. Given the possible options, the question about "why a particular course of action is chosen" needs to be addressed. Although philosophically and ethically the course of action posed by Carter (2002) and Mahan (1996) may be viewed as the preferred, it may necessitate major changes in program outreach efforts, costs, and program availability that far exceed available resources. Considering the two extremes suggested, a middle-of-the-road option may surface as the preferred alternative, an example being the sentencing of pregnant women to drug-free prenatal treatment programs. Garcia (1993), in addressing maternal drug abuse "asserts that ethical concepts and legal tenets must be combined to develop new paradigms designed to minimize conflict and to achieve just and therapeutic balances between the rights and needs of those involved. [She strongly supports] . . . attempts to achieve balances that are just and promote positive consequences" (p. 1311).

As noted previously, the worker not only has responsibilities to the clients—the mother and unborn child—but also has responsibilities to society. In looking at responsibility to overall society, the worker must not only assess the impact of the mother's drug use on her fetus, but also the long-term costs the infant's health poses to society in general. Whose rights have priority: At what point do clients' rights become secondary, or tertiary, or temporarily placed on hold?

Like the other ethical dilemmas presented here, the treatment of pregnant drug users is another example of the challenges confronting social workers employed in the area of substance use and abuse. The answers do not flow easily; however, the tools are available to help in the formulation of ethically sound solutions.

Control of Advertising for Alcohol, Tobacco, and Prescription Drugs

Because legal drugs, including alcohol, tobacco, and prescription drugs, have such strong potential to adversely affect an individual's well-being, the question is frequently raised about the control of their promotion (Goldberg, 1998). In 1994, in a court decision *(Overton v. Anheuser-Busch),* the Michigan Supreme Court ruled that the dangers of drinking alcohol are well known and television ads are viewed as suggesting fantasies and are not taken seriously by viewers (Parker, 1998). Parker's work included numerous research studies supporting the contrary. General consensus was that advertising frequently supports the fantasies of viewers; however, its influence is difficult to measure. Some of the fantasies suggested by beer ads, in particular, include the following: beer as a reward for hard work or play, beer as being useful in gaining social acceptance, beer as leading to positive peer bonding, beer as facilitating interaction between the sexes, and beer as an avenue to true friendship (Parker, 1998).

Tobacco advertising is another area of concern. Tobacco frequently is viewed as a "gateway" drug, or one whose use is positively correlated with later use of other potentially more dangerous illegal drugs. Pollay (1997; reprinted in Goldberg, 1998), strongly believes that tobacco advertising should be regulated, that frequently advertising presents misleading impressions about the glamour of smoking while overlooking the physical dangers related to the use of tobacco. The same holds true for alcohol. Young people, in their quest for maturity, are especially vulnerable to advertising tactics. Even if the long-term implications of use are highlighted in the advertising, it is questionable whether youths, with their heavy emphasis on immediate gratification and strong response to peer pressure, would seriously entertain considering the potential negative consequences.

Some, such as Dority (1997; reprinted in Goldberg, 1998), question the connection between advertising and smoking. Her thinking could be expanded to include advertising and the use of alcohol or advertising and the use of prescription drugs. She strongly believes that limiting such advertising is a strict violation of the First Amendment. Within certain age restrictions and medical requirements, prescription drugs, alcohol, and tobacco are all legal entities. Therefore, these products should be advertised without impunity or control. Any control should be offered in the form of education or strong personal example by key role models.

Goldberg (1998) raised serious question about the advertising of tobacco: Does it really encourage smoking? Would its limitation decrease smoking? Does the advertising of alcohol increase its use? Would a reduction in advertising diminish its use?

The Public Health Cigarette Smoking Act of 1970, which banned the advertising of tobacco on television and radio, did not result in a significant reduction in tobacco sales. What it did was to force tobacco companies to develop alternative means of advertising (Goldberg, 1998). Pollay (1997) contended that advertising gives tobacco (and alcohol) a degree of "friendly familiarity." Seeing repeated situations involving tobacco (and alcohol) gives the impression that the use of such substances is the modus operandi or an expected parameter of behavior. Although tobacco companies (and the producers of alcohol) contend that the bulk of their advertising is not directed toward youths, rather toward adults who might switch brands, all one has to do is look at the models in the advertisements to realize the population being addressed. One sees attractive, successful, and YOUTHFUL people—or cartoonlike characters portraying the merits of tobacco and alcohol use in a youthful fashion to a youthful contingent. Pollay reminds us that typically new, young users are a more attractive market, given their potential for long-time use and commitment.

In addition to marketing and advertising efforts for tobacco and alcohol, David Kessler and colleagues (1994; reprinted in Goldberg, 1998), offer comparable opinions about the advertising of prescription drugs. To retain their competitive edge and increasing market share, drug companies must actively sell drugs. Initially their advertising campaigns were directed toward physicians responsible for prescribing their drugs. More recently, advertising has been directed to the actual consumer who can prompt his or her physician to prescribe a specific product. All one has to do is leaf through a popular magazine, turn on the television, or connect to the Internet to see the full array of drug advertisements reaching out to a consumer.

Matthews (2001) strongly stressed that the advertising of prescription drugs in popular venues leads to an informed consumer who is better prepared to address his or her medical needs and possible treatment choices with his or her physician. Langreth and Herper (2006) emphasized that advertising does not lead to more informed consumers, but, rather, to increased revenues for the pharmaceutical companies. They contend that instead of advertising, the drug manufacturers should be spending those resources on research and new product development. Kessler et al. (1994) questioned whether most consumers can fully appreciate the appropriateness of any particular drug for their respective medical conditions. The views reflected in many prescription ads include fantasies of peaceful sleep-filled nights, alert wakeful mornings, easy weight loss, removal of all pain resulting in perfect balance, the ability to dance like a professional, increased capacity for socialization, or a life based on close friendships and enhanced interpersonal relationships including great sexual relationships, all of which seduce or convince consumers to beg their physicians for the "perfect" pill. More recently, because of some negative fallout such as that generated by Vioxx, the pharmaceutical companies have added risk-management statements to their advertising, such as "if one does suffer from drug-related complications," "tell your physician if you have any of these pre-existing conditions" or " tell your physician immediately if you experience any of the following . . . if taking this product."

Goldberg (1998) reminds us that "with the exception of alcohol . . . prescription drugs cause more accidents in the workplace than illegal drugs" (p. 180). Is the consumer really educated sufficiently to filter the content of advertisements, assess risks, and ask for the prescription drugs that are more appropriate? Kessler and colleagues (1994) do not believe the consumer is adequately prepared and as such should be protected. They also suggest that frequently risks are not adequately spelled out. In addition, companies use celebrity figures to enhance credibility in the eyes of the consumer.

Rubin (1991; reprinted in Goldberg, 1998), disagreed, arguing that there are many advantages inherent in the current broad-based advertising of prescription drugs: The consumer becomes more aware of benefits, risks, and side effects; the consumer learns of new possibilities for addressing his or her medical problems; and the consumer can request less costly alternatives.

Although Dority (1997) strongly agrees with those who deplore tobacco, she believes that restricting advertising is an infringement on individual rights or freedom. She strongly contends that it is unconstitutional to restrict the advertising of legal substances—and strongly opposes any action in that direction. If the advertising of such legal products as tobacco and alcohol can be restricted, then the advertising of other products and services can be restricted as well. Government censorship would become a way of life.

Ethical questions and dilemmas surface in the area of advertising. Should priority be given to protecting the client from its lure or influence? Because many believe that the consumer is not sophisticated or strong enough to act freely and judiciously in response to advertising, is it the social worker's responsibility to intervene, to push for a ban or limitation on the advertising of potentially dangerous legal substances? Or would the more responsible action be the protection of individual freedom of speech, for example, the freedom to advertise? Or would the desirable action be a compromise position, such as one involving increased education of the consumer and more accurate and complete advertising content detailing the pros and cons? A major concern would continue to be "how much the consumer denies possible problems with the mind-set that 'it [bad outcomes] could never happen to me.'" Like other ethical dilemmas, one definitive answer does not surface. The worker must weigh the options in light of his or her professional convictions, answering key questions in the process: Is it legal? Is it balanced? How will it make me feel? (Blanchard & Peale, 1988).

Additional Practice-Related Issues

Unique ethical challenges emerge from the broad range of dual relationships that exist in the field of ATOD (Abbott, 1997, 2003a; Alcoholism & Drug Abuse Weekly News for Policy and Program Decision-Makers, 2008; Kaplan, 2005). Some of them stem from recovering ATOD workers attending AA meetings with clients or with their supervisors, or the changing role of some individuals from that of client to service provider within the very program in which they previously received treatment. Some ATOD programs encourage physical contact among clients and workers, something that is discouraged among many professions, including social work. Additional challenges arise from the hinging of services to abstinence or the ongoing debate surrounding abstinence versus controlled use.

As noted previously, not all professionals come to the playing field sharing a common set of values and ethical principles. Professionally educated social workers have a clearly defined code of ethics and a well-developed mechanism for peer review and adjudication (Abbott, 2008) designed to protect the rights of clients and to help ensure professional compliance with the code of ethics. State licensing boards also help to contribute to high-quality professional social work practice. Most professions, including medicine, nursing, and psychology, have professional codes of ethics, with mechanisms designed to encourage adherence. On the whole, the codes support such aspects as client confidentiality, but are not as specific as they are in such areas as dual relationships, sexual misconduct, and impaired professionals. In 1987, the National Association of Alcoholism and Drug Abuse Counselors (NAADAC, 1987) adopted a code of ethics. Overall, that NAADAC code of ethics is compatible with that of NASW. Increased certification of addictions counselors is contributing to greater awareness of and compliance with professional ethical standards. Where differences may be noted, the more stringent alternative is suggested.

Major challenges frequently surface in the ethical socialization and commitment of paraprofessionals working in the field. They do not always understand the professional obligation to adhere to ethical practice, nor do they suffer the same repercussions stemming from ethical violations.

In addition to struggling for a common ethical base, challenges emerge from concerns such as patient–treatment matching, support of controlled drinking or drug use, and response to restrictions on care, such as those posed by the managed care community.

Patient–Treatment Matching

The literature raises a series of questions about the viability of patient–treatment matching, or the assigning of clients to particular methods of treatment on the basis of various client characteristics. Over the past 25 years, many professionals involved in ATOD treatment found that different types of clients benefited from different treatment programs. For example, several researchers found coping-skills training to be more effective than interactional therapy in preventing substance abuse relapse among psychiatric or sociopathic clients (Cooney, Kadden, Litt, &

Getter, 1991; Kadden, Cooney, Getter, & Litt, 1989). Koenig and Crisp (2008) identified the unique needs of older women who misuse substances. Whittinghill (2002) found that clients responded more favorably when family therapy was used as a major component of treatment. Other professionals tended to fit clients into available treatment options, many times acting as if "one size fits all." For example, frequently women were placed in programs designed primarily by and for white men (Abbott, 1994), with no regard for their unique needs and resulting in little treatment success. More recently, social support was identified as being more crucial to successful treatment than actual treatment protocol (Longabaugh et al., 1993).

The concern about patient–treatment matching was examined by Project Match, a project supported by the National Institute on Alcohol Abuse and Alcoholism (NIAAA, 1997), in which a national sample of over 1,700 patients was randomly assigned to three treatment protocols. The findings illustrate that patient–treatment matching is less important than many previously conceived. The results also show that drinking and related consequences declined for all participants, regardless of treatment option.

A dilemma is posed by conflicting research findings. The important ethical challenge is not to jump on the bandwagon, acting as if the latest findings present the definitive answer. In culling through the research literature, one can find studies that support patient–treatment matching and others that refute its value. The key question or concern for social workers is how can the rights of the client be protected and what can be done to ensure the best possible treatment. Yes, research should be used to guide practice; however, the worker must promote examination or consideration of the full gamut of research studies, use findings to guide program development and treatment assignment, and also listen to the unique needs and interests of the clients. In addition to the three questions raised by Blanchard and Peale (1988) to guide practice, the question raised by Wells (1986), recognizing the client's point of view, should definitely be considered.

Restriction of Care–Managed Care and Cost Containment

Managed care, driven by cost containment, poses new challenges for social workers employed in the area of ATOD treatment. Frequently workers are forced to select treatment options that are driven by monetary restrictions, rather than client treatment needs. At times workers are tempted to change clients' diagnoses to ones that qualify for enhanced or longer treatment. Although modifying a diagnosis may seem like a viable alternative to serve a client, it represents a legal and ethical breach. Recall the two "mandatory" standards identified by Corey and colleagues

(2007)—law and professional codes. To misdiagnose for the sake of receiving additional services for a client not only represents an ethical violation, but also constitutes fraud, or stealing from a health care overseer or insurance company.

Examples of more appropriate and ethically responsible courses of action would be confronting the managed care provider for purposes of procuring additional services for the client; helping the client address the managed care system on his or her own behalf; or helping others organize to confront the system, whether it be the managed care company or legislation.

Using the general decision-making model suggested by Dolgoff and colleagues (2009) should help the worker arrive at a suitable and effective course of action.

The primary challenge is not solely an ethical one; rather, it is an ethical and legal conundrum that poses temptation because frequently the managed care company, in its restriction of service, appears to be the enemy, rather than a watchdog of efficiency or a proponent of cost containment and quality care.

Confidentiality and Informed Consent

Additional challenges to confidentiality are present in the ATOD treatment setting. Because of the broad range of individuals providing treatment, a common definition of "confidentiality" rarely exists. Professional standards or expectations for confidentiality are frequently put to the test. Many treatment components involve groups of clients, many of whom are not bound to maintain confidentiality, only requested to do so. Jeopardy for the client is increased because of the illegal nature of many substances used. New challenges to confidentiality are being generated by the increased use of technology, especially in the maintenance of client records, including insurance data and client billing.

The challenge to the social worker requires not only acting in an ethically responsible fashion in carrying out the expectations for confidentiality, but also instructing others about its parameters, instituting policies designed to guarantee its presence, and warning clients about limitations and potential glitches in the system (see Houston-Vega & Nuehring, 1997; Reamer, 2001b). It also is critical for social workers to document the ethical issues addressed and the rationale for violating confidentiality. To do less would be ethically irresponsible.

Another area of ethical concern involves that of informed consent. Some examples include the right to have information shared or withheld from others (typically the client owns case record information and has the right to determine where and to whom that information will be sent, unless demanded by law). This is of special concern to those working with minors. Although Brody and Waldron (2000) spoke specifically to issues related to adolescent participation in substance abuse research, their ideas introduce major ethical concerns for both research and treatment providers. "Adolescent substance abuse treatment research presents challenges to the moral principle of autonomy via issues related to the informed consent process" (p. 218). Can adolescents agree to participate in treatment or research without parental consent? What information will remain confidential and what is required to be shared with family members, primarily parents?

The preceding is an example that refreshes the emphasis of Corey and colleagues (2007) to focus on the guiding framework consisting of two mandatory standards—laws and professional codes. What does the law state about the rights of minors to treatment and informed consent? What does the code state? How does the worker move forward based on the guidance provided by both and in light of previous experience and consultation with others?

Harm Reduction

There is general agreement that excessive use of ATOD can adversely affect the users as well as their families and the communities in which they reside. One method of addressing the problems resulting from drug use has been referred to as "harm reduction" (Duncan et al., 1994; Mancini et al., 2008; Marlatt, 1998). It focuses on reducing or minimizing the negative consequences stemming from the use of drugs. An ongoing debate surrounds the concept of harm reduction. However, there are philosophical issues that add support to both sides of the harm-reduction argument (Kleinig, 2004). Many contend that it is more appropriate to address all efforts toward abstinence or toward reducing the supply of drugs (Evans-Whipp, 2007). Others contend that the elimination of drugs, or the goal of abstinence, is an impossible dream, that resources would be better spent on reducing the problems or harm resulting from drug use. Still others, in addressing such ethical issues as harm reduction, argue that it depends. Kleinig (2004), quoting John Stuart Mill (1848), strongly states "the only purpose for which power can be rightfully exercised over any member of a civilized community, against his will, is to prevent harm to others" (2004, pp. 372–373); however, in citing Ritchie (1894), Kleinig reminds us that "the human freedom we prize is not a freedom that can be enjoyed by one man or one set of men at the cost of loss of freedom to others" (p. 374). If this is the case, should harm-reduction efforts be imposed on individuals, or should they remain an option for users? It is a challenge to decide whether the actions of one or many are truly interfering with the rights, actions, and freedom of others. Will harm reduction lead to overcontrol of some without resulting in the increased safety or freedom of others?

Needle-exchange programs intended to stop the spread of HIV caused by the sharing of infected needles would be one example of harm reduction (Springer, 1991). Teaching users to clean their "works" (needles, syringes, and so forth) is another example. Additional efforts included attempts to reduce harm in the form of violence associated with drug use and to increase prevention, education, and treatment programs designed to reduce harm (Goldberg, 1998).

Goldberg (1998, 2008) raised both sides of the debate surrounding the use of harm-reduction strategies, as does Kleinig (2004). He highlights the work of Reuter and Caulkins (1995) who "support efforts to reduce the violence and disease associated with drugs and the drug trade" (Goldberg, 1998, p. 104) and that of Rosenbaum (2004) who believes "that because many teens experiment with drugs, a message to reduce harms associated with drugs is necessary . . . a problem with the abstinence-only message is that teens have no one to turn to if they experience problems with drugs" (Goldberg, 2008, p. 441). Supporters of harm reduction believe that drug use and drug users are not bad; rather, that the results of or risks associated with drug use are bad (Springer, 1991). In addition to attempting to reduce harm, they also stress the importance of use reduction. They contend that focusing only on the latter—use reduction—does not adequately recognize the full extent of damage associated with drug use. Harm reduction includes a perspective that recognizes the broad impact.

Opponents of the harm-reduction model believe that such a philosophy does not get at the root of the problem—drugs—rather, focusing primarily on the impact of drugs, may, in fact, divert attention from restriction and control of drug use (DuPont & Voth, 1995). Some contend that the harm-reduction philosophy even serves to support the use of drugs. Harm-reduction advocates remind us that approximately only 10 percent of people who use drugs experience difficulties, with the remaining 90 percent being relatively problem free.

Historically, the concept of harm reduction pertained to drug use. It was developed in England in the mid-1980s in response to the spread of HIV through the use of shared needles by injection drug users. The needle-exchange program was developed in light of the belief that the prevention of the spread of HIV takes priority over the elimination or prevention of drug use (Springer, 1991). Abstinence from drug use would continue to be the top goal; however, if people could not abstain, it was essential that programs be developed to reduce the harmful effects of their drug use. In addition to reducing the risk of spreading HIV, needle-exchange programs provide an opportunity for users to connect with the treatment system, hopefully generating commitment to seeking treatment, and eventually resulting in abstinence.

Controlled Drinking and Drug Use versus Abstinence

Although harm reduction was primarily developed as a strategy to reduce the harmful effects of illegal drug use, its concepts can and have been applied to the full range of substances—alcohol, tobacco, prescription drugs, even food. It reflects a paradigm shift from a strategy based on use prevention to one accentuating abuse prevention (Duncan et al., 1994). Controlled drinking is a form of harm reduction. Debates similar to those surrounding controlled use of drugs have developed, pitting abstinence against self-control.

The concept of controlled drinking peaked in the 1970s (Peele, 1987; Sobell & Sobell, 1978), only to resurface in the late 1980s, 1990s, and carried into the 21st century (Byrd, 1997; Holmila, 1993; Kishline, 1996; Marlatt, Larimer, Baer, & Quigley, 1993; Miller, 1992; Miller, Walters, & Bennett, 2001; Morgan, 2003: Nathan, 1992; Peele, 1987, 1992; Stockwell, 1988). Proponents of abstinence (Byrd, 1997) believe that some individuals are "powerless" against alcohol and that unless they abstain from its use they will fall totally under its influence. It is believed that such individuals must learn how to abstain each time the urge to drink surfaces. This is the basic model endorsed by many treatment programs and also by AA. Proponents of controlled drinking (Kishline, 1996; Peele, 1992) believe control or moderation is a viable, in fact desirable, alternative. Certain treatment programs, such as Rational Recovery and various cognitive therapy approaches, support the controlled drinking concept and emphasize a change in beliefs accompanied by a change in drinking behavior. Those emphasizing the merits of controlled drinking believe that excessive drinking is a learned behavior, rather than a disease, and can be replaced by other more appropriate learned behavior (Kishline, 1996). Kishline referred to this new behavior as moderation management.

Some individuals attempt controlled drinking only to discover that it does not work for them. They, in turn, may choose to move in the direction of total abstinence. The attempt at controlled drinking or moderation management may have served a useful role in preparing or facilitating the next step. If so, its intent—harm reduction—would have been realized.

An additional ethical challenge surrounds the controlled administration of alcohol for research and treatment purposes (Modell, Glaser, & Mountz, 1993). Although some professionals contend that the administration of alcohol leads to relapse, Modell and colleagues presented evidence indicating that controlled experimental administration of alcohol does not lead to "uncontrolled drinking, relapse, or other adverse effects on recovery" (p. 189). Rather, it leads to enhanced knowledge about the impact of alcohol and may help clients more fully understand their alcohol use and dependence.

The debates surrounding both harm reduction and controlled drinking continue to challenge us. The challenge for the social worker is to determine where to place one's support along the continuum. Should one endorse abstinence, or should one emphasize controlled drinking or moderation management? Or should one not favor any single approach but, rather, try to find the combination that best fits the individual client? Should one support needle exchange or should one fight it as a contributor to increased use of injection drugs? There is no correct answer; the challenge confronting the social work practitioner is to determine, on the basis of knowledge and ethical conviction, which positions to support. Using the general decision-making model as a guide , one can identify the overall problem, assess potential solutions, determine the necessary supports, and attempt to support the best course of action. In addition, it is incumbent on the worker to identify relevant professional values and ethics and to protect, to the greatest extent possible, the rights of clients as well as the rights and welfare of others; to minimize potential conflicts; and to select the alternatives that will result in the least harm possible. To do this, the worker must have not only knowledge of the specific issues, but also working familiarity with the values and ethical standards of the profession. He or she must recognize the influence of personal beliefs and act in light of professional expectations.

Summary

The ethical dilemmas and challenges confronting the social worker dealing with ATOD treatment are numerous and complex. A few of the major challenges have been identified here: the legality of drugs, the treatment of pregnant drug users, the support for tobacco-free environments, the concept of controlled drinking versus abstinence, and the use of drug testing in the workplace, to name a few. A range of alternative solutions have been suggested; however, it remains for the worker to arrive at his or her own solution, based on technical and ethical knowledge.

The ethical challenges presented here reflect but a tip of the iceberg. The worker must rely on his or her knowledge of how to address dilemmas and to improve that knowledge, when a noted lack is identified. Some areas that have not been mentioned but could easily come to the attention of a social worker include the issue of controlled medical prescribing of heroin to users. Although this approach is not popular in the United States, it has been used effectively in Great Britain, Canada, Spain, Germany, Switzerland, and the Netherlands (Sheldon, 2008; Walker, 2008).

Other less controversial areas of practice, but ridden with ethical issues, are treatment of adolescents involving the consent of minors versus consent of parents, informed consent for research, confidentiality, and release of information (Brody & Waldron, 2000). Unique ethical considerations relate to use of family therapy in ATOD treatment (Whittinghill, 2002). What if an individual is denied treatment because a family member is not available or unwilling to participate in a mandated family aspect of a treatment program? What if a member of the treatment team using family therapy is not sufficiently trained in the dynamics and protocols of family intervention? What if the professional providing family treatment is adequately prepared in the area of family but insufficiently prepared to deal with common ATOD issues and dynamics? Alcohol, illegal drug, and prescription drug misuse is increasing among older adults (Moos, Brennan, Schutte, & Moos, 2004). What if professionals who are trained in the area of ATOD are not prepared to tackle the challenges unique to our burgeoning older population? The same concern would surface if they lack knowledge of family intervention in a program demanding expertise in that area. The NASW *Code of Ethics* (2008) clearly spells out professional responsibilities that demand competence in the expected area of practice. Thus, the worker should be knowledgeable of aging, of adolescents, of family therapy, if the situation calls for such skills, and knowledgeable and willing to address lacks in himself or herself or others reporting to him or her.

Most dilemmas are not answered in isolation. The sophisticated worker is never reluctant to seek consultation surrounding any dilemma or challenge; it is the neophyte who believes that he or she can simplify and address complexities on his or her own. The skilled worker also is comfortable with and committed to documenting his or her assessment of a dilemma and the decisions growing out of his or her deliberations. Guidelines have been presented here to foster ethical decision making. With solid commitment to enhance the quality of social work treatment, social workers should be able to provide ethically sound services to clients in need of help with problems involving ATOD.

References

Abbott, A. A. (1988). *Professional choices: Values at work.* Silver Spring, MD: NASW Press.

Abbott, A. A. (1992, March). NASW vote: Meet the officer candidates. *NASW News,* p. 6.

Abbott, A. A. (1994). A feminist approach to substance abuse treatment and service delivery. *Social Work in Health Care, 19*(3–4), 67–83.

Abbott, A. A. (1997). Social work in ATOD settings: Testing our ethical foundation. *Issues of Substance, 2*(2), 1, 13, 15.

Abbott, A. A. (2002). Health care challenges created by substance abuse: The whole is definitely bigger than the sum of its parts [Guest Editorial]. *Health & Social Work, 27,* 162–165.

Abbott, A. A. (2003a). Understanding transference and countertransference: Risk management strategies for preventing sexual misconduct and other boundary violations. *Psychoanalytic Social Work, 10*(2), 21–41.

Abbott, A. A. (2003b). Meeting the challenges of substance misuse: Making inroads one step at a time [Editorial]. *Health & Social Work, 28,* 83–88.

Abbott, A. A. (2008). Professional conduct. In T. Mizrahi & L. Davis (Eds.-in-Chief), *Encyclopedia of social work* (20th ed., pp. 418–423). Washington, DC, and New York: NASW Press and Oxford University Press.

Alcoholism and Drug Abuse Weekly News for Policy and Program Decision-Makers. (2008, July 21). Ethics and supervision key to preventing sexual exploitation in treatment programs: Allegations involving Odyssey House ex-counselor raise questions. Author, *20*(28), 1–4.

Andrews, A. B., & Patterson, E. G. (1995). Searching for solutions to alcohol and other drug abuse during pregnancy: Ethics, values, and constitutional principles. *Social Work, 40,* 55–64.

Banks, S. (1995). *Ethics and values in social work.* London: Macmillan.

Bina, R., Harnek Hall, D. M., Mollette, A., Smith-Osborne, A., Yum, J., Sowbel, L., & Jani, J. (2008). Substance abuse training and perceived knowledge: Predictors of perceived preparedness to work in substance abuse. *Journal of Social Work Education, 44,* 7–20.

Black, P. N., Hartley, E. K., Whelley, J., & Kirk-Sharp, C. (1989). Ethics curricula: A national survey of graduate schools of social work. *Social Thought, 15*(3–4), 141–148.

Blanchard, K., & Peale, N. V. (1988). *The power of ethical management.* New York: Wm. Morrow.

Brody, J. L., & Waldron, H. B. (2000). Ethical issues in research on the treatment of adolescent Substance abuse disorders. *Addictive Behaviors, 25*(2), 217–228.

Burke, A. C., & Clapp, J. D. (1997). Ideology and social work practice in substance abuse settings. *Social Work, 42,* 552–562.

Byrd, T. (1997). *Lives written in sand: Addiction awareness and recovery strategies.* New York: Hallum.

Carter, C. S. (2002). Prenatal care for women who are addicted: Implications for empowerment. *Health & Social Work, 27,* 166–174.

Congress, E. P. (1999). *Social work values and ethics: Identifying and resolving professional dilemmas.* Chicago: Nelson-Hall.

Cooney, N. L., Kadden, R. M., Litt, M. D., & Getter, H. (1991). Matching alcoholics to coping skills and interactional therapies: Two-year follow-up results. *Journal of Consulting and Clinical Psychology, 59,* 598–601.

Copas, J. B., & Shi, J. Q. (2000). Reanalysis of epidemiological evidence on lung cancer and passive smoking. *British Medical Journal, 320,* 417–418.

Corey, G., Corey, M. S., & Callanan, P. (2007). *Issues and ethics in the helping professions* (7th ed.). Belmont, CA: Brooks/Cole.

Council on Social Work Education Commission on Accreditation. (1994). *Handbook of accreditation standards and procedures* (4th ed.). Alexandria, VA: Author.

CSWE Commission on Accreditation. (2008). *Educational policy and accreditation standards.* Alexandria, VA: Author.

DeCew, J. W. (1994). Drug testing, balancing privacy, and public safety. *Hastings Center Report, 24*(2), 17–23.

Dolgoff, R., Loewenberg, F. M., & Harrington, D. (2009). *Ethical decisions for social work practice* (8th ed.). Belmont, CA: Thomson Higher Education.

Dority, B. (1997). The rights of Joe Camel and the Marlboro man. *Humanist, 57*(1), 34–36.

Duncan, D. F., Nicholson, T., Clifford, P., Hawkins, W., & Petosa, R. (1994). Harm reduction: An emerging new paradigm for drug education. *Journal of Drug Education, 24*(4), 281–290.

DuPont, R. L., & Voth, E. A. (1995). Drug legalization, harm reduction, and drug policy. *Annals of Internal Medicine, 123,* 461–465.

Englesman, E. (1989). Dutch policy on the management of drug-related problems. *British Journal of Addictions, 84,* 211–218.

Evans-Whipp, T. J. (2007). School, parent, and student perspectives on school drug policies. *Journal of School Health, 77*(2), 138–146.

Fullilove, M. T., & Dieudonne, I. (1996). Substance abuse in pregnancy. In *Hatherleigh guide to treating substance abuse, Part II* (pp. 93–188). New York: Hatherleigh Press.

Garcia, S. A. (1993). Maternal drug abuse: Laws and ethics as agents of just balances and therapeutic interventions. *International Journal of the Addictions, 28,* 1311–1339.

Goldberg, R. (1998). *Taking sides: Clashing views on controversial issues in drugs and society* (3rd ed.). Guilford, CT: Duskin/McGraw-Hill.

Goldberg, R. (2008). *Taking sides: Clashing views on controversial issues in drugs and society* (8th ed.). New York: McGraw-Hill.

Gorman, P. (2006). *Veteran cops against the drug war.* Retrieved May 5, 2009, from http://worldandijournal.com

Haas, L. J., & Malouf, J. L. (1989). *Keeping up the good work: A practitioner's guide to mental health ethics.* Sarasota, FL: Professional Resource Exchange.

Hall, W., & Kimber, J. (2005). Being realistic about benefits of supervised injecting facilities. *Lancet, 366,* 271–272.

Harwood, H. (2000). *Updating estimates of the economic costs of alcohol abuse in the United States: Estimates, update methods and data.* Bethesda, MD: National Institute on Alcohol Abuse and Alcoholism.

Harwood, H., Fountain, D., & Livermore, G. (1998). *The economic costs of alcohol and drug abuse in the United States, 1992* (NIH Publication No. 98–4327). Rockville, MD: National Institute on Drug Abuse.

Hill, M., Glaser, K., & Harden, J. (1995). A feminist model for ethical decision making. In E. J. Rave & C. C. Larsen (Eds.), *Ethical decision-making in therapy: Feminist perspectives* (pp. 18–37). New York: Guilford Press.

Holmila, M. (1993). Heavy drinking women: Drinking patterns and resources for controlled drinking. *Addiction Research 1*, 119–130.

Houston-Vega, M. K., & Nuehring, E. M. (with Daguio, E. R.). (1997). *Prudent practice: A guide for managing malpractice risk*. Washington, DC: NASW Press.

Inciardi, J. A., & Harrison, L. D. (2000). Introduction: The concept of harm reduction. In J. A. Inciardi & L. D. Harrison (Eds.), *Harm reduction: National and international perspectives* (pp. vii–xix). Thousand Oaks, CA: Sage Publications.

Inciardi, J. A., & Saum, C. A. (1996). Legalization madness. *Public Interest, 123*, 72–82.

International Federation of Social Workers & International Association of Schools of Social Work. (2004). *Ethics in social work, statement of principles*. Bern, Switzerland: Author.

Judge, W. J. (1993). Drug testing: The legal framework. In R. S. Wright & D. G. Wright (Eds.), *Creating and maintaining the drug-free workforce*. Guilford, CT: McGraw-Hill.

Kadden, R. M., Cooney, N. L., Getter, H., & Litt, M. D. (1989). Matching alcoholics to coping skills or interactional therapies: Posttreatment results. *Journal of Consulting and Clinical Psychology, 57*, 698–704.

Kaplan, L. E. (2005). Dual relationships: The challenges for social workers in recovery. *Journal of Social Work Practice in the Addictions, 5*(3), 73–90.

Kern, J., Gunja, F., Cox, A., Rosenbaum, M., Appel, J., & Verma, A. (2006). *Making sense of student drug testing: Why educators are saying no* (2nd ed.). Santa Cruz, CA: ACLU and New York: Drug Policy Alliance.

Kessler, D. A., Rose, J. L., Temple, R. J., Schapiro, R., & Griffin, J. P. (1994). Therapeutic-class wars—Drug promotion in a competitive marketplace. *New England Journal of Medicine, 331*, 1350–1353.

King, M. J. (2009, January 12). Decriminalize drugs, free up city jail space. *Philadelphia Inquirer*, Sect. A, p. ll.

Kishline, A. (1996). *Moderate drinking*. New York: Harmony Books.

Kleber, H., & Califano, Jr., J. A. (1995). *Legalizations: Panacea or Pandora's box* (White paper). New York: Columbia University, National Center on Addiction and Substance Abuse.

Kleinig, J. (2004). Ethical issues in substance use intervention. *Substance Use & Misuse, 39*, 369–398.

Kleinig, J. (2008). The ethics of harm reduction. *Substance Use & Misuse 43*, 1–16.

Koenig, T. L., & Crisp, C. (2008). Ethical issues in practice with older women who misuse substances. *Substance Use & Misuse, 43*, 1045–1061.

Langreth, R., & Herper, M. (2006, May 8). Pill pushers: How the drug industry abandoned science for salesmanship. *Forbes, 1*(10), 94–102.

Levy, C. S. (1973). The value base of social work. *Journal of Education for Social Work, 9*, 34–34.

Levy, C. S. (1976). *Social work ethics*. New York: Human Sciences Press.

Levy, C. S. (1982). *Guide to ethical decisions and actions for social service administrators*. New York: Haworth Press.

Levy, C. S. (1984). Values and ethics. In S. Dillick (Ed.), *Value foundations of social work* (pp. 17–29). Detroit: Wayne State University, School of Social Work.

Loewenberg, F. M., & Dolgoff, R. (1996). *Ethical decisions for social work practice* (5th ed.). Itasca, IL: F. E. Peacock.

Logli, P. A. (1990). Drugs in the womb: The newest battlefield in the war on drugs. *Criminal Justice Ethics, 9*(1), 23–39.

Longabaugh, R., Beattie, M., Noel, N., Stout, R., & Malloy, P. (1993). The effect of social investment on treatment outcomes. *Journal of Studies on Alcohol, 54,* 465–478.

Mahan, S. (1996). *Crack cocaine, crime, and women: Legal, social, and treatment issues.* Thousand Oaks, CA: Sage Publications.

Mancini, M. A., Linhorst, D. M., Broderick, F., & Bayliff, S. (2008). Challenges to implementing the harm reduction approach. *Journal of Social Work Practice in the Addictions, 8,* 380–408.

Marcellus, L. (2004). Feminist ethics must inform practice: Interventions with perinatal substance users. *Health Care for Women International, 25*(8), 730–742.

Marlatt, G. A. (1998). Basic principles and strategies of harm reduction. In G. A. Marlatt (Ed.), *Harm reduction: Pragmatic strategies for managing high risk behaviors* (pp. 49–68). New York: Guilford Press.

Marlatt, G. A., Larimer, M. E., Baer, J. S., & Quigley, L. A. (1993). Harm reduction for alcohol problems: Moving beyond the controlled drinking controversy. *Behavior Today, 24,* 461–504.

Matthews, M., Jr. (2001). Advertising drugs is good for patients. *Consumers Research Magazine, 84*(8), 15–21.

Miller, W. R. (1992). Building bridges over troubled waters: A response to "Alcoholism, politics, and bureaucracy: The consensus against controlled-drinking therapy in America." *Addictive Behaviors, 17,* 79–81.

Miller, W. R., Walters, S. T., & Bennett, M. E. (2001). How effective is alcohol treatment in the US. *Journal of Studies on Alcohol, 62,* 211–220.

Modell, J. G., Glaser, F. B., & Mountz, J. M. (1993). The ethics and safety of alcohol administration in the experimental setting to individuals who have chronic, severe alcohol problems. *Alcohol & Alcoholism, 28*(2), 189–197.

Moos, R. H., Brennan, P. L., Schutte, K. K., & Moos, B. S. (2004). High-risk alcohol consumption and late-life alcohol use problems. *American Journal of Public Health, 94,* 1985–1990.

Morgan, T. J. (2003). Behavioral treatment techniques for psychoactive substance use disorders. In F. Rotgers, J. Morgenstern, & S. T. Walters (Eds.), *Treating substance abuse: Theory and technique* (2nd ed., pp. 190–216). New York: Guilford Press.

Nadelmann, E., & Wenner, J. S. (1994, May 4). Toward a sane national drug policy. *Rolling Stone, 681,* 24–26.

Nathan, P. E. (1992). Peele hasn't done his homework—Again: A response to "Alcoholism, politics, and bureaucracy: The consensus against controlled-drinking therapy in America." *Addictive Behaviors, 17,* 63–65.

National Association of Alcoholism and Drug Abuse Counselors. (1987). NAADAC code of ethics. *Counselor, 5*(5), 13–16.

National Association of Social Workers. (2005). *NASW standards for social work practice with clients with substance use disorders.* Washington, DC: Author.

National Association of Social Workers. (2008). *Code of ethics of the National Association of Social Workers.* Washington, DC: Author.

National Institute on Alcohol Abuse and Alcoholism (NIAAA). (1997). Patient–treatment matching. *Alcohol Alert, 36,* 1–3.

Office of National Drug Control Policy (ONDCP). (1992). Needle exchange programs: Are they effective? *ONDCP Bulletin, 7.*

Office of National Drug Control Policy. (2006). Principals claim testing brings a wealth of benefits. *Strategies for Success: New Pathways to Drug Abuse Prevention, 1*(1), 1–2.

Parker, B. J. (1998). Exploring life themes and myths in alcohol advertising through a mean-based model of advertising experiences. *Journal of Advertising, 27*(1), 97–112.

Peele, S. (1987). Why do controlled-drinking outcomes vary by investigator, by country, and by era? Cultural conceptions of relapse and remissions in alcoholism. *Drug and Alcohol Dependence, 20,* 173–201.

Peele, S. (1992). Alcoholism, politics, and bureaucracy: The consensus against controlled-drinking therapy in America. *Addictive Behaviors, 17,* 49–62.

Pollay, R. W. (1997). Hacks, flacks, and counter-attacks: Cigarette advertising, sponsored research, and controversies. *Journal of Social Issues, 53*(1), 53–74.

Reamer, F. G. (1990). *Ethical dilemmas in social service: A guide for social workers* (2nd ed.). New York: Columbia University Press.

Reamer, F. G. (1995). *Social work values and ethics.* New York: Columbia University Press.

Reamer, F. G. (1997). Does professional education adequately prepare students to resolve ethical problems of practice? In E. Gambrill & R. Pruger (Eds.), *Controversial issues in social work ethics, values, and obligations* (pp. 169–174). Boston: Allyn & Bacon.

Reamer, F. G. (2001a). *Ethics education in social work.* Alexandria, VA: Council on Social Work Education.

Reamer, F. G. (2001b). *The social work ethics audit: A risk management tool.* Washington, DC: NASW Press.

Reamer, F. G. (2006a). *Ethical standards in social work: A review of the NASW Code of ethics* (2nd ed.). Washington, DC: NASW Press.

Reamer, F. G. (2006b). *Social work values and ethics* (3rd ed.). New York: Columbia University Press.

Reuter, P., & Caulkins, J. P. (1995). Redefining the goals of national drug policy: Recommendations from a working group. *American Journal of Public Health, 85,* 1059–1063.

Rosenbaum, M. (2004). *Safety first: A reality-based approach to teens, drugs, and drug education.* New York: Drug Policy Alliance.

Rubin, P. H. (1991). What the FDA doesn't want you to know. *American Enterprise, 2*(3), 18.

Scheck, J. (2009). Heroin program's deadly toll: Needle exchange may exact high price from workers. *Wall Street Journal, 252*(8), 1, 8.

Sheldon, T. (2008). More than a quick fix. *British Medical Journal, 336*(2), 68–69.

Siegel, D., Green, J., Abbott, A. A., & Mogul, M. (2007). Welfare leavers and returners: Correlates of quality of life. *Journal of Human Behavior in the Social Environment, 15*(1), 69–97.

Sobell, M. B., & Sobell, L. C. (1978). *Behavioral treatment of alcohol problems.* New York: Plenum Press.

Springer, E. (1991). Effective AIDS prevention with active drug users: The harm reduction model. *Journal of Chemical Dependency Treatment, 4*(2), 141–157.

Stockwell, T. (1988). Can severely dependent drinkers learn controlled drinking? Summing up the debate. *British Journal of Addiction, 83,* 149–152.

Strom-Gottfried, K. (2007). *Straight talk about professional ethics.* Chicago: Lyceum Books.

Substance Abuse and Mental Health Services Administration (SAMHSA), Office of Applied Statistics. (2008). *Results from the 2007 National Survey on Drug Use and Health: National findings* (NSDUH Series H-34, DHHS Publication No. SMA 08–4343). Rockville, MD: Author.

U.S. Department of Health and Human Services, Office of Public Health and Science. (2006). *The health consequences of involuntary exposure to tobacco smoke: A report of the surgeon general.* Rockville, MD: Author.

Walker, T. (2008). Giving addicts their drug of choice: The problem of consent. *Bioethics, 22,* 314–320.

Wells, C. C. (with Masch, M. K.). (1986). *Social work ethics day to day: Guidelines for professional practice.* New York: Longman.

Whittinghill, D. (2002). Ethical considerations for the use of family therapy in substance abuse treatment. *Family Journal: Counseling and Therapy for Couples and Families, 10*(1), 75–78.

4

Dynamics and Physiology of Drug Use

Raymond Bolden, Jr.

The dynamics and physiology of drug use is a distinct area of knowledge that social workers must possess to better serve their clients. Drug use and its impact on human growth and pathology is important information not only for social workers who treat drug disorders, but also for all social workers who deal with the needs of individuals, families, or communities. Social workers must understand that drug misuse introduces neurochemical, social, medical, and cultural differences that are distinct from nondrug disorders.

Drugs are defined as "any substance, natural or artificial, other than food that by its chemical nature alters the structure or function within a living organism" (Ksir, Hart, & Ray, 2006, p. 6). Substances such as alcohol and caffeine may be described as food, especially in the form of their delivery mechanism into the body through wine, beer, coffee, or chocolate. However, in this chapter they will be treated as drugs.

These substances provide benefits or risks to the user based on the quantity and frequency of the substance taken and with which other substances it is consumed. Without such an understanding, problem prevention and intervention strategies for misusers and abusers of alcohol, tobacco, and other drugs (ATOD) may be inappropriately applied. The term "misuse" refers to the inappropriate use of prescription drugs whereas "abuse" refers to the use of both legal and illegal drugs in ways that result in social, mental, and, or physical impairment. This chapter intends to provide the social worker with information on the nature and effect of the most commonly misused and abused drugs.

Classification and Identification of Drugs of Abuse

Drugs are usually grouped together or classified according to the effects they have on the central nervous system (CNS). Some act as depressants or as stimulants, others relieve pain, and some produce unusual sensory perceptions. Table 4.1 delineates drugs of abuse by category and effect, greater details of which are presented in the text that follows.

Depressants

Depressants, or downers as they are often called, have the effect of decreasing the neural activity of the brain, slowing the CNS. Alcohol, whether in the form of beer, wine, or hard liquor; sedatives such as the barbiturates (phenobarbital, amobarbital, and secobarbital); and tranquilizers (valium, xanax, and librium) are examples of depressants. These depressants may be administered orally (alcohol, sedatives, and tranquilizers) or injected (sedatives, tranquilizers). Inhalants, such as paints, gasoline, glue, or solvents, produce a similar depressant effect when breathed (Ksir et al., 2006). Low dosages of depressants appear to depress the inhibitory parts of the brain that may lead to disinhibition or relaxation. As the dosages and frequency of the depressants used continues, the possible effects may be slurred speech, disorientation, staggering, and drunken behavior. The effects of overdosing are shallow respiration, cold and clammy skin, weak and rapid pulse, coma, and possible death. Withdrawal from depressants may result in anxiety, insomnia, tremors, delirium, convulsions, and possible death.

Stimulants

Drugs that increase alertness, wakefulness, a sense of energy, and euphoria are referred to as stimulants that can be sniffed, smoked, injected, or swallowed. Cocaine, caffeine, amphetamines (speed), and methylphenidate (Ritalin) are examples of the most commonly abused stimulants. In addition to increased excitation, alertness, and euphoria, stimulants increase the pulse rate and blood pressure, cause insomnia, and loss of appetite. Overdosage produces agitation, increased body temperature, hallucinations, convulsions, and possible death. Withdrawal from stimulants may severely depress the mood and cause apathy, disorientation, and prolonged sleep.

Opioids

Opioids are a class of drugs also known as analgesics or painkillers. Opiates specifically come from a resin taken from the seed pod of the opium poppy, and they include opium, morphine, and codeine. Opioids include synthetic and semisyn-thethic opiatelike drugs: heroin, oxycodone, methadone, meperidine (Demerol), and fentanyl. Methadone, is used in the treatment of heroin addicts because it prevents withdrawal symptoms for as much as a day. LAAM (L-alpha-acetylmethadal), brand name Orlaam, has also been approved for treating heroin addicts.

Heroin, a morphine derivative, introduced by the German-based Bayer company in 1898, is no longer available for its originally intended medical use (Levinthal, 2008); however, its use as an illegal substance has continued to increase in popularity. Fentanyl was introduced in 1968 as a surgical anesthetic that can be administered by intravenous injection, through the skin by patch form or laced in candy and given to children to calm them before surgery or to lessen a woman's pain during childbirth. Fentanyl is a powerful opium analog, at least 50 to 100 times more potent than heroin, and because it does not have to be injected, its abuse potential is great (Doweiko, 2008).

Oxycodone is a synthetic opioid used as a medication for pain relief in its most widely known continuous-release formulation as the brand name OxyContin. The increased use of oxycodone has resulted in an increased pattern of abuse in recent years (Jaffe & Strain, 2005). Codeine is approved as a medication in the form of a syrup or tablet to relieve mild to severe pain, coughing, and diarrhea. However, chronic use can cause physical dependency to occur as with other opioids.

Opioids alter the user's perception of pain, producing a relaxed, dreamlike state and, at moderately high dosages, sleep can be induced and even death. For some users, opioids appear to have the capacity to ameliorate certain types of depression, reduce anxiety, control anger, and to blunt paranoia (Knapp, Ciraulo, & Jaffe, 2005). When opioids are injected, the user feels an immediate "rush" or surge of euphoric pleasure. Users may go "on the nod," going back and forth from feeling alert to drowsy. The unpleasant effects may include restlessness, nausea, and vomiting.

Nicotine

Nicotine, the psychoactive drug in tobacco, is a powerful drug with neurobiological effects similar to those of other drugs of abuse. Although some list it as a stimulant (Ksir et al., 2006), it can stimulate or relax and has rewarding effects such as mood and cognitive elevated effects and reduced bodyweight (Vleeming, Rambali, & Opperhuizen, 2002). Nicotine is an alkaloid that exerts diverse, often subtle, effects on the CNS. Cigarette smoking has been the most prevalent method of taking nicotine, involving over 25 percent of the U.S. population in 2005 (Levinthal, 2008), down from 42.4 percent in 1965 (Schmitz & Delaune, 2005). However,

TABLE 4.1: Most Commonly Misused/Abused Drugs

Drugs	Medical Names	Slang Names	Medical Uses	Forms
Depressants				
Alcohol	Ethyl Alcohol	Booze	None	Liquid
Sedatives	Secobarbital, phenobarbital, Seconal	Barbs, reds, downers, killers	Sedative, Anticonvulsant, Anesthetic	Capsules, tablets, powder
Tranquilizers	Valium, Librium	Downers	Antianxiety, Sedative	Capsules, tablets
Inhalants	Acetone, Benzene, etc.		None	Liquid, paste, aerosol
GHB	Gamma hydroxybutyrate	Grievous "G" Bodily Harm	Narcolepsy	Liquid, tablet, powder
Ketamine	Derivative of phencyclindine hydrochloride	"Special K"	Anesthetic for surgery & Veterinary medicine	Liquid, powder
Stimulants				
Caffeine	Xanthine		Asthmatic conditions	Liquid, tablets, powder,
Cocaine	Cocaine	Coke, rock, crack, snow, flake	Local anesthetic	Powder, rock
Amphetamines	Dexedrine, Benzedine	Speed, bennies	Hyperkinesis, Narcolepsy, Weight control, Mental disorders	Tablets, capsules, liquid, powder
Ritalin	Methylphenidate		Attention deficit/hyperactivity disorder	Tablets, powder

Route of Administration	Effects Sought	Possible Effects	Overdose
Swallow	Anxiety reduction, mood alteration	Increased dependency, depression	Loss of concentration, unconsciousness, death
Inject, swallow	Anxiety reduction, euphoria, sleep	Loss of concentration, slurred speech, depression, dependency	Dependency, severe withdrawal, toxic psychosis
Swallow	Anxiety reduction, euphoria, sleep	Loss of coordination, sluggishness, slurred speech, disorientation, dependence	Cold and clammy skin, dilated pupils, weak and rapid pulse, coma, death
Inhaled	Anxiety reduction, euphoria, sleep	Loss of coordination, sluggishness, slurred speech, disorientation, dependence	Cold and clammy skin, dilated pupils, weak and rapid pulse, coma, death
Swallow	Euphoria, sedation, lower inhibitions	Dizziness, nausea, severe headache	Lack of consciousness, amnesia, coma, death
Injection, snort, smoke	Intense psychological and somatic state (K-hole)	Dissociated state and sensory deprivation, amnesia	Disorientation, coma, death
Swallow	Alertness, improved performance	Osteoporosis, panic attack	Caffeinism (extreme nervousness, twitching, insomnia)
Inject, smoke, inhale	Euphoria, excitation	Increased alertness, blood pressure, excitation, insomnia, loss of appetite	Agitation, convulsions, death
Swallow, inject	Alertness, activeness	Increased alertness, pulse rate, blood pressure, excitation, insomnia, loss of appetite	Agitation, increase in body temperature, hallucinations, convulsions, death
Swallow, snort	Euphoria, excitation	Nervousness, insomnia	Vomiting, tremors, seizures, death

(continued)

TABLE 4.1 *(continued)*

Drugs	Medical Names	Slang Names	Medical Uses	Forms
Opioids				
Heroin	Diacetylmorphine	China white, smack, horse, H	Research	Powder
OxyContin	Oxycodone	Killers	Pain relief	Tablet, powder, solution
Codeine			Pain, cough, diarrhea	Liquid, tablets
Nicotine	Nicotine	Butt, chew, smoke, cig, plug, pinch	None	Pipe, cigar, cigarette, Snuff
Hallucinogens				
PCP	Phencyclidine	Angel dust, monkey dust, jet fuel	None	Tablets, powder
LSD	d-lysergic acid diethylamide	Acid	Research	Crystalline form, liquid
MDMA	3,4, methylenediarymethamphetamine	Ecstasy	None	Tablet
Mescaline	3, 4, 5-trimethoxyphenethylamine	Mesc	Ritualistic use by some Native American tribes	Tablet, powder
Cannabis, Marijuana	Tetrahydrocannabinol	Pot, weed, grass, reefer, ganja, dope	Research	Plant particles

Route of Administration	Effects Sought	Possible Effects	Overdose
Inject, swallow	Euphoria, prevent withdrawal, sleep	Euphoria, drowsiness, sleep, nausea, respiratory depression, dependency	Clammy skin, slow breathing, convulsions, coma, death
Swallow, inhaled, injected	Euphoria	Euphoria, sleep, nausea	Clammy skin, slow breathing, seizures, coma, death
Swallow	Euphoria	Euphoria, Sleep, nausea	
Sniff, chew, smoke	Relaxation	Respiratory difficulties, high blood pressure, dependency, heart attacks	Confusion, convulsions, coma, death
Smoke, swallow	Distortion of senses, insight, exhilaration	Illusions and hallucinations, distorted perception of time and distance	Longer or more intense episodes, psychosis, convulsions, death
Swallow	Distortion of senses, insight, exhilaration, trip	Hallucination, increased heart rate, elevated blood pressure, nausea	Psychological reaction that can lead to dangerous & life-threatening behavior, bad trip
Swallow	Relaxation, euphoria	Stimulates & possesses hallucinogenic properties	Possible heart attack, stroke, seizure
Swallow, snort	Distortion of the senses, insight	Dizziness, irrational thoughts, hallucinations	Convulsions, heart failure, death
Smoke, swallow	Relaxation, euphoria, increased perception	Relaxed inhibitions, euphoria, increased appetite, disoriented behavior and perceptions	Fatigue, paranoia

tobacco may also be sniffed, chewed, and placed in the jaw as means of absorbing nicotine. Smokers often give reasons for their tobacco use, such as reducing body-weight, reducing anxiety and stress, and enhancing positive mood states. Recent findings, however, indicate that smoking tobacco appears to reverse, to some extent, anxiety and stress found in smokers who were deprived of tobacco but does not promote the attainment of beneficial moods (Schmitz & Delaune, 2005). Respiratory difficulties and ailments, high blood pressure, fatigue, lung cancer, and heart attacks are possible long- and short-term tobacco use effects (Ksir et al., 2006). Tolerance, withdrawal, and dependency can occur, but there is no evidence of overdosing unless combined with several other nicotine products.

Hallucinogens

Hallucinogens are drugs that are capable of replacing the present world with a world of fantasy—visual and other sensory distortions and altered perceptions of one's own body. Because hallucinogens also produce increased emotionality, over-doses may result in prolonged episodes that resemble psychotic states. The most commonly used hallucinogens are phencyclidine (PCP), often referred to as "angel dust," d-lysergic acid diethylamide (LSD), the less potent psilocybin and mescaline, and 3, 4 methylenedioxy methampetamine (MDMA), also known as "ecstasy" on the street.

Marijuana, a psychoactive drug originating from the cannabis plant, is the most frequently used illicit drug in the United States (Levinthal, 2008). The cannabis plant has more than 400 different compounds; however, only one of these is thought to account for most of marijuana's effect: THC (delta-9-tetrahydro-cannabinol). Marijuana smokers frequently feel drowsy, sleepy, and dreamy, and if THC concentration is high enough, sleep can be induced (Leventhal, 2008). Another behavioral outcome dependent on the direct function of THC levels is diminished focus of concentration and impairment of both short- and long-term memory tasks. The greater the THC concentration, the greater the magnitude of memory task impairment.

When smoked, marijuana is often referred to as "reefer," "weed," or "joint." Although smoking is the predominant form of administration, cannabis may be ingested orally. Its possible effects are euphoria, released inhibitions, increased appetite, impaired memory and attention. Marijuana has been referred to as a "gateway drug" because of its association with other drug use. The likelihood of people who have never used marijuana using cocaine or heroin is rare; the likelihood of using alcohol and illicit drugs increases as marijuana use increases (Grinspoon, Bakalar, & Russo, 2005).

Forms, Methods of Use, and Ingestion of Drugs

How drugs will affect the body chemistry of a user will depend on the dosage and effects, composition, frequency of use, how it is administered, and interactions with other drugs. All of these factors influence the body's response.

Dosage and Effects

When a drug is introduced into the body, it produces effects that are dependent on the amount and strength of the dosage. The relationship between the drug and the effect is called the dose–response relationship. When a drug produces no noticeable effect, the dosage has not reached the noticeable effect or threshold for that person. Maximum effect is reached by increasing the dosage. For example, if after taking a 325-milligram analgesic tablet for a headache and the pain does not lessen, the sufferer may increase the dosage to two tablets (650 milligrams) to get relief or the desired effect. Effects are said to be of two types—therapeutic or adverse. For instance morphine's therapeutic effect is pain relief, and lithium is intended to help alleviate depression; if other effects occur, they are considered adverse.

Adverse effects include side effects, allergic reactions, idiosyncratic reactions, and toxic effects. Side effects are reliable anticipated adverse effects that the drug may produce, such as upset stomach, depression, or euphoria. Often a side effect such as the euphoria resulting from opioid pain relievers becomes the effect sought by drug misusers. Allergic reactions differ from side effects in their predictability and in their frequency of occurrence. An allergic effect depends on the particular host. For example, some individuals may develop a skin rash or have difficulty breathing after drinking a vodka Collins. This reaction, not common to, or expected of most vodka Collins drinkers, is an allergic reaction.

Idiosyncratic reactions are highly unusual, unanticipated, and unreliable reactions to a drug, which cannot be attributed either to side effects or allergic reactions. For a particular person, the use of an opioid such as heroin may produce a paradoxical effect of excitation and overstimulation instead of the "mellowing out" effect common to most heroin users. Toxic drug effects (overdosages) are the lethal or near-lethal dosages, which can result in coma or death.

Ksir and colleagues (2006) remind us that potency is one of the most misunderstood concepts in the area of drug use. The dosage of a drug refers to the amount of drug that must be taken to get a certain effect. The less the amount needed to get the effect, the more potent the drug. Potency relates to the level of effect a drug can produce. Alcohol is a rather impotent drug because ounces or grams of it are required to produce noticeable effects. The hallucinogen LSD is very potent because dosages are measured in micrograms or millionths of grams. However, the effects of LSD are relatively limited—It does not lead to overdose deaths the way alcohol does. Alcohol, although less potent, has more powerful effects than LSD, even though in terms of the dose required to produce a psychological effect LSD is thousands of times more potent (Ksir et al., 2006).

Composition

The tablets, pills, and other forms of pharmaceutical preparations are composed of active and inactive ingredients. Inactive ingredients may be binders, fillers, coloring compounds, dissolving agents, coatings, and even flavorings. These inactive ingredients are not intended to affect the user, but some people can react adversely to them. Thus, two apparently identical compounds can have different effects depending on the inactive ingredients used. Illicit drugs are not subjected to quality controls as are over-the-counter (OTC) and prescription drugs. Street drugs vary in quality, quantity, and purity. That is, the composition of the drug may be different from what it is alleged to be. For example, when heroin was introduced in the 1990s with purity rates of 90 percent, which were often 10 times greater in purity than typical on the streets of New York in the 1980s, spikes in overdosage incidents occurred. Street cocaine with similar purity levels may be "cut with" an added white, flaky, or sparkling ingredient such as talcum powder, strychnine, boric acid, or phencyclidine, which in themselves can have an effect on the user.

Frequency of Use

A drug will produce changes in an individual from one use episode to the next; the first cocktail changes the drinker so that the second cocktail is experienced differently. If a drug is used frequently enough, its accumulation in the body changes the metabolism of the body. If consumption of a drug is so rapid that the body cannot excrete it faster than it is being ingested, intoxication or even death can occur. However, to maintain a certain level of a drug in the bloodstream, dosages must be "serialed" in such a way to maintain that desired level. Prescription drug use patterns are designed to achieve and maintain a certain level of the drug in the bloodstream. Individuals using a stimulant to maintain a "high" will space their dosages to achieve the desired results.

How It Is Administered

The specific way in which a drug is administered will have an effect on the speed with which that drug can be distributed throughout the body. There are numerous routes for administering drugs; only those most frequently used will be discussed.

The three most common methods are swallowing (oral and sublingual), injecting (subcutaneous, intramuscular, and intravenous), and inhaling (smoking) and snorting.

Swallowing. Tablets, capsules, and liquids are the most common forms of orally taken drugs. Alcohol is the best example of a liquid drug of abuse taken orally. Drugs sublingually taken are absorbed through the blood-rich tissues under the tongue. Fentanyl is absorbed by this method. However, other drugs of abuse are rarely administered by the sublingual method (Doweiko, 2008).

Injection. Three methods are used for injecting drugs directly into the body—subcutaneous, intramuscular, and intravenous. When a drug is injected just under the skin, the method is called subcutaneous. Subcutaneously injected drugs are absorbed more slowly than those injected into muscles or veins. Heroin users often used subcutaneous methods, a process called "skin popping." The intramuscular injection of a drug (injection into blood-rich muscles) allows for more rapid absorption into general circulation. The most rapid and direct method of depositing a drug into circulation is through IV injection. Heroin, cocaine, and amphetamines are drugs of abuse often administered by IV injection.

Inhalation. Inhalation is a very efficient way to deliver a drug (Ksir et al., 2006). It is the method of preference for nicotine, marijuana, and crack cocaine as well as for glue, paints, gasoline, solvents, and aerosols. Smoking cigarettes allows nicotine to reach the brain in seven to 19 seconds of puffing; similar results occur with the smoking of cocaine. Inhalation is also used medically to introduce various anesthetics. The onset of an inhaled drug's effect is rapid, its peak is high, and the effect is of relative short duration.

Drug Interactions

There are basically three forms of drug interactions when drugs are administered in close proximity to one another: additive, synergistic, and antagonistic. Additive interactions occur when two drugs in combination produce an effect that is greater than the effect of either drug taken alone (Levinthal, 2008). For example, when two depressants such as alcohol and the sedative Valium are consumed in close proximity to each other, an additive effect occurs. In some instances, when two depressants are combined, the effect can become hyperadditive, more than the sum of the individual drugs. Respiratory depression, drug overdose, or even death may occur. Any hyperadditive effect is referred to as synergistic. In synergistic combinations one drug may double or even triple the effect of another. It is also possible that one drug administered alone may have little or no effect but in combination with the other have its effect considerably enhanced. For example, amphetamines taken with a class of antidepressants known as monoamine oxidase inhibitors has the potential to create a hypertensive crisis.

In antagonistic interactions, the drugs counter each other's effects—The effect of one drug is diminished to some degree when administered with another. This can be caused by the antagonist drug taking control of the receptors and blocking the effect of the other drug. Some drugs are perfectly antagonistic to each other, one cancels out the effect of the other. Naltrexone when administered with injected opiates will block the euphoric effect of the injection, yet, produces no effects of its own (Doweiko, 2008; Lewis, Dana, & Blevins, 2001). Naltroxone was approved by the Federal Drug Administration in 1994 for use as an antagonist to reduce the craving for alcohol.

Physiology of Drug Use and Effects on the Body

Transportation of Drugs in the Body

After a drug enters the body, unless it is injected into the site of action, it must travel to the site, through the circulatory system, as a foreign substance that is taking advantage of the body's chemical distribution system. The speed at which the drug is distributed depends on the efficiency and health of the circulatory system; it also depends on the means by which it was taken. There are several ways a drug can use the circulatory system to reach the site of action. If it is water soluble, it will mix freely with the blood plasma and travel throughout the entire body to all blood-rich organs, including the brain, assuming it has the ability to cross the blood brain barrier. Alcohol is an excellent example of a water-soluble drug that distributes itself throughout the body.

Drugs such as barbiturates are lipid soluble because they bind to fat molecules in the blood, known as lipids. Because lipids are used to build cell walls, they move quickly out of the bloodstream into the body's tissue. Thus, they are distributed throughout the body, especially to those organs with high concentrations of lipids, such as the brain (Cooper, Bloom, & Roth, 1996).

Inhaled drugs are taken directly into the lungs through the nostrils and nasal cavity or mouth, larynx, and trachea. The lungs have a large, rich blood supply. On inhalation of a substance to the surface area of the lungs, the substance easily enters the bloodstream and travels to the brain very rapidly.

Biotransformation

Because drugs are foreign substances to the body, its natural defenses attempt to eliminate them. For elimination to be accomplished, in most cases, the drug's chemical structures must be modified. The liver is the primary site breaking down a molecule structure into simpler forms by the actions of enzymes; that is, the liver engages in a process that alters a drug to form a new and often inactive one that can be more readily eliminated. This transformation process is usually referred to as metabolism or more accurately, as biotransformation (Levinthal, 2008). The new chemical that emerges is a metabolite of the original or parent drug. The liver, although the prime source of biotransformation, is not the only organ that carries out this function. Some alcohol is biotranformed in the stomach before it is absorbed into circulation. Most drugs go through biotransformation before they are eliminated.

Eliminating Drugs

Sometimes small percentages of drugs can be eliminated in exhaled breath, sweat, feces, saliva, or breast milk. The most common means of eliminating drugs from the body, however, is through excretion of urine. The process that leads to urinary secretion is a series of actions in the liver and kidneys. The sequence of metabolic events begins with the biotransformation process described earlier—the transformation of the original drug into metabolites. If these metabolites are water soluble, they pass through the kidneys and are excreted into the urine. If they are less water soluble, they are reabsorbed into the intestines and excreted through feces.

The factors that may influence the biotransformation rates are a function of the drug's concentration in the blood; the larger the quantity of drug in the bloodstream, the faster the body will try to eliminate it. The exception is alcohol, for which the rate of biotransformation is constant regardless of the amount ingested (Levinthal, 2008). The presence of other drugs may also increase or decrease the work of liver enzymes. Factors such as age, ethnicity, and gender, discussed in a later section of this chapter, may also affect biotransformation and elimination rates.

Fat-soluble drugs have slower elimination rates than those that are water soluble because they are absorbed and stored in fat tissue. Elimination rates are often gauged by a half-life index. This index refers to the amount of time it takes for a drug in the bloodstream to decline to 50 percent of its original level. The half-life is a measure of the drug's duration of action. Drugs with long half-lives tend to remain biologically active for longer periods of time. Drugs like nicotine and cocaine have half-lives of only a few hours; marijuana, however, has a much longer half-life. How drugs are eliminated from the body must be of interest and understood by practitioners if drug testing procedures to detect the presence of misused and abused drugs are to be appropriately developed and used.

The Primary Site of Action

The primary site of action for mood-altering drugs is the CNS, located along the central axis of the body and consisting of the spinal cord and the brain. The brain, with its 100 billion specialized neurons, is the focus of our attention here. These neurons are where psychoactive drugs do their work. Neurons are cells with membranes that are semipermeable, meaning that some agents can move in and out of these cells; other agents can be held inside or kept out. It is this characteristic that makes it possible for messages (electrical charges) to be transported across the membrane. The generation of the electrical charge is referred to as the nerve impulse (Levinthal, 2008).

The job of neurons is to receive and transmit messages through electrochemical processes. This is done through three major components: (1) the cell body, which is the bulk of the neutron, including the nucleus; (2) the dendrites, which are short appendages extending out of the cell body that receive messages from the outside; and (3) the axon, a long appendage, which at its end diverges like a tree trunk with smooth buttonlike structures with ends called synaptic knobs. When a nerve impulse from the cell body is generated, it follows along the axon to the knob; the impulse causes the neurotransmitters to be released and cross the intervening gap or synapse. The neurotransmitter is accepted by or binds with the receptor on the dendrites. Once the initiating neuron releases the neurotransmitter molecules, it responds in several ways. It reabsorbs, by a process known as reuptake, as many free-floating molecules as possible for reuse while simultaneously producing more neurotransmitters for future use; or the released molecules are broken down or inactivated through enzymatic action known as metabolization. In either case, the action prepares the neurotransmitter for subsequent impulses. (See Figure 4.1 for a depiction of the basic structure of a neuron.)

Receptors (sites on the membranes of dendrites on the other side of the synapse) have shapes that match the external shape of neurotransmitters, which allow for a neurotransmitter and a receptor to bind, completing a chemical communication. When such a fit takes place, an electrical charge occurs in the membrane of the receiving neuron, and electrical communication occurs within that neuron. The message is either to excite (continue firing nerve impulses) or inhibit (reduce the number of nerve impulses per second). Whether it is to excite or to inhibit will depend on the specific neurotransmitter that is present at the receptor.

Six prominent neurotransmitters are involved in the misuse and abuse of psychoactive drugs. The first, acetylcholine, the most widely distributed neurotransmitter, sometimes excites and sometimes inhibits nerve impulses. These

Figure 4.1: Basic Structure of a Neuron

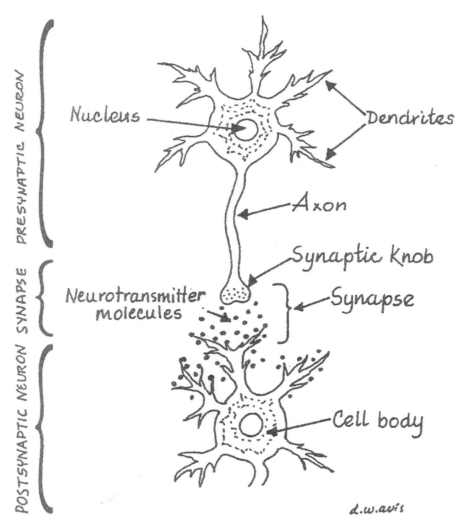

neurotransmitters are involved in motor activity, learning and memory, sleep, and food and water intake (Lewis et al., 2001). Acetylcholine receptors are sensitive to nicotine; some antinicotine drugs such as poison curate, affect the motor neurons to the extent that the body can become paralyzed within seconds (Levinthal, 2008).

The second neurotransmitter, norepinephrine, is important for regulating waking and rapid eye movement sleep. It is perhaps norepinephrine that induces wakefulness (Ksir et al., 2006). This neurotransmitter also regulates mood states; drugs that boost the levels of norepinephrine help to relieve symptoms of depression (Levinthal, 2008). Drugs such as methamphetamines boost levels of norepinephine.

The third neurotransmitter, dopamine, is concerned with the ability to start and stop motor activity by choice and to execute movement with smoothness and precision. Deficiencies in this neurotransmitter are seen in symptoms of Parkinson's disease (Levinthal, 2008).

The fourth neurotransmitter, serotonin, is involved in arousal and mood modification processes and is important for deep sleep. Drugs that relieve mood swings—mania and depression—act on the serotonin-releasing neurons. Some hallucinogens also stimulate the release of serotonin (Levinthal, 2008). Tricyclic antidepressant drugs relieve mood swings through serotonin.

The fifth neurotransmitter of importance here is gamma-aminobutyric acid (GABA), the main inhibitory neurotransmitter of the brain. Antianxiety and sedative drugs in general tend to stimulate the GABA receptors of the brain and provide reduction in feelings of fear and stress. GABA deficiencies are also associated with the tendency to suffer epileptic seizures (Levinthal, 2008).

The sixth neurotransmitter, endorphins, are opioidlike chemicals that play a role in pain relief. Morphine, heroin, and codeine stimulate these receptors in the spinal cord and the brain. There has been some speculation that endorphins play a role in creating drug dependency. Ksir and colleagues (2006) caution that as yet there is no strong evidence to assume this association.

Drugs affect neurotransmitters by altering their pathways. This can happen in one or a combination of the following ways: destroying neurons; altering neuron membranes; affecting the enzymes that help neurons synthesize neurotransmitters; destroying neurotransmitters and creating false neurotransmitters; mimicking neurotransmitters and creating false neurotransmissions; blocking receptors; and changing receptor's sensitivity, thus enhancing or retarding the neurotransmitters' actions on the receptors (Lewis et al., 2001).

Influence of Physiological, Psychological, and Social Characteristics of Drug Effects on Drug Users

Variation in the effects drugs have on users may be attributed to the particular physiological, psychological, and social characteristics of the person taking the drug, rather than the drug itself (Levinthal, 2008). People's bodies respond to and process drugs differently (Lewis et al., 2001). Characteristics such as body weight, gender, age, ethnicity and race, genetics, expectations, biorhythms, emotional mood, and social environment influence drugs effects.

Body weight (or body mass). A frequently used variable by medical personnel to adjust drug dosages, body weight is an indicator of several variables, fat and protein proportions, volume of blood, and cardiovascular function (Lewis et al., 2001). In general, a heavier person will require a greater amount of a drug than a lighter person to acquire the same drug effect.

Gender differences. Variations in drug effects are influenced by gender even when other characteristics, such as weight, are controlled. Women and men differ in body composition and sex hormones. Men's bodies have higher water content and lower fat-to-muscle ratios. Gender differences in the proportion of body fat and water influence blood alcohol concentrations and also have an effect on the impact of psychoactive drugs (Blume & Zilberman, 2005).

Age. Another factor that leads to variability of drug effects on users is age. Drug dosages have historically been adjusted according to the age of the user. Pediatric and geriatric dosages have been established for many drugs. Cardiologic, metabolic, excretory, and neurological functions vary with age, as does body weight and a number of psychosocial functions.

Ethnicity and race. Factors that may directly or indirectly influence the effects of drug use are ethnicity and race. About 50 percent of the people of Asian descent carry a gene that lessens the effectiveness of their liver's aldehyde dehydrogenase (Ksir et al., 2006). When they consume alcohol, there is a buildup of a toxic byproduct of alcohol metabolism, acetaldehyde, which leads to an increase in heart rate, facial flushing, sweating, and nausea. Caucasians metabolize antipsychotic and antianxiety medications faster than Asians and hence end up with relatively lower concentrations of these drugs in the bloodstream. Another example of racial variations influencing drug effects is the higher levels of cotinine (a nicotine metabolite) found in black smokers than found in white smokers because of the differences in nicotine metabolism and cotinine excretion (Wagenknecht et al., 1990). Socioeconomic factors such as income, education, and employment also varied along racial lines in a 10-year study by Kiefe and colleagues (2001) of changes in smoking among young adults.

Genetics or heredity. Also shown to play a role in the susceptibility and immunity to various drugs is genetics. The sensitivity Asians show to alcohol ingestion has been linked to two protective enzymes, aldehyde dehydrogenase and alcohol dehydrogenase that work independently of each other to metabolize alcohol (Luczak, Glatt, & Wall, 2006). Research evidence from studies of twins and adoptees indicate the importance of genetic influence on alcoholism risks. In a reanalysis of adoption and twin studies, Heath (1995) concluded that the influence of genetics on alcoholism has been found to be consistent across studies, across groups born in different time periods, and regardless of gender. The generalizability of the twin and adoptee studies' findings to people of non-European ancestry is yet to be determined as these studies' samples were drawn from groups who were predominately of European origin (Heath, 1995).

Expectations. Not all of the effects of a drug depend on the interaction of the drug with the body's physiology. The impact of psychological factors on the variability of drug effects is increasingly being understood. The most prominent psychological factor is the influence of expectations on the part of the person consuming the drug (Levinthal, 2008). Expectations about the drug's effect are derived from a variety of sources: settings, previous personal experiences, mass media, the experiences of friends, education, and professionals. To "have a better time," "get energy up," "mellow out," and "forget" are often-heard motives for using a mood-altering drug. Placebo studies provide clear illustrations of the influence of expectations on drug effects not dependent on chemical interactions. Placebo effects are produced by an inactive chemical (placebo) that the user believes to be a drug. Users have reported cognitive, sensory, and emotional changes related to the use of a placebo. Such effects are related to the user's beliefs, rather than the drug's chemistry.

Biorhythms. It is clear that variations in the responses individuals have to drugs may be influenced by the particular characteristics of the person taking the drug, rather than the drug itself. In addition, different effects from the same drug administered in the same way may occur for different users and for the same user on different occasions. Cyclical processes or biorhythms such as time of day, menstrual cycles, periods of alertness, fatigue, hunger, and states such as sexual arousal can influence the variability of a drug's effects in the same users and among different users.

Emotional mood. The emotional mood of the user not only contributes to the motives for drug use, but also determines how the drug will influence subsequent moods. An angry or depressed person may use a drug to forget or elevate his or her mood, a happy individual may use it to celebrate. The motive for use and context in which it is used are factors that must be included in predicting the present and future effects of drug use on behavior.

Social environment. People, places, and things that make up the social environment influence the effect drugs may have on the user. Germain and Bloom (1999) suggested that it is important not to separate physical and social environments because physical arrangements can shape the nature of social arrangements and the interactions that then occur. The physical setting prescribes and proscribes the types of people found there and the ways in which they interact. It is difficult, if not impossible, to engage in certain behaviors when the props are missing. A drug will result in very different behavior when used in a medical setting than when used at a party (Lewis et al., 2001).

Classification of Substance Disorders

The American Psychiatric Association (APA, 2000) and the World Health Organization (WHO, 2007) have both developed classification systems for defining problems associated with drug-taking behaviors. The *Diagnostic and Statistical Manual of Mental Disorders—Text Revision*, 4th edition (DSM-IV-TR) (APA, 2000) and the *Tenth Revision of the International Classification of Disease* (ICD-10) (WHO, 2007) both have sections on substance-related disorders, which consist of two parts: (1) substance use disorders, which include abuse and dependence; and (2) substance-induced disorders, which include, among others, intoxication, withdrawal, and substance-induced mental disorders. Each section is divided into general drug categories under which specific mood-altering drugs are listed and criteria are provided so the disorders attributable to particular drugs can be identified and coded.

Dependence

The substance use disorders sections of both classification systems have criteria that greatly overlap, particularly the items for substance dependence. Both systems define dependence as occurring with or without physiological features. According to the DSM-IV-TR (APA, 2000), tolerance or withdrawal must be present for dependence with physiological features to be the diagnosis. The absence of both of these features and the presence of three or more of the other criteria are necessary for dependence without physiological features to be the classification. No such sub-typing of dependence exists in the ICD-10 system (Cacciola & Woody, 2005). Dependence can be diagnosed for both systems when at least three dependence criteria are present. Comparison of the dependence criteria for the DSM-IV-TR and the ICD-10 are presented in Table 4.2.

Abuse and Harmful Use

The most prominent difference between the DSM-IV-TR (APA, 2000) and the ICD-10 (WHO, 2007) classifications systems is the use of the term "abuse" in the DSM-IV-TR and the term "harmful use" in the ICD-10. The DSM-IV-TR defined substance abuse in social terms such as failure in role obligations, use in physically hazardous situations, and recurrent substance-related legal problems, in the absence of compulsive use, tolerance, and withdrawal. ICD-10 has been reluctant to apply social criteria to define disorders because ICD-10 must be applicable to a wide range of cultures; what is acceptable social behavior in one culture may not

TABLE 4.2: Comparison of DSM-IV-TR and ICD-10: Items for Dependence

DSM-IV-TR Three or More	ICD-10 Three or More
(1) tolerance	(IV) tolerance
(2) withdrawal	(III) withdrawal
(3) substance often taken in larger amounts or over longer period than was intended	(II) difficulties controlling substance-taking behavior in terms of onset, termination, or levels of use, no corresponding ICD category
(4) any successful efforts or a persistent desire to cut down or control substance use	(V) part one—increased amounts of time necessary to obtain or take the substance or recover from its effects
(5) great deal of time spent in activities to obtain substance or recover from effect	(V) part two—progressive neglect of alternative pleasures or interests
(6) important social, occupational, or recreational activities reduced or given up because of substance use	(VI) persisting with substance use despite evidence of overly harmful problem consequences
(7) continued substance use despite knowledge of having had persistent physical or psychological problems caused or exacerbated by substance use, no corresponding DSM category	(I) a strong desire or sense of compulsion to take the substance

Notes: DSM-IV-TR = *Diagnostic and Statistical Manual of Mental Disorders*-IV-Text revision. ICD = *International Classification of Disorders*.
Source: Cacciola, J., & Woody, G. E. (2005). Diagnosis & classification: DSM-IV-TR and ICD-10. In J. H. Lowinson,, P. Ruiz, R. B. Millman, & J. G. Langrod (Eds.), *Substance abuse: A comprehensive textbook* (4th ed., p. 560). Philadelphia: Lippincott, Williams & Wilkins.

be in another. For instance, the drinking of alcohol in Western cultures is woven into the social fabric, whereas in Moslem cultures such a practice will have adverse social consequences (Cacciola & Woody, 2005). Therefore, the harmful use category in the ICD-10 is limited to physical or mental harm. The DSM-IV-TR defines abuse as problematic behavior, social impairment that does not meet the compulsive use, tolerance, and withdrawal criteria of dependence. The differences in DSM-IV-TR concept of "abuse" and the ICD-10 "harmful use" category are presented in Table 4.3.

TABLE 4.3: Comparison of Abuse and Harmful Use

DSM-IV-TR	ICD-10
Abuse One or more of the following occurring over the same 12-month period: 1) recurrent substance use resulting in a failure to fulfill major role obligations at work, school, or home 2) recurrent substance use in situations in which it is physically hazardous 3) recurrent substance-related legal problems 4) continued substance use despite having persistent or recurrent social or interpersonal problems caused or exacerbated by the effects of the substance Never met criteria for dependence	**Harmful Use** Clear evidence that the substance use was responsible for (or substantially contributed to) physical or psychological harm, including impaired judgment or dysfunctional behavior

Notes: DSM-IV-TR = *Diagnostic and Statistical Manual of Mental Disorders IV*-Text revision. ICD = *International Classification of Disorders.*
Source: Cacciola, J., & Woody, G. E. (2005). Diagnosis & classification: DSM-IV-TR and ICD-10. In J. H. Lowinson, P. Ruiz, R. B. Millman, & J. G. Langrod (Eds.), *Substance abuse: A comprehensive textbook* (4th ed., p. 562). Philadelphia: Lippincott, Williams & Wilkins.

Substance-Induced Disorders

The substance-induced disorders section of both classification systems provides for each substance a brief description of the clinical manifestations of induced disorders such as intoxication, withdrawal delirium, and amnestic, psychotic, mood, and sleep disorders. Not all substances are capable of inducing the same number and type of disorders. For example, a few substances such as LSD do not induce clinical intoxication and withdrawal manifestations, whereas alcohol and opioids such as heroin may be associated with a wide range of induced disorders (Cacciola & Woody, 2005). The DSM IV-TR (APA, 2000) provides considerable detail on drug-induced disorders.

These two classification systems suggest a continuum of drug use from nonproblematic to dependence. An overview of the continuum is presented in Table 4.4. Viewing drug use as a continuum is not meant to imply that all people who have drug use problems will progress to dependence. The inevitable progression from nonproblematic to problems, to increase in severity, and finally dependence

TABLE 4.4: Drug Use Continuum

Experimental Use	Recreational Use	Abuse	Dependence
Uses a few times for fun, curiosity	Continues to use, desires repetition of psychological effect	First signs of loss of control, due to use (oversleeping, thinking about use, absence from school or work)	Maladaptive behavior; continues to use despite negative consequences

lacks sufficient empirical evidence. Social workers, however, must be able to discern the physiological, psychological, and social manifestations that correlate with the various stages along a specific drug use continuum to institute appropriate interventions.

Societal Trends in Drug Use

This section presents an overview of the societal trends, patterns, and manifestations of the more commonly misused and abused drugs in the United States.

The influence of peers and social supports on young people's values, behavior, and attitudes is evident in both risk factors and protective factors. Deviant friends tend to promote acceptance of deviant behavior, including the use of alcohol and other drugs, whereas strong social supports act as protective factors and decrease one's vulnerability to substance use and abuse (Hesselbrock & Hesselbrock, 2006). Protective factors such as supportive parents, positive educational experiences, and high self-esteem act independently of each other but serve as buffers against deviant peers, the availability of drugs, or a negative personal event that could lead to the use of such substances (Levinthal, 2008).

Peer influence is found across racial and cultural groups of white, African American, and Hispanic youths. However, trends in drug use among adolescent minorities document less ATOD use by African American than white or Hispanic peers (Henderson, Xuegin Ma, & Shive, 2002).

White people typically begin using tobacco and alcohol at an earlier age than African Americans. White men have the highest proportion of heavy drinkers, which peaks between 18 and 25 years old and declines with age. African American men's drinking is consistently lower at each age compared with Hispanic men. Alaska Natives report the highest levels of alcohol-related depression and the earliest age of onset of alcoholism (Hesselbrock & Hesselbrock, 2006) whereas Asian drinkers of non-Japanese origin have the most moderate drinking patterns of all the racial and ethnic groups (Holder, 2006).

The U.S. culture encourages individualism, whereas immigrant Hispanic culture emphasizes family obligations over personal desires. This uncomfortable clash of cultures can lead Hispanic teenagers toward substance use. Hispanic teenagers with low levels of self-regulation and behavioral control are similar to white teenagers in that they are more likely to engage in heavy drinking and marijuana use (Pantin et al., 2007). Mexican Americans and Puerto Ricans are more likely than Cuban Americans to have ever used marijuana, cocaine, inhalants, or sedatives, but the overall number of Hispanic women who use substances is disproportionately low. Alcohol is the most prominent drug of abuse among Hispanics, resulting in a high rate of alcohol-related disease (Castillo & Henderson, 2002).

There is a high rate of heavy drinking among Native Americans compared with the entire U.S. population. This includes both chronic drinking in which men are six times more likely than Native American women to be chronic drinkers, and binge drinking in which Native American men binge drink at a rate of 28 percent compared with 21 percent for men of all races (Zahnd, Holtby, & Crim, 2002).

Women are less likely than men to consume alcohol and when they do, they drink less than men (Hesselbrock & Hesselbrock, 2006). Because women have lower body water content than men, their alcohol is not diluted to the same extent that it is in men. Therefore women have higher blood alcohol levels than men even if both are the same weight and consume the same amount (Levinthal, 2008).

Classic Drugs

Classic drugs are those drugs that have been used for a good deal of time in the past but may have fallen out of favor and been replaced by other substances. But these drugs always seem to have a second life, particularly for those who have not yet been exposed to their effects.

Alcohol. Because much of the research on drug disorders has been done by those studying alcohol use and because alcohol use directly or indirectly affects more people, with the exception of nicotine and caffeine, than any of the other drugs, it provides a good starting place for understanding use patterns and clinical manifestations at various continuum points. Also, clinical experience and studies of alcohol use imply that other drug use follows a prognosis similar to that for alcohol (N. S. Miller, 1995).

The majority of people who drink do so without negative consequences. They neither drink to excess (intoxication), nor experience physical, mental, or social problems because of their drinking. These drinkers usually confine their consumption to social settings and govern their behavior by social rules. Problems with alcohol arise when alcohol use begins to have undesired effects on the lives of drinkers or the lives of others with whom drinkers come in contact. Drinking until impaired or intoxicated can lead to aggression, accidents, medical problems, and other adverse psychological and social consequences.

Sobell and Sobell (1996) in their analysis of studies on the progression of alcoholism found most studies were biased in their design or used retrospective data from severely dependent alcoholics. In these studies severe alcoholics reported experiencing less severe problems in their pasts. The Sobells contended that such reporting failed to address the issues of progression—whether drinkers who had an alcohol problem at one time and continue to drink will have a worse problem at a later time. In their examination of studies that tracked people identified as having alcohol problems, a minority of cases, about 25–30 percent, showed a progressive development of alcohol problems. The Sobells concluded that most people move in and out of alcohol problems of varying severity that are separated by periods of either abstinence or of drinking without problems. Individual variations also occur in the rapidity of onset of dependence and the progression and severity of symptoms (N. S. Miller, 1995).

Nicotine. The progression from experimental use to dependence on nicotine may not be totally understood, but as is true for other drugs, tobacco use is not constant from initiation on because the process could take months or even years. Researchers collecting data from the United States found that in 2007 nearly 71 million Americans age 12 and older had used a tobacco product at least once in the previous month (Substance Abuse and Mental Health Services Administration [SAMHSA], 2008). Approximately 80 percent of all tobacco use initiation occurs among people less than 18 years of age (Henderson et al., 2002). The younger the age at which a young person starts smoking, the more likely it is that he or she will never quit. The social events that accompany passages to adulthood have, until very recently, been supportive and promotive of nicotine use. Colleges, the military, and the work arenas into which high school graduates and high school dropouts enter have, until recently, widely accepted smoking and even created smokers. The smoking bans in public places passed in many states are a product of local criminal and occupational safety and health laws and the 2006 Surgeon General's report *The Health Consequences of Involuntary Exposure to Tobacco Smoke* (U.S. Department of Health and Human Services [HHS], 2006).

Caffeine. Caffeine is the most frequently consumed drug in the world. Over the past 10 years there has been great interest in coffee as a way to consume caffeine from fine drip coffee to lattes to cappuccinos. More recently the "power drink," containing great amounts of caffeine and sugar has exploded onto the scene.

Caffeine levels peak in the CNS in two hours, and half of it remains in the bloodstream three to seven hours later (Levinthal, 2008). Caffeine addiction, especially in the form of coffee, has shown to have a genetic predisposition (Luciano, Kirk, Heath, & Martin, 2005; Svikis, Berger, Haug, & Griffiths, 2005). Some noted that caffeine consumption does not fit a perfect profile of addiction (Oberstar, Bernstein, & Thuras, 2002; Satel, 2006), whereas others (Juliano & Griffiths, 2004; Nehlig, 2004) believe it does. Levinthal (2008) stated that the strongest case for caffeine being a drug is the withdrawal symptoms of headache, impaired concentration, drowsiness, irritability, muscle aches, and other flulike symptoms.

Caffeine-rich energy drinks such as Red Bull, Monster Energy, Full Throttle, and one of the newest drinks called Cocaine are being consumed in growing numbers by adolescents and young adults. The market for these drinks exceeds 5 billion dollars and is increasing at over 50 percent annually (K. M. Miller, 2008) with no reduction in sight. Dangerous risks are being taken predominately by males with a "toxic jock identity" (K. M. Miller, 2008) with links to problem drinking, unsafe sex, and interpersonal violence. With the addition of alcohol to these energy drinks, the probability of the development of alcohol dependence becomes much higher (Oteri, Salvo, Caputi, & Calapal, 2007), and the ability to perceive a headache, the impairment of motor coordination, and weakness is significantly reduced (Ferreira, deMelo, Pompeia, & de Souza-Formigoni, 2006).

However, more recently, the negative effects of strong doses of caffeine in these products have led some manufactures to turn to liquid B12 (Cyanocobalamin) at 500 mg (8,333 percent over the daily value) and B6 (Pyridoxine Hydrochloride) at 40 mg (2,000 percent over the daily value) as dietary supplements. These five-hour energy and six-hour energy drinks are advertised as "hours of energy" without the "crash" and "no caffeine."

Marijuana. Marijuana is the most widely used of the illicit drugs. Its pattern of use varies and is dependent on social, cultural, and personality factors. Many young people experiment with the drug then relegate it to a peripheral status in their lives or cease to use it completely. Others continue to use it intermittently at special social occasions such as parties and concerts. Regular smokers include those who use the drug three to five times per week; chronic users are those who smoke every day, often throughout the day to maintain intoxication (McDowell, 2005).

The problems that define drug dependence—preoccupation with the drug to the exclusion of most other things, increasing the dose to recapture the original sensation, intoxication, recovery from the effects, work impairment, interruptions with family life, physical and mental health impairments, and numerous attempts to cut down or stop use—affect proportionally fewer marijuana smokers than users of alcohol, tobacco, heroin, and cocaine. Even heavy users in countries like Greece, Jamaica, and Costa Rica do not seem to be dependent in this damaging sense (Grinspoon et al., 2005). Regular use of marijuana is often associated with psychopathology or some sort of emotional and mental deterioration. The problem of distinguishing causes from symptoms is particularly complex with this drug.

Grinspoon and colleagues (2005) analyzed studies that assessed the effects of marijuana on users. They concluded that the evidence did not substantiate the commonly held belief that the amotivational syndrome (passivity, apathy, uncommunicativeness, and lack of ambition) and other personality conditions such as anxiety, depression, and feelings of inadequacy were the result of heavy marijuana use. In some cases heavy marijuana use may cause these emotional and mental states, but, often, marijuana use is a symptom of pre-existing psychological disorders. For example, some people may smoke marijuana to decrease symptoms of anxiety or depression. Sometimes users may be seeking distance from their symptoms and derive some comfort from the idea that their symptoms are drug induced.

In the United States almost everyone who has used an illicit drug has used marijuana first, just as almost everyone who smokes marijuana has drunk alcohol first (Grinspoon et al., 2005). Hence, marijuana has been labeled a "gateway drug"; alcohol and tobacco also have a similar correlation with other drug use. This correlation does not imply cause and effect. Anyone using any given drug is more likely to be interested in others. Smoking marijuana does not mean that the inevitable next step is use of another illicit drug. The gateway metaphor is not based on evidence one way or the other. Although the acquisition and use of marijuana encourages association with others who have access to other drugs, most marijuana smokers use neither heroin nor cocaine. Grinspoon and colleagues (2005) implied that the gateway hypothesis suggests it would be more difficult to develop an interest in cocaine if no one smoked marijuana. Clearly marijuana has been used without other illicit drugs and other drugs have been used without first using marijuana.

Cocaine. The mere possession of drugs such as cocaine, heroin, and marijuana is problematic because of their illegality. However, not all people who use them will become dependent on them. In describing the process that leads to dependence, Coombs and Howatt (2005) suggested that a person's body gradually develops a tolerance for the substance and may sometimes experience painful detoxification for three to five days for the relatively short-acting drug such as cocaine. The "crash," or feeling of depression after the initial high has dissipated, may lead to headaches, dizziness, and accompanying muscle spasms. As a result of cocaine's action on the brain, the increased impulses activate the reward system. But with continued use of the drug, the normal positive reinforcement of pleasure from the natural world such as food and sex eventually dissipates. What remains is the cocaine to maintain those feelings. But this will usually happen over a period of time from experimental use to recreational use to abuse and finally dependence.

Signs of loss of control and maladaptive behavior begin to emerge—such as irritability, sleeplessness, restlessness, hypervigilance, talkativeness, grandiosity, missing work, lateness, and so forth as someone moves from experimental to recreational use. Cocaine use may be episodic and infrequent, occurring around payday or a special event or holiday, and lasting for a few hours or days of high dosage use. Abusers may have longer periods (weeks or months) of occasional, nonproblematic use, or abstinence (APA, 2000). When the need for the potent euphoric effects increases, accompanied by both an increase in time spent on drug-obtaining behaviors and an increase in the number of maladaptive behaviors despite the knowledge of negative consequences, dependence occurs. The movement from experimental to recreational to abuse and finally to dependence, although not inevitable, can easily occur, particularly with crack cocaine because of its high dependence potential.

Opioids. It has been difficult to study the course of opioid use and dependence potential as only a minority of abusers can be studied effectively (those who enter treatment); however, some generalizations can still be made. The vast majority of opiate users are between the ages of 20 and 50. Although they come from all races, ethnicities, and socioeconomic strata, in the United States, African Americans and Hispanic users are overrepresented (Dilts & Dilts, 2005). Opiate dependence, characterized by relapse and remission, seems to abate in middle age (Dilts & Dilts, 2005). It is now known that just a fraction of those who experiment with these illicit opioids develop serious problems. However, for those who used opioids heavily, such as once a day, dependence can become chronic. The overall death rate is 20 times that of the general population, because of overdose, use-related infections, suicide, homicide, or accidental death (Jaffe & Strain, 2005). Multiple-drug use is common with this population; almost all are nicotine dependent; and many may have serious alcohol-related problems, use stimulants such as amphetamines and cocaine, and smoke marijuana (Dilts & Dilts, 2005).

Hallucinogens. Hallucinogens are a group of natural and synthetic drugs that alter consciousness and change the perceptions of the user. Their mind-altering or transcendent effects inspired the label "psychedelic" (mind revealing) for this class of drugs. The psychedelic drugs most commonly abused in Western society are PCP, LSD, psilocybin, Mescaline, and new "designer drugs" (chemical psychedelic analogues) such as MDMA, the chemical cousin of amphetamines, known as "ecstasy." Ritual and recreational use of the naturally occurring hallucinogens dates back to antiquity (McDowell, 2005). Mescaline (found in the buttons of the peyote cactus [and psilocybin] found in over 100 related species of mushrooms) is still being used ritualistically by certain Native American tribes. Hallucinogens are generally used by young people at celebration events, parties, and concerts. Some adolescents use them more regularly, sometimes every day, but the pattern is generally short lived. When used in this way the hallucinogen effects are decreased because of tolerance (McDowell, 2005).

OTC drugs. Most OTC drugs are from the stimulant, analgesic, depressant, and sedative drug classification. Analgesics such as aspirin, acetaminophen, naproxen, and ibuprofen are quite effective in controlling mild and moderate pain without the side effects of narcotic analgesics. Stimulants such as No Doz and Vivarin are caffeine-based products sold to restore wakefulness and alertness. Weight-loss products, especially those containing phenylpropanolamine, involve sympathetic nerve stimulation; they are designed to suppress appetite but can also contribute to an increase in blood pressure. Sedatives such as Nytol and Compos, used to produce drowsiness and aid sleep, are depressants and will potentiate the effect of alcohol and other depressants. Cold and cough remedies are intended to relieve cold symptoms and are the second-largest OTC category after analgesics (Levinthal, 2008). These remedies often contain an antihistamine, which could produce drowsiness, and alcohol, which could increase that drowsiness.

OTCs have the potential to promote health and the potential for misuse and abuse. When taken with other drugs, toxic reactions may occur because for some individuals using even normal or slightly above-normal dosages may produce such reactions. Liver and kidney damage is also possible with chronic, above-normal dosing. Suicide attempts have involved OTC analgesics, in combination with other drugs or sometimes alone.

Party Drugs

The popularity of "party drugs" ingested before, during, and after all-night parties or raves has been a phenomenon of both private and public bars and dance clubs across the country. This is where the intake of dangerous drugs takes place and where uneducated users suffer life-threatening consequences (Maxwell, 2005). Among these drugs are MDMA, GHB (gamma-hydroxybutyrate), and ketamine.

MDMA. MDMA is a synthetic, psychoactive drug that stimulates and possesses hallucinogentic properties. It has been available since the early 1980s, reached its peak in 2001, and has since declined among all age groups (Johnston, O'Malley, Backman, & Schulenberg, 2006a, 2006b).

GHB. GHB is a CNS depressant with intoxicating effects and anesthetic properties if taken in high enough doses (Nicholson & Balster, 2001). It produces euphoria, often with the lowering of inhibitions. The use of GHB has varied across the nation and age groups since it began in the early 1990s and is often used as a "date rape" drug. In Miami, Detroit, and San Francisco, use was reported down in 2003 (Maxwell & Spence, 2005). Although use by eighth and 10th graders has gone down in the early 2000s, use by 12th graders varied (Johnston et al., 2006a) and use was reported to be even lower in young adults and adults (Johnston et al., 2006b).

Ketamine. Ketamine is an anesthetic derivative of phencyclidine hydrochloride approved for human and animal use in surgery and veterinary medicine. Ketamine produces a dissociative state and sensory deprivation (Wolf & Winstock, 2006). A "K-hole" is desired by some injection users in which they experience an intense psychological and somatic state (Lankenau & Sanders, 2007). Its misuse has been reported since the early 1990s and its use has decreased since 2003 in all age groups (Johnston et al., 2006a, 2006b).

Multiple-Drug Dependence

Drug-taking behavior involving the simultaneous use of two or more drugs is becoming increasingly common. Historically, there has been a close association between nicotine dependence and alcoholism. Alcohol use was reported by 66.9 percent of current cigarette smokers compared with 46.1 percent of nonsmokers (SAMHSA, 2008). Marijuana is also highly associated with other types of illicit drug use and dependence. Assessment, treatment, and relapse prevention must, in many cases, not only address the primary drug of choice, but also the secondary and tertiary ones. People dependent on cocaine, for example, may not only need help with reducing dependence on that drug, but also may need tobacco, marijuana, and alcohol cessation or reduction intervention as well.

Health Impacts from Drug Use

Research studies over the past century have determined that a great many health risks, including death, are possible from the use and misuse of drugs. Increased levels of substance use by children and adolescence can interfere with the development of cognitive, emotional, and social competence and compromise later functioning in important adult domains such as marriage, parenting, and gainful employment. The earlier the substance use, the more likely it is to progress to substance abuse and the more negative its effects are likely to be (Pantin et al., 2007). There is concern about the malleability of the developing brain during childhood and adolescence, which is supported by animal studies (Adriani et al., 2003).

Schuckit (2005) reported that 90 percent of the U.S. population consumed at least one alcoholic drink, with some beginning their drinking in their early to mid-teens. By the end of high school 80 percent of students have had a drink and 60 percent of them have been intoxicated at least once (Schuckit, 2005).

Health problems associated with alcohol use contribute to a variety of diseases, health conditions, and high-risk behaviors such as liver disease, mental health conditions, and traffic injury and deaths. The WHO (2008) reported that there is a strong link between alcohol misuse and interpersonal violence and that both act as catalysts for each other. Alcohol use and violence is found particularly in domestic violence where 67 percent of people victimizing intimate partners were found to be under the influence of alcohol (Hesselbrock & Hesselbrock, 2006).

Pregnant women and their fetuses are at increased risk because of exposure of drugs. Maternal drinking that results in fetal alcohol syndrome is associated in infants with increased risk of maltreatment by caregivers and the development of delinquent problems later in life (Kelly, Day, & Streissguth, 2000). In addition, a second-generation study of prenatal cocaine-exposed women showed heightened vulnerability and decreased resilience to environmental risks of children 12 to 36 months of age born to these women and those burdens may become more pronounced as the child ages (Lewis, Misra, Johnson, & Rosen, 2004). Prenatal exposure that results in fetal alcohol syndrome is associated in infants with increased risk of maltreatment by caregivers and the development of delinquent problems later in life (Kelly et al., 2000).

The role of drugs in the spread of sexually transmitted diseases is reflected in the transmission of HIV. The majority of women who are HIV-positive are between 13 and 39 years of age, with half of them being injection drug users and frequently heavy alcohol drinkers. Heavy drinking in women can also lead to higher rates of cardiovascular disease and gastrointestinal diseases (Blume & Zilberman, 2005).

Ethnic minority groups typically use fewer drugs than do white people, but major causes of morbidity and mortality in ethnic minority communities include substances such as tobacco and alcohol. Generally, African Americans have the greatest drug-related health problems among minority groups (Henderson & Xue-gin Ma, 2002). Advertising for alcohol and tobacco products is heavy in many minority neighborhoods.

Research over the past century determined that cigarette smoking is linked to cancer and other diseases. The first U.S. Surgeon General's Report on smoking and health finally made that determination in 1964, and people have been informed of its dangers since 1966 when the risks were required to be printed on all packaged tobacco products (Levinthal, 2008).

The adverse effects of tobacco use are seen in cardiovascular disease (coronary heart disease and arteriosclerosis), respiratory disease (chronic bronchitis and emphysema), and cancer (lung cancer, leuloplakia, and erythroplakia). Smoking-related deaths account for at least one out of every five deaths in the United States each year, 1,200 per day (Levinthal, 2008).

Marijuana use can lead to the same diseases as nicotine because smokers tend to inhale more deeply and hold it longer than cigarette smokers. However, marijuana users can have impairments of cognitive functioning, including lasting memory loss (Coombs & Howatt, 2005). Intravenous drug use has its own health risks related to "dirty" needles that include HIV/AIDS, hepatitis B and C, and any other disease that may be transmitted from sharing needles. Heroin users who regularly consume through injection have a higher risk of death than nondrug users of the same age range. Chronic heroin users may also develop infection of the heart lining and valves, abscesses, liver disease, and pulmonary complications (Coombs & Howatt, 2005).

Because the strength of a heroin dosage may be unknown at the time of intake, the risk of an overdose is quite possible. Overdoses from heroin and other drugs such a depressants that lead to emergency room treatment and even death are a major health risk for many, especially inexperienced drug users and those attempting suicide.

Harm reduction is a public health philosophy that uses various strategies to reduce drug-related harm, such as needle-exchange programs, drug substitution therapies, and abstinence-oriented programs. Empirical studies support harm-reduction approaches to alcohol problems that are as effective as abstinence-oriented programs in reducing alcohol-related consequences (Coombs & Howatt, 2005). For example, abstinence from ATOD during pregnancy can increase the chances of a woman having a healthy baby.

For those who stop taking drugs, the benefits of cessation are great. Smokers who quit can have the effect of carbon monoxide levels in their blood drop to normal in eight hours or have the risk of coronary heart disease cut in half in a year, and within 10 years a former smoker's lung cancer death rate can be cut in half (Levinthal, 2008).

The benefits are similar for other drugs. The sooner the substance is reduced and eventually eliminated, the sooner a healthier life may be pursued.

Detoxification from Drugs

Only a small percentage of the U.S. population has problems with drugs of abuse. It is estimated that 19.9 million people age 12 years and older (8 percent of total U.S. population) are classified with dependence on or abuse of illicit drugs or alcohol (SAMHSA, 2008). Even the use of cocaine, crack cocaine, and heroin does not automatically lead to compulsive and destructive use; many use it a few times a week or less (Ksir et al., 2006). To understand how drug use can progress from nonproblematic use to overwhelming involvement leading to dependence, two key processes must first be defined: the development of tolerance and the phenomenon of withdrawal.

Tolerance occurs with many drugs (Ksir et al., 2006). It refers to the capacity of a drug dose to have a diminished effect on the user as that drug is repeatedly taken. The same amount of alcohol that previously produced a specific effect is no longer adequate; a higher amount is necessary. The saying "holding one's liquor" is an illustration of this process. Another illustration is the effect of caffeine in coffee. Some individuals may drink four or five cups of coffee during the afternoon and early evening and still be able to sleep comfortably because of having developed high levels of caffeine tolerance, whereas others who drink caffeinated beverages less frequently will be awake throughout the night. The tolerance phenomenon has been suggested as a key component in many definitions of drug dependence.

A second key component when speaking of drug dependence is withdrawal. The major recreational drugs of abuse will, if used long enough, result in some form of withdrawal syndrome once usage is interrupted (Doweiko, 2008). Withdrawal refers to maladaptive behavioral changes with physiological and cognitive concomitants that occur when blood or tissue concentrations of a substance decline in an individual who has maintained heavy drug use. To relieve the unpleasant effects created by withdrawal, the same or similar drug is often used. The common saying "give me the hair of the dog who bit me" typifies the withdrawal syndrome— unpleasant symptoms, which occur when a heavily used drug is no longer taken and the user seeks to eliminate or reduce these symptoms by re-dosing.

The nature of the withdrawal will vary depending on the class of drug. Each class of drug will produce certain physical symptoms when a person no longer takes the drug. Depressants (alcohol and sedatives) and, to a lesser extent, opiates, produce the most severe physical withdrawal symptoms, whereas stimulants such as cocaine and amphetamines produce less apparent physical signs and symptoms. The presence of physical symptoms, although they may vary in degree and kind according to the drug being withdrawn, point to some kind of physical need perhaps as far down as the cellular level (Levinthal, 2008).

Based on the DSM-IV-TR (APA, 2000), the criteria for substance withdrawal include the development of a substance-specific syndrome because of the cessation of, or reduction in, use that has been heavy and prolonged. In addition, it causes clinically significant distress or impairment in social, occupational, or other important areas of functioning. Finally, the symptoms are not because of a general medical condition and are not better accounted for by another mental disorder.

The need to avoid unpleasant physical withdrawal symptoms is not, however, a complete explanation for continued drug use. Hallucinogens and marijuana do not produce physical withdrawal symptoms, yet consistent use can occur. The relapse rate among heroin and alcohol users would not be as high if avoidance of physical withdrawal symptoms were the only viable explanation for continual use. What is needed is a broader explanation of why many individuals dependent on a drug become redependent after completing the withdrawal process.

There are factors beyond the chemical effects of withdrawal that help to explain drug dependence. Psychological or behavioral terms help to broaden our understanding of drug dependence. Psychological dependence refers to the drug user being motivated by the craving—strong subjective drive to use a substance—for the pleasurable effects of the drug. This may explain why after several years of being heroin free some former users still have to fight the desire for the drug. Empirical evidence of psychological dependence is found in studies showing that animals and humans would self-administer drugs despite the fact that the drugs did not usually produce physical symptoms during withdrawal. The data from such studies indicate that reinforcement is the unifying feature of drug abuse and dependence, with tolerance and withdrawal being viewed as related but not as critical phenomena (Gold & Jacobs, 2005; Ksir et al., 2006).

An abrupt detoxification from drugs can lead to withdrawal symptoms of a physiological and cognitive nature dependent on the drug. Alcohol, for instance, may put an individual into an alcohol withdrawal syndrome that may include insomnia and a severe hangover followed by tremors, nausea, and vomiting. This stage can reach its peak in 24 to 36 hours and be completed in two days. A less common but more dangerous stage is delirium tremors in which severe tremors, fever, and disturbing nightmares can take place. These effects can peak in three to four days, and the threat of heart failure and suicide may be present. Complete hospital observation must take place at this stage, with normally only antianxiety medication used to treat symptoms (Levinthal, 2008).

Pharmacological interventions for detoxification from drugs have expanded to include Librium and Valium for both alcohol and benzodiazepine detoxification, and a benzodiazepine (Clonazepam) and phenobarbital for benzodiazepine detoxification. Medications for opiate detoxification include suboxone (Subutex), clonidine, naltrexone, and methadone. Bromocryptine and amantadine are used for stimulant detoxification, with Wellbutrin (another benzodiazepine) used for cannabis detoxification.

Pharmacological Interventions for Treatment Management

Pharmacological interventions for treatment management have come a long way in the past several years. Even though a multitreatment approach may be the most effective way to assist someone dependent on alcohol, tobacco, or other drugs, including therapy, counseling, and support groups, it is important to note the historic changes in this area to more fully understand its future potential (see Table 4.5).

The widespread use of methadone to treat opioid abuse over the past several decades was the first step toward the research and development of similar drugs and the increasing use of pharmacological interventions for treatment management. Methadone is used to treat heroin dependence and is not intoxicating when prescribed and used properly. One dose can last six times as long as heroin (Coombs, 2004).

Methadone is the most widely empirically proven medication treatment for opiate dependence; however, other medications have been approved by the U.S. Food and Drug Administration (FDA) for use. LAAM was approved in 1993 for heroin addiction. It has an advantage over methadone because it can be taken as infrequently as three times a week in comparison to a daily dose.

Naltrexone and naloxone block the effects of morphine, heroin, and other opioids. Naltrexone is used to prevent relapse by blocking the pleasurable effects of heroin, whereas naloxone is used as an antidote to heroin overdoses. Naltrexone is also used as a medication in addressing alcohol dependence.

Buprenorphine was approved for use in 2000 and is a much milder treatment than methadone or LAAM, therefore limiting its overdose effects. It is approved for use by those dependent on OxyContin and heroin.

The best success in use of these pharmacological interventions for addiction management comes from a combination of drugs and psychosocial treatment. That is why most often treatment of this kind was administered in facilities such as a

TABLE 4.5: Classification of Drugs for Addiction Management

Drug	Brand Name	Addictive Drug	Medical Use
Methodone	Avinea, Roxanol	Heroin-Opioids	Addiction management
LAAM (levo-alpha-acetyl-methadol)	Orleen	Heroin-Opioids	Addiction management
Naloxone	Suboxone	Heroin	Antidote to heroin overdoses
Naltrexone	Vivitrol	Heroin-Opioids-Alcohol	Prevent relapse/ Medication management
Buprenophine	Subutex	Heroin-Opioids	Heroin abuse treatment/ Opioid detoxification
Acomprosate	Campral	Alcohol	Reduce cravings and prolonged withdrawal syndromes
Naltrexone	Vivitrol	Alcohol-Opioids	Reduction of cravings/ Addiction management
Nicotine Replacement Therapy (NRT) Products	Various Brands: Gum, inhaler, nasal spray, patch, lozenge	Nicotine	Tobacco dependence
Bupropion	Zyban	Nicotine	Withdrawal symptoms Smoking cessation
Varenicline Tartrate	Chantix	Nicotine	Withdrawal symptoms
Clonidine	Catapres	Opioids-Nicotine	Opioid detoxification/Anti-hypertensive medication
Bromocryitine	Parlodel	Stimulants	Detoxification
Amantadine	Symmetrel	Stimulants	Detoxification
Benzodiazepine Phenobarbital	Clonazepam	Benzodiazepine	Detoxification
Benzodiazepine	Wellbutrin	Cannabis	Detoxification
Benzodiazepine	Librium	Alcohol-Benzodiazepine	Detoxification

methadone clinic where drugs and therapy are both provided. However, based on the Drug Addiction Treatment Act of 2000, private physicians' offices may be used for some pharmacological treatment options. This not only reduces the stigma associated with addiction, but also provides an additional option for users who may not otherwise attempt to get clean. Psychosocial treatment as an accompaniment to the pharmacological intervention is the appropriate course of action. This may be done in the physician's office or at another facility providing such services.

Acomprosate is used as a medication to control alcohol dependence. It serves to reduce cravings and prolonged withdrawal syndromes. Vivitrol is also used to address symptoms of withdrawal.

Nicotine replacement therapy is used for nicotine dependence. Chantix is a medication that works directly in a smoker's brain to ease withdrawal symptoms. It also blocks the pleasurable effects of nicotine if the person is tempted to light up again. Recently the FDA reported Chantix may be linked to psychiatric problems, including suicidal behavior and vivid dreams. These reports are based on the number of reported cases of serious drug reactions, including deaths during January to March of 2008 (Alonso-Zaldivar, 2008).

Conclusion

This chapter has focused on helping the social worker to understand the nature of drugs of abuse and their effects on users. The properties and characteristics of the major drugs of misuse and abuse were briefly discussed. The influence of physical, psychological, and environmental manifestations on how drugs may variously affect users was explored. Emphasis was placed on the classification of substance disorders, societal trends, the health impacts of addictive drug use, detoxification, and pharmacological interventions. Social workers, to intervene from prevention or treatment perspectives, must be knowledgeable about the neurochemical, social, medical, and cultural differences that distinguish drug problems from other types of problems and must be capable of working with other professionals in addressing the challenges posed by ATOD misuse and abuse.

Note

The author wishes to thank and recognize Patricia C. Dunn for her contributions to an earlier version of this chapter, major portions of which are included here, and that appear in the first edition of *Alcohol, Tobacco, and Other Drugs*.

References

Adriani, W., Spijker, S., Deroche-Gamonet, U., Lavcola, G., LeMoal, M., Smit, A. B., & Piazza, P. V. (2003). Evidence for enhanced neurobehavioral vulnerability to nicotine during preadolescence in rats. *Journal of Neuroscience, 23,* 4712–4716.

Alonso-Zaldivar, R., (2008, October 23). Drug reaction reports set mark. *Philadelphia Inquirer,* p. A10.

American Psychiatric Association. (2000). *Diagnostic and statistical manual of mental disorders* (4th ed., text rev.). Washington, DC: Author.

Blume, S. B., & Zilberman, M. L. (2005). Alcohol and women. In J. Lowinson, P. Ruiz, R. B. Millman, & J. G. Langrad (Eds.), *Substance abuse: A comprehensive textbook* (4th ed., pp. 1049–1063). Philadelphia: Lippincott, Williams & Wilkins.

Cacciola, J., & Woody, G. E.(2005). Diagnosis and classification: DSM-IV-TR and ICD-10. In J. Lowinson, P. Ruiz, R. B. Millman, & J. G. Langrod (Eds.), *Substance abuse: A comprehensive textbook* (4th ed., pp. 559–563). Philadelphia: Lippincott, Williams & Wilkins.

Castillo, M., & Henderson, G. (2002). Hispanic substance abusers in the United States. In G. Xueqin Ma & G. Henderson (Eds.), *Ethnicity and substance abuse: Prevention and intervention* (pp. 191–206). Springfield, IL: Charles C Thomas.

Coombs, R. H. (Ed.). (2004). *Handbook of addiction disorders: A practical guide to diagnosis and treatment* (2nd ed.). Hoboken, NJ: John Wiley & Sons.

Coombs, R. H., & Howatt, W. A. (2005). *The addiction counselor's desk reference.* Hoboken, NJ: John Wiley & Sons.

Cooper, J. R., Bloom, F. E., & Roth, R. H. (1996). *The biochemical basis of neuropharmacology* (7th ed.). New York: Oxford University Press.

Dilts, S. L., Jr., & Dilts, S. L. (2005). Opioids. In R. J. Frances, S. I. Miller, & A. H. Mack (Eds.), *Clinical textbook of addictive disorders* (3rd ed., pp. 138–156). New York: Guilford Press.

Doweiko, H. E. (2008). *Concepts of chemical dependency* (7th ed.). Belmont, CA: Brooks/Cole.

Ferreira, S. E., de Mello, M. T., Pompeia, S., & de Souza-Formigoni, M.L.O. (2006). Effects of energy drink ingestion on alcohol intoxication. *Alcoholism: Clinical and Experimental Research, 10,* 598–605.

Germain, C. B., & Bloom, M. (1999). *Human growth and the social environment: Ecological view.* New York: Columbia University Press.

Gold, M. S., & Jacobs, W. S. (2005). Cocaine (and crack): Clinical aspects. In J. Lowinson, P. Ruiz, R. B. Millman, & J. G. Langrad (Eds.), *Substance abuse: A comprehensive textbook* (4th ed., pp. 218–251). Philadelphia: Lippincott, Williams & Wilkins.

Grinspoon, L., Bakalar, J. B., & Russo, E. (2005). Marijuana: Clinical aspects. In J. Lowinson, P. Ruiz, R. B. Millman, & J. G. Langrad (Eds.), *Substance abuse: A comprehensive textbook* (4th ed., pp. 263–276). Philadelphia: Lippincott, Williams & Wilkins.

Heath, A. C. (1995) Genetic influences on alcoholism risk. *Alcohol Health & Research World, 19,* 166–171.

Henderson, G., & Xueqin Ma, G. (2002). Concepts of addiction in ethnic minority populations. In G. Xueqin Ma & G. Henderson (Eds.), *Ethnicity and substance abuse: Prevention and intervention* (pp. 5–18). Springfield, IL: Charles C Thomas.

Henderson, G., Xueqin Ma, G., & Shive, S. E. (2002). African American substance users
and abusers. In G. Xueqin Ma & G. Henderson (Eds.), *Ethnicity and substance abuse:
Prevention and intervention* (pp. 59–86). Springfield, IL: Charles C Thomas.

Hesselbrock, V. M., & Hesselbrock, M. N. (2006). Developmental perspectives on the risk
for developing substance abuse problems. In W. R. Miller & K. M. Carroll (Eds.),
Rethinking substance abuse: What the science shows and what we should do about it (pp.
97–114). New York: Guilford Press.

Holder, H. D. (2006). Racial and gender differences in substance abuse. In W. R. Miller &
K. M. Carroll (Eds.), *Rethinking substance abuse: What the science shows and what we
should do about it* (pp. 153–181). New York: Guilford Press.

Jaffe, J. H., & Strain, E. C. (2005). Opioid-related disorders. In B. J. Sadock & V. A. Sadock
(Eds.), *Kaplan & Sadock's comprehensive textbook of psychiatry* (8th ed., pp. 1265–1290).
Philadelphia: Lippincott, Williams & Wilkins.

Johnston, L. D., O'Malley, P. M., Backman, J. G., & Schulenberg, J. E. (2006a). *Monitoring
the future: National survey results on drug use, 1975–2005. Volume I: Secondary school
students, 2005.* Bethesda, MD: National Institute on Drug Abuse.

Johnston, L. D., O'Malley, P. M., Backman, J. G., & Schulenberg, J. E. (2006b). *Monitoring
the future: National survey results on drug use, 1975–2005. Volume II: College students
and adults ages 19–45, 2005.* Bethesda, MD: National Institute on Drug Abuse.

Juliano, L. M., & Griffiths, R. R. (2004). A critical review of caffeine withdrawal: Empirical
validation of symptoms and signs, incidence, severity and associated features. *Psychopharmacology, 176,* 1–29.

Kelly, S. J., Day, N., & Streissguth, A. P. (2000). Effects of prenatal alcohol exposure on
social behaviour in humans and other species. *Neurotoxiciology and Teratology, 22,*
143–149.

Kiefe, C. I., Williams, O. D., Lewis, C. E., Allison, J. J. Sekar, P. S., & Wagenknecht, L. E.
(2001). Ten-year changes in smoking among young adults: Are racial differences
explained by socioeconomic factors in the CARDIA study? *American Journal of Public
Health, 91,* 213–218.

Knapp, C. M., Ciraulo, D. A., & Jaffe, J. H. (2005). Opiates: Clinical aspects. In J. Lowinson,
P. Ruiz, R. B. Millman, & J. G. Langrad (Eds.), *Substance abuse: A comprehensive textbook* (4th ed., pp. 180–194). Philadelphia: Lippincott, Williams & Wilkins.

Ksir, C., Hart, C., & Ray, O. (2006). *Drugs, society, and human behavior* (112th ed.). Boston:
WGB/McGraw-Hill.

Lankenau, S. E., & Sanders, B. (2007). Patterns of ketamine use among young injection drug
users. *Journal of Psychoactive Drugs, 39,* 21–29.

Levinthal, C. F. (2008). *Drugs, behavior, and modern society* (8th ed.). Needham Heights,
MA: Allyn & Bacon.

Lewis, J. A., Dana, R. Q., & Blevins, G. A. (2001). *Substance abuse counseling* (3rd ed.). Belmont, CA: Brooks/Cole.

Lewis, M. W., Misra, S., Johnson, H. L., & Rosen, T. S. (2004). Neurological & developmental outcomes of prenatally cocaine-exposed offspring from 12–36 months. *American Journal of Drugs and Alcohol, 30,* 299–320.

Luciano, M., Kirk, K. M., Heath, A. C., & Martin, N. G. (2005). The genetics of tea and coffee drinking and preference for source of caffeine in a large community sample of Australian twins. *Addiction, 300,* 1510–1517.

Luczak, S. E., Glatt, S. J., & Wall, T. L. (2006). Meta-analysis of ALDH2 and ADHIB with alcohol dependence in Asians. *Psychological Bulletin, 132,* 607–621.

McDowell, D. (2005). Marijuana, hallucinogens, and club drugs. In R. J. Frances & S. I. Miller (Eds.), *Clinical textbook of addictive disorders* (3rd ed., pp. 157–183). New York: Guilford Press.

Maxwell, J. C. (2005). Party drugs: Properties, prevalence, patterns and problems. *Substance Use & Misuse, 40,* 1203–1240.

Maxwell, J. C., & Spence, R. T. (2005). Profiles of club drug use in treatment. *Substance Use & Misuse, 40,* 1409–1426.

Miller, K. M. (2008). Wired: Energy drinks, jock identity, masculine norms, and risk taking. *Journal of American College Health, 56,* 481–489.

Miller, N. S. (1995). *Addiction psychiatry.* New York: John Wiley & Sons.

Nehlig, A. (2004). Dependence upon coffee and caffeine: An update. In A. Nehlig (Ed.), *Coffee, tea, chocolate and the brain* (pp. 133–145). Boca Raton, FL: CRC Press.

Nicholson, K. L., & Balster, R. L. (2001). GHB: A new and novel drug of abuse. *Drug Alcohol Dependence, 63,* 1–22.

Oberstar, J. V., Bernstein, G. A., & Thuras, P. D. (2002). Caffeine use and dependence in adolescents: One-year follow-up. *Journal of Child & Adolescent Psychopharmacology, 109,* 85–91.

Oteri, A., Salvo, F., Caputi, A. P., & Calapal, G. (2007). Intake of energy drinks in association with alcoholic beverages in a cohort of students of the School of Medicine of the University of Messina. *Alcoholism: Clinical and Experimental Research, 31,* 1677–1680.

Pantin, H., Schwartz, S. J., Coatsworth, J. D., Sullivan, E. B., & Szapocznik, J. (2007). Familias unidos: A systemic, parent-centered approach to preventing problems behavior in Hispanic adolescents. In P. Tolan, J. Szapocznik, & S. Sambrano (Eds.), *Preventing youth substance abuse: Science-based programs for children and adolescents* (pp. 211–238). Washington, DC: American Psychological Association.

Satel, S. (2006). Is caffeine addictive?—A review of the literature. *American Journal of Drug and Alcohol Abuse, 32,* 493–502.

Schmitz, J. M., & Delaune, K. A. (2005). Nicotine. In J. Lowinson, P. Ruiz, R. B. Millman, & J. G. Langrad (Eds.), *Substance abuse: A comprehensive textbook* (4th ed., pp. 387–403). Philadelphia: Lippincott, Williams & Wilkins.

Schuckit, M. A. (2005). Alcohol-related disease. In B. J. Sadock & V. A. Sadock (Eds.), *Kaplan & Sadock's comprehensive textbook of psychiatry* (8th ed., pp. 1168–1188). Philadelphia: Lippincott, Williams & Wilkins.

Sobell, M. B., & Sobell, L. C. (1996). *Problem drinkers: Guided self-change treatment.* New York: Guilford Press.

Substance Abuse and Mental Health Services Administration (SAMHSA). (2008). *National survey on drug use and health 2007*. Rockville, MD: U.S. Department of Health and Human Services.

Svikis, D. S., Berger, N., Haug, N. A., & Griffiths, R. R. (2005). Caffeine dependence in combination with family history of alcoholism as a predictor of continued use of caffeine during pregnancy. *American Journal of Psychiatry, 162*, 2344–2350.

U.S. Department of Health and Human Services. (2006). *The health consequences of involuntary tobacco smoke: A report of the surgeon general*. Rockville, MD: Author.

Vleeming, W., Rambali, B., & Opperhuizen, A. (2002). The role of nitric oxide in cigarette smoking and nicotine addiction. *Nicotine and Tobacco Research, 4*, 341–348.

Wagenknecht, L., Cutter, G. Haley, N., Sidney, S., Manolio, T., Hughes, G. & Jacobs, D. (1990). Racial differences in serum continine levels among smokers in the coronary artery risk development in (young adults) study. *American Journal of Public Health, 80*, 1053–1056.

Wolf, K., & Winstock, A. R. (2006). Ketamine from medicine to misuse. *CNS Drugs, 20*, 199–218.

World Health Organization. (2007). *Tenth revision of the International classification of disease* (ICD-10). Geneva: Author.

World Health Organization. (2008). *WHO interpersonal violence and alcohol policy briefing*. Geneva: Author.

Zahnd, E., Holtby, S., & Crim, D.K.D. (2002). Trends in drug abuse among Native Americans. In G. Xeuqin Ma & G. Henderson (Eds.), *Ethnicity and substance abuse: Prevention and intervention* (pp. 249–269). Springfield, IL: Charles C Thomas.

5

Tobacco Use and Nicotine Dependence

Raymond Bolden, Jr.

Tobacco use and nicotine dependence constitute the deadliest combination in existence today. Legally sold across all 50 states and around the world, tobacco is, in many instances, a "cash cow" to business and a "cash burden" to insurance companies and states that have the responsibility for the health care of users who succumb to the diseases resulting from years of tobacco and nicotine use.

Introduction

History

Tobacco has been used in the United States since the earliest Native Americans were the sole occupants. Tobacco possessed a spiritual power for many tribes who used it as a bridge from this world to the next. The explorers to the new world of North America, from Christopher Columbus to John Smith, did not fully understand the spiritual nature of tobacco for Native Americans, but observed it being smoked, chewed, snuffed, drunk, and often used as an analgesic for wounds.

Some tribes smoked pipes, whereas others preferred an early form of cigarettes. The nicotine intake of the Native Americans was accomplished through the most potent tobacco they could cultivate (Hughes, 2003). It was not long before these new inhabitants began to grow and use their own form of tobacco. By the mid-16th century pipe smoking tobacco became widely used. Tobacco plantations in the Virginia colonies and elsewhere prospered. Sir John Rolf cultivated a tobacco that was much milder than that of the Native Americans but it still seemed too strong for European tastes. Sir Walter Raleigh popularized the idea of plantations and tobacco smoking from the Virginia colonies to England.

The cost was high enough to attract the higher classes of people, and by the 1700s the custom of snuffing overtook smoking as the dominant form of tobacco use, especially among the aristocratic men and women of France (Levinthal, 2008). For the first few decades, only the more affluent in society could afford to smoke because tobacco was expensive. However, as supplies increased, prices fell and smoking became popular for all levels of society (Hughes, 2003). Tobacco use was strongly associated with drinking, and taverns were common places for smokers to congregate, and, at the same time, cheaper homegrown varieties made it easier for the middle and lower classes to enjoy tobacco.

Rolling papers to make cigarettes became popular in Europe in the 19th century, whereas rolled leaves to make cigars were the major choice for the United States. Cigarette smoking in America was slower to catch on, especially with the strong opposition of the cigar industry. Later that same century, the patented cigarette machine generated a greater supply of cigarettes and the price dropped to affordability for most people.

In the 20th century, women began to venture into smoking. Although the idea of women smoking was frowned on in most circles, and many women who smoked were viewed in a nonfeminine manner, it continued in popularity with them. Increased advertising and competition for cigarette smoking by companies in the 20th century expanded that demand.

Both World War I and World War II further popularized the practice of tobacco consumption by servicemen to relax and to cool their nerves brought on by the stresses of combat. In the 1950s, as a way to lessen the number of toxins in the body, filtered cigarettes became an alternative, although at first they were considered an alternative for women rather than men.

Legality and Economics

Tobacco is a legally sold product within the bounds of federal and state laws, even though its use has been found to be one of the most unhealthy and deadly substances to the consumer and others in their surroundings.

The parent companies of the five major U.S. tobacco manufacturers, known as "Big Tobacco," are required to report cigarette sales, advertising, and promotional expenditures annually to the U.S. Federal Trade Commission (FTC). Those manufacturers include the Altria Group, Inc. (the ultimate parent of Philip Morris); Houchens Industries, Inc. (the ultimate parent of Commonwealth Brands, Inc.); Loews Corp. (the ultimate parent of Lorillard Tobacco Co.); Reynolds American, Inc. (the ultimate parent of R. J. Reynolds Tobacco Co. and Santa Fe Natural Tobacco Company, Inc., and that acquired Brown and Williamson Tobacco Corp.

in 2004); and Victor Group, Ltd. (the ultimate parent of Liggett Group, Inc. and Victor Tobacco, Inc.) (FTC, 2007a).

The total number of cigarettes sold or given away decreased by 4.2 billion (1.1 percent) from 2003 (367.6 billion cigarettes) to 2004 (363.4 billion cigarettes), with a decrease of 8.8 billion (2.4%) from 2004 to 2005 (354.6 billion cigarettes) (FTC, 2007a).

Cigarette advertising and promotional expenditures by Big Tobacco domestically were estimated to be $361,000 in 1970, $2.4 billion in 1985, and $8.24 billion in 1999. By 2003, these expenditures had increased to $15.5 billion, the highest expenditures ever for cigarette advertising and promotion. However, in 2004, they were down to $14.15 billion, a decline of $1.04 billion, and in 2005 expenditures declined again to $ 13.11 billion (FTC, 2007a).

The FTC Smokeless Tobacco Report for the years 2002–2005 (FTC, 2007b) contains the domestic smokeless tobacco sales (for example, chewing tobacco, snuff, and snus), advertising, and promotional activities. The five major domestic manufacturers of smokeless tobacco are the North Atlantic Trading Company, Inc.; Swedish Match North America, Inc.; Swisher International Group, Inc.; UST, Inc.; and Conwood LLC. Sales revenues increased each year since 1985 through 2004 ($2.62 billion) before declining in 2005 ($2.61 billion), even though sales and marketing expenditures increased from $234.65 million in 2002 to $231.08 million in 2004 and $250.79 million in 2005 (FTC, 2007b).

An example of one of the most successful advertising campaigns of the past was conducted by Philip Morris to sell Marlboro cigarettes. The Marlboro country campaign, with the "Marlboro Man" cowboy as the centerpiece, went on for well over 30 years as the longest-running advertising campaign for both television and print media in the 20th century (Kluger, 1996). It reflected the wide-ranging independent thinking and ruggedness that Philip Morris wanted the Marlboro brand to project. The campaign succeeded for several years even through the period when television advertising for tobacco products was banned.

In 1964, the per capita consumption of cigarettes began to decline as a result of the U.S. Surgeon General's *Report on Smoking and Health* (U.S. Department of Health Education and Welfare [USDHEW], 1964). Once released, the report had an effect of reducing per capita consumption of tobacco by 25 percent (Levinthal, 2008). By 1966, warning labels were put on tobacco packages, and by 1971 all tobacco advertising on television was banned. The tobacco industry never fully recovered from this initial step to inform the public about the health consequences of smoking.

For years, cigarette makers held off serious government restrictions by firming up their political alliances, challenging the scientific case, confusing the public, reassuring their customers and their own conscience by lowering tar and nicotine yields of their products. This defense strategy was continued to make the public perceive smoking as a smoker's right, even if it kills the smoker (Kluger, 1996).

In the 1990s, the tobacco industry was presented with a series of suits from individuals, as well as challenges from government agencies, based on the negative health effects of tobacco products. Congressional hearings were held on the basis of information that tobacco companies withheld their own research findings from the 1970s that found cigarette smoking was bad for the smoker's health. A year earlier the U.S. Environmental Protection Agency (EPA) determined that lung cancer can be caused by secondhand smoke.

As a result of this pressure, U.S. tobacco companies entered into a settlement agreement on November 23, 1998, with 46 states to compensate them for the cost of treating residents with smoke-related illnesses. The settlement provided these states with $206 billion until the year 2023. Four additional states made individual settlements with the tobacco companies. In return the tobacco industry won protection against future lawsuits.

The federal Government Accountability Office data analysis conducted by the Associated Press identified 46 states, between 2000 and 2006, spending only 30 percent of their $61.5 billion on health care, with less than 4 percent spent on antismoking efforts. States were using these funds to fund everything from a museum in Alaska and college scholarships in Michigan to tax breaks in Illinois. "Over the last several years about two dozen states have sold their annual tobacco-settlement payments for up-front money, sometimes for pennies on the dollar" (Leblanc & Smyth, 2008, p. A4). As states eye their economic crisis of 2009 and beyond, it is expected that more states will propose to dip into the tobacco money to cure their economic ills.

States, as well as the federal government, have used taxes on tobacco products to fund a number of programs and to add to the general fund of governmental entities. For example, on February 5, 2009, President Barack Obama signed a reauthorization of the State Children's Health Insurance Program, which continued health insurance to 7 million children and expanded services to another 4.1 million. The approved increased spending was $32.8 billion to be funded by boosting the federal excise tax on a pack of cigarettes from 62 cents to $1.01 ("Obama Signs Children's Health Bill," 2009).

Tobacco Ingredients and Use

Tobacco Ingredients

Tobacco is a manufactured product from tobacco leaves of the nicotiana plant. It is a cultivated crop used as an organic pesticide, in some forms of medicine, and by humans as a stimulant and agent of relaxation. There are a number of species of tobacco, including Virginia tobacco that is grown in fertile lowlands, burley tobacco used primarily for cigarette production, shade tobacco that is cultivated in northeastern states, and Y1, which is a tobacco with high nicotine content that was developed by the Brown and Williamson Company in the 1970s.

Nicotine is a toxic, dependence-producing, psychoactive drug found only in tobacco and the nightshade family of plants. It is an oily compound that could kill a healthy adult with a pure drop of 60 mg and is a major ingredient in pesticides of all kinds (Levinthal, 2008). It is named after the tobacco plant *(Nicotiana tabacum),* which was named for Jean Nicot who first sent tobacco seeds from South America to France in 1560 as a medical treatment. Nicotine was first isolated from tobacco in 1828 by the German chemists Posselt and Reimann (Hughes, 2003).

Tobacco Smoke

Tobacco from a smoked cigarette contains over 4,000 separate components that are oxidized and released through mainstream smoke that travels directly into a smoker's body and contains 60 chemicals that meet the stringent criteria for listing as known carcinogens (American Cancer Society [ACS], 2009a). The R. J. Reynolds Tobacco Company is the second largest tobacco company in the United States, with approximately 28 percent of cigarette sales. Their Website contains a full list of tobacco ingredients used in its manufactured brands. The list contains over 200 chemicals and their maximum levels of use from acetanisole to wheat absolute (an aromatic compound) (R. J. Reynolds Tobacco Company, 2009).

Tar is a sticky black liquid derived from the smoke of tobacco. The amount of tar in cigarettes varies from 6 mg to 16 mg; however, the last third of a cigarette contains 50 percent of the total tar. The sticky quality of tar has the ability to adhere to cells and clogs the lungs and pulmonary system, allowing dangerous carcinogenic compounds to accumulate in healthy tissue.

Carbon monoxide is an odorless, colorless, tasteless, toxic gas that is formed when tobacco burns because oxidation is incomplete. It can attach itself to hemoglobin, the protein inside red blood cells that assist in the transport of oxygen from the lungs to the rest of the body. However, carbon monoxide continues to accumulate and asphyxiate the body over time from the reduction in oxygen (Levinthal, 2008).

Forms and Methods of Tobacco Use

The major forms of tobacco intake are cigarettes, cigars, pipes, and smokeless tobacco. Cigarette smoking is the most common form of tobacco consumption. The tobacco industry manufactures cigarettes and adds hundreds of substances not found in either tobacco or nicotine. These additives are provided to enhance the cigarette's mild to strong taste. Cigarettes are normally provided in packs of 20 each and in cartons of 10 individual packs. To lower the price, some individuals prefer to "roll their own" from large bags of tobacco, cigarette papers, and filters purchased separately.

Cigars are made with air-cured or dried tobacco leaves that are aged about a year and then fermented for months. Cigar smoke is usually inhaled into the mouth and exhaled, rather than taken into the lungs. Cigars are produced in a number of sizes such as the Cigarillo (small), Corona (medium), and Robusto (large). The taste and smell of a cigar can be strengthened by the continued fermenting of each leaf beyond the normal fermenting process.

Pipe smoking is conducted by putting tobacco into the bowl of a pipe, lighting it, and drawing it through the stem to the mouthpiece and into the mouth of the smoker. Pipes are made from briar, meerschaum, wood, and a variety of other materials. Pipe tobacco is manufactured and processed not only for its taste, but also for its aroma. Pipe tobacco is a mixture of various blends, including an American Burley tobacco to which artificial sweeteners and flavorings are added.

Smokeless tobacco includes chewing tobacco, snuff, and snus. Chewing tobacco is tobacco furnished in long strands and whole or coarsely shredded leaves and consumed by placing it between cheek and gum or teeth, commonly referred to as dipping. It must be crushed by teeth to release flavor and nicotine. Unused chew is spit out. Snuff is either dry or moist. Dry snuff is ground tobacco that is inhaled or snuffed through the nose. Moist snuff is loose, fine tobacco put between the cheek and gum or lower lip and is available in small contained pouches.

Snus, a moist powdered tobacco product that is not fermented, is made from air-cured tobacco, water, salt, and flavorings. It is consumed by placing a small pouch under the lip. It is a form of snuff used in a fashion similar to dipping tobacco, but it is contained in small premeasured packets. It is also spitless and smokeless.

One final method of tobacco delivery is the electronic cigarette, which delivers nicotine without tobacco smoke. The electronic cigarette is a battery-powered device that provides inhaled doses of nicotine by a vaporized delivery system.

Prevalence and Incidence of Use

The Centers for Disease Control and Prevention (CDC) reported the prevalence of smoking declined from a high of 42.2 percent among adults in 1965 to 25.5 percent in 1990 and then remained fairly steady into this century (Schmitz & DeLaune, 2005). The CDC (2008a) reported that in 2007 there were 43.4 million adult (19.8 percent) smokers, whereas in 2008 there were 46 million (20.6 percent) (CDC, 2009). This includes 23.1 percent of men and 18.3 percent of women. In 1980, 51 percent of all U.S. military personnel smoked; by 1998 that percentage was reduced to 29.9 percent but increased to 33.8 percent in 2002, and by 2005 it was reduced again to 32.2 percent (Joseph, Muggli, Pearson, & Lando, 2005; Peterson et al., 2007).

In 2004 the CDC reported that 3 percent of adults were current users of smokeless tobacco. This includes six percent of men and 1 percent of women (CDC, 2006). More than one in three major league baseball players used smokeless tobacco, mainly moist snuff (Severson, Klein, Lichtenstein, Kaufman, & Orleans, 2005). Military personnel are more than twice as likely as civilians to use smokeless tobacco, with 16.8 percent as users (Peterson et al., 2007).

Age, Socioeconomic, Cultural, and Ethnic Trends in Use

According to Delnevo and Bauer (2009), the tobacco industry has a history of marketing its products disproportionately to minority communities that have become increasingly diverse in the United States. There are also differences in smoking rates among ethnic groups such as Asians (9.6 percent) and Hispanics (13.3 percent) with the lowest rates, and Native Americans and Alaska Natives (36.4 percent) with the highest. White Americans were at 21.4 percent, whereas the rate for African Americans was 19.8 percent in 2007 (CDC, 2008a).

The overall prevalence of cigarette smoking among African Americans decreased from 37.3 percent to 26.5 percent between 1980 and 1995, and smoking cessation increased from 26.8 percent to 35.4 percent in the same period. Fifty-eight percent of all deaths among African Americans are caused by smoking-related diseases. In general, African Americans tend to start smoking later in life and smoke fewer cigarettes a day than white Americans, although they tend to smoke higher tar and nicotine brands (Pederson, Ahwailia, Harris, & McGrady, 2002).

Tobacco use in adolescents occurs mainly from cigarette smoking. The Youth Risk Behavior Surveillance Survey, done to study prior health risk behavior from October 2004 to January 2006, found 54 percent of students nationwide had ever tried cigarette smoking. Of those, 23 percent had smoked a cigarette during the preceding 30 days (CDC, 2006). Nationwide, 20 percent of high school students and 6 percent of middle school students indicated smoking in 2007 (CDC, 2008b). Boys initiate smoking a few months before girls for white Americans and African Americans only, and the prevalence of adolescent subgroups, including ethnic and racial subgroups, mirrored those of adults. For example, smoking among Native Americans or Alaska Natives was the highest at 27.9 percent and among the Japanese the lowest at 5.2 percent (Caraballo et al., 2006).

There is a negative correlation between smoking and education. Those with advanced degrees had the lowest levels of smoking at 8.4 percent, whereas the highest rates of smoking (47.2 percent) were among those who had GED degrees. People between 18 and 44 years of age had the highest rate of smoking; those over 64 had the lowest (Schmitz & DeLaune, 2005).

Addictive Properties of Nicotine

Reports of the Surgeon General

Research on the negative effects of smoking began to accumulate early in the 20th century. That eventually led the U.S. Surgeon General Leroy E. Burney, in 1957, to publish the official position of the U.S. Public Health Service that there was a relationship between smoking and cancer. The first full report of the surgeon general in relationship to smoking was the 1964 *Report on Smoking and Health* (USDHEW, 1964). That report was initiated from collaborative efforts among the ACS, the American Heart Association, the National Tuberculosis Association, and the American Public Health Association.

This alliance of advocates wrote to President John F. Kennedy in 1961 requesting the establishment of a national committee on smoking with a goal to seek a solution to the health problem. The Kennedy administration responded to the request, as well as to the number of research studies on cigarette smoking, the following year by convening a committee of experts. The then-Surgeon General Luther L. Terry convened a commission of 10, including representatives from a variety of related fields, such as medical, pharmacology, and statistics, who had not taken a previous stand on tobacco use (USDHEW, 1964).

After 15 months of meetings, review of over 7,000 related articles, and with the assistance of 150 consultants, the report was issued on a Saturday, January 11, 1964, to minimize the negative effects on the stock market. The news was instantaneous in informing the public of the negative consequences of smoking. The tobacco industry began to see reduced profits immediately, never to see the same profitability again.

The report stated smokers had 10 times the risk of lung cancer compared with nonsmokers and heavy smokers had a 20-time risk. In addition, smoking was viewed as important in causing chronic bronchitis, a correlation with emphysema, and heart disease (USDHEW, 1964). However, they viewed nicotine as a habit, rather than an addiction, because at the time the impact and ingredients of nicotine were still not fully known. The former, *habit,* meaning something willfully chosen often, and the latter, *addiction,* implying the user has limited control usage.

Over the next 45 years there have been 29 surgeon general reports on smoking and health. In 1986, for example, Surgeon General C. Everett Koop issued the first report on *The Health Consequences of Involuntary Smoking: A Report of the Surgeon General* (U.S. Department of Health and Human Services [HHS], 1986). By then the causal link between inhaling secondhand smoke and the risk of cancer, as well as the effects of smoking by parents on their nearby children, were supported by a good deal of research. The latest report on *The Health Consequences of Involuntary Exposure to Tobacco Smoke: A Report of the Surgeon General* was issued in 2006. That report is backed by a tremendous amount of research on the involuntary effects of smoking on children and adults that include cancer and cardiovascular and respiratory disease. It also reviews the epidemiologic evidence on the health effects of involuntary exposure to tobacco smoke (HHS, 2006).

Neurophysiology

As nicotine enters the body, it moves quickly through the bloodstream to the brain. Inhaling nicotine through smoking is the quickest method of entry to the brain because it flows to the lungs and to the blood–brain barrier within a few seconds. The amount of nicotine released through tobacco smoke is only a fraction of what exists in each cigarette; however, the amount of nicotine in chew, dip, or snuff tends to be greater because individuals can control the amount by the force of crushing their teeth.

Nicotine activates molecules called nicotine acetylcholine receptors (nAChRs) in the mesocorticolimic dopaminergic system that projects from the ventral tegmental area to the nucleus accumbens and the pre-frontal cortex. A variety of reinforcing effects occur, particularly release of dopamine, which is a neurochemical effect shared by other drugs that also serve as positive reinforcement. The preponderance of data points to the critical role of the midbrain dopamine system. These reward circuits activate feelings of pleasure (Schmitz & DeLaune, 2005).

At the same time there is a release of adrenaline that causes increased heart rate, blood pressure, and respiration. Cotinine is a major byproduct of nicotine metabolism that can remain in the bloodstream for 48 to 72 hours after use of any nicotine product, and it can be detected in body fluids as one indicator of a person's exposure to nicotine (Ebbert et al., 2007).

Classification and Criteria of Nicotine Dependence

DSM-IV-TR Diagnostic Criteria for Nicotine-Related Disorders

Most smokers use tobacco because they are dependent on nicotine, and their behavior meets the diagnostic criteria for nicotine-related disorders in the DSM-IV-TR (American Psychiatric Association [APA], 2000). The DSM IV-TR criteria include the following: tolerance; withdrawal; used in large amounts or over a longer period than intended; persistent desire or unsuccessful efforts to cut down or quit; a great deal of time spent using the substance; giving up important social, occupational or recreational activities because of substance abuse; and continued use despite knowledge of medical problems related to use (Schmitz & DeLaune, 2005).

It is important to be reminded that most smokers try to quit a number of times before they are successful. As smokers begin to stop smoking, many experience nicotine withdrawal symptoms as defined by the DSM-IV-TR. Those symptoms include cravings, impaired performance on some tasks, increased appetite, weight gain, and for some, depression and difficulty sleeping (APA, 2000).

Because it may take two or more times for smokers to successfully quit, they will return to smoking, or relapse, quite a few times before full abstinence occurs. Hymowitz (2005) reported that those former smokers who are able to sustain their nonsmoking routine for more than three months are more likely not to relapse, although the potential may stay there for many years.

The Smoker

A *smoker* is one who smokes the gaseous products of burning materials, especially of organic origin, visible by the presence of small particles of carbon or the suspension of particles in a gas (Merriam-Webster, Inc., 2008). A smoker's first smoke is a well-documented experience, with people reporting feelings of nausea and other physical discomfort, as well as even many remembering that they enjoyed it. Each day more than 6,000 teenagers under 18 years of age try their first cigarette. More than half will become daily smokers. This adds up to more than 1 million new smokers a year (Cordry, 2001). Hughes (2003) reported that, over time, smokers begin to smoke more frequently and in a more stable manner as tobacco-using practices begin to settle into a more consistent pattern.

Standardized Nicotine Addiction Instrument

A number of instruments are used to assess chemical dependency. However, the diagnosis of nicotine dependence for adults begins with the admittance that they consume a tobacco product containing nicotine, which is normally not a difficult task to determine because most adult users admit to daily consumption of tobacco. Teenagers may not consume nicotine daily, or their daily consumption may be less than that of adults. In either case a determination of the degree of nicotine dependence is necessary to gauge the severity of the problem and the method of intervention.

The Agency for Healthcare Research and Quality developed the Treatment Tobacco Use and Dependence (TTUD) guidelines that provide an assessment and intervention model for the treatment of nicotine dependence. Pbert and colleagues (2004) present the National Cancer Institute's five As as an evidence-based treatment strategy follow-up that incorporates TTUD: Ask (about the person's smoking status), Advise (the person to stop smoking), Assess (their willingness to quit), and Assist and Arrange (for brief a intervention and follow-up).

An individual's level of physiological dependence and a recommendation for pharmacotherapy can be made without a formal evaluation of physiological dependence. The Fagerstrom Tolerance Questionnaire, developed by Karl Fagerstrom in 1978, is the most widely used self-report measure of nicotine dependence and has spawned other widely used modified versions such as the Fagerstrom Test for Nicotine Dependence (FTND). The FTND is a subjective measure of nicotine dependence with an original purpose to gauge the amount of energy smokers expend to achieve and maintain a blood nicotine level for desired effects (Richardson et al., 2008). A smoker with significant withdrawal symptoms, prior unsuccessful quit attempts, and high scores on FTND typically indicates nicotine dependence.

Health Impacts of Tobacco Use

Major Health Risks for Users

As far back as 1671, Francesco Redi, a Florentine scientist and physician, discovered that extracted "oil of tobacco" would kill an animal if injected into the bloodstream (Hughes, 2003). Tobacco use has caused more than 15 million deaths in the United States since 1965, the year after the first U.S. surgeon general's report of smoking and health (Armour et al., 2005). That reflects approximately 440,000 deaths a year, that costs men about 14.5 years of life, and women 13.2 years (Schmitz & DeLaune, 2005).

The major health risks for users of tobacco products include nicotine dependence, diseases of the cardiovascular and respiratory systems, and cancers in many areas of the human body. According to the ACS (2009a), cigarette smoking accounts for approximately 30 percent of all cancer deaths and is the major cause of cancer of the lung, larynx, mouth, pharynx, bladder, and esophagus. Smoking is also linked to other cancers of the pancreas, cervix, kidney, stomach, and some leukemias (ACS, 2009a).

Smokeless tobacco is not a safe substitute for smoking. Besides nicotine dependence, the risks include mouth cancer, pancreatic cancer, leukoplakia (cancerous sores in the mouth), receding gums, and tooth loss (ACS, 2009a).

Risks from Secondhand Smoke

Secondhand smoke, or involuntary smoke, is inhaled smoke that is a mixture of sidestream smoke released by the smoking cigarettes and the mainstream smoke that is exhaled by a smoker. Sidestream smoke tends to have higher concentrations of many of the toxins found in cigarette smoke because it is not filtered. This smoke is a complex mix of chemicals—formaldehyde, cyanide, carbon monoxide, ammonia, and nicotine, many of which are known carcinogens (HHS, 2006).

Risks from secondhand smoke include acute respiratory tract illnesses, asthma, chronic respiratory symptoms, and ear infections, among other conditions. *The Health Consequences of Involuntary Exposure to Tobacco Smoke: A Report of the Surgeon General* (HHS, 2006) details the research on the involuntary effects of smoking on children and adults that include cancer, cardiovascular disease, and respiratory disease. It also reviewed the epidemiologic evidence of the health risks of secondhand smoke.

It is estimated that 126 million people are exposed to secondhand smoke annually (HHS, 2006). The EPA estimates that each year at least 3,000 non-smoking adults die of lung cancer resulting from secondhand smoke. The EPA also estimates 150,000 to 300,000 children under one and one-half years of age get bronchitis or pneumonia as a result of breathing secondhand smoke (Cordry, 2001).

The major conclusion then is that secondhand smoke continues to cause premature death and disease in children and adults who do not smoke. Exposure of adults to secondhand smoke causes coronary heart disease and lung cancer, and millions of Americans are still exposed to secondhand smoke despite substantial progress in tobacco control.

Risks from Thirdhand Smoke

Thirdhand smoke is residual tobacco smoke contamination that remains after the cigarette or other tobacco product is extinguished. Thirdhand smoke can take place when the toxins from tobacco smoke accumulate in the hair and clothing of a smoker and are passed on to others through touch. The toxins from tobacco smoke can affect infants and other young children as they crawl and play where these chemicals have settled, such as rugs, play mats, and even cribs. Pediatricians see a real danger because particulate matter from smoke is linked to brain function problems, even at low levels (Winickoff et al., 2009).

The same poisonous gases, chemicals, and metals included in tobacco smoke that create risks of secondhand smoke are accumulating onto materials to make thirdhand smoke. According to the National Toxicology Program, there are 250 of these materials in smoke, including arsenic, lead, and the radioactive polonium-210 compound (Winickoff et al., 2009). In a large nationally representative sample, Winickoff et al. found that those families who believed secondhand and thirdhand smoke are health issues that will harm their children and others address the problem by implementing smoking bans in their homes. These no-smoking policies in the home have led to lower levels of biochemical and tobacco exposure, resulting in lower health risks in nonsmokers.

Prenatal Risks

Tobacco use can damage a woman's reproductive health beginning with her being less likely to become pregnant. Smoking can cause problems during pregnancy that will present difficulties for mothers and their infants. Smokers have a higher risk of the placenta growing too close to the opening of the uterus, early membrane ruptures, bleeding, premature birth, and emergency cesarean sections. It is also predicted that 5 percent of infant deaths would be prevented if pregnant women did not smoke (ACS, 2009b).

Breastfeeding mothers who smoke can pass toxins on to their babies in their milk. Even mothers who quit smoking or who never smoked come in contact with others who do and are capable of carrying thirdhand smoke back to their infants.

Pregnancy-specific stress is another predictor of early birth and, therefore, indirectly contributes to the lower birth weight of newborns. Pregnancy-specific stressors includes physical symptoms, parenting concerns, relationship strains, bodily changes, anxiety about labor and delivery, and concerns about the baby's health. These stressors were associated with cigarette smoking, caffeine consumption, and an unhealthy diet. In fact, cigarette smoking can be a good predictor of lower birthweight and subsequent developmental difficulties (Lobel et al., 2008).

Wakschlag et al. (2002) reported that the body of evidence is consistently supportive of an etiologic role for prenatal exposure to nicotine in the onset of severe antisocial behavior of offspring. The possibility of women smoking during pregnancy playing a causal risk in the development of antisocial behavior in their offspring is consistent with existing knowledge that prenatal insults and exposures have long-term effects on health.

Treatments for Nicotine Dependence

Cognitive–Behavioral Therapy

Cognitive–behavioral therapy (CBT) has been used to address drug abuse related to many substances such as alcohol, cocaine, and nicotine. Like cognitive therapy,

CBT emphasizes patient education, case conceptualization, collaboration, structure, and standard CBT techniques. It is also one of the most empirically studied and used approaches to treating substance abuse (Beck, Liese, & Najavits, 2005).

In CBT, thoughts are seen as playing major role in dependence behavior, negative emotions, and physiological responses. It is believed that substance abuse behavior is learned and can be unlearned (modified) through the CBT processes. The aim is to modify thoughts associated with substance use brought on through people's core beliefs such as helplessness, loneliness or failure, that they have been conditioned to believe since childhood, and that they think they have no control over.

Comorbidity disorders such as nicotine dependence and a psychiatric disorder such as depression, based on the DSM-IV-TR, should have a treatment plan that addresses both conditions. Beck and colleagues (2005) suggested several steps in the plan, including the following: identifying the person's motivation for change; identifying his or her socialization to the cognitive model, such as actions stemming from his or her perceptions of situations; and specifying the person's problems and concrete steps to address them. A referral to a psychiatrist for medication consultation and monitoring may also be a necessary element of the treatment plan.

Nicotine Replacement Therapy

The FDA approved five different nicotine replacement therapy (NRT) products for the treatment of tobacco dependence: nicotine gum, nicotine inhaler, nasal spray, lozenge, and the transdermal patch. All five products have been found to have equal effects as pharmacological approaches to smoking cessation (Ebbert et al., 2007; Schmitz & DeLaune, 2005).

NRT helps the nicotine-dependent person to abstain from tobacco by replacing the nicotine usually obtained from a tobacco product. NRT reduces the general or prominent withdrawal symptoms so the person can function normally while he or she learns to live without cigarettes, reduces the reinforcing effects of tobacco-delivered nicotine, provides some desirable mood states, and enhances the ability to handle stress (Hymowitz, 2005).

The quit rate for NRT is twice that of placebo-controlled studies for both short- and long term. When combined with behavioral counseling and follow-up, quit rates can reach 40 percent to 50 percent after one year (Hymowitz, 2005). The quit rates of over-the-counter NRT products seem to mirror those of NRT products prescribed by a physician, but the long-term efficacy is still in question. The extended use of NRT, beyond the recommended time frame, may be an effective strategy to forestall continued tobacco use; however, the combination of two or more NRT delivery systems is still questionable.

Psychopharmacological Medications

Bupropion SR is a benzodiazepine medication, approved in 1997 by the FDA, as the first nonnicotine medication shown to be effective for smoking cessation. Bupropion SR, marketed as Zyban, works directly in a smoker's brain to ease withdrawal symptoms and can be combined with Wellbutrin, when there is an indication of depression.

Bupropion SR minimizes weight gain, reduces withdrawal symptoms, and is effective for both men and women. Hymowitz (2005) reported that a continuous abstinence rate of up to one year, or double that of placebos, is possible and that both bupropion SR treatments are superior to patch treatments. However, there is less evidence to support the combination of bupropion SR medications with NRT to enhance quit rates.

Chantix is another psychopharmacological medication that has been used for smoking cessation; it operates by blocking the pleasure effects of nicotine in the brain if the person attempts to smoke. But the FDA reported a link to psychiatric problems with Chantix that include suicidal behavior and vivid dreams. These reports are based on reported cases of serious drug reactions, including death, during January to March 2008 (Alonso-Zaldivar, 2008).

The Importance of Social and Environmental Support

Most people who successfully quit smoking do so on their own (80 percent), without the help of specialized programs or formal treatments. People who quit usually make two to three unsuccessful attempts before achieving abstinence (Pederson et al., 2002). However, the support of family, friends, coworkers, and other environmental supports during these periods is underestimated.

The social and environmental supports have a positive effect on a smoker's ability to stop smoking. People who experience more social supports for cessation and who also have fewer smokers in their environment are more likely to succeed in stopping smoking (Pbert, Ockene, & Reiff-Hekking, 2004). In particular, a person trying to quit smoking who experiences stress or other pressures may need the help of family, coworkers, friends, and other environmental supports to be successful.

For example, churches play an important role in many communities, including the African American community, and a wide range of health-related interventions have been implemented and evaluated in such settings. Pederson and colleagues (2002) found, in reviewing several studies in African American communities, that quitting was significantly associated with smoking fewer cigarettes per day and being married, and those who attended church were more likely to quit than those who did not.

Insurance Costs and Health Benefits

The proportion of Americans who smoke has decreased from 42.4 percent in 1965 to 20.6 percent in 2008; however, smoking is still the leading cause of preventable diseases and death in the United States. Smoking adds well over $165 billion to health care and disability costs annually, with up to $92 billion of that in lost productivity (Fitch, Iwasaki, & Pyenson, 2006). The CDC reports that smoking costs companies $3,400 per smoking employee annually, or about $7.18 per pack of cigarettes, in health care bills, reduced productivity, and absenteeism (Tomsho, 2009). Therefore, if smokers quit, the savings to the health care industry and to employers who underwrite much of the health care costs would decrease substantially.

Because the cost of smoking cessation programs can be as little as $0.50 per person per month, the impact on employer-sponsored health insurance programs is minimal. It is estimated that for each employee and dependent who quits smoking at least $210 in short-term annual medical and life insurance costs would be saved immediately (Fitch et al., 2006). That does not count the smoking causes of cancer that can take years to develop but can be much more costly to address.

A study led by a team from the University of Pennsylvania, School of Medicine, tracked 878 General Electric Company (GE) employees for 18 months during 2005 and 2006. Participants were smokers who divided up into two groups, and both were provided with smoking-cessation information. Members of one group were provided $750 in cash over 18 months as they continued not to smoke. Members of the other group were not provided a cash incentive. The group provided cash had a 14.7 percent rate of smoking cessation compared with the other group with 5 percent. At the end of the study, 9.4 percent of the paid group was still abstaining, compared with 3.6 percent of the other group (Volpp et al., 2009). GE is now planning to institute an incentive plan for all of its 152,000 U.S. employees (Tomsho, 2009). This is a way for GE to save the $50 million a year it pays in extra health insurance and other costs for smoking employees. It can also be used as a model for other employers as a way to save health insurance costs and develop healthier, more productive employees.

Synergy of Nicotine Dependence and Alcohol and Other Drug Dependence

Alcohol- and Other Drug-Involved People as Special Tobacco Users

Alcohol and nicotine are two of the oldest and most commonly used drugs, and they are frequently used together. Both are legally available, and that contributes to their concurrent use. Alcohol is usually classified as a depressant, whereas tobacco is primarily a stimulant. Nicotine acts on the brain by binding to receptors, but alcohol does not bind to receptors. However, there is evidence that both substances may act on a common target in the brain that is responsible for the reinforcing effects of both drugs. There is also strong evidence, through research with twins, of a genetic basis for the co-use of alcohol and tobacco (Funk, Marinelli, & Le, 2006).

The Substance Abuse and Mental Health Services Administration (2008) reported that in the past month alcohol use was reported by 66.9 percent of current cigarette smokers compared with 46.1 percent for those who said they did not use cigarettes in the last 30 days. There was also a noted association between binge drinking, in that 45 percent of current cigarette users binge drink, whereas only 16.4 percent of nonsmokers do. Current smokers also represent more heavy drinkers (16.4 percent) than do nonsmokers (3.8 percent).

Adolescents with alcohol and other drug problems smoke tobacco at about 1.5 times the rate of their counterparts; however, despite smoking's health risk, substance abuse treatment programs often do not target smoking or nicotine dependence. Griffin and colleagues (2007) examined youths at 10 alcohol and other drug dependence treatment programs and found adolescents who recovered had significantly lower rates of smoking than youths who did not recover. Adolescents who did poorly in treatment may have additional health risks with continued high rates of smoking and other substance abuse after treatment. It may be prudent for alcohol and other drug treatment centers to put more emphasis on smoking cessation.

Synergistic Health Impacts

Alcohol, tobacco, marijuana, and other drugs, such as amphetamines, may be used separately or in pairings as a result of a person attempting to address depression, anxiety, or peer pressure. Unfortunately, the effects of comorbidity, drug dependence, physical symptoms, and mental health issues may interfere with any attempts at treatment for one or more of these drug dependencies and make it even more difficult to quit smoking. Totally eliminating any one of these substances can lead to bouts of depression, irritation, and even panic attacks. However, even a reduction to the point of moderation can become difficult because several drugs, such as marijuana, have no safe level of use.

Alcohol use of three or more drinks a day and cigarette smoking share similar effects on some forms of cardiovascular diseases, including increased blood pressure, increased levels of triglycerides in the blood, higher rates of stroke, and congestive heart failure (Mukamal, 2006). However, there is little evidence that they act synergistically or that the effects are worse when smoking and drinking occur together than would be expected from their independent effects.

▼
▼
▼

Mukamal's (2006) work determined in most cases moderate drinking of perhaps one drink a day does not share the same negative cardiovascular risks and may have effects opposite of those for smoking. However, the idea of one drink a day for positive health benefits has been challenged by the work of Allen and colleagues (2009) in a study of 1.3 million middle-aged women in the United Kingdom. They found that low to moderate alcohol consumption increased the risk for breast, liver, and rectal cancers. This risk may account for nearly 13 percent of those cancers. They found no difference between wine drinkers and consumers of other alcohol products. In addition, they found that alcohol use was strongly predictive of cancer of the upper oral-digestive tract (mouth and throat), but only for women who currently smoked.

Approaches by Substance Abuse Treatment Professionals

The substance abuse treatment professional is charged with duties relevant to the assessment, clinical evaluation, treatment, or referral of clients identified or suspected to be in need of assistance related to their abuse of drugs. Ongoing study and evaluation of drug treatment methodologies and evidence-based practice is necessary to maintain the most current, appropriate, and available services.

Most drug treatment professionals do not recommend one treatment approach for their clients. There are too many differences among substance users and abusers, and the treatment ranges are too vast to encompass all the different substances and combinations a client is likely to be dependent on. The levels of treatment range from the simple to the more complex, based on the physical, behavioral, medical, and psychological impacts.

Regardless of the treatments used, some people relapse after treatment. For example, it is not uncommon for individuals treated for nicotine dependence to relapse five to six or more times before they are successfully free of nicotine dependence. In general, the more varied the treatment approaches attempted, even without success, the closer the person will become to reaching the specific treatment or combinations of treatments that will work.

The professional may ask the client to add a formal support system to his or her treatment beyond the immediate family, especially if there seems to be a change in the family structure, or former supports are no longer able to supply the needed encouragement necessary for the client to quit smoking or using smokeless tobacco products.

The decision on a treatment approach is often the result of an agreement between the social work professional and the client. Once both social worker and client are aware of the problem, such as a dependency on both alcohol and nicotine, a recommendation is made by the social worker that the client may or may not agree to implement. Deciding on a treatment approach is not only difficult for the professional, when taking into consideration any number of factors, but also difficult for the client as well because it is often confusing with the number of factors they must consider. Sometimes a second opinion is the best course of action, and that should be encouraged if an agreement cannot be made on which treatment path to pursue.

Programs, Initiatives, and Resources to Prevent or Lessen Tobacco Use

Prevention Education

Most youths who begin to smoke do not fully understand nicotine use as potentially leading to drug dependence as challenging as the use of heroin, cocaine, or alcohol; they truly underestimate the health consequences. CDC guidelines for school-based prevention programs include a number of areas—policy, instruction, curriculum, training, family involvement, tobacco cessation efforts, and evaluation (Cordry, 2001). Among the number of strategies advocated by the CDC in these areas is a zero tolerance for tobacco at school and school functions; development of student problem-solving skills; instruction and reinforcement of prevention education and training; promotion of discussions at home about tobacco use; provision of access to cessation programs; and assessment of the tobacco-use prevention programs at regular intervals (Cordry, 2001).

Other education programs include providing information, psychological approaches, mass media campaigns, and community coalition approaches. Information provided includes the health risks and harmful effects of tobacco, such as the chronic disease, morbidity, and mortality associated with tobacco use. Psychological approaches include learning about the impact of positive and negative peer pressure, the development of refusal skills, and the social consequences of smoking. Mass media campaigns are normally used in conjunctions with other methods of prevention, including school-based programs that reinforce the antismoking advertisements put forth in schools, television, and online. Community coalitions involve parents, churches, police, and the larger community that target changing the social norms, raise public awareness, and work together to focus on tobacco as a public problem.

For example, the Great American Smokout has taken place across the country the third Thursday of November each year since 1977. It spotlights the dangers of tobacco use and asks people to give up smoking for a day and take that opportunity to make a long-term plan to quit for good.

Societal Trends in Restriction of Tobacco Use

Federal, state, and local governments have issued laws to restrict smoking tobacco products in and around government buildings, hospitals, restaurants, bars, and other public places. In 1997, pursuant to Executive Order 13058 signed by President Bill Clinton, smoking was prohibited in all interior spaces owned, rented, or leased by the executive branch of the federal government, as well as in front of intake ducts in any outdoor areas under executive branch control (Federal Register, 1997).

Since California first adopted smokeless laws in 1994, half the states have issued smoking prohibitions in public places and elsewhere. Most states were responding to the 2006 surgeon general's report *The Health Consequences of Involuntary Exposure to Tobacco Smoke* (HHS, 2006). This report gave new life to the smoke-free laws because of its conclusion that secondhand smoke was a health hazard to children and nonsmoking adults. Although some states barred smoking completely in public buildings, others extended it to hospitality venues such as restaurants, bars, and shopping malls.

Delaware passed its smoking bans in 2002 in all public buildings, including workplaces, bars, restaurants, and casinos. Several New England states followed. Ohio went smoke free in 2006. New Jersey's smoking prohibition began in 2006, and a smoking ban compromise for Atlantic City casinos went into effect in 2007. New Mexico's ban in 2007 includes nearly all indoor workplaces and public places. Pennsylvania passed a smoking ban in 2008 that banned cigarettes, cigars, and pipe smoking in restaurants, schools, sports arenas, theaters, and bus and train stations. Wyoming has, so far, limited their smoking prohibitions to certain locations in state buildings.

Bangor, Maine, was one of the first places to take the step to prohibit smoking in vehicles with young children in 2002, followed by Rockland County, New York. Louisiana and Arkansas have extended their smoking restrictions to privately owned vehicles with children aboard.

On June 22, 2009, President Obama signed the Family Smoking Prevention and Tobacco Control Act (P.L. 111-31) into law. The law gives the FDA the authority to oversee the science-based regulation of tobacco products, stop youth-focused marketing, provide full disclosure of ingredients and additives, and strengthen warning labels (White House, 2009).

A major shift is expected over the next several years that will result in a reduction in youth and adult smoking as well as an increase in the protection of the public health of those presently consuming tobacco products and the recipients of secondhand and thirdhand smoke.

As more research on the risks of secondhand and thirdhand smoke continue to grow, states and other governmental entities will see the value of reduced health care costs and a healthy citizenry. That will, no doubt, add even more restrictions on smoking.

Cessation Support Programs

Smokers who are ready to stop smoking should develop a treatment plan with their physician, clinician, or social worker. That plan may include CBT, NRT, or psycho-pharmacological medications. Of course, social and environmental supports can have a positive effect on a smoker's ability to quit smoking.

There are many national and local smoking cessation support programs to further assist those who want to quit. Quitnet is a quit-smoking support program that can be joined online at http://www.quitnet.com. Quitnet provides science-based resources, tips and advice, 24/7 support, and a directory of local programs. It also is able to tailor smoking cessation and corporate wellness programs for public and private organizations. Smokefree.gov was created by the National Cancer Institute and has an online guide (http://www.smokefree.gov) that provides support for the first year of smoking cessation, as well as print resources, studies, and local telephone quitlines. The American Lung Association's Freedom From Smoking online site (http://www.lungusa.org) provides information through seven modules that explores one's readiness to quit, helps individuals get prepared for quit day, and informs them about long-term strategies for maintaining a smoke-free lifestyle.

Because young adults potentially have lower levels of nicotine dependence, it would seem to be much easier for them to stop smoking in a cessation support program. However, they may have as difficult a time quitting as their adult counterparts. Unfortunately, young people who decide to quit smoking are just as likely as adults to relapse. Youths can use Smokefree America's Web site (http://www.anti-smoking.org). Its mission is to motivate youths to stay tobacco free and to empower youth smokers to quit. Smokefree America is an in-house program to fight tobacco use at the local, regional, and national levels. It uses Web sites, school-based educational programs, and other support efforts to assist youths suffering from nicotine dependence.

Resources Available to the Social Worker

Social workers offer a broad range of services to help evaluate a person's strengths, resources, and support systems. They offer social and emotional supports and counseling services for individuals and groups, and develop specific plans for clients to assist them in meeting their own needs. Social workers also have a number of resources that can guide their work with clients who use tobacco and have nicotine dependence.

Conclusion

This chapter has focused on helping social workers understand the nature of tobacco use and nicotine dependence so that they are better prepared to address a variety of issues related to tobacco use. The history, economics, and availability of tobacco were presented, along with the methods and prevalence of its use. The dependence-producing properties of nicotine and other related toxins that relate to neurophysiology, assessment, and diagnosis were explored. A good deal of emphasis was placed on the major health risks, treatment methods, and the synergy between nicotine, alcohol, and other drugs. Finally, program initiatives and resources to prevent and lessen tobacco use were outlined. Armed with knowledge, social workers will be better equipped to prevent, assess, and treat tobacco use and nicotine dependence.

References

Alonso-Zaldivar, R. (2008, October 23). Drug reaction reports set mark. *Philadelphia Inquirer*, p. A10.

Allen, N. E., Beral, V., Casabonne, D., Sau Wan Kan, Reeves, G. K., Brown, A., & Green, J. (2009). Moderate alcohol intake and cancer incidence in women. *Journal of the Natural Cancer Institute, 101*, 296–305.

American Cancer Society. (2009a). *Cigarette smoking.* Retrieved March 9, 2009, from http://www.cancer.org/docroot/PED/content/PED_10_2X_Cigarette_Smoking_and_Cancer.asp

American Cancer Society. (2009b). *Women and smoking.* Retrieved March 9, 2009, from http://www.cancer.org/docroot/PED/content//PED_10_2X_Women_and_Smoking.asp

American Psychiatric Association. (2000). *Diagnostic and statistical manual of mental disorders* (4th ed., text rev.). Washington, DC: Author.

Armour, B. S., Woolery, T., Malarcher, A., Pechacek, T. F., & Husten, C. (2005). Annual smoking-attributable mortality, years of potential life lost, and productivity losses-United States, 1997–2001. *Morbidity & Mortality Weekly Report, 54*, 625–628.

Beck, J. S., Liese, B. S., & Najavits, L. M. (2005). Cognitive therapy. In R. J. Frances, S. I. Miller, & A. H. Mack (Eds.), *Clinical textbook of addictive disorders.* (3rd ed., pp. 474–501). New York: Guilford Press.

Caraballo, R. S., Yee, S. L., Gfroerer, J. C., Pechacek, T. F., & Henson, R. (2006). Tobacco use among racial and ethnic population subgroups of adolescents in the United States. *Preventing Chronic Disease, 3*, 1–12. Retrieved April 2, 2009, from http://www.cdc.gov/pcd/issues/2006/Apr/toc.htm

Centers for Disease Control and Prevention. (2006). Youth risk behavior surveillance—United States, 2005. *Morbidity & Mortality Weekly Report, 55,* 1–108.

Centers for Disease Control and Prevention. (2008a). Cigarette smoking among adults—United States, 2007. *Morbidity & Mortality Weekly Report, 57,* 1221–1226.

Centers for Disease Control and Prevention. (2008b). Smoking-attributable mortality, years of potential life lost and productivity losses, United States, 2000–2004. *Morbidity & Mortality Weekly Report, 57,* 1226–1228.

Centers for Disease Control and Prevention. (2009). *Cigarette smoking among adults and trends in smoking cessation—United States, 2008.* Retrieved November 18, 2009, from http://www.cdc.gov/mmwr/preview/mmwrhtml/mm5844a2.htm

Cordry, H. V. (2001). *Tobacco: A reference handbook.* Santa Barbara, CA: ABC-CLIO.

Delnevo, C. D., & Bauer, U. E. (2009). Monitoring the tobacco use epidemic III, The host: Data source and methodological challenges. *Preventive Medicine, 48,* S16–S23.

Ebbert, J. O., Dale, L. C., Severson, H., Croghan, I. T., Rasmussen, D. F., Schroeder, D. R., et al. (2007). Nicotine lozenges for smokeless tobacco use. *Nicotine & Tobacco Research, 9,* 233–240.

Family Smoking Prevention and Tobacco Control Act, P.L. 111-31, Stat. 1776–1858.

Federal Register. (1997). Executive order 13058—Protecting employees and the public from exposure to tobacco smoke in the federal workplace (Vol. 62, pp. 43451–43452). Washington, DC: U.S. Government Printing Office.

Federal Trade Commission. (2007a). *Federal trade commission cigarette report for 2004 and 2005.* Retrieved March 9, 2009, from http://www.ftc.gov/reports/tobacco/cigarettes 2004-2005.pdf

Federal Trade Commission. (2007b). *Federal trade commission smokeless tobacco report for the years 2002–2005.* Retrieved March 9, 2009, from http://ftc.gov/reports/tobacco/02-05smokeless0623105.pdf

Fitch, K., Iwasaki, K., & Pyenson, B. (2006). *Covering smoking cessation as a health benefit: A case for employers.* New York: Milliman.

Funk, D., Marinelli, P. W., & Le, A. D. (2006). Biological processes underlying co-use of alcohol and nicotine: Neuronal mechanisms, cross-tolerance, and genetic factors. *Alcohol Research and Health, 29*(3), 186–192.

Griffin, B. A., Ramchand, R., Harris, K., McCaffrey, D., & Morral, A. (2007). Smoking rates among adolescents in substance abuse treatment programs. *Psychiatric Services, 58,* 1528.

Hughes, J. (2003). *Learning to smoke: Tobacco use in the west.* Chicago: University of Chicago Press.

Hymowitz, N. (2005). Tobacco. In R. J. Frances, S. I. Miller, & A. H. Mack (Eds.), *Clinical textbook of addiction disorders* (3rd ed., pp. 105–137). New York: Guilford Press.

Joseph, A. M., Muggli, M. M., Pearson, K. C., & Lando, H. (2005). The cigarette manufacturer's efforts to promote tobacco to the U.S. military. *Military Medicine, 170,* 874–880.

Kluger, R. (1996). *Ashes to ashes: America's hundred-year cigarette war, the public health, and the unabashed triumph of Philip Morris.* New York: Alfred A. Knopf.

Ksir, C., Hart, C., & Ray, O. (2006). *Drugs, society and human behavior* (11th ed.). Boston: WGB/McGraw-Hill.

Leblanc, S., & Smyth, J. C. (2008, November 21). Cash from tobacco settlement is funding unrelated topics. *Philadelphia Inquirer,* p. A12.

Levinthal, C. F. (2008). *Drugs, behavior and modern society* (8th ed.). Needham Heights, MA: Allyn & Bacon.

Lobel, M., Cannella, D. L., Graham, J. E., DeVincent, C., Schneider, J., & Meyer, B. A. (2008). Pregnancy-specific stress, prenatal health behaviors, and birth outcomes. *Health Psychology, 27,* 604–615.

Merriam-Webster, Inc. (2008). *Merriam-Webster's collegiate dictionary* (11th ed.). Springfield, MA: Author.

Mukamal, K. J. (2006). The effects of smoking and drinking on cardiovascular disease and risk factors. *Alcohol Research and Health, 29,* 199–202.

Obama signs children's health bill. (2009). *U.S. News & World Report.* Retrieved February 5, 2009, from http://www.health.usnews.com/aticle/health/healthday/2009/02/05/

Pbert, L., Ockene, J. K., & Reiff-Hekking, S. (2004). Tobacco. In M. Galanter & H. D. Kleber (Eds.), *Textbook of substance abuse treatment* (3rd ed., pp. 217–234). Washington, DC: American Psychiatric Publishing.

Pederson, L., Ahwailia, J. S., Harris, K. J., & McGrady, G. A. (2002). Smoking cessation among African Americans. In G. Xueqin Ma & G. Henderson (Eds.), *Ethnicity and substance abuse: Prevention & intervention* (pp. 87–123). Springfield, IL: Charles C Thomas.

Peterson, A. L., Severson, H. H., Andrews, J. A., Gott, S. P., Cigrang, J. A., Gordon, J. S., et al. (2007). Smokeless tobacco use in military personnel. *Military Medicine, 172,* 1300–1305.

Richardson, L., Greaves, L., Jategaonkar, N., Bell, K., Pederson, A., & Tungohan, E. (2008). Rethinking an assessment of nicotine dependence: A sex, gender and diversity analysis of the Fagerstrom test for nicotine dependence. *Journal of Smoking Cessation, 2,* 59–67.

R. J. Reynolds Tobacco Company. (2009). *Full list of tobacco ingredients.* Retrieved March 9, 2009, from http://www.rjrt.com/smoking/ingredientsRJRList.asp

Schmitz, J. M., & DeLaune, K. A. (2005). Nicotine. In J. Lowinson, P. Ruiz, R. B. Millman, & J. G. Langrad (Eds.), *Substance abuse: A comprehensive textbook* (4th ed., pp. 387–403). Philadelphia: Lippincott, Williams & Wilkins.

Severson, H. H., Klein, K., Lichtenstein E., Kaufman, N., & Orleans, C. T. (2005). Smokeless tobacco use among professional baseball players: Survey results, 1998–2003. *Tobacco Control, 14,* 31–36.

Substance Abuse and Mental Health Services Administration. (2008). *National survey on drug use and health 2007.* Rockville, MD: U. S. Department of Health and Human Services.

Tomsho, R. (2009, February 12). More smokers quit if paid, study shows. *Wall Street Journal,* pp. D1, D6.

U.S. Department of Health Education and Welfare (USDHEW). (1964). *Smoking and health: Report of the advisory committee to the surgeon general of the public health service.* Washington, DC: Author.

U.S. Department of Health and Human Services, Centers for Disease Control and Prevention. (1986). *The health consequences of involuntary smoking: A report of the surgeon general.* Atlanta: Author.

U.S. Department of Health and Human Services, Public Health Service. (2006). *The health consequences of involuntary exposure to tobacco smoke: A report of the surgeon general.* Rockville, MD: Author.

Volpp, K. G., Troxel, A. B., Pauly, M. V., Glick, H. A., Puig, A., Asch, D. A., et al. (2009). A randomized controlled trial of financial incentives for smoking. *New England Journal of Medicine, 360,* 699–709.

Wakschlag, L. S., Pickett, K. E., Cook, Jr., E., Benowitz, N. L., & Leventhal, B. L. (2002). Maternal smoking during pregnancy and severe antisocial behavior in offspring: A review. *American Journal of Public Health, 92,* 966–974.

White House. (2009). *Fact sheet: The family smoking prevention and tobacco control act of 2009.* Retrieved June 22, 2009, from http://whitehouse.gov/the_press_office/fact-sheet-and-expected-attendees-for-todays-Rose-Garden-bill-signing

Winickoff, J. P., Friebely, J., Tanski, S. E., Sherrod, C., Matt, G. E., Hovell, M. F., & McMillen, R. C. (2009). Beliefs about the health effects of "thirdhand" smoke and home smoking bans. *Pediatrics, 123,* 74–79.

6

The Challenges of Co-Occurring Disorders

Laura Blankertz and Gwenelle S. O'Neal

Introduction

The goal of this chapter is to introduce a type of client, one with co-occurring disorders (CODs; one or more mental health disorders and one or more substance-related disorders that are independent of each other), that has been recognized by the federal government as a special service priority (Co-Occurring Center for Excellence [COCE], Overview Paper 1, 2007; see COCE Overview Papers listed in Resources). Over the years a number of names have been attached to individuals with this condition: MICA (mentally ill chemical abusers), dual diagnosis, dual disorder, and comorbidity. Currently, the term most frequently used is co-occurring disorders, or COD. These individuals, whose numbers are widespread and often difficult to determine, present a major service challenge. Both disorders and their interaction need to be treated at the same time, mandating the development of new methods of treatment. Currently, there are many individuals with COD who are receiving no treatment. This service need has caused the federal government to focus on helping the substance abuse and mental health systems integrate and develop special programs to meet the needs of these clients.

This chapter introduces the range of characteristics of individuals with COD, methods to identify these individuals, types of programs necessary to treat them, specific interventions that are needed to help individuals with COD, several models or programs that have been established as evidence-based practice, and the unique needs of specific populations, such as lesbian, gay, bisexual, transgender or transsexual, or questioning (LGBTQ) clients, or older adults. Because of the large numbers of COD clients, many helping professionals will meet them in their work and will need to know how to engage them or how to make appropriate referrals.

Characteristics and Service Needs of Individuals with COD

An individual with CODs has one or more mental health disorders and one or more substance-related disorders (COCE, Overview Paper 1, 2007). "A diagnosis of COD occurs when at least one disorder of each type can be established, independent of the other, and is not simply a cluster of symptoms resulting from the one disorder" (Center for Substance Abuse Treatment [CSAT], 2005, p. xvii). Although independent, the mental health and substance-related disorders interact with each other. This interaction, as well as each disorder, must be treated.

The duality ranges in complexity and severity as it reflects moderate to severe levels of psychiatric or emotional distress combined with various substances used, including alcohol, tobacco, marijuana, cocaine, crack, methamphetamine, prescribed medicines (Ziedonis et al., 2005), and other less frequently used substances (for example, glue, oxygen, paint). The interactions of the illnesses affect the course and prognosis of each (National Institute on Drug Abuse [NIDA], 2008).

Attention has also been focused on the need for services for the triply diagnosed: HIV, substance abuse, and mental illness (Bouis et al., 2007). The presence of two or more CODs generally depicts a more challenging pathway to recovery than does either mental illness or substance abuse alone.

The interest in substance use and co-occurring mental disorders is a growing national and international health concern. CODs were first recognized in the 1970s, and during the 1980s and 1990s, a few innovative programs with integrated treatment were developed. However, it was not until the beginning of the 21st century that COD individuals were recognized as a priority service need by the federal government (COCE, Overview Paper 6, 2007). In 2002, the U.S. Department of Health and Human Services (HHS), at the request of Congress, submitted a *Report to Congress on the Prevention and Treatment of Co-Occurring Substance Abuse Disorders and Mental Disorders* (Substance Abuse and Mental Health Services Administration [SAMHSA], 2002). In 2005, *Transforming Mental Health Care in America: The Federal Action Agenda: First Steps* was released by SAMHSA with recommendations for transforming both the mental health care system and substance abuse treatment system to address CODs.

Two factors contributed to this recognition: (1) the severe negative consequences associated with the lack of treatment for co-occurring disorders and (2)
the prevalence of these disorders.

> Co-occurring disorders, in their most severe form, can evoke strong nega-
> tive consequences. People with dual disorders are at high risk for many
> additional problems such as symptomatic relapses, hospitalization, finan-
> cial problems, loss of contact with families, homelessness, suicide, vio-
> lence, sexual and physical victimization, incarceration, serious medical ill-
> ness such as HIV, hepatitis B, or C, and early death." (SAMHSA, 2003, p. 2)[1]

Individuals with severe mental health and substance-related disorders can be
very challenging to serve. "They are difficult to engage. Often they are noncom-
pliant with medication and treatment plans and frequently enter the service system in crisis" (Blankertz & Cnaan, 1993, p. 100). Many have been homeless and
present with childhood sexual or physical abuse, and other forms of victimization
(Blankertz, Cnaan, & Freedman, 1993).

In addition, the number of potential clients possessing CODs is startling.
Without proper treatment, they make extensive use of emergency services and, as
a result, are a very high-cost subpopulation. It is estimated that more than 5 million individuals in United States have CODs (SAMHSA, 2006). Providing a definite
prevalence rate is difficult. Data collection, using national representative samples,
has been conducted for different purposes, with many projects using different definitions of mental illness (CSAT, 2005). Convenience samples taken at substance
abuse or mental health treatment settings suggest that 20 percent to 50 percent of
mental health clients had a lifetime co-occurring substance use disorder (SUD) and
50 percent to 70 percent of those in substance abuse treatment had a lifetime co-
occurring mental health disorder (COCE, Overview Paper 8, 2007). Severe mental
illness (SMI) is highly correlated with substance abuse and dependence. An amount
of substance use that would have little or no effect on someone without mental illness can cause harmful outcomes for individuals with mental illness (Osher, 2005).

From the mental health point of view, it is the severity of the symptoms, rather
than the specific diagnosis, that is important. (Indeed, it is not unusual for individuals to have several mental health diagnoses). Many psychiatric disorders listed
in the *Diagnostic and Statistical Manual of Mental Disorders* (fourth edition, text
revision) (DSM-IV-TR (American Psychiatric Association [APA], 2000) may coex-
ist with substance abuse or dependency. The relevant ones are identified primarily
by which service sectors are designated to pay for care. The major relevant mental

health disorders are schizophrenia, other psychotic disorders, mood disorders, anxiety disorders, and personality disorders (APA, cited in COCE, Overview Paper 1, 2007). The existence of mental illness often precedes the connection to substance abuse, but that is not always the case. Substance abuse or dependency may precede mental illness or may develop simultaneously over time, triggered by curiosity, peer pressure, or the need to self-medicate (Khantzian, as cited in Hall & Queener, 2007).

Role functioning, as well as the duration of the illness, is used as the basis for the ratings of severity of each disorder (COCE, Overview Paper 1, 2007). For mental illness, the criteria include the degree to which the symptoms impede the roles needed for independent living and self-sufficiency over time. Substance abuse refers to abuse of alcohol and other drugs, including prescription medications. Often individuals with COD will be poly-substance abusers. For substance abusers, the key criteria are failure to fulfill roles for which they are responsible and the use of substances in the face of serious physical and psychological consequences (COCE, Overview Paper 1, 2007).

There can be a wide range of combinations of the two disorders, when they are assessed by the severity of each disorder. The National Dialogue on Co-Occurring Mental Health and Substance Abuse Disorders conference (1999) created a conceptual framework, a typology of quadrants, to understand the range of the disorder and the level of coordination of service systems needed to treat each subtype. The Quadrant Model is presented in Figure 6.1. Although this typology has not been empirically validated, it is has been accepted as useful by COCE (Overview Paper 1, 2007) and CSAT (2005, tip 42).

This four-quadrant model (NASMHPD & NASADAD, as cited in COCE, Overview Paper 1, 2007) offers guidance for services to consumers from Quadrant I, low addiction and low mental illness severity; Quadrant II, low addiction and high mental illness; Quadrant III, high addiction and low mental illness; and Quadrant IV, high addiction and high mental illness. "This model provides a framework and structure to coordinate consultation, collaboration, and integration among system services and providers with the goal of providing appropriate care to every client" (COCE, Overview Paper 1, p. 5).

Drake has found that provision of integrated treatment over a sufficient length of time "result(s) in significant reductions of substance use and improvement in a range of other outcomes" (Osher, 2005, p. 8). The critical problem is that very few of the individuals with CODs have received integrated treatment for their problems. In 2004, among COD individuals (with SMI and an SUD), 18 years and older, 34.3 percent received only mental health treatment, 4.1 percent received substance abuse-only treatment, 8.5 percent received both mental health and substance abuse

Figure 6.1: Quadrant Model for Guiding Services Co-Occurring Disorders

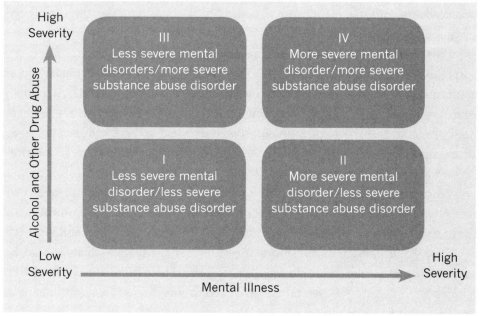

Source: NASMHPD and NASADAD, 1993.

treatment, and 53 percent received no treatment (SAMHSA, 2006). More recent SAMHSA data indicate that of the population experiencing CODs, 33.3 percent received mental health care only, 2.8 percent received treatment for substance use problems only, 10.4 percent received both mental health care and substance use care, and 53.5 percent did not receive any care (COCE, Overview Paper 8, 2007). Clearly, the unmet need is huge.

The lack of treatment for CODs is expensive. "Mental health systems spend most of their resources on a small percentage of individual[s] with difficult problems, often consumers with dual disorders. Mental health services for these consumers cost, on average, nearly twice as much as for clients with single disorders" (SAMHSA, 2003).

Why Have We Not Had the Integrated Treatment We Need?

Traditionally the mental health and substance abuse systems have been separate and distinct. They have had different administrations, funding streams, treatment systems, policies, procedures, and certification of workers. On the mental health

▼
▼
▼

side, the public health system included hospitals, community mental health centers, residential programs, and, more recently, consumer self-help organizations. Mental health therapists were required to be certified as professionals with specialized academic training. Medication to control the symptoms of the illness has been a major component of care.

The substance abuse system has consisted of detoxification (hospital-like care), outpatient care (often called clinics), residential programs (most frequently therapeutic communities), and consumer-run self-help groups (for example, Alcoholics Anonymous and Al-Anon). The treatment philosophy suggested that any medications given outside of detoxification presented a hazard to recovery. The substance abuse counselors, although certified, were often former users themselves. Confrontation was often used in treatment

When a person with CODs came for help, he or she was often treated separately by each system, either in parallel or sequentially, with no communication or coordination between systems. In addition, each system had a different approach to the problem. Substance abuse providers often felt that individuals should be sober before they received mental health treatment. Mental health systems often ignored the substance abuse and concentrated on mental health symptoms only. The implicit treatment philosophy was that if the mental health issues were dealt with, the substance abuse would diminish (that is, self-medication). Individual with CODs were left to make their way between systems, which typically were geographically separate. The result was a high attrition rate from treatment, often leading to hospitalization, incarceration, or homelessness.

Problems Within the Mental Health and Substance Service Delivery System

Development of Integrated Systems and Services: Background

Until recently, there were few integrated programs. The ones that did exist either had special funding at the state or county level or were experimental studies funded by the federal government, and not the result of systems or service integration. The challenges brought to providers by people experiencing CODs have prompted stronger advocacy for this population. The separation of systems that has prevailed in community settings is usually tied to separate block grants, fiscal resources, and funding lines. Existing federal policy issues, clinical guidelines, and suggested practices have impeded clear definitions and service pathways that would allow for accommodation of CODs at any facility. In 1998, the National Dialogue on Co-occurring Mental Health and Substance Abuse Disorders (NASMHPD, 1999) conference offered state alcohol and drug abuse program directors and other health care professionals an opportunity to discuss issues related to CODs. This conference resulted in identifying an agenda for structuring care for those with CODs. The findings of this conference and the success of early integrated programs, as well as the severity and extent of the COD problem, sparked recognition by the federal government that there needed to be a structure or mechanism to provide integrated services, so that CODs could be treated concomitantly and effectively.

Over the past decade, SAMHSA has moved forward in addressing the needs of people with CODs (COCE, Overview Paper 6, 2007). Funding state incentive grants for CODs, establishing a technical assistance and cross-training center, creating an evidence-based practices (EBPs) toolkit, expanding the National Registry of Evidence-Based Programs, and releasing an updated Treatment Improvement Protocol on CODs have been implemented. These resource materials are available through Web sites listed in the Resources section of this chapter.

Systems Integration

If integrated services are to be widespread, they must be preceded by integrated systems. *Systems* can be defined as states, regions, counties, or communities. Systems set up the infrastructure within which services are delivered. They "determine funding, standards of care, licensing, and regulation" (CSAT, 2005, p. 34). To develop integrated services, the mental health system and the substance abuse system must work individually and collaboratively to develop structures and mechanisms to meet the needs of individuals with COD (COCE, Overview Paper 7, 2007). These might include memoranda of understanding, training on CODs, designated funding streams, and policies about entry into the systems. Systems integration itself does not ensure integrated treatment and programs, but it is a necessary mechanism, or facilitator, for collaborative development to occur (COCE, Overview Paper 6, 2007). Through systems integration, organizational boundaries can be eliminated as obstacles, and philosophical differences between the mental health and substance abuse systems can be resolved so that sequential or parallel models do not occur (COCE, Overview Paper 6, 2007).

Systems integration is a form of organizational change (COCE, Overview Paper 7, 2007). The field is still discovering the best way to accomplish this goal. The Co-Occurring State Incentive Grants (awarded by the federal government to states in five phases from 2003 to 2007) were developed to fund different forms of systems integration. Nineteen states participated in this program, most of which have adopted integrated screening, assessment, and treatment planning throughout their respective systems.

One example of systems integration is the adoption of the policy by the mental health and substance abuse systems of "no wrong entry." This policy states that no individual with a COD who attempts entry at any point in the system will be refused services because the specific entry point does not provide the appropriate service; instead, the individual will be provided with referral to an appropriate service.

At the same time that federal direction is aimed at providing specific services for individuals with CODs, practitioners in many community settings are faced with additional challenges associated with providing services to specific demographic groups. Specific populations of adults, women, children, youths, seniors, sexual minorities, and those with specific combinations of mental illness and substance-related disorders are often neglected in the organizational policy formulation processes of agencies.

To support success of systems integration, "cross-training" has been initiated. Through this mechanism, each system offers training about the practices and interventions of the other system to all of its providers through training sessions, videos, or manuals. The Integrated Dual Diagnosis Toolkit (mental health) (SAMHSA, 2003) and the Substance Abuse Treatment for Persons with Co-Occurring Disorders (substance abuse) (CSAT, 2005, TIP 42) are good examples that can be used to facilitate successful cross-training. In addition, providers will also need specific training in work with various populations, such as those mentioned earlier.

Services Integration

Services integration is defined as "the participation of providers trained in both substance abuse and mental health services to develop a single treatment plan to address both sets of conditions and their continued formal interaction and cooperation to reassess and treat the client" (Osher, 2005, p. 4).

There are two levels of services integration, *integrated programs* and *integrated treatment*. Integrated programs occur at the organizational level. Integrated programs consist of policies, procedures, and activities that occur among providing facilities. Integrated programs provide the mechanisms or arrangements to ensure that both mental health and substance abuse services are provided and coordinated.

For example, as a result of interagency cooperation, a client with severe substance abuse and mild mental health problems could receive integrated services by having treatment within a substance abuse program but with the substance abuse staff having regular contact with a mental health agency on mental health issues. A client with severe mental health and mild substance abuse in a large integrated agency could go for mental health services on a daily basis and, for substance abuse treatment, to a program within the same agency, one day a week.

Integrated treatment occurs at the client–clinician level. (COCE, Overview Paper 6, 2007). This is what distinguishes integrated services from integrated programs. *Integrated treatment* is the application of knowledge, skills, and techniques by providers to comprehensively address both mental health and substance abuse issues in people with CODs. Treatment can be provided by either one clinician or a team (COCE, Overview Paper 6, 2007). Although integrated treatment can be provided across agencies, it is best for those with the most severe disabilities if it is provided at one site. For these individuals, treatment in multiple settings is associated with a rapid and significant decrease in treatment retention (Hellerstein, Rosenthal, & Miner, 1995). Limited research has been devoted to assessment of service integration for those with less severe disorders (Osher, 2005).

Although service integration is most commonly thought of as involving the mental health and substance abuse communities, according to client needs, other services such as physical health, housing, and legal issues, must be integrated into the treatment plan (see Figure 6.2).

Services Assessment from Various Delivery Settings

The provision of services to people whose needs may be assessed at various points along the continuum of low to high severity occurs at a variety of entry points (COCE, Overview Paper 4, 2007). In the process of screening and assessment, the practitioner must determine the most appropriate individualized plan for treatment

Figure 6.2: Characteristics of Concern and Entry Points for Persons with Co-Occurring Disorders

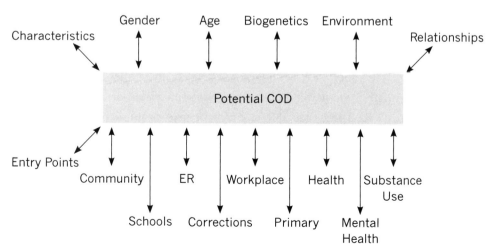

(See Chapters 7 and 8 for additional information on screening and assessment; also see Resources.) Client issues may be observed and possibly treated in or referred to the following: primary health care settings, school-based clinics, workplace services, public welfare offices, places of worship, food programs, other community programs, mental health programs, substance abuse services, state hospitals, jails, prisons, forensic units, or homeless services. A large proportion of people experiencing multiple disorders receive no care at all. An illustration of the possible points of service connection and characteristics of people experiencing CODs, all of which may reflect different needs and require different services is presented in Figure 6.2.

Although people in need may appear at a variety of settings, the more typical locations for services when people with CODs need assistance are mental health agencies and substance abuse programs. In other instances, client needs may be identified in a broad range of agencies. Providers will all need to be aware of referral sites for appropriate services. In many instances, a referral to integrated services for CODs will place clients in a context that will be best prepared to address their multiplicity of needs.

EBPs for CODs

Several terms have been used to describe practices that typically result in positive outcomes. These terms include consensus-based practices, science based, best, promising, emerging, effective, and model. The COCE has refrained from inferring that any one practice is the best or most effective. The COCE was established as a five-year project, which ended on March 27, 2009 (COCE, Overview Paper 5, 2007). Its mission was to receive, generate, and advance substance abuse and mental health treatments, guide infrastructure innovations, and foster adoption of EBPs and organizations for co-occurring disorders.

Provision of Integrated Treatment to COD Clients

COCE in Overview Paper 3 (2006) suggested a set of principles to guide system development and treatment interventions so that integrated services and treatment can be provided. These principles can also be used to guide provider activity. Because social workers will often encounter COD clients in their work, associated implications for social workers are presented below.

1. CODs must be expected when evaluating any person, and clinical services should incorporate this assumption into all screening, assessment, and treatment planning.

Implication for social workers—all must be able to screen for COD, coordinate assessments, and know the appropriate programs for client referral.

2. Within the treatment context, both CODs are considered primary.

Implication for social workers—When monitoring progress of a client referred to COD service, the social worker should know that both disorders should be the focus of treatment and be continually assessed. The relationship between the two disorders must also be evaluated and managed.

3. Empathy, respect, and belief in the individual's capacity for recovery are fundamental provider attitudes.

Implication for social workers—The social worker may be the first point of contact for a COD patient. For the client to accept a referral, the social worker must establish a trusting, empathic relationship, and convey hope for recovery.

4. Treatment should be individualized to accommodate the specific needs, personal goals, and cultural perspectives of the unique individual in different stages of change.

Implication for social workers—When initially working with a client, the social worker must know what stage of motivation and change the client is in as this may affect screening and referral efforts. Being sensitive to client needs and cultural differences may help the worker establish a relationship so that the client can accept a referral for treatment.

5. The special needs of children and adolescents must be explicitly recognized and addressed in all phases of assessment, treatment planning, and service delivery.

Implication for social workers—The special needs of children and adolescents are determined by their developmental stage. Special interventions are needed for each stage; use of interventions developed for adults may not be appropriate.

Skills and Knowledge about COD that Social Workers Need

The social worker must not only know how to screen for COD, but also be familiar with the characteristics of good integrated treatment and referral.

Integrated Screening

Integrated screening should be done when the client first has contact with the human services system. Given the policy of "no wrong entry," screening can occur at any entry point within the system. *Screening* is defined as "determining the likelihood that a client has co-occurring substance use and mental disorders or that his or her presenting signs, symptoms, or behaviors may be influenced by co-occurring issues" (COCE, Overview Paper 2, 2007, p. 1). Screening does not make a formal diagnosis but establishes the need for an in-depth assessment (COCE, Overview Paper 2, 2007). The goal is to identify anyone who might have COD and also to explore other possible service needs such as medical, housing, victimization, or trauma.

The screening process has two goals: to gain information about service needs and to establish a connection with the client. "Such a connection may be important in motivating the client to accept a referral for assessment, if needed" (COCE, Overview Paper 2, 2007, p. 3). Information is gathered using screening instruments (see chapter 8 for in-depth information about substance abuse assessment, including instruments and the Web site for COCE documents, especially Overview Paper 2, listed in Resources, for mental health assessment and CODs), laboratory tests, clinical interviews, and personal contact. Although screening instruments are an efficient and reliable means of gathering information, they should not be the only source of information. The screening process must be flexible so that the cultural and other special needs of the clients are taken into account.

Licensed social workers may be involved in the next step that occurs after integrated screening, which is an integrated assessment. There are four purposes for an integrated assessment: (1) establish a formal diagnosis, (2) evaluate the client's level of functioning, (3) determine the client's readiness for change, and (4) make initial decisions about the appropriate level of care (COCE, Overview Paper 2, 2007). "The assessment process should be client-centered in order to fully motivate and engage the client in the assessment and treatment process" (COCE, Overview Paper 2, 2007, p. 3). The client's perception of his or her problem and desired goals is critical. Information should be gathered on strengths and cultural needs, as well as other service needs. The ACT toolkit (SAMHSA, 2008) has a number of good assessment tools that can help set the stage for a treatment plan that meets the multiple needs and goals of individuals with CODs.

A treatment plan should emerge from the assessment information. Table 6.1 offers a matrix for contemplating individualized service plans written in conjunction with the consumer. This ecological framework sets the stage for examining the multiple factors that affect the problem and can be used to influence the solution.

(See chapters 7 and 8 in this text for screening and assessment tools and chapters 9 through 11 for treatment intervention strategies.) Screening resources from the COCE (Overview Paper 2, 2007) are also listed at the end of this chapter. A multiple method paradigm simultaneously includes individual therapy, group therapy, psychopharmacology, and the coordination of services with medical, behavioral health, social services, and educational providers, as noted in Table 6.1.

TABLE 6.1: An Ecological Framework for Contemplating Individualized Services

Biological Issues	Substance Use	Psychological Issues	Social Issues	Spiritual
Medical illness	Types	Problems	Gender	Sense of belonging
Current medications	Denial	Past and current diagnoses	Age	Sense of self
Awareness of risky behaviors	Goals for change	Thoughts of death, suicide	Legal issues/ corrections status	Ability to forgive
	Stages of change for each substance	Current symptoms	Education	Strengths
		Worldview	Transportation	
		Trauma experiences	Safe environment	
		Grief and loss issues	Quality of relationships	
		Motivation and readiness for change	Presence and development of social support network	
		Strengths	Employment/ Economics	
			Stigma	
			Strengths	

Components of Good Integrated Treatment

Most of the research on the effectiveness of integrated services has been done with quadrant 4 individuals, those with SMI and severe substance abuse. Little research has been done on less severe combinations (Osher, 2005). CSAT (2005) asserted that for publicly funded programs, a state's definition of the target population as SMI may limit provision of mental health services to less severely ill individuals with substance abuse disorders and suggested that this group is best served in the substance abuse programs that have integrated treatment. Regardless of the quadrant in which the client falls, the same basic intervention components can be used.

The specific interventions that are used in integrated treatment have been drawn from both the mental health and substance abuse fields. From the mental health side come the stages of treatment, psychoeducation, and a focus on each disorder having a separate course. From the substance abuse side come techniques such as motivational interviewing, stages of change, cognitive–behavioral therapy, and self-help groups.

Stages of Treatment

Stopping the use of substances, or attaining abstinence, is a very large change in a person's life. Making this change is a process, which can best be described as a series of stages, first in the person's attitude toward change, and then in the behavioral steps that the individual takes to attain it (Prochaska & DiClemente, 1992). Attaining a major change like abstinence can take a long time. Progress may be slow and nonlinear (for example, an individual may revert back to a previous stage many times) (SAMHSA, 2003). (The stages of change [pre-contemplation, contemplation, preparation, action, and maintenance] are described in detail in chapter 7.) Because people interact differently with the treatment system at each stage, they need different interventions at each stage of change. Thus, each stage of change can be associated with a stage of treatment (Drake et al., 1998).

The relationship of each stage of treatment to the stages of change is shown below (See Table 6.2).

1. *Engagement*—The person has no relationship with the treatment provider and does not recognize that there is either a mental health or a substance abuse problem. It is the provider's job to develop a working alliance or positive relationship with the person. The provider needs to demonstrate empathy and respect. He or she needs to listen to understand the client's worldview. It is often very helpful to demonstrate his or her care by helping the client with material needs, such as housing or medical care. The provider

Table 6.2: Stages of Change and Treatment

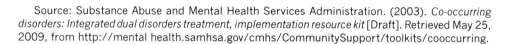

Precontemplation – Engagement
Contemplation and Preparation – Persuasion
Action – Active treatment
Maintenance – Relapse prevention

Source: Substance Abuse and Mental Health Services Administration. (2003). *Co-occurring disorders: Integrated dual disorders treatment, implementation resource kit* [Draft]. Retrieved May 25, 2009, from http://mental health.samhsa.gov/cmhs/CommunitySupport/toolkits/cooccurring.

does not confront the client about either set of problems, but spends time getting to know the client enough so an assessment can be conducted.

2. *Persuasion*—This stage is marked by the client having regular contact with the provider. "The clinical task is to help the client think about the role of substance use in her or her life" (SAMHSA, 2003, p. 31). This is accomplished by continuing to build the working relationship, asking the client about his or her goals and previous experiences, and integrating cultural supports. Motivational interviewing can be very helpful.

3. *Active treatment*—At this stage, the client recognizes that substance use is a problem and decides to reduce or stop use. The provider needs to help the person gain the skills and supports to avoid the use of substances.

4. *Relapse prevention*—At this stage, a plan is developed to help maintain abstinence by identifying triggers and identifying strategies to combat them.

Motivational Interviewing

As noted previously, motivational interviewing is a counseling technique that is used to help clients develop the motivation to make changes in their lives, such as reducing or stopping the use of substances or entering mental health treatment (Miller & Rollnick, 1991). "It helps clients clarify goals and commit to change" (CSAT, 2005, p. 112). This approach has been useful for very difficult clients with severe symptoms.

Motivational interviewing is used in the engagement and persuasion stages of treatment. The five principles of motivational interviewing are as follows:

1. *Express empathy with the client.* This step is actually part of the engagement process. The counselor uses reflective listening. "The goals of reflective listening are to understand the world through the client's eyes and to build trust by being a good listener and demonstrating that understanding"

(SAMHSA, 2003, p. 64). The counselor does not give advice or attempt to have the client change.

2. *Develop discrepancy.* The goal of this step is to help the client to outline goals for his or her life, and to outline steps that might have to be taken to get these goals. The role of the counselor is to help the client examine the pros and cons of substance abuse and how the use of substances affects being able to take the steps to reach the goals. Hopefully, the client will see the discrepancy between substance use and the goals and voice concern over the use of substances (the underlying psychological mechanism is cognitive dissonance). The counselor uses reflective listening to build on and accept any ambivalence, any recognized discrepancy, and any voiced desire for change.

3. *Avoid argumentation.* The technique of motivational interviewing avoids arguments, in general, and any confrontation, for several reasons. First, arguments only make the client defend his or her views, rather than consider change. Second, the counselor's goal is to have a relationship with the client that demonstrates trust, respect, and an understanding of the world as the client sees it. The client will only change if he or she sees discrepancies in his or her goals and substance abuse, not because change is the goal of the counselor.

4. *Roll with resistance.* If a client does not want to discuss a certain topic, do not make him or her do so; rather let him or her express his or her feelings. Try to discuss or work on a different goal in the treatment plan and, perhaps by examining this, the client will realize that the first topic, such as substance abuse or not taking medication, may prevent success in the other area.

5. *Support self-efficacy.* Self-efficacy is the belief that one can succeed at change. Many individuals with CODs have low self-efficacy because of extensive past failures. Self-efficacy can be enhanced by helping the client achieve small successes. Thus, early goals should not be too large.

The following case example (Case Example 6.1) shows how respect for the individual in his or her current state, active engagement in the community, and motivational interventions can be used to help develop a willingness to accept mental health treatment and to reduce substance use (taken from SAMHSA, 2003).

Psychoeducational Groups

The mental health system has offered the concept of psychoeducational groups to the COD field. The goal of these groups is to provide information about the basic

CASE EXAMPLE 6.1: The Case of Kevin

Kevin is a 57-year-old Irish American, unemployed, divorced father of five grown children. He was diagnosed with posttraumatic stress disorder, psychotic disorder not otherwise specified, and alcohol dependence. He has been living at the homeless shelter and receiving outreach services from the assertive community treatment team.

Kevin worked as a heavy equipment operator until five years ago. Since his discharge from the Marines 20 years ago, he has experienced symptoms of racing thoughts, flashbacks, anxiety, and social avoidance. He has used alcohol and marijuana since adolescence. As his use of alcohol and marijuana has increased over time, he has become more and more paranoid. Kevin has been arrested a number of times for criminal threatening and assault.

Five years ago, Kevin was in an automobile accident and sustained a brain injury. He was charged with driving while intoxicated, lost his driver's license, and lost his job as a heavy equipment operator. Since then, he has not had stable housing, has not worked, and has experienced poor memory and concentration in addition to his other symptoms. He refused treatment at the local Veterans Administration (VA) Hospital and at the local mental health center, but was willing to meet with team members at the homeless shelter.

Kevin's case manager began meeting with Kevin at the homeless shelter every day. They usually went for a walk and had coffee. Over the next month, they had many conversations. The case manager started by asking Kevin what he thought about the judge's order. Kevin thought "he has it in for me" and refused to go to the mental health center. The case manager offered to meet with him at the shelter or a coffee shop, and Kevin agreed. Asked about the good things in his life right now, Kevin identified having a warm, dry place to sleep, his five children, his drinking buddies, and a good disability income check from the VA. The case manager then asked Kevin what was "not so good" in his life right now. Kevin listed the judge's order requiring him to be in treatment, living with the "crazy" people in the shelter, and running out of money during the month. The case manager asked Kevin to tell him more about his concern about living with the "crazy" people and running out of money during the month. He learned

(continued)

CASE EXAMPLE 6.1 *(continued)*

that Kevin wanted to have his own place, but that his confidence in being able to keep housing was low. With his case manager's help, Kevin listed the following pros and cons of having his own apartment.

Pros	Cons
Privacy	Trouble managing his money
Nothing gets stolen	Isolation and loneliness
Control of when to sleep, eat, etc.	Drinks more
Something that is his	Friends want to move in
	No money for furnishings
	Not eligible for housing supplement

After looking over the list, Kevin began to talk more about his use of substances and how much he has lost because of his drinking. When he was taking medication, he was able to concentrate better and felt more hopeful about life. Kevin's case manager said that Kevin was presenting an interesting picture and wondered if Kevin would like feedback on his impressions, noting that the feedback could be taken or thrown out. Kevin agreed to hear the feedback. The case manager suggested that there could be a connection between Kevin's use of substances, taking medication, and his capacity to live on his own. The case manager also wondered if Kevin's desire to be in control has actually left him out of control in most areas of his life. He then asked for Kevin's reaction to the feedback. Kevin agreed he wanted control of his life and that until recently he believed he was in control.

Kevin's case manager asked him what he wanted to do next. Kevin decided to begin working on a plan that included reducing his drinking to every other day, attending a money management group once, and thinking about opening a bank account to work on saving money for housing.

After four months, Kevin was taking medication. After two more months, he decided to apply for and got into a residential treatment setting where he was able to stop substance use, take some classes, and become involved in Alcoholics Anonymous. He stayed there for two years and then transitioned into his own apartment. He had reconnected with a daughter and was proud to be involved with her family.

facts of substance abuse and mental health, what medications can do, how side effects can be managed, and how the two disorders can interact. Because COD clients may present with cognitive disorders, these groups offer the chance to present the information slowly, using different types of media (verbally, with pictures, or with simple written material). The repetition of the groups and chance to hear other people's views and experiences may help with the processing of the information. These groups may also serve as persuasion groups in which clients can explore the pros and cons of treating their disorders.

Specialized Dual Disorder Groups

Three types of groups (persuasion, action, and self-help) are useful at different stages of treatment. In all three, the discussion among the clients is the most valuable element. Clients will believe other clients who have been in similar situations (SAMSHA, 2003). For individuals who are not yet ready to change their patterns of substance abuse, persuasion groups offer the chance to talk about their use of substances with their peers in a nonjudgmental environment. As others talk about their use, clients can begin to look at the pros and cons of use and learn about the interaction of drugs and mental illness.

Action groups can help those who have made the commitment to stop using substances. These groups may be co-facilitated by a substance abuse counselor and a mental health counselor, and they provide strategies to handle cravings and to avoid risky situations. Self-help groups typically consist of individuals working toward recovery with people who share the same problems. They offer strategies for coping, role modeling, and personal support. They can be used to supplement other treatment or to serve as treatment itself. Some self-help groups focus on specific drugs, such as alcohol, narcotics, or cocaine. Other groups focus on dual disorders. Self-help groups should only be used if the client feels comfortable in the group and wants to attend. The group attended should be compatible with the needs of the individual.

Best Practice Models

Three specific models of integrated treatment have been suggested as best practices: Integrated Dual Disorders Treatment (IDDT), Assertive Community Treatment (ACT), and Modified Therapeutic Communities (MTC). Both IDDT and ACT are evidence-based practices based within the mental health system, and they have integrated substance abuse interventions. Both are outpatient programs. The MTC is a residential model within the substance abuse community. It has modified the traditional model of a therapeutic community to meet the needs of individuals with SMI.

ACT has been declared an evidence-based practice by the Cochrane Collaboration, meaning that it has reached the highest state of evidence—randomized trials that have been synthesized into a meta-analysis. The Cochrane Collaboration (2009) does not consider IDDT an evidence-based model (because of variation in which components are presented in different programs). However, most researchers consider it effective as long as a program follows the basic principles of the model. Toolkits have been developed by SAMHSA for both ACT and IDDT (see Resources).

These toolkits are aimed at disseminating the two evidence-based practices. They have brief introductions and tips for all of the stakeholders (mental health administrators, agency management, program supervisors, clinicians, consumers, and family members), an extensive training manual for clinicians and supervisors, videotapes, outcomes measures, and fidelity scales, which can be used to monitor how closely an actual program is following the ideal model. All instruments are carefully explained. The training manuals contain vignettes and tables that list the key points of the chapter section.

IDDT

IDDT is a program that provides integrated treatment in which one person or a team delivers mental health and substance abuse treatment. It follows the stages of treatment model and uses assessment, motivational treatment, and substance abuse counseling. After the stages of engagement and persuasion, a substance abuse action plan is established to help each client cease or reduce the use of substances.

A substance abuse action plan is developed with the client to provide skills, strategies, and supports to deal with situations and feelings that lead to substance abuse. Cognitive–behavioral counseling, planned coping strategies, and external supports are used to help the client avoid or cope with internal clues and external situations that lead to substance abuse (SAMHSA, 2003).

The critical elements of IDDT, as listed in the IDDT Workbook (SAMHSA, 2003) and measured by a fidelity scale, include the following:

1. *Multidisciplinary team with an integrated substance abuse specialist.* In addition to an experienced substance abuse counselor, the team should consist of at least two other individuals, such as a case manager, psychiatrist, nurse, rehabilitation specialist, or social worker. These team members can help meet the client's other needs, such as housing, employment, health, or reestablishing family contact. Individuals with CODs have multiple problems that need to be addressed while working on their substance abuse.

2. *Stagewise interventions.* These are the stages of treatment that were described earlier. Each stage responds to a stage of planned change as the individual with COD moves from denial to abstinence.

3. *Access for clients to comprehensive dual diagnosis services.* This may be done by referral. Such services include supported housing, supported employment, illness management and recovery, family psychoeducation, and assertive community treatment.

4. *Time–unlimited services.* This holds true for all rehabilitation services, not just substance abuse treatment.

5. *Outreach.* Team members seek out individuals with COD in the community, both to offer services and to provide the services in vivo that meet their needs.

6. *Motivational interventions.* This refers to motivational interviewing and to persuasion groups. Motivational interviewing helps the client to develop a willingness to change. Persuasion groups let individuals explore their drug use as it affects their lives and goals.

7. *Substance abuse counseling.* This mode of counseling identifies the internal and external triggers that can cause an individual to take drugs and provides methods to avoid or cope with the triggers.

8. *Group dual diagnosis treatment.* Groups could include family, persuasion, or dual recovery.

9. *Family psychoeducation on dual diagnosis training.* This approach focuses on educating the family about CODs and how they can support the family member in recovery from both disorders.

10. *Participation in alcohol and drug self-help groups.* These groups are best suited for clients in the action stage or the relapse prevention stage. They can be regular substance abuse groups or specialized dual recovery groups.

11. *Pharmacological treatment.* Medication can be used for mental health disorders or to reduce addiction cravings.

12. *Interventions to promote health.* These may include diet, exercise, safe housing, and avoidance of high-risk behaviors and situations. "The intent is to directly reduce the negative consequences of substance abuse using methods other than substance use reduction itself." (SAMHSA, 2003, p. 23).

13. *Secondary interventions for substance abuse treatment nonresponders.* These are more intensive interventions, such as special medications, trauma interventions, or long-term residential care.

The overall goal of the training manual is to focus on providing information about substance-related disorders to mental health providers and to introduce them to interventions often used in the substance abuse field, such as motivational interviewing. It also provides descriptions of how each of the critical elements should be implemented and an instrument (called a Fidelity Scale) that can be used to measure how well each program is implementing each element. A protocol on how to use the Fidelity Scale also is included.

Assertive Community Treatment

ACT, an evidence-based practice, has been implemented in 35 states, Canada, England, Sweden, Australia, and the Netherlands. It is a service delivery model that focuses on individuals with SMI who are most in need, that is, those whose symptoms will not remit with medication and who have functional impairments that prevent them from living independently (inability to perform practical tasks to function in the community, inability to be consistently employed or to carry out a homemaker role, inability to maintain a safe living situation) (SAMHSA, 2008). Often these individuals have a history of high service needs, are difficult to engage, and abuse substances. ACT provides treatment in the community to promote recovery and provide the skills that can help prevent hospitalization and promote independent living. Although many of the substance abuse and rehabilitation components are similar to IDDT programs and other intensive case management programs, the method of service delivery is markedly different. It is characterized by:

1. *A transdisciplinary team approach.* The team consists of professionals from different specialties (for example, psychiatrist, nurse, substance abuse counselor, mental health counselors, social workers, vocational support counselor) who work with the client as part of the team to develop a treatment plan that is carried out by all team members.

2. *Service is provided in vivo, where the client lives in the community.* This enables the team to teach the skills that are needed in the situation in which they will be used. It also promotes active engagement and improves the quality of life of the client by helping to ensure housing stability and medication adherence.

    Providing services is not simply doing things for consumers. Rather, the ACT team works closely with consumers to teach them how to develop and carry out strategies to reduce the negative effects of their mental illness and associated impairments in cognitive and social functioning (SAMHSA, 2008, p. 2).

3. *There is a small caseload for the team as a whole and responsibility for the caseload is shared by all workers.* This permits team members to know all clients (which avoids disruption at vacation and turnover); it prevents burnout and lets all of the team members receive on-the-job training from specialists in areas different from their own.

4. *Services are time unlimited.*

5. *There is flexible service delivery.* Services are tailored to meet the needs of a client, rather than a set program format. Teams meet daily so that interventions can be monitored and modified.

6. *The team is on call 24/7* to ensure that crises are met.

7. *There is fixed responsibility.* The team is responsible for directly providing all services, rather than brokering them. If a service cannot be provided, such as mental or physical health hospitalization, the team stays in constant contact with the medical providers and the client.

The substance abuse treatment that ACT provides is fully integrated into the total treatment plan. The specific interventions that are used are the ones listed above and used by IDDT.

Modified Therapeutic Community

A third best practice is the MTC (Sacks, Sacks, & DeLeon, 1999). This is a residential program that is used in the substance abuse system. This program has been deemed an evidence-based practice by consensus and by the National Register of Evidence-based Programs and Practices. (It should be noted that the requirements to receive this designation are less rigorous than those used by the Cochrane Collaboration.) It also should be noted that "although improved psychological functioning has been reported, differential improvement in mental health functioning using the MTC approach in comparison to more standard treatment has yet to be demonstrated" (CSAT, 2005, p. 178). This model provides integrated treatment within a therapeutic community that has been modified to meet the needs of COD clients. The mission of a therapeutic community is to provide "treatment based on community–as-method, that is, the community is the healing agency. The goal is to develop a culture where clients learn mutual self help and affiliation with the community to promote change" (CSAT, 2005, p. 173).

There are three different types of interventions: *community enhancement* (meeting of all participants about house business); *therapeutic education* (individual counseling, psychoeducational classes, conflict resolution groups, medication monitoring that partially relies on observations from other clients), and *a set of rules and regulations to order conduct* (including corrective learning experiences [if a client does not behave in a way that meets the standards of the program] and vocation development [peer work to perform necessary day-to-day functioning of the community, psychoeducational groups about work]). Clients progress through a series of stages, each with more privileges, while they are in the program.

To modify the therapeutic structure for COD clients, there are three fundamental alterations: increased flexibility; decreased emotional intensity, such as that typically observed in traditional encounter groups; and greater individualization. Specifically, there is more staff contact and guidance, more individualized counseling, reduced intensity of interpersonal interaction, and individualized progress through the stages of the program. Manuals and principles of implementation have been developed for the MTC programs (Sacks, DeLeon, Bernhardt, & Sacks, 1998; Sacks et al., 1999; Sacks & Peters, 2002).

Needs of Special Populations

Role of Gender

Men and women bring different characteristics that must be planned for in developing treatment plans. Assessment and intervention are planned, depending on the diagnosis and assessment of the biological, psychological, social, cultural, economic, and spiritual characteristics of clients. For example, for young men, considering the provision of information in high school orientation sessions as well as legal reference points may be critical for education and awareness. Peer support groups for high school freshmen may be a place to offer opportunities to dialogue about the potential pathways of development over their high school years. Understanding the role of unresolved stress, the differences between appropriate and destructive coping mechanisms, and possible alternatives and resources could affect their lives, resulting in more positive choices.

Individuals working with women with COD must also consider the women's caregiver functions in the family and their capacity for reproduction. When this is the case, these dynamics urge the provision of more specialized services that incorporate people who may help care for the family when a woman is in treatment, as well as focus on the impact on children or future pregnancies. These factors require multiple levels of consideration and development. In other cases, a woman experiencing CODs may have her children removed by child welfare. This scenario requires consideration of how the well-being of her children may play a role in her treatment and recovery. Gender-specific services in the New Directions for Families program were found to be more effective when the unique needs, including mental health, substance abuse, trauma, and those of dependent children were considered (VanDeMark, Brown, Bornemann, & Williams, 2004). Women who have been victims of abuse and violence, and who have substance-related problems and mental health issues, may also experience challenges protecting and meeting the needs of their children (Smyth, Miller, Mudar, & Skiba, 2003).

Role of Trauma

Service needs should be modified on the basis of assessment that incorporates childhood risk factors, childhood abuse history, family history of mental illness, perceived quality of relationships with family, and age of onset of substance use (Miles, Kulstad, & Haller, 2002). Women with substance abuse problems often have histories of physical or sexual abuse as children or rape and domestic violence as adults (Markoff et al., 2005). There are models that assist women to deal with their trauma symptoms and to refrain from substance abuse (Markoff et al., 2005).

The histories of major trauma that many women with substance abuse problems have experienced emphasize the role of victim. Victimization is a core event that influences a survivor's sense of self, coping skills, relationship with others, worldview, and overall emotional regulation (Markoff et al., 2005).

Women with histories of psychiatric disorders and substance use have often encountered enormous structural barriers to effective treatment. The consequences of early relational trauma point to the lack of capacity for emotional self-regulation and problems with affect. However, the process and potential of healing through the trauma have been observed to be transformational and do improve quality of life (Levine & Fredericks, 1997). Interventions that coordinate these elements may provide awareness and important structure.

Najavits, Schmitz, Gotthardt, and Weiss (2005) indicated men experience higher lifetime rates of trauma than do women. Men with posttraumatic stress disorder (PTSD) are at higher risk for comorbid SUD, with rates of alcohol and other drug dependence disorders estimated at about 52 percent and 35 percent, respectively. Trauma and PTSD among men are associated with hard drug use and have been associated with more behavioral problems and high-risk behaviors than among women. The probability of dying among veterans with psychiatric illness and co-occurring substance dependence was 55 percent higher than among those without substance dependence. Substance-related illnesses and overdoses accounted for almost 30 percent of these deaths (Rosen, Kuhn, Greenbaum, &

Drescher, 2008). The need to address safety for men is an important area of focus in providing services to this population.

The incidence of PTSD and substance use among male and female military veterans is especially disconcerting. With more than 38,000 documented cases in the past five years, providing appropriate services is critical (NIDA, 2008). Among the female veterans participating in a PTSD COD group, reports of sexual assault (M. Ngo, personal communication, April 1, 2009) and subtle coping mechanisms in groups dominated by men (T. Ryan, personal communication, April 7, 2009) have been observed.

Importance of Recognizing Cultural Needs in Addressing Trauma

Multicultural literature can be useful in helping both men and women connect to role models and characters with similar histories to overcome trauma and move forward to accomplish their goals (O'Neal & Reid, 1999). Services informed by individual narratives of trauma are important in determining individualized treatment strategies (Savage, Quiros, Dodd, & Bonavota, 2007). Using literature with culturally similar role models in group work provides opportunities to stimulate thinking and engage in mutual aid and discussion, without immediate self-disclosure (O'Neal, 2006). With guided facilitation, group work process can protect participants in dealing with sensitive issues. For example, some women with a history of trauma may be willing to discuss Ntozake Shange's poem "With No Immediate Cause" about the frequency of abuse on women without discussing the details of their own experiences. (A link to the poem can be found in the Resources.) Excerpts from *The Street,* by Ann Petry, may offer scenarios in which life chances result in choices that put children at risk. This kind of discussion could provide opportunities to identify how to make other choices that provide more protection for children.

Role of Religion and Spirituality

Studies of the religious involvement of alcohol- and other drug-dependent women with CODs have also demonstrated some positive results. Negative religious coping was associated with greater PTSD and depressive symptoms, whereas positive coping and involvement with organized religion were associated with positive mental health outcomes (Conners, Whiteside-Mansell, & Sherman, 2006).

One should not avoid considering the importance of religious and spiritual support in helping men or women deal with their CODs. The possibility should always be introduced as a vehicle of support and change.

Fallot and Heckman's (2005) study of women trauma survivors with CODs urged more attention to the spirituality of trauma survivors. Women who experienced sexual abuse in childhood had higher levels of negative religious coping than those whose abuse occurred in adulthood. Severity of posttraumatic and other mental health symptoms were significantly related to negative spiritual coping. However, a stronger association of positive religious coping style, which offered spirituality as a supportive, strengthening, and collaborative force, was observed among the women with fewer mental health symptoms.

Factors associated with co-occurring substance abuse or dependence and borderline personality disorders include a concern with childhood maltreatment (Gratz et al., 2008). Although the areas covered earlier generally address challenges among the adult population of consumers, a word about the potential of young people to develop CODs is triggered by this reference to what happens to people (maltreatment) at a young age. The development of disorders when young also urges consideration of health promotion and prevention strategies.

The co-occurrence of substance abuse or dependence with borderline personality disorder, or antisocial personality disorder appears to be associated with increased ongoing use of substances (Straussner & Nemenzik, 2007). "An individual can meet the criteria for more than one personality disorder" (Straussner & Nemenzik, 2007, p. 8). Prescribing appropriate medications for these disorders is complicated. The lack of cross-training for health professionals to work with these CODs is an obstacle. A major challenge for people in these diagnostic groups is teaching them new coping skills. Much more work is needed in this area.

Impact of CODs on Family Members

Family caregivers dealing with women with substance abuse and co-occurring mental disorders reported clearly the family burden caused by this kind of situation (Biegel, Ishler, Katz, & Johnson, 2007). The literature on family involvement in substance abuse cases typically looks at client outcomes and not mental health impacts on the family itself or predictors of the mental health of the family members (Biegel et al., 2007). Family caregivers experienced moderate levels of burden after two to three years. Studies show participation of family members in care tends to help reduce rates of substance use. Needs of the family caregivers themselves should be addressed in the substance abuse treatment system (Biegel et al., 2007). Triage should assess not only the identified client, but also the family caregiver (parent, spouse, or sibling).

Lack of perceived social support, formal and informal, has been the most important variable that predicts burden. If treatment is to be expected to proceed and continue, the extended family must be supported and encouraged to become involved in the assessment, planning, and treatment processes (Biegel et al., 2007).

Youth Issues

Adolescent experiences with mental health problems and alcohol and other substance use are particularly important with respect to improving life pathways. People who use alcohol, cigarettes, and cannabis in high frequency as adolescents are likely to use later (Bonomo et al., 2004). There are groups of adolescents, in which risk may be higher, who are likely to be neglected by existing services, such as LGBTQ clients.

In general, current service systems are inadequately prepared to provide the needed interventions (Hawkins, 2009). Without effective intervention, youths with CODs are at increased risk of serious medical and legal problems, incarceration, suicide, school difficulties and dropout, unemployment, and poor interpersonal relationships.

In a study of adolescent juvenile detainees, the examination of offense, substance use, and mental illness characteristics is associated with high risk among female detainees (Hussey, Drinkard, & Flannery, 2007). Over two-thirds of the juvenile justice population is estimated to comprise individuals with CODs.

Incorporating techniques that reduce substance use, improve mental health, integrate accessibility, and are culturally relevant are important in working with youths. Adolescents have responded well to culturally sensitive approaches (Gil, Wagner, & Tubman, 2004). The identification of evidence-based practices regarding ethnic-sensitive approaches is limited, but cultural responsiveness must be a priority in evaluation of assessment and practice outcomes (Aisenberg, 2008).

The most promising approaches among adolescents include multisystem therapy (MST), brief strategic family therapy (BSFT), and cognitive–behavioral therapy (CBT). MST targets key factors including peers, attitudes, family. BSFT targets family interactions. CBT works to modify beliefs and behaviors (NIDA, 2008). These techniques can target mental health issues and substance use in structured formats. The strategies should be developed with respect to the ecological framework and the needs that are identified in the screening and assessment process. (These approaches will be discussed in greater detail in chapter 11. Additional resources for working with adolescents with CODs are listed in the Resources section of this chapter.)

One area that frequently surfaces in relation to youths and substances involves the use of stimulants in the treatment of attention deficit hyperactivity disorder (ADHD). Several studies have documented an increased vulnerability of drug use disorders among youths with ADHD that have not been treated (NIDA, 2008). ADHD is a category with prominent symptoms of inattention, hyperactivity, or impulsivity (see http://www.Psychiatry Online.com). A recent study by Arias and colleagues (2008) examined the prevalence of psychiatric and substance dependence disorders in participants with ADHD. Their study concluded that among cocaine or opioid users, ADHD was associated with greater substance use and psychiatric comorbidity, and a more severe course of illness. However, among some studies of youths who received early treatment intervention with stimulants, there was no evidence that medication use increased risk of later substance use (Biederman et al., 2008).

Older Adults

According to Farkas (2008), over 1 million adults over age 50 are dependent on substances, and that number is expected to increase. For many social workers, aging and substance use have not been focal points and there are few programs that reach out to this group. At the same time, among this group, mental health disorders occur in about 26 percent of the population, 9.9 percent live below the poverty line, and their absolute numbers among the homeless population have grown (COCE, 2006). Although the research on these combinations is limited, the possible differences in substance consumption and health patterns require attention (Satre & Arean, 2005). An intervention with the older population that provides information regarding health consequences is a likely focal point to address potential co-occurring problems.

LGBTQ

Issues of co-occurring disorders appear to be relatively high among persons who identify as LGBTQ (Cochran, Sullivan, & Mays, 2003). Historically marginalized, members of the LGBTQ community often exhibit internalized homophobia that predicts poor mental health outcomes and substance use (Cochran, Sullivan, & Mays, 2003). Cochran, Peavy, and Cauce (2007) examined attitudes about LGBT people in urban and rural communities. Their findings suggest that sexual minorities benefit from treatment programs that acknowledge the "likelihood that societal stigma contributes to their problems" (Cochran et al., 2007, p. 202).

Special Needs of the Providers Working with Clients with CODs

With respect to the provision of service as it exists, the challenges that practitioners face daily need to be recognized and appreciation extended to those who work in this field. The need for supportive, engaging relationships with people with CODs is critical. For those who enter health, mental health, and substance abuse services and provide assistance to people experiencing CODs, this advocacy and ongoing support are essential.

Simultaneously, the ongoing presence of person-to-person and person-in-society struggles takes a toll on service providers. Improving the service delivery process through redesigned program formats, support from the agency management to develop and implement multicultural models, and listening to the consumers all contribute to the professionals' sense of recognition and progress on the job and to the overall quality of service to clients–consumers.

Future Trends

The issue of unmet needs among the population of people with CODs includes perceptions of need that reflect problems in accessing services and problems that influence help-seeking behavior, such as stigma, motivation, and dissatisfaction with past services (Urbanoski, Cairey, Bassani, & Rush, 2008). Educational and organizational systems are beginning to respond to the service gaps. Compton, Galaway, and Cournoyer (2005) identified the need for social work students to be encouraged to identify informal and formal resources in developing support systems for consumers.

The COCE efforts have led several states to develop action plans to address CODs (see state plans in Resources). These plans are individualized with respect to state definitions of CODs and needs. The possible components include certification and licensure, evaluation and monitoring, evidence- and consensus-based practices, financing mechanisms, screening assessment, treatment planning, information sharing, services integration, systems change, workforce development, and special features, for example, cultural competence and early intervention. For example, New Jersey, New York, and Pennsylvania are in various stages of developing assessment and intervention protocols and training practitioners for transitioning to a service delivery system that integrates substance use and mental health.

Conclusions

Working to reduce the discomfort created by CODs is a huge task. Providing services to consumers and their families must incorporate multiple theoretical and service delivery concepts. Program development recommends a learning culture that encourages and sustains transforming services for increased effectiveness. Providing services for persons experiencing CODs requires focus in these areas:

1. mental health
2. substance misuse
3. family support and modification
4. relapse prevention

In addition, community education would be useful, especially in the areas of

- role and potential of individuals and families in their own development, prevention of life-damaging occurrences, and guided self-change
- organizational development that supports the learning process and cross-training in flexible and structured promising interventions and practices
- ongoing monitoring, evaluation, and follow-up of people participating in our service systems.

Program development involves attention and planning for screening and prevention, wellness and recovery plans developed by the consumers and their families, EBPs, use of community resources, self-help groups, and multicultural resources. Awareness of the multiple mental health and health issues, environmental stressors, exclusion, and the social stigmas associated with CODs challenges professionals and consumers to build a well-structured, coordinated, tolerant, and flexible community to embrace those affected.

Social workers are moving forward to develop supportive evidence-based practices for CODs, and advocate pathways for health promotion and prevention at the earliest possible intervention points. Implementing evidence-based practices and planning with consumers within the ecological framework should benefit those who experience mental health, alcohol, other drug, and primary health disorders.

Note

1. This document is part of an EBP implementation resource kit developed through a contract (No. 280–00–8049) from the SAMHSA Center for Mental

Health Services (CMHS), a grant from the Robert Wood Johnson Foundation (RWJF), and support from the West Family Foundation. These materials are in draft form for use in a pilot study. No one may reproduce, reprint, or distribute this publication for a fee without specific authorization from SAMHSA.

Resources

1. COCE SAMHSA's Co-Occurring Center for Excellence, USDHHS: www.samshsa.gov
   - COCE Mission and Vision, http://coce.samhsa.gov/images/vision_clip_image004L.gif
   - Strategies and Assessment Instrumentation, http://coce.samhsa.gov/products/overview_papers.aspx
   - Overview Papers: Definitions, Principles, Evidence-Based Practices and other information:
   - Overview Paper 1—Definitions and Terms Relating to Co-Occurring Disorders
   - Overview Paper 2—Screening, Assessment, and Treatment Planning for Persons with Co-Occurring Disorders
   - Overview Paper 3—Overarching Principles to Address the Needs of Persons with Co-Occurring Disorders
   - Overview Paper 4—Addressing Co-Occurring Disorders in Non-Traditional Service Settings
   - Overview Paper 5—Understanding Evidence-Based Practices for Co-Occurring Disorders
   - Overview Paper 6—Services Integration for Persons with Co-Occurring Disorders
   - Overview Paper 7—Systems Integration Relevant to Co-Occurring Disorders
   - Overview Paper 8—The Epidemiology of Co-Occurring Substance Use and Mental Disorders.
2. Office of Applied Studies Substance Abuse and Mental Health Statistics: http://www.oas.samhsa.gov/
3. National Alliance on Mentally Illness: http://www.nami.org/
   - The National Alliance on Mental Illness (NAMI) has launched a new Web site, www.nami.org/soloist, as part of a social action campaign with Participant Media surrounding *The Soloist,* starring Jamie Foxx and Robert Downey, Jr.

- "The movie will help humanize people who live with schizophrenia and are homeless," said NAMI executive director Mike Fitzpatrick. "It will help people look beyond stereotypes and create better understanding of the challenge for treatment and recovery."

4. SAMHSA Vision of Integrated Services: http://www.samhsa.gov/about/background.aspx
   - Locating Services: http://findtreatment.samhsa.gov/ufds/abusedirectors

5. COD Research and Monthly Resources, Screening, Brief Intervention and Referral to Treatment Resources, August 2008: http://coce.samhsa.gov/products/monthly_reviews.aspx

6. Screening and Assessment Procedures
   - Co-Occurring Center for Excellence (COCE): http://www.coce.samhsa.gov/cod_resources/PDF/ScreeningReportRevised6-23-08.pdf
   - Screening and assessment of adolescents: www.scattc.org; http://www.attcnetwork.org/regcenters/specialtopics.asp?rcid=14
   - Screening and assessment of adolescents with emphasis on juvenile justice population: www.ncmhjj.com (Go to Publications)

7. Evidence-Based Practices: Shaping Mental Health Services Toward Recovery
   - Co-Occurring Disorders: Integrated Dual Disorders Treatment (IDDT): http://mentalhealth.samhsa.gov/cmhs/CommunitySupport/toolkits/cooccurring/, retrieved May 28, 2009
   - Assertive Community Treatment (ACT): http://mentalhealth.samhsa.gov/cmhs/CommunitySupport/toolkits/community/

8. Screening and Assessment for Co-Occurring Disorders in the Justice System: www.gainscenter.gov
   - *Treating adolescents with co-occurring disorders.* Hills, H. A. (2007). Treating adolescents with a co-occurring disorders. Florida Certification Board/Southern Coast ATTC Monograph Series #2, August. http://coy.state.va.us/Conference/Pauley%20Tuesday%20Workshop2.pdf retrieved 5/18/09

9. COCE State Action Plans: http://coce.samhsa.gov/cod_resources/PAChart.aspx

10. Multicultural Resources
    - Ntozake Shange, With No Immediate Cause: http://iambecauseweare.wordpress.com/2006/09/09/with-no-immediate-cause-byntozake-shange/
    - Petry, A. (1998). *The Street.* New York: Houghton Mifflin Harcourt.

11. Hazelden Foundation: www.cooccurring.org

References

Aisenberg, E. (2008). Evidence-based practice in mental health care to ethnic minority communities: Has its practice fallen short of its evidence? *Social Work, 53,* 297–306.

American Psychiatric Association. (2000). *Diagnostic and statistical manual of mental disorders* (4th ed., text rev.). Washington, DC: Author.

Arias, A., Gelernter, J., Chan, G., Weiss, R., Brady, K., Farrer, L., & Kranzler, H. R. (2008). Correlates of co-occurring ADHD in drug dependent subjects: Prevalence and features of substance dependence and psychiatric disorders. *Addictive Behaviors, 33*(9), 1199–1207.

Biederman, J., Monuteaux, M. C., Spencer, T., Wilens, T. E., MacPherson, H. A., & Faraone, S. V. (2008). Stimulant therapy and risk for subsequent substance use disorders in male adults with ADHD: A naturalistic controlled 10-year follow-up study. *American Journal of Psychiatry, 165,* 597–603. Retrieved April 14, 2009, from http://www.health.harvard.edu

Biegel, D. E., Ishler, K. J., Katz, S., & Johnson, P. (2007). Predictors of burden of family caregivers of women with substance use disorders or co-occurring substance and mental disorders. *Journal of Social Work Practice in the Addictions, 7*(1–2), 25–49.

Blankertz, L. E., & Cnaan, R. A. (1993). Serving the dually diagnosed homeless: Program development and interventions. *Journal of Mental Health Administration 20*(2), 100–112.

Blankertz, L. E., Cnaan, R. A., & Freedman, E. (1993). Childhood risk factors in dually diagnosed homeless adults. *Social Work, 38,* 587–596.

Bonomo, Y., Bowes, G., Coffey, C., Carlin, J., & Patton, G. C. (2004). Teenage drinking and the onset of alcohol dependence: A cohort study over seven years. *Addiction, 99,* 1520–1528.

Bouis, S., Reif, S., Whetten, K., Scovil, J., Murray, A., & Swartz, M. (2007). An integrated, multidimensional treatment model for individuals living with HIV, mental illness, and substance abuse. *Health & Social Work, 32,* 268–278.

Center for Substance Abuse Treatment. (2005). *Substance abuse treatment for persons with co-occurring disorders* (Treatment Improvement Protocol [TIP] Series 42, DHHS Publication No. [SMA] 05–3992). Rockville, MD: Substance Abuse and Mental Health Services Administration.

Cochran, B. N., Peavy, K. M., & Cauce, A. M. (2007). Substance abuse treatment providers' explicit and implicit attitudes regarding sexual minorities. *Journal of Homosexuality, 53*(3), 182–203.

Cochran, S. D., Sullivan, J. G., & Mays, V. M. (2003). Prevalence of mental disorders, psychological distress and mental health services use among lesbian, gay, and bisexual adults in the US. *Journal of Consulting and Clinical Psychology, 71,* 1, 53–61.

Cochrane Collaboration. (2009). *Psychosocial interventions for people with both severe mental illness and substance misuse.* Retrieved May 25, 2009, from http://www.cochrane.org/reviews

Compton, B., Galaway, B., & Cournoyer, B. R. (2005). *Social work processes.* Belmont, CA: Brooks/Cole.

Conners, N. A., Whiteside-Mansell, L., & Sherman, A. C. (2006). Dimensions of religious involvement and mental health outcomes among alcohol and drug dependent women. *Alcoholism Treatment Quarterly, 24,* 89–108.

Co-Occurring Center on Excellence (COCE). (2006). *Co-occurring disorder related quick facts–Elderly.* Retrieved March 13, 2009, from http://coce.samsha.gov.cod_resources/ PDF/Elde

Drake, R. E., Mercer-McFadden, C., Mueser, K. T., McHugo, G. J., & Bond, G. R. (1998). Review of integrated mental health and substance abuse treatment for patients with dual disorders. *Schizophrenia Bulletin, 24,* 589–608.

Fallot, R. D., & Heckman, J. (2005). Religious/spiritual coping among women trauma survivors with mental health and substance use disorders. *Journal of Behavioral Health Services & Research, 32*(2), 215–226.

Farkas, K. (2008). Aging and substance use, misuse and abuse. *CSWE Gero-Ed Center, Aging Times, 4*(2), 1.

Gil, A., Wagner, E. F., & Tubman, J. G. (2004). Culturally sensitive substance abuse intervention for Hispanic and African American adolescents: Empirical examples from the alcohol treatment targeting adolescents in need (ATTAIN) project. *Society for the Study of Misuse, 99*(Suppl. 12), 140–150.

Gratz, K. L., Tull, M. T., Baruch, D. E., Bornovalova, M. A., & Lejuez, C. W. (2008). Factors associated with co-occurring borderline personality disorder among inner-city subjects: Intensity/reactivity, and emotion dysregulation. *Social Comprehensive Psychiatry Abstracts, 49,* 603–615.

Hall, D., & Queener, J. (2007). Self-medication hypothesis of substance use: Testing Khantzian's updated theory. *Journal of Psychoactive Drugs, 39*(2), 151–154.

Hawkins, E. H. (2009). A tale of two systems: Co-occurring mental health and substance disorders treatment for adolescents. *Annual Review of Psychology, 60,* 197–227.

Hellerstein, D. J., Rosenthal, R. N., & Miner, C. R. (1995). A prospective study of integrated outpatient treatment for substance-abusing schizophrenic patients. *American Journal on Addictions, 4*(1), 33–42.

Hussey, D. L, Drinkard, A. M., & Flannery, D. J. (2007). Comorbid substance use and mental disorders among offending youth. *Journal of Social Work Practice in the Misuses, 7,* 117–136.

Levine, P., & Fredericks, A. (1997). *Walking the tiger, healing trauma: The innate capacity to transform overwhelming experiences.* Berkeley, CA: North Atlantic Books.

Markoff, L. S., Reed, B. G., Fallot, R. D., Elliot, D. E., & Bjelajac, P. (2005). Implementing trauma-informed alcohol and other drug and mental health services for women: Lessons learned in a multisite demonstration project. *American Journal of Orthopsychiatry, 75,* 525–539.

Miles, D., Kulstad, J. L., & Haller, D. L. (2002). Severity of substance abuse and psychiatric problems among perinatal drug-dependent women. *Journal of Psychoactive Drugs, 34,* 339–346.

Miller, W., & Rollnick, S. (1991). *Principles of motivational interviewing.* New York: Guilford Press.

Najavits, L. M., Schmitz, M., Gotthardt, S., & Weiss, R. D. (2005). Seeking safety plus exposure therapy: An outcome study on dual diagnosis men. *Journal of Psychoactive Drugs, 37*, 425–435.

National Association of State Mental Health Programs Directors and National Association of State Alcohol and Drug Abuse Directors. (1999, March). *National dialogue on co-occurring mental health and substance abuse disorders.* Washington, DC: U.S. Department of Health and Human Services, SAMHSA, CSAT.

National Institute on Drug Abuse (NIDA). (2008). *Research report news series* (National Institutes of Health Publication No. 08-5771). Washington, DC: U.S. Department of Health and Human Services.

O'Neal, G. S. (2006). Using multicultural resources in groups. *Groupwork, 16*(1), 48–68.

O'Neal, G. S., & Reid, J. C. (1999). Parent education groups: Using cultural literature in the engagement phase. *Groupwork, 11*(2), 138–141.

Osher, F. C. (2005, November 29). *Integrated mental health/substance abuse responses to justice involved persons with co-occurring disorders.* Paper presented at the Evidence-Based Practice for Justice-Involved Individuals: Expert Panel Meeting, Bethesda, MD.

Prochaska, J. O., & DiClemente, C. C. (1992). Stages of change in the modification of problem behavior. In M. Hersen, R. Eisler, & P. M. Miller (Eds.), *Progress in behavioral modification* (pp. 184–214). Sycamore, IL: Sycamore Publishing.

Rosen, C., Kuhn, E., Greenbaum, M., & Drescher, K. (2008). Substance abuse-related mortality among middle-aged male VA psychiatric patients. *Psychiatric Services, 59*(3), 290–269.

Sacks, S., DeLeon, G., Bernhardt, A. I., & Sacks, J. Y. (1998). *Modified therapeutic community for homeless mentally ill chemical abusers: Treatment manual.* New York: National Development and Research Institutes.

Sacks, S., & Peters, J. (2002, October). *Modified TC for MICA offenders: Description and interim findings.* Paper presented at the GAINS Center National Conference, San Francisco.

Sacks, S., Sacks, J. Y., & DeLeon, G. (1999). Treatment for MICA: Design and implementation of modified TC. *Journal of Psychoactive Drugs 31*(1), 19–30.

Satre, D. D., & Arean, P. A. (2005). Effects of gender, ethnicity, and medical illness on drinking cessation in older primary care patients. *Journal of Aging and Health, 17*(1), 70–84.

Savage, A., Quiros, L., Dodd, J., & Bonavota, D. (2007). Building trauma informed practice: Appreciating the impact of trauma in the lives of women with substance abuse and mental health problems. *Journal of Social Work Practice in the Addictions, 7*, 91–115.

Smyth, N. J., Miller, B. A. Mudar, P. J., & Skiba, D. (2003). Protecting children: Exploring differences and similarities between mothers with and without alcohol problems. *Journal of Human Behavior in the Social Environment, 7*, 37–58.

Straussner, S. L., & Nemenzik, J. M. (2007). Co-occurring substance use and personality disorders: Current thinking on etiology, diagnosis and treatment. *Journal of Social Work Practice in the Addictions, 7*, 5–23.

Substance Abuse and Mental Health Services Administration (SAMHSA). (2002). *Report to Congress on the prevention and treatment of co-occurring substance abuse disorders and mental disorders.* Rockville, MD: Author.

Substance Abuse and Mental Health Services Administration. (2003). *Co-occurring disorders: Integrated dual disorders treatment, implementation resource kit* [Draft]. Retrieved May 25, 2009, from http://mentalhealth.samhsa.gov/cmhs/CommunitySupport/toolkits/cooccurring

Substance Abuse and Mental Health Services Administration. (2005). *Transforming mental health care in America. Federal action agenda: First steps.* Rockville, MD: Author.

Substance Abuse and Mental Health Services Administration. (2006). *Results from the 2005 National Survey on Drug Use and Health: National findings* (Office of Applied Studies, NSDUH Series H-30, DHHS Publication No. SMA 06–4194). Rockville, MD: Author.

Substance Abuse and Mental Health Services Administration. (2008). *Assertive community treatment: Training frontline staff* (DHHS Publication No. SMA–08–4344). Rockville, MD: U.S. Department of Health and Human Services, Center for Mental Health Services, Substance Abuse and Mental Health Services Administration.

Urbanoski, K. A., Cairey, J., Bassani, D. G., & Rush, B. R. (2008). Perceived unmet need for mental health care for Canadians with co-occurring mental and substance use disorders. *Psychiatric Services, 59*(3), 283–289.

VanDeMark, N., Brown, E., Bornemann, A., & Williams, S. (2004). New directions for families: A family oriented intervention for women affected by alcoholism and other drug abuse, mental illness and trauma. *Alcoholism Treatment Quarterly, 22,* 141–160.

Ziedonis, D. M., Smelson, D., Rosenthal., R. N., Batki, S. L., Green, S., L., Henry, R., Montoya, I., Parks, J., & Weiss, R. D. (2005). Improving the care of individuals with schizophrenia and substance use disorders: Consensus recommendations. *Journal of Psychiatric Practice, 11*(5), 315–339.

The Journey of Planned Change

Sharon C. Lyter and Ann A. Abbott

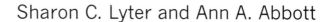

"A journey of a thousand miles begins with a single step."
—Lao-tzu, *The Way of Lao-tzu*,
Chinese philosopher (604 BC–531 BC)

Overview and Introduction

The journey of planned change may be a long and arduous one—especially for the individual with an alcohol, tobacco, or other drug (ATOD) history. The client may be exquisitely sensitive to the vision of an onerous trip, filled with heavy baggage, delays, wrong turns, missteps, and communication mishaps. The thought spinning through the client's mind might well be: "At least what I have now is familiar, even if it appears chaotic to others! If nothing else, I have the few moments of intoxication bliss. Please don't expect me to give that up."

We look to social work as a profession that is well positioned to take on this complex challenge. Social work has historically sought out the most challenging and vulnerable of populations and has a record of service on those very long, hard journeys. Social workers bring a common set of roles and functions that are applied to a variety of venues, including chemical dependency, mental health, child welfare, aging, and corrections. The helping professions share the mission of providing counseling services, but "social work, more than other professions, has expansive boundaries" (Gibelman, 2004, p. 1). Within the chemical dependency field, substance abuse is intertwined with all aspects of human functioning—biological, psychological, social, and spiritual. "As the largest allied health profession in the United States, social workers regularly encounter individuals, families, and communities faced with substance use disorders" (National Association of Social Workers [NASW], 2005, p. 6). At the generalist level of practice, social workers use a range of intervention methods. At an advanced level of practice, social workers may specialize in work with a specific population, synthesizing and applying "a broad range of interdisciplinary and multidisciplinary knowledge and skills" (Council on Social Work Education [CSWE], 2008, p. 8).

Social Workers as Agents of Change

Social workers function in a capacity that allows them to bring their knowledge of person and environment to address the complex array of concomitants that arise, serving as screeners, gatekeepers, referral agents, group workers, counselors, and therapists. They address chemical dependency issues, directly or indirectly, in mental health centers, schools, employment settings, medical centers, and child welfare agencies, as well as in substance abuse treatment centers. They may work directly with substance abusers and with family members or they may work with those systems designed to address substance abuse.

> Guided by a person and environment construct, a global perspective, respect for human diversity, and knowledge based on scientific inquiry, social work's purpose is actualized through its quest for social and economic justice, the prevention of conditions that limit human rights, the elimination of poverty, and the enhancement of the quality of life for all persons. (CSWE, 2008, p. 1)

Importance of the Social Work Perspective

This philosophy aptly prepares social workers to join ATOD clients on their journey of change. The underlying theoretical assumptions, the ethical code, and the practice behaviors of social work fit well with "best practices" of the field of ATOD. Salient concepts in social work include "being where the client is" and respect for the "right of clients to self-determination" (NASW, 2008). These concepts fit well with prominent contemporary approaches to substance abuse, including "harm reduction," "motivational interviewing," and the "transtheoretical stages of change model."

"Harm reduction" is regarded by many as a promising paradigm (Marlatt, 1998), a set of strategies that have a substantial effect in the reduction of the negative consequences of substance abuse. Although some oppose it as a political statement, positing that it contributes to the medicalization of political and social problems through cost containment (Gordon, 2005), its merits as a public health model are clear. Harm reduction strategies include access to safe syringes, access to medical care without penalty, and access to treatment programs that do not impose the goal of total abstinence. Harm reduction concepts have gained popularity in social work practice. Bigler (2005) described harm reduction as "ideally suited as a guide to practice in virtually all social work settings and reflects fundamental values and beliefs of the social work profession including the inherent worth and dignity of individuals, client self-determination, and the strengths perspective" (Bigler, p. 1).

Miller and Rollnick (1991) introduced and popularized "motivational interviewing." Its principles are consistent with social work values and ethics and meet the social work standard of evidence-based practice. Compatible with social work, it has application not only in substance abuse treatment, but also in domestic violence, health care, co-occurring disorders, eating disorders, and child welfare (Wahab, 2005). It is a collaborative approach that is focused and client centered, designed to elicit behavioral change by accepting and managing ambivalence in the counseling relationship. It assumes that "each person possesses a powerful potential for change" and helps to "get the person unstuck," with the client regarded as "an ally rather than an opponent" (Miller & Rollnick, 1991, p. 62).

The embracing of motivational interviewing may have ended the reign of the notorious and unbridled use of aggressive methods of confrontation as a tool in ATOD treatment. Many believed that aggression was in fact critical to the process of breaking through a client's denial system. Yet aggressive tactics are not in line with most ethical codes and find little support from the outcomes research literature. According to Polcin, the "free flowing" (2003) confrontation, often using personal attacks, common to therapeutic communities of the past has little support. A detailed analysis suggests that a more nuanced use of confrontation can produce the desired results. The more effective use of confrontation is conceptualized as containment (Polcin, Galloway, & Greenfield, 2006) and provides compelling individual feedback that stems from a variety of systems, not just from the clinician: the criminal justice system; the canons and ideologies of religion and peer support and therapy groups; and in the compassionate statements of fact from the treatment professional. This wide array of sources contributes to a consistent message that allows the client to find benefit in confrontational exchanges, helping them "examine and contain addictive behaviors" (Polcin et al., 2006, p. 379).

The "transtheoretical stages of change model"—a model of behavior change—applies a six-stage process of planned change through which individuals progress: pre-contemplation, contemplation, preparation, action, maintenance, termination.

In their pivotal book *Changing for Good,* Prochaska, Norcross, and DiClemente (1994) described the model that encourages understanding client readiness for change and the application of relevant and matched intervention strategies.

The Process of Planned Change

The ideals and values of the social work profession include primacy of the client, social justice, a valuing of the therapeutic relationship, and a belief in empowerment (Plionis, Bailey-Etta, & Manning, 2002). The broad base of social work micro practice requires the positioning of a scaffold or foundation for the climb through the complex processes of assessment and intervention. A planful, systematic procedure is offered by Kirst-Ashman and Hull (2009) in their delineation of planned change. (See *Understanding Generalist Practice*). The planned change model provides a comprehensive approach that guides the worker to apply values, ethics, knowledge, and skills, using multiple methods and with awareness of the larger implications of "the public ills of society" (Plionis, Bailey-Etta, & Manning). It involves the systematic application of change principles, with a beginning, middle, and end.

The steps of the planned change process—engagement, assessment, planning, implementation, evaluation, termination, and follow-up—are grounded in a systems perspective and require assessment of micro, mezzo, and macro systems, facilitating intervention and problem solving at various levels. *Micro systems* here are defined as individuals, *mezzo* as families and groups, and *macro* as organizations and communities. Knowledge and skills of best practices in interviewing are necessary, and workers must be skillful in applying the concepts of empowerment, empathy, warmth, genuineness, and mutuality. Planned change is atheoretical, requiring the worker to impose another layer of knowledge with respect to evidence-based models of interviewing and counseling practice that encompass an array of strengths-oriented methods, including crisis, interpersonal, cognitive–behavioral, narrative, solution-focused, psychodynamic, and humanistic.

Compton, Galaway, and Cournoyer (2005) remind us that planful approaches to processes of change proceed in a fairly predictable process, sequential and interactional, more spiral than linear—in fact, never purely linear. They describe their approach to planned change, termed *problem solving,* as

> a squirming, wriggling, living process that embraces the social reality between our clients and ourselves and the systems within which we operate. Occasionally it may be difficult to identify and track each phase in the sequence or to discern the logic of the process. (p. 76)

Importance of Cultural Competence

Social work brings another tool to this epic journey, that of cultural competence. Social work places major emphasis on diversity awareness and cultural competence (see NASW, 2001). The ethical positioning (NASW, 2008) is very clear. Social workers are obligated to recognize the strengths that exist in every culture; to have knowledge of and be sensitive to the cultures of clients served; and to understand the potential for oppression "with respect to race, ethnicity, national origin, color, sex, sexual orientation, gender identity or expression, age, marital status, political belief, religion, immigration status, and mental or physical disability" (p. 9, section 1.05).

The worker must respect "therapeutic boundaries, taking into consideration gender, culture, and ethnic differences" (NASW, 2005, p. 14). The idea, though, of matching clinicians and clients on the basis of culture is highly controversial. "The available research does not show that matching on the basis of race, ethnicity, or sexual orientation is necessary for conducting a successful interview" (Kadushin & Kadushin, 1997, p. 343). Language barriers, however, can be a significant obstacle. This can be addressed in part through maintaining a staff that represents the languages common to the region.

"Culturally competent practitioners will utilize their knowledge and skills differently within each of the stages of the planned change process" (Kirst-Ashman & Hull, 2009, p. 420). In the engagement phase, the worker must be aware of obvious differences of culture and language—perhaps requiring use of interpreters—but alert to an individual's experiences of and history with diversity, oppression, and marginalization. The individual brings his or her own heritage and associated practices. If his or her culture differs from the dominant culture, the client may have at least some identification and practices related to the dominant one. The ATOD user often has identification with the perceived peer group—the other smokers huddled around the dumpster at break time, the familiar faces on the adjacent bar stools, and the associates in illicit drug use. Social inclusion questions and the right to hope for a better life may not be expressed openly but are often of paramount importance to the client. The client may frequently wonder: "Where do I fit? Do I belong? Does anyone care about me?" The worker cannot overlook other pertinent layers of diversity—spirituality, sexual orientation, age, gender, multi-culturalism.

A strengths-oriented diversity assessment brings awareness of the potential for resources and supports within each and every culture. Indeed, the "dumpster peer group" has been described by many as a place of respite and safety. Mindful of the importance of peers and the common phenomenon of alienation of close family members, the clinician then begins, in collaboration with the client, to find alternative sources of support. This array can include religious organizations, neighbors, extended family, and cultural centers.

A pictorial may be a powerful tool here for the client—social workers often use ecomaps that represent the environmental context and display all of the relevant systems. An individualized ecomap (see Figure 7.1) can serve as a lifeline that a client consults to find alternative support, particularly during periods of intense challenge on his or her journey. The ecomap depicts the actual links from client to system, a reminder to the client of concrete options, rather than abstract conceptualizations.

In the last stages of planned change—evaluation, termination, and follow-up—the worker continues to incorporate diversity awareness by applying measures of overall effectiveness that ensure inclusion of diverse groups and by measuring

Figure 7.1: Example of a Client Ecomap

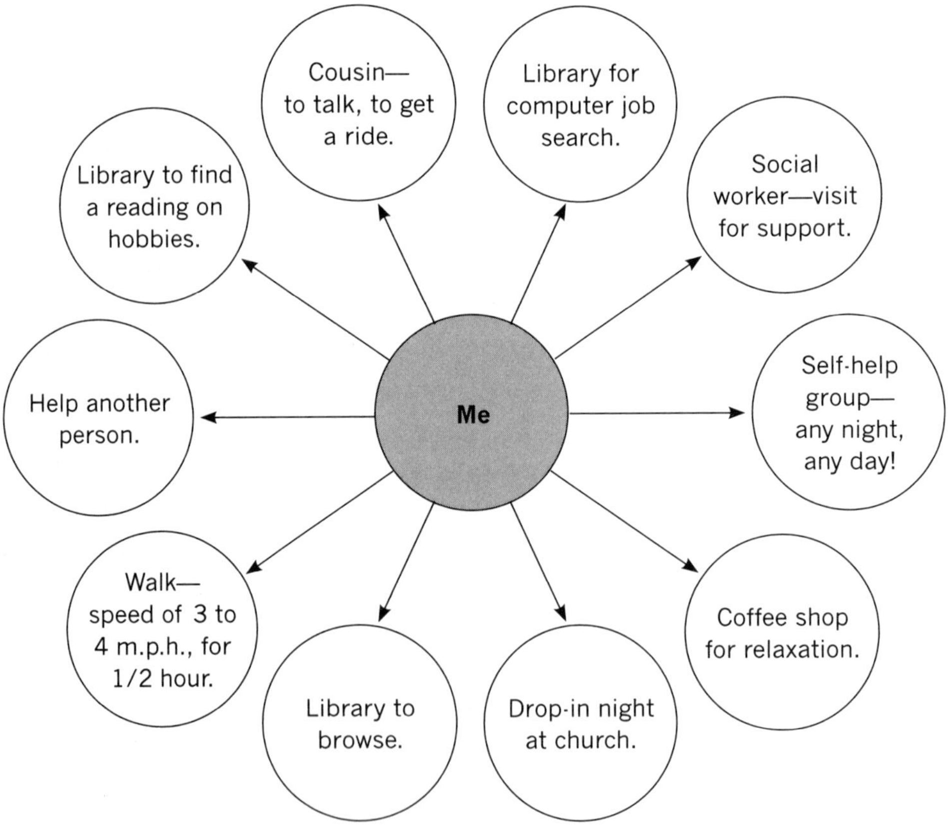

Cousin—to talk, to get a ride.

Library for computer job search.

Library to find a reading on hobbies.

Social worker—visit for support.

Me

Help another person.

Self-help group—any night, any day!

Walk—speed of 3 to 4 m.p.h., for 1/2 hour.

Library to browse.

Drop-in night at church.

Coffee shop for relaxation.

There is always hope. Here are my resources.

individual practice effectiveness in a manner that integrates both qualitative and quantitative methods. Through the entire journey, the worker must be open to constructive criticism and moreover must be willing to engage in painstaking and meticulous self-critique in an ongoing manner. Only in that atmosphere can the client feel free to express concerns about cultural insensitivity and become an informant and educator to the agency and the worker.

This chapter will walk us through the journey of planned change described above, with attention to the skills needed and pitfalls encountered at each level, and with recognition of the need to use critical thinking to evaluate each decision and knowledge that effective practice requires the "recognition of the importance of scientific research and its application to intervention or treatment services for clients" with substance use disorders (NASW, 2005, p. 14).

Engagement

The clinician proceeds as follows in the process of engaging, or joining, with the client (Kirst-Ashman & Hull, 2009):

1. Greet the client.
2. Demonstrate effective attending skills.
3. Discuss services and client expectations.
4. Decide whether the clinician can help.
5. Offer services to the client.
6. Orient client to the helping process.
7. Complete required documentation.

According to Kirst-Ashman and Hull (2009), engagement is the springboard to addressing needs and problems effectively. The worker is establishing rapport, a working relationship, through verbal and non-verbal communication (eye contact, facial expression, body positioning), with actions coinciding with expressions. The worker conveys warmth, empathy, and genuineness—the core conditions of practice. This relationship provides the client a foundation from which to safely evaluate the impact of his or her current behavior on all aspects of life: relationships, employment, social activities, family, and health.

The social work literature is rich with research and guidance on the theme of engagement. According to Kadushin & Kadushin (1997), "Research has identified a positive relationship as the most consistent and ubiquitous factor associated with positive outcomes in human service helping" (p. 133). The elements of that relationship include: "acceptance, empathy, genuineness and authenticity, self-determination, confidentiality, individuality, interest, warmth, trust, and respect" (p. 133). A positive relationship acts "as an anesthetic to the sharing of painful material" (p. 100). This positive and productive relationship provides the client with the confidence necessary to identify weaknesses, to practice new and unfamiliar behaviors, and to divulge painful experiences that are inhibiting growth and change. This foundation allows the client to feel comfortable disclosing vulnerabilities and confident in attempting new patterns of behavior.

For alcohol and other drug treatment to produce positive results, it is necessary for clients to become engaged in the treatment process and remain engaged for a time sufficient to support behavior change. Engagement is a necessary but not sufficient condition for a positive treatment outcome. Engagement is not enough; the clinician also must reflect competence and "technical skill" (Kadushin & Kadushin, 1997).

Glicken (2005) asserted that competence and effectiveness are predicated on evidence based practice, that a therapeutic relationship has been demonstrated to be one in which power differences are neutralized and communication is safe and sincere. Effective outcomes are fostered by the "bond developed between two or more people for the purpose of helping people resolve social and emotional difficulties" (p. 112). The bond stems from the belief in the idea of a "caring, facilitative, and change-oriented partnership" (p. 112). Bisman (1994) promoted a similar notion in her description of "belief bonding" as the process through which clinician and client come together. Each brings something to the table: The worker brings competence and hope, and the client brings hope and, often, anxiety. The joining of competence and hope results in the shared vision of the prospect of change, with both client and worker believing that change is possible, anticipating a successful outcome. "Most clients cycle through the change stages several times, sometimes spiraling up and sometimes down, before they settle into treatment or stable recovery" (Center for Substance Abuse Treatment [CSAT], 1999, p. 139). Even those clients with a history of failed attempts can take some hope from the phenomenon of the cumulative effect. Recovery can be a long-term process and may require multiple episodes of treatment before the client achieves stabilization and restoration of functioning.

The beliefs and feelings of the client must be acknowledged with understanding and compassion. Bemoaning the client's feelings as a hindrance will do little to further the engagement. It is not unusual for a mandated client to express anger about being ordered to attend counseling. Many adults resent being told what they need by an agency that does not know them. However, the clinician should not assume that all mandated clients are angry. To accurately assess clients' feelings, it is suggested that the clinician simply ask clients how they feel about participating in treatment

(Newman, 1997). If the client is angry, the clinician should allow him or her to express this anger. Acknowledging clients' feelings of frustration and anger suggests that the clinician empathizes with them. Allowing the client to express her or his anger during the beginning sessions of treatment will reduce the likelihood that unexpressed anger will underlie and perhaps undermine future treatment sessions.

The Role of Anxiety and Discomfort

Many of these clients need help getting past the blaming and moralizing of others. It is important for the clinician to respect the client and demonstrate a positive regard for the client. In many instances, the client requests treatment when he or she experiences enough discomfort in life to trigger help seeking. The cons of using substances may at times outweigh the pros of using, and anxiety is often the result. The anxiety that the client brings can be a special challenge and is often misinterpreted as an obstacle to be overcome rather than managed. The clinician works with the anxiety, alleviating extreme anxiety yet not removing anxiety that motivates the client. The wise clinician understands the benefits of both hope and discomfort, and strives to find the right balance that will propel the client forward.

To reduce excessive anxiety, the clinician can educate the potential client about what this treatment will entail, what the client can expect during the process, what the client is expected to do during each session, and what the client can expect from the clinician. By offering the client a preview of what to expect, the clinician can minimize anxieties about the unknown. In addition, with anxiety management in mind, the clinician must apply the same effective interviewing micro skills that pertain throughout the process of planned change: attentive listening, eye contact, body positioning; expression of warmth, empathy, and genuineness; and cultural competence. It is worthy of note here that the clinician must be hopeful yet realistic. Worker expectations and self-care will be discussed further in the evaluation section of this chapter.

According to the CSAT (2006), the early phases are crucial and many clients drop out of treatment. CSAT recommends that these elements be included: a welcoming environment, a site accessible by public transportation, supportive intake interviews, sensitivity to cultural differences, assurances of privacy, rapid response to client initial inquiry, and respectful attitudes from both professional and clerical staff. The agency must strive to overcome barriers that discourage the client and may lead to early dropout, and must convey respect for the client's efforts in connecting with the system. "Matching clients to the least intensive and restrictive treatment setting that can support recovery effectively" (p. 59) is a tool that helps to minimize dropout, along with fitting the program to the client, rather than forcing the person into a predefined program.

Importance of the Therapeutic Alliance

The therapeutic alliance has transcended the era of practitioner authority. The client is not viewed as the inferior party who is directed through change. Instead, the autonomy and authority of the client must be recognized, with both the client and clinician having a voice—each voice then participating in the language of change (CSAT, 1999). The clinician, together with the client, acknowledges the obstacles, and, indeed, benefits that the substance use has had for the client (CSAT, 1999). Only then can the client and worker, with mutuality and optimism for the future, go on to partialize the problems and needs into manageable components.

Value of the Strengths Perspective

There has been a steady shift from a medical, pathology oriented perspective to a more empowering, humanistic model that assumes that all clients have underlying strength and the ability to change, and that both individuals and environments can transform. According to Saleebey (2009), successful engagement is promoted by specific strategies. Talking to people is more likely to bring success than "interviewing" them, with the worker striving to bring genuine caring, so that the reluctant and potential client is given a voice in the process, enabling him or her to achieve trust and not just compliance. That trust leads to acceptance of the possibility for growth and change. Accepting and validating the client, the worker's belief:

> that you can do better and prevail through your tribulations translates into the recrudescence of hope, the revival or birth of a dream—no matter how modest. A focus on possibility, an eye cast to a better future, and the creation of justifiable optimism all promote movement toward one's aspirations. (pp. 95–96)

As the worker assesses the client, the client, likewise, is assessing the worker. The use of a strengths assessment reassures the client of the worker's competence and establishes such realities as where the client will sleep tonight, what financial supports are available or need to be explored, and if natural resources such as friends and family are available. Finding housing is likely to take precedence over the client's commitment to other aims, such as abstinence or even a short respite from substance use.

Overcoming Resistance

The worker moves the work forward when he or she uses some disclosure of things in common with the client and even in some instances sharing an activity such as taking a walk, discussing sports, having coffee together. Lastly, Saleebey (2009) reminds the worker of the critical need for understanding and acceptance of the client's cultural background, taking on the role of the learner with the client as the informant and educator.

Families cannot be overlooked and programs need to assert the belief that families are important to recovery (CSAT, 2006). To further engagement of significant others, the agency may offer incentives for attendance such as food and transportation vouchers. Family members could be included in the intake or in group events for families, especially family education.

Empowerment themes have also transformed another compelling issue—that of "client resistance." All clients are involuntary at least in part, but some are court mandated for treatment. Some clients have selected treatment, rather than jail, when given the choice by a court. Others seek treatment after being strongly encouraged to do so by spouses, other family members, or employers. "Involuntariness," as such, exists along a continuum, with clients expressing resistance in various ways (CSAT, 1999). They may argue repeatedly with the clinician, interrupt when the worker or other clients are speaking, ramble, or, conversely, ignore and disengage. They may use silence in a hostile manner. The client may blame others or may become defeatist about self. Some clients question clinician competence, pointing a finger at the worker as the "cause" of the client's actions. Some use the defense mechanism of intellectualization, in which they continually "test" the worker on knowledge of theory, or talk endlessly about what they have read or their philosophies of life.

Another potential example of resistance is the overly compliant client—one who does everything that is expected of him or her, verbalizes what he or she thinks the clinician wants to hear, voices appropriate opinions and comments, but internalizes little or nothing from the treatment experience. The best method of resistance, of course, is to pretend compliance.

The Negative Impact of Shaming and Blaming

According to Saleebey (1997), blaming and shaming are commonly applied to those with substance problems, the stigma perhaps outweighing that applied to those with mental disorders. The associated stigma "requires special attention to empowerment and advocacy" (NASW, 2005, p. 20). The shaming may be rooted in part in the popular media, where "virtually every reference to substance abusers is framed in the context of problems, chaos, and pathology" (p. 78), with little consideration of the ramifications of poverty and hopelessness. Resistance then is framed as the likely result of both clinician and client factors, with both denial and resistance emerging as artifacts of the helping process. Saleebey suggests that strength-based interventions reduce attrition and encourage client compliance and positive outcomes, heightening the responsibility of the client by affirming past successes and abilities, and building a bridge to responsibility.

Innovative Strategies of Engagement

Innovative strategies of engagement are sometimes more successful than traditional ones. Recognized as one of the top 10 CNN heroes of 2008, Anne Mahlum pioneered a project titled "Back on My Feet" in which she recruits joggers from local homeless shelters in Philadelphia. Participants are required to live in an affiliated shelter facility and remain free of alcohol and other drugs for 30 days. They receive running shoes and clothing, and they run early in the morning as part of a club. This approach has already engaged 54 individuals, with the plan to expand. Mahlum acknowledged that running has been her personal strategy for dealing with alcoholism within her own family of origin (CNN, 2008).

Even those clients mandated into treatment are not necessarily in direct opposition to the demands and expectations of treatment. Burman (2004) reminds us that the social control aspect of affiliation with the court system is an important variable to consider. Burman examined the mandated client phenomenon and concluded that clinical outcomes may be limited when the clinician is forced to simultaneously address dual obligations—to clients and society. "Consideration should also be given to altering current policies and standards that would assist in resolving dilemmas, when role activities yield disparate crossed purposes" (Burman, 2004, p. 205).

Rather than framing "the resistant client" as a standalone, isolated phenomenon, in this chapter we instead regard hesitation and resistance as expectable considering the inherent dynamics of substance abuse and the planned change process. Instead, we offer an emphasis on understanding the client. Two strategies have emerged as well suited to client resistance: options and fit.

Miller and Rollnick (1991) recommended that the client be offered a set of options, a "menu of alternative strategies," with the belief that allowing the clients to have a choice, to have options, is more likely to be motivating, resulting in engagement. Likewise, the fit, or match, between the method and the client's readiness must be considered. Engagement is more likely to be accomplished if the intervention method is matched to the individual's present stage of change and readiness (CSAT, 1999).

Transtheoretical Stages of Change

The transtheoretical stages, as described here, have special meaning in the engagement phase, but the clinician should refer back to this section for consideration throughout the process of planned change. It is not unusual for clients to enter treatment at the "pre-contemplation" stage. Those in pre-contemplation are not yet considering change, not within the next six months, and as such the task of the clinician is to create doubt and evoke concern. Expressing concern, the clinician moves forward cautiously, with permission, to establish trust and rapport. At some point, doubts can be raised through discussion of the pros and cons of substance use, with an attempt to envision alternatives to current behaviors. A person at this stage of change may resent any attempt by the clinician to label the substance-using behavior as problematic, and labeling may increase the level of resistance and defensiveness. Research suggests that "labeling someone an alcoholic or drug addict has a detrimental, not facilitative, effect on help-seeking" (Marlatt, Tucker, Donovan, & Vuchinich, 1997, p. 45). To engage the pre-contemplative client, the clinician should consider assigning the client the task of defining his or her own level of substance use. If the client will be involved in group treatment, describe the group process and explain that the client will receive feedback from similarly situated peers so that the client can place himself or herself along the substance-using continuum. Informing the client that she or he will be responsible for defining his or her own use empowers the client, recognizes his or her capabilities as an adult, and minimizes the likelihood that the client will become defensive.

As the client begins to understand more about addiction, he or she may move into the "contemplation" stage. Those in the contemplation phase acknowledge concern but are uncertain. They consider the idea of change initiation, with the possibility that such a process could begin within one to six months. The client begins to assess her or his own use of alcohol and other drugs and compares the benefits of changing the using behavior with the benefits of continuing the use (DiClemente & Scott, 1997; Marlatt et al., 1997; Miller & Rollnick, 1991). The client is more willing to look at the substance-using behavior and the clinician can provide the client with information about the impact of alcohol and other drug use on the client's physical, family, social, and employment functioning. The task of the clinician is to promote a picture in which the advantages of change outweigh the disadvantages. Strategies can include normalizing ambivalence, empowerment and emphasis on self-efficacy, and eliciting self-change statements. The clinician should consider advising the client about the need for change (DiClemente & Scott, 1997; Marlatt et al., 1997; Miller & Rollnick, 1991).

In the "preparation" phase, the client is committed and planning to begin the change process in the near future, possibly within the next month. The clinician can assist the client to identify an acceptable change strategy, to negotiate a plan and, perhaps, a change contract. The clinician offers options, helps the client to find natural resources and supports, and helps the client to assess challenges such as child care needs and employment interruptions. The objectives subsumed within the overall goal should be SMART—specific, manageable, attainable, realistic, and time specific (Whitten, 2005). Lastly, the clinician encourages the client to announce the change plan; positive pressure from peers and family can enhance plan compliance. Once a strategy is identified, the client moves into the "action" stage and the plan or strategy for change is implemented. In the action phase, usually lasting three to six months, the client commits to the process and actively engages in fulfilling the plan identified. The task of the clinician is to support the client's efforts to change and to navigate the new terrain. The clinician helps the client to remove barriers and find reinforcement for change. Behaviors here take precedence over thoughts and feelings. The clinician acknowledges the challenges and difficulties encountered and reminds the client of the coping strategies already identified.

If the desired change is achieved, the client moves into the "maintenance" stage. In the maintenance stage, usually lasting at a minimum six months, the client has achieved initial goals such as abstinence and is now working to maintain those gains. The task of the clinician is to support the lifestyle changes and to reinforce awareness of sustaining options such as a support group in the community. The clinician helps the client identify triggers for substance use and to plan a course of action that overcomes those triggers. Client self-efficacy is reinforced. If a slip occurs, the client needs an escape or emergency plan so that a recurrence is not catastrophic. The client is then in a position to reenter the cycle of change, with the assumption that the client as such would be farther along on the learning curve. The client, then, is not likely to free-fall all the way back to pre-contemplation but should be able to regain some of the growth. The clinician reminds the client that change is rarely linear, that for change to have a sustained effect, it may require a more circular path.

The "termination" stage is that point at which the client no longer perceives the threat of temptation. Controversy remains as to whether this is a goal that can be achieved; indeed, many are more likely to see themselves as "in recovery," rather than free of the temptation to use. If relapse does occur, the clinician can assist the client to renegotiate these stages of change. As the client begins these stages again, the clinician can remind the client of his or her previous success (DiClemente & Scott, 1997; Marlatt et al., 1997; Miller & Rollnick, 1991; Prochaska & DiClemente, 1982). Rarely is change a truly linear, straightforward process (Prochaska et al., 1994). Relapse remains the rule and not the exception. Many people do not fall back all the way to pre-contemplation; rather, they may return instead to contemplation, suggesting that a better term to apply might be "recycle" rather than "relapse" (Prochaska et al., 1994).

We acknowledge that engagement is critical, that "the way in which a clinician interacts with clients appears to be nearly as important as—perhaps more important than—the specific approach or school of thought from which he or she operates" (Miller & Rollnick, 1991, p. 4). An engaged client is more than one who is punctual and attends all scheduled sessions. An engaged client is one who actively participates in both the selection of therapeutic goals and in each therapeutic activity. In other words, an engaged client is one who is invested in the entire treatment process. We acknowledge that engagement is necessary but not sufficient. Once the client is engaged, the journey of planned change moves on from engagement to assessment.

Assessment

The clinician proceeds as follows in the process of assessing the client and environment, attending to micro, mezzo, and macro system levels (Kirst-Ashman & Hull, 2009):

1. Identify the client.
2. Assess the client-in-situation from the following perspectives—micro, mezzo, macro.
3. Assess aspects of diversity with special attention to strengths.
4. Cite information about client problems and needs—micro, mezzo, macro.
5. Identify client strengths—micro, mezzo, macro.

As the journey shifts from the engagement phase into the assessment phase, the worker is setting the stage for the client to move into task-oriented activities of responding to questions and assisting in gathering relevant data, setting goals, and collaborating in the setting of a treatment plan. The thorough biopsychosociocultural assessment is accompanied by an explanation of program rules and expectations (CSAT, 2006).

An informal style of interviewing may be more appropriate at this time, using the sandwich technique in which formal, standard screening and assessment queries are "sandwiched" between less formal questions. This strategy may evoke client views, "gaining cooperation, and defusing potential resentments or hostilities" (CSAT, 2006, p. 62), shifting from a more conversational tone to a more directive, formal tone as needed. Simultaneously, the clinician is conveying empathy, giving empowerment and hope messages and affirming and supporting statements of self-efficacy. Probing is used gently, watching for non-verbal expressions. Assessment findings must be presented to the client, in a straightforward manner, without judgment. The sharing of assessment feedback is an opportune time to elicit change talk from the client.

ATOD problems do not discriminate. Problems related to ATOD afflict every ethnic and cultural group, both sexes, the age range from grade school children to older adults, and all socioeconomic strata. Almost every social work practitioner, in the course of regular practice in whatever agency or private context, is likely to encounter people for whom ATOD are playing some role in the "presenting" problem for which they are seeking help. The ATOD abuse can either be implicated causally in the presenting problem (for example, in the marital couple whose fights are often about one spouse's drinking), or be exacerbating the presenting problem and making it more difficult to solve.

The clinician's role is dependent on setting and agency function. Screening for ATOD problems is more likely to occur in an agency providing general services or in a primary care medical setting. Screening is a lower level assessment in that it broadly identifies a potential problem. According to NASW (2005), screening includes "awareness, active listening, and observation of behaviors" (p. 16), and should consider current and recent substance use, previous treatment, health problems, criminal history, mental disorders, drug test results, family issues, employment, housing, and financial status.

True assessment is more comprehensive and provides a more precise appraisal and measurement of the extent of the problem. Assessment should include information that can be collected with standardized instruments (see chapter 8 for a detailed description of a wide variety of ATOD assessment instruments) and interviewing, resulting in a decision about the need for further intervention or possible referral. The information should include general health, medical and dental issues, and the presence of infectious diseases such as hepatitis or HIV. History of drug use and treatment is assessed in detail, with review of the types of substances used and routes of administration; symptoms of withdrawal or tolerance; loss of control and secrecy; family and peer relationships; job and school status; legal and socio-economic status; mental disorders; risk of suicide; family history; social supports or barriers; cultural and spiritual issues; and client motivation and readiness.

The client seen in those community agencies that are not specialized ATOD treatment facilities may already have an ATOD problem of such severity that referral to a specialized resource may be in order. But there are many more people who "abuse" ATOD than there are people who develop severe "dependence" (as those terms are defined in the DSM-IV-TR [American Psychiatric Association, 2000]). ATOD-dependent people are more likely to show up in ATOD-specialized agencies than are clients whose problems are at the abuse stage. Although it is not true that every ATOD abuser will inevitably progress to the stage of severe dependence, ATOD abuse itself wreaks great damage on many people's lives. It is not the professional in an ATOD-specialized treatment agency, but, rather, the practitioner in a community agency—such as a mental health center, family service agency, hospital, school, or other youth service agency, or a service for older adults—who is more likely to identify problems of ATOD abuse that are impairing the client's family relationships, work, finances, or health.

ATOD abuse is frequently a variable in child neglect or abuse, or other forms of intrafamilial abuse such as spousal violence and elder abuse. It can be a factor in marital conflict, even when physical violence is not occurring. Alcohol or other drugs may be involved in sexual performance problems. ATOD abuse may be a factor in behavioral or learning problems of children and adolescents. There is a high incidence of ATOD problems in people referred by the court system and probation. Older adults often abuse prescription and nonprescription medications, and a disturbing number of older adults abuse alcohol, even people who never previously had a drinking problem. The older adult who falls frequently or suffers blackouts may have a medical condition causing these symptoms—or they may be caused by ATOD. Similarly, the "accident-prone" younger person who frequently shows up in the emergency room may actually have an ATOD problem. The health care social worker meets patients with medical disorders that might possibly be related to ATOD abuse and who need to be evaluated for this. (Likewise, their physicians may need help in recognizing the need for such evaluation; physicians, unfortunately, may also assume that the well-dressed executive or suburban homemaker could not possibly have an ATOD problem. People with chronic painful conditions may try to "self-medicate" with alcohol or other drugs. Psychiatric patients, unfortunately, often prefer alcohol or other drugs to their prescribed medications, thereby exacerbating the original problem and adding a new one. Similarly, those who are prescribed medications for a psychotic disorder may be attempting to address side effects of that medication with other drugs of their own choosing. Pregnant women are not always sufficiently aware of the dangers to their babies caused by ATOD.

The list goes on. The practitioner, in whatever agency context, needs to incorporate into usual practice an exploration of whether, and to what degree, ATOD may be playing a role in whatever is the presenting problem. One way of doing this might be a routine questionnaire administered to all clients at intake that not only requests the usual "face sheet" information, including the client's brief statement of the presenting problem, but also inquires about patterns of ATOD use, including prescribed medications. Such a routine, generalized instrument may be perceived by the client as less personalized and thus less threatening. (See chapter 8 for samples of standardized assessment instruments.) The practitioner may also question the client directly about ATOD use, in the course of developing information about the presenting problem. This can be done quite directly if it is also tactful and nonaccusatory—for example, if preceded by a comment that the practitioner has found that use of alcohol or other drugs may be a complication in problems such as the one the client is experiencing, and so the practitioner would find it helpful to explore this a little with the client. Quite frequently, the client is really not aware that intake of ATOD is implicated in the problem with which the client is struggling. It should be noted that a presenting problem by the client or family may include intermittent or lasting memory impairment related to substance use. This impairment may influence ability to clearly describe the details of the problem, as would being under current influence of a substance.

To launch into treatment of the marital problem or sexual performance problem or child abuse or whatever without this vital knowledge of the role of a concomitant ATOD problem will, in all probability, doom to failure treatment of the presenting problem—because nothing is being done to change this vital component of the problem situation. In some cases, work on the ATOD problem could go on concurrently with work on the presenting problem—but, in many cases, the focus should shift to the ATOD problem to attempt to control it before any positive change can be expected to happen with the presenting problem. Some clients may refuse to admit that their ATOD abuse has anything to do with the presenting problem; the practitioner may then have to go ahead with attempting to help with, say, the presenting marital problem as a way of letting the client learn experientially that no progress can really be made on this as long as ATOD abuse is part of that problem.

According to Kirst-Ashman and Hull (2009), within the planned change process *assessment* is defined as "the investigation and determination of variables affecting an identified problem or issue as viewed from micro, mezzo, or macro perspectives" (p. 34). Even though client participation may not be fully voluntary, both the client and the family are likely to be integral to the process and likely to receive the benefits of the assessment and treatment efforts. A comprehensive, systemic perspective is therefore essential.

On the micro-level, the review includes bio-psycho-socio-cultural-spiritual aspects of the client, with regard to how health and psychology interface with social and cultural characteristics. Critical problems and needs—both immediate and longer term—and strengths are identified. What is the client's physical and medical condition? Are there potential medical emergencies? Psychiatric and psychological screening includes assessment of appearance, alertness, and affect; speech and communication; cognition in terms of orientation to person, place, time, and condition; capacity for insight, judgment, and ability to problem solve; coherence in terms of delusions, hallucinations; risk of violence or suicide; and history of mental disorders.

Does the client identify any religious or spiritual beliefs or practices? Even those who deny any specific religiosity often describe a sense of ennui or a "spiritual emptiness" (CSAT, 2005, p. 111) and benefit from attention to a spiritual self and to the search for purpose in life. The clinician is wise to elicit the client's views on faith, spirituality, and religion and those definitions held by that individual. Stewart and Koeske (2005) found that spirituality changed significantly during treatment for substance abuse, even among those who did not express strong ties to religion. The authors described a highly compelling transformation: a change from "a 'guilty' spirituality to a positive spirituality characterized by perceiving themselves as being able to be forgiven by God and by other people, and as being better able to forgive others" (p. 335).

Mezzo aspects include religious and cultural affiliations and any social group connections, recognizing that some associations for the client are healthier than others. Family aspects are assessed although, clearly, individuals with a substance abuse history may have strained family relationships. Some having fully "burned their bridges" to family members and must turn to any willing friends and extended family. The client may need to reach out for peer support from nonfamily groups such as those offered by Alcoholics Anonymous. It must be assumed that a seeming paradox may occur, with family members moving into crisis just as the client seems to be moving toward improved health. Family crises often erupt or family coping deficits become exacerbated by the process of treatment seeking. The family member may be provoked emotionally by the glimmer of hope. This can result in an attempt by the family member to force a crisis that would reinforce the leverage or to leap forward in expectations that change will come quickly. In addition, family members may experience conscious or unconscious resistance to change, with the realization that patterns that have been established to help the substance-affected family cope may now have to change. A prime example of this is the adolescent whose parent's inadequacies resulted in freedom for the teenager. That teenager now may have to respond to parental authority.

Macro aspects include a review of the services available to the client. Is transportation available? Child care? What is the economic status of the client? Does the client have a work history? What are the policies that may influence the client's status and access to care? What is the attitude in the community? Diversity and any potential for discrimination must be evaluated. What is the cultural heritage, age, gender, sexual orientation of the client? Is the client at risk of bias, of institutional oppression?

Assessment is not without its challenges. Barriers to treatment may appear, such as evidence that the client is coming in intoxicated or has withdrawal symptoms that require care. Concrete needs such as shelter, food, transportation (and driver privileges), child care, and employment must be recognized as requiring attention. They are not merely entries on an intake form but, rather, very real and current demands.

Helpful Instrumentation Pertaining to Readiness for Change

Two very useful instruments in the public domain are readily available to clinicians: the Stages of Change Readiness and Treatment Eagerness Scale (SOCRATES) and the Readiness Ruler (see CSAT, 1999). The 19-item SOCRATES (Miller & Tonigan, 1996) addresses problem drinkers and their readiness to change, using three related factors: problem recognition, ambivalence, and taking steps toward change. SOCRATES can be used as a pretreatment tool and also during treatment to measure treatment impact. The Readiness Ruler, developed by Rollnick (CSAT, 1999), is a rough measure of readiness to engage in treatment. It is simply a graphic of a ruler, labeled from 1 to 10, with the low end (1–3) anchored as "Not Ready," the middle (4–7) as "Unsure," and the high end (8–10) as "Ready" (see Figure 7.2). The client is asked, at different intervals in time, to identify where he or she falls on the ruler. This can be used not only to measure treatment progress but also to determine readiness for action. In this context, at the screening or assessment stage, it can provide some indication to the worker as to what steps to take next. Is the client

Figure 7.2: Readiness Ruler

Readiness Ruler									
1	2	3	4	5	6	7	8	9	10
Not Ready					Unsure				Ready

Source: Rollnick as cited in Center for Substance Abuse Treatment (CSAT). (1999). *Enhancing motivation for change in substance abuse treatment* (Treatment Improvement Protocol [TIP] Series, Number 35, DHHS Publication No. [SMA] 08–4212). Rockville, MD: Substance Abuse and Mental Health Services Administration.

ready to move on? How cooperative will the client be in the specifics of planning, in setting goals and objectives?

Planning and Implementation

Given that engagement has been achieved and there is willingness and cooperation on the part of the client to move to the next level, the planned change process proceeds to goal setting and intervention (Kirst-Ashman & Hull, 2009):

1. Work with the client.
2. Prioritize problems (problem 1, problem 2, and so forth).
3. Translate problems into needs (problem 1 → need 1, problem 2 → need 2, etc.).
4. Identify alternatives, solutions, and evaluation plans for each need, at micro, mezzo, and macro system levels.
5. Consider the pros and cons of each alternative.
6. Identify and reinforce client strengths.
7. Establish goals and specify objectives.
8. Specify action steps; for each step, identify: Who? Will do what? By when? How will you measure success?
9. Formalize a contract.
10. Follow the plan (micro, mezzo, macro levels of implementation).
11. Monitor progress.
12. Revise plan, when necessary.
13. Complete plan to the greatest extent possible.

The planned change journey (Kirst-Ashman & Hull, 2009) moves on the path from assessment through to planning and implementation of that plan. The clinician works with the client, reinforcing engagement and continuing to apply the core conditions of warmth, empathy, and genuineness. Throughout, client strengths are emphasized. Problems are prioritized, then translated into needs so that the solutions can be identified. The level of intervention is evaluated for each need: micro, mezzo, or macro. The clinician identifies alternatives and proposes solutions. Pros and cons are reviewed for each option. Goals are then established, providing direction as to how to proceed. These are operationalized through specific objectives and action steps that are tied to each goal. Each action specifies who will do the task, what the task or action entails, and the timeline. Objectives need to be met for goals to be achieved.

During the implementation and intervention phase, the client and the worker carry out the action plan. As planned change proceeds, some goals and objectives may need to be revised, new ones added, and those with unanticipated negative consequences deleted. The worker should be mindful of how to elicit information from the client, using both closed-ended and open-ended questions aimed at assessing the client's feelings about the treatment experience. Closed-ended reach for "clearly defined answers" whereas open-ended questions reach for "the client's thoughts, ideas, and explanation for answers" (Kirst-Ashman & Hull, 2009, p. 67). The worker—an attentive listener—creates a zone of safety and encourages the client to feel free to elaborate and provide details.

An example of a closed-ended question is:
Where are you now on the Readiness Ruler?

Examples of open-ended questions are:

How would you describe your progress?
What has this experience been like for you?

The client's goals may include issues of abstinence, lifestyle improvements, and relapse prevention. Client history may be significant here. What has the client tried in the past? What does the client want and expect now? Is detoxification necessary? Should medication be provided? How cooperative and compliant with treatment has the client been in the past? (CSAT, 2006). Depending on the amount of substances used, age of first use, and earlier drug treatment history, clients are referred to long-term inpatient, short-term inpatient, intensive outpatient, or short-term outpatient treatment services. ATOD clients often have problems in addition to their substance abuse and may be in need of, for example, marriage or family therapy; anger management; or therapy for posttraumatic stress syndrome, for self-mutilation behaviors, or for deviant sexual behavior. Brokering and the referral of clients elsewhere can be best accomplished if the agency negotiates alliances with other treatment facilities, health clinics, emergency service providers, GED and vocational training centers, and the complete range of support groups. Practitioners are ethically bound to undertake only those goals that are commensurate with their competence and to refer clients who require services for which they are not qualified to deliver (NASW, 2008).

Agencies that provide logistical services, such as transportation and child care, to their clients may be better able to engage their clients than are agencies that do not provide such services. Because transportation is not an unusual problem for this population, substance abuse treatment agencies should have offices within a reasonable walking distance from public transportation. The agency should also offer treatment sessions on a variety of days and at different times so that clients can choose sessions that are convenient and make public transportation an easier option.

In addition to transportation problems, the lack of adequate child care can also present difficulties for clients. "Concerns about . . . accessing child care services discourage individuals from seeking treatment" (Rockhill, Green, & Newton-Curtis, 2008, p. 86). If these parents are working during the day and attending treatment during the evening, traditional child care is not usually an option because there are few centers that provide evening child care.

Progress measurement varies by goal and by client. For example, in this case illustration, Emma's consistent attendance in group could be one measure of success. But considering Emma's high degree of motivation, they opted for more direct measures overall of sobriety, parenting, and workplace. They chose to use Goal Attainment Scaling (GAS), an individualized instrument, to help to maintain Emma's motivation and to measure progress. Here, the GAS serves as a treatment plan or client–worker contract. The variables they chose are number of days choosing alternatives to alcohol, times per day at home that voice is raised in anger, and workplace schedule modifications. It is noted on the GAS matrix (see Table 7.1) that the client is beginning at the −2 level. The contract may be formal or informal, written, oral, or implicit. However, there is evidence that use of instruments such as GAS do motivate change (Kiresuk, Smith, & Cardillo, 1994).

The clinician "intercedes in an individual's internal, family, group, and/or environmental life" to achieve goals (NASW, 2005, p. 9). Social work scholars (Compton et al., 2005; Kirst-Ashman & Hull, 2009) and researchers in the ATOD field stress the importance of formulating clear goals to facilitate change (Marlatt, 1998; Miller & Rollnick, 1991). Goal setting is used to help clients implement changes in

CASE EXAMPLE 7.1: The Case of Emma

The clinician works with the client to prioritize the problems identified and to identify the levels of intervention appropriate for each need. For example, let us consider the case of a 40-year-old woman, Emma, a single parent with a four-year-old daughter, Becca, and an eight-year-old son, Jay. Emma was successful several years ago in undergoing treatment for alcohol dependence and has been abstinent from alcohol for five years. However, Emma began drinking again recently when her job became more demanding, her daughter Becca began to protest going to her usual day care center, and Jay became obstinate and irritable. Chaos in the household had become the norm, with Emma using rebukes and shouting as her primary method of discipline and parenting. Along with the need to resume her sobriety, Emma needs help in acquiring more effective parenting techniques around discipline. Emma's sobriety—which she and the social worker have agreed is need number one—was successfully maintained in the past with telephone support from Women for Sobriety, and she has agreed to resume this sobriety strategy. The parent–child relationship issues, which they have identified as need number two, may be best met in this example in a mezzo (group) setting, with a group facilitator conducting parenting education for women seeking sobriety. Last, the employment issue—need number three—is examined. The supervisor has been demanding more and more of Emma's time and has indicated that she has little interest in allowing Emma to adjust her schedule to attend to family and personal responsibilities. The clinician and Emma agree that the best option for now for addressing the employer challenge is to plan and role play a discussion with the supervisor. Both realize that the supervisor may not be willing to make any changes, so other interventions at the macro level may need to be considered, such as contacting the union. The overall goals are broken down into specific objectives and action steps. Finally, the contract is established: Who will do what? By when? How will progress be measured? The worker reinforces the client's strengths, and the belief that bonds them together is that the client will find success. The progress is monitored. Indeed, Emma has little success with seeking help from her supervisor. The decision finally is made to contact the trade union, and that revision is made to the contract.

TABLE 7.1: Example of Goal Attainment Scale Used with ATOD Client, Emma

Level of expected outcome	Objective 1: Number of days choosing alternatives to alcohol	Objective 2: Times per day at home that voice is raised in anger	Objective 3: Workplace schedule modifications
Rating			
Much more than expected (+2)	All 7 days per week	No longer raises voice in anger	Schedule is modified to allow a flexible schedule, with weekly changes allowed
More than expected (+1)	From 5 to 6 days per week	Raises voice in anger from 1 to 2 times per day	Schedule is modified to allow a flexible schedule, with monthly changes allowed
Most likely outcome (0)	From 3 to 4 days per week	Raises voice in anger from 3 to 4 times per day	Schedule is modified to allow four 10-hour workdays
Less than expected outcome (−1)	From 1 to 2 days per week	Raises voice in anger from 5 to 9 times per day	Schedule is inflexible but supervisor will consider occasional requests for changes
Much less than expected (−2)	Zero days per week	Raises voice in anger 10 times or more per day	Schedule is inflexible

thoughts, behaviors, and environments. Clear goals help to ensure that practitioners stay focused and do not wander into areas that are not germane to their clients' problems, and serve as criteria for evaluating the effectiveness of specific helping interventions. Goals also help practitioners and clients to monitor progress.

Standards of performance involve quality and accuracy (how well), quantity (how often), when (how soon), and may include duration (how long). Is the goal achieved if the client uses his or her old route home from work one day and stops by the dealer's house for a small pack of heroin but uses the new route the other four days of the work week? When should the client cease smoking altogether? The answers to goals should be built into the performance objective by the practitioner and the client.

Goals should be positive and stated in terms of gains rather than losses or deficits to enhance motivation and minimize negativity (Hepworth et al., 2006). For example, if a client states that his goal is: "I will no longer drink in the evening to help me sleep," the practitioner can help the client turn this into a positive goal statement such as: "During the next week, I will practice my meditation exercises in the evening, drink decaffeinated coffee at dinner, and take a soothing bath to help me sleep." The emphasis should be on what is to be gained rather than what is to be given up. When goals are positively stated, they focus on the desired outcome instead of the problem, fostering a sense of hope that the situation can be changed.

According to Miller and Rollnick (1991), it is better to acknowledge the client's own goals than to insist a priori that the client accept a particular goal such as total abstinence. It is far better for client movement that the goals of treatment be negotiated rather than prescribed. When working with individual clients who have or are affected by ATOD problems, the focus may involve intrapersonal subsystems (such as emotional dysregulation), as well as interaction with the social and physical environment (such as job loss and subsequent intersection with unemployment services) (Hepworth et al., 2006). Goals directed to individual clients focus on covert and overt behaviors. Examples can be changes in cognitive functioning (reducing the number of negative thoughts about self), changes in emotional functioning (reducing the intensity of depressing feelings), or behavioral changes (eliminating the use of cocaine). Goals may also be directed to interpersonal behaviors such as spending time with people who do not use cocaine. What are circumstances in which the client is expected to order ginger ale instead of a cocktail? When does the problem behavior most likely occur? Under what circumstances do negative thoughts relevant to the target problem appear? What routes should the client take to and from work to avoid the temptation to stop by the former drug dealer's apartment? All of these are illustrations of the circumstances in which performances specified in objectives are to be accomplished.

Making objectives explicit and operational from the beginning effectively reduces failure (Hepworth et al., 2006). Goals are usually general statements of intent that need to have the steps for their achievement clearly specified. The steps that lead to goal accomplishment are referred to as objectives. There are times when a client's goal is so clear and uncomplicated that it is synonymous with an objective. However, in many cases, goals must be translated into objectives. Failure for the worker, in consultation with the client, to facilitate defining how a goal can be accomplished contributes to lack of forward movement. Objectives address how a client can accomplish a goal. What should the client be doing and thinking? Each objective has actions that move the client closer to the goal. Vague objectives lead to unrealistic aspirations and to repeated shifts in direction. As noted previously, useful objectives are SMART—specific, measurable, attainable, realistic, and time specific (Whitten, 2005).

Clear objectives present clients with specific "word pictures" of the changes that are to occur in their behaviors and thoughts. Word pictures are adjectives and verbs that describe the desired change. Examples of such objectives are: "To walk for 20 minutes at least four days each week"; "Have only one drink once per day at meal time—for example, 4 ounces of red or white wine." The client and the practitioner must both be clear about the changes to be accomplished; they should be attainable by and realistic for the client, and should be stated in a way that is measurable. Frequently used time frames are by "the next session," "by the end of the week," "within three months," and "by the end of treatment."

If questions about what is expected arise, the language may be too vague or fuzzy and should be restated using more precise wording. Sometimes objectives must be revised to more elementary levels. In the example in the preceding paragraph, the effort to increase days sober may need to be measured instead with number of contacts made with Women for Sobriety.

There are going to be instances when practitioners do not agree with the goals clients propose. The client may wish to pursue moderate drinking when there are strong medical reasons for abstinence. Clients may also have nonmedical risks that are too great for them to continue use of other drugs despite their wish to simply cut back use, for example, loss of job, marital conflict, or risk of losing their children. In such situations, the practitioner should advise the client about the risks of following through with their presenting goal. Information from research on situations similar to the client's, considerable emotional support, and helping to identify alternatives that address the client's wants and needs all help the client shift to more feasible goals.

Throughout the journey the client and the social worker benefit from graphic representations that show movement and accentuate behavioral measurement. The treatment plan progress can be dipicted as a map of the journey, how the client moved from point A to point B to point C (see Figure 7.3). In this example, the client shows progress on the first goal and a setback on the second goal. Coupled with the GAS matrix and done with care, this map fosters rapport and motivation. Getting from A to B is facilitated by goals and objectives that specify both substance-related and other contextual factors. As with the example given in Table 7.1, the individual could have a goal of substance use moderation along with a goal associated with parenting education.

▼
▼
▼

Figure 7.3: Client Journey Map

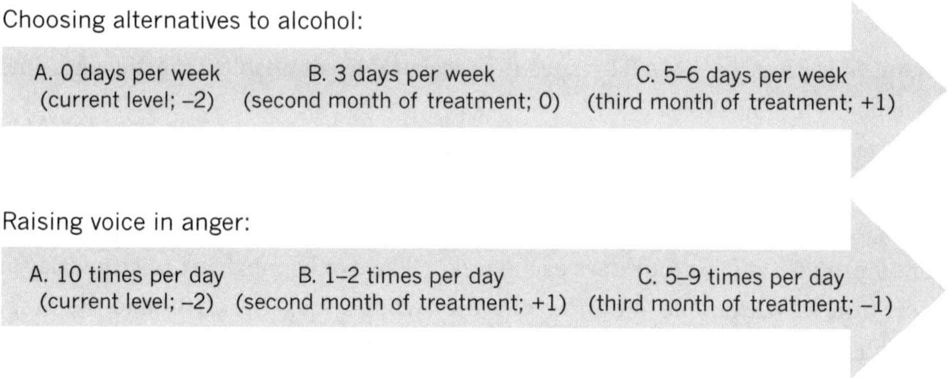

Choosing alternatives to alcohol:

A. 0 days per week   B. 3 days per week   C. 5–6 days per week
(current level; –2)   (second month of treatment; 0)   (third month of treatment; +1)

Raising voice in anger:

A. 10 times per day   B. 1–2 times per day   C. 5–9 times per day
(current level; –2)   (second month of treatment; +1)   (third month of treatment; –1)

The planned change contract is now complete and should be coupled with agreement on the part of both the worker and the client. Flexibility, however, is recommended: The contract should be "formal enough to clarify expectations but informal enough to let the worker respond flexibly to the client's changing needs or conditions" (Kirst-Ashman & Hull, 2009, p. 40). Progress is monitored, the plan is revised as necessary, and the plan is implemented through to its completion.

Counseling perspectives and theories are important here as well. The planned change model is, in essence, atheoretical. As such, the clinician applies the theoretical models appropriate to his or her training and style and to the needs of the client. Examples include cognitive–behavioral, humanistic, solution-focused, and social constructionist models.

Practitioners who view alcoholism as a progressive disease are likely to promote abstinence as the only acceptable goal. Those practitioners who view alcohol use as falling along a continuum with no clear dividing line might feel that a possible beneficial outcome would be controlled drinking. Harm reduction is yet another approach, meeting clients where they are and helping them to understand and minimize the risks involved in their behavior. Although harm reduction recognizes abstinence as an ideal outcome, it accepts alternatives that reduce harm (Marlatt, 1998). Practitioners must keep in mind that their particular theoretical view of ATOD abuse and dependence will, in general, influence the goal-setting process and implementation of the plan (Ksir, Hart, & Ray, 2008).

"No single treatment approach is appropriate for all individuals" (NASW, 2005, p. 18). Rather, effective practice requires "a variety of theoretical approaches and practical skills to plan and deliver a combination of interventions and supportive services during the course of treatment and recovery" (p. 19). Intervention strategies include counseling, medication, parenting instruction, vocational rehabilitation, and social and legal services. The worker should be knowledgeable about self-help and peer-support groups and navigating the complex network of services and resources, advocating for the client as needed.

Effective practice requires that the worker "strive to maintain knowledge of existing and emerging theories and interventions in addiction and the recovery process" (NASW, 2005, p. 28). Substance abuse treatment is regarded by many to be "stuck" in the past, often guided as much by dogma as by evidence. Current research findings and implications for clinical application should be studied to determine whether changes should be made in approaches to treatment, continuing to emphasize evidence-based practice confirmed by sound research.

Evaluation, Termination, and Follow-Up

The clinician moves from implementation into the final stages of evaluation, termination, and follow-up (Kirst-Ashman & Hull, 2009):

1. Review all that has transpired.
2. Review the extent to which each goal is achieved.
3. Identify any remaining issues.
4. Make a decision to either reassess the plan (and revise and endorse the plan) or to terminate.
5. Apply research principles and measure clinician and program accountability.
6. Assess client satisfaction.
7. Re-examine the client's situation after the intervention to monitor ongoing effects.

The journey of planned change does not end with the intervention. Rather, the planned change process culminates in the evaluation and termination of services, using research methods to determine the extent to which the planned change intervention has met the goals identified. Scientific rigor counters the offering of beliefs and opinions that may be based in bias or tradition, rather than in evidence of best practices. Likewise, the client, according to the transtheoretical stages of change model (Prochaska & DiClemente, 1982), is shifting from action to maintenance. In the maintenance stage, the clinician helps the client identify triggers for substance use and plan a course of action that overcomes those triggers.

Effective planned change includes evaluation and requires the "identification and use of appropriate tools to measure clinical outcomes and client satisfaction" (NASW, 2005, p. 25). The evaluation phase "includes a planned process of disengagement through which clients and workers may conclude their work together and say their goodbyes" (Compton et al., 2005, p. 75). "Ideally, the evaluation phase results in a clear, mutual understanding of the nature and extent of progress toward goal achievement, what and how the client-and-worker attempted to attain those goals, and a satisfactory conclusion to the process" (Compton et al., 2005, p. 75). Evaluation assists practitioners and clients in determining if a particular activity is yielding the intended results. In some cases "evaluation data reveal unexpected results that lead to major revisions in the service agreement" (Compton et al., 2005, p. 75). For example, with reference to Emma and the GAS matrix (see Table 7.1 and Figure 7.3), her movement on Objective 2—Times per day at home that voice is raised in anger—actually reverted to the minus 1 (−1) level. Emma revealed to the social worker that she believed her parenting challenges were in part because of her own history of trauma in her family of origin. She found herself reverting to an aggressive style used by her own parent, and acknowledged the need to address the early trauma in therapy. Thus, the intervention plan was amended to include psychotherapy with a social worker specializing in trauma work.

In the aftermath of evaluation, "the partners may modify the action plan, reformulate the problem definition, or perhaps revise goals, if necessary" (Compton et al., p. 75). Evaluation is used to reinforce goals and objectives, to redirect the focus of work, or to change various objectives.

Ideally, termination is planned, and it occurs as a natural consequence of achievement of goals. In that situation, the worker and client celebrate the achievements and solidify the client's ongoing plans. On the basis of evaluation results, "the client-and-worker may terminate service because they decide the goals have been accomplished, determine they are unlikely to be accomplished, or decide that another worker or agency may better serve the client" (Compton et al., 2005, pp. 75–76). If the plan has met success, celebrating the client's accomplishments often affords the client the courage to take the next step, to practice unfamiliar and uncomfortable behaviors. Sometimes, however, the termination is not ideal. The client may not return and may or may not provide any additional information about his or her decision and current status. In some situations, clients' appraisal of the situation is that they achieved their own aims, even though they did not comply with the plan. Sometimes clients fail to continue because of medical trauma, family crisis, or lack of funding.

According to the transtheoretical model, termination occurs when the client no longer perceives the threat of temptation. A more common and traditional theme is that of remaining "in recovery," rather than "cured" or "recovered," that is driven by theoretical orientation and by client views and beliefs. If relapse should occur, the clinician should encourage the client to renegotiate the stages of change, warning against catastrophic thinking that could plunge the client into despair.

The transition into maintenance and stabilization requires that triggers be identified, thus enabling the client to avoid specific people, places, or events that could pose a risk. This anticipates problems before they arise and establishes a "repertoire of alternative strategies" (CSAT, 1999). This assessment extends to family and friends as well. Some pose more of a risk than others. The professionals help the client find the "holes" in the "network of support" and to identify activities and reinforcers for the future. Will the client attend an ongoing community support group, participate in the church, hold a job? Perhaps the client will pursue a hobby or get involved with volunteer work.

The GAS strategy used as an example (see Table 7.1) includes aspects of engagement, assessment, planning, and evaluation. It provides a measurement matrix through which the client and the worker lay out the preferred aims and assign a quantitative correlate of the degree to which the aim is achieved. As such, the client's progress is systematically tracked, depicting the progress toward meeting the objectives of the helping relationship. This strategy is useful for a number of reasons. First, completing the GAS sheet facilitates clarification of goals for client and worker, and desired outcomes are clearly identified. Second, discussion of and reflection on the goal sheet as the work progresses can provide positive reinforcement, encouragement, and a demand for work. Third, data regarding goal completion can be easily tabulated using GAS. These data can be statistically analyzed to provide empirical evidence of client success or can identify areas of helping in which changes are required. As the service draws to a close, GAS helps the clinician and client carefully evaluate the achievement of objectives and their related goals and determine when and if the services to the client should be terminated.

Most human services providers are expected to follow the tenets of accountability. Social work practice emphasizes evidence-based practice, with the directive to "critically analyze, monitor, and evaluate interventions" (CSWE, 2008, standard 2.1.10[d]]) and "evaluate their own practice" (standard 2.1.6).

Follow-up is the "reexamination of a client's situation at some point after the intervention is completed"—"its purpose is to monitor its ongoing effects" (Kirst-Ashman & Hull, 2009, p. 42). Often agencies do not have time and funding to do this. Unfortunately, the lack of sufficient follow-up contributes to fragmentation for clients and to inadequate measurement of client service outcomes.

Client satisfaction can be measured in a variety of ways. Many agencies have a uniform instrument that is used at termination or as a follow-up, allowing for anonymity. An individual worker can ask a client for verbal feedback and might use a standard instrument as a way of structuring the feedback. However, in that case, anonymity is sacrificed and the client may not be frank in answering. In some cases, clients highly resistant to treatment may respond in a manner that reflects their opposition to what they view as social control (Kirst-Ashman & Hull, 2009), and the findings must be interpreted with that possibility in mind. In most cases, if a client chooses to participate, the client may not be highly resistant but, rather, displeased with the results.

Substance abuse is still regarded overall as a "chronic, relapsing disorder that may not resolve for months or even years" (NASW, 2005, p. 6). Relapses take their toll on clients, their families, and workers alike. Disappointment is part of any helping profession, but every clinician in this field will encounter the phenomenon of relapse and must be prepared with coping mechanisms (Tims, Leukefeld, & Platt, 2001). Moreover, clinicians must recognize the potential for vicarious suffering and compassion fatigue, sometimes termed "burnout" (Compton et al., 2005), and recognize as well the importance of worker self-care. As discussed, success is measured with attention to goals and objectives, but also with realization of the cyclical nature of change and the fact that the journey of planned change is not purely linear. The frustration experienced is well illustrated by a classroom vignette: In a field seminar taught by one of the chapter authors, a social work student was assigned to a field practicum in a child welfare agency. One of his clients was a man with a history of alcoholism. The student was armed with information, having studied substance abuse rather extensively. He had participated in classroom exercises that reviewed stories of relapse designed to inoculate learners to the realities of the work. He attended and learned about peer support groups in the community. Hoping to avoid the use of leverage in the form of mandated treatment, the student worked arduously to assemble a list of strategies tied to the client's apparent state of "pre-contemplation." The client failed to respond to the interventions offered. The student arrived at seminar, clearly agitated and needing support from his peers. His succinct and passionate remark well summarized his dismay: "This man is completely infuriating!" Faculty and agencies alike need to attend to the risks to the worker in a field that is filled with the potential for disappointment.

Summary

The showdown with substances appears so daunting that many surrender before they begin. It is utter humility, then, that one must bring while taking that first step on the thousand-mile journey. The clinician confirms for the traveler that the journey is indeed likely to be arduous, that one step forward is sometimes followed by two steps backward. Yet at the same time the clinician reassures the traveler, confirming that the journey's map is grounded in the best evidence available and that the clinician is a skilled planned-change tour guide. The planned change process is designed to serve the clinician and the client as they systematically navigate the journey, both of them fueled by the strengths orientation. It is a tool that is orderly yet allows for flexibility. With its clear guidelines, the planned change process provides a coherent and practical protocol that directs the helping process. Suitably applied, the process can result in realistic satisfaction for both client and worker and any others involved in or influenced by the journey.

Note

The authors wish to thank and recognize Patricia C. Dunn and Christine Boyle for their contribution to related chapters, which appear in the first edition of *Alcohol, Tobacco, and Other Drugs,* portions of which were used in this chapter.

References

American Psychiatric Association. (2000). *Diagnostic and statistical manual of mental disorders* (4th ed., text rev.). Washington, DC: Author.

Bigler, M. (2005). Harm reduction as a practice and prevention model for social work. *Journal of Baccalaureate Social Work, 10*(2), 69–86.

Bisman, C. (1994). *Social work practice: Theory and principles.* Pacific Grove, CA: Brooks/Cole.

Burman, S. (2004). Revisiting the agent of social control role: Implication for substance abuse treatment. *Journal of Social Work Practice, 18,* 197–210.

Center for Substance Abuse Treatment (CSAT). (1999). *Enhancing motivation for change in substance abuse treatment* (Treatment Improvement Protocol [TIP] Series, Number 35. DHHS Publication No. [SMA] 08–4212). Rockville, MD: Substance Abuse and Mental Health Services Administration.

Center for Substance Abuse Treatment. (2005). *Substance abuse treatment: Group therapy* (*Treatment Improvement Protocol [TIP] Series 41,* DHHS Publication No. [SMA] 05-3991). Rockville, MD: Substance Abuse and Mental Health Services Administration.

Center for Substance Abuse Treatment. (2006). *Substance abuse: Clinical issues in intensive outpatient treatment* (TIP Series 47, DHHS Publication No. [SMA] 06–4182). Rockville, MD: Substance Abuse and Mental Health Services Administration.

CNN. (2008, October 7). *Runner gets homeless on right track.* Retrieved December 29, 2008, from http://www.cnn.com/2008/LIVING/04/02/heroes.mahlum/index.html#cnnSTCText

Compton, B., Galaway, B., & Cournoyer, B. (2005). *Social work processes.* Belmont, CA: Brooks/Cole.

Council on Social Work Education. (2008). *Educational policy and accreditation standards.* Alexandria, VA: Author.

DiClemente, C. C., & Scott, C. W. (1997). Stages of change: Interactions with treatment compliance and involvement. In L. S. Onken, J. D. Blaine, & J. J. Boren (Eds.), *Beyond the therapeutic alliance: Keeping the drug-dependent individual in treatment* [Research Monograph 165] (pp. 181–206). Rockville, MD: National Institute on Drug Abuse.

Gibelman, M. (2004). *What social workers do* (2nd ed.). Washington, DC: NASW Press.

Glicken, D. (2005). *Improving the effectiveness of the helping professions: An evidence-based approach to practice.* Thousand Oaks, CA: Sage Publications.

Gordon, R. (2005). Harm reduction as paradigm: Is better than bad good enough? The origins of harm reduction. *Critical Public Health, 15*(3), 243–250.

Hepworth, D. H., Rooney, R. H., Dewberry-Rooney, G., Strom-Gottfried, K., & Larsen, J. A. (2006). *Direct social work practice: Theory and skills* (7th ed.). Belmont, CA: Brooks/Cole.

Kadushin, A., & Kadushin, G. (1997). *The social work interview: A guide for human service professionals* (4th ed.). New York: Columbia University Press.

Kiresuk, T. J., Smith, A., & Cardillo, J. E. (Eds.). (1994). *Goal attainment scaling: Applications, theory, and measurement.* Hillsdale, NJ: Lawrence Erlbaum.

Kirst-Ashman, K. K., & Hull, G. H. (2009). *Understanding generalist practice* (5th ed.). Belmont, CA: Thomson.

Ksir, C., Hart, C. L., & Ray, O. (2008). *Drugs, society, and human behavior* (12th ed.). New York: McGraw-Hill.

Marlatt, G. A. (Ed.). (1998). *Harm reduction: Pragmatic strategies for managing high-risk behaviors.* New York: Guilford Press.

Marlatt, G. A., Tucker, J. A., Donovan, D. M., & Vuchinich, R. E. (1997). Establishing and maintaining a therapeutic alliance with substance abuse patients: A cognitive therapy approach. In L. S. Onken, J. D. Blaine, & J. J. Boren (Eds.), *Beyond the therapeutic alliance: Keeping the drug-dependent individual in treatment* (Research Monograph 165, pp. 181–206). Rockville, MD: National Institute on Drug Abuse.

Miller, W. R., & Rollnick, S. (1991). *Motivational interviewing: Preparing people to change addictive behavior.* New York: Guilford Press.

Miller, W. R., & Tonigan, J. S. (1996). Assessing drinkers' motivations for change: The Stages of Change Readiness and Treatment Eagerness Scale (SOCRATES). *Psychology of Addictive Behaviors, 10*(2), 81–89.

National Association of Social Workers. (2001). *Standards for cultural competence in social work practice.* Washington, DC: Author.

National Association of Social Workers. (2005). *Standards for social work practice with clients with substance use disorders.* Washington, DC: Author.

National Association of Social Workers. (2008). *Code of ethics of the National Association of Social Workers.* Washington, DC: Author.

Newman, C. F. (1997). Establishing and maintaining a therapeutic alliance with substance abuse patients: A cognitive therapy approach. In L. S. Onken, J. D. Blaine, & J. J. Boren (Eds.), *Beyond the therapeutic alliance: Keeping the drug-dependent individual in treatment* (Research Monograph 165, pp. 181–206). Rockville, MD: National Institute on Drug Abuse.

Plionis, E. M., Bailey-Etta, B., & Manning, M. (2002). Implementing the generalist model in practice: Implications for curriculum and best practices. *Journal of Teaching in Social Work, 22*(3–4), 103–119.

Polcin, D. L. (2003). Rethinking confrontation in alcohol and drug treatment: Consideration of the clinical context. *Substance Use & Misuse, 38,* 165–184.

Polcin, D. L., Galloway, G. P., & Greenfield, T. K. (2006). Measuring confrontation during recovery from addiction. *Substance Use & Misuse, 41,* 369–392.

Prochaska, J. O., & DiClemente, C. C. (1982). Transtheoretical therapy: Toward a more integrative model of change. *Psychotherapy: Theory, Research, and Practice, 19,* 276–288.

Prochaska, J. O., Norcross, J. C., & DiClemente, C. C. (1994). *Changing for good.* New York: William Morrow.

Rockhill, A., Green, B. L., & Newton-Curtis, L. (2008). Accessing substance abuse treatment: Issues for parents involved with child welfare services. *Child Welfare, 87*(3), 63–93.

Saleebey, D. (1997). *The strengths perspective in social work practice* (2nd ed.). New York: Longman.

Saleebey, D. (2009). The strengths approach to practice. In D. Saleebey (Ed.), *The strengths perspective in social work practice* (5th ed., pp. 49–57). Boston: Pearson.

Stewart, C., & Koeske, G. F. (2005). Spiritual change in treatment of substance dependence. *Social Work & Christianity, 32*(4), 321–340.

Tims, F. M., Leukefeld, C. G., & Platt, J. J. (2001). *Relapse and recovery in addictions.* New Haven, CT: Yale University Press.

Wahab, S. (2005). Motivational interviewing and social work practice. *Journal of Social Work, 5,* 45–60.

Whitten, L. (2005). S.M.A.R.T. treatment planning. *NIDA Notes, 20*(1).

8

Assessment

Tools for Successful Navigation

of Planned Change

Ann A. Abbott

Screening for Possible ATOD Problems

The next phase in the journey through planned change is that of assessment. The client-in-situation is assessed with respect to micro, mezzo, and macro system levels, citing information about both client needs and client strengths. Simultaneously, the clinician is aware of aspects of diversity and how those aspects influence the assessment process.

As noted in chapter 7, much information can be garnered through the contact practitioners have with clients; however, significant pieces of information related to substance use and misuse often goes unsaid in those professional encounters. The ability and willingness on the part of consumers to share such information frequently depends on where they are in their journey of planned change. Self-awareness and the ability to share depend not only on the quality of the therapeutic relationship, but also on the client's anxiety, denial, and readiness to change.

For many workers dealing with individuals in the throes of change, and for the individuals themselves, the use of assessment instruments facilitates the sharing of information. This also may be the case for family members or significant others who are reluctant or unable to describe directly the substance-related behaviors they have witnessed with their family members or friends.

Brief instruments such as the Alcohol Use Disorders Identification Test (AUDIT), the shortened version of the Michigan Alcoholism Screening Test (MAST) (the SMAST), the MAST–G (geriatric version), or the CAGE are examples of instruments that may be useful, either by themselves or incorporated into a regular intake questionnaire; these and other relevant instruments will be discussed in more detail later in this chapter.

In the course of gathering information about the presenting problem, the practitioner may question the client directly about ATOD use. This can be done quite directly if it is tactful and non-accusatory—for example, if preceded by a comment that the practitioner has found that use of alcohol or other drugs may be a complication in problems such as the one the client is experiencing, and so the practitioner would find it helpful to explore this a little with the client. Quite frequently, the client is really not aware that his or her intake of ATOD is implicated in the problem with which he or she is struggling.

To launch into treatment of the marital problem, or sexual performance problem, or child abuse, or whatever, without this vital knowledge of the role of a concomitant ATOD problem will, in all probability, doom to failure treatment of the presenting problem—because nothing is being done to identify and change this vital component of the problem situation. In some cases, work on the ATOD problem could go on concurrently with work on the presenting problem—but, in many cases, the focus should shift to the ATOD problem to attempt to control it before any positive change can be expected to happen with the presenting problem. Some clients may refuse to admit that their ATOD use has anything to do with the presenting problem; the practitioner may then have to go ahead with attempting to help with, say, the presenting marital problem as a way of letting the client learn experientially that no progress can really be made on this as long as ATOD use is part of that problem.

Identifying the Problem

An important first step in the diagnostic assessment of any presenting client problem should be exploration of whether ATOD is a contributing or confounding factor in that problem. If an ATOD problem is identified, the practitioner next needs to assess whether its severity warrants referral to an ATOD-specialized resource, or whether the community agency practitioner can continue to work with the client toward its resolution. In the case of a co-occurring mental health problem, the practitioner needs to assess, or arrange for a mental health assessment, and treat or refer the client out for treatment of the co-occurring disorder.

Instrumentation for Identification and Screening of ATOD Problems and Assessment of Their Severity

A number of instruments have been designed for identifying ATOD problems. The ones suggested here, and summarized in Table 8.1, are those most commonly used by practitioners and those most easy to administer. For the most part, the instruments identified are simple screening tests that can be administered either by a clinical or non-clinical interviewer, or, in many cases, by the client (Nilssen & Cone, 1994). The list includes some instruments that are specific to alcohol, others that are designed to focus on drug use, some that address both, and some that were developed for use with specific populations.

Some assessment instruments focus on current quantity, frequency, and effect of substance use; other instruments put greater emphasis on a historical accounting. The historical approach, which can use either a calendar or summary format requesting day-by-day consumption information or a summary format requesting "typical" day usage, produces a developmental perspective. A quantity-frequency approach produces a more recent accounting of usage. Typically, the historical format involves more time to administer; the quantity-frequency approach is more time efficient. Recent studies indicate that both foci can be effective in providing reasonable appraisals of problematic consumption (Grant, Tonigan, & Miller, 1995).

The practitioner is reminded that the suggested tests are useful in identifying ATOD problems; however, they should be used with caution and typically in conjunction with other measures of assessment, including interviews with clients and significant others and, when appropriate, physical tests for substance use.

In additional to the instruments suggested here, the clinician is encouraged to search the resources of SAMHSA (http://www.samhsa.gov) for access to instruments that are available in the public domain and can be used at no cost.

Specific Tests for Identification of Alcohol-Related Problems

The three most commonly used instruments for identification of alcohol abuse are the CAGE, the MAST, and the AUDIT.

CAGE. The CAGE, developed by Ewing and Rouse (1970; see also, Ewing, 1984; Mayfield, McLeod, & Hall, 1974), is the most widely used test in clinical practice. The test, consisting of four questions aimed at identifying alcohol dependence, can be administered in one to two minutes. If clients respond affirmatively to two out of four questions, they are determined to be at risk of being alcohol

TABLE 8.1: Commonly Used Instruments for Screening and Assessing ATOD Problems

Test Name	Number of Items	Time Required (minutes)	Administration	Specific Focus or Group
CAGE	4	1–2	Social worker	Alcohol (could be revised for TOD)
T-ACE	4	1–2	Social worker	Variation of CAGE for pregnant women
TWEAK	5	1–2	Social worker	Variation of CAGE for pregnant women
MAST	25	3–4	Client	Lifelong drinking patterns
SMAST	13	3–4	Client	Shortened version of MAST
BMAST	10	3–4	Client	Shortened version of MAST
SASST	35	7–8	Client	Expanded version of MAST
AUDIT	10	3–4	Client	Early alcohol misuse warning signs
ASISA	14	4–5	Computer administrated	Combined CAGE and AUDIT
HSO	5	5–6	Client	Alcohol use and other health issues
HSI		5–6	Client or social worker	Alcohol use and other health issues
PDS	16	5–6	Social worker	Emphasis on frequency of alcohol use
HSS	9	5–6	Social worker	Alcohol use and other health issues
ACI	17 (CSC) 3 (MHQ)	10	Client or social worker	Alcohol use and general medical history
MAC	49	20	Social worker	Incorporated Into MMPI
DAST	10	3–4	Client	Drug use
DUSI	149	15	Client	Severity of alcohol and drug use
DLSI	4 sections	10	Social worker	Drug use
ASI		30 plus	Social worker	Overall substance abuse
SAPC	377	30 plus	Client	Overall substance abuse
SASSI	78	15–20	Client	Overall substance abuse (adolescent version available)
ADI	24	8–10	Client	For use with adolescents
CAST		2–4	Client	Children and adolescents in alcoholic families
DPDS	16	4–5	Client	Discomfort with partner's ATOD use

dependent, and further assessment is warranted. The four questions frame the acronym for this test:

C—Have you ever felt you should *Cut down* on your drinking?

A—Have people *Annoyed* you by criticizing your drinking?

G—Have you ever felt *Guilty* about your drinking?

E—*Eye Opener*: Have you ever had a drink first thing in the morning to steady your nerves or to get rid of a hangover?

(Although designed to assess alcohol use, by altering the content of the four CAGE questions, this instrument could be modified to assess the risk of tobacco and other drugs).

Of importance in selecting any instrument or test is the degree of sensitivity (its ability to correctly identify alcohol dependency) and specificity (its ability to correctly identify [or rule-out] problematic alcohol use). Studies of the CAGE produced sensitivity scores ranging from 60 percent to 95 percent and specificity scores ranging from 40 percent to 95 percent.

Some limitations of the CAGE revolve around the fact that it does not include specific questions about the frequency of alcohol use, the level of consumption, or information about episodes of heavy drinking, factors useful in identifying early stages of alcohol difficulties (Nilssen & Cone, 1994). Studies have found that although the CAGE provides "a substantial amount of information quickly ... more reliable and valid information can be obtained with the Short MAST [a shortened version of the MAST—the SMAST] or AUDIT measures, either of which requires an additional 1 to 2 minutes to administer" (Hays, Merz, & Nicholas, 1995, p. 277). A brief description of these two alternatives follows. However, before launching into a description of the MAST and the AUDIT, it is important to mention several variations of the CAGE—the CAGE–AID (Adapted to Include Drugs) (Brown & Rounds, 1995) and the TWEAK (a special instrument designed for use with pregnant women) (Russell et al., 1991).

The CAGE–AID expands the CAGE to include drug use in addition to alcohol use:

1. Have you felt you ought to cut down on your drinking or drug use?
2. Have people annoyed you by criticizing your drinking or drug use?
3. Have you ever felt bad or guilty about your drinking or drug use?
4. Have you ever had a drink or used drugs first thing in the morning to steady your nerves, get rid of a hangover, or get the day started? (Brown & Rounds, 1995)

TWEAK is a screening tool for identifying pregnant women with alcohol problems. The acronym stands for

T—Tolerance: How many drinks can you hold?

W—Have close friends or relatives Worried or complained about your drinking in the past?

E—Eye-Opener: Do you sometimes take a drink in the morning?

A—Amnesia: Has a friend or family member ever told you about things you said or did while you were drinking that you could not remember?

K(c)—Do you sometimes feel the need to Cut Down on your drinking?

(Russell et al., 1991)

On the tolerance question, two points are given if a woman reports that she can consume more than five drinks without falling asleep or passing out. A positive response to the worry question yields two points, and positive responses to the last three questions yield one point each. A score of two signals an at-risk drinker. TWEAK has been found to be highly sensitive in identifying women who are at-risk drinkers.

MAST. The second most commonly used instrument, the MAST (Michigan Alcoholism Screening Test) developed by Selzer (1971), consists of 25 questions designed for self-appraisal of drinking habits (Nilssen & Cone, 1994). In addition to questions regarding specific drinking habits are ones related to a range of problems associated with heavy drinking, such as work-related, family, and social difficulties. A score of seven or more is viewed as indicative of a serious drinking problem; a score of five or six indicates a borderline situation; and a score of four or less indicates a nonproblematic situation. Identified sensitivity scores for the MAST range from 86 percent to 96 percent, and specificity scores from 81 percent to 95 percent (Nilssen & Cone, 1994).

A major limitation of the MAST stems from the wording of the questions, which tends to cause respondents to focus on lifetime drinking patterns rather than current alcohol-related problems. This focus may restrict the ability of the MAST to detect early symptoms of emerging alcohol dependence (Magruder-Habib, Durand, & Frey, 1991). Like the CAGE, the MAST fails to address issues of frequency of drinking, quantity of drinking, and, more specifically, binge drinking (Fleming, 1993). They both tend to focus on lifelong drinking patterns, with little emphasis on recent behavior. However, as noted previously (Hays et al., 1995), investigators have found the MAST to be more reliable, with stronger validity than the CAGE.

Several variations of the MAST should be mentioned, including the SMAST. (See Appendix 8.1 for a copy of the SMAST.) These variations include, but are not restricted to, the BMAST (Brief MAST), comprising 10 selected MAST questions (Pokorny, Miller, & Kaplan, 1972); the SMAST, comprising 13 selected MAST questions (Selzer, Vinokur, & Van Rooijen, 1975; also see Fisher, 2008); and the SAAST (Self-Administered Alcohol Screening Test), comprising 35 items consisting of the 25 MAST items plus 10 additional items (Swenson & Morse, 1975). These variations were developed in response to noted shortcomings of the MAST, coupled with testing needs of specific populations.

AUDIT. Unlike the CAGE and the MAST, which cannot differentiate harmful alcohol use or other early warning signs, the AUDIT, developed by a collaborative project sponsored by the World Health Organization (WHO) (Babor, de la Fuente, Saunders, & Grant, 1989; Saunders & Aasland, 1987; Saunders, Aasland, Amundsen, & Grant, 1993; Saunders, Aasland, Babor, de la Fuente, & Grant, 1993), and the third most frequently used alcohol assessment instrument, can be helpful in identifying early warning signs of alcohol dependence (Babor & Grant, 1989). It was designed to assess alcohol use and alcohol-related problems occurring over the previous 12 months as well as over a lifetime. In addition, the AUDIT was developed from a six-country multi-cultural WHO project and tested on multi-cultural samples, a factor that makes this instrument particularly appealing for use with the diverse populations with which practitioners tend to work and contributes to the global reach of social work practice. (See Appendix 8.2 for a copy of the AUDIT.)

Responses to the 10-item AUDIT questionnaire are scored from 0 to 4, with a maximum total score of 40. (Note: Chan [1993] recommends that nine out of 10 items be scored 0–4 and the 10th item scored 0–5, with a maximum score of 41.) In either version, a score of 8 or greater indicates problem drinking and the need for a more in-depth assessment. Research has reconfirmed the suitability of a cutoff score of 8 for maximum discrimination between individuals with alcohol-related problems and those without (Conigrave, Hall, & Saunders, 1995). Overall AUDIT sensitivity scores of 92 percent and specificity scores of 93 percent to 94 percent have been identified (Babor & Grant, 1989; Saunders, Aasland, Babor, et al., 1993), both of which indicate satisfactory sophistication of the AUDIT in differentiating alcohol-related difficulties.

A criticism of both the CAGE and the MAST—their inability to detect emerging or less severe drinking problems—has been addressed by the AUDIT. Its target is the detection of problem drinkers at "the less severe end of the spectrum, rather than . . . persons with established dependence or alcoholism. [In addition] it places considerable emphasis on hazardous consumption and frequency of intoxication compared with drinking behavior and adverse consequences" (Saunders, Aasland, Babor, et al., 1993, p. 799).

The 10 items of the AUDIT are such that they can be embedded in a general health survey, thereby, disguising their true intent. It should be noted, however, that although the embedding of AUDIT items within larger questionnaires may facilitate more accurate information, their predictive validity under such circumstances has yet to be sufficiently tested.

Other Testing Alternatives

The CAGE, MAST, AUDIT, or some variation of these three most frequently used tests, may be appropriate in the majority of initial screening situations. For other situations, additional alternatives, such as the following, may prove useful.

ASISA. The Alcohol Screening Instrument for Self-Assessment, which combines the CAGE and the AUDIT into a composite instrument designed for computer administration (Rathbun, 1993), is a useful alternative for reaching a large number of individuals in a relatively labor-free context. It by no means substitutes for an in-depth evaluation, but it offers a mechanism for assessing the overall alcohol use status of a pool of individuals, such as a university or high school community.

HSQ. The Health Survey Questionnaire uses a quantity–frequency scale focused on assessing consumption during the previous seven days (Wallace & Haines, 1985). It also contains questions about four other areas of lifestyle—smoking, exercise, dieting, and weight. In addition to specific questions about quantity and frequency related to alcohol use, it incorporates the four questions that constitute the CAGE (Mayfield et al., 1974). Because it is self-administered, Wallace and Haines (1985) found the HSQ to be much easier to administer than a detailed history interview. However, they noted that its usefulness is dependent on the accuracy of the answers given.

In a later study involving larger samples, Cutler, Wallace, and Haines (1988) compared the use of the HSQ with a Health Survey Interview (HSI), the latter being a detailed interview developed specifically for their study. In comparing the two formats, Cutler and colleagues found individual agreement between the HSQ and the HSI to be poor, but on a sample-wide basis the measures were comparable. For women, the percentages of excessive drinkers were comparable (2.7 percent for HSQ compared with 2.9 percent for HSI); however, for men, greater disparity was noted (7.6 percent for HSQ compared with 11.7 percent for HSI). On the whole, the HSQ tended to underestimate consumption or to generate a more conservative estimate of consumption. The HSQ was found to be effective if the definition for excessive drinking was expanded to include not only those who indicated a heightened level of consumption, but also those who expressed concern about their drinking.

In addition, it was found that indication of cigarette smoking was an important additional determinant of excessive drinking. Using the modifications mentioned in the preceding paragraph, overall, the HSQ was found to be a fairly effective instrument for detecting excessive drinkers (and smokers). It is economical, easy to oversee, and applicable to a wide variety of patients in a wide range of settings.

PDS. The Problem Drinking Scale (Vaillant, 1980) incorporates both physiological (for example, hospital, clinic, or AA visit; morning tremors or drinking; tardiness or sick leave) and sociological (for example, marital problems, multiple job losses) components in defining or identifying alcohol-related problems. Scoring on four or more out of 16 problems indicates problem drinking or alcohol dependence. In many ways, the PDS is similar to the MAST; however, the PDS puts greater emphasis on frequency of the problem than does the MAST.

HSS. One alternative is the nine-question "life style" Health Screening Survey (Fleming & Barry, 1991), which focuses on the previous three months by asking questions about both use of three types of alcohol (beer and wine coolers, wine, hard liquor) and emerging problem drinking patterns. HSS focuses not only on recent drinking patterns and experiences, but also on health-related behaviors, including exercise, smoking, and weight control (National Institute on Alcohol Abuse and Alcoholism, 1993).

The HSS is similar in format to the HSI mentioned earlier. It examines overall health risks but disguises the focus on alcohol use. The HSS has been found to be particularly useful in primary care settings, including mental health facilities.

ACI. Another useful scale, which includes both substance use and physical health components, is the Alcohol Clinical Index (Skinner & Holt, 1987; Skinner, Holt, Sheu, & Israel, 1986). The ACI consists of two components: a 17-item Clinical Signs Checklist (CSC) and a 13-item Medical History Questionnaire (MHQ). The former is designed to elicit information about a number of physical characteristics that are found to be present to a greater extent among alcohol-dependent individuals than among nondependent individuals. The medical history portion contains items related to alcohol use that cannot readily be recognized as such by clients completing the scale. Sensitivity and specificity scores for both portions of the ACI fell between 88 percent and 97 percent, supporting its value as a screening instrument (Skinner & Holt, 1987; Skinner et al., 1986). Later research on the ACI (Alterman, Gelfand, & Sweeney, 1992) raised some questions about the ability of the ACI to sufficiently differentiate between alcohol dependent and nondependent individuals. This latter research found greater merit in the use of the MHQ portion than the CSC and strongly recommended the use of the MHQ in conjunction with the CAGE and the MAST.

MAC. It is not surprising that researchers have developed subscales for detecting alcohol dependence within the most frequently administered personality test—the Minnesota Multiphasic Personality Inventory, or the MMPI (Hathaway & McKinley, 1951). Of the six identified MMPI-based subscales for detecting alcohol dependence, the most well known is the 49-item MacAndrew Alcoholism Scale, or the MAC (MacAndrew, 1965). The items address substance abuse indirectly by identifying areas of personal maladjustment frequently common among substance users: sleeping difficulties, eating disturbances, and sexual inadequacies (Weinstein & Slaght, 1995).

Preng and Clopton (1986) described the findings from many studies designed to examine the usefulness of the MAC in differentiating between alcohol-dependent and nondependent individuals. They concluded that, although many researchers support the MAC's ability to discriminate between the two, additional studies need to be undertaken with the intent of clarifying the extent to which the MAC is truly able to detect problematic alcohol use.

As noted earlier, other MMPI variations for the detection of substance dependence have been developed. For example, Conley and Kammeier (1980) identified seven MMPI items that appear useful in the detection of alcohol dependence. Another variation developed by Hoffman, Lumry, Harrison, and Lessard (1984) contains 13 MMPI items, four of which are also contained in the seven-item Conley and Kammeier (1980) scale.

These latter two scales are not only shorter and easier to administer than the MAC, but also were derived using normal populations. The MAC, however, was developed using non-alcohol-dependent psychiatric outpatients and alcohol-dependent outpatients and appears to be more effective for those populations than for discriminating between alcohol-dependent and nondependent individuals within a normal population. MacAndrew (1981), however, noted that the MAC can accurately detect alcohol problems before the onset of psychiatric difficulties, but not necessarily alcohol dependence following the onset of psychiatric problems.

It is important to note that men and women frequently score differently on the MAC; however, if separate gender-based cut-off scores are used, the MAC is able to differentiate between both male and female alcohol-dependent and their nondependent counterparts (Conley & Kammeier, 1980; Svanum, Levitt, & McAdoo, 1982).

Overall, Hoffman and colleagues (1984) found the following specificity rates for the MAC: 70 for men and 81 for women, and sensitivity rates of 82 for men and 66 for women. They raise serious concern about its low rate of sensitivity for women. Specificity rates for the Conley and Kammeier (1980) and the Hoffman Scale (Hoffman et al., 1984) exceeded 85 for both men and women, and sensitivity rates for both exceeded 90, thus adding support for the use of these two shorter MMPI-based scales.

Specific Tests for the Identification of Drug-Related Problems

Instruments for the identification of drug problems are less prevalent and less sophisticated than those for the identification of alcohol problems. In part, this may be because of a greater reliance on the use of tests designed to detect physical evidence of drug use. However, some quick tools akin to those used for identification of alcohol problems are available.

DAST. Like the MAST, the DAST (Drug Abuse Screening Test) (Skinner, 1982b, 1984) is a 20-item self-administered inventory designed to identify problems related to drug abuse. A review of the literature reveals limited research involving the DAST; overall sensitivity scores of 85 percent were reported (Gavin, Ross, & Skinner, 1989); alpha coefficients range from .88 (Saltstone, Halliwell, & Hayslip, 1994) to .92 (Skinner, 1982b).

DUSI. The Drug Use Screening Inventory (Tarter, 1990; Tarter, Laird, Bukstein, & Kaminer, 1992) was designed to examine the severity of alcohol and drug use by quantifying the severity of disturbance or the consequences of substance usage. The DUSI measures disturbance within 10 domains: substance use, psychiatric disorder, health status, behavior problems, peer relations, social competence, family, school, work, and leisure. The DUSI, which can be self-administered, consists of 149 yes–no items. Findings indicate that the scale has adequate validity, reliability, and discriminatory ability (specificity and sensitivity).

DLSI. The Drug Lifestyle Screening Inventory (Walters, 1994, 1995) uses measures of four behavioral dimensions associated with drug use (irresponsibility or pseudo-responsibility, stress or coping imbalance, interpersonal triviality, and social rule breaking or bending) to validate serious drug misuse. Adequate inter-rater reliability, internal consistency, and concurrent validity have been reported (Walters, 1995); however, predictive validity remains uncertain.

ASI. The Addiction Severity Index (Carson-Dewitt, 2001; McLellan, Luborsky, Woody, & O'Brien, 1980) examines the client's use of both drugs and alcohol. The ASI does not rely on self-reports; rather, it is administered by professionals and takes at least 30 minutes to administer. A detailed description of the ASI is presented in the *Encyclopedia of Drugs, Alcohol, and Addictive Behavior* (Carson-Dewitt, 2001). The ASI has been modified for use with a variety of clients, many examples of which are available on the Internet.

SAPC. The Substance Abuse Problem Checklist (Carroll, 1984) is another useful self-administered screening instrument (Fisher, 2008). The 377 items included in the instrument represent eight different problem categories: mental and physical health problems, personality problems, social and family relationship problems, job-related problems, legal problems, spiritual or religious conflicts, motivation for treatment issues, and use of leisure-time activities. Collectively these items facilitate comprehensive assessment and enhance the development of more client-appropriate treatment initiatives. The specific approach reflects the orientation of AA and Narcotics Anonymous (NA) toward client involvement and responsibility. The SAPC has been found to have high levels of reliability and is easy to administer.

SASSI. The Substance Abuse Subtle Screening Inventory (Miller, 1983) contains 52 true–false items designed to assess chemical dependency. The items, which are independent of key demographic variables such as age and socioeconomic status, generate five scales: Obvious Attitudes (OAT), Subtle Abuse (SAT), Denial (DEN), Personal-Family (FAM), and Alcohol/Drug Preference (ALD) (Cooper & Robinson, 1987). Miller's studies reported sensitivity (ability to correctly identify substance abusers) ranging from 89 percent to 97 percent and specificity (ability to correctly identify, or rule out, nonabusers) of 90 percent to 95 percent (Miller, 1983). Typically, the SASSI is completed by the client. A later factor analysis of items reconfirmed its strength as an assessment alternative (Gray, 2001). A study by the SASSI Institute (2001) also confirmed its relevance as an assessment instrument for adolescents (SASSI–A2) 12 to 18 years old (Fisher, 2008).

Special Populations

Specific mention should be made of the numerous variations or adaptations to the earlier mentioned scales for use with special populations. For example, the ASISA (Rathbun, 1993), based on a combination of the CAGE and the AUDIT, was developed specifically for members of the University of Michigan community to examine their own drinking patterns via computerized format. A version of the DUSI was developed specifically for use with adolescents (Kirisci, Mezzich, & Tarter, 1995; Tarter, Mezzich, Kirisci, & Kaczynski, 1994).

In addition, a number of scales were developed with specific populations in mind. For example, the Adolescent Drinking Inventory, or ADI (Harrell, Sowder, & Kapsak, 1988; Harrell & Wirtz, 1989), the Personal Experience Screen Questionnaire, or PESQ (Winters, 1988), the Rutgers Alcohol Problem Index, or RAPI (White & Labouvie, 1989), the Perceived Benefits Scale, a perceived-benefit-of-drinking scale (Petchers & Singer, 1987; Petchers, Singer, Angelotta, & Chow, 1988) are but a few of the scales developed specifically for adolescents.

CAST. The Children of Alcoholics Screening Test (Jones, 1982) was developed with the intent of identifying children and adolescents living in families with members who are alcohol dependent. The test, which can be self-administered, asks about respondents' perceptions of, experiences with, reactions to, and concerns about family drinking. It also can be reframed to assess family drug use. The test has been useful in identifying the children of alcohol- and other drug-dependent parents.

DPDS. The Drinker's Partner Distress Scale (Crisp & Barber, 1995) is an example of an assessment instrument developed to measure level of discomfort with a partner's drinking and drug use. It encourages assessment and feedback from significant others in the user's life and can also be used to illustrate to the user the amount of distress his or her substance use is causing. All of the earlier mentioned scales are useful tools in aiding the process of assessment. Their value is only as great as their validity, their reliability, the truthfulness of the respondent, the respondent's ability to provide accurate information, and the reviewer's ability to evaluate and interpret. The skill of the practitioner comes into play in selecting the instruments, and in his or her ability to interpret the findings and to use them in developing the most effective avenues of intervention.

The Process of Assessment with an ATOD Problem

Because a book like this must attempt to offer an orderly presentation, we are focusing in this chapter on the assessment process. We do not want, however, to create the false impression that assessment is a one-time event—that early in the case the practitioner conducts a diagnostic assessment and then moves away from this completely to other processes. In actuality, like the engagement process addressed in the previous chapter, and like goal setting, contracting, and the other processes, assessment takes place over the life of the case (see chapter 7). Assessment may indeed be emphasized more in beginning contacts with the client, but throughout the relationship the practitioner is modifying the early assessment on the basis of new information and the client's response to intervention.

Beginning practitioners are often overly focused on learning intervention techniques, as if that were the essence of practice skill, or as if intervention techniques have a magical power of their own. This leads to "applying" intervention techniques learned from a book or in a classroom in a rigid, non-individualized, and not specifically targeted way. The result is often disappointment and confusion for both practitioner and client.

To the contrary, the intervention must be solidly based on an understanding of the factors involved in the problem, and therefore on those factors that are both changeable and need to be changed to resolve or ameliorate the problem. In short, accurate ongoing assessment is imperative for successful intervention. This may seem like a self-evident truism, and indeed it is. It would seem obvious that wildly flailing about, trying one unfocused intervention technique after another without a fundamental understanding of the problematic situation one is trying to change, has little chance of success. There is another sense in which the assessment process is crucially important. Assessment is indeed an early intervention—the first stage in actual intervention—in that it is designed to engage the client in examining, with the social worker, what his or her problem is all about. The assessment provides the client with some needed emotional distance from the problem, and thus some degree of objectivity in thinking about it and how to resolve it, rather than a panicky sense of being confused, guilty, defensive, and overwhelmed. The way in which the client is involved in the assessment also sends the message that client and practitioner are expected to be partners, and that the client has an important and coequal responsibility in the problem-solving effort. If ATOD dependence has been identified, either as the presenting problem itself, or as a factor in some other presenting problem, the assessment process involves the client in thinking about triggers for his or her ATOD use, negative influences leading to ATOD abuse, and possible resources for help. By engaging with the worker in the process of assessment, the client is thereby actually beginning the stage of what Prochaska, Norcross, and DiClemente (1994) called "contemplation" of his or her ATOD abuse, shifting the balance toward "motivation" to do something about it.

The Purpose of Assessment

There are five major purposes for the assessment process:

1. To help the practitioner *and the client* to understand as fully as is possible the nature of the ATOD problem (given the time available and whatever constraints may exist in the context in which client and practitioner are meeting). They cannot work together effectively on trying to resolve the problem unless and until they have some understanding of what it is they are attempting to change.
2. To help the practitioner *and the client* to recognize and to evaluate the role that intra-psychic, interpersonal, and environmental or situational factors may be playing in continuing or exacerbating the ATOD problem, or whether any of these factors might actually be resources in the struggle for sobriety.

3. To help the practitioner *and the client* to make the best decisions about matching the intervention to the needs of this unique client and his or her life situation.

4. To help the practitioner *and the client* to identify the client's unique triggers for ATOD abuse, as an early start for later relapse prevention planning.

5. To provide the practitioner *and the client* the baseline necessary to later determine the outcome of treatment, that is, whether or not treatment has been successful.

Note that the purpose of assessment is not to identify "the" cause of the ATOD problem. Practitioners new to the ATOD field sometimes buy into the pop-psychology myth that there is one unitary, underlying factor in the problem, and that sobriety depends on discovering what that factor is. To the contrary, an ATOD problem usually comes about, over time, growing out of a variety of interrelated factors. Even if one underlying incident, or predisposition, or other factor does exist, it is probably buried in the mists of time and is inaccessible to easy immediate recall. Furthermore, even if such a factor could be identified, its discovery by no means automatically guarantees resolution of the problem—that is, knowing the ultimate cause of something does not mean the person necessarily can do anything about it. It is important that the practitioner not waste his or her (and the client's!) valuable energy, time, and possibly money in fruitless searches for the one factor or personality "trait" responsible for the problem. The focus must remain squarely on understanding the nature of the problem and doing something about it in the here and now. Many times trauma plays a significant role. When someone is haunted by memories of sexual or combat trauma or abuse, the worker has to help the client acknowledge the trauma that is in the person's awareness and yet not allow him or her to use the trauma as justification for continuing use.

The Sequential Nature of Assessment

Assessment can be divided into a series of substages. As noted earlier, the initial stage is identifying whether an ATOD problem exists—what is called *screening*. If such a problem is identified, then practitioner and client must assess whether its severity, duration, and medical, psychiatric, legal, or other complications are such that treatment in a specialized resource should be a priority. Although a single-scale instrument is often used for screening, multi-scale instruments are more useful for assessment of where treatment should be obtained.

If the practitioner decides to continue with treatment of the ATOD problem rather than refer the client to a specialized resource, detailed information about ATOD usage must be obtained. The kind of substances used is obviously important. In this connection, it should be noted that people who abuse alcohol or use street drugs are often also heavy tobacco users. The practitioner then needs to assess the level of use, the pattern of use, and the history of use. The level of use has to do with the amounts of the substance used (at different times; this may mean day to day, over a week, over a month) and how this use may differ from past usage. The pattern of use may be related but different: Is the client a "binge" user, or does he or she need a steady supply? In this connection, it should be noted that people who drink alcohol to excess but spaced out over the course of the day are less likely to become severely intoxicated than people who consume several drinks in rapid succession. The client who does not experience severe intoxication may be more likely to sincerely deny the problem, because he or she does not get as visibly drunk (although the client may be taking in as much of the substance as the person with the alternate pattern). The pattern of use relates also to what the client and the practitioner, together, can identify as situations, emotions, or experiences that trigger ATOD use. The tobacco user, for example, can frequently identify needing a cigarette in combination with coffee, or after a meal. Or a client may feel the need for a drink when feeling anger that he or she cannot express appropriately to the marital partner or boss, or when self-conscious in a social situation, or just when habitually stopping off at a neighborhood bar with coworkers after work. The cocaine or crack user may "hang out" with other users.

The history of ATOD use elicits information about the duration of the problem and whether the client has tried to stop or curtail usage in the past and with what results. The client's presence in the practitioner's office now is obviously evidence that these past attempts at sobriety did not work, and the client is probably feeling helpless and inadequate because of these past failures. It is important to help the client to see that, although he or she did not accomplish everything that he or she hoped for, stopping or curtailing usage for even a short time was a partial success rather than a total failure. Client and practitioner can now gain valuable information about what piece of it worked at the time, and what were the triggers that led to relapse.

In terms of history, it is useful for the client to look at the ATOD history of family members, because an active hypothesis in the field involves genetic predisposition to alcohol dependence. This may be useful information especially for the client who perceives his or her ATOD problem as proof of weak character.

Some of the assessment instruments previously described are also useful in gathering a historical accounting of ATOD usage. The ASI (McLellan et al., 1980) and the DUSI (Tarter, 1990) both include detailed questions about the frequency and intensity of drug and alcohol use. In addition to focusing on quantity of intake or use, the DAST (Skinner, 1982b, 1984) provides a detailed history of the consequences related to drug misuse. Several other scales use a retrospective focus interview (Grant et al., 1995) designed to provide a useful historical accounting. Some examples include the Lifetime Drinking History (LDH) (Skinner, 1982a, 1984); the Comprehensive Drinker Profile (CDP) (Marlatt & Miller, 1984); the Time-Line Follow-Back Interview (TLFB) (Sobell & Sobell, 1992); the Alcohol Use Inventory (AUI) (Horn, Wanberg, & Foster, 1983); and the Alcohol Dependence Scale (ADS) (Skinner, 1984; Skinner & Allen, 1982; Skinner & Horn, 1984). The CDP and the TLFB examine the developmental phases of a person's drinking career; the AUI, ADS, and LDH all measure the severity of impairment related to increased substance use and the development of dependency. In addition, the MHQ (Skinner & Holt, 1987; Skinner et al., 1986) portion of the ACI is useful for eliciting overall health information.

The majority of scales do not include questions about smoking and cigarette use. Thus, additional questions about smoking should also be included, in conjunction with the instruments described earlier. One example is the Fagerström Test for Nicotine Dependence (Heatherton, Kozlowski, Frecker, & Fagerström, 1991).

Assessing the consequences of ATOD use is an important part of the assessment. Although this is also addressed later in our discussion of the "three dimensions" of assessment, we can note here in the context of assessment of the ATOD problem itself that information is needed about what consequences—positive and negative—the client has experienced as a result of ATOD use. What is the result of ATOD use? What is the client facing in giving up using? What positive results does the client get from ATOD use?

It is important that the practitioner not gloss over the positive results or derogate them. They indeed are positive results; otherwise it is likely that the client would not use ATOD. It is important to note that some users are overtly self-destructive, in that they indeed are provoking a destructive process because of some perhaps unconscious wish to punish oneself. Although many traditional addictions counselors like to believe so, ignoring some profound wound, for example, a history of trauma, does not work when that person cannot imagine a life without this self-deprecating, harmful process. What is facing the client is his or her giving up these positive consequences, and that seems, to the client, to be a great deal to give up.

The worker needs to sensitively recognize and respect this perception of the client, because it indeed is "true." After doing so, the practitioner then needs to help the client move on to looking at the negative consequences of ATOD use. It is important that the practitioner at this stage not preach, not scold, not imply in any way that the client is a stupid or inadequate person for not appreciating how bad the ATOD is for him or her. It is equally important that the practitioner lead the client to identify the negative consequences of the ATOD use. Has the ATOD usage brought about, or exacerbated, marital or other family problems, or sexual problems, or problems at work, or financial problems, or legal problems, or medical problems, or psychiatric problems? If the client has experienced profound wounds, has the ATOD use solved them? The purpose of this part of the assessment is not only to supply needed information, but also to help tip the balance for the client from contemplation (or, perhaps, even denial) toward the decision to try to change.

The Multidimensional Nature of Assessment

Now that an ATOD problem has been located—its general "shape" identified in terms of its severity, duration, drug(s) of choice; its medical, psychiatric, and legal complications ascertained; and the decision made not to refer to another resource—the practitioner and client must undertake a more detailed assessment of the factors in the client's life that either are contributing to ATOD dependence or might be resources for recovery.

Because the client's life situation is multi-dimensional, this assessment must also be multi-dimensional. In chapter 2, we discussed the dangers of the practitioner's narrowing his or her view to the tenets of some particular theory. This caveat applies to assessment as well as to intervention. The practitioner should not look only for material highlighted in a favorite theory, because this may result in ignoring other data that may be more relevant and important for accurate understanding of the problem and, thus, for effective intervention.

In the beginning years of ATOD treatment programs, the approach in use was this kind of "univariate" focus, meaning that it concentrated on single biological or psychological or environmental factors, and gave little weight to the others. The dominance of the medical model in all forms of psychotherapy also led to an almost exclusive concern with the psychology of the individual client, with the client's material situation, family, and work and social environment perceived more vaguely as something "out there." More recently, the ATOD field has shifted to a multivariate or bio-psycho-social-cultural-spiritual perspective, which recognizes the interplay of all of these factors in the development of the ATOD problem and in its resolution.

Social workers may well wonder what is new about this "biopsychosocialculturalspiritual" viewpoint, because social work has always emphasized an ecological perspective on person-in-situation. This social work perspective means seeing the case as a total "field of action where the client is in transaction with a variety of social and physical environments—with all of these being important sources of information" (Peterson, 1979, p. 590). The focus is on the nature of those transactions, whether they are contributing to, exacerbating, or perpetuating the ATOD problem, or whether they represent present or potential resources for the client to use in his or her struggle toward recovery.

In assessment, the practitioner and the client, together, are looking at the ATOD problem itself plus three other areas, or dimensions, of the client's life situation to see whether and how they have relevance to the ATOD problem—either as a factor in that problem or as a possible resource to help in recovery. These three dimensions are the intra-personal dimension, the interpersonal dimension, and the environmental or situational dimension or context.

Dimension 1. The environmental or situational context. Note that we are reversing the order of the dimensions given above, to start with the client's ecological surround rather than with his or her internal psychology. This is also the reverse of the focus of most psychology, psychiatry, and psychotherapy generally. But the old social work maxim "start with the outside of the case and work in" still makes practical sense (see, for example, Braverman, 1986; Geismar & Wood, 1989; Mailick, 1977; Sheffield, 1931; Siporin, 1970, 1972; Zimbalist, 1952). Starting with the intra-psychic dimension carries certain risks. For one, the practitioner's focus may get stuck there. Because every client (as every person) has some intra-psychic pathology or past trauma, and because most practitioners find these fascinating, the practitioner may overly focus on these psychodynamics and ignore aspects of the client's interpersonal or environmental situation that may have as much, or possibly more, relevance to the ATOD problem. Furthermore, exclusive interest in the inner world strips a client of context, and thus distorts understanding of that inner world because it is inherently connected to interpersonal and environmental reality.

The practitioner is interested in understanding something about the material circumstances of the client: housing, neighborhood, job or school, and money. Do these represent stressors and pressures, or might they be resources? For example, does the client live in a neighborhood, or work in a job, or go to a school, where he or she is surrounded by ATOD use? Is the employer aware of the ATOD problem? Is the client's job at risk? Is this nonproductive stress, or might it add to motivation to do something about the problem? Or is the workplace willing to cooperate with the client while he or she struggles to get the problem under control? What personal satisfactions does the job offer, or is it mindless and dehumanizing? Is a young client having academic or social problems in school or college? Do recent changes in the welfare law mean that a client is at risk of being thrown off the rolls, but with inadequate education and skills to get a job? Is there a job training program available that would be an important component in the overall ATOD treatment plan? Or is this a homeless person who cannot concentrate on the ATOD problem as long as tonight's meal and place to sleep are unknown? The socioeconomic status of the client is relevant, particularly if it involves experience of discrimination on the basis of race, gender, sexual orientation, socioeconomic status, or education. Of course, the practitioner should not conclude that a client with a good education and a well-paying career job cannot also have ATOD problems and should be aware that sometimes the work environment of stockbrokers or lawyers can include heavy use of ATOD. Even with a high income, perhaps the client is trying to live beyond his or her means, or the drug use has gotten the person into a deep financial hole.

> *Dimension 2. The interpersonal dimension.* Who are the people who are important to the client (for good or for ill): family members, including extended family (some individuals of which may be more important to the client than nuclear family); friendship network, including drinking or drugging buddies; coworkers or classmates; fraternities, sororities, clubs, church, and other groups; perhaps a clergyperson or family doctor; the neighborhood bartender or drug dealer, and so forth. Which of these people know of the client's ATOD problem, and what is their attitude toward it? The practitioner needs to explore the nature of these relationships, at least as much as determining if the people involved are knowingly or unwittingly exacerbating the client's problem, or if they might be helped to be constructive partners to the client in his or her struggle for recovery. A marital partner, or the parents of a young person, usually plays a major role in the client's life, and a good deal more about the nature of those relationships needs to be assessed. Do certain interactions with these people represent triggers for ATOD use; what skills does the client need to learn to avoid them? What interactions could possibly facilitate recovery? Will the

client give permission for major role players, such as a marital partner or a parent, to be seen by the practitioner? In many such cases, the practitioner may have to carefully explain to the client why this is necessary, and forthrightly discuss what will and will not be held confidential.

In terms of confidentiality, the client referred for ATOD treatment by the justice system has a right to know if the practitioner is required to file a report on the client's progress and just what that report will contain.

Assessment of the interpersonal field of the client should include assessment of his or her social interactive skills. Some treatment programs have found the teaching of social skills, preferably in a group context, to be an important component in the effectiveness of treatment (for example, Chick, Ritson, & Connaughton, 1988; Ferrell & Galassi, 1981).

The best way for the practitioner to obtain information describing the dimensions of the client's interpersonal life is through the skillful in-depth interview—a process based on sound interviewing principles and practices. In addition to establishing essential rapport, the worker must guide the interview with the intent of developing a better understanding of the client's interpersonal relationships and how they affect and are affected by the client's ATOD problems and the search for effective treatment.

Dimension 3. The intrapersonal dimension. This dimension includes consideration of the client's physical status, age, medical problems, and psychiatric problems. The treatment approach to a 75-year-old widower will obviously have to be different, at least in some respects, than to that of a 15-year-old adolescent. Medical problems, whether or not they are related to the ATOD use, may need to be brought under as much control as possible before treatment of the ATOD problems can progress.

Clients with certain psychiatric diagnoses—particularly schizophrenia, affective disorders, and borderline personality disorders—appear to be especially vulnerable to development of ATOD problems. Furthermore, they sometimes turn to ATOD as an alternative self-medication to their prescribed psychiatric medication, thereby exacerbating the psychiatric problem and adding a new problem. Such clients need to have their psychiatric medications reviewed as the first order of business, and, when indicated, adjusted or reinstated to render them accessible to ATOD intervention. The course of ATOD treatment will also have to adapt to any cognitive or affective impairments that arise from the psychiatric diagnosis.

The intra-personal dimension also includes the intra-psychic world of the client. Here, the practitioner is interested in the client's view of his or her reality: the ATOD problem, current life situation, values and attitudes, dreams and fears for the future. What are the client's ethnic, cultural, social, and religious characteristics; are any aspects of these conducive to ATOD use, or are they resources for help? The issue for the practitioner is whether and how to use these beliefs and attitudes in the service of recovery, although in some cases they may need to be respectfully challenged if they are supporting the ATOD problem.

All of the foregoing intra-personal aspects of the client can be said to constitute his or her "personality." This term, however, is too broad and too vague to be really useful. The practitioner's interest is more narrowly focused on identifying behavior patterns, beliefs, and attitudes that may affect which treatment approaches or modalities the client may find more useful and which the client will reject, and what kind of relationship with the practitioner will best fit the client. For example, clients who hold strong opinions and are highly organized tend to prefer therapy that is not highly structured, whereas clients who are less structured internally may prefer structured programs such as Alcoholics Anonymous (AA) (Institute of Medicine, 1990, p. 244). According to Annis and Chan (1983), clients with a very negative view of themselves cannot tolerate confrontational types of therapy and indeed may be iatrogenically harmed by them; however, some clients may react most favorably to confrontation. Clients who are especially fragile because of a co-occurring mental health disorder also may be extremely vulnerable to confrontation.

We should note here that when assessing the client's personality, the practitioner is not interested in determining whether the client has an "addictive personality." Despite decades of research, no valid profile of such a personality has ever been found. People with ATOD problems do not run to type: They are as different from each other as are individuals who do not have ATOD problems. The practitioner is interested in the individual characteristics of the specific client.

Evaluation of a client's intelligence, and level of cognitive functioning, is needed. There may have been some cognitive impairment as a result of the ATOD use. Some treatment approaches require a good ability to process information at a high level of abstraction. If this is beyond the client's capability, other treatment approaches may need to be initiated, at least in the earlier stages.

The practitioner needs to be aware that the client's denial of the presence or extent of the ATOD problem is not a character problem but, rather, a psychological defense mechanism; it is the practitioner's responsibility to establish an atmosphere within which the client can be helped to move at his or her own pace toward the decision to change.

Clients with an ATOD problem usually are suffering from very low self-esteem, because they blame the problem on their poor character or lack of will power. This applies even to those who deny the existence of the problem—or perhaps especially to such clients, because the denial is an obvious defense against the pain of the self-criticism that is just under the surface, and it also can be a device used to protect the continued use of ATOD. Likewise, the grandiose behaviors of some clients—the boastful, supercilious language—suggest a profound lack of self-confidence.

In addition to informing the client that having an ATOD problem says nothing about one's basic moral character, the practitioner needs to engage the client in assessing his or her own strengths and capabilities. It is important that this not be perceived by the client as a shallow pep talk by the practitioner, but, rather, that the practitioner move sensitively, at the client's own pace, to engage the client in assessing his or her strengths. For many clients, this is probably better accomplished if the practitioner adopts a rather businesslike attitude rather than one that drips with empathy. Such an approach enhances the client's ability to better objectify his or her strengths. Clients with an ATOD problem characteristically see their glass as half-empty and overly focus on their negatives; it is important for building the client's motivation for him or her to begin to believe in his or her own strengths and capacities. For many clients, it may be helpful to review with them the successes they have experienced, the tough times and challenges they have met, and even the failures they have survived. In this, it is important that the practitioner not label the successes and strengths as such, but, rather, that the practitioner lead the client to do so.

Throughout the entire interaction with the client, the practitioner should remain constantly aware that ATOD "treatment" is not actually treatment by the practitioner but, rather, self-treatment by the client. Only the client can do something about the problem; the practitioner cannot "treat" it away. The practitioner's job is to enable the client to start and to help and support the client in his or her faltering steps to health.

A repeat of a caveat is appropriate here. In assessing the intra-personal dimension and in working with the client over a period of time, the practitioner will probably become aware of some intra-psychic or personality difficulties of the client. The temptation will be to divert attention from the focus on the ATOD problem to attempt psychotherapy of these difficulties. This is warranted only if clear evidence exists that such difficulties are an integral part of the ATOD problem, or that they have to be ameliorated before progress can be expected on the ATOD situation. The latter may be the case, for example, for the client with very poor social skills, which in turn are making the client turn to ATOD to relax in social situations; here, teaching social skills may well be a necessary component of the ATOD treatment package.

If, however, such evidence does not exist, switching focus away from the ATOD may only confuse the client and contribute to the failure of ATOD treatment.

Certain instruments mentioned earlier in this chapter provide an assessment of psychiatric difficulties associated with ATOD problems. For example, the MAC (MacAndrew, 1965) and scales by Conley and Kammeier (1980) and Hoffman and colleagues (1984) are based on items from the MMPI (Hathaway & McKinley, 1951), one of the most widely used personality assessment instruments. The ASI (McLellan et al., 1980) also incorporates a psychiatric assessment component within the context of an assessment of drug and alcohol use.

In addition, many treatment facilities and programs, as part of standard intake assessment, provide an overall psychiatric assessment based on the DSM-IV-TR (American Psychiatric Association, 2000), which also recognizes the critical inter-active relationship among psychiatric difficulties, ATOD use, interpersonal relationships, and community-based challenges.

Summary

Numerous studies of the effectiveness of various ATOD treatment approaches indicate that effectiveness depends, in large part, on how well the treatment fits the client as an individual, and on whether it takes into account the context of the client's life situation. The client should feel a certain ownership in arriving at a treatment plan with the worker.

This chapter defines the context of ATOD assessment, highlighting a biopyscho-social–cultural–spiritual or person-in-environment approach. It recognizes the importance of skillful interviewing coupled with the use of appropriate diagnostic and assessment instruments.

Making choices about treatment depends on a solid multivariate diagnostic assessment. Successful treatment is dependent on skillful accurate assessment. Assessment is not a one-time event; rather, it is an ongoing process that incorporates new data as the worker and client proceed together along the challenging path to effective treatment outcomes.

Note

The author wishes to recognize and express thanks to Katherine M. Wood, who contributed significantly to portions of this chapter related to the multi-dimensional nature of assessment as it initially appeared in the first edition of *Alcohol, Tobacco, and Other Drugs*.

APPENDIX 8.1: The Short Michigan Alcoholism Screening Test (SMAST)

Directions: The following is a list of questions about your past and present drinking habits. Please answer "yes" or "no" to each question by placing an "x" in the appropriate column next to each question. When you are finished answering the questions, please add up how many "yes" responses you checked.

#	Question	Yes	No
1.	Do you feel you are a normal drinker (drink as much as or less than others)?		
2.	Does your wife, husband, a parent, or other near relative ever worry or complain about your drinking?		
3.	Do you ever feel guilty about your drinking?		
4.	Do friends or relatives think you are a normal drinker?		
5.	Are you able to stop drinking when you want to?		
6.	Have you ever attended a meeting of Alcoholics Anonymous (AA)?		
7.	Has your drinking ever created problems between you and your wife, husband, a parent, or near relative?		
8.	Have you ever gotten into trouble at work because of your drinking?		
9.	Have you ever neglected your obligations, your family, or your work for 2 or more days in a row because you were drinking?		
10.	Have you ever gone to anyone for help about your drinking?		
11.	Have you ever been in a hospital because of drinking?		
12.	Have you ever been arrested for drunken driving, driving while intoxicated, or driving under the influence of alcoholic beverages?		
13.	Have you ever been arrested, even for a few hours, because of other drunken behavior?		

Note: There are two methods for scoring the SMAST: The Ross Method uses one point for each question answered "yes." A score of four or fewer is considered to be a normal score. A score of five or more indicates potential alcohol dependence. The Seltzer Method uses one point for a "no" answer to questions 1, 4, and 5, and each "yes" response to the other questions. Two points indicate a possible problem. Three points indicate a probable problem.

Source: Selzer, M. L., Vinokur, A., & van Rooijen, L. (1975). A self-administered Short Michigan Alcoholism Screening Test (SMAST). *Journal of Studies on Alcohol, 36,* 124.

APPENDIX 8.2: Alcohol Use Disorder Identification Test (AUDIT)

How often do you have a drink containing alcohol?
[   ] Never (0)
[   ] Monthly or less (1)
[   ] 2 to 4 times a month (2)
[   ] 2 to 3 times a week (3)
[   ] 4 or more times a week (4)

How many drinks containing alcohol do you have on a typical day when you are drinking?
[   ] None (0)
[   ] 1 or 2 (1)
[   ] 3 or 4 (2)
[   ] 5 or 6 (3)
[   ] 7 or 9 (4)
[   ] 10 or more (5)

How often do you have six or more drinks on one occasion?
[   ] Never (0)
[   ] Less than monthly (1)
[   ] Monthly (2)
[   ] Weekly (3)
[   ] Daily or almost daily (4)

How often during the last year have you found that you were unable to stop drinking once you had started?
[   ] Never (0)
[   ] Less than monthly (1)
[   ] Monthly (2)
[   ] Weekly (3)
[   ] Daily or almost daily (4)

How often during the last year have you failed to do what was normally expected of you because of drinking?
[   ] Never (0)
[   ] Less than monthly (1)
[   ] Monthly (2)
[   ] Weekly (3)
[   ] Daily or almost daily (4)

How often during the last year have you needed a first drink in the morning to get yourself going after a heavy drinking session?

[   ] Never (0)
[   ] Less than monthly (1)
[   ] Monthly (2)
[   ] Weekly (3)
[   ] Daily or almost daily (4)

How often during the last year have you had a feeling of guilt or remorse after drinking?

[   ] Never (0)
[   ] Less than monthly (1)
[   ] Monthly (2)
[   ] Weekly (3)
[   ] Daily or almost daily (4)

How often during the last year have you been unable to remember what happened the night before because you had been drinking?

[   ] Never (0)
[   ] Less than monthly (1)
[   ] Monthly (2)
[   ] Weekly (3)
[   ] Daily or almost daily (4)

Have you or someone else been injured as the result of your drinking?

[   ] Never (0)
[   ] Less than monthly (1)
[   ] Monthly (2)
[   ] Weekly (3)
[   ] Daily or almost daily (4)

Has a relative, friend, or a doctor or other health worker been concerned about your drinking or suggested you cut down?

[   ] Never (0)
[   ] Less than monthly (1)
[   ] Monthly (2)
[   ] Weekly (3)
[   ] Daily or almost daily (4)

Record the total of the specific items. [   ]

References

Alterman, A. I., Gelfand, L. A., & Sweeney, K. A. (1992). The Alcohol Clinical Index in lower socioeconomic alcohol-dependent men. *Alcoholism: Clinical and Experimental Research, 16,* 960–963.

American Psychiatric Association. (2000). *Diagnostic and statistical manual of mental disorders* (4th ed., text rev.). Washington, DC: Author.

Annis, H. M., & Chan, D. (1983). The differential treatment model: Empirical evidence from a personality typology of adult offenders. *Criminal Justice & Behavior, 10,* 159–173.

Babor, T. F., de la Fuente, J. R., Saunders, J. B., & Grant, M. (1989). *AUDIT—The Alcohol Use Disorders Identification Test: Guidelines for use in primary health care.* Geneva: World Health Organization.

Babor, T. F., & Grant, M. (1989). From clinical research to secondary prevention: International collaboration in the development of the Alcohol Use Disorders Identification Test (AUDIT). *Alcohol Health and Research World, 13,* 371–374.

Braverman, L. (1986). Social casework and strategic therapy. *Social Casework, 67,* 234–239.

Brown, R. L., & Rounds, L. A. (1995). Conjoint screening questionnaires for alcohol and drug use. *Wisconsin Medical Journal, 94,* 135–140.

Carroll, J. F. (1984). The Substance Abuse Problem Checklist: A new clinical aid for drug and/or alcohol treatment dependency. *Journal of Substance Abuse Treatment, 1*(1), 31–36.

Carson-Dewitt, R. (Ed.). (2001). *Addiction Severity Index (ASI), encyclopedia of drugs, alcohol, and addictive behavior* (2nd ed.). Retrieved May 18, 2009, from http://www.enotes. com/drugs-alcohol-encyclopedia/addiction-severity-index-asi

Chan, A. W. K. (1993). Recent developments in detection and biological indicators of alcoholism. *Drugs and Society, 8*(1), 31–67.

Chick, J., Ritson, B., & Connaughton, J. (1988). Advice versus extended treatment for alcoholism: A controlled study. *British Journal of Addiction, 83,* 159–170.

Conigrave, K. M., Hall, W. D., & Saunders, J. B. (1995). The AUDIT questionnaire: Choosing a cut-off score, *Addiction, 90,* 1349–1356.

Conley, J. J., & Kammeier, M. L. (1980). MMPI item responses of alcoholics in treatment: Comparisons with normals and psychiatric patients. *Journal of Consulting and Clinical Psychology, 48,* 668–669.

Cooper, S. E., & Robinson, D.A.G. (1987). Use of the Substance Abuse Subtle Screening Inventory with a college population. *Journal of American College Health, 36,* 180–184.

Crisp, B. R., & Barber, J. G. (1995). The Drinker's Partner Distress Scale: An instrument for measuring the distress caused by drinkers to their partners. *International Journal of Addictions, 30,* 1009–1017.

Cutler, S. F., Wallace, P. G., & Haines, A. P. (1988). Assessing alcohol consumption in general practice patients: A comparison between questionnaire and interview (findings of the Medical Research Council's general practice research framework study on lifestyle and health). *Alcohol & Alcoholism, 23,* 441–450.

Ewing, J. A. (1984). Detecting alcoholism: The CAGE questionnaire. *JAMA, 252,* 1905–1907.

Ewing, J. A., & Rouse, B. A. (1970, February). *Identifying the hidden alcoholic.* Paper presented at the 29th International Congress on Alcohol and Drug Dependence, Sydney, Australia.

Ferrell, W. L., & Galassi, J. P. (1981). Assertion training and human relations training in the treatment of chronic alcoholics. *International Journal of Addictions, 16,* 959–968.

Fisher, M. S. (2008). Substance abuse assessment tools for improving clinical outcomes. *Alcohol, Tobacco & Other Drugs, Section Connection, 2,* 9–11.

Fleming, M. F. (1993). Screening and brief intervention for alcohol disorders. *Journal of Family Practice, 37,* 231–234.

Fleming, M. F., & Barry, K. L. (1991). A three-sample test of a masked alcohol screening questionnaire. *Alcohol and Alcoholism, 26*(1), 81–91.

Gavin, D. R., Ross, H. E., & Skinner, H. A. (1989). Diagnostic validity of the Drug Abuse Screening Test in the assessment of DSM-III drug disorders. *British Journal of Addiction, 84,* 301–307.

Geismar, L. G., & Wood, K. M. (1989). *Families at risk: Treating the multiproblem family.* New York: Human Sciences Press.

Grant, K. A., Tonigan, J. S., & Miller, W. R. (1995). Comparison of three alcohol consumption measures: A concurrent validity study. *Journal of Studies of Alcohol, 56,* 168–172.

Gray, B. T. (2001). A factor analytic study of the Substance Abuse Subtle Screening Inventory (SASSI). *Educational and Psychological Measurement, 61,* 102–118.

Harrell, A. V., Sowder, B., & Kapsak, K. (1988). *Field validation of Drinking and You: A screening instrument for adolescent problem drinking* (Contract No. ADM 281–85–0007). Rockville, MD: National Institute on Alcohol Abuse and Alcoholism.

Harrell, A. V., & Wirtz, P. W. (1989). Screening for adolescent problem drinking: Validation of a multidimensional instrument for case identification. *Psychological Assessment, 1*(1), 61–63.

Hathaway, S. R., & McKinley, J. C. (1951). *The Minnesota Multiphasic Personality Inventory manual* (rev.). New York: Psychological Corporation.

Hays, R. D., Merz, J. F., & Nicholas, R. (1995). Response burden, reliability, and validity of the CAGE, Short MAST, and AUDIT alcohol screening measures. *Behavior Research Methods, Instruments, and Computers, 27*(2), 277–280.

Heatherton, T. F., Kozlowski, L. T., Frecker, R. C., & Fagerström, K. O. (1991). The Fagerström Test for Nicotine Dependence: A revision of the Fagerström Tolerance Questionnaire. *British Journal of Addictions, 86,* 1119–1127.

Hoffman, N. G., Lumry, A. E., Harrison, P. A,, & Lessard, R. J. (1984). Brief Minnesota Multiphasic Personality Inventory scales to screen for substance abuse. *Drug and Alcohol Dependence 14,* 209–214.

Horn, J. L., Wanberg, K. W., & Foster, F. M. (1983). *The Alcohol Use Inventory.* Baltimore: Psych Systems.

Institute of Medicine. (1990). *Broadening the base of treatment for alcohol problems.* Washington, DC: Academic Press.

Jones, J. W. (1982). *Preliminary test manual: The Children of Alcoholics Screening Test.* Chicago: Family Recovery Press.

Kirisci, L., Mezzich, A., & Tarter, R. (1995). Norms and sensitivity of the adolescent version of the Drug Use Screening Inventory. *Addictive Behaviors, 20*(2), 149–157.

MacAndrew, C. (1965). The differentiation of male alcoholic outpatients from nonalcoholic psychiatric patients by means of the MMPI. *Quarterly Journal of Studies on Alcohol, 26,* 238–246.

MacAndrew, C. (1981). What the MAC Scale tells us about men alcoholics: An interpretive review. *Journal of Studies on Alcohol, 42,* 604–625.

Magruder-Habib, K., Durand, M. A., & Frey, K. A. (1991). Alcohol abuse and alcoholism in primary health care settings. *Journal of Family Practice, 32,* 406–413.

Mailick, M. (1977). A situational perspective in casework theory. *Social Casework, 58,* 401–411.

Marlatt, G. A., & Miller, W. R. (1984). *Comprehensive drinker profile.* Odessa, FL: Psychological Assessment Resources.

Mayfield, D. G., McLeod, G., & Hall, P. (1974). The CAGE questionnaire: Validation of a new alcoholism screening instrument. *American Journal of Psychiatry, 131,* 1121–1123.

McLellan A. T., Luborsky, L., Woody, G. E., & O'Brien, C. P. (1980). An improved diagnostic evaluation instrument for substance abuse. *Journal of Nervous and Mental Disease, 168,* 26–33.

Miller, C. A. (1983). *Cross-validation of measures to differentiate chemical abusers from general responsible chemical users and non-abusing psychiatric clients.* Unpublished research proposal.

National Institute on Alcohol Abuse and Alcoholism. (1993). *Eighth special report to the U.S. Congress on alcohol and health* (NIH Publication No. 94–3699). Bethesda, MD: National Institutes of Health.

Nilssen, O., & Cone, H. (1994). Screening patients for alcohol problems in primary health care settings. *Alcohol Health & Research World, 18*(2), 136–139.

Petchers, M. K., & Singer, M. (1987). Perceived-benefit-of-drinking: An approach to screening for adolescent alcohol abuse. *Journal of Pediatrics, 110,* 977–981.

Petchers, M. K., Singer, M., Angelotta, J. W., & Chow, J. (1988). Revalidation and expansion of an adolescent substance abuse screening measure. *Journal of Developmental and Behavioral Pediatrics, 9*(1), 25–29.

Peterson, K. J. (1979). Assessment in the life model: A historical perspective. *Social Casework, 60,* 586–596.

Pokorny, A. D., Miller, B. A., & Kaplan, H. B. (1972). The Brief MAST: A shortened version of the Michigan Alcoholism Screening Test. *American Journal of Psychiatry, 129,* 342–345.

Preng, K. W., & Clopton, J. R. (1986). The MacAndrew Scale: Clinical application and theoretical issues. *Journal of Studies on Alcohol, 47,* 228–236.

Prochaska, J. O., Norcross, J. C., & DiClemente, C. C. (1994). *Changing for good.* New York: Avon Books.

Rathbun, J. (1993). Development of a computerized alcohol screening instrument for the university community. *Journal of American College Health, 42,* 33–36.

Russell, M., Martier, S. S., Sokol, R. J., Jacobson, S., Jacobson, J., & Bottoms, S. (1991). Screening for pregnancy risk-drinking: Tweaking the tests. *Alcoholism Clinical and Experimental Research, 15*(2), 368.

Saltstone, R., Halliwell, S., & Hayslip, M. A. (1994). A multivariate evaluation of the Michigan Alcoholism Screening Test and the Drug Abuse Screening Test in a female offender population. *Addictive Behaviors, 19,* 455–462.

SASSI Institute. (2001). *Summary of the consistency and accuracy of the Adolescent SASSI-A2 for non-statisticians.* Springville, IN: Author.

Saunders, J. B., & Aasland, O. G. (1987). *WHO collaborative project on the identification and treatment of persons with harmful alcohol consumption. Report on Phase I: Development of a screening instrument.* Geneva: World Health Organization.

Saunders, J. B., Aasland, O. G., Amundsen, A., & Grant, M. (1993). Alcohol consumption and related problems among primary health care patients. WHO Collaborative Project on Early Detection of Persons with Harmful Alcohol Consumption—I. *Addiction, 88,* 349–362.

Saunders, J. B., Aasland, O. G., Babor, T. F., de la Fuente, J. R., & Grant, M. (1993). Development of the Alcohol Use Disorders Identification Test (AUDIT): WHO Collaborative Project on Early Detection of Persons with Harmful Alcohol Consumption—II. *Addiction, 88,* 791–804.

Selzer, M. L. (1971). The Michigan Alcoholism Screening Test: The quest for a new diagnostic instrument. *American Journal of Psychiatry, 127,* 1653–1658.

Selzer, M. L., Vinokur, A., & Van Rooijen, L. (1975). A self-administered Short Michigan Alcoholism Screening Test (SMAST). *Journal of Studies on Alcohol, 36*(1), 117–126.

Sheffield, A. E. (1931). The situation as the unit of family case study. *Journal of Social Forces, 9,* 465–474.

Siporin, M. (1970). Social treatment: A new-old helping method. *Social Work, 15*(3), 13–25.

Siporin, M. (1972). Situational assessment and intervention. *Social Casework, 33,* 91–109.

Skinner, H. A. (1982a). *Development and validation of a lifetime alcohol consumption assessment procedure* (Substudy No. 1248). Toronto: Addiction Research Foundation.

Skinner, H. A. (1982b). The Drug Abuse Screening Test. *Addictive Behaviors, 7,* 363–371.

Skinner, H. A. (1984). Instruments for assessing alcohol and drug problems, *Bulletin of the Society of Psychologists in Addictive Behaviors, 3,* 21–33.

Skinner, H. A., & Allen, B. A. (1982). Alcohol dependence syndrome: Measurement and validation. *Journal of Abnormal Psychology, 91,* 199–209.

Skinner, H. A., & Holt, S. (1987). *The Alcohol Clinical Index: Strategies for identifying patients with alcohol problems.* Toronto: Alcoholism and Drug Addiction Research Foundation.

Skinner, H. A., Holt, S., Sheu, W. J., & Israel, Y. (1986). Clinical versus laboratory detection of alcohol abuse: The Alcohol Clinical Index. *British Medical Journal, 292,* 1703–1708.

Skinner, H. A., & Horn, J. L. (1984). *Guidelines for using the Alcohol Dependence Scale.* Toronto: Addiction Research Foundation.

Sobell, L. C., & Sobell, M. B. (1992). Timeline follow-back: A technique for assessing self-reported alcohol consumption. In R. Z. Litton & J. P. Allen (Eds.), *Measuring alcohol consumption: Psychological and biological methods* (pp. 41–72). Totowa, NJ: Humana Press.

Svanum, S., Levitt, E. E., & McAdoo, W. G. (1982). Differentiating male and female alcoholics from psychiatric outpatients: The MacAndrew and Rosenberg alcoholism scales. *Journal of Personality Assessment,* 81–84.

Swenson, S. M., & Morse, R. M. (1975). The use of a Self-Administered Alcoholism Screening Test (SAAST) in a medical center. *Mayo Clinic Proceedings, 50*(4), 204–208.

Tarter, R. (1990). Evaluation and treatment of adolescent substance abuse: A decision tree method. *American Journal of Drug and Alcohol Abuse, 16,* 1–46.

Tarter, R., Laird, S., Bukstein, O., & Kaminer, Y. (1992). Validation of the adolescent Drug Use Screening Inventory: Preliminary findings. *Psychology of Addictive Behaviors, 15,* 65–75.

Tarter, R., Mezzich, A., Kirisci, L., & Kaczynksi, N. (1994). Reliability of the Drug Use Screening Inventory among adolescents alcoholics. *Journal of Child & Adolescent Substance Abuse, 3*(1), 25–36.

Vaillant, G. E. (1980). Natural history of male psychological health, VIII: Antecedents of alcoholism and "orality." *American Journal of Psychiatry, 137,* 181–186.

Wallace, P. G., & Haines, A. P. (1985). The use of a questionnaire in general practice to increase the recognition of patients with excessive alcohol consumption. *British Medical Journal, 290,* 1949–1953.

Walters, G. D. (1994). Discriminating between high and low substance abusers by means of the Drug Lifestyle Screening Interview. *American Journal of Drug and Alcohol Abuse, 20,* 19–33.

Walters, G. D. (1995). Predictive validity of the Drug Lifestyle Screening Interview: A two-year follow-up. *American Journal of Drug and Alcohol Abuse, 21,* 187–194.

Weinstein, B. A., & Slaght, E. (1995). Early identification of alcoholism: A new diagnostic tool for clinicians. *Alcoholism Treatment Quarterly, 12*(4), 117–125.

White, H. R., & Labouvie, P. W. (1989). Towards the assessment of adolescent problem drinking. *Journal of Studies on Alcohol, 50,* 30–37.

Winters, K. (1988). *Personal Experience Screen Questionnaire manual.* Minneapolis: Adolescent Assessment Project, University of Minnesota.

Zimbalist, S. E. (1952). Organismic social work versus partialistic research. *Social Casework, 33,* 3–10.

9

New Strategies for Intervention with Individuals

Langdon Holloway

The alcohol and drug treatment field is a demanding and rapidly changing area of treatment. The traditional approach of a single standardized program is changing to a more comprehensive and individualized counseling approach. The development of different clinical theories in several disciplines has yielded therapeutic options for the practitioner. However, social workers seeking outcome studies on the most effective treatment approaches for a particular population find the supporting evidence limited. The criteria for evidence-based practice form a hierarchy in which quasi-experimental design, comparison groups, randomization, and multiple sites are highly recommended (Rubin, 2008). Long-term follow-up periods are needed for treatment outcome studies. These standards are not consistently met. For instance, the Cochrane Collaboration, an online site (http://www.cochrane.org), reviews studies on treatment for abuse of alcohol, cannabis, cocaine, stimulants, and opiates (see http://www.cochrane.org). Their conclusions most often include statements concerning substantive methodological limitations to the reviews that lead the comparative studies to be equivocal. The research criteria require an investment of time and money that inhibits long-term outcome research comparing multiple treatment approaches.

Substance abuse in the United States has evidenced some slight declines among various age groups from the 1990s. At the same time, the culture tolerates beliefs that contribute to substance misuse. We tend to expect immediate gratification for our desires, relief from pain, and the use of medications or chemicals to change our appearance, enhance our recreation, and alter our moods. There has been increased advertising of medications and supplements in the media and on the Internet. These values contribute to a culture prone to substance misuse and abuse. Parents may expect adolescents to experiment with nicotine, alcohol, and drugs; some consider it integral to the college experience. At the same time, epidemiological studies indicate that increased drinking is prevalent for youths who enter the workforce (Muthen & Muthen, 2000).

Social work interventions in the field of addictions include the ecological approach, the cognitive–behavioral approach, and the behavioral approach. The medical model has long focused on the need for a pharmacological treatment, initially with the use of disulfiram, followed by methadone maintenance, and more recently with nicotine replacement therapy and opioid agonists such as buprenorphine, and buprenorphine-naloxone. Therapeutic communities, detoxification, and relapse prevention intervention have developed in the substance abuse field. Brief solution-focused therapy and dialectical behavioral therapy (DBT) are recent theoretical additions to the range of possible services. Adjunctive therapies, including acupuncture and hypnosis, have been incorporated into some treatment settings. Furthermore, the use of drug courts is a community-based innovation that is demonstrating success in reducing recidivism.

Harm reduction approaches and drinking moderation are controversial philosophies in the addiction treatment community. The efficacy of these approaches for reducing criminal behavior and the transmission of HIV and hepatitis is gaining recognition. The question of viewing harm reduction and reduced risk drinking as part of a continuum of social work interventions will be considered.

With the expansion of treatment modalities, and research about its effectiveness, social workers have the responsibility to establish the habit of constantly upgrading their knowledge with Internet resources. The U.S. government has a number of excellent sites that provide information on new research (for example, Substance Abuse and Mental Health Services Administration [SAMHSA] at http://www.oas.samhsa.gov, National Institute on Drug Abuse at http://www.nida.nih.gov, and National Institute of Alcohol, Abuse, and Alcoholism [NIAAA] at http://www.niaaa.nih.gov). SAMHSA provides tips on guidelines for best practice for clinical social workers. Professional organizations such as the National Association of Social Workers, the American Psychological Association, and the American Psychiatric Association have informative Web sites (http://www.socialworkers.org, http://www.apa.org, and http://www.psych.org, respectively). These Web sites can be used when developing treatment plans.

History of Substance Abuse Treatment

As a preface to understanding the evolution of models and strategies, a brief synopsis of the history of substance abuse treatment will be presented. Because of the public stigma accompanying alcoholism and other drug misuse, federal funding for treatment and professional assistance for recovery occurred long after the help provided for other human maladies. The initial source of hope for the rehabilitation of these individuals was not professional treatment, but the development of a self-help movement (Alcoholics Anonymous [AA]) in 1935. AA is based on the belief that alcoholics must concentrate on supporting each other in their quest for sobriety. Since then other self-help groups, developed from the AA approach, have been formed to address alcohol and other drug issues that affect individuals and families (L'Abate, Farrar, & Serritella, 1992).

The professional treatment of alcoholism in the United States had its beginnings in the 1940s (Gomberg, White, & Carpenter, 1982), incorporating both individual and group therapies. World War II had a prominent impact on the increasing numbers of people needing psychological treatment and counseling, particularly in the returning military, leading to training and treatment programs using group methods. The focus was on serving large numbers of patients at the least cost (Lubin, 1983). Along with other disabling ailments, the abuse of alcohol was recognized as problematic, requiring medical and psychological assistance. Addiction professionals recognized "the importance of group therapy in working with alcoholics became clear, and alcoholism treatment agencies were among the first to use group therapies" (Gomberg, 1982, p. 200). (See chapter 10 for more detailed information on working with groups.) This was manifested by the significance of social rehabilitation in the group context, coupled with the recognition of the positive influence of AA as a self-help group organization.

With the growing acceptance of the disease concept of alcoholism (Jellinek, 1952, 1960) by the American Medical Association and the American Hospital Association in the 1950, funding sources for substance abuse research and treatment and increasing health insurance coverage emerged (Blume, 1983; Strug, Priyadarsini, & Hyman, 1986). As recovering alcoholics became an integral part of treatment rehabilitative programs, the disease model and AA Twelve Step Principles and Traditions gained prominence in intervention orientations (Burman, 1994).

The expansion of delivery services incorporated a variety of methods in subsequent years. Within the last several decades, family therapy has been established as an important part of treatment with the acknowledgment of the interactional effects of drug use on the family unit. (see chapter 11 for more detailed information on working with families.) Managed care, the policy of reducing health care costs by oversight of insurance companies and brief interventions, has resulted in increased use of substance abuse services by identified employees, under pressure of job loss. Social workers in private practice have provided early assessment and brief intervention, operating as external Employment Assistance Programs. In this capacity, their expertise in co-occurring mental illness with substance abuse has been beneficial. When substance dependency is identified, the social worker refers the client to the appropriate community agency, detoxification (detox), or inpatient treatment facility. Based on a medical model, managed care has limited the length of counseling for alcohol and drug use problems. Traditionally, residential programs were labeled "30-day treatment" programs; now the average length of stay is less than 20 days. Partial care programs and intensive outpatient treatment provide substance abuse treatment on an outpatient basis. Partial care provides individual and group counseling during the day, as well as psychosocial and vocational services. Intensive outpatient programs, providing similar services, usually meet in the evening, requiring attendance four nights a week.

Another influence on the provision of substance abuse counseling has been the disparity in reimbursement for substance abuse treatment in comparison with mental health treatment. Recent legislation has corrected this parity issue.

Self-help support groups have proliferated throughout the country. All indicate the significance of viewing recovery of the individual in the context of the group structure. In addition, the importance of social influences in the quest toward recovery is recognized. Alcoholism and other drug misuse are no longer seen solely as an "individual problem," but one that affects many facets of familial and societal functioning (Burman, 1993).

Treatment for Special Populations

This chapter is divided into two main sections: treatment for special populations, and a review of specific treatment approaches.

Adolescents

Adolescence may be a period of experimentation that may include experimenting with substances such as cigarettes, alcohol, marijuana, and other drugs. Accessibility to each of these has a substantial impact on the likelihood that the adolescent will try them. Families who have cigarettes, alcohol, or other drugs in the home have higher rates of initiation of these substances (Resnick et al., 1997).

Demographers have learned that there are patterns of initiating with different substances. This gateway hypothesis has become popularized, but the earlier stepping stone concept has more explanatory value. The stepping stone theory spells out which substances are tried first: cigarettes, or for some, alcohol, and marijuana.

"Gateway drugs" is a term that implies that once an adolescent uses one substance, he or she will catapult into other drug use. Many readers will reflect on their own youthful experimentation and note that they did not progress to problematic substance use, providing their own individual, albeit non-confirmatory, evidence to refute the gateway drug theory.

Neurological research has focused on the immaturity and mutability of the adolescent brain, explicating some of the behaviors that mystify adults. Areas of the brain responsible for abstract thinking, discerning other's emotions, and self-control are still developing throughout adolescence. Therefore adolescents have a difficult time anticipating the consequences of their behavior.

Hawkins, Catalano, and Miller (1992) completed an extensive literature review of studies of risk and protective factors for adolescent substance abuse and misuse. The quality of the parent–child relationship, a connectedness, was a protective factor. Likewise school connectedness, good grades (Resnick et al., 1997), and involvement in school activities diminish alcohol and drug use. Other protective factors include religion and ethnicity (being African American) (Johnston, O'Malley, & Bachman, 2004; Wallace, Brown, Bachman, & Laveist, 2002). Risk factors can be delineated: early childhood aggression, conduct disorder, rejection from peers, having been left back in school, and truancy. Accessibility of substances in the neighborhood or within the home increases the likelihood of substance use.

Social learning theory posits that parental role modeling of behavior contributes to adolescent substance use. The role of the older sibling has been found to have a major impact on initiation. However, in a study of biological children and adoptees, McGue, Pickens, and Svikis (1992) found that genetic factors are strongly predictive of a vulnerability to alcoholism and addiction. The influence of the peer group, as well as the perception that friends or the popular peer leader were using cigarettes, alcohol, and drugs, is associated with use of these substances, a finding that is well documented (Epstein, Botvin, Diaz, & Schinke, 1995).

In the National Longitudinal Study of Adolescent Health (Resnick et al., 1997), family factors accounted for 6 percent to 9 percent of substance use. The influence of parents, in particular, the influence of parental monitoring (Barnes, Farrell, & Dintcheff, 1997; Webb, Bray, Getz, & Adams, 2002) and the impact of parents on peer selection, has been studied (Rodgers-Farmer, 2000; Steinberg, Fletcher, & Darling, 1994). Initiation is strongly affected by monitoring and association with nonusing peers.

School factors account for another 4 percent to 6 percent in explaining predictors of substance use (Resnick et al., 1997). Furthermore, recent findings from the

National Survey of American Attitudes on Substance Abuse (Center for Addiction and Substance Abuse [CASA], 2007) found smaller school size to be associated with less availability to alcohol and drugs. Schools have increased services offered to students with substance use problems. Student assistance counselors are in many schools to address a range of student issues, but generally are involved in addressing substance-related problems. They function as both prevention specialists and counselors for those already involved with substances, providing individual and group services. Peer mentoring programs are used in preventive efforts concerning substances and high-risk sexual behavior.

Studies of predisposing factors to alcohol and drug use are considered useful in developing therapy to assist those who have alcohol and drug problems. Therefore, family therapy is considered key to treatment for adolescents with substance abuse problems. Using systems theory, therapists recognize that both parents and adolescent need to develop skills to improve the parent–child relationship. Systems theory views the situation as interdependent, thereby decreasing the tendency to blame the adolescent for the behavior. Attention is refocused on problems experienced in the marital dyad and problems in maintaining authority in the parent–child relationship. Change in one part of the family system leads to change in another part. Results from a recent meta-analysis (Waldron & Turner, 2008) did not find support for family intervention on family relations variables. Inclusion criteria for the studies in the meta-analysis were randomization, manual-guided interventions, and long-term follow-up periods. Comparing the effect sizes across 17 studies, they found that no one treatment was clearly more efficacious than other treatment approaches. Most studies had found a modest effect size of the outcomes of one treatment compared with another. In conclusion, multi-dimensional family therapy and functional family therapy were considered to meet standards for "well-established" therapy, the highest ranking.

Case Example 9.1 exemplifies the need to build trust with adolescents and the struggle to recognize the client's self-determination when it counters accepted practice.

Cognitive–Behavioral Therapy (CBT) for Adolescents

Results from a recent meta-analysis (Waldron & Turner, 2008) the efficacy of cognitive–behavioral treatment using a group modality is considered well established. However, within each treatment type, there was high variability on individual outcomes. This result focuses on the need for more research on subgroups of adolescents and the necessity of improving the skill in implementing these techniques. Another research recommendation based on this meta-analysis was the issue of *dosage*, defined as the intensity of the intervention. For example, techniques to increase

CASE EXAMPLE 9.1. An Adolescent Male: Is Abstinence from One Drug Enough?

Kirk is an 18-year-old male, high school senior, and part-time dishwasher. Mrs. O. called to request an appointment for her son, stating he was smoking marijuana daily and under-performing in school. She said that she was calling because he was in school but assured the social worker that it was Kirk who wanted the appointment. (At 18, Kirk did not need his mother's permission to receive social work services.)

In a brief meeting with both Kirk and his mother, the mother expressed caring and pride in her son. She believes that the marijuana and association with friends who appeared not to have any future ahead of them were two things that had a negative impact on Kirk. The worker briefly reviewed whether any health or developmental factors were contributing to Kirk's current performance. Kirk and Mrs. O. live in a lower-middle-class suburb. The mother provides the major income working as a dental assistant.

Kirk informed the worker that his reason for counseling was discontent in his situation. He feels that his life is going nowhere. A mental status assessment was made with no symptoms or signs of depression or suicidality. He knows his mother loves him and he has a close relationship with his stepfather. This man is the mother's fourth husband. When Kirk was eight his mother divorced his father, her second marriage. There was a brief third marriage, and when he was 12, the mother married her current husband. He sees his father and an older brother about twice a year, but says they are close. His current stepfather is in recovery for alcoholism, has no other children, and delegates parenting responsibilities to Kirk's mother.

Kirk disagrees about his school performance as being under-performance. He likes his English class. No other class motivates him. What he likes is his job at a diner. He is never late, works hard, and finds satisfaction from it. Having money has allowed him to buy a car and pay the insurance, leaving some money for spending.

He has a group of friends who just "hang out" for recreation. Mostly they smoke pot. The type of friends is an issue between Kirk and his mother, as he values their comradeship. He has no other interests. He states he is heterosexual, but is not sexually active or interested. He

(continued)

CASE EXAMPLE 9.1. *(continued)*

denies any sexual trauma. There is no girlfriend to whom he attributes his being considered a "loser" at school and in with the "wrong" crowd.

Kirk completed an outpatient after-school drug program two years ago after he failed a drug test at school. He and his friends thought the program was a joke. It was not helpful; he did not decrease his marijuana use. The social worker, challenged by hearing his disdain, began motivational interviewing to increase his acknowledgement of areas affected by the drug use. Kirk denied that there was any connection between the marijuana and his performance or discontentment. An initial treatment plan focused on what he wanted to change: complete homework assignments, improve grades, manage his money, and start feeling better about himself. The client refused to contract on discontinuing marijuana, except to abstain from marijuana if he was driving. The intent on the social worker's part was to engage the client and discuss the effect of the marijuana use in the immediate future sessions. Kirk signed the plan.

Kirk attended counseling regularly and reported improvement in homework and grades. Prior to the fourth session, the mother called to report that Kirk had informed her that he was using cocaine, "free-basing." Kirk explained to the social worker that he and friends were driving to the poor urban community to get the cocaine weekly. He stated that he knew this was affecting his health (stomach problems), his schooling, his socializing, and his self-concept, and he was putting himself in danger of arrest or car accident. He had intended to tell his mother and the counselor for the past four weeks. The social worker and Kirk made a contingency contract for him to stop using cocaine or his mother would be contacted and Kirk would be referred to a higher level of service. He

client motivation and engagement are recommended. However, one well-regarded approach, motivation enhancement therapy, did not compare well with treatment as usual with the adolescent population (Waldron & Turner, 2008).

Drug Courts

In the late 1980s a number of states developed the model of drug courts for youths and for adults. Drug courts combine immediate adjudication, elements of court proceedings, supervision by the legal system, and elements of drug treatment. A wide was given a Cocaine Anonymous (CA) meeting schedule, and a plan for attendance was developed.

Kirk maintained all appointments in counseling; he did not relapse on cocaine. He attended CA weekly and had contact with an assigned sponsor from the group. The social worker and Kirk were able to refocus on his desire to socialize with non-drug-using friends and increase self-esteem. At 10 weeks, they discussed his future goals. A particularly difficult point was the recommendation that Kirk commit to a four-week trial abstinence period, to demonstrate that he was not dependent on marijuana. He did not comply. There had been significant improvement on his goals, socially, functionally, and educationally. With Kirk's permission, the mother was contacted and she reported satisfaction with his behavior at school and socially. In the worker's opinion the continuation of marijuana, even if substantially reduced, required termination. The termination process began.

A booster session took place in May. Kirk remained free of cocaine, limited his marijuana use, and was dating a classmate. He had decided that his best opportunities were in the army and planned to attend basic training after graduation. (He would graduate!) This case example presents a realistic portrayal of working with adolescents. With active engagement the young man was able to admit to cocaine use and a desire to stop. Using the philosophy of harm reduction, the social worker tried a two-step approach to stop the cocaine use with the intent to motivate Kirk to abstain from marijuana. He did not agree to discontinuing marijuana but he did fulfill some adolescent developmental tasks, such as high school graduation, socializing, and sexual identity formation.

variety of models for drug courts and for implementation of treatment services have been identified. Some courts include components of a self-help meeting in conjunction with a Twelve Step philosophy, the encouragement of a support group within the court, recitation of the Serenity Prayer, and acknowledging those who complete drug court successfully. The implementation of drug courts has required the collaboration of local drug treatment agencies with the court and probation departments. The participating staff members of the drug courts are specifically trained in community resources, Twelve Step premises, and alcohol and drug treatment.

Adolescent drug use co-occurs with a number of other individual problems, such as conduct disorders; attention deficit disorder; mental health problems; lower educational achievement and motivation; vocational problems; and early, risky sexual behavior. (See chapter 6 for more detailed information on co-occurring disorders.) Other significant problems are problems in the community and schools and ongoing family issues. Adolescents who are arrested report higher levels of physical and sexual abuse (Belenko & Dembo, 2003). Furthermore, there are problems in service delivery in the health field, mental health counseling, and educational and vocational services. Mental health problems appear to be more prevalent for female adolescents (Amaro, Blake, Schwartz, & Flinchbaugh, 2001; Belenko & Dembo, 2003). Systemic problems in the community have affected the viability of the juvenile drug courts, resulting in limited treatment slots for adolescents, unsympathetic schools, vocational problems, and few agencies specializing in family intervention.

Drug courts screen the adolescents who have been arrested. For those who are accepted, there are individualized treatment plans, involving wraparound services. The drug court sentence is specified for a period of time requiring regular return to drug court. As stated, the protocol in the drug court begins with a drug court member (arrestee) reading the Twelve Steps of Narcotics Anonymous (NA) or AA and recitation of the Serenity Prayer. The drug court judge reviews the progress, urinalysis or drug screening, probation department's report, school attendance, and the treatment agency's notation of progress toward the treatment goal, including the family's cooperation with family counseling and other needed services, and then the judge makes a decision concerning the adolescent continuing in treatment and Twelve Step programs. It is the judge's decision about when the client has met his or her treatment goals. When there is successful completion, the court erupts in cheers.

Criticisms of the drug court model focus on the arrestee's rights and the requirement of a plea of guilty for admission to the drug court program. When an arrestee "fails," he or she may be sentenced to jail and required to serve the original sentence, meaning that the client serves more time by participating in drug court, and in fact, could serve an indeterminable sentence term. However, there are preplea and postplea models that address this criticism and offer an incentive to the arrestee to participate without extending his or her sentence. Preplea courts determine the length of the sentence if one successfully completes treatment, and in postplea courts, with successful completion the sentence can be reduced or a guilty plea expunged. The preplea or postplea models have been found to have slightly better outcomes on recidivism than models that do not designate sentencing criteria. These "ad hoc" models leave the final sentencing on the authority of the judge and result in less clarity of the benefits for the arrestee (D. B. Wilson, Mitchell, & MacKenzie, 2006). Other criticisms are that there is a need for cultural training and adequate funding for services for female teenagers (Belenko & Dembo, 2003).

In a meta-analysis of drug courts, D. B. Wilson et al. (2006) aggregated the results from studies of juvenile and adult drug courts. Drug courts did increase the length of stay in treatment, and the most stringent studies had a slight statistical positive effect on lowering recidivism (14 percent), the outcome most commonly studied. D. B. Wilson and colleagues conclude that the null hypothesis, that drug courts are not effective in reducing crime, has not been proven false. There was support for a model that links treatment to a single provider, or alternatively, that a single provider controls for the quality of the treatment received (D. B. Wilson et al., 2006). CBT was the most commonly used approach.

Juvenile drug courts have become popular as an alternative to incarceration. Studies indicate that there are lower recidivism rates for adolescents in drug court programs (Belenko & Dembo, 2003) and for adults (Fielding et al., 2002). However, outcome research on juvenile drug courts is limited and does not meet standards for evidence-based practice, such as randomization, comparison groups, an adequate follow-up period, and a control for selectivity of admissions to drug court programs (Belenko & Dembo, 2003). The best studies are limited to studies of recidivism of arrests, rather than the substance use itself. The availability of family treatment has been judged uneven (Belenko & Dembo, 2003). Therefore, it is recommended that standardized research on the components of treatment in the drug court model be undertaken (Belenko & Dembo, 2003; D. B. Wilson et al., 2006).

Women and Addiction

Addiction researchers and practitioners concur that women have special needs in treatment. In addition to drinking more often as a reaction to environmental influences, experiencing more stress in the environment, and experiencing more stigma for problem drinking and drug use (Burman & Allen-Meares, 1991), there are specific issues regarding pregnancy, child care responsibilities, victimization from sexual abuse and domestic violence, health issues, and reproductive disorders resulting from sexually transmitted diseases (STDs). For instance, estimates of the prevalence of sexual abuse in women with substance abuse disorder range from 11 percent to as high as 80 percent. Lifetime prevalence of domestic violence is between 14 percent and 50 percent. Comorbid rates of posttraumatic stress disorder (PTSD) and substance abuse range from 32 percent to 66 percent for women with a history of physical or sexual assault. High rates of lifetime traumas have been documented for women living in inner-city neighborhoods (Najavits, Weiss, Shaw, & Muenz, 1998).

Women are more likely to experience co-occurring mental health problems. Women are more likely to use licit drugs than men (Nelson-Zlupko, Kauffman, & Dore, 1995). Other differences between men and women include women being at a disadvantage in terms of less education and fewer vocational skills, contributing to lower economic status and economic instability.

Grella, Scott, Foss, and Dennis (2008) determined that women had more problems but were twice as likely to complete treatment in a women-only center. However, other studies have concluded that women with a history of childhood neglect and abuse, including sexual abuse, had lower completion rates of mental health counseling, a finding that is supported by the study of Latina women in substance abuse residential programs and low-income pregnant women with PTSD (Amaro, Nieves, Johannes, & Cabeza, 1999). In contrast, women receiving prenatal care and child care following delivery had higher retention rates (Clark, 2001).

The physiology of women means that the progression of alcoholism is faster. The ratio of body fat to water in women is lower, which leads to alcohol entering the woman's system at a less diluted level (Brick & Erickson, 1998). Symptoms including neurological, heart problems, and depression occur after fewer years of drinking. Women metabolize alcohol differently than men, resulting in intoxication from fewer drinks. Alcohol and drugs affect the hormonal system and menstruation, impair metabolism, and reduce appetite, contributing to poor nutrition in girls and women (Sun, 2004). Long-term effects are more physiological damage over a shorter period of time, referred to as "telescoping."

Pregnancy and alcohol use may result in fetal alcohol syndrome. Drugs are not metabolized by the fetus and may affect fetal development. Cocaine has been attributed to irritable response in infants; however, the early fear of long-term consequences for "crack babies" has been mitigated (Lyons & Rittner, 1998). Opioid withdrawal, including the use of methadone, is not life threatening, but medical detoxification is recommended.

Legal sanctions for pregnant women using illegal drugs have been imposed on women, but not the prospective fathers. In addition, these laws have a disproportional impact on ethnic minority women in arrest rates as well as intervention by child welfare authorities (Paltrow, 1991).

Furthermore, there are differences in treatment availability and reasons for agreeing to treatment. Men are more likely than women to be referred by the legal system and encouraged to seek treatment by family members (Weisner, Matzger,

Tam, & Schmidt, 2002). Women participate in and benefit from self-help more as a path from substance use to treatment and recovery (Grella et al., 2008).

Treatment for Women Only

Issues such as the aforementioned have resulted in an expansion of women-only treatment programs since the 1980s. In addition to sexual abuse, the unequal dynamics of intimate relationships between women and men, the self-perception of shame in behavior that led to substance use or provided the means of financing continued use (that is, prostitution and "being prostituted" by male pimps), sexual identification as lesbian, self-esteem, and pregnancy and child care needs are best addressed in women-only facilities. With female staff or nonsexist male staff, women do not experience subjugation by men or become emotionally and sexually involved with male peers. Women-only facilities provide a safe environment in which women do not recreate behavior patterns that had proven destructive in the past. This objective was incorporated into the implementation of block grants in 1984, and additional implementation came from funding from the Center for Substance Abuse Treatment for women and children beginning in 1991 (Sun, 2006).

A meta-analysis on the effectiveness of women-only treatment demonstrates that, in general, these programs have better outcomes in reduced substance abuse, reduced crime, improved health of the mothers and children (Ashley, Marsden, & Brady, 2003), and improved social functioning of the women participants. Characteristics of the programs are as follows: being a single-sex facilities; providing onsite child care; providing case management services; counseling for mental health, education, finances, and vocational training. A number of women-only programs included counseling for sexual abuse, acceptance of sexual orientation, pregnancy-related health care, and HIV and AIDS prevention. Given the broad range of interventions, and the differences in outcome measures, these reviews did not attempt to make statistical comparisons. Programs that demonstrate innovations or services placed under the auspices of the same agency (one-stop shopping) were viewed favorably.

Bride (2001) studied the effect of transforming a mixed-gender day treatment program into two single-sex treatment units. The gender-specific treatment did not ensure improved treatment completion by women or men. Bride concluded that single-sex treatment needs to be augmented by specific new approaches for women to result in improved retention. The small effect on retention for men is interpreted that men are not in need of specialized single-sex counseling approaches because current treatment models are based on the needs for men.

Treatment for Comorbid Substance Abuse, Trauma, and PTSD

Amaro et al. (2007) completed a quasi-experimental study of women entering an integrated, comprehensive treatment program designed to address substance abuse and mental health issues concurrently. The integrated program included mental health and trauma assessment and intervention, and case management and skills training. A comparison group received a treatment-as-usual protocol. Differences between the two groups were controlled for in the statistical analyses. There was improvement in abstinence for alcohol and drug use, improved mental health, and reduced symptoms of PTSD in the treatment group. Significant differences between the two groups were observed for abstinence from drugs, improvement in mental health, and reduction of PTSD symptomatology at the 12-month follow-up. Significant differences between the intervention group and the control group were not present for abstinence from alcohol use. Although not statistically different, the population that displayed the strongest benefits in terms of drug use severity and mental health was the non-Hispanic white group. This study provides direction for specialized services for women targeting trauma as a comorbid factor. (See chapter 6 for more detailed information on co-occurring disorders.)

Outcome Studies on Women

Sun (2006), in a systematic review of 35 published articles, identified treatment intensity or dose, provision of child care, centralized case management, supportive staff, and individual counseling as elements of effective programs. Treatment intensity, case management, and child care increased retention but did not affect outcomes. However, Sun (2006), in support of other reviewers (Morgenstern & Longabaugh, 2000; Waldron & Turner, 2008), stated that there are research design and methodological limitations to the studies reviewed: the lack of randomization, no comparison groups, selection bias, interplay of treatment components, self-reported substance use measures, and not testing for alcohol and drug use outcomes. It is difficult to determine if the differences relate to the type of drug used, the delivery of case management services, or treatment provided in a single-sex setting. The intensity of the program and the length of stay further confound the effect of single-sex treatment.

Acknowledging the methodological limitations, there is a continued need for a feminist orientation to counseling that values the individuality of each client and requires cultural competency. Self-in-relation theory posits that the primacy of relationships for women and empowerment are critical aspects of recovery. Women deserve a safe environment within the treatment milieu in which to explore their relationships without repeating old patterns of dependent behavior or fear of sexual harassment. It is important for women to receive the child care and case management services. Program attributes that can increase access to treatment is a laudable goal. Results by Bride (2001) reiterate that gender-specific services need a specialized theoretical approach, in addition to a single-sex program.

Gay and Lesbian Clients

Research on substance use in the gay community has been based on convenience samples primarily. The result has been that samples are more likely to be white, male, and well educated. These demographic characteristics reflect characteristics of a population that has higher drinking rates than the general population. Cochran, Keenan, Schober, and Mays (2000) analyzed responses to the National Household Survey on Drug Abuse to ascertain actual alcohol use in a sample more representative of the general population. Cochran and colleagues learned that gay men had similar drinking patterns to heterosexual men. However, women who were lesbian reported a higher frequency of drinking, drinking larger amounts on a drinking day, more occasions of feeling drunk, more alcohol dependency, and greater use of treatment than women who were heterosexual. There were significant differences on the indicator of heavy drinking (drinking five or more drinks on an occasion on five or more days in the past month), with 7 percent of the homosexual women reporting heavy drinking compared with 2.7 percent of heterosexual women. A lesser measure, binge drinking, did not indicate a significant difference between the two groups.

Studies of the gay and lesbian population have theorized that the differences when present can be accounted for by different drinking norms, social stigma and discrimination, stress related to identity conflicts, and problems in family relationships. However, it could be argued that those drinking at higher levels risk developing problem drinking (Cochran et al., 2000). Specific long-term research will need to be designed to determine if lifestyle or life stress predicts alcohol and other drug-related problems.

At present, the treatment needs of gay men and lesbians need to be considered to ensure a tolerant and bias-free therapeutic environment. In group settings, other clients may be homophobic; practitioners, themselves, may harbor these attitudes and feelings. Gay and lesbian clients are often highly sensitive to these attitudes, stemming from their prior experiences of homophobia. Social workers need to increase their knowledge of working with this population, including transgendered individuals, bisexual individuals, and those beginning to question their sexual orientation. Questions concerning sexual orientation and sexual identity need to be standard in the assessment protocol. Follow-up questions concerning the degree to which this population experiences stress from discrimination and stigma should be included. Assuming that substance abuse results from stigmatization for all gay and lesbian clients may lead to overlooking other contributing factors and the unique experiences of each client. Currently, many programs address cultural sensitivity to the homosexual community by employing openly gay and lesbian staff members as a policy of being diverse and responsive to clients.

Many gay men and lesbians address their sexual identity in their young adult years. One task is acceptance of a loss of expected roles prescribed by society. Coming out to family and old friends can mean rejection, or at the least, a period of strain in the relationships. Substance use may have been a means of coping with intense feelings of depression, anxiety, and the obstacles that exist in accepting one's own image and identity. Therefore, besides recovery goals, acceptance of self and reconnecting with family are important objectives. With this in mind, significant others and partners should be included in family sessions, in addition to the intimate support network that nurtures the gay person. Fortunately, there are resources available in gay and lesbian communities, such as specialized AA meetings, that should be used.

The research based on the general population appears to be most helpful in making comparisons between straight and gay groups. More research is needed on substances other than alcohol. The popular media tends to inflate drug use in the gay community, a tendency that needs to be met with empirical studies, either quantitative or qualitative.

Older Adults

Services for older adults have centered on improved screening for alcohol abuse, educational interventions, such as doctor's advice, motivational interviewing, and age-specific interventions. For many older adults, drinking is done privately and is difficult to uncover. Statistics indicate that drinking decreases with age. For those ages 50 to 64 years, binge drinking—equal to five or more drinks at a sitting—at least once in the past 30 days, ranges from 21 percent to 14 percent, compared with 7.6 percent of those over 65 who report binge drinking (SAMHSA, 2007). Heavy drinking, which is the same quantity as that for binge drinking but on five days or more in a month, approximated 5 percent to less than 3 percent for the 50 to 64 age group. Almost 1.5 percent of those over 65 report the heavier drinking rates.

The influence of alcohol abuse is a medical concern for older adults because of changes in metabolizing alcohol, other physical conditions, and interactions with prescriptions or over-the-counter medications. Physical indicators of abuse are similar to other problems with aging (for example, loss of appetite, memory loss, depression, confusion, falls and broken bones), and therefore doctors may not ask about drinking patterns. Alcohol use in the elderly population has been character-ized as early onset, most commonly before age 50, and late onset alcohol use. Late onset is related to life transitions and changes in social supports, such as death of a spouse or retirement.

Gender roles and drinking behavior in the older adult are consistent with pat-terns of drinking at younger ages. Men drink more than women, have an earlier onset, are married or divorced, and are more likely to be employed. Women, who are more likely to be the late onset type, tend to be widowed. Women have a high risk for alcohol problems because they are more likely than men to use or abuse prescriptions (Gomberg, 1996).

There is a need to learn more about different drinking problems in minority communities. African Americans drink less but have more severe health conse-quences related to drinking (Hanson & Gutheil, 2004). Hispanic Americans report drinking patterns similar to those of white Americans (SAMHSA, 2007). The inter-est in research on alcohol in the older population is stimulated by the demographic fact that older adults will become a growing proportion of the population as the baby boom population reaches 65. This cohort may bring a different attitude about drinking, and about social use of other drugs, stemming from their drug experi-mentation in their youth. A laissez-faire attitude about alcohol and drug use may lead to an escalation in problematic use.

Research on treatments for the older adult demonstrates similar methodologi-cal problems as research in other areas of alcohol and drug treatment: non-stan-dardized assessment tools, samples of one ethnicity, and limited follow-up periods. In a study comparing middle-aged treatment recipients and older adult treatment recipients, Oslin, Slaymaker, Blow, Owen, and Colleran (2005) learned that both groups improved with treatment. The treatment studied was the Minnesota model. The older adults in this sample had less severe alcohol problems and less comor-bid conditions than those in middle age. They were less likely to engage in formal aftercare services and less likely to contact a sponsor over the one-month follow-up period. Results also indicated that there was a significant difference in the report of improved quality of life following treatment, with fewer older adults reporting an improvement compared with the middle-aged adults.

In another study, Blow, Walton, Chermack, Mudd, and Brower (2000) com-pared abstaining older adults with two other groups, those with a binge drink-ing pattern and those with fewer drinks per drinking occasion but regular drink-ing that was problematic. The drinkers were treated on an inpatient unit with an older adult-specific program. The approach included pharmacotherapy, supportive individual and group therapy without a confrontational style, cognitive–behavioral interventions, a slower pace, and encouragement of a therapeutic alliance with the counselors. At a six-month follow-up, those who completed treatment had reduced their drinking, improved health, and decreased pain; 55.9 percent maintained abstinence. In this study, psychiatric comorbidity and severity of alcohol problem were not associated with the outcome status. Reasons for relapse were feeling social pressure, especially within the family, and negative emotions, such as grief and loss. The older adults, in retrospect, reported using prescription medication on their drinking days. The category of binge drinkers, unlike those drinking slightly less, did not experience a decrease in psychological symptoms with reduced drinking. The authors recommend that future research examine this finding in more depth. Overall, it would appear that a modified treatment program for older adults has potential long-term benefits.

Others have looked at educational intervention by doctors, cognitive behavior treatment for older adults, and motivational interviewing. A doctor's advice, coupled with follow-up phone calls, proved to lead to decreased frequency and quantity of drinking, and less drinking to intoxication (Fleming et al., 1999). Hanson and Gutheil (2004) reviewed successful components of motivational interviewing and concluded that these components may prove helpful with older drinkers. Motivational interviewing relates the presenting problem to questions about drinking. The concern that a person brings to the interview becomes a motivating factor to address the drinking. Physical complaints, memory impairment, depression, and isolation may be why an older person comes to counseling, and these issues may indicate both social drinking and drinking in private. Information from doctor's visits and laboratory reports will support the effects of drinking on health. One should use the client's terminology to connect the concerns with the behavior (Hanson & Gutheil, 2004). Educating the older adult on the influence of alcohol on aging can result in reduced drinking. The social worker needs to be sensitive to the values of the older adult in terms of privacy and shame, but at the same time use self-awareness about his or her own discomfort and cultural biases in confronting an older person about drinking.

In a follow-up study that included 42 older alcoholics, Rice, Longabaugh, Beattie, & Noel (1993) compared relationship enhancement therapy, CBT, and an occupational therapeutic approach. All three provided a functional analysis of precursors and consequences of drinking, but the cognitive–behavioral approach focused on cognitive restructuring, assertion training, problem solving, and responses to relapse (Rice et al., 1993). They found that CBT for the older age group (50 years old or more) to be more effective than the occupational intervention in reducing the number of days drinking and the days of heavy drinking. Reduced drinking was present for the older adults participating in the relationship enhancement group, but the difference between it and the occupational group did not reach significance.

There is a continued need to examine treatments, alcohol and drug use severity, and linkage to aftercare for this older population. We need to learn more about age-specific programs, building social supports (Rice et al., 1993), and effective engagement of minority problem drinkers. Natural supports and community supports like senior citizen programs should be used. The baby boom generation presents upcoming challenges: Their youthful acceptance of illegal drug use may mean more older adults with drug abuse; women of that generation may demonstrate substance use patterns more similar to men, requiring attention to serious health problems in their later years; and widespread use of antianxiety medications may result in increased risk of prescription drug misuse.

To summarize the research on special populations across the life span, there are effective interventions for each of these groups. The addiction field has recognized that treatment approaches need to be varied and targeted to each group. In recognition of the diversity, the field is receptive to interventions representing different theoretical perspectives. Case Example 9.2 is an example of an older client who resists standard treatment.

Treatment Approaches

The following sections provide an overview of different treatment approaches. Descriptions of the components of each approach are followed by reviews of meta-analyses and independent empirical studies that support or qualify the treatment approach. Some of these approaches are consistent with a medical model of alcoholism. However, social work practice in the addictions includes the influence of AA, social learning theory, and the holistic approach labeled biopsychosocial–cultural–spiritual perspective. The approaches reflect this diversity.

Advances in Medication in Conjunction with Individual Treatment

Medications for Alcoholism Treatment

There has been continued research in pharmacology to develop an agonist or antagonist for alcohol and other drugs. The biochemical research is based on findings about what systems in the brain are responsible for the euphoric feelings after

▼
▼
▼

CASE EXAMPLE 9.2. An Older Adult: How Does Family Support Abstinence?

At the age of 71, Mr. E. was experiencing marked deterioration of his health and emotional stamina. He had been a heavy drinker and smoker most of his life, cutting down on alcohol intermittently when it seemed to be interfering at work. Yet he never had the desire to quit either drinking or smoking, considering them as "important as food." He stated, "they helped me relax, and booze to socialize and forget my troubles." He enjoyed the camaraderie with the guys at the clubs; and alcohol was the key to join in and be accepted. He had no understanding of those "younger kids" and their preoccupation with other drugs. To him, they were in another class—tripping into an illegal and mind-altering lifestyle that was beyond his comprehension. The drugs he used were an extensive part of his family background—all the men (and some women) drank and smoked. His father, grandfathers, and uncles even made their own "home spirits." Although his wife and children complained about his drinking and smoking, they inadvertently overlooked the consequences of these activities by not actively confronting excessive usage, and sometimes even encouraging it when his mood was at a low point.

When he had a mild stroke and heart attack, and tests showed liver damage, his physician warned him about the necessity to quit alcohol and cigarettes. Mr. E.'s denial of the source of these physical problems was challenged when the social worker gathered the family together to make an intervention with the goal of having him enter an inpatient treatment program. His decision to attend was not an easy one, for at this point, he was still at the pre-contemplation stage of change. What was so evident to others—that these drugs were the precursors of the ills that were threatening his life—was totally eluding him. The initial task of treatment was to alter his belief system and motivate him to make ample changes that would prolong his life.

drinking, the craving for alcohol, and brain functioning that cause withdrawal symptoms. Thus, the dopamine system is being studied, in addition to the neurotransmitter responsible for inhibitory responses, gamma-amnobutyric acid (GABA), and the neurotransmitter, glutamate, that becomes overstimulated in chronic drinkers (Swift, 2007).

Because of Mr. E.'s resistance to the label of alcoholic and the stigma it produced, it was decided that a more effective approach would be a direct, educational presentation of the facts depicting his physical condition in light of his long-term drinking and other possible precipitating factors. The damage to his body through smoking was also emphasized. A behaviorally oriented focus was on the cost–benefit of using these drugs. Family therapy prodded communication concerning the members' fears of Mr. E. dying; this brought tears and emotional upheavals from all. In addition, a systems approach, exploring the function that alcohol serves within the interactional context of the family and the external environment, was developed. It was determined that alcohol had taken on a life of its own, directing the actions and activities of the participants in this family sage. This was reinforced by selective, outer influences where alcohol was dominant. Communication often centered on drinking; photos of drinking parties were displayed on the walls of the household.

Closely monitoring withdrawal symptoms, the rehabilitation team's supplemental efforts were focused on helping Mr. E. and his family substitute meaningful goals in their daily routines that did not include alcohol and smoking. Health-oriented activities were planned, with non-alcoholic refreshments being served. Supportive structures, such as a senior citizen group that scheduled interesting activities, became a major time-consuming and pleasurable pastime. In time, alcohol and cigarettes took a "back-seat" to the new found diversions. The possibility of relapse, always of concern, was attended to by including Mr. E. in aftercare groups of older problem drinkers. A surprising comment he made during the group showed his attitude change, "Think of all the money I'm saving, now that I'm not drinking or smoking; and I've added years to my life!"

Disulfiram, or Antabuse, has been available for a long time, but its use is limited to a small population of problem drinkers. Disulfiram, taken daily, acts to produce nausea when someone drinks alcohol. There are contraindications for many people with chronic diseases, such as coronary disease, hepatic cirrhosis, and diabetes mellitus, and the daily dosage requires the individual to be motivated to stop drinking. A group of medications is now in use; the medications have varying degrees of effectiveness in changing drinking behavior. Naltrexone acts on the natural opioid receptors, the reward system in the brain, to decrease one's craving for alcohol. Acamprosate is thought to affect the neurotransmitters, GABA, and glutamate. Topiramate is an anticonvulsive that does not have U.S. Food and Drug Administration approval for treatment of alcoholism but is being prescribed "off-label." Other medications, including the selective serotonin reuptake inhibitors, are in experimental study for potential to decrease heavy drinking and relapses.

Naltrexone reduces cravings for alcohol. Studies report fewer drinking days and less relapse for patients receiving naltrexone than those receiving a placebo (Kranzler, Wesson, & Billot, 2004; O'Malley et al., 1992). The COMBINE study has several comparison groups with results supportive of combining naltrexone and counseling for alcohol treatment (Zweben, 2001). In particular, a combined behavioral intervention, including motivational counseling, cognitive behavior treatment, and relationship enhancement therapy resulted in improved outcomes. Naltrexone can also be used in an injectable, extended-release form. This injectable form addresses the problem of adherence to a medication regimen of taking the pill daily. The injectable method avoids the situation of requiring the client to decide if he or she wishes to remain abstinent on a daily basis.

The COMBINE research team also examined the counseling interventions and acamprosate. Acamprosate and medical management did not prove as effective as a placebo or naltrexone (Anton et al., 2006). These results differed from European studies in which acamprosate was effective (Swift, 2007). Given the equivocal results and rapid advancement in new medications, it is recommended that social workers remain informed about the productive use of medication and counseling.

A third medication, topiramate, an anticonvulsive, has demonstrated success with reduced drinking and more abstinence. It has not been approved for use in treatment yet. Two other anticonvulsive medications with mood-stabilizing properties are being tested: carbanazepine and valproate.

Medications that affect the serotonin system have been tested for use in alcoholism treatment. Although there are reduced drinking effects, there are limitations because of adverse reactions to the medications or efficacy limited to certain subgroups, such as men and lower risk drinkers.

Medications for Treatment for Opioids

Methadone is familiar to social workers as an opioid agonist—that is, a chemical that blocks the euphoric effects of opioids. LAAM, L-alpha-acetylmethadol, is a second agonist that can be prescribed for withdrawal and maintenance. Newer drugs used in the treatment of opioid addiction are buprenorphine and buprenorpnine-naloxone. Buprenorphine acts to affect neural receptors as an agonist, blocking the reception, and an antagonist, acting in opposition to the abused drug. Buprenorphine is used in detoxification and maintenance. It has been shown to lead to less opioid use and greater patient retention in comparison with a low-dose methadone maintenance program (Johnson et al., 2000). Several studies were reviewed by Boothby and Doering (2007) in which buprenorphine, buprenorphine-naloxone, and methadone were found to have similar outcomes in reducing opioid use.

The question arises about the efficacy of joining the medication management with counseling interventions. The Cochrane collaboration, in a systematic review, determined that psychosocial treatment, in addition to medication, improved attendance, increased the number of patients completing treatment, and increased abstinence (Amato et al., 2008). Meier and Patkar (2007) raised concerns about the administration of the newer medications in doctor's offices without a counseling component. They noted that insurance coverage for the medication rarely includes coverage for office visits or counseling visits. Furthermore, there are other barriers to in-office treatment with these medications, such as limitations on the doctor's caseload size and prevailing stigmatization of the drug addict. They recount that patients feel better with buprenorphine, have the convenience of fewer office visits, and, therefore, do not recognize the need for treatment for emotional problems. The lethargy that results from methadone lifts and alters the patient's relationship with family, one's life goals, and one's self-assessment. There are psychosocial needs for the recovering user, but he or she may have trouble accepting the need for ongoing counseling. Meier and Patkar endorse counselor–doctor partnerships to facilitate initiation of appropriate psychosocial treatment (see Case Example 9.3).

Research is ongoing for different medications for opioids and other drugs. There will be continuing studies of the effectiveness of "talk" therapy. The NIAAA has made several recommendations that demonstrate the flux that the pharmacological research in the addictions is in: Follow-up periods should be two years or more; studies need to occur in various treatment settings; psychosocial interventions need to be standardized; treatment outcomes should be consistent; and more research is needed on the different patient subgroups (NIAAA, 2008).

Because alcoholism and drug abuse affect many different people, and because it is hypothesized that there are multiple pathways in the brain that foster continued use of such substances, the medication management approach is just one alternative to other therapies. Crucial transition points in seeking treatment can benefit from social work interventions: initiation and screening, adherence to a medication regimen, retention in treatment, and long-term aftercare. Therapies

CASE EXAMPLE 9.3. A Patient on Opioid Agonists: Buprenorphine and Naloxone. How Can Counseling Complement Medication?

Michele is a 32-year-old woman. She has two children placed outside the home: a son who is seven years old and a son who is two years old. The seven-year-old son is in kinship care, but the younger son is in foster care.

A psychosocial history revealed that Michele was raised in an intact family. However, her parents' relationship was volatile. She began drinking at age nine. She reports several physical and mental traumas starting in childhood. She has a history of two sexual assaults between the ages of nine and 16. She used marijuana, cocaine, and hallucinogens. She "fell in love" with heroin after skin-popping. At age 14 she began using heroin intravenously. Her recent use cost $1,000 daily.

Her involvement with the legal system also started at a young age. She has a history of 10 overdoses from multiple drug use. She had one failed treatment episode at a methadone clinic and was put on Suboxone (a combination of buprenorphine and naloxone) prior to a long-term women's and children's program. Her longest period of living drug free was nine months while in the long-term program. She reports she was relatively happy during this period. On discharge, the pressures of returning to her former life without supports resulted in relapse. She had been using heroin intravenously daily for four months when she applied for outpatient treatment at the New Innovations program. She was admitted to a detoxification and rehabilitation facility.

In past attempts to reduce her heroin use, she had purchased Suboxone on the street. She was aware that the new medications are helpful in managing withdrawal symptoms, and requested it at intake. Michele was highly motivated to get clean. She was eager to be reunited with her two sons. Prior to receiving her first dose, she needed to be in a mild to moderate withdrawal. After two days in a treatment facility, she was ready to be placed on a maintenance dose of Suboxone. She was scheduled for medication monitoring and regular urine drug screens for opioids and other drugs.

New Innovations requires that the client participate in counseling to continue on Suboxone. During the first three months Michele was drug free other than the medication. She attended group counseling regularly. The groups included cognitive–behavioral therapy, social skills training, and a women's group. She found a job and began to put money aside for her own apartment. When she attended medication monitoring around the holiday season, Michele confided that she was worried about her upcoming custody hearing. One month later, at her medication review, the urine tests indicated that she had used crack cocaine. She reported that she was drinking over the weekend and used crack with a friend. She was very remorseful.

The social worker and Michele discussed her relapse and the pressures that precipitated her choice of dealing with her problems in the old pattern of drug use. A level of care change was discussed and Michele decided to stay in her groups. She agreed to increase attendance at Narcotics Anonymous meetings with the contingency that she will go to intensive outpatient treatment if she has emotional instability or fears of a relapse. In response to Michele's focus on the child custody hearing, the worker was clear that the drug use will be considered in the judge's decision and was empathic about how upsetting the consequences were to her. The worker understood that there may be ambivalence regarding custody of her children. Michele had returned to her habit of dealing with her interpersonal problems by dulling her feelings with drugs. She and her worker will need to deal with her fear of not being able to face her responsibilities drug free. She needs to approach a sponsor so she will have a plan to deal with her cravings. Developing a support system, attending parenting classes, and confronting issues related to a different lifestyle that includes the care of her children are priorities. Michele faces difficult challenges because of her history of early drug use. The social worker will be challenged to address the client's needs in several domains: skill building, lifestyle change, and emotional growth.

such as motivational interviewing, relationship enhancement therapy, coping skills training, and other CBTs are encouraged (Zweben, 2001). These specific treatment approaches will be described next within the broad treatment categories.

Behavior Theory

Behavior therapy is based on observations of how people develop new behaviors, or continue using self-defeating behaviors, and the factors that reinforce behaviors. Classical conditioning is the technique commonly associated with Pavlov's training of dogs to salivate on hearing a bell, the stimulus, before seeing the food. Operant conditioning is the term used to describe how more complex behavior is developed and maintained. There are several different behavioral techniques that therapists have used to change behavior. Some of the methods will be reviewed with particular attention to how they operate in relation to drug- and alcohol-using behaviors.

The theoretical formulation of addiction from the behaviorist's viewpoint is that drinking and drug use is a learned behavior, evolving from social learning precepts such as modeling, cue exposure, and positive reinforcement. One of the ways that substance use differs from other negative behaviors is that the drug itself is reinforcing for positive effects. Recognizing the biochemical reinforcement of the drug, behaviorists note that there are also behavioral principles acting in the environment that functions to maintain the behavior.

Reinforcement and rewards are often thought of as behavioral components. It is necessary to designate these reinforcers and their active components more specifically. Rewards are positive events that occur subsequent to the behavior. However, rewards are not thought to influence the occurrence or continuation of a behavior. What is reinforcing is positive reinforcement, a pleasant event that occurs at or near the timing of the event and acts to encourage repetition of the behavior. Another technique to encourage reoccurrence of the behavior is negative reinforcement. Negative reinforcement, like a noxious environmental stimulus, is repeated but is withdrawn if the desired behavior occurs. One can think of the obnoxious buzzing of the car door when it is open with the car keys in the ignition. The desired behavior is to remove the keys, and the noxious noise ends. A simplistic illustration would be the noxious stimulus of a nagging spouse for the alcoholic; cessation of the nagging would be the outcome when the alcoholic is not drinking.

Punishment

Punishment is also divided into positive and negative types. Positive punishment is a required behavior demanded following an event. For instance, after experiencing an urge to drink, the client writes 50 times "I can overcome this." A negative punishment is taking away something desirable (demanding a fine that exacts money from the person), or giving a consequence, such as performing an unpleasant task. Punishment tends to be used infrequently in preference to positive and negative reinforcement.

The behavioral therapist uses these techniques after analyzing the client's problem behavior and the client's desired outcome. The client is an active participant in the treatment goals and the interventions. When the behavior has been adequately analyzed, the therapist develops hypotheses about how the behavior is maintained and how it can be changed. Together the therapist and the client develop a behavioral contract. Baseline measurement of the frequency of the behavior and the context are measured. Interventions need to be individualized to be reinforcing. Operant conditioning needs to be immediate and carried out over a sufficient period of time to affect behavior. Following this period, there can be intermittent reinforcement.

Another technique is shaping behavior. Once the desired behavior is determined, a planned strategy of positive reinforcement is activated until the behavior ends or desired behavior is maintained. Two incompatible behaviors cannot occur simultaneously, so the preferred behavior is reinforced. For instance, relaxation cannot occur with anxiety or drink-seeking behavior.

Additional treatment behavior approaches that are used with drug and alcohol-related problems are aversion therapy, contingency management, covert sensitization, and counter conditioning (relaxation). A "contingency management" technique uses a direct consequence of the behavior that is perceived as negative for the client. For instance, one can contract with the client that if he or she relapses a letter will be sent to his or her employer, or other significant person, declaring the clients drug use. This kind of technique has been proven effective during the time that the contingency is in effect.

"Aversion therapy" is the technique of linking a negative behavior with alcohol use. The aversive agent has been a noxious chemical to induce vomiting, electric shocks and methods to produce apnea, or a paralyzed breathing sensation (Rimmele, Miller, & Dougher, 1989). Most behaviorists have changed aversion therapy to covert sensitization techniques. Covert sensitization has proven to be more effective than aversion therapy (G. T. Wilson, 1978). In covert sensitization, the client imagines drinking while a noxious stimulus is linked to an unwanted conditioned response. The objective in covert sensitization is to evoke strong feelings other than nausea, perhaps disgust, anxiety, or embarrassment, followed by a detailed guided imaging of pouring the drink down the drain, thus alleviating the negative feelings (Rimmele et al., 1989). Jayasinghe (2005) in discussing hypno-aversion therapy, specifies that the aversive stimuli is to be connected to a precursor to the drinking behavior, not the drinking itself.

An expert behaviorist needs to supervise and train the therapist in the behavioral assessment, choice of interventions, and implementation of the treatment. Some techniques may need special consideration, such as the aversion techniques. Ethical considerations concerning the client's full understanding of the choice of treatment have been a subject of criticism. For example, is it ethical to induce nausea during the covert desensitization?

CBT

Cognitive–behavioral methods in substance abuse treatment have offered practitioners and clients a number of varying strategies that have been empirically tested and validated. No other approach has produced such a consistent number of studies that serve to judge its effectiveness. It is important to be aware that the significance of AA and other self-help groups to recovery is recognized in this mode of therapy and is often recommended to clients (McCrady & Miller, 1993). As Miller and Kurtz explained,

> [AA] clearly has important social, behavioral, and cognitive components. . . . It is not a treatment, but a way of living and being. Although its sole purpose is to help alcoholics become and stay sober, the program attends to much more than the mere imbibing of alcohol. . . . Practice of the 12 steps brings a recovery characterized by growth in character traits such as honesty, humility and patience. (1994, p. 161)

"Cognitive therapy . . . attempts to reduce excessive emotional reactions and self-defeating behavior by modifying the faulty or erroneous thinking and maladaptive beliefs that underlie these reactions" (Beck, Wright, Newman, & Liese, 1993, p. 27). This is, in large part, based on the pioneering work of Albert Ellis's (1971) rational emotive therapy that challenged irrational and, therefore, dysfunctional thought processes, which created negative emotions and subsequent self-defeating behaviors. Ellis conceptualized our thinking processes as an activating event (A), which leads to thoughts about the event (B), resulting in an emotional response (C). This ABC model characterizes the cognitive–behavioral premise that thoughts lead to emotions. Over time, irrational thoughts develop into rigid schemata of "musts" and "shoulds" that impair healthy functioning. The treatment approach is designed to teach clients how to identify the "shoulds," dispute faulty thinking and develop new ways of interpreting the activating events.

Beck and colleagues (1993) elaborated on the ABC model and structured irrational beliefs, also referred to as automatic thoughts, into a list that can be shared with the client. Clients can identify three or four of their habitual thinking patterns and develop knowledge of their core beliefs and worldview.

In CBT, the counselor normalizes the beliefs by explaining that they derive from early thinking patterns, before the child had developed abstract thinking abilities. Automatic thoughts are universal. Among the strategies developed by cognitive researchers and practitioners that can be useful when working with substance-abusing clients are the following: cost–benefit analysis, Daily Thought Record (DTR), Daily Activity Schedule (DAS), relaxation and stress management, imagery, role modeling and behavioral rehearsal, and social skills training (Beck et al., 1993).

Cost–Benefit Analysis

Most clients will be ambivalent about having to give up drugs that have been functional for them. It could be argued that all behavior is purposeful, even that which is self-destructive and may be incomprehensible. Many reasons have been made for using (for example, relief from emotional pain, boredom, loneliness; the unwanted reality of living conditions; desire to lose inhibitions; enjoyment with friends). None should be discounted, for they can relate a great deal about the client's circumstances, emotional composure, and social interactions. To demonstrate the negative consequences of drug use to motivate change, eliciting from the client the advantages and disadvantages of drinking and drugging can be very enlightening.

A four-cell matrix, listing some of the advantages and disadvantages of stopping and not stopping, is displayed in Figure 9.1. This illustration can initiate challenges

FIGURE 9.1: Cost–Benefit Analysis of Stopping and Not Stopping to Misuse Substances

	Stopping	Not Stopping
Advantages	Improved health Better relationship with family More productive at work (won't lose job)	Keep drug-using friends Pain/stress relief Don't give up source of pleasure/enjoyment
Disadvantages	Lose some friends Can't relax/forget problems DTs/painful withdrawal	Poor health Continued fights with family May lose job

to and re-evaluations of detrimental behavioral patterns in the context of viewing the costs versus the benefits they have produced.

The next task with the client is weighing the positives with the negatives that should lead to formulating constructive treatment goals. The strategy is to point out the deleterious effects of drug use and suggest alternative coping mechanisms (for example, socializing with nonusing people, acquiring pleasurable hobbies and activities) to allay fears of stopping. This should be done while reinforcing the benefits of change. From this demonstration, the client can obtain an objective outlook on the toll of his or her self-defeating behaviors, increase the motivation to quit, and facilitate abstinence with mutually designed strategic plans to obtain that goal.

DTR

What occurs in counseling sessions is, of course, the beginning of the continuation of the change process. So when we consider that these sessions make up a relatively short period of time in the life of the client, strategies outside of the meeting that reinforce learning and motivation should also be conducted. This is accomplished by a variety of homework assignments, one of which the DTR (see Figure 9.2) that serves to monitor negative moods and thoughts that could result in drug use. By listing situations that occur daily (for example, those that create cravings), the thoughts and emotions that follow, and the rational thought responses that will counteract self-defeating beliefs and attitudes and respective consequences, the client becomes aware how negative thoughts that trigger corresponding emotions can be altered to produce positive outcomes. It is important to set aside a portion of the following session (usually at the beginning to formulate strategies and tasks) to review the DTR with the client, discussing the affirming and constructive rational responses and posing for consideration other alternative positive thoughts that will not trigger drug use.

Boredom, loneliness, and a desire for pleasure and excitement often serve as a stimulus for drug usage. Filling time productively and pleasurably can help to resist urges. By recording daily activities hour by hour, with a notation designating the degree of mastery and pleasure experienced, this homework assignment will illuminate those activities that bring satisfaction without a drug focus and, conversely, those that resembled or initiated previous drug-related activities. A DAS is easily constructed with columns for each day and rows for each hour (Beck et al., 1993). Figure 9.3 is an example of a DAS for the older adult client illustrated by Case Example 9.2. As with the DTR, these schedules should be examined in sessions, affording both the client and the practitioner to devise activities of interest and enjoyment. Many times, clients are unaware of what brought them pleasure

FIGURE 9.2: Daily Thought Record

Directions: When you notice your mood getting worse, ask yourself, "What's going through my mind right now?" and as soon as possible, jot down the thought or mental image in the Automatic Thought Column.

DATE/ TIME	SITUATION: Describe: 1. Actual event leading to unpleasant emotion 2. Stream of thoughts, daydreams or recollection, leading to unpleasant emotion, or 3. Distressing physical sensations.	AUTOMATIC THOUGHT(S) 1. Write automatic thought(s) that preceded emotion(s) 2. Rate belief in automatic thought(s) 0–100%.	EMOTION(S) 1. Specify sad, anxious, angry, etc. 2. Rate degree of emotion 0–100%.	RATIONAL RESPONSE 1. Write rational response to automatic thought(s). 2. Rate belief in rational response 0–100%.	OUTCOME 1. Re-rate belief in automatic thought(s) 0–100%. 2. Specify and rate subsequent emotions 0–100%.
Friday	Alone at home. Coworkers have invited me to meet them at a restaurant.	"I'll make a fool of myself." (75%) "I don't know how to act around people." (85%) "I'll be alone for the rest of my life." (50%)	Nervous (75%) Anxious (85%) Sad (45%)	"I'm generally quiet when I go out, not foolish." (100%) "I know how to be polite toward others." (90%) "If I take risks, I'll meet someone eventually." (75%)	1. "Fool" (25%) 2. "Relieved" (65%) 1. "Don't know how to act." (25%) 2. "Relieved" (65%) 1. "Alone for life." (35%) 2. "Hopeful" (50%)

Questions to help formulate the rational response: (1) What is the evidence that the automatic thought is true? Not true? (2) Is there an alternative explanation? (3) What's the worst that could happen? Could I live through it? What's the best that could happen? What's the most realistic outcome? (4) What should I do about it? (5) What's the effect of my believing the automatic thought? What could be the effect of changing my thinking? (6) If————(friend's name)——was in this situation and had this thought, what would I tell him/her?

Source: Beck, A. T., Wright, F. D., Newman, C. F., & Liese, B. S. (1993). *Cognitive therapy of substance abuse.* New York: Guilford Press.

FIGURE 9.3: Daily Activity Schedule

Time Period	Sunday	Monday	Tuesday
6—7	Walk dog	Walk dog	Walk dog
7—8	Breakfast	Y exercise	Breakfast
8—9	News	Dress	News & Dress
9–10	Dress	Psycho-Education Group	Photography Sr. Center
10–11	Church		"
11–12	Church	"	"
12—1	Family dinner	Group lunch	Food Pantry
1—2		Special time with wife	"
2—3	Family time	"	"
3—4	Family	"	Clean up
4—5	TV/exercise	News	"
5—6	"	Dinner	Dinner
6—7	Dinner	Set up for group problem-solving	
7—8	TV	Group	Scrabble practice
8—9	TV/ relax	"	"
9—10	Meditate Serenity Prayer	Meditate	"
10–11	Sleep	Sleep	Sleep
11–12			
12—6			

Source: Beck, A. T., Wright, F. D., Newman, C. F., & Liese, B. S. (1993). *Cognitive therapy of substance abuse.* New York: Guilford Press.

Wednesday	Thursday	Friday	Saturday
Walk dog	Walk dog	Walk dog	Walk dog
Y exercise	Breakfast	Drive children to school	Breakfast
Dress		Breakfast with C.	Chores
Done workin' club	Psycho-education group	Babysit with Mom	Volunteer
"	"	Babysit	"
"	"	Babysit	"
Lunch	Lunch	Pick up children	Lunch
Budgeting	Mall/museum	Lunch out	Outdoor work
"	"	Swim	or photo outing
Write minutes/ club	"	Swim	Biweekly trip
Read news	"	Home	"
Friends/dinner	Pizza	Dinner	"
"	Walk	Groceries or night out	Dinner out
Optional group	Scrabble	Movie/friends	Socialize with friends
"	"	"	Cards/chess
Home	Home	"	"
Sleep	Slccp	Sleep	"
			Meditate Sleep

and feelings of mastery and efficacy before their drug usage began. Tapping these memories can instill the motivation to rekindle interests and activities that interrupt associations with drug-using behaviors. The next step is to actually plan and schedule favorable activities with the assignment of again filling out the DAS to demonstrate the significance of using time productively to achieve goals.

By using these homework sheets, one develops a detailed description of the behaviors, automatic thoughts, and resulting emotions. This functional analysis has practical results for research also. Operationalizing variables for research becomes easy, and CBT has been extensively tested.

Studies on CBT have been completed for the major drugs. The Cochrane collaboration has reviewed six randomized studies on marijuana (Denis, Lavie, Fatseas, & Auriacombe, 2006), determining that CBT using individual counseling is effective in reducing the frequency of marijuana use and symptoms of dependency. However, although there was some support that CBT is effective in reducing cocaine and stimulant use compared with treatment as usual, the Cochrane review concluded that there is not sufficient support for any one treatment approach in preference to others.

Furthermore, there are outstanding questions about what components of CBT are the salient mechanisms by which the therapy achieves improved alcohol and drug outcomes. Morgenstern and Longabaugh (2000) examined the extent to which studies had tested for the mechanisms and the relationships between an increase in theorized skills and alcohol or drug use. Their thorough examination determined that little is known of the mechanisms. Many studies have confirmed that CBT increases a skill, such as coping skills, but a subsequent link to substance use has not been established. Long-term outcomes of substance use were not studied; however, other methodological problems with the studies were reviewed. The outcomes from Project MATCH, an extensive study that placed clients in one of three treatments on the basis of their characteristics indicated that CBT was more effective than Twelve Step programs for clients who scored low on alcohol dependence (Babor & Del Boca, 2003). However, other client subgroups did not benefit in CBT over either the Twelve Step programs or Motivational Enhancement therapy. Notwithstanding the research challenges, CBT has been used as the comparison therapeutic group in other studies (see Waldron & Turner, 2008).

Relapse Prevention

Strategies based on cognitive–behavioral precepts are incorporated into relapse prevention programs. One challenge for social workers working in alcohol, tobacco, and other drugs treatment is the frequency of relapse. Of participants in AA, 50 percent to 70 percent do not continue long term. One cannot conclude that those individuals are not abstinent, but one can imagine that many are not. Therefore, counseling approaches that enhance abstinence have been developed. Researchers have focused on multiple factors contributing to relapse in an effort to improve outcomes. Combining behavioral and cognitive behavioral approaches, Marlatt and Gordon (1985) developed relapse prevention. Among factors contributing to relapse are the environmental stimuli, ideas of self-efficacy, and positive and negative effect. Among the slogans Twelve Step programs use are "once an alcoholic, always an alcoholic." In contrast, in relapse prevention, efforts are directed toward thoughts that increase self-efficacy, such as "I can handle being in a drinking situation," or "one drink is a lapse, not an inevitable return to abusive drinking patterns." A lapse has been defined as a single incidence of drinking, "a valuable learning experience in the trial-and-error process of building a life free of former addiction" (George, 1988, p. 129).

Relapse prevention begins with an assessment of situations that the client perceives to present risk. These risky situations should cover multiple domains including interpersonal encounters (people), environmental factors (places and things), and emotional states (Annis & Davis, 1989). To the client the relapse appears to be an event, happening without warning; however, relapse is actually a process (Gorski, 1988). The more details the client can relate about the precursors to a relapse, the more he or she can anticipate the relapse and develop a plan to curtail it. It is important that the precursors be individualized. Evidence shows that both pleasant and negative emotions can trigger a relapse. While reviewing a hierarchy of risky situations, the client is asked to review how he or she has used his or her strengths to avoid some risks, his or her coping responses, such as logical thinking, and who can be contacted for assistance. Different interventions associated with new coping skills become the focus of relapse prevention. The client develops plans and discusses how confident he or she feels with his or her ability to stop drinking urges and the relapse. Scheduling homework of dealing with the risky situations, with the easiest situations first, increases self-efficacy, according to Annis and Davis (1989). Monitoring self-efficacy, noting success and the degree of effort, among other indicators, contributes to the evaluation of successful treatment.

Gorski (1988), in a widely used relapse prevention program, emphasized that affect, in addition to automatic thoughts, constitutes drinking triggers. After a functional analysis, education on post-acute withdrawal symptoms, and descriptions of at-risk drinking situations, the client is asked to examine how he or she can identify when his or her thinking leads to an emotional state that leads to a relapse. Repeatedly, the client is asked to examine more deeply what the emotional state is that becomes a precursor, until the client identifies a strong emotional state, such as shame or fury. The in-depth examination provides an understanding of the steps, which without the examination, appears automatic. More than one client has described the combined spiral of thinking and feeling as "ballistic."

Social skills training has been an important component of relapse prevention, initially based on the work of Marlatt (1978). Incorporating three groups (skills training, feelings discussion, controls receiving routine alcohol treatment) in a study of the attributes of social skills training in high-risk situations, Chaney, O'Leary, and Marlatt (1978) reported that those in the social skills training group had a significant reduction in the duration and severity of relapses compared with those in other groups after a one-year follow-up. Assertiveness training was taught both to address social situations that contribute to stress for the client and to deal with high-risk situations. Clients are taught how to improve their communication skills, decrease dependent behavior, and practice skills within a safe counseling or group environment.

Studies cited in the previous paragraph have focused on individuals who are alcohol dependent. Relapse prevention techniques have been used with other substances. In a meta-analysis, Irvin, Bowers, Dunn, and Wang (1999) reviewed 26 relapse prevention studies with alcohol and other drugs. Overall they learned that relapse prevention interventions reduced substance use and resulted in improved functioning. In analyzing four studies in which medication was provided, medication with counseling increased the effectiveness of alcohol treatment. There were no differences in treatment effect for individual counseling in comparison with group interventions. Nor were there differences in inpatient programs as compared with outpatient programs. The results of this meta-analysis should be interpreted with care given that the studies on alcohol accounted for a disproportionate amount of the results. It is interesting that the alcohol outcome studies used unverified self-report, whereas the nicotine and cocaine studies used verified self-report or laboratory results. In this analysis, relapse prevention, compared with other treatment interventions, was not preferable over the other interventions. However, the researchers conclude that the costs of relapsing to habitual alcohol and drug use may be so great that continued use of relapse prevention interventions may still be beneficial (see Case Example 9.4).

Treatment Modalities: Partial Care Programs and Intensive Outpatient Care

Relapse prevention interventions are popular in partial care programs and intensive outpatient programs. The programs are an outgrowth of the medical model

CASE EXAMPLE 9.4. Relapse Prevention: Do Relationships Lead to Relapse?

Aubrey, an African American woman, age 32, has two years of college and currently works as a bank teller. She lives with her daughter, age 10, in an apartment building in a safe, but poor neighborhood. Aubrey's sexual orientation is homosexual, an identity with which she is comfortable.

She began drinking alcohol and smoking marijuana at age 12. At age 16 she was using cocaine and experimenting with other street drugs. Her crack use has escalated. She sought treatment at age 21 in a 28-day rehabilitation program for women. The rehabilitation program included educational groups, supportive group counseling, individual therapy, and Twelve Step participation. She completed the program and has maintained abstinence from all drugs and alcohol for 11 years.

Aubrey requested drug counseling because she felt that she was at risk of relapse and was experiencing conflicts with sexual partners. She had had past long-term sexual relationships, but had not been in a serious relationship for four years. She started a relationship, but after a few months she became dissatisfied with the partner, leading to major interpersonal conflicts. At this time she "dates" one particular female friend, but frequents a dance club for lesbians. She identifies several problems with this socializing: alcohol and drugs are available, she experiences frustration and diminished self-esteem when she does not meet a new sexual partner, and the flirtations with others create significant conflicts with the woman she is dating. She reports mood swings, difficulty meeting her commitments, like her job, and cravings for cocaine.

The treatment plan developed with her social worker included exploring what she wants from a relationship, tracking her drug cravings, and learning assertiveness skills. She attended counseling with regularity. Although she conceded that socializing in a drugging environment ran counter to maintaining recovery, she rejected attempts to select an alternative social scene. Mood swings were associated with drug cravings.

A crisis with her primary partner resulted in her relapsing. The next day she contacted her sponsor and her counselor. The sponsor assisted with a daily schedule of NA meetings and supportive contact with her as well as other NA members. The social worker and Aubrey developed a

(continued)

▼
▼
▼

CASE EXAMPLE 9.4. *(continued)*

contract including NA attendance, contact with the sponsor, and informing the social worker if there is a relapse. They reassessed her readiness
to maintain a drug-free lifestyle, then recontracted about motivation to
address what triggered relapse and drug cravings. They discussed an
intensive relapse prevention program but, based on her long period of
abstinence, they agreed on individual relapse prevention counseling.
Using the strengths perspective, the social worker and Aubrey discussed
how she had managed sobriety for an extended period. Important family
relationships were explored and contracted for more leisure time with
her mother and siblings. Her parenting skills were supported. Concern
for her daughter prompted Aubrey to contact friends in NA to initiate a
teenage Nar-Anon meeting. Aubrey and the social worker rehearsed a
conversation with her off-and-on partner about new ways to de-escalate
conflict at its inception. Four specific relapse interventions were (1) knowing who to contact when fearing a relapse; (2) in-depth analysis of feelings, using the Gorski approach (1988)—"I know I am in trouble with my
addiction when I . . ."; (3) anger management skills; and (4) discussion
of dependency issues. A more comprehensive assessment concerning
other areas of her life was included: the importance of family, a desire
to find a spiritual place that was welcoming to gay people, establishing
an exercise program, and limiting socializing to a drug-free environment,
like NA social groups.

and partial hospital departments of community mental health centers. Programs
have expanded to incorporate the Minnesota model philosophy (abstinence and
Twelve Step program facilitation), motivational interviewing, behavioral, and cognitive–behavioral approaches. Partial care programs are scheduled for three or
more days a week, for five or more hours, and serve substance abusers with histories of multiple relapsing. Criteria for acceptance can include a comorbid mental
health diagnosis or personality disorder. There are individual and group counseling sessions, activities of daily living, recreation, social skills training, and prevo-
cational training. Intensive outpatient treatment programs have similar services,
but for fewer hours and fewer days a week. Intensive outpatient programs may be
scheduled for evening hours. Group treatment strategies are used with a variety

of specific treatment approaches, such as the stress management techniques to be discussed in the next section.

Stress Management Techniques

Strategies such as stress management training, systematic desensitization, and biofeedback, coupled with relaxation techniques, have shown equivocal outcomes on the reduction of drinking behavior. Milkman and Sederer (1990) had positive results, but a study by Miller, Taylor and West (1980) found no overall effect on drinking measures. Brady and Sonne (1999) did not find empirical studies of stress management isolating stress management as the salient technique contributing to effectiveness in the substance abuse field. Currently, mindfulness in meditation is gaining more widespread use. Mindfulness in meditation is being aware of distractions in the environment, accepting the thoughts or emotions, and returning one's attention to the meditation practice. Mindfulness is a step in the process of objectifying negative thoughts and emotions, which serves to break the automatic linkage with the desire to use drugs. In mindfulness, one notes negative thoughts in conjunction with their "transient nature" (Breslin, Zack, & McMain, 2002). Mindfulness is based on behavioral principles of conditioned response, cue exposure, memory network, automatic drug-use action plans, and extinction.

In the substance abuse field we are familiar with the concept of triggers, words or other stimuli in the environment that generate a craving or negative affective state. Memory is activated by the triggers, including the memory of an action plan to secure the craved-for drug. Action plans, whether to secure the drug or to initiate behaviors to maintain abstinence, are stimulated. However, the new abstinence action plan is weaker than the automatic habitual drug-seeking pattern. Paying attention to the trigger is helpful in breaking the automatic response. In this way, mindfulness proves to be more helpful than ignoring the trigger or ignoring negative emotions connected to the trigger. Awareness of high-risk situations can facilitate greater coping responses. In the long term, breaking the link between the triggers and the drug seeking may result in extinction of that conditioned response.

Mindfulness that attends to negative emotional states, but without destructive pre-occupation on the feelings, further aids the process of interrupting the automatic response of drug seeking (Breslin et al., 2002). The mindfulness meditation approach synthesizes the cognitive response and the influence of negative affective states in a complex theoretical implementation of behavioral therapy techniques.

To learn to effectively use mindfulness meditation, the therapist begins with triggers of moderate intensity, coaches the client to use mindfulness meditation in the situation, and over time, progresses to more difficult triggers. This therapeutic process is equivalent to counterconditioning.

Few studies have been conducted on the efficacy of mindfulness meditation with alcohol and drug problems, but results have been supported for those with a diagnosis of depression and borderline personality disorder. Mindfulness-based cognitive therapy has some evidence of reducing relapse for depressed patients. With pharmacotherapy and DBT (discussed below), borderline clients learn both "acceptance and control of negative affect" to reduce substance use (Linehan et al., 2002). Which component in DBT contributes to outcome remains unclear, so the effectiveness of mindfulness as a stand-alone therapy is unclear.

One criticism of mindfulness meditation is that to benefit, one needs adequate time to learn the method. It would require special training for those clients who have difficulty with meditation. Furthermore, some clients do not respond to what may appear to be a passive and cognitive intervention.

Hypnosis

Hypnosis is an approach to treating substance abuse that uses guided imagery after a hypnotic state has been induced. Hypnosis can be used to assess the individual's motivation for change and for the therapeutic change itself. Hypno-aversion therapy uses the same techniques as covert sensitization by linking nausea imagery with the precursor to taking a drink (Jayasinghe, 2005). Jayasinghe described another method, Hypno-Rational Emotive Behavior Therapy, in which the client assesses the effect of alcohol on his or her life, visualizes the negative effects of the drinking, and then imagines a future state without alcohol. This process is followed while the client is under hypnosis. There is limited empirical research on hypnosis. The hypno-aversion therapy is intensive and lengthy. For instance, Jayasinghe initiates the therapy when the client is hospitalized, and requires frequent reexposure to the therapy for a year after hospitalization.

Dialectical Behavior Therapy

DBT was developed for individuals with borderline personality disorder and a history of self-destructive behavior, including self-mutilation and multiple suicide attempts. The name derives from the dialectical tensions that disturbed clients have, as well as the attention to both thoughts and behavior (Linehan et al., 2002). The approach has now been adapted to other diagnostic categories including those with chemical dependency. It is a problem-oriented technique with a dual emphasis on validating the client and changing dysfunctional behavior. Behavioral techniques are used, such as positive and negative reinforcement and aversive consequences for nonadaptive behavior. There is a positive orientation to the growth potential and the practice of listening to the "wise mind" that is within each person. In addition to validation and behavioral techniques, DBT uses psycho-education and weekly groups for skill training, particularly focused on emotions and interpersonal effectiveness. Differing from CBT, the objective of DBT is to teach the clients to manage emotional trauma, not to reduce the negative emotions. In the weekly groups, group members increase their tolerance to distress and their ability to regulate their emotions. Other group skills are interpersonal communication and mindfulness.

In DBT for alcohol- and drug-dependent individuals the goal is abstinence. Skills related to relapse prevention are taught in recognition of the challenges of this population to achieve abstinence without early relapses. The role of the therapist emphasizes reciprocal communication and self-disclosure. Therapists use warmth, genuineness, and responsiveness, including accessibility on weekends and during non-office hours.

Marsha Linehan, the originator of DBT, has completed much of the research on the approach. In the research of her collegial group, DBT has been found to improve substance abuse behavior compared with treatment as usual. In a recent study to determine the salient components of the approach for women with borderline personality disorder and opioid dependence, Linehan et al. (2002) compared DBT with another therapeutic approach using individual, group supportive counseling, and Twelve Step programs. For both the experimental DBT group and the control group, LAAM, an opioid agonist, was prescribed to the clients. At 12 months the DBT group had less frequency of opioid use. At 16 months there was no difference in either substance abuse or psychopathology. Caution should be used in interpreting the results because there was significantly better retention in the alternative group, compared with the DBT group, which numbered nine completers. Therefore, given similar long-term results for those completing treatment in either group, treatment costs and the extensive training for DBT needs to be weighed.

In other research on DBT not associated with Linehan and colleagues, van den Bosch, Verheul, Schippers, and van den Brink (2002) did not show a treatment effect for decreased substance abuse for DBT compared with treatment as usual at an extended follow-up period of 18 months. Van den Bosch and colleagues had several recommendations in regard to DBT. They concluded that DBT is an excellent therapy for specific behaviors, whether suicidal behavior, binge eating, or substance abuse, but it has not demonstrated efficacy over traditional therapies for multiple behaviors. They recommended that substance abuse should be considered as serious a destructive behavior as suicidal behavior on the DBT assessment hierarchy. In addition, therapist training in DBT needs to incorporate training in substance abuse counseling because of the frequency with which these illnesses co-occur. Based on this literature review, it is not possible to conclude that DBT results in more successful treatment outcomes for substance abuse for women with borderline personality disorder than other comprehensive therapeutic approaches.

Brief Solution-Focused Therapy

Solution-focused therapy, developed to address the need for short-term intervention, validates the client and works with the strengths that the client brings. It contrasts with earlier social work approaches in that it does not delve into the problems that the client relates, it does not look for causative factors that contribute to the problem, and it is atheoretical. Like strengths-based theory, it maintains that a focus on how things go wrong for the client or the family promotes concern for the problem and sends the meta-message that the client is deficient, the client is the problem. Instead, the objective of solution-focused therapy is to focus on the existing health-enhancing behaviors of the client.

Solution-focused therapists compliment the client on making a decision to enter counseling and ask what coping skills have been used to date that have maintained him or her in the positive condition (compared with being worse off). The relationship between the client and the social worker is collaborative. One hallmark of solution-focused therapy is the asking of the miracle question. The intent of the miracle question is to visualize how one would behave if the problem is solved. The miracle question is:

> Suppose tonight, after our session, you go home, and fall asleep, and while you are sleeping, a miracle happens. The miracle is that the problem[s] that brought you here today are solved! But you don't know that the miracle has happened, because you are asleep. When you wake up in the morning, what will be some of the first things you will notice that will be different to tell you that this miracle has happened? (Tohn & Oshlag, 1995, p. 54)

The miracle question short-circuits rational, right-brain thinking, allowing the client to envision outcomes that would be satisfying to him or her. The client is asked to describe what his or her behavior would look like, who would notice the behavior, and what else would result. Questions elicit a detailed description of the behavior, the surrounding circumstances, and the responses of significant people so that it can become the solution to the problem. It enables the client to move toward that same behavior.

In solution-focused therapy one assesses the readiness for counseling, not unlike the transtheoretical stages of change model (Prochaska & DiClemente,

1988). The relation of the client to the worker is characterized as a customer–seller, complainant–listener, or visitor–host relationship (Tohn & Oshlag, 1995). In the visitor–host relationship, the client does not perceive that there is a problem, and is visiting. Sometimes it is possible to alter the relationship to a customer, but if not, then one is hospitable and invites the client to return. The complainant, an appropriate appellation, is frequently interested in the counselor changing another person's behavior. The customer recognizes that he or she has a problem, to which the counselor responds with "selling" solutions. In addition, solution-focused counselors use scaling to determine how far along the goal the person is. The counselor uses imagining questions to enhance how the person envisions what it is like to achieve his or her goal. These techniques are effective in avoiding intellectualization.

Solution-focused therapists look for "exceptions" to the behavior and prescribe doing more of what is successful. Or they prescribe a hypothetical situation, like a coin toss, and suggest that the client pretend that the behavior is right. When clients have stopped their behavior for days prior to the first appointment, the therapist and the client examine the conditions that have led to this change. In this way, the client finds his or her own treatment objectives.

Although theory and diagnosis are denied, the prescriptions are based on the work of Milton Erickson, using the behavioral patterns of individuals. Erickson considered "'utilizing' a patient's own mental processes in ways that are outside his usual range of intentional or voluntary control" (Erickson, Rossi, & Rossi, 1976, p. 19). de Shazer (1988) expanded that idea to "utilizing whatever the client does that is somehow 'right,' 'useful,' 'effective,' 'good,' or 'fun' for the purpose of developing a solution" (p. 140). For example, for one couple in which the husband is the drinker, the "fun" events are surprises. The therapist links the wife's creating a surprise to the drinking in a double-bind situation in which the husband can either enjoy the special pleasure of the relationship or continue to drink. When she surprises him with a six-pack, he opts to stop drinking. No negative consequences are incorporated in the solution. An example in which more of the same behavior is prescribed is recounted in *Working with the Problem Drinker* (Berg & Miller, 1992). The prescription to a problem drinker is to continue drinking, but one drink at a time, and to walk to a bar at a considerable distance from the first bar for the second drink.

Both of these examples show how solution-focused techniques appear to challenge traditional alcohol and drug counseling. First, there is no goal of abstinence and no direction to attend self-help meetings. There is no diagnostic period to learn the causes of the addiction, periods of abstinence, or comorbid factors. There is no psychoeducational component or motivational interviewing. However, one technique that compliments relapse prevention is "flagging the minefield" (Homrich &

Horne, (2000). Clients review what could interfere with continuing the new behavior. Thus, they anticipate possible obstacles and ways to avoid them. The metamessage is that they have changed the behavior and have power over old behavior patterns (Homrich & Horne, 2000).

This method requires advanced training, high levels of supervision, and input from a reflecting team. Given the dramatic differences in the approach and the other methods we have reviewed, it is understandable that there is skepticism of the method. Support for the approach derives from the research (McKeel, 1996), the success of the approach with other mental health problems, the ability to engage the client, working with decreased resistance, and high validation of the actions of the clients.

Elements of solution-focused therapy have been incorporated into Strengths-Oriented Referral for Teens (SORT), a child–parent group intervention for teenagers with drinking and drug problems (Smith & Hall, 2007). The substance abuse and other problem behaviors are assessed in an earlier session with the adolescent and the parent.

Motivational interviewing (Miller & Rollnick, 2002) is the technique practiced. The SORT counselor meets with the adolescent and the parents separately, and then together. Their strengths are detailed, as well as the recommendations from the assessment, linking concerns and strengths by reflecting the adolescent's (and parents') answers from the assessment. Like solution-focused therapy, the counselor uses empathy, praise, and questions, such as "What does your probation officer have to see you doing differently in order to feel confident that you no longer need probation?" (Smith & Hall, 2007, p. 71) Scaling questions are used, and mutual agreements between adolescent and parent are concluded. Thus, SORT is an integrated model that provides an example of how solution-focused therapy can be implemented in substance abuse treatment. There is a need for empirical research to confirm the efficacy of the model.

Self-Help Groups

With the anonymity of self-help groups, often it is assumed that research in this area cannot be accomplished. This is erroneous, as studies of AA have dated as far back as 50 years ago (Kurtz, 1993). Early research was conducted by qualitative methods of attentive listening to AA members within and outside of meetings, with an analysis of the collected data. More recent studies have been quantitatively oriented. (See chapter 11 for more detailed content on self-help groups.)

It was reported that between 50 percent and 70 percent of participants leave after brief contact with AA, but for those who maintain their memberships, better drinking-related outcomes are evident (Emrick, 1987). A prospective study from Australia (Toumbourou et al., 2002) provides support for the value of NA on drinking outcomes. They determined that stable attendance at NA and having a service role (for example, being sponsored or chairing a meeting) was associated with lower alcohol use for one year. Controlling for indicators of stability, such as completion of secondary education, confirmed that the model of self-help meeting participation led to reduced alcohol use and marginal support for reduced marijuana use. The results from Project MATCH (Babor & Del Boca, 2003), a research project that matched clients to treatment options, indicated no significant differences among CBT, motivational enhancement therapy, and Twelve Step facilitation groups. For individuals with high severity, an aftercare program experience and little support to stop drinking had favorable outcomes with higher AA participation. However, Ferri, Amato, and Davoli (2006) in a review of eight studies, concluded that there is no definitive support for self-help groups for the outcomes of the number of drinks on drinking days. The methodological limitations across the studies, including small sample sizes, hamper comparisons from these studies.

The support of AA and other Twelve Step programs is endorsed by treatment programs in the United States. Securing a sponsor, and regular attendance, is considered necessary for the relapse prevention approaches previously described.

Harm Reduction

Harm reduction approaches have greater influence in Europe than in the United States. Historically, in the United States, we tend to adhere to both the moral and the disease models of alcoholism. The moral model suggests that people with addictions cannot be helped, because of their moral turpitude. The disease model implies that alcoholism and addiction are progressive diseases, treatment for which can only be abstinence. The influence of recovering people in leadership positions in the addiction treatment field has resulted in less openness to changing beliefs about goals. In the 1990s, the Institute of Medicine (1990) emphasized the societal benefits of reduced crime and incarceration from methadone maintenance. Several other factors contributed to acceptance of limited harm reduction approaches, such as the spread of disease, sexually transmitted diseases (STDs), HIV/AIDS, tuberculosis, and hepatitis. The increased research on nicotine addiction and the harmful effects of secondhand smoke led to the popular acceptance of the nicotine patch.

Harm reduction approaches for those using opioids target the administration of the drug and blocking the neuron receptors. Opioid agonists, such as LAAM (L-alpha-acetymethadal) and buprenorphine, stop the craving for heroin or other opioids. Doctors are now able to prescribe these agonists in their offices, a contrast to the government-regulated and stigmatizing distribution method of methadone as it was implemented in the 1960s.

A different harm reduction approach is the needle-exchange approach. Trained community outreach workers, some in recovery themselves, provide unused needles without judging or asking questions about drug use. They present themselves as knowledgeable about resources if the individual makes a decision to stop heroin use.

Research on the effectiveness of harm reduction approaches is limited. An interesting qualitative study of the perceptions of case managers, working with dual diagnosis clients, illustrates that although there is support for the measures, there is still ambivalence and controversy in the treatment community (Mancini, Linhorst, Broderick, & Bayliff, 2008).

Moderate drinking can be described as a secondary prevention approach, rather than a harm reduction approach. Since the 1970s, there have been studies and advocates for including reduced drinking as a treatment method for a sub-population of problem drinkers who would not engage in abstinence-only treatment. There has been limited research on moderate drinking, controlled drinking, or reduced drinking in the past decade. Elements that support reduced drinking as a treatment approach include research that clients respond to having choices about their treatment, consumers themselves seek counseling that does not stigmatize or label them as "alcoholics," non-abstinent goals are sensible for some populations, such as adolescents and older adults, and clinicians' successful use of motivational interviewing techniques. Ambrogne (2002) suggested that addiction treatment needs to be conceived of as a continuum of approaches, not a dichotomy of no treatment or abstinence-only treatment. She recommended that definitive guidelines be developed and tested to assist counselors. For instance, there are guidelines for physicians, developed by NIAAA. Her recommended guidelines are as follows: (1) assessment of risks, drinking patterns, and context of drinking; (2) a written contract denoting quantity and frequency of drinking; (3) emergency plans; and (4) coping plans if a return to heavier drinking occurs. There are specific conditions that preclude the use of reduced drinking, such as medical conditions, pregnancy, medications, failed attempts at reduced drinking, and indications of lack of commitment to a reduced drinking goal (Ambrogne, 2002). Further research can bring empirical support to the efficacy of these guidelines.

Conclusion

This review of new treatment approaches has sought to demonstrate that the substance abuse treatment field faces the challenge of improved empirical methods.

Some treatments approach the acceptable criteria of evidence-based practice but many need more study on the salient components of treatment. Extended follow-up periods are needed before we can say the approach has empirical support. A source of bias in most studies is the sample of those in treatment, which often reflects how treatment is funded, not the population of individuals in need of services. Outcomes of specific approaches have not resulted in unequivocal support for one approach compared to others. Effective approaches that best serve adolescents, individuals with PTSD, the growing senior population, and different minority groups, need to be examined. Such outcomes studies are critical for program development and funding. Research results need to be disseminated to the treatment community expeditiously. Given the social worker's ethical responsibility to use the best practice methods available, we must seek collaboration of practice experts and researchers to develop productive research.

Note

The author is greatly indebted to Sondra Burman, who authored the chapter on intervention with individuals for the first edition of *Alcohol, Tobacco, and Other Drugs*. The current author has used some material from Dr. Burman's chapter, including some case examples. This chapter highlights a review of the current literature, examining treatment approaches when empirical evaluation is present. However, in-depth analyses of the research reports are beyond the intent of the chapter.

References

Amaro, H. Blake, S. M., Schwartz, P. M., & Flinchbaugh, L. J. (2001). Developing therapeutic-based substance abuse prevention programs for young adolescent girls. *Journal of Early Adolescence, 21*(3), 256–273.

Amaro, H., Dai, J., Arevalo, S., Acevedo, A., Matsumoto, A., Nieves, R., et al. (2007). Effects of integrated trauma treatment on outcomes in a racially/ethnically diverse sample of women in urban community-based substance abuse treatment. *Journal of Urban Health, 84,* 508–522.

Amaro, H., Nieves, R., Johannes, S. W., & Cabeza, N. M. L. (1999). Substance abuse treatment: Critical issues and challenges in the treatment of Latina women. *Hispanic Journal of Behavioral Science, 21,* 266–282.

Amato, L., Minozzi, S., Davoli, M., Vecchi, S., Ferri, M.M.F., & Mayet, S. (2008). *Psychosocial and pharmacological treatments versus pharmacological treatments for opioid detoxification.* Retrieved August 26, 2009, from the Cochrane Database of Systematic Reviews (Issue 4, Art. No., CD005031). DOI: 10.1002/14651858.CD005031.pub3

Ambrogne, J. A. (2002). Reduced-risk drinking as a treatment goal: What clinicians need to know. *Journal of Substance Abuse Treatment, 22,* 45–53.

Annis, H. M., & Davis, C. S. (1989). Relapse prevention. In R. K. Hester & W. R. Miller (Eds.), *Handbook of alcoholism treatment approaches: Effective alternatives* (pp. 170–182). New York: Pergamon Press.

Anton R. F., O'Malley, S. S., Ciraulo D. A., Cisler R. A., Couper D., Donovan, D. M., et al. (2006). Combined pharmacotherapies and behavioral interventions for alcohol dependence: The COMBINE study: A randomized control trial. *JAMA, 295,* 2003–2017.

Ashley, O. S., Marsden, M. E., & Brady, T. M. (2003). Effectiveness of substance abuse treatment programming for women: A review. *Journal of Drug and Alcohol Abuse, 29,* 19–54.

Babor, T. F., & Del Boca, F. K. (2003). *Treatment matching in alcoholism.* Cambridge, England: Cambridge University Press.

Barnes, G. M., Farrell, M. D., & Dintcheff, B. A. (1997). Family socialization effects on alcohol abuse and related problem behaviors among female and male adolescents. In R. W. Wilsnack & S. C. Wilsnack (Eds.), *Gender and alcohol* (pp. 156–175). New Brunswick, NJ: Rutgers Center of Alcohol Studies.

Beck, A. T., Wright, F. D., Newman, C. F., & Liese, B. S. (1993). *Cognitive therapy of substance abuse.* New York: Guilford Press.

Belenko, S., & Dembo, R. (2003). Treating adolescent substance abuse in juvenile drug court. *International Journal of Law and Psychiatry, 26*(1), 87–110.

Berg, I. K., & Miller, S. D. (1992). *Working with the problem drinker: A solution-focused approach.* New York: W. W. Norton.

Blow, F. C., Walton, M. A., Chermack, S. T., Mudd, S. A., & Brower, K. J. (2000). Older adult treatment outcome following elder-specific inpatient alcoholism treatment. *Journal of Substance Abuse Treatment, 19,* 67–75.

Blume, S. B. (1983). The disease concept of alcoholism. *Journal of Psychiatric Treatment and Evaluation, 5,* 471–478.

Boothby, L. A., & Doering, P. L. (2007). Buprenorphine for the treatment of opioid dependence. *American Journal of Health-System Pharmacists, 64*(1), 266–272.

Brady, K. T., & Sonne, S. C. (1999). The role of stress in alcohol use, alcoholism treatment, and relapse. *Alcohol Research and Health, 23*(4), 263–271.

Breslin, F. C., Zack, M., & McMain, S. (2002). An information-processing analysis of mindfulness: Implications for relapse prevention in the treatment of substance abuse. *Clinical Psychology, Science, and Practice, 9,* 275–299.

Brick, J., & Erickson, C. K. (1998). *Drugs, the brain, and behavior: The pharmacology of abuse and dependence.* New York: Haworth Medical Press.

Bride, B. E. (2001). Single-gender treatment of substance abuse: Effect on treatment retention and completion. *Social Work Research, 25,* 223–232.

Burman, S. (1993). Chemically-dependent women in treatment: A study of the experiences in and responses to different treatment models (Doctoral dissertation, University of Illinois at Urbana-Champaign, 1993). *Dissertation Abstracts International, 54,* 05A.

Burman, S. (1994). The disease concept of alcoholism: Its impact on women's treatment. *Journal of Substance Abuse Treatment, 11,* 121–126.

Burman, S., & Allen-Meares, P. (1991). Criteria for selecting practice theories: Working with alcoholic women. *Families in Society, 72,* 387–393.

Center for Addiction and Substance Abuse (CASA). (2007). *National survey of American attitudes on substance abuse, XII: Teens and parents.* New York: Author.

Chaney, E. F., O'Leary, M. R., & Marlatt, G. A. (1978). Skill training with alcoholics. *Journal of Consulting and Clinical Psychology, 47,* 1092–1104.

Clark, H. W. (2001). Residential Substance Abuse Treatment for Pregnant and Postpartum Women and Their Children: Treatment and Policy Implications. *Child Welfare, 80,* 179–198.

Cochran, S. D., Keenan, C., Schober, C., & Mays, V. M. (2000). Estimates of alcohol use and clinical treatment needs among homosexually active men and women in the U.S. population. *Journal of Consulting and Clinical Psychology, 68,* 1062–1071.

Denis, C., Lavie, E., Fatseas, M., & Auriacombe, M. (2006). *Psychotherapeutic interventions for cannabis abuse and/or dependence in outpatient settings.* Retrieved August 26, 2009, from the Cochrane Database of Systematic Reviews (Issue 3, Art. No. CD005336). DOI: 10.1002/14651858. CD005336.pub.2

de Shazer, S. (1988). *Clues: Investigating solutions in brief therapy.* New York: W. W. Norton.

Ellis, A. (1971). *Growth through reason.* North Hollywood, CA: Wilshire Books.

Emrick, C. D. (1987). Alcoholics Anonymous: Affiliation processes and effectiveness as treatment. *Alcoholism: Clinical and Experimental Research, 11,* 416–423.

Epstein, J., Botvin, G., Diaz, T., & Schinke, S. (1995). The role of social factors and individual character in promoting alcohol use among inner-city minority youths. *Journal of Studies on Alcohol, 56,* 39–46.

Erickson, M. H., Rossi, E., & Rossi, S. (1976). *Hypnotic realities.* New York: Irvington.

Ferri, M. M. F., Amato, L., & Davoli, M. (2006). *Alcoholics Anonymous and other 12-step programmes for alcohol dependence.* Retrieved August 26, 2009, from Cochrane Database of Systematic Reviews (Issue 3, Art. No. CD005032). DOI: 10.1002/14651858. CD005032.pub2

Fielding, J. E., Tye, G., Ogawa, P. L., Imam, I. J., & Long, A. M. (2002). Los Angeles County drug court programs: Initial results. *Journal of Substance Abuse Treatment, 23,* 217–224.

Fleming, M. F., Manwell, L. B., Barry, K. L., Adams, W., & Stauffacher, E. A. (1999). Brief physician advice for alcohol problems in older adults. *Journal of Family Practice, 48,* 378–384.

George, W. H. (1988). Marlatt and Gordon's relapse prevention model: A cognitive–behavioral approach to understanding and preventing relapse. In D. C. Daley (Ed.), *Relapse: Conceptual, research and clinical perspectives* (pp. 125–152). New York: Haworth Press.

Gomberg, E. L. (1982). Alcoholism: Psychological and psychosocial aspects. In E. L. Gomberg, H. R. White, & J. A. Carpenter (Eds.), *Alcohol, science & society revisited* (pp. 186–204). Ann Arbor: University of Michigan Press.

Gomberg, E. S. L. (1996). Women's drinking practices and problems from a lifespan perspective. In J. M. Howard, S. E. Martin, P. D. Mail, M. E. Hilton, & E. D. Taylor (Eds.), *Women and alcohol: Issues for prevention research* (pp. 185–214). Bethesda, MD: National Institutes of Health.

Gomberg, E. L., White, H. R., & Carpenter, J. A. (1982). *Alcohol, science and society revisited*. Ann Arbor: University of Michigan Press.

Gorski, T. (1988). The CENAPS model of relapse prevention planning. In D. C. Daley (Ed.), *Relapse: Conceptual, research and clinical perspectives* (pp. 153–169). New York: Haworth Press.

Grella, C. E., Scott, C. K., Foss, M. A., & Dennis, M. L. (2008). Gender similarities and differences in the treatment, relapse and recovery cycle. *Evaluation Review, 32,* 113–134.

Hanson, M., & Gutheil, I. A. (2004). Motivational strategies with alcohol-involved older adults: Implications for social work practice. *Social Work, 49,* 364–372.

Hawkins, J. D., Catalano, R. F., & Miller, J. Y. (1992). Risk and protective factors for alcohol and other drug problems in adolescence and early adulthood: Implications for substance abuse prevention. *Psychological Bulletin, 112,* 64–105.

Homrich, A. M., & Horne, A. M. (2000). Brief family therapy. In A. M. Horne (Ed.), *Family counseling and therapy* (pp. 243–271). Itasca, IL: F. E. Peacock.

Institute of Medicine. (1990). *Broadening the base of treatment for alcohol problems.* Washington, DC: National Academy Press.

Irvin, J. E., Bowers, C. A., Dunn, M. E., & Wang, M. C. (1999). *Efficacy of relapse prevention: A meta-analytic review. Journal of Consulting and Clinical Psychology 67,* 563–570. Retrieved August 15, 2008, from http://psycnet.apa.org/index

Jayasinghe, H. B. (2005). Hypnosis in the management of alcohol dependence. *European Journal of Clinical Hypnosis, 6*(3), 12–16.

Jellinek, E. M. (1952). Phases of alcohol addiction. *Quarterly Journal of Studies on Alcohol, 13,* 673–684.

Jellinek, E. M. (1960). *The disease concept of alcoholism.* New Haven, CT: Hill House Press.

Johnson R. E., Chutuape, M. A., Strain, E. C., Walsh, S. L., Stitzer, M. L., & Bigelow, G. E. (2000). A comparison of levomethadyl acetate, buprenorphine, and methadone for opioid dependence. *New England Journal of Medicine, 343,* 1290–1297.

Johnston, L. D., O'Malley, P. M., & Bachman, J. G. (2004). *Monitoring the future.* Retrieved September 15, 2008, from http://oas.samhsa.gov

Kranzler, H. R., Wesson, D. R., & Billot, L. (2004). Naltrexone depot for treatment of alcohol dependence: A multicenter, randomized, placebo-controlled clinical trial. *Alcohol, Clinical, & Experimental Research, 28,* 1051–1059.

Kurtz, E. (1993). Research on Alcoholics Anonymous: The historical context. In B. S. McCrady & W. R. Miller (Eds.), *Research on Alcoholics Anonymous: Opportunities and alternatives* (pp. 13–26). New Brunswick, NJ: Rutgers Center of Alcohol Studies.

L'Abate, L., Farrar, J. E., & Serritella, D. A. (Eds.). (1992). *Handbook of differential treatments for addictions.* Boston: Allyn & Bacon.

Linehan, M. M., Dimeff, L. A., Reynolds, S. K., Comtois, K. A., Welsh, S. S., Heagherty, P., & Kivlahan, D. R. (2002). Dialectical behavior therapy versus comprehensive validation therapy plus 12-step for the treatment of opioid dependent women meeting criteria for borderline personality disorder. *Drug and Alcohol Dependence, 67*(1), 13–26.

Lubin, B. (1983). Group therapy. In I. B. Weiner (Ed.), *Clinical methods in psychology* (2nd ed., pp. 389–446). New York: John Wiley & Sons.

Lyons, P., & Rittner, B. (1998). The construction of the crack babies phenomenon as a social problem. *American Journal of Orthopsychiatry, 68,* 313–325.

Mancini, M. A., Linhorst, D. M., Broderick, F., & Bayliff, S. (2008). Challenges to implementing the harm reduction approach. *Journal of Social Work Practice in the Addictions, 8,* 380–408.

Marlatt, G. A. (1978). Craving for alcohol, loss of control, and relapse: A cognitive–behavioral analysis. In P. E. Nathan, G. A. Marlatt, & R. Loberg (Eds.), *New directions in behavioral research* (pp. 271–314). New York: Plenum Press.

Marlatt, G. A., & Gordon, J. R. (1985). *Relapse prevention: Maintenance strategies in the treatment of addictive behaviors.* New York: Guilford Press.

McCrady, B. S., & Miller, W. R. (Eds.). (1993). *Research on Alcoholics Anonymous: Opportunities and alternatives.* New Brunswick, NJ: Rutgers Center of Alcohol Studies.

McGue, M., Pickens, R. W., & Svikis, D. S. (1992). Sex and age effects on inheritance of alcohol problems: A twin study. *Journal of Abnormal Psychology, 101,* 3–17.

McKeel, A. J. (1996). A clinician's guide to research on solution-focused brief therapy. In S. D. Miller, M. A. Hubble, & B. L. Duncan (Eds.), *Handbook of solution-focused brief therapy* (pp. 251–271). San Francisco: Jossey-Bass.

Meier, B. R., & Patkar, A. A. (2007). Buprenorphine treatment: Factors and first-hand experiences for providers to consider [Electronic version]. *Journal of Addictive Disease, 26*(1), 3–14.

Milkman, H. B., & Sederer, L. I. (1990). *Treatment choices for alcoholism and substance abuse.* New York: Lexington Books.

Miller, W. R., & Kurtz, E. (1994). Models of alcoholism used in treatment: Contrasting AA and other perspectives with which it is often confused. *Journal of Alcohol Studies, 55,* 159–165.

Miller, W. R., & Rollnick, S. (2002). *Motivational interviewing: Preparing people to change addictive behavior.* New York: Guilford Press.

Miller, W. R., Taylor, C. A., & West, J. C. (1980). Focused versus broad-spectrum therapy for problem drinkers. *Journal of Consulting and Clinical Psychology, 48,* 590–601.

Morgenstern, J., & Longabaugh, R. (2000). Cognitive–behavioral treatment for alcohol dependence: A review of evidence for its hypothesized mechanisms of action. *Addiction, 95,* 1475–1490.

Muthen, B. O., & Muthen, L. K. (2000). The development of heavy drinking and alcohol-related problems from ages 18–37 in a U.S. national sample. *Journal of Studies on Alcohol, 61,* 290–300.

Najavits, L., Weiss, A., Shaw, S., & Muenz, W. (1998). Seeking safety: Outcome of a new cognitive–behavioral psychotherapy for women with posttraumatic stress disorder and substance dependence. *Journal of Trauma Stress, 22,* 437–456.

National Institute of Alcohol Abuse and Alcoholism (NIAAA). (2008). *Pharmacology for alcohol dependence: Summary of evidence report.* Retrieved August 26, 2009, from www.ahrq.gov/clinic/epcsums/alcosumm.htm

National Institute of Alcohol, Abuse, and Alcoholism (NIAAA). (2005). *Helping patients who drink too much: A clinician's guide.* Retrieved August 27, 2009, from http://www.niaaa.nih.gov/Publications/EducationTrainingMaterials.html

Nelson-Zlupko, L., Kauffman, E., & Dore, M. M. (1995). Gender differences in drug addiction and treatment: Implications for social work intervention with substance-abusing women. *Social Work, 40*, 45–54.

O'Malley, S., Jaffe, A., Chang, G., Schottenfeld, R., Meyer, R., & Rounsavillle, B. (1992). Naltrexone and coping skills therapy for alcohol dependence: A controlled study. *Archives of General Psychiatry, 49*, 881–887.

Oslin, D. W., Slaymaker, V. J., Blow, F. C., Owen, P. L., & Colleran, C. (2005). Treatment outcomes for alcohol dependence among middle-aged and older adults. *Addictive Behaviors, 30*, 1431–1436.

Paltrow, L. (1991). Perspective of reproductive rights attorney. *Future of Children, 1*(1), 85–91.

Prochaska, J. O., & DiClemente, C. C. (1988). Toward a comprehensive model of change. In W. R. Miller & N. Heather (Eds.), *Treating addictive behaviors: Processes of change* (pp. 3–27). New York: Plenum Press.

Resnick, M. D., Bearman, P. S., Blum, R. W., Bauman, K. E., Harris, K. M., Jones, J., et al. (1997). Protecting adolescents from harm. Findings from the National Longitudinal Study on Adolescent Health. *JAMA, 278*, 823–832.

Rice, C., Longabaugh, R., Beattie, M., & Noel, N. (1993). Age group differences in response to treatment for problematic alcohol use. *Addiction, 88*, 1369–1375.

Rimmele, C. T., Miller, W. R., & Dougher, M. J. (1989). Aversion therapies. In R. K. Hester & W. R. Miller (Eds.), *Handbook of alcoholism treatment approaches* (pp. 128–140). New York: Pergamon Press.

Rodgers-Farmer, A. (2000). Parental monitoring and peer group association: Their influence on adolescent substance use. *Journal of Social Service Research, 27*, 1–18.

Rubin, A. (2008). *Practitioner's guide to using research for evidence-based practice.* Hoboken, NJ: John Wiley & Sons.

Smith, D. C., & Hall, J. A. (2007). Strengths-oriented referrals for teens (SORT): Giving balanced feedback to teens and families. *Health & Social Work, 82*, 69–72.

Steinberg, L., Fletcher, A., & Darling, N. (1994). The vicissitudes of autonomy in earlier adolescence. *Child Development, 57*, 841–851.

Strug, D. L., Priyadarsini, S., & Hyman, M. M. (1986). *Alcohol interventions: Historical and sociocultural approaches.* New York: Haworth Press.

Substance Abuse and Mental Health Services Administration (SAMHSA). (2007). *N.S.D.U.H. national findings.* Retrieved November 26, 2008, from http://www.oas.samhsa.gov/nsduh/2k7nsduh/2k7Results.cfm

Sun, A.-P. (2004). Principles for practice with substance-abusing pregnant women: A framework based on the five social work intervention roles. *Social Work, 49*, 383–394.

Sun, A.-P. (2006). Program factors related to women's substance abuse treatment retention and other outcomes: A review and critique. *Journal of Substance Abuse Treatment, 30*, 1–20.

Swift, R. (2007). Emerging approaches to managing alcohol dependence. *American Journal of Health-System Pharmacy, 64*(1, Suppl. 3), 512–522.

Tohn, S. L., & Oshlag, J. A. (1995). *Crossing the bridge.* Natick, MA: Solutions.

Toumbourou, J. W., Hamilton, M., U'Ren, A., Stevens-Jones, P., & Storey, G. (2002). Narcotics Anonymous participation and changes in substance use and social support. *Journal of Substance Abuse Treatment, 23,* 61–66.

van den Bosch, L.M.C., Verheul, R., Schippers, G. M., & van den Brink, W. (2002). Dialectical behavior therapy of borderline patients with and without substance use problems. Implementation and long-term effects. *Addictive Behaviors, 27,* 911–923.

Waldron, H. B., & Turner, C. W. (2008). Evidence-based psychosocial treatments for adolescent substance abuse. *Journal of Clinical Child & Adolescent Psychology, 37*(1), 238–261.

Wallace, J. M., Brown, T. N., Bachman, J. G., & Laveist, T. A. (2002). The influence of race and religion on abstinence from alcohol, cigarettes and marijuana among adolescents. *Journal of Studies on Alcohol, 64,* 843–848.

Webb, J. A., Bray, J. H., Getz, J. G., & Adams, G. (2002). Gender, perceived parental monitoring, and behavioral adjustment: Influences on adolescent alcohol use. *American Journal of Orthopsychiatry, 72,* 392–400.

Weisner, C., Matzger, H., Tam, T., & Schmidt, L. (2002). Who goes to alcohol and drug treatment? Understanding utilization within the context of insurance. *Journal of Studies on Alcohol, 63,* 673–682.

Wilson, D. B., Mitchell, O., & MacKenzie, D. L. (2006). A systematic review of drug court effects on recidivism. *Journal of Experimental Criminology, 2,* 459–487.

Wilson, G. T. (1978). Alcoholism and aversion therapy: Issues, ethics, and evidence. In G. A. Marlatt & P. E. Nathan (Eds.), *Behavioral approaches to alcoholism* (pp. 90–113). New Brunswick, NJ: Rutgers Center of Alcohol Studies.

Zweben, A. (2001). Integrating pharmacotherapy and psychosocial interventions in treatment of individuals with alcohol problems. *Journal of Social Work Practice in the Addictions, 1*(3), 65–80.

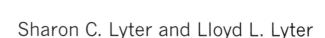

10

Group Strategies in ATOD Treatment

Sharon C. Lyter and Lloyd L. Lyter

Theoretical Foundations

This chapter examines the powerful and prominent role of groups in the treatment of individuals who misuse alcohol, tobacco, and other drugs (ATOD). Groups predominate in the self-help community and "groups form the crux" (Center for Substance Abuse Treatment [CSAT], 2006) of many professional treatment programs. Why do groups play such a critical role for ATOD misusers? How is it that professionally led groups flourish alongside self-help groups?

The proponents of "groupness" and group experiences see the advantages of groups as varied and profound and as appropriate for a range of human tribulations. Small groups are a common method of service delivery in professional social work, created for purposes that include therapy, personal growth, mutual support, and goal achievement (Anderson, Carter, & Lowe, 1999). Group has the potential to "provide for a range of human needs" (p. 137) that include the need to be accepted by others, for validation from others, for sharing of experiences, and to work with others who have common goals. In addition, a well-trained group leader can serve as a role model and a guide.

Substance abuse groups have demonstrated benefits that include structure and routine, communication and socialization that occur in the absence of the substance effect, and sharing of experiences that can both support positive behaviors and confront negative ones. Members have reported the attraction of peer support and group pressure, of the feeling of partnership in darkness, and the gradual defusing of defense structures that lead to self-examination and personal epiphany. What all groups have in common is an opportunity to reconstruct or revive abilities to relate to others and an appreciation of the healing power of connection with other human beings. In those groups with professional leadership, that expertise is a benefit in the form of providing information and clinical guidance that is specific to substance abuse (CSAT, 2006). The cost factor cannot be overlooked; groups bring the economy of scale associated with multiple clients served simultaneously. Clearly, the group milieu has advantages.

According to the CSAT (2005) Treatment Improvement Protocol 41, research studies provide evidence that group therapy and treatment of addiction are a powerful combination. People who abuse substances are often more likely to stay sober and committed to abstinence when treatment is provided in groups, apparently because of rewarding and therapeutic benefits such as affiliation, confrontation, support, gratification, and identification. Facilitated by trained leaders, five therapeutic group models are used: psychoeducational, skills development, cognitive–behavioral, support, and interpersonal process.

Since the 1980s, Motivational Interviewing (MI)—and its incorporation of the transtheoretical stages of change (Prochaska, Norcross, & DiClemente, 1994)—is a model that has emerged as one of the most promising and well-researched in substance abuse treatment. The application of MI in the group milieu does not have as much empirical evidence as does work with individuals (Velasquez, Stephens, & Ingersoll, 2006), but interest is growing. "The MI approach begins with the assumption that the agency for change is within the client, so the counselor's task is to assume a collaborative and encouraging role to enhance client motivation" (p. 30). This method is congruent with social work traditions and values: perspective of person-in-environment, meeting the client where he or she is in the process of change, a strengths orientation, and client empowerment (Kirst-Ashman & Hull, 2009).

But what explains the popularity of groups that convene in the absence of professionals? Why would people who misuse substances seek out peers rather than professionals? "The emergence of self-help groups may reflect a societal response to failures" (Félix-Ortiz et al., 2000, p. 340) within the helping professions. The professional community may have taken approaches that were ineffective and inconsistent with the needs of those who misuse substances, and many misusers regard the professions (e.g., social work, medicine, psychology) as superfluous at best or iatrogenic at worst. According to Flores:

> [Alcoholics Anonymous] (AA) would have never come into existence if it had not been for the failure of the professional healthcare system to offer

the kind of help alcoholics desperately needed. AA, as a social phenomenon, is an example of how a certain portion of an inflicted population
banded together in a unity of help because society's sanctioned mode of
treatment was inadequate. (1988, p. 21)

In the United States, the conventional routes to relief from illness and dysfunction did not produce a consistent package of remedies for those suffering from substance misuse. The professional community, to some extent, relinquished leadership
to the lay community; and many of the attempts at providing relief must be credited
to the lay community and not to the professionals. The group context—particularly
that of peer support—evolved quite naturally from the vacuum created by a lack,
extending over decades, of coherent and effective professional policies and practices.
Fortunately, there now seems to be a rapprochement, more of a collaboration in
finding the best of the fellowship phenomenon and the best of the empirical evidence to produce methods that are effective and affordable. Self-help groups can
complement the work of the treatment professionals and reduce overall costs.

As with other modes of treatment, evidence-based practice (EBP) tenets must
be considered with regard to group. EBP is a research-guided and knowledge-
guided approach to practice that "tries to organize a way of providing the best possible service to clients" (Glicken, 2005, p. 15). The efforts to apply EBP to substance
abuse continue, but there is considerable controversy over the validity of studies on
this topic, because of methodological flaws. The group experience is not one easily subject to scientific design, and the challenge remains to tailor the intervention
to the client, considering contextual factors and the cooperation and "substantial
involvement of clients in decision making" (Glicken, 2005, p. 15).

This chapter supports the view asserted that "clients with substance use disorders should be treated by qualified professionals and that mutual-help groups
should serve as adjuncts to a treatment plan" (CSAT, 2006, p. 4). Indeed, the formula of combining professional program treatment with mutual help programs
continues to have strong support (CSAT, 2006).

Social workers are trained to weigh the findings borne of EBP, and yet to bring
a holistic view that methodically and strategically tailors the fit of available treatments to the specific individual. This matching allows for consideration of both
"norms" to be expected and "idiosyncrasies" to be uncovered. Assigning ATOD
misusers to groups, and conducting groups, cannot be done purely on the basis of
empirical research. So far, this is not a pure science. This matching effort requires
the knowledge, wisdom, and sensitivity that the social worker can bring (Buelow
& Buelow, 1998).

This chapter identifies the available research findings, with the understanding that social workers and other clinicians must use judgment and discretion in their professional decisions. Clearly, further scientific inquiry is required, and findings should be assessed and incorporated into practice as they emerge.

It is important to acknowledge here that the reader may see this book as replete with narratives of pathology and loss. Indeed, one cannot address ATOD abuse matters without acknowledging risks and deficits. Undeniably, social work is a profession that targets for service those populations that are most at risk and have multiple deficits. Yet, although risk factors cannot be ignored, social work has discovered increased effectiveness when we expand our understanding not just of risk factors, but also of strengths, moderating influences, protective factors, and resilience. An orientation toward strengths brings into better balance the hope and discomfort that every client brings. A belief in the inherent ability of each human to grow and change extends a message of hope to every client, giving a clear message of empowerment. The findings of the authors' previous research on protective factors in the family and implications for parenting (Lyter & Lyter, 2003) emphasized parenting models that promote resilience and infuse the child's world with "connections and bonds, order and discipline, and hopes and dreams" (p. 20).

Given the confluence of macro exigencies (managed care, cost awareness, and increasing emphasis on empiricism) and the confluence of micro exigencies (biological, psychological, social, cultural, and spiritual characteristics of the individual misuser), social workers are in a unique position to guide treatment decisions. Social work recognizes that misusers do not merely have a pathology to be conquered, but are complex individuals with an array of challenges to be addressed (O'Neill, 1999). Social work brings compassion and the person-in-environment perspective, both of which support the complexities of ATOD treatment.

Types of Groups

For the purposes of this chapter, we will refer to two overriding categories—(1) professionally facilitated therapeutic groups and (2) self-help groups. The professionally facilitated groups are those within treatment settings, inpatient and outpatient. The self-help groups are the fellowship assemblies of peers such as those based on a Twelve Step format and others that bring together people with similar problems and goals.

A variety of group types can be identified in the literature, but the overlap in style and goals prevents definitive classification. The Association for the Advancement of Social Work with Groups (AASWG, 2006) categorized groups as treatment, support, psychoeducational, task, and community action groups. CSAT (2006) reviewed an array that includes psychoeducational groups, skills development groups, cognitive–behavioral groups, support groups, and group psychotherapy. In psychoeducational groups, clients learn about the facts of substance misuse and the related dynamics through the use of structured lectures and instruction. They emphasize the use of structure to teach members about the facts of substance misuse, about using problem-solving skills, and being alert to the cues of relapse. In skill development groups, clients practice new behaviors such as tolerating anxiety, identifying relapse triggers, and managing stress. In support groups, clients in the same phase of recovery work on similar problems.

Traditional therapy groups are conducted by professionals who may use such approaches as psychodynamic, cognitive behavioral, confrontational, supportive, or client centered. Psychodynamic groups typically have an interpersonal focus; they subscribe to the view that ATOD misuse is the "solution" to the problem of psychological vulnerability and that self-medication is used to relieve deficits in ego capacities. Psychodynamic and interpersonal groups are more oriented to relationships, insight, and the group process itself. Group, from this point of view, is a path to heighten awareness of self and change characteristic patterns of handling vulnerabilities (Golden, Khantzian, & McAuliffe, 1994). A cognitive–behavioral group may seek to inform and, moreover, to achieve changes in cognitions and, subsequently, behaviors. Some groups actually combine elements.

Krentzman (2007) defined a *self-help group* as a "non-professional organization of individuals who share a common problem and come together to help one another cope" (p. 29). Many of these nonprofessional self-help groups are based on the quest for abstinence and a mutual-support philosophy similar to that of Alcoholics Anonymous (AA), such as AA itself, Secular Organizations for Sobriety, Cocaine Anonymous, Narcotics Anonymous (NA), Nicotine Anonymous (NicA), and Dual Disorders Anonymous. Parallel to the self-help groups for misusers would be the groups for families and significant others, such as Al-Anon, Nar-Anon, Alateen, and Co-Dependents Anonymous. A hybrid category is those groups that have blended features and may have principles that are counter to those of AA, the prime examples of which are Women for Sobriety (WFS), SMART (Self-Management and Recovery Training) Recovery, Moderation Management (MM), and Rational Recovery (RR). [RR, however, no longer provides group meetings; this will be discussed in more detail further on.]

Self-help groups are available for a wide range of purposes. During the last half century, those groups dedicated to countering problems associated with substance abuse have flourished and gained prominence worldwide. Exceptions to this principle will be noted further on in this chapter, but many of those groups support total abstinence from substances for those in recovery. Self-help groups do not have professional leadership, although professional organizations may provide space for these groups to meet and provide some sponsorship for them. These groups vary in the extent to which an individual takes on the role of leader, serving to convene the group, direct the discussion, and provide role modeling.

The next two sections of this chapter outline three examples of professionally facilitated therapeutic groups (harm-reduction groups, MI groups, and therapeutic groups for significant others) and several self-help groups. Each type will be described in terms of its themes, rules, membership, and power and leadership structure; its services to families and significant others; and its outcomes, evidence of effectiveness, and costs.

Professionally Facilitated Therapeutic Groups

When groups are facilitated by a professional, that individual brings expertise and information. The group's outcomes are advanced by knowledge of group development and dynamics. The power of mutual aid can be harnessed by a group leader who understands group work principles and practices.

Effective group leaders must have a range of skills and abilities: self-confidence, empathy for others, the ability to listen actively, flexibility, the ability to manage and regulate affect and emotional extremes within the group, the ability to motivate and stimulate interaction, and the finesse to use confrontation appropriately. The leader must keep in mind that those with ATOD problems often have coexisting mental and emotional problems, including depression, anxiety, anger, shame, and some degree of cognitive impairment. Moreover, the leader must practice cultural competence and ensure the safety of everyone in group.

The leadership role in a therapeutic group is highly demanding. The wise group leader prepares herself or himself for the onslaught of challenges and the continuous limit testing of the group members. The clinician must understand and tolerate the defensive structures of the misusing person, combining knowledge of chemical dependence and mental health. (See chapter 6 for more detailed information on co-occurring disorders.) There is more structure in psychoeducational and cognitive-behavioral groups; psychodynamic and interpersonal groups are less structured and, thus, need more active leadership to establish and maintain the group norms. The clinician may experience anger toward some clients as a natural result of the repeated limit testing and behavioral challenges, and needs to self-examine any tendency to indirectly discriminate against or punish a client. In addition, the leader must prepare for the likelihood that the individual in recovery will suffer the frustration of relapses and must be aware of the effects of such relapses on the group cohort (Vannicelli, 1995).

The clinician must observe and react to issues of transference and counter-transference, the primitive defenses of denial and splitting, and the risk of triangulation in the group. These issues, if left unchecked, could seriously disrupt the group equilibrium. The clinician must be sensitive to the dynamic of group that evokes and provokes the polarities of dependence and control, and of grandiosity and shame.

The leader needs to be aware of potential roadblocks, including those that relate to her or his own recovery. Some leaders have their own histories of family or personal ATOD misuse and may bring skewed or biased views and beliefs to the group, expecting others to have similar goals and problem-solving paths. The leader must find a balance of familiarity with the topic and respect for the perspectives of others and for boundaries, and allow for individualized client goals and means. A leader with a "history" can easily fall into a trap of excessive self-disclosure, personal war stories, and the hardened belief that his or her path to recovery is the only path. In addition, the leader who presents herself or himself as a model of recovery needs to be prepared to acknowledge her or his own relapses even when there is a desire and a benefit to being seen as successful. Many programs do employ individuals who are in recovery from substances themselves. However, there is little evidence that there is any difference in effectiveness based on the variable of one's substance history (CSAT, 2005).

Placement of clients in groups requires consideration of several variables. Although most people can benefit from a heterogeneous group, it is essential that clients in a group have similar needs (CSAT, 2005). It is generally wise to separate high-functioning from low-functioning clients, and to screen out those with severe paranoia (Vannicelli, 1995).

Indeed, some people are not appropriate for group settings. Those who cannot honor group norms and rules, and those with no impulse control, are unlikely to function well in a group and may do harm to others. A group agreement specifies and affirms the rules of the group, expectations about behavior, the need for group members to respect privacy and confidentiality, refraining from sharing personal information of group members outside the group. These ground rules must be reviewed by the members as the group begins. This allows for the creation of a safe place in which members can begin the work of the group—moving from engagement to productivity and problem solving, creating a group culture and a culture of recovery (however that is defined for the group)—and proceed to termination.

The clinician must teach the individuals to be group members and establish the group contract: establish the rules of confidentiality, attendance, promptness, and abstinence; state the shared norms (commitment to talking about feelings and problems, acknowledge possible regression to behaviors such as slips and childish acts); and provide hope and a vision of progress and recovery. The group will usually have rules established on various common topics: clarification about whether there is a goal of abstinence; the concept of relapse—often reframed as "slips" and often with cautions against over-reaction; how to handle a situation in which a member arrives intoxicated; assurances for the safety of all members; and parameters for the use of problem solving to address group interaction impasses and disruptive behaviors of individual group members (Vannicelli, 1995).

Words take precedence over actions inside the group. The quest for recovery includes learning to live a less precarious life outside of the group, for example, by avoiding dangerous friends and dangerous situations and avoiding the use of substances and other maladaptive coping acts. The group context offers a constant place in their lives that helps members find alternative ways to cope with the feelings and functional disruptions that their misuse has fueled. The drugs themselves are no longer doing the job of medicating the fears and worries that accompany the problems. Words and the process of the mutual sharing of words and ideas help those with poor judgment and those who are self-destructive to gain a new tool.

Safety—psychological and physical—in the group is ultimately the responsibility of the leader. Proper preparation and setting of ground rules is the first step to attaining an environment of safety. Acceptance, respect, and cooperation set an atmosphere that discourages disruptive behaviors. The effective group leader will acknowledge the anxiety and discomfort that are concomitants of being in a group; members should be encouraged to participate, but not at the expense of their major ego defense structure. Resistance and denial are expectable responses to drug misuse and also to the prodding and probing of other group members. The capable group leader guides the group probing and disclosure in such a way that premature self-disclosure is discouraged as members slowly build trust for one another and slowly but willingly give up maladaptive defenses that keep them stuck. Confrontation kept at a tolerable level, and balanced with mutual support, is key. Confrontation delivered with compassion is a powerful force in uncovering the obstacles to recovery. However, the group members must be protected from verbal attacks that are more likely to provoke shame than self-awareness.

The leader always needs to promote and protect his or her own safety as well. The group leader, who in many ways becomes the conscience or superego for the group members, is perpetually at risk of becoming the focus of anger and dependency. It is worthwhile for the leader not only to be involved in continuing education, but also to remain in supervision with a more experienced clinician or to participate in group peer supervision that will allow examination of the typical experiences and challenges to group leadership. Because of the complexity of groups, in some groups, it is advisable to have a coleader. For a group to be successful, the development of group cohesion must be considered. Strategies to promote group cohesion include preparing clients for the group, using group rituals, creating a symbol or emblem that represents the group, and processing emotional material such as that generated by the premature termination by a group member (CSAT, 2006). The degree of cohesiveness of the group helps to determine the sense of belonging that it creates; a group with numerous "no shows" and early dropouts does not boast a cohesive membership. In some groups the cohesiveness may grow in a perverse way around the mutuality of identification with misuse and rejection of conventional social norms. The group that prides itself on the extent of its violations of social rules and laws is stuck in a tradition of dysfunction, and members may fear seeing themselves as "regular folks." They will rather display the banner of upheaval than see themselves as ordinary, common, and dull. Many misusers grew to adulthood in a world of abuse, neglect, and dysfunction, and they do not have the ability to create mental images of more conventional lives. The clinician must be alert to disruptions to the group cohesion and to threats to safety by not only demonstrating compassion and concern, but also setting limits and enforcing group rules (Vannicelli, 1995).

Conflict in group therapy is to be expected; however, the facilitator needs to assess when the conflict needs to be reigned in. The group facilitator has the challenging task of shifting group control to the members themselves yet simultaneously maintaining order and managing any disruptive behaviors in the group. Disruptive behavior cannot be tolerated; the wise facilitator can often harness the power of the group to address it openly. In addition, the facilitator needs to be aware of individual maladaptive behaviors, such as chronic lateness, dominating the discussion in the group, interrupting others, or remaining silent (CSAT, 2005).

Groups move through phases that reflect the stages of treatment. In ATOD treatment, groups will progress according to the aims of the group. For those transitioning through recovery, in the early phase the tasks begin with engagement within the group and identifying resistance to change. As cognitive functioning makes some gains and clients move into a middle phase, the culture of recovery begins to take hold. In the late phase, there is an increasing readiness for clients to begin to tackle issues other than their substance use, such as marital problems, parenting deficits, and emotional trauma, which can be factors triggering or maintaining use.

▼
▼
▼

Those groups that do address the concomitant personal problems associated with substance use often serve as surrogate families. An ideal outcome is when that surrogate family provides reparative personal and family experiences, sometimes termed a "corrective experience." Conversely, a potential negative outcome is that the experience recreates the same negative dynamics of the earlier life events, or that the leader may foster destructive interchange, with pathology overshadowing strengths, or with a particularly troubled group member either explicitly or implicitly taking control of the group. Clearly, skilled leadership is required in groups that address such profound and complex matters.

Group treatment has multiple benefits (CSAT, 2005). The group milieu for those who abuse substances can provide peer pressure that is constructive, using group expectations and confrontation in a manner that motivates rather than alienates. It reduces isolation, provides nurturance, corrects misperceptions, brings structure and discipline, teaches social skills, and provides encouragement in the face of fear. Groupness promotes hope for the future, especially when a member observes growth and change within the cohort and points this out to the group.

The group member learns that participation in a therapeutic group is governed by implicit and explicit rules and expectations. Membership requires member accountability: regular attendance and prompt arrival, notification in advance of and following absences, active participation in the group process, and notification of termination. The group experience often includes exploration of group process itself, group discussion of mutual issues—not just monologues from each member—and a focus on feelings and development of clear communication. Being a group member can be an epiphanic, transformative experience.

Harm Reduction Groups

"Harm reduction" is a concept embraced by social work, public health, and other disciplines.

The goal of harm reduction is to "reduce the amount of personal and/or societal harm directly or indirectly" by substance misuse (Witkiewitz, 2005, p. 202).

> Harm reduction is solely designed to meet an individual "where he/she is at" and develop treatment strategies based on the motivation, strengths and limitations of each client. For example, consider an individual who is drinking heavily four nights a week, not willing to quit drinking, and most concerned about hangovers resulting in poor performance at work. From a harm reduction perspective the practitioner might work with the client

toward a goal of not drinking on work nights. This is not to say that abstinence is ruled out for this particular client, rather it is not identified as a primary treatment goal. (Witkiewitz, 2005, p. 197)

This approach eschews dogmatic definitions of success such as those promoted by AA in which total abstinence is given a lofty designation as the only acceptable goal. "Harm reduction is a 'come as you are' approach that welcomes drug users into a helping relationship that allows them to set their own short *and* long-term goals" (Little, 2006, p. 70) and to "start where they are." Harm reduction incorporates theoretical underpinnings from social work and its person-in-environment, biopsychosocial-cultural-spiritual perspective; cognitive–behavioral intervention; the transtheoretical model of change (including motivational interviewing [MI] and the stages of change); and public health.

Harm reduction groups support the strengths of their members and welcome them without judgment. They provide education about the substance misuse, the processes of change, and the power of a group experience. Abstinence is introduced as one option in a repertoire of options. Clearly, the range of individuals in these groups is wide and they fit along a wide continuum in terms of readiness to change. Little (2006) affirms that the facilitator of a harm reduction group must be capable of welcoming diversity and a variety of challenges. The facilitator must have the capacity for fully integrating the ethical standard of self-determination of the *Code of Ethics* (National Association of Social Workers [NASW], 2008) into attitudes toward group members. The facilitator must be able to tolerate anxiety of group members and the inevitable ambivalence and resistance of group members. Some members may arrive at the group meeting under the influence, and the leader will need to make a decision about the ability of the individual and the group to function under those circumstances. The leader must be able to accept that each member of the group sets his or her own path and to trust in the power of free will and inherent strength. Last, the leader must practice neutrality and understand the concept of equifinality, that is, many paths to a solution.

MI Groups

MI and stages of change are now key concepts used in a variety of treatment settings, particularly in inpatient and outpatient ATOD treatment. As noted, this method is harmonious with social work practice (Kirst-Ashman & Hull, 2009), operationalizing concepts of person-in-environment, being with the client, self-determination, and client strength in a manner that fosters motivation for change (Velasquez et al.,

2006). Miller and Rollnick (2002) identified four principles of counseling that fit well with social work traditions. "Develop Discrepancy" is a strategy to emphasize the inconsistencies in the client's story, the mismatch between the client's intentions and their actions. As in social work practice, the clinician attempts to use respect and logic to engage the client in collaboration on setting the course in treatment. This is in contrast to more traditional methods of aggressive confrontation. "Roll with Resistance" is a strategy in which the clinician recognizes the client's pulling back from the worker; the social worker strives to work with, not against, the client, and holds client self-determination in high regard. The worker reframes the matter such that the hope and discomfort in the client come into better balance and anxiety is tempered. "Express Empathy" is a strategy of engagement familiar to social workers, in which the clinician prepares an understanding of the client and the client's needs and attempts to put oneself into the shoes of the client without judgment. "Support Self-Efficacy" is a strategy in which the worker honors the client and shows respect for self-determination and the power of the client to find strength within self. The worker provides information but collaborates with the client in identifying options and making a plan.

The group facilitator addresses possible conflicts that could arise in the philosophy of the group, including that of powerlessness versus empowerment. Many individuals find the self-help philosophy of acknowledging personal failure and powerlessness as having advantages in terms of making a conceptual shift. However, the facilitator can promote the notion of diversity as being a strength of group (Kirst-Ashman & Hull, 2009; Velasquez et al., 2006).

The facilitator should arrange the group members into a circle to emphasize the egalitarian nature of the group. The acronym "OPEN" is shorthand that can help the facilitator in initiating and engaging the group members, bringing an understanding to the group members of the rules for the group

Open with group purpose: to learn more about members' thoughts, concerns, and choices.

Personal choice is emphasized.

Environment is one of respect and encouragement for all members.

Non-confrontational nature of the group. (Velasquez et al., 2006, p. 35)

The group leader uses reflective listening and encourages "change talk." "Change talk" is described by Miller and Rollnick (2002) as talk coming from the client—unfiltered by the worker—that reflects the desire to change, the need to change, and the reasons for changing. This is an indication that the client's motivation is in place, that the worker and client are operating in tandem, and that the client is moving from one stage of change to another.

The MI group facilitator uses methods that are familiar to social work group workers (AASWG, 2006), adapted specifically to the unique needs of the person with a substance abuse history. For example, the facilitator can address resistance in the group by showing "Respect for persons and their autonomy" (p. 4), using empathy and validating personal choice and responsibility (Velasquez et al., 2006), and by responding to hostile comments from a group member by selectively emphasizing the positive components of the comment. The worker manages resistance in the group in part by remembering "The importance of diversity in relationship to how a group attains its goals" (AASWG, 2006, p. 13), and affirming that the diversity within the group is actually a strength. The facilitator shows "Knowledge of groups and small group behavior" (p. 6) by encouraging members to help each other, using mutual aid; this parallels the MI strategy of encouraging group members to listen carefully to each other, responding and reflecting among each other in a non-judgmental manner. Exercises in group decisional balance impel the group to brainstorm both the good things about drug use and the bad (Velasquez et al., 2006); a "playful twist is for one facilitator to use the group's list to argue against change and invite the rest of the group to take up counterarguments about why change would be a good thing" (p. 41). This is a much more realistic approach than dogmatic attacks from the facilitator on the desire to use drugs.

The stages of change—pre-contemplation, contemplation, preparation, action, and maintenance—are a critical factor in the implementation of MI. Group members should receive some instruction on stages of change and be able to identify their own stage and readiness for change (Velasquez et al., 2006). This comports with the group work standard of the "competency-based assessment" and reassures each group member that differences in readiness are acceptable.

As noted earlier in this chapter, MI is a model that is well researched in work with individuals. The generalization of MI to the group milieu in substance abuse treatment does not yet have as much empirical evidence as does work with individuals (Velasquez et al., 2006), but it holds great promise.

Therapeutic Groups for Significant Others

Therapeutic groups are also available for family members and significant others associated with those who are substance involved. These groups include psycho-educational or informational sessions, couples groups (in which both the misuser and the partner attend), groups for relatives and significant others (in which the substance-affected family member or partner attends without the misuser), and groups for adult children raised in households that were substance affected (such as Adult Children of Alcoholics). Adult children's groups are prevalent. They are distinguished by the definition of the immediacy of the problem; they deal with past issues as well as those in the present.

In the group for adult children, the group leader should be alert to some common themes. For example, adult children may ignore or deny their own ATOD issues; assessment should be done first to fully explore the extent to which the individual is currently using. The adult child is vulnerable to "blame polarities," that is, she or he may affix blame to the misuser in total or, conversely, may engage in total self-blame. The group process allows an opportunity for the adult child to sort through "assignment of blame" and to arrive at more productive motivation for change. This devotion to assignment of blame may have been a life-long obsession, and may be displayed in the group in the form of resistance to the role of client, in lengthy monologues or war stories, and in a re-creation of the original family patterns in the group itself, with members taking on rigid family roles (complete with the acting-out identified client and the supporting roles of substance-affected family members). The group leader will strive to shift the focus from blame assignment to expression and exploration of feelings and to here-and-now problem solving. The leader must identify such scenarios and dynamics and open them to group discussion.

Multiple-family groups are offered by many inpatient and outpatient programs and are lauded in the form of clinical anecdotes. More research is needed, but some studies have documented the efficacy of this method. "Multifamily groups can be thought of as microcosms of the larger community" (CSAT, 2006, p. 100); they provide cross-learning, mutual support, and the reduction of stigma. In a study examining home-based family services, Zarski, Aponte, Bixenstine, and Cibik (1992) explored the dynamics of family systems theory with at-risk families. They reported that in their use of multiple-family therapy with this population, the families found acceptance; "this validation helps to attenuate the stigma often associated with multiproblem families" (Zarski et al., p. 12). Clearly, bringing families with common challenges together can result in a reduction of isolation (McKay, Gonzales, Stone, Ryland, & Kohner, 1995).

Crnkovic and DelCampos (1998) reported that multiple-family groups are an important facet of recovery in outpatient treatment for chemical dependency, providing education about the disease process, a support network, and camaraderie.

The families also participate in numerous group exercises regarding healthy communication, cessation of enabling behaviors, and co-dependency. All of the educational exercises are facilitated in an atmosphere of acceptance and emotional safety in order to allow for learning in a relaxed, less intense setting. (pp. 33–34)

The multiple-family group is one method used by the author (L.L.L.) during his tenure as director of an inpatient AOD (alcohol and other drugs) treatment facility. See Case Example 10.1 for an illustration of a therapeutic group for significant others.

Self-Help Groups

To make prudent decisions about a treatment plan for someone with a substance abuse problem, a clinician must be knowledgeable about both professionally facilitated therapeutic groups and self-help groups. This section provides a review of several of the self-help options, including AA and Al-Anon. Adaptations to the AA prototype have been achieved by several groups, including WFS, RR, SMART Recovery, and MM. They are discussed, along with an option for smokers, NicA. Last, information is provided for those who prefer cyberspace over a face-to-face option.

A practitioner should have some firsthand experience about the self-help phenomenon. As such, it has been the policy of the authors to include a visit to an AA or other self-help group meeting as part of the social work ATOD classroom curriculum. Case Example 10.2 includes an excerpt from a student reaction paper submitted to the author (S.C.L.).

According to Wuthnow (1996),

At present, four out of every ten Americans belong to a small group that meets regularly and provides caring and support for its members. These are not simply informal gatherings of neighbors and friends, but organized groups: Sunday school classes, Bible study groups, Alcoholics Anonymous and other twelve-step groups, youth groups and singles groups, book discussion clubs, sports and hobby groups, and political or civic groups. (p. 4)

Wuthnow (1996) declared that "The small-group movement has been effecting a quiet revolution in American society" (p. 2) and "is beginning to alter American society, both by changing our understandings of community and by redefining spirituality" (p. 3). A popular interpretation of the movement toward mutual help "was that self-help groups were a response to the breakdown of traditional informal

▼
▼
▼

CASE EXAMPLE 10.1: Multiple-Family Group

Both clients and their family members ("family" was defined by the program as those people whom the individual clients identified as important in their lives) attended a weekly group session with constantly evolving membership based upon clients currently in the treatment program and what family members were available to attend each week.

The group, frequently as large as 25 to 30 members, with primary and assistant therapists, focused on allowing individual families to confront their own issues from the past and plans for the future. Frequently, the issues of one family struck a chord with other families, even though the other families may not have been active, verbal participants in the group session. Non-using partners or other family members often could understand the using partners or family members from other families in a way that they could never hear or understand their own significant other, and vice versa. Because they were not emotionally involved in the situations, relating to these "strangers," they were much more open to listening in a nonjudgmental way. The experiences of one family often became the lesson needed for other families to understand each other.

Because the membership was constantly changing on the basis of the client population and available family members, some families attended as few as one session and others as many as four. The number of sessions attended seemed relatively less important for making change than the intensity of the experience.

The numbers of group members and the level of intensity necessitated not only a primary therapist, but one and possibly two assistant therapists. Frequently, debriefing sessions with individual families had to be conducted after the group session to process the experience and incorporate their learning.

support systems such as the family and local community" (Makela, 1996, p. 12). Tracing the origins of current self-help groups to medieval guilds, trade unions, and religious orders, he concluded that this linkage with the past, in fact, gives credence to the idea that shattered lives can only be rebuilt in the company of others.

Although definitive answers have not emerged, the evidence of effectiveness will be examined here in the context of clinical decision making. Given the state of the art and science, Glicken's (2005) advice has merit. In the text on evidence-based practice (EBP), the author responded to this question, "Would you refer a client to a self-help group?" Cautioning the reader that some groups are likened to cults, the author replied, "Yes, but only after meeting with the group leader and evaluating the group objectives" (p. 278).

Various terms are found in the literature that describe the joining together of individuals to solve a common problem: self-help groups, mutual support groups, mutual-aid groups, mutual self-change groups, mutual help movement, and fellowship groups. For our purposes, we will rely on the term "self-help."

AA and Al-Anon

The common U.S. ancestor of self-help in the ATOD arena is AA. Most fellowship groups to some degree comply with the original underpinnings of AA, and other forms, conversely, as polarities of AA.

AA boasts a rather long history, having been founded in 1935 by two alcoholics, Bill Wilson and Dr. Bob Smith, who saw value in the idea of mutual support. Its ideology can be traced to various influences including the Washingtonians (a temperance group), the Oxford Group (an evangelical Christian fellowship), transcendentalists and existentialists (for example, Camus, Sartre, and Nietzsche), Carl Jung (a European psychoanalyst who contributed mysticism and the notion of a conversion experience), William James (a U.S. psychologist and philosopher, an advocate of pragmatism and functionalism), and Calvary Episcopal Church in New York. The founders of AA discovered that their comradeship—characterized by the sharing of stories of a personal, spiritual, and inspirational nature—spurred their own recovery. The establishment of the Twelve Steps (see Appendix 10.1) distinguished this grassroots movement as driven by common and profound principles.

Vaillant (1995) identified four essential components of treatment of an "ingrained habit": a non-chemical substitute dependency for alcohol, ritual reminders that even one drink can lead to pain and relapse, repair of medical and social damage, and restoring self-esteem (p. 367). He posited that this combination could be fashioned from a mix of group therapy, church attendance, disulfiram, and vocational rehabilitation, but that AA and other self-help groups are the simplest, most direct route to the four components.

The 1996 *Alcoholics Anonymous Member Survey* (Alcoholics Anonymous World Services [AAWS], 1997) found more than 96,000 groups throughout the world, and the 2007 membership survey (AAWS, 2008) reported more than 113,000. Although all groups are autonomous, they subscribe to the original principles. Anyone who has a desire to stop drinking is welcome to attend. In North

CASE EXAMPLE 10.2. Classroom AA Meeting Attendance Assignment

I dreaded this assignment because I was afraid of how other people would feel about me intruding on their meeting. I followed your instructions and I chose an open meeting, and I explained who I was so that I was not hiding anything. I sat toward the back of the room, and tried to observe without seeming too overly curious. Everyone was drinking coffee, and the group leader came and offered me some, but I declined. I just wanted to be as unobtrusive as possible. A guest speaker got up and spoke about her experiences when she was actively drinking. She was a wonderful storyteller, and I was intrigued by her ability to hold everyone's attention. I remember most her illustration of the primacy that alcohol held in her life. She spoke about a night in her life when the weather was treacherous—a thunderstorm was whirling through her neighborhood and there was a warning that a tornado was likely. Her husband, after a recent dispute, had angrily disposed of her last bottle of vodka; when the electricity went off, she sought out the bottle to get herself through the storm and realized there was nothing left. She bolted from the apartment with nothing but a few dollars in her pocket. She found trees and electrical wires down all around her, and literally stepped over live wires to get to the nearest place to buy her booze. She literally risked her life for a bottle of vodka! Everyone in the group seemed to understand, in a very personal way, what that desperation was like. They supported her in her abstinence from alcohol—she had been sober for about 12 years at that point—and I was stunned by the power of their relatedness that night. After the formal part of the meeting, everyone came and welcomed me, and several people offered to serve as a resource to me in my study of this topic. Not one person seemed to resent my being there, and in fact I can say I have never felt the warmth that I felt that night. It occurred to me that I have to acknowledge what is missing in my own life—belonging, being part of something. I began to have the crazy thought that maybe I should pretend to be alcoholic so I could find something like this for myself! That would give me reason to continue attending meetings and have that sense of connection. What I can conclude from that memorable night is the power inherent in the support available in fellowship groups. I don't think it's an exaggeration to say that the event for me was a turning point in my life.

America, it was reported that 33 percent of AA members were women, and that the average age of AA members was 47, with only 13.6 percent less than 31 years old; 85.1 percent were described as "white" (AAWS, 2008).

AA as an organization retains independence from all other organizations, whether they are political, social, professional, or other kinds. These peer support groups often meet in public places such as churches and community centers, but may also hold regular sessions within ATOD treatment facilities and rehabilitation programs. Many professional treatment programs and clinicians choose to incorporate the philosophy of the Twelve Steps and Traditions into their treatment methods. Nevertheless, AA maintains a stance of noninterference from and with other organizations. The fellowship is elevated to a position over anything else, including professional treatment services. Followers are cautioned about the well-meaning but naive interference of non-followers, such as ill-informed physicians, social workers, counselors, and family members who do not fully comprehend the movement (Wallace, 2006).

Although AA is often compared with other treatments for alcohol misuse, it is not designed as a treatment but rather as a social movement. It does not contain the typical elements of formal treatment—engagement, assessment, planning, intervention, evaluation, termination, and follow-up. Wallace (2006) referred to AA as an informal bio-psycho-social-spiritual model of ATOD treatment, something akin to folk psychotherapy.

AA believes in a disease model—etiological and descriptive—and expects followers to admit to powerlessness over the drug, and to turn their will and their lives over to a power greater than themselves. Followers are taught to move from a destructive higher power to a constructive one, to overcome self-centeredness and grandiosity with commitment to spiritual growth.

These aims are achieved through self-scrutiny and self-criticism, setting priorities, and embarking on an orderly and systematic sequence of change. AA also fosters phenomenology and use of narrative through the telling and sharing of life histories. This process of discovery and change requires one to seek abstinence by dealing with the drug problems themselves, using credos and behavioral problem solving strategies, staying focused on the present, rather than the past or the future, recognizing triggers to relapse, getting proper rest and nutrition, and avoiding the environmental stimuli (people, places, things) that can prompt drug misuse.

Members learn that AA doctrine expects that followers will learn to deal more effectively with anxiety; rather than react to pain with alcohol use, the member is expected to "sit still and hurt," to learn that pain and suffering are features of life that require effective coping strategies.

▼
▼
▼

Most who suffer from dependence on chemicals have discovered the ability to achieve one day without use of the drug, and AA sustains that belief in today and prevents rumination about the terror of "no drug tomorrow."

AA perpetuates altruism and service to fellow sufferers; the 12th step, known as the missionary step, encourages those in recovery to give something back to the AA community, often in the form of serving as a sponsor to others new to recovery. Clinicians have long recognized a link between altruism, self-esteem, and mental health; the founders of AA recognized, possibly in an intuitive way, the benefits of a mission of redemption.

Many treatment professionals over the past decades have speculated about those aspects of AA—the active ingredients—that actually produce the desired effect. Various aspects have been heralded as those most significant. They include the self-help orientation, freedom from commercial or political affiliations, the spiritual element, anonymity, the disease concept, the willingness to use the label of "alcoholic," the concept of humility and powerlessness, the emphatic quest for abstinence, the concept of recovery as a lifelong process, the belief that reuse equals relapse, the idea of redemption, and commitment to altruism.

Others have cited the importance of the introduction of ceremony and ritual. The rituals promoted by AA often serve to replace the almost complete lack of observation of social rituals in the lives of many alcoholics. A symptom commonly reported by families of alcoholics is a failure to celebrate and systematize meaningful life events such as birthdays, holidays, and even family mealtime. Those events were often marked by absence of ceremony or, indeed in some cases, by chaos and violence. Another way in which AA introduces behavioral rituals is through the use of slogans and mottoes, including:

One drink is too many and a thousand not enough.

Keep the plug in the jug.

Fake it till you make it.

Utilize, don't analyze.

Sit down, shut up, and listen.

Let go and let God.

Expect miracles.

First things first.

Easy does it.

One day at a time.

Keep it simple.

Don't get too hungry, or too angry, or too lonely, or too tired (H.A.L.T.).

Live and let live.

What you hear and see here stays here. (Makela, 1996, p. 122)

In contrast to psychotherapy groups, many followers regard AA as according more power to the client. The clout of the AA group is tempered by the philosophy that is often quoted as "Take what you need and leave the rest." This credo encourages the novice to retain control over her or his fit with the group. This permission to self-direct, it can be argued, is not accorded as fully in the dyad of the therapist–client as it is in the mutual aid group. In addition, some maintain that respect for misusers and for their right to self-determination is demonstrated in the permission to concentrate on the problem itself—"one day at a time," "utilize, don't analyze"—isolating it as the problem and avoiding the deep shame and guilt that could accompany fuller analysis of the issues and of one's history. This allows the group member to tackle the ATOD misuse with tactics and strategies that will help her or him to reach a place (one of sobriety) in which further self-examination and exploration of complex issues can proceed.

These characteristics of self-help groups—mutual aid, open membership, common experiences, run by and for members, voluntary, nonprofit status—have proven to be factors that have helped the groups sustain themselves. They allow a place where individuals can learn the effects of drugs on others and can be instilled with hope while watching others who are further along in the process of recovery. Last, they have evolved into one of the few places where social status or other special identifiers are de-emphasized, a context approximating a classless microcosm. Even the leadership is egalitarian, with individuals coming forward who have achieved sobriety and have gained the trust of fellow members, telling their stories as models of hope and recovery.

The belief system of Twelve Step programs includes the conviction that someone who is addicted is pre-occupied to the extent of pathological obsession with something, whether it be alcohol, narcotics, food, or the addict him- or herself. Al-Anon operates on the premise that the family members of the alcoholic indeed are habituated to a preoccupation with the addict, and must learn to free themselves from preoccupation with the alcoholic drinker and that person's problems, catastrophes, and needs.

Fellowship groups for family members closely followed the creation of the original fellowship groups for misusers. Most began with the notion that the misuser had to admit powerlessness over the substance, but the family member had to admit powerlessness over the behavior of the alcoholic or substance abuser. Most groups have the aim of helping family members learn to stop enabling or helping the user to continue using and to detach and "let go" of the delusion of being able to solve the problem. Detach, in this belief system, does not mean taking away the love and compassion, but preserving the integrity and mental health of the family.

Al-Anon Family Groups was formed in 1935 by Lois Wilson, wife of Bill Wilson, in response to a demand for a parallel support network for the families of alcoholics, using similar steps (see Appendix 10.2). Al-Anon guides its members in a process of admitting their powerlessness over the alcoholic and the unmanageability of their lives. Al-Anon encourages personal recovery from the dependency on the alcoholic. This philosophical guideline of "detachment," or release with love, encourages the family member to stop taking responsibility for the alcoholic and as a result relieves the family member from feelings of guilt.

Nar-Anon, likewise, was formed to benefit those in relationships with drugs other than alcohol. Other off-shoots of Al-Anon have emerged, such as Alateen, which is specifically for the teenage children of alcoholics, and similar groups have formed in some communities for children of different ages, including Ala-Tot for pre-teenage children.

Although these collateral support groups did not propose the term itself, their orientation to the concept of "enabling" laid the foundation for the notion of "codependency." Codependency is described as the relationship dynamic in which the family member engages in behaviors that serve to sustain the dysfunctional behaviors of the misuser. Codependent people, it is asserted, enable the misuser to maintain harmful patterns by making excuses for the misuser, trying to control the misuser, and otherwise participating in a destructive cycle. By taking care of and watching over the misuser, he or she is prevented from fully feeling the consequences of abusive alcohol or other drug use. Some psychoanalytic interpretations propose that, for some, these behaviors represent unconscious wishes to maintain the unhealthy status quo. However, more inclusive, enlightened models view codependency behaviors as well-intentioned but ineffective attempts at interrupting the cycle of harm. Even this more benign point of view has been countered further by feminist and social work empowerment conceptualizations.

These paradigms question the validity of such assertions and call into question the notion that helping and nurturing behaviors, traditionally termed as "feminine," are in some way pathological. These concepts of codependency also imply that women who are involved with a misuser are "asking for it," that in some way they are acting out their own self-destructive tendencies. The term "codependent" is generally applied to females or to children of misusers.

Codependency models are unacceptable to many service providers because they suggest that "family members are 'part of the problem' and are themselves suffering from a condition—codependency" (Orford, Templeton, Velleman, & Copello, 2005, p. 1612). As stated by Collins: "Social workers should not foster models of personal betterment that suggest women must label themselves as sick, addicts, or diseased to challenge the context that disempowers them" (1993, p. 474). Opponents to the codependency notion maintain that these individuals are oppressed, not diseased, supporting the credo: "I didn't cause it, I'm not to blame, and I have nothing from which to recover." Bepko and Krestan (1985) reframed the codependency concept into reciprocal patterns of over- and underresponsible behavior transmitted intergenerationally through modeling and learning.

Sociopolitical ramifications notwithstanding, the significance of the opportunity to disengage from the cycle of dysfunction cannot be overlooked. The clinician who is aware of these risk factors, moreover, can more ably promote change and growth for ATOD-affected families.

The peer support group phenomenon has enjoyed a long-standing, formidable, and dominant reputation in the recovery community. For example, Humphreys (1997) reported that 79.4 percent of substance abuse patients in the veterans health care system were referred to AA following treatment. Peer support is regarded as providing destigmatization, and as an antidote to depersonalization, dehumanization, and alienation from society. The peer group provides an arena for identity, collective willpower, and constructive action toward goals. Many regard the peer group phenomenon as an alternative to the hierarchy and bureaucracy that are characteristic of professional authority.

These beliefs became more "legitimate" in the eyes of the professional community when the then-Surgeon General C. Everett Koop of the United States sponsored the Surgeon General's Workshop on Self-Help and Public Health in September 1987. Koop provided credence for a movement from which he benefited in a very personal way after the death of his own son and his participation in Compassionate Friends (Powell, 1990). The Compassionate Friends (see http://www.compassionate friends.org), founded in 1969, is a national non-profit support organization that offers friendship and understanding to families who are grieving the death of a child of any age, from any cause, which, they maintain, can best be understood by another bereaved parent.

The controversy over what methods really produce the desired yield has been stalled many times because of the factors that threaten and inhibit attempts at rigorous research. This is a special problem in terms of the self-help groups. Krentzman (2007) affirmed the challenges to studying groups such as AA, citing lack of systematic recording of data and lack of rigorous controls. Yet in a review of the existing empirical findings, Krentzman makes the observation that "countless testimonials support the idea that 12-step programs offer something profound to its members" (p. 28) and to society at large as well. Indeed, Krentzman concluded that clinicians need to involve clients in AA early in the process of treatment, reiterating that AA is free of charge.

Emrick (1994) advised cautious optimism with regard to AA and other Twelve Step programs. Because of methodological flaws and other limitations, Emrick concluded that the evidence is not sufficient to say that AA is a method that is proven. Humphreys and Moos (1996) calculated that self-help groups helped to reduce substance-abuse-related treatment costs by $1,826 per person. Moreover, they found that outcomes were essentially equal between those who voluntarily chose self-help and those who chose professional outpatient treatment, lending support not only to cost containment, but to the benefits of choice.

Vaillant (1995) argued in support of AA:

> Research during the last 15 years has revealed growing indirect evidence that AA is an effective treatment for alcohol abuse. One difficulty is that the subject of AA, like the subject of controlled drinking and the subject of whether alcoholism is a disease, evokes adversarial argument rather than dispassionate reflection. (p. 265)

Vaillant maintained that indirect evidence that supports AA is that AA continues to attract believers both in the United States and abroad and its membership increases, now including individuals from a variety of groups, regardless of age, gender, socioeconomic status, and race, not just those from the groups more traditionally known as AA attendees. He refuted the notion that AA is only effective with those often viewed as the typical AA member: males with the most severe alcohol problems.

Some researchers suggest that participation alone in AA does not guarantee good outcome and that more precise subtyping needs to be pursued to determine for whom AA might in fact be effective. Those variables most associated with positive outcome (as measured by change in drinking behavior) were having an AA sponsor, engaging in 12th-step work, leading a meeting, increasing one's degree of participation in the organization compared with a previous time, sponsoring other AA members, and working the last seven of the 12 steps. These associations were weak and do not allow for strict conclusions, but they do support the need for a more precise analysis (Emrick, Tonigan, Montgomery, & Little, 1993).

Emrick et al. (1993) performed a meta-analysis of the effectiveness of combining AA and professional treatments. The very limited data available led them to conclude only that "AA may not always be 'enough' for the person with an alcohol-related problem, particularly when AA is introduced *before* the professional treatment" (p. 58). In addition, they questioned the common practice of many professionals to encourage (and sometimes coerce) clients to join AA, inasmuch as current findings cannot justify such a dramatic position. The effect of AA on other aspects of life, besides drinking behavior, is not fully supported, although the authors asserted that "AA appears to be at least not harmful to affiliates, with one area even showing measurable benefits" (p. 61). That one area was improvement in psychological adjustment (see Case Example 10.3).

The 2007 AA Membership Survey (AAWS, 2008) noted that 39 percent of members said they were referred to AA by a "health care professional." In addition, the survey reported that most AA members did in fact receive "additional help" outside of AA: 63 percent of members received treatment or counseling prior to coming to AA (with 74 percent of those saying this outside help "played an important part in directing them to AA"); 63 percent of members received treatment or counseling after coming to AA (with 86 percent of those saying this additional help "played an important part in their recovery from alcoholism").

Many clinicians and scholars have sought to isolate those characteristics and features of individuals that most correlate with AA attendance and with good outcomes from AA attendance. Emrick et al. (1993) reviewed the existing research on AA and found it difficult to describe the "typical [AA] affiliate." Weak, yet intriguing, correlations were found with many variables. The strongest one to surface was that of using external sources of support to stop drinking. The authors speculated about a likely composite profile of an AA affiliate, who could be described as someone who suffers from a relatively strong degree of alcohol problem characterized by losing control of drinking behavior and losing control of one's behavior when drinking, drinking larger amounts of alcohol on the days when drinking occurs, having more worry and anxiety about one's drinking, being more pre-occupied with and compulsively involved with drinking, more often espousing beliefs about how alcohol use improves one's ability to functional mentally, and having sought out external sources of help.

CASE EXAMPLE 10.3. The Case of Patrick

Patrick (fictitious name) is a 28-year-old white male with a long history of multiple-drug use (since the age of 14) that included alcohol, marijuana, Valium, cocaine, and IV methamphetamine. His family of origin, of Irish heritage, included six children, clustered by age into two groups of three, each with an older male and two younger females, with Patrick as the younger of the two males and the fourth-oldest overall. The family history included much alcohol and other drug misuse. Patrick had been attending Twelve Step programs, both Alcoholics Anonymous (AA) and Narcotics Anonymous (NA), for approximately two years, attempting to gain sobriety. His record was one of remaining totally drug free for up to 60 days, relapsing for short periods, and then repeating this cycle. A fellow AA and NA member had witnessed this process for some time and believed that Patrick needed something more than what the 12-step programs had to offer him. He suggested working with a therapist, because Patrick seemed to spend too much time "intellectualizing" and being "in his head," meaning that Patrick tried too hard to analyze, understand, and question rather than "accept."

I (L.L.L.) became Patrick's therapist. He seemed sincerely motivated both in gaining sobriety and in working through his "secret." Patrick very quickly acknowledged keeping a family secret he felt was so terrible that to divulge it in the Twelve Step meetings would cause such shock that all in attendance would leave or reject him. He said his difficulty in gaining sobriety in the "rooms" was that he could attend without addressing personal issues for some time, but he would ultimately reach a point where both he and others felt he should be sharing his story. It was at these times that his concerns about the secret would arise, he feared the rejection, and he would relapse.

Patrick presented as a very intelligent individual who appeared to be responding to some internalized sense of extreme concern over his secret. What was seen by his friends in the rooms as being negative, intellectualizing and being in his head, I felt could be turned to his advantage by utilizing a cognitive-behavioral approach. He seemed a likely candidate for the approach utilized in Rational Recovery (RR). As no RR or SMART meetings were readily available at that time, I began a series of approaches with him that are based on cognitive–behavioral precepts.

As sensitive issues arose, Patrick would examine his beliefs about those issues. I became a sounding board for him, paraphrasing and repeating back to him his comments as he presented them to me. Similarly, I gave him homework assignments to work on outside of our sessions and report back on later. Rather quickly, he began to laugh at me as I would repeat back his statements. He was able to realize that hearing the secret from someone else caused it to seem much less threatening, and that his concern over it was greatly exaggerated. We then used the sessions to review his feelings and thoughts about each of the individual people in his family and to practice telling his story.

Essentially, Patrick was able to "dispute" his prior belief system, and develop new beliefs that allowed him to shed his earlier shame and guilt over the secret. He returned to the rooms and freely told his story.

The secret that Patrick was protecting was that his parents, and his paternal uncle, were problem drinkers or alcoholic and that they spent every weekend in Patrick's family home drinking together, with the uncle staying over. At some point after the birth of the older three children, Patrick's parents become uninvolved intimately, and his mother and uncle became intimate and were, in fact, the biological parents of the three younger children, including Patrick, even though the married couple continued to live as a couple, and the uncle still came around only on weekends. Even though everyone in the family apparently knew the truth, they tried to keep it a secret from the outside world, and all of the children treated the couple as their biological parents and the father's brother as an uncle. In the process of his own therapy, Patrick was able to acknowledge that lifelong comments from friends and neighbors clearly indicated that the family "secret" was really common knowledge. As part of his dispute of the irrational beliefs, Patrick actually gave his "uncle" (biological father) a Father's Day card that year. Although they had no further discussion of the issue at that time, he reported his "uncle" was very pleased with the recognition.

Initially, Patrick attempted to apply two AA slogans to his recovery process, "Bring the body and the mind will follow" and "Fake it till you make it." However, his belief in the power of the secret scuttled his ability

(continued)

▼
▼
▼

CASE EXAMPLE 10.3 *(continued)*

to gain sobriety in the rooms. Until his intellectualization and being in his head were dealt with, issues seen as negatives in 12-step programs, but positives when dealt with using a cognitive–behavioral approach, he was unlikely to succeed in achieving sobriety.

Drawing on his natural tendencies to analyze and process, this choice of methods seemed obvious. Although Patrick was ultimately able to return to AA and NA, he likely would have benefited from an ongoing relationship with RR, had a group been available and, given his tendency to analyze, process, and change his belief system, may well have incorporated the RR precept of "recovered," as opposed to the AA precept of "recovering," and ultimately divorced himself from group completely. For the next several years, Patrick would call me on the anniversary of his sobriety to let me know he was still abstinent. It is worth noting that Patrick may have benefited at that time from the current web-based support offered through RR, now the only approach used by RR.

It is also important to acknowledge the importance of culture in Patrick's case. As a frequent visitor to Ireland and a student of treatment practices in the Republic of Ireland and in Northern Ireland, I was aware of the hypothesized genetic predisposition to alcoholism among the Irish. Furthermore, over the years I had observed what many have romanticized as a sort of melancholy among Irish males, especially those alcohol affected, and was aware that there might have been a tendency in Patrick to carry—and perhaps to nurture or dwell on—shame and guilt. I believe my awareness increased my ability to engage this client and to remain engaged over a period of years.

Clearly, social workers and other clinicians must make referrals on the basis of individual client needs, capabilities, and appropriateness of match with available resources. Although successful for many over its history, AA is not a suitable match for everyone, and in the case of Patrick it may have been necessary but not sufficient. It has been criticized as having a male bias; for having a Christian, religious base; for fostering its own form of dependence; and for demanding self-disclosure and sharing one's history—all issues that may make it an inappropriate referral for some individuals.

Vaillant (1995) identified the following variables significantly associated with the use of AA by those who had achieved abstinence at some time: Irish ethnicity; 8+ symptoms on the Problem Drinking Scale; alcohol-dependent as per the *Diagnostic and Statistical Manual of Mental Disorders* (3rd ed.) (American Psychiatric Association, 1980); blackouts; morning drinking; binge drinking; maternal neglect; and verbal IQ less than 80.

The controversy rages onward in the debate over how to improve the outcomes in ATOD treatment. Many people hold very strong views about the effectiveness of peer support as compared with other intervention methods. Opponents of AA level the charge that fellowship groups flourish despite a lack of scientific evidence, and that indeed their members are threatened by a potentially dangerous atmosphere of fanaticism and zeal. They warn of dogmatism and extremism, citing examples of groups that are not welcoming to women, groups that expect singularity (for example, many AA groups disdain those who have used other drugs in addition to alcohol), and groups that appear cultlike and promote religious fundamentalism.

Signs of cooperation and collaboration can be found, however. Both the professional community and AA acknowledge—and there is a growing recognition of this idea—that Twelve Step and other fellowship approaches are not the only avenue to recovery but can serve as a strong complement to professional treatment. For example, the American Society for Addiction Medicine (ASAM) promotes a policy wherein "Addiction treatment professionals and programs should develop cooperative relationships with self help groups" (ASAM, 2005, p. 2). The prevailing view that is emerging is that a variety of elements should be available on an array or menu of options.

Corrigan (1983), in her classic study of alcoholic women in treatment in the 1970s, found that "entry into treatment from an A.A. group contributed significantly to abstinence, whereas 'only A.A. treatment' contributed little and 'any outpatient treatment' was negatively correlated with abstinence" (p. 117). In her lectures while serving as an educator at Rutgers University, Corrigan often referred to this finding as the "AA plus 1" principle. She suggested that in the absence of more powerful evidence, the clinician should consider recommending that the client pursue involvement in both AA and in some sort of formal treatment. Ouimette, Moos, and Finney (1998) studied a group of veterans suffering from a range of substance disorders and found that patients receiving a combination of outpatient treatment and Twelve Step group participation fared better at one-year follow-up. A peer support group and a therapy group can be attended simultaneously.

However, it must be recognized that AA and therapeutic groups have substantial differences. It is useful for the leader to recognize some of the special characteristics and dynamics that the AA or NA member may bring to this experience. There may be resistance by such individuals to certain therapeutic group rules and methods, such as examining how the past gets repeated in the present. AA emphasizes that focus should be "just for today" rather than exploring early history. In addition, these members may use lingo and slogans of AA as a defense against any new demands of the therapeutic group. Members who are concurrently in AA or NA (or Al-Anon or Nar-Anon) groups may push others to do the same and need to be reminded that different paths work for different people.

Self-help groups with a history are highly organized in their structure and goals and can boast of a depth of accumulated experience. Few can deny the power of the group leader who has a success story to tell to the desperate and frightened novice. Although not fully validated under the principles of logical positivism, AA has the potential to enhance outcomes for certain types of clients. Considering the rather spotty history of the professional treatment community, and the stigma bestowed by an "unacceptable social problem," it is an expectable result that fellowship and folklore-based methods would be viewed as superior to, or an equal partner with, professional treatments. The question is how to help each client make the determination of the fit or mix of professional and fellowship methods, and how to best assess the potential risks and benefits.

Women for Sobriety

Dr. Jean Kirkpatrick, founder of Women for Sobriety (WFS), died in June of 2000 at the age of 77. About three years prior, the author of this section (S.C.L.) had the honor of a private meeting with this pioneer, held on September 9, 1997, in the offices of WFS in Quakertown, Pennsylvania. Information updates have been provided by current WFS leadership.

Kirkpatrick originally tried to form a women-only AA group but found that the core themes of AA were not appropriate for women and, in fact, could further contribute to their sense of shame and powerlessness. As a result, WFS—founded in 1975—blends the precepts of feminism, cognitive psychology, meditation, nutrition, and group dynamics. The group eschews powerlessness, with more focus on the present than the past, empowering women to tap their inner strength to make positive changes. Any woman with a sincere desire to achieve lasting recovery is welcome. Members introduce themselves by stating "I am a competent woman" and close meetings with the words "we are capable and competent." Kirkpatrick stated that self-help only works if there is a "desire to quit using alcohol and to apply use of self, for those who want to think and use cognitive process." Men are not welcome but may form their own chapters, known as Men for Sobriety.

Current membership figures are described by WFS leadership as "several hundred thousand women." In several hundred locations in the United States, Canada, and other countries across the globe, WFS offers face-to-face groups. Meetings are conducted by certified volunteer moderators—who have at least one year of sobriety—guided by a structured format and the Thirteen Statements of the New Life Acceptance Program of WFS (see Appendix 10.3), with emphasis on empowerment, ego strength, self-esteem building, emotional maturation, and achievement. The moderator is expected to be knowledgeable about the philosophy of the program, how it differs from other programs, and how to facilitate a group. Many AA group members use caffeine and nicotine during their recovery, but WFS meetings are smoke free, and members are encouraged to avoid caffeine and sugar. These WFS face-to-face meetings are not open to the public—only to women in recovery—so visitors are generally not permitted. This ensures privacy and confidentiality and also the comfort of the group members. According to the WFS representative, a growing number of treatment facilities offer the WFS program as a treatment alternative by holding in-house WFS meetings for their women clients. For women who do not wish to join a group or do not have access to a group in their geographic area, WFS has designed a self-help program to use at home. The WFS Web site (www.womenforsobriety.org) offers detailed information on how to start a group, information about their conferences, a complete description of the Women for Sobriety New Life Program, suggestions for using the program in daily recovery, and several articles. In addition, it provides an online bookstore and shop with items featuring their "W" logo (representing WFS).

Telephone support is available as well from women volunteers who use WFS and are willing to share their own personal experiences in their sobriety journey. The WFS monthly newsletter, "Sobering Thoughts," provides positive messages, practical tips, and insights into the recovery process. It is written by women in recovery for women in recovery. The WFS online community (http://www.women forsobrietyonline.com) was created in 1998 to serve as a forum to provide encouragement. Its chat groups are reported to be used by thousands of members daily.

WFS believes that the needs of women in recovery vary by individual and that each woman's personal preference should decide which recovery alternatives work best for her. Dependency is discouraged. For example, WFS does not provide sponsorship in which one member shepherds another through recovery, it does not require belief in a higher power, and it does not expect lifelong attendance at meetings. WFS encourages women to address and work through the problems and stressors that first led to their substance misuse, in contrast to AA, which focuses more on the substance itself as the problem. "AA absorbs everything" stated Kirkpatrick, but in WFS "once we learn how to cope with the problems of life, we won't need a group any longer." Women are welcome to leave the ties of the group after a period of recovery.

Kirkpatrick noted that she was "uncomfortable with the idea of codependency" and "addiction to an addicted person." Family members are not served directly by WFS groups. However, WFS does provide educational literature directed to significant others, with information and ideas that are similar to those of Al-Anon.

WFS does not oppose competing fellowship groups and does not discourage women from receiving professional help. Kirkpatrick expressed dismay at the anecdotes told to her by WFS participants that their involvement with WFS is often criticized by AA members. Many WFS members find satisfaction in participating in AA as well, and WFS encourages women to "get as much help as possible." When questioned about the Moderation Movement (discussed later in this chapter), Kirkpatrick expressed skepticism and doubt about the notion of controlled substance use, but did acknowledge that controlled use may be possible for a small segment of the population. She went on to say that in WFS, those who wish to continue using drugs are advised that WFS would not be an appropriate avenue for them and that those women for whom their primary drug is not alcohol, particularly if it is heroin, should seek help elsewhere. However, WFS now welcomes not only women with alcohol problems, but also those with other ATOD issues (WFS spokesperson, personal communication, August 15, 2008).

Financial support for WFS comes from individual and group donations, the annual conference, and the sale of literature. Membership is free of charge. In the face-to-face meetings, moderators collect a voluntary free-will donation. No group member is turned away if she cannot afford to give a donation.

Formal research on program effectiveness has not been conducted and is not permitted by outside parties. WFS takes the position that this would breach participant confidentiality. Kirkpatrick noted considerable testimony of good results in correspondence from followers and that the literature distributed by WFS is requested by consumers worldwide. WFS is described by their leadership as having grown steadily in the last decades as a recognized secular treatment alternative to religious-based programs.

Rational Recovery and SMART Recovery

According to CSAT (2006), providing support group options that include SMART and RR as alternatives to Twelve Step programs empowers clients to make informed decisions. Both SMART and RR were developed on the "foundation of cognitive-behavioral theory" (CSAT, 2006). Cognitive–behavioral methods are viewed by many in the mental health treatment field as one of the most promising and evidence-based methods of treatment (Buelow & Buelow, 1998).

Few current studies are available that use rigorous scientific methods, but some promising exploratory research and commentary provide support for the options of RR and SMART Recovery. RR has been found to be successful in helping clients achieve openness and decrease their denial (Schmidt, Carns, & Chandler, 2001). The relative success of these alternatives to AA contradicts the assumption that AA is the right fit for everyone and reminds clinicians of the variability and diversity among clients (Buddie, 2004).

RR is identified as a philosophy that is more appropriate than AA for those who "wish to keep their personal beliefs outside of the structured recovery process or who consider themselves non-spiritual" (Brown, Whitney, Schneider, & Vega, 2006, p. 656) or are "unwilling to deal with its spiritual orientation" (Galanter, Egelko, & Edwards, 1993, p. 509). RR is now an online experience, an Internet-based program without groups, emphasizing self-efficacy and personal responsibility. RR has evolved beyond its original link to Rational Emotive Therapy and Albert Ellis, and eschews ties to any psychological theory (Trimpey, 2009c), including cognitive–behavioral.

RR (see Appendix 10.4), sometimes referred to as a mirror image of AA, emphasizes choice and reaffirms faith in one's own rational self-efficacy, rather than in a higher power. According to the RR Web site (http://www.rational.org), the founder (Trimpey, 2009b) offers a strong admonition against recovery groups: "Stay away from recovery groups of all kinds; you can't possibly recover there. They'll never let you go, and you'll be 'in recovery' forever." Instead, he recommends following the method "to permanently abstain from alcohol and other drugs," the Addictive Voice Recognition Technique (AVRT). AVRT can be accessed by following the online prompts (free of charge) to the Internet crash course and to the literature; by subscription; or by attending face-to-face instruction at the RR headquarters. The *addictive voice* is defined as "any thinking that supports or suggests the possible future use of alcohol and other drugs" (Trimpey, 2009a, ¶ 4).

The Web site addresses families through the Zero-Tolerance Ultimatum for the Addicted Spouse or Significant Other (ASS) in Your Family. In this statement, Trimpey (2009d) further asserted the iconoclastic position, opposing Al-Anon for fostering group dependence, stating that "we take a rather old-fashioned view of the addiction as willful misconduct, voluntary and for the purpose of physical pleasure" (¶ 3).

> We suggest that the *addicted spouse* or *significant other* be thought of in the shortened tag, ASS, *an ass who is betraying others for the sheer pleasure produced by alcohol and other drugs.* Accordingly, we tend to view the family of addicted people as *suckers,* because the family's ASS takes advantage of everyone's better nature in order to build tolerance for more self-intoxication, especially those little planned, personal parties called, "relapses."

Trimpey (2009d) opposes the strategy of using "interventions" as well, positing that professional "interventionists" are costly and offer a "marginally legal service, which is essentially forceful recruitment into the recovery group movement via a health care setting." Trimpey (2009d, ¶ 2) used strong statements: "Addiction is a state of chemically-enhanced stupidity which can be overcome by abstinence." He asserted that the most serious addictions often are associated with the easiest recovery experiences, even for those who begin with minimal motivation.

SMART Recovery (see Appendix 10.5) offers both face-to-face and online "mutual help groups" (SMART Recovery, 2008), to help in recovery from "all types of addictive behaviors, including: alcoholism, drug abuse, substance abuse, drug addiction, alcohol abuse, gambling addiction, cocaine addiction, and addiction to other substances and activities." The SMART Web site reports more than 300 face-to-face meetings globally and more than 16 online meetings weekly, and that SMART Recovery is recognized by "the American Academy of Family Physicians, the Center for Health Care Evaluation, The National Institute on Drug Abuse (NIDA), US Department of Health and Human Services, (and the) American Society of Addiction Medicine."

SMART Recovery claims to offer tools to address motivation for abstinence; management of urges, thoughts, feelings, and behaviors; lifestyle balance; and problem solving. It claims to have scientific underpinnings rather than a spiritual base and to promote self-reliance, viewing addiction as a bad habit rather than a disease. Lifelong meeting attendance is not expected, real dialogue is expected in the meetings, and labeling is discouraged.

Moderation Management

Conventional fellowship groups almost exclusively favor total abstinence as the desired goal for the ATOD misuse, and this is certainly the view of AA. However, there is increasing disagreement in the treatment community as to what constitutes a desirable outcome for the alcohol misuser. Vaillant (1995) asserted that abstinence "is justifiable as a treatment goal only if moderate drinking is not a viable alternative" (p. 277). The moderation movement boasts many adherents who recommend a consideration of moderation—controlled use of alcohol—as an acceptable alternative to abstinence, but determining for whom this is an acceptable alternative is difficult.

The MM group has attracted a significant degree of controversy, and its history is marked by tragedy. Yet support for this point of view comes from an array of notables: Frederick Rotgers (associate professor and associate director of clinical training, Psychology Department, Philadelphia College of Osteopathic Medicine); Archie Brodsky (senior research associate, Harvard Medical School); Stanton Peele (2007) (author of many books, including *Addiction-Proof Your Child: A Realistic Approach to Preventing Drug, Alcohol, and Other Dependencies*); and G. Alan Marlatt (director, Addictive Behaviors Research Center).

Proponents of this movement maintain that individuals with serious alcohol problems become more easily identified and most treatment efforts are targeted to them. Those with less serious problems—typically termed "problem drinkers"—often do not come to the attention of treatment professionals but nonetheless would benefit from methods to reduce their substance intake. Many more problem drinkers may exist than those with alcoholism and more apparent multi-level disturbances. Critics express caution about the notion of moderation; moderation may be "the best hope for problem drinking in America or the most threatening form of self-delusion" (Shute, 1997, p. 57).

Audrey Kishline, author of *Moderate Drinking: The Moderation Management Guide* (1994) and at that time the foremost proponent of the moderation option, maintained that "problem drinkers" create more of a burden on society than those with more severe alcohol dependency problems. They are, she posited, quite capable of self-help through control of their drinking. Ironically and tragically, Kishline—the founder of MM—pleaded guilty in the 2000 killing of two people while driving drunk, further fueling the controversy surrounding the notion of moderation as a legitimate option. (After her release from prison, Kishline and coauthor Maloy, the woman whose husband and child had been killed by Kishline, published a book about this tragedy.) Careful examination of the symbolism and meaning of the event is imperative; nonetheless, the tragic actions of this high-profile individual do not in themselves invalidate the potential merits of moderation for some people.

According to the MM Web site,

> MM is a behavioral change program and national support group network
> for people concerned about their drinking and who desire to make positive

lifestyle changes. MM empowers individuals to accept personal responsibility for choosing and maintaining their own path, whether moderation
or abstinence. (MM, 2008)

The membership of MM is largely white, female, college educated, and upper
middle class, with a mean age of 44 years (Kosok, 2006). The research described
MM as "a mutual aid support group that helps problem drinkers reduce drinking to
non-harmful levels" (Kosok, 2006, p. 295) and asserted that MM is a viable option
for drinkers.

MM does not offer programs that are addressed specifically for family members of problem drinkers. In an e-mail communication asking about the group's
point of view on family members and loved ones, Executive Director Ana Kosok
stated that Al-Anon or private therapy might be recommended (personal communication with Ana Kosok, February 9, 2009).

The philosophy of self-determination promoted by MM is attractive to the
social work profession and to many other clinicians. Moderation, in fact, is a
method devised of necessity by many who never interface with the treatment system, those who struggle on their own to succeed or fail in the battle with their own
alcohol and other drug problems. In the United States, the cultural popularity of
AA has created an atmosphere of "one-size-fits-all" thinking in which many clients
are coerced into AA attendance. Many institutions host AA meetings or provide
an AA-like component as a required part of treatment; as a result, the majority of
those who engage in formal treatment experience at least a facsimile of AA, even if
that is not a useful match. This alternative support group may provide a midrange
solution for this subpopulation and for those who favor personal responsibility.
(See Appendix 10.6 for additional information on MM.)

Most MM members are categorized as having "low-severity alcohol problems,
high social stability, and little interest in abstinence-oriented interventions" (Humphreys, 2003, p. 622).

Tragedies such as the deaths in the car accident involving Audrey Kishline
can occur when alcoholics fail to abstain, but they can also occur when
nondependent problem drinkers are denied assistance because they have
not deteriorated enough to become committed to a goal of abstinence.
(Humphreys, p. 622)

MM is described by the author as a worthwhile option and a benefit to public
health, "given the demonstrated realities that there are many more nondependent drinkers than alcoholics, that nondependent drinkers underutilize existing

interventions, and that alcoholics were attempting controlled drinking long before MM existed" (Humphreys, 2003, p. 622). The author went on to suggest, however, that MM, as an organization, needs to develop a stronger statement that would advise those with more severe problems that MM is not the correct option for them.

NicA and Other Peer Support Options for Smokers

Tobacco is the most neglected area of inquiry about misuse of substances. Most course work and textbooks on chemical dependency treatment fail to include information about smoking cessation, and yet the cost to individual health and to society is clearly significant. (See chapter 5 for more detailed information on nicotine and related problems.) Many experts regard smoking as the "world's most prevalent and recognizable health risk" (Prochaska, Norcross, & DiClemente, 1994, p. 242). "Indeed, it is difficult to identify any other condition that presents such a mix of lethality, prevalence, and neglect, despite effective and readily available interventions" (Agency for Healthcare Research and Quality Technical Reviews and Summaries, 2008).

In the United States in 2006, nearly 30 percent of the population over age 11 were categorized as current users of tobacco, the vast majority of which were cigarette smokers (Substance Abuse and Mental Health Services Administration [SAMHSA], Office of Applied Studies [OAS], 2008). Furthermore, nicotine dependence is associated with increased risk of alcohol and other drug use; the tar in cigarettes is associated with increased risk of lung cancer, emphysema, and bronchial disorders; and the carbon monoxide in smoke is associated with risk of cardiovascular diseases. Secondhand smoke is associated with lung cancer in adults and increases the risk of respiratory illnesses in children (National Institute on Drug Abuse [NIDA], 2006). According to the Surgeon General (U.S. Department of Health and Human Services [HHS], 2004), smoking kills approximately 440,000 Americans each year. The annual cost to society exceeds $157 billion each year, with $75 billion in direct medical costs and $82 billion in lost productivity.

An association between cigarette smoking and alcoholism is in evidence in the smoke-filled rooms of many AA meetings where alcoholics are in recovery. Nicotine for many is the first drug ever used and the first on which they became dependent. Some professionals believe that in fact many who are in recovery from and abstaining from alcohol and other drugs are substituting one symptom—nicotine dependence—for the former symptom, and that many in recovery from other drugs have "romanticized" the use of caffeine and nicotine (Hoffman & Slade, 1993).

Group treatment for smokers offers peer support and encouragement and the sharing of suggestions and strategies for how to accomplish the task of abstinence. Prochaska's theoretical stages of change model posits that smokers who relapse but eventually have success learn from their failures; rather than going in circles, they spiral up toward an effective outcome (Prochaska, 1991). The group context may help those attempting change to observe that spiral effect in others. Those who are quitting smoking should be taught to continue to use support resources after the active treatment phase and to motivate the awareness of significant others about the need to support subjects during the maintenance phase. Relapse prevention that included group support and discussion fared better than a sample that received only a non-social-contact method (Mermelstein et al., 1986), but Velicer, Prochaska, and Redding (2006) advocated for tailoring interventions and following specific principles with smokers, including reaching out proactively, thus, making treatment more accessible through in-home computer and telephone access to help.

NicA (www.nicotine-anonymous.org) is described as a fellowship of men and women helping each other to live their lives free of nicotine. (Refer to Appendix 10.7 for Twelve Steps of NicA.) Similar to AA, and with attribution given to AA, they refer to sharing of experience, strength, and hope in the quest to be free of a powerful addiction, with the only requirement for membership being a desire to stop using nicotine. Meetings are available around the world, and newcomers are encouraged to form new groups in their communities. There are no dues or fees for NicA membership. Some online assistance is provided through email. Similar factors pertain; for example, those uncomfortable with the spiritual emphasis of AA may object to the parallel practices and beliefs in AA, and those taking medications for smoking cessation may find some group members to be intolerant of anyone not dedicated to total substance abstinence.

According to Liechtenstein (1999), NicA originated in the 1980s in Los Angeles, California, with the first meetings consisting of recovering alcoholics. The author described NicA as having the structure that typically characterizes a "stable, national organization" (p. 61), including an elected Board of Directors, by-laws, a national clearinghouse (Nicotine Anonymous World Services), a Web site, a book titled *Nicotine Anonymous: The Book* (Nicotine Anonymous World Services, 2008) that outlines its principles, an annual global conference, and a newsletter.

Coverage for smoking cessation still varies among insurance policies but has steadily increased in recent years (Agency for Healthcare Research and Quality Technical Reviews and Summaries, 2008). The American Cancer Society Web site lists a number of cost-free options, including those sponsored by the National

Cancer Institute, the American Heart Association, the American Lung Association, and the Centers for Disease Control and Prevention Office on Smoking and Health. A collaborative program offered online—http://www.smokefree.gov—represents a collation of the National Cancer Institute, the Centers for Disease Control and Prevention, NIDA, and HHS. This site encourages smokers to consider getting support from others, including finding a support group. Local hospitals and medical centers often offer no-cost or low-cost options as well.

The impact of smoking on family life is not regarded to be as extreme as that of abuse of alcohol and illicit drugs (Liechtenstein, 1999). Alcoholism, for example, is associated with a greater degree of family and social disruption, employment disruption, and legal problems. However, Nicotine Anonymous (NicA) encourages members to consider the effects of secondhand smoke, which is clearly a demonstration of concern for loved ones. Step 8 is stated as: Make a list of all persons we had harmed, and become willing to make amends to them all.

Christakis and Fowler (2008) reported that smoking cessation appears to have a strong group component. That is, people exposed to such influences as cigarette taxes and smoking-cessation campaigns appear to be heavily influenced by "groupness" and by "person-to-person spread." Peer pressure is key. As entire groups moved toward abstinence from cigarettes together, interpersonal contact was a key feature. The social marginalization that is created for the smoker can be devastating for those without the ability to form bonds with others, but for many it leads to the benefit of joining together, in concert moving toward freedom from nicotine and, subsequently, influencing others to quit. People appear to march to nicotine addiction en masse and, according to the authors, it follows logically that smoking cessation proceeds in a like manner.

Groups in Cyberspace

Online self-help groups are available 24 hours a day, seven days a week, to those who have access to a computer. The peer-support movement is now considered a global phenomenon. The geographic span is limited only by language. Self-help groups are voluntary and offer the opportunity to receive support in a non-judgmental manner, but online groups also provide anonymity and confidentiality. Stofle and Harrington (2002) concluded that the Internet and its promise of anonymity can further the initiation of treatment for those struggling with shame and embarrassment about their substance misuse. Although face-to-face groups admonish members to practice confidentiality, there are no guarantees that individual members will honor that.

In addition to face-to-face meetings, each of the groups mentioned in this chapter has a website, and most of these websites are rich with information. RR is the exception, now providing Web-based support only, with no face-to-face groups.

Directories of these online groups can be searched via Google or other search engines. Yahoo! Groups is available at http://groups.yahoo.com. Some people develop a new e-mail account for use with support sites, an additional measure to ensure anonymity and security.

Cultural Competence and Special Populations

In the earlier edition of this text, the need for diversity awareness was foreshadowed. "As the 21st century approaches, cultural competence, like computer literacy, is a necessity" (CSAT, 1994, p. ix). It is now quite clear that every clinician must attend to diversity issues as keenly as they do to treatment theories (NASW, 2001). This has helped to diminish the tendency to generalize findings indiscriminately from one group to another, such as assuming that research and existing literature on white males and alcoholism can be applied equally to all populations. Every individual presents with a constellation of characteristics that places her or him in a variety of special populations, and it is that interface that should dictate the individualized treatment protocol.

According to NASW (2005), the worker must strive to "understand the history, traditions, expectations, values, and attitudes of diverse groups" in treatment planning for those with substance use disorders (p. 5) and to "conduct self-examinations of their own biases and stereotyping of clients that may affect their practice" (p. 29). The clinician takes on that responsibility—regardless of one's own history and regardless of one's own characteristics—male or female, African American or Caucasian, old or young. The worker may be a member of a non-dominant population herself or himself, but nonetheless is obligated to put the client first. "The treatment provider—not the person seeking treatment—is responsible for ensuring that treatment is effective for diverse clients" (CSAT, 2006, p. 180).

The assumption is made that, in discussing special populations, the reference is to clearly identifiable typing schemas that are based on race, ethnicity, gender, religion, and so on. Although those classifications are useful, a referent described by many individuals in recovery is that of the "culture of recovery." Clinicians cite anecdotes that lend credence to this notion that the recovery culture may carry equal or greater weight in the self-identity. This cultural entity is exemplified by the networking and the belief system perpetuated by those engaged in the peer support movement. This culture can be observed at events such as the Summer Alcohol

Studies program sponsored by the Center of Alcohol Studies at Rutgers University, and would be worth further examination.

It must be noted that there is inherent risk in the fellowship dynamic when that conceptualization fosters an indifference to victimization by dominant systems. Those subpopulation members who immerse themselves in seeking internal answers to political issues may be less alert to macro-level influences. This orientation to the personal over the political helps to absolve systems in power from their responsibility for creating and maintaining oppressive conditions. The power of the fellowship may lull individuals into an attitude of indifference to larger sociopolitical realities, with the result that there is less demand on those systems to address their part in creating an atmosphere where ATOD misuse can flourish. This chapter, however, is not intended to provide analysis of institutional and political influences.

There is a risk in arbitrarily labeling one section as distinct—"special populations"—as this implies that "mainstream" information does not apply to the groups that are "special." The task of the clinician is to select from the evidence that applies—that which is dominant, or mainstream, and that which is specific to the individual in her or his cultural context.

Special, underserved, and particularly vulnerable groups may include: Native Americans, Hispanics, Latinos, African Americans, Asian Americans, Pacific Islanders, gay, lesbian, and transgendered people, adolescents, older adults, people of color, people with HIV/AIDS, people with physical disabilities (incl. brain and spinal cord injury which may be the result of substance misuse), and people with mental illnesses. Acknowledging their vulnerability, clinicians must nonetheless recognize the heterogeneity of every subpopulation.

With respect to ethnic and racial heritage, the groups reported (Office of Applied Studies, 2001) to be at highest risk in terms of nicotine were American Indians and Alaska Natives, with rates of 42.3 percent on past month use of cigarettes, compared with white people at 25.9 percent, black people at 23.3 percent, and Hispanics/Latinos at 20.7 percent. The groups reported to be at highest risk in terms of illicit drug use (Office of Applied Studies, 2001) were again American Indians and Alaska Natives, with rates of 12.6 percent compared with white and black people at 6.4 percent and Hispanics at 5.3 percent. With respect to "past month" alcohol use (Office of Applied Studies, 2001), white people reported use of alcohol at 50.7 percent, Hispanics at 39.8 percent, and black people at 33.7 percent. According to Tighe and Saxe (2006), white people were more likely to receive treatment for their substance abuse problem, with Hispanics three times and African Americans four times less likely to receive treatment. Overall, Hispanics and African Americans experienced a "greater unmet need for alcoholism, drug abuse, and mental health treatment" (Wells, Klap, Koike, & Sherbourne, 2001, p. 2030) along with inferior quality of care.

The literature is rich and constantly evolving on the topic of special populations. The clinician is urged to remain current and consult contemporary materials. The remainder of this section on the potential of group modalities for special populations will use diversity exemplars within these four categories: race–ethnicity (Latinos and African Americans), age (adolescents and older adults), sexual orientation (gay, lesbian, or bisexual), and gender (women and men).

Latinos

At 13 percent of the population, Latinos (used interchangeably with the term Hispanics in census data) are the largest ethnic minority in the United States (U.S. Census Bureau, 2001) and are clearly a heterogeneous group.

At risk for problems related to poor physical health and mental health, undereducation, underemployment, and poverty, Latinos as a group underuse services that would be available to them (Gutiérrez, Yeakley, & Ortega, 2000). Defining factors such as language proficiency, specific national origin, issues of undocumented status, level of education, gender, acculturation and assimilation, and socioeconomic status must be considered in tailoring methods for specific individuals (Delgado & de Saxe Zerden, 2007). Nonetheless, for most Hispanics one variable that is quite common across the subpopulation is that of a collective orientation and commitment to family—sometimes termed as "familism" (Gutiérrez et al., 2000), which may be the single most highly valued component of life. Group treatment opportunities in the community allow for attention to substance misuse while preserving the opportunity for the individual to remain fully involved and connected with family.

"Within social work practice, the 'person in environment' perspective is a seminal framework practitioners employ to more fully appreciate the lives and contexts in which people live" (Delgado & de Saxe Zerden, 2007, p. 139). The authors advocated for a "cultural assets paradigm" in which a shift occurs, moving the focus from a "deficit-driven" view to one that emphasizes strengths (p. 138). A cultural asset paradigm is described by Delgado (2007) as " a construct that represents the beliefs, traditions, principles, knowledge, and skills that effectively help people, particularly those who are marginalized economically and socially by a society, to persevere and succeed in spite of immense odds against them" (p. 20).

An orientation toward group work and family-based work may fit well with the familism and preferences for the collective over the individual. A collective orientation also suggests that group work or family treatment may be more consonant with *Latino* cultural values than individual work may be (Gutierrez & Ortega, 1991; Gutiérrez et al., 2000). The group environment helps Latinos develop new attitudes and explore the possibility of social change; a group work setting "could be quite effective when the goal is to empower Latinos" (Gutierrez & Ortega, p. 39). "For Latinos, the group setting provides an opportunity for members to establish contact with others, particularly those members who maintain social isolation as a retreat from or consequence of negative experiences with their social world" (p. 40). The group offers the promise of mutual support, acceptance, and consensual validation of experiences. Latinos, who quite ably celebrate mutuality, spirituality, and interdependence, often seek support and problem-solving among natural support networks—their friends and relatives—and many find comfort in a group that promotes mutual aid.

African Americans

The Office of Applied Studies (2001) reported that African Americans at 33.7 percent are less likely than both white Americans at 50.7 percent and Hispanics/Latinos at 39.8 percent to use alcohol. In terms of illicit substances, African Americans and white Americans are the same at 6 percent, slightly surpassing Hispanics/Latinos at 5 percent (Office of Applied Studies, 2001).

Those who identified as black or African American (alone) composed about 12 percent of the population according to the U.S. Census 2000 (U.S. Census Bureau, 2001). As with the Latino population, this group is diverse; connections can be traced to various places, including Africa and the Caribbean. This group, however, is often distinguished from the Latino population in terms of the extent to which many of its members have been victimized by racism. African American youths appear to be at greater risk in terms of the consequences of substance abuse even though their consumption of illicit substances is on a par with or lower than that of white youths (Sharma & Atri, 2006). The deficits in addressing the needs of this population and the concomitant effects of oppression are due, in part, to a lack of research designed specifically to explore the African American population. Furthermore, the existing literature largely ignores and demonstrates a lack of understanding about intragroup diversity.

> The first subgroup consists of the blacks that have been living in the country for three or four generations or longer. The second subgroup is comprised of individuals that have migrated from the Caribbean countries. The third subgroup is made up of individuals who are first generation immigrants

from Africa, which too has a lot of diversity. The final subgroup consists of multiracial individuals, many of whom are often misclassified as African Americans. (Sharma & Atri, 2006, p. 3)

African Americans in the United States have a long history of self-care and self-help, often in affiliation with local churches (O'Donnell, 1994). Evidence of the significance of professionally facilitated group work with African Americans is sparse, but one small study (DeCarlo & Hockman, 2003) found favorable outcomes in advancing prosocial behavior among a sample of 21 African American male adolescents, using an innovative strategy titled RAP therapy. In a study of chemically dependent African American women, the participants were reported to benefit in terms of progress in self-efficacy and stress reduction and in a more highly developed sense of community (Washington & Moxley, 2003).

AA provides a brochure titled *AA for the Black and African American Alcoholic* (AAWS, 2001). According to this document, the first African Americans attended AA meetings in 1940 and since then "thousands have found a welcome and recovery" (p. 6). Testimonials are provided from individual members of color. For example, according to Larry, "AA has worked tremendously fine for me," (p. 34) and according to Palmer, "I am an unflinching advocate of a healing faith and of Alcoholics Anonymous" (p. 25). Links between African Americans and the church date back generations in the United States. The spiritual elements of AA may continue to be viewed as attractive to African Americans in the 21st century.

Adolescents

Adolescents in substance abuse treatment are often regarded as adultlike in terms of their exposure to the hazards of the life cycle. This custom seems to conflict with the developmental realities. We all want the answer to this question: Given the very "adult" problems of these adolescents, should they be referred to peer support groups often associated with adults and older adults, such as AA and NA? There is considerable controversy—the research evidence and opinions are mixed (Kelly & Myers, 2007).

Adolescents are often referred to AA groups and NA groups as if they will have equal opportunity for benefit, without regard for developmental differences. However, some research findings (Lyter, 1993; Pandina, 1978) point to the notion that adolescent behaviors are multi-determined and that various demographic and social factors can contribute to abstinence behaviors or drug use that, although experimental, does not become problematic. In attempts to counter the hazards and pitfalls encountered by our youths, social work theory emphasizes the infusion into the child's world of the benefits of "connections and bonds, order and discipline, and hopes and dreams" (Lyter & Lyter, 2003, p. 3), with the aim of elevating orientation toward strength over that of pathology. In contrast to adults, prediction of risk for the adolescent misuser or must be tempered with consideration of psychosocial protective factors. Assignment of adolescents to peer support groups such as AA or NA may neglect consideration of those developmental realities, and may propel the youth toward identification with a stage of development that underestimates the power of hope.

Adolescents may benefit more from cultivation of the effectiveness of their parents' parenting skills, from habilitation, and from the development of "personal abilities"; these factors can help to inoculate the child from becoming a misuser or contribute to mitigation of problematic use. Fragmentation of both the adolescent self and services do little to address the whole child. This suggests that attention to development of the adolescents' and the parents' skills would be superior to referral to fellowship groups that tend to focus more on powerlessness over the drug and require a commitment to chronic recovery.

Adolescents are different; they "experience many developmental changes, may require habilitation rather than rehabilitation, may be considered dependents legally, and may require parental consent for treatment" (CSAT, 2006, p. 171). Professionally facilitated group work in general with adolescents has some support in the literature and in one study (DeCarlo & Hockman, 2003) was found to be favorable in promoting prosocial behavior.

Group therapy for adolescents continues to be a highly recommended treatment option (DeCarlo & Hockman, 2003) but evidence of the support for group work specific to substance abuse has limited evidence to draw from. Practice wisdom suggests that same-gender groups may be safer; that groups' rules must be clear and posted; that stories of nostalgia for substances should be prohibited; that a signed confidentiality statement should be used; and that groups should take into consideration the attention span of the youth (CSAT, 2006). Recreational and sports-related group activities can help to promote the development of personal abilities and routines.

Older Adults

As the baby boom population ages, it is expected that the number of older adult substance abusers will more than double by 2020 (SAMHSA, OAS, 2007a). Poly-drug problems are significant because of use of alcohol in combination with prescription and over-the-counter medications (Memmott, 2003). In ATOD treatment, older adults are sometimes stigmatized with pessimistic expectations, with many holding the belief that treatment outcomes are especially limited with this population. Surprising to many is that smoking cessation at age 65 or older can reduce by nearly 50 percent a person's risk of death as a result of smoking (HHS, 2004).

Treatment barriers for this age group include denial, the presence of multiple disorders, transportation, limited social and family support, time demands if they are caregivers for others, and insurance coverage, but perhaps the barrier of most significance to the clinician is that of ageism, the tendency to "dismiss older adults' problems as a function of aging rather than to investigate possible medical, social, or psychological causes" (CSAT, 2005, p. 12), assuming that treatment will not be a cost-effective endeavor.

According to CSAT (1998), treatment success with this age group is quite possible, but more empirical studies need to be conducted and special accommodations must be incorporated. Group-based approaches are identified as particularly beneficial for older adults; older adults appear to bond more quickly in group settings than do younger adults. Groups for older adults can include educational groups in which clients benefit from information about processes of chemical dependency and recovery; socialization groups, in which they have the opportunity to form relationships that counter isolation and practice their new skills with others who are in recovery; and also therapy groups, where group leaders facilitate feedback among group members and provide factual information about recovery. In addition, many older adults are referred to self-help groups such as AA.

Group facilitators need to prepare to address the special needs of some older adults (CSAT, 1998). Because of some sensory decline, this population benefits from use of both audio and visual presentations of material, minimizing noise and glare interference. Endurance and stamina limitations can be addressed by limiting session time to 55 minutes, and by allowing clients to set the pace in the group. The group session can be supplemented with homework or one-to-one booster sessions. The possibility of hidden literacy problems should be considered. Integration may require more time and older adults should be assisted in practicing how to use new information. New information may be especially helpful and older adults need to be kept abreast of new findings especially in the area of pharmacology. Last, it is wise to warn older clients about differences that they might expect in peer support groups. For example, AA groups may be more confrontational than groups in a professional treatment setting and may include young adults who speak very frankly about their experiences and may use profane language. Age-specific groups may be available and may promote more camaraderie, but many clinicians see benefits in the broader representation of age-mixed groups (Sorocco & Ferrell, 2006).

Lesbians, Gay, Bisexual, and Transgender Individuals

Attention to sexual orientation gender identity within the rubric of ATOD treatment improves as awareness is raised about treatment for lesbian, gay, bisexual, and transgender (LGBT) clients (CSAT, 2001), with an emphasis on sensitizing providers to unique issues pertaining to this population in a manner that is culturally competent. Further studies will help workers identify the incidence and prevalence rates of substance abuse by LGBT individuals. In recent history, few studies asked for respondents to identify their sexual orientation. However, it is estimated that when compared with the general population, "LGBT people are more likely to use alcohol and drugs, have higher rates of substance abuse, are less likely to abstain from use, and are more likely to continue heavy drinking into later life" (p. xiii).

Clearly, heterosexism can contribute to substance misuse among the LGBT population. Bias, homophobia, and shaming influence individuals to internalize negativity and guilt, causing "some members of the marginalized community to manage these additional stressors by using mind-altering substances" (p. xv). This negativity may come from family members as well as others. "Substance use, especially alcohol use, is a large part of the social life of some segments of the LGBT community" (p. xv).

The clinician must give special attention to application of the group modality to this population. There is a potential for bias among other group members; as such, the facilitator must ensure that homophobia and prejudice will not be tolerated. Only the LGBT client has the authority to make the decision about relating sexual orientation with group members. Efforts should be made to ensure the client's emotional safety, but it would be unfortunate to deny the individual the opportunity to be exposed to the power of groupness, where tolerance and acceptance in a heterogeneous group has the potential to "accelerate healing" (CSAT, 2001, p. xv). Significant others and domestic partners—sometimes termed "family of choice"—should be considered as well because LGBT individuals may have life partners who do not meet legal definitions of family. For example, diverse multiple-family groups are a service that could be of benefit.

Women and Men

In the earlier edition, a separate section on issues of women was included; in this edition, the focus was shifted to attend to both women and men. Although it is true that women's issues suffered from neglect for many years and that more focused attention on the concerns of women has been crucial, we also recognize the risk of polarization when women and men are considered in isolation. There is growing recognition that social work, in its zeal to serve the underserved, has overlooked the health needs of men. Kosberg (2002) asserted, "Social work literature has mainly focused upon females and gay males" (p. 51); social work research, practice, and education need to "focus upon males; no more, but certainly no less, than females" (p. 66). Referring to the heterosexual male population as neglected, Kosberg (2002) found in a review of the prominent social work publications that "when males are discussed they were, in the main, discussed as gays or if heterosexuals, discussed in negative ways" (pp. 51–52). The potential for group modalities are reviewed here with regard to both women and men.

"Even though women and men who have substance use disorders have many similarities, they differ in some important ways" (CSAT, 2006, p. 158). Gender imbalances in diagnosis and treatment are often attributed to a greater propor- tion of the male population suffering from substance misuse and to the tendency for women to maintain secrecy about their misuse. It is the job of the clinician to understand both the comparisons and the contrasts.

For 2006, it was reported that the rate of substance dependence or abuse for males over the age of 11 was twice that for females (12.3 compared with 6.3 per- cent) (SAMHSA, OAS, 2007c). With regard to past month rates of drinking in 2004 and 2005 (SAMHSA, OAS, 2007b), men exceeded women on each measure: any alcohol use, 57.5 percent for men and 45 percent for women; binge drinking, 30.8 percent for men and 15.1 percent for women; and heavy alcohol use, 10.5 percent for men and 3.3 percent for women.

Similarly, men accounted for three-fourths of admissions for abuse of alcohol alone (75 percent) and for abuse of alcohol with secondary drug abuse (74 percent) (SAMHSA, OAS, 2006). According to Tighe and Saxe (2006), women were less likely to receive needed treatment than men—seven times less likely. Some authors have suggested that gender differences in use of treatment may be the result of bar- riers to treatment for women, such as financial, accessibility, child responsibilities, and a higher level of stigma applied to women (Greenfield, 2002). These same bar- riers may affect outcome.

A report from CSAT (1994) concluded that clinicians must consider issues of recovery that may be particularly relevant to women, such as self-esteem, sexual- ity, sexual abuse and violence, cultural roles and cultural identity, communication skills, assertiveness, stress management, family and other relationships, and health. Women may be disengaged or estranged from family, and yet many retain respon- sibility for minor children. Women who misuse substances often have a history of trauma. In one intriguing example, Duffy (2007) described the introduction of a therapeutic group activity—a knitting program—that appeared to address some of the issues of trauma experienced by women; the use of such innovations in group may assist in group bonding and, according to Duffy, affect management. Knitting became both a positive habit and a method of soothing self.

Many women are tied to the home because of child care responsibilities or because of a lack of linkages with the community. A support group or support system of other recovering women may serve as a new "family," facilitated by regular meetings and daily phone contacts. Groups can help women to join with peers, practice newfound skills of coping and abstinence, and maintain treatment gains. This may be best attained in the woman's own cultural and geographic community, with services that include child care during treatment and during recovery, parent training, and a 24-hour hotline to help with relapse problems. CSAT (1994) noted that because services are home based, certain adaptations should be available, such as a telecommunications device (TDD) for deaf women and, when necessary, transportation for handicapped women.

CSAT (1994) reported the benefits of securing volunteers to serve as temporary sponsors or "big sisters" for women reentering the community after treatment. Sororities, women's leagues, and support groups for abused women are good resources for this type of pairing. CSAT also recommended advocating for women-only groups that are part of AA, Adult Children of Alcoholics, Co-Dependency Anonymous, WFS, and groups specific to populations such as lesbians, adolescents, and older women. Professional assistance can be offered to help women to locate meeting space and to encourage social events for clients, alumnae, and their sponsors to meet and socialize with recovering women.

Some research posits that women who misuse alcohol, tobacco, and other drugs are perceived in ways that are more judgment-laden than men who do the same (Blume, 1998). "Women alcoholics," for example, "are often stranded by their spouses and scorned by their children" (Burman & Allen-Meares, 1991, p. 388). Women alcoholics report lower self-esteem and suffer social stigma to a greater degree. The stereotypes applied to women include an array of images that connote such qualities as a lack of femininity or wickedness.

Treatment methods and programs traditionally were predicated on research on men. Many clinicians believe that women have unique needs and that treatment should be gender specific and sex segregated. As noted by McCrady and Raytek, "specialized treatment programs for women seem to result in better treatment outcomes than mixed-sex units" (1993, p. 332).

Kosberg (2002) pointed out that men as well have some extraordinary challenges. They are heavily influenced to "exemplify stoicism, independence, self-reliance, and strength" and to refrain from having problems, showing sadness, and getting help (p. 63). Moreover, providers must acknowledge the special needs of men (Kosberg, 2002) from minority groups.

Men and women of color, including Latinos/Latinas, Native Americans, and African Americans, share a power deficit by virtue of both their gender and their race or ethnicity. They are over-represented in terms of social disadvantages—lower levels of education and of employment status—and women especially are underrepresented in positions of power and authority (Gutierrez, 1990). Collective powerlessness contributes to vulnerability to substance misuse and to an inability to cope with issues of treatment and recovery. In addition, some treatment strategies define pathology as located within an individual, ignoring the need for change within environmental sources of dysfunction. Gutierrez (1990) suggested that social workers need to make an effort to increase power, especially for women of color, by promoting self-efficacy; bolstering ego functioning; promoting a sense of group consciousness or "shared fate" among minority women; reducing the self-blame that leads to immobilization; accepting the client's definition of the problem; identifying potential client strengths and power resources; and teaching problem solving and life skills such as parenting, personal safety and preservation, social skills, and collaborative advocacy.

Because Twelve Step programs emphasize giving oneself over to a higher power and powerlessness over the drug, it is important for providers to recognize the jeopardy this may pose for those—men or women—who already see themselves as powerless and to incorporate a feeling of collaboration in the helping relationship. Group support can be a crucial resource. Gutierrez (1990) cited small groups as the "ideal modality for empowering interventions" (p. 151) and McCrady and Raytek (1993) described group support as enabling disengaged women to begin to build a social and support network.

Stereotyping and bias may be at work with males as well, assigning expectations and characteristics to them as well that put them at risk. Demands to display stoicism and self-reliance interfere with the display of emotion and vulnerability and, perhaps, with help-seeking behavior. "Accordingly, there are significant challenges facing professionals who wish to assist males with their psychological, social, and interpersonal problems" (Kosberg, 2002, p. 63).

It is a popular notion that AA pertains more to white, middle-class men and is less welcoming and less beneficial for racial and ethnic minorities, for non-Christians, and for women. From this belief, variations on the traditional theme, such as WFS, have emerged, as have specialized AA groups. Female membership has remained the same since the previous membership survey a decade ago; for North America, AAWS (2008) reported that 33 percent of AA members were women.

AA promotes the notion of admission of powerlessness over alcohol and submission to a higher authority or power. Feminists assert that, for some women, this ideology or doctrine can exacerbate a sense of hopelessness, rather than provide the empowerment that would encourage the development of self-sustaining behaviors and beliefs. Likewise, women who join Al-Anon may be persuaded to a way of thinking that promotes self-blame in their "addiction to the alcoholic."

Controversy abounds regarding the extent to which traditional male-oriented programs can be generalized to women. As noted by Makela (1996), the AA literature has a "patriarchal flavor, and many AA groups still seem to be based on very traditional sex roles" (p. 175). Abbott (1994) contended that the underlying philosophy of AA has been questioned by feminists, and indeed may not be appropriate for many women. She identified self-help group models that are more in line with feminist modifications of the AA philosophy: WFS, RR, Secular Organization for Sobriety/Save Our Selves, and Kasl's Sixteen Steps for Discovery and Empowerment. Conversely, Beckman (1993) drew a startling and contrary conclusion from her review of the existing research on women and AA:

> I now believe that AA, a fellowship originally designed by and composed primarily of men, appears to be equally or more effective for women than men. There is no clear empirical evidence to suggest that certain types of women would fare better in other types of alcoholism treatment. (p. 246)

Likewise, in a subsequent study, Sanders (2006) reported a more optimistic view of the fit of women with AA. In a study of 167 women, all of whom attended women-only AA meetings, and many of whom attended mixed gender meetings as well, Sanders found that women were able to create a comfortable space for themselves, to adapt the steps to their own needs, "putting to rest the concerns of certain feminist scholars that AA and the recovery culture are invidious to women" (p. 28).

Stocker (1998), in a review of NIDA-funded studies, reported that women are at less risk of relapse in drug abuse treatment than men in part because they are more likely to attend group counseling and to attend more total sessions than men, supporting the belief that the intensity of participation is associated with better outcomes. Women are more likely, in general, to seek professional help; the hesitance of men to do so leads to less desirable outcomes overall.

The reputation of Al-Anon is that its membership is primarily female; indeed the 2006 Al-Anon Membership Survey reported that, as in the previous survey, 85 percent of members were female (Al-Anon Family Group Headquarters, 2007). As such, men who are involved with someone who is an ATOD misuser may not perceive that they have an equal opportunity for access to this particular group. Men who have attended report that their singularity in the group can deprive them of male role models and can place them in a position of special attention in the group.

"AA, Al-Anon, and later Alateen developed around modern nuclear family roles, AA being primarily for the father, Al-Anon for the mother, and Alateen for the child" (Makela, 1996, p. 171).

The Clinician's Mission

Social work is one of the largest allied health profession in the United States, and it is crucial that social workers acquire knowledge, skills, and values that will enable them to work effectively with issues of ATOD abuse. "Social workers shall be knowledgeable about" the concept of "openness to various approaches to recovery" (NASW, 2005, p. 14) and "integrating multiple intervention strategies into practice including . . . self/mutual-help programs" (p. 19). Clinicians need to know how to engage in planned change with their clients, how to match clients with appropriate interventions, and how to properly prepare clients for the group experience.

The clinician must sift through complex and sometimes contradictory evidence about treatment and about the role of group process in chemical dependency. Groups, as with any modality of change, have risks and deficits as well as benefits. Armed with knowledge and awareness of possible risks, the professional can more ably and responsibly guide the client. Usually the benefits outweigh the risks, but no treatment is totally safe. Glicken (2005) observed that "self-help groups, just like professional help, have the potential for doing harm" (p. 278) such as creating a cultlike atmosphere, using group pressure to impose belief systems, promoting the notion of lifelong alcoholism, and encouraging dependency. Although overall self-help groups have advantages, such as the cost factor, Glicken concluded, there is less risk posed by groups led by professionals than by peer-facilitated groups.

Galinsky and Schopler (1994) conducted research to investigate the potential negative effects of support groups, specifically in cancer support. Their exploration identified such effects and issues as the risk of not feeling accepted, irregular attendance, members at different stages, premature termination, lack of participation, disruptive members, unclear goals, inappropriate composition, inappropriate behavior, interpersonal conflicts, and violation of confidentiality or of group rules. Wuthnow (1996) found the following as the most common complaints about group: disagreements among group members, feeling shy or reluctant to share feelings, finding it hard to make time for the group, feeling uncomfortable, and feeling pressure from the group to do something.

Anecdotes and narratives provide similar evidence of the variety of obstacles that the change seeker may encounter in a group composed of substance misusers. Some group members may be more seriously "damaged" or may be lacking in superego, with little regard for the needs of cohorts. Group members may behave in a grandiose manner and may act out character flaws in the group. Some members may be inappropriately medicated by their physicians, and their behavior may be additionally disrupted or disruptive. Manipulation, splitting, and violation of group rules may occur. Violations of boundaries and of the group contract include trying to do group business outside the group with other clients or with clinician leaders. Sometimes cliques form that can make some members feel alienated or can detract from group cohesiveness.

Some groups may be biased toward a population cohort and may not be welcoming to women, certain ethnic or racial groups, or gay men and lesbians. Moreover, some groups are intolerant of misuse of specific substances; for example, an AA group may not welcome an individual who has misused both alcohol and illicit drugs. An intolerance of professionals or a position that "all drugs are bad" can also be a hindrance; for example, an individual taking lithium for bipolar disorder and receiving individual counseling may be persuaded to instead commit to the saving powers of the group and forgo the use of the therapist and prescribed medication. An atmosphere that fosters suspicion of professionals may perpetuate sharing of misinformation that cannot be challenged.

To make the most of a group experience, it is often expected that one must share openly and honestly. However, some cultures value privacy and discourage public airing of personal issues. A group environment may in fact pose some special threats to someone who feels shame about public display of personal issues. Individuals in groups may feel intimidated by others to reveal more than they wish; each has right to privacy, and although sharing can be part of the process of healing, individuals should not be forced to share intimacies before they are ready (CSAT, 2005). Clients must be advised that confidentiality cannot be guaranteed in a group milieu.

Many misusers see themselves as controlled by external events, promoting a picture of themselves as continually victimized by an uncaring world. Grandiosity alternates in a dramatic manner with inadequacy and dependency, enmeshment with isolation and withdrawal, bravado with shame, expressions of emotionality with constricted affect. These polarities are disconcerting not only to the misuser, but also to cohorts and the group leader. These swings in mood, affect, and cognition sometimes result in the misuser attacking and devaluing others in an attempt to deflect attention from his or her own shortcomings. Many misusers bring to group their typical crisis-prone, volatile, disruptive behaviors. Often unmotivated to do things in a planful way, they will act first rather than reflect. In response, the group leader may at times feel depressed, angry, puzzled, and overwhelmed (Golden et al., 1994).

Group members who are early in their recovery may be especially vulnerable. Most clients are not functioning substance-free at optimal cognitive levels until they have achieved months of abstinence (Schuckit, 1999). In these early months, the client may benefit less from the group experience and more from information about specific behavioral strategies for dealing with such challenges as sleep problems, anxiety, and mood swings. Any existing pathology in cohorts or the group system may be especially harmful to the novice. Some group members may go as far as to prey on or victimize the more vulnerable newcomers.

Veteran fellowship group members often believe in the concept of altruism and wish to give something back to the other group members. Although well-meaning, payback from veterans in the recovery process may subject others to endless storytelling that may not be beneficial. Moreover, those who have found some personal success may believe that their method should be the right one for everyone. Some veterans indeed become dependent on the newcomers and on the group instead of moving on with their lives. Some seem to thrive on or can only survive by continually "rescuing" others. In some particularly disturbing situations, a person with severe mental or emotional disturbance may take control of a group. That person may manipulate the scenario and exert an undue influence on the group dynamics, the group process, and the other members.

Groups pose some risks and challenges to the leaders as well. "Leaders should expect that people with substance abuse histories will have learned an extensive repertoire of intimidating, shaming, and other harmful behaviors. Because such conduct can make group members feel unsafe, the leader should use interventions that deflect the offensive behavior without shaming the shamer" (CSAT, 2005, p. 101). Substance-misusing individuals bring special needs and dynamics that demand attention. Many ATOD misusers, particularly those with severe and multiple substance problems, have character flaws or personality extremes that serve as obstacles to communication and relationships with others. Their group behaviors may be characterized as manipulative and resistant, even as they crave and yet reject intimacy. Other descriptors include charming, seductive, aloof, hypersensitive, deferential, demanding, and ruthless. In some cases, they may pose a danger to self and others, acting out anxiety and aggression. Violation of boundaries and doing group business outside the group disrupt the group cohesion and alter the complex inter-relationships of members and of the group leader.

Groups as a social microcosm, however, have the potential to produce character change, to counter prevailing cultural pressures, and to counter denial and resistance. Groups compel clients to deal with the here and now, to learn strategies for change, to use and benefit from empathy, to relate to others and to work through fears about intimacy and contact, and to address psychological vulnerabilities. The group event provides the individual with an experiential learning milieu that promotes the sharing of practical problem solving strategies. The benefits of group can include advocacy, special emotional bonds, reassurance of the universality of the struggle, and the opportunity to observe a successful role model (Powell, 1990). From a sociopolitical point of view, groups can promote democratic thinking, tolerance, and diversity. This is of special relevance to subpopulations that may be victimized by dominant mainstream groups. Particularly in the United States, a group experience may provide a counterbalance to a national philosophy of rugged individualism, a factor that indeed may help to maintain substance misusing behaviors. Observers of social trends note a breakdown of the family and the loss of the sense of community; these effects of alienation to some extent are countered by group experiences.

In assessing the wisdom of prescribing a group experience, the clinician needs to keep an open mind about the risks and benefits of group, putting biases and rivalries aside. The practitioner must be alert to her or his own resistance. The clinician must allow for the possibility that a group, even a group of which the clinician is not the leader, might be beneficial for the client. The treatment professional may perceive a fellowship group, however, as a threat to her or his own self-esteem. The engaging qualities of a group may be more appealing to a client than the demands of a one-to-one relationship, and the client may stray away from individual treatment. The clinician must process such circumstances and be prepared, when needed, to recognize the merits of the alternatives to one-on-one treatment.

Likewise, the clinician must also be ready to accept that not every client is ready and not every client is capable of benefiting from fellowship support. The principle of equifinality holds: many different paths can lead to a positive outcome.

The authors have had the experience of teaching graduate social work courses in ATOD dependency and treatment. The curriculum requires that the student attend open meetings of fellowship groups such as AA and Al-Anon, then report about their experiences in a phenomenological manner. This provides an opportunity for the student to carefully analyze the many elements of the experience in a very personal way, and to prepare for the self-awareness that is required of treatment professionals in the ATOD field. Their responses are always varied and compelling, some profound and some practical. Following are some representative quotes, collected over years of classroom instruction.

- I feared that someone would see me—a neighbor or acquaintance, or a co-worker—and I felt I needed to be prepared with some sort of story to explain myself.
- I was overwhelmed by the smoke in the room [at an AA meeting that was not smoke free]—I wondered did they trade alcohol for nicotine and caffeine.
- I discovered that what brought me to that Al-Anon meeting was not the classroom assignment, but the personal desire to resolve the profound sadness I still carried with me about my ex-husband's alcoholism and abusive behavior. I was rid of him but not the tragedy of our time together.
- I became one with the group [an AA meeting]. I had never felt so welcome anywhere—The warmth was very attractive even for someone without a substance problem!
- There's something not right about teenagers sitting around with a bunch of older men, bragging about all of their exploits and being on the brink of death. I know that some of these kids have had really horrifying experiences, but some of them just seem to have lost their way. All the talk of death and powerlessness just seemed to turn them off.
- I really resent this assignment. You forced me into a room where I felt like the odd person out. Should I tell the truth about who I am?
- This seems wonderful for some of the people [AA meeting]. But I was put off by all the religious stuff. It's clear that they push you to believe in God, even though they don't exactly say that.
- I felt surrounded by dogma and folklore—This ain't science.
- I attended an Al-Anon meeting. I think I was lucky to get out of there without being evicted! When I introduced myself and explained that I am interested in becoming a social worker who specializes in substance abuse treatment, it was as if I unleashed all of the anger that anyone in that room harbored against the treatment community. One woman sobbed loudly and shrieked at me, stating that the counselor that her son had worked with actually made things worse. Although I was frightened at the time, I've had some time to think. Now I am mostly awed by the intensity and magnitude of that mother's feelings.

The responses reported from students give a beginning understanding of the variety of issues that the clinician must perceive to individualize treatment successfully. The professional can facilitate the fellowship resource by helping the client to make good choices. To do this, the clinician must know not only the resources available, but also how to help the client to prepare herself or himself for the event. The clinician should become familiar with the support groups in the community and learn something about their reputations and goals. In addition to having current schedules of meetings available, the clinician can develop a network of members or participants who could help ease the way for a novice. The clinician should have had the experience of attending open meetings, and should be knowledgeable about features and characteristics that would help in determining a good fit between client and group.

Many times the client needs to try more than one meeting, and may find that certain neighborhoods or communities may be more congruent with personal interests and needs. For example, a group that allows smoking may be uncomfortable for a non-smoker, or a group with women only may not feel welcoming to a man. The clinician who knows the nature of the various groups can help guide the client to select the best target group and to experiment with others if necessary.

Examination of human issues requires acknowledgment of the multivariate nature of such inquiry, and it customarily falls to the clinicians to use not just scholarly knowledge but also to use good clinical judgment and common sense. ATOD treatment research has not produced a simple yes–no dichotomy to answer the question of the suitability of group methods. The client must be thoroughly assessed, and the clinician helps the client to match treatment options with client needs, to find strategies for individualizing the care plans (CSAT, 2006). With knowledge of the needs of the individual client, the professional has the opportunity to capitalize on the strengths of the group experience in a variety of ways: by referral to an existing group (peer or therapy); by combining peer group with counseling that will directly and intentionally complement the group experience; by educating the client about how to make the most of the group experience; or by providing a therapeutic group experience that addresses the needs of clients with similar characteristics.

Regardless of personal opinions about fellowship and self-help groups, the treatment professional should not underestimate the depth and breadth of the influence of such groups or the perceptions of the public about their meaning and worth. The professional should be aware of and sensitive to the effects of the peer support movement. Many clients have formulated more thorough and complete views about fellowship groups than they have about professional treatment. They may be more likely to visualize themselves in the role of peer group member than that of "client." Accordingly, a task for the clinician should be to help to minimize the deficits and maximize the benefits of fellowship groups, enhancing and facilitating the client's group experience.

There is more awareness now of the merit of client choice among a variety of options. Social workers promote the achievement of client self-determination and hold in high regard the dignity that empowerment bestows on the individual. "Patients who participate in choosing their own treatment approach from among alternatives show more motivation, compliance, and better outcomes than patients only offered a single approach" (Hester, 1994, p. 42). This assertion is contrary to the more traditional practice in the treatment community of "one size fits all." Typically it was believed that most clients, as a result of their denial and resistance, need to be confronted with the truth and persuaded to see the views of the clinician or of recovery cohorts, regardless of their own views or wishes.

The spiral nature of the transtheoretical stages of change model (Prochaska, 1991; Prochaska et al., 1994) refutes another popular notion—that is, that change occurs in a systematic, linear manner. Instead, because smoking and other addictions are chronic rather than acute behaviors, people who change successfully do so in a non-linear upward spiral. Each attempt at change, each program attended, may move individuals toward the goal, with occasional slips backward, until they eventually circle around and upward, accumulating experiences that lead to a conclusion that is satisfactory. According to Vaillant (1995), "we may need to recognize that the recovery process in alcoholism is best catalyzed not by a single episode of treatment but by fostering natural healing processes over time" (p. 359). This process may involve years of trial and error, numerous efforts on the part of clinicians and fellow changers to help the individual make the best choices along the way.

The frontier of change is predicated on, according to Prochaska (1997), the maximal package, which is likely to include some sort of group experience along with access to the precision offered by computer assistance. For example, in his weight control program, clients participate in group support and also in a computer program that allows the individual to progress through a change process that matches the individual's stage of and readiness for change with the techniques that will best facilitate growth and change. There is no conclusive empirical evidence that group treatment methods are superior to other methods, chance alone, or the passage of time alone. Some empirical evidence calls into question the effectiveness of self-help group methods as a stand-alone strategy, but the support among those in the recovery community has been unwavering. In light of the conflicting forces of evidence versus popularity, professionals are faced with an awesome and thankless task: to weigh the "scientific" evidence against the prevailing views of a powerful and influential consumer movement. The testimony presented by participants in Twelve Step programs has persuaded many professionals of the potency of peer support. A responsible scientist-practitioner may feel forced to choose between conflicting sides to reconcile dissonant views. "No one should be *required* to attend AA" but "everyone should be encouraged to *try*" (Glaser, 1993, p. 392). Given the persuasive arguments, this idea of encouraging most people to at least consider peer fellowship is sound.

Moreover, those who serve as group leaders or group consultants can work to ameliorate and prevent some negative effects. For example, the leader can carefully provide direction about structure and format, teach the group to use problem solving, handle disruptions as they arise, use structured exercises and activities, and engage in group work education and ongoing consultation or supervision. It behooves the treatment professional, as with any treatment intervention, to secure informed consent from the client, with notification of potential risks and benefits.

Fellowship groups are widely available, seven days a week, live or online, at no cost; similarly, therapy groups often are less costly than individual treatment. Groups may be an intervention method that is less intensive, less intrusive, and less disruptive than inpatient methods, and for many people may be as effective. Affordable outpatient services, especially in a group format, can serve larger numbers of people at less cost and fewer hours of professional labor. Clients may find that "sharing the costs" with others in group is a more budget-effective way to maximize their treatment dollars.

We propose that the evidence is quite convincing that groups—those facilitated by peers and those by professionals—can be effective for many and that the ultimate goal of treatment effectiveness comes in an acknowledgment of the complex interplay of variables. It is counterproductive to ignore the extensive network of self-help groups if it can be useful for some clients. In sum, the clinician should strive to make the most effective recommendations for linking clients with interventions, to guide the client to maximize treatment opportunities, and to help the client to minimize costs and potential negative outcomes.

In a study by Moos and Moos (2005), "compared with individuals who participated only in professional treatment," those who participated in both AA and professional treatment "were more likely to achieve remission" (p. 1858). Although it is still far from being definitive, it may be the closest that we have to a formula for sound ATOD treatment. The compelling combination of professional help plus self-help continues to give promise.

APPENDIX 10.1: The Twelve Steps of Alcoholics Anonymous

1. We admitted we were powerless over alcohol—that our lives had become unmanageable.
2. Came to believe that a Power greater than ourselves could restore us to sanity.
3. Made a decision to turn our will and our lives over to the care of God *as we understood Him.*
4. Made a searching and fearless moral inventory of ourselves.
5. Admitted to God, to ourselves and to another human being the exact nature of our wrongs.
6. Were entirely ready to have God remove all these defects of character.
7. Humbly asked Him to remove our shortcomings.
8. Made a list of all persons we had harmed, and became willing to make amends to them all.
9. Made direct amends to such people wherever possible, except when to do so would injure them or others.
10. Continued to take personal inventory and when we were wrong, promptly admitted it.
11. Sought through prayer and meditation to improve our conscious contact with God *as we understood Him,* praying only for knowledge of His will for us and the power to carry that out.
12. Having had a spiritual awakening as the result of these steps, we tried to carry this message to alcoholics, and to practice these principles in all our affairs.

Source: Alcoholics Anonymous World Services, http://www.alcoholics-anonymous.org. The Twelve Steps are reprinted with permission of Alcoholics Anonymous World Services, Inc. (AAWS). Permission to reprint the Twelve Steps does not mean that AAWS has reviewed or approved the contents of this publication, or that AAWS necessarily agrees with the views expressed herein. A.A. is a program of recovery from alcoholism only—use of the Twelve Steps in connection with programs and activities which are patterned after A.A., but which address other problems, or in any other non-A.A. context, does not imply otherwise.

APPENDIX 10.2. The Twelve Steps of Al-Anon Family Groups

1. We admitted we were powerless over alcohol—that our lives had become unmanageable.
2. Came to believe that a Power greater than ourselves could restore us to sanity.
3. Made a decision to turn our will and our lives over to the care of God *as we understood Him.*
4. Made a searching and fearless moral inventory of ourselves.
5. Admitted to God, to ourselves, and to another human being the exact nature of our wrongs.
6. Were entirely ready to have God remove all these defects of character.
7. Humbly asked Him to remove our shortcomings.
8. Made a list of all persons we had harmed, and became willing to make amends to them all.
9. Made direct amends to such people wherever possible, except when to do so would injure them or others.
10. Continued to take personal inventory and when we were wrong, promptly admitted it.
11. Sought through prayer and meditation to improve our conscious contact with God *as we understood Him,* praying only for knowledge of His will for us and the power to carry that out.
12. Having had a spiritual awakening as the result of these Steps, we tried to carry this message to others, and to practice these principles in all our affairs.

APPENDIX 10.3. Women for Sobriety: "New Life" Acceptance Program

1. I have a life-threatening problem that once had me.
   We now take charge of our life and our disease. We accept the responsibility.
2. Negative thoughts destroy only myself.
   Our first conscious sober act must be to remove negativity from life.
3. Happiness is a habit I will develop.
   Happiness is created, not waited for.
4. Problems bother me only to the degree I permit them to.
   We now better understand our problems and do not permit problems to over-whelm us.
5. I am what I think.
   I am a capable, competent, caring, compassionate woman.
6. Life can be ordinary or it can be great.
   Greatness is mine by a conscious effort.
7. Love can change the course of my world.
   Caring becomes all important.
8. The fundamental object of life is emotional and spiritual growth.
   Daily I put my life into a proper order, knowing which are the priorities.
9. The past is gone forever.
   No longer will I be victimized by the past. I am a new person.
10. All love given returns.
    I will learn to know that others love me.
11. Enthusiasm is my daily exercise.
    I treasure all moments of my new life.
12. I am a competent woman and have much to give life.
    This is what I am and I shall know it always.
13. I am responsible for myself and for my actions.
    I am in charge of my mind, my thoughts, and my life.

To make the Program effective for you, arise each morning 15 minutes earlier than usual and go over the Thirteen Affirmations. Then begin to think about each one by itself. Take one statement and use it consciously all day. At the end of the day, review the use of it and what effects it had that day for you and your actions.

APPENDIX 10.4. Rational Recovery

Below is a comprehensive, 200-word description of AVRT, providing enough information for you to end your addiction, *right now*.

> Observe your thoughts and feelings, positive and negative, about drinking or using. Thoughts and feelings which support continued use are called the Addictive Voice (AV); those which support abstinence are you. When you recognize and understand your AV, it becomes not-you, but "it," an easily-defeated enemy that has been causing you to drink. All it wants is pleasure. "I want a drink," becomes, "It wants a drink." Think to yourself, "I will never drink again," and listen for its reaction. Your negative thoughts and feelings are your AV talking back to you. Now, think, "I will drink/use whenever I please." Your pleasant feelings are also the AV, which is in control. Recovery is not a process; it is an event. The magic word is "Never," as in, "I will never drink/use again." Recognition defeats short-term desire, and abstinence soon becomes effortless. Complete separation of "you" from "it" leads to complete recovery and hope for a better life. The only time you can drink is now, and the only time you can quit for good is right now. "I will never drink/use again," becomes, "I never drink now." It's not hard; anyone can do it.

http://www.rational.org/html_public_area/course_avrt.html

APPENDIX 10.5. SMART Recovery

SMART Recovery® Purposes and Methods Statement

1.   We help individuals gain independence from addictive behavior.
2.   We teach how to
     —enhance and maintain motivation to abstain
     —cope with urges
     —manage thoughts, feelings and behavior
     —balance momentary and enduring satisfaction
3.   Our efforts are based on scientific knowledge, and evolve as scientific knowledge evolves.
4.   Individuals who have gained independence from addictive behavior are invited to stay involved with us, to enhance their gains and help others.

Commentary:
1.   We assume that addictive behavior can arise from both substance use (e.g., psychoactive substances of all kinds, including alcohol, nicotine, caffeine, food, illicit drugs, and prescribed medications), and involvement in activities (e.g., gambling, sexual behavior, eating, spending, relationships, exercise, etc.). We assume that there are degrees of addictive behavior, and that all individuals to some degree experience it. For some individuals the negative consequences of addictive behavior (which can involve several substances or activities) become so great that change becomes highly desirable.

     To individuals who are, or think they may be, at this point, we offer our services. Our groups are free of charge (although a donation is requested). Our Internet listserv discussion group is free to those who can access it. There is a nominal charge for our publications.
2.   Gaining independence from addictive behavior can involve changes that affect an individuals entire life, not just changes directly related to the addictive behavior itself. Consequently there appear to be as many roads to gaining independence from addictive behavior as there are individuals. For many the road will lead somewhere other than using our services. We recommend they follow the direction they have chosen, and we wish them well. They are always welcome to return.

     Individuals who have been successful in gaining independence from addictive behavior appear to have made changes in all four areas we teach about. These four areas could also be described as maintaining motivation, coping with craving, thinking rationally, and leading a balanced lifestyle. Although we teach important information in each of these areas, ultimately it is the individual's determination and persistence to keep moving forward that will determine how much success is achieved.

Our services are provided for those who desire, or think they may desire, to achieve abstinence. Individuals unsure about whether to pursue abstinence may observe in our group discussions how abstinence can be achieved, and how it can help. Even those whose ultimate goal is moderated involvement with their substances or activities may benefit from participation in abstinence-oriented discussions. Benefit could occur if the individual aims to engage in selected periods of abstinence, or frames the goal as abstaining from over- involvement (as opposed to all involvement).

Much of the information imparted by us is drawn from the field of cognitive-behavioral therapy (CBT), and particularly from Rational Emotive Behavior Therapy, as developed by Albert Ellis, Ph.D. In general, CBT views addictive behavior more as a complex maladaptive behavior than as a disease. Use of the CBT perspective allows us to use a rich and easily accessible body of ideas, techniques, and publications. Some of these publications we are able to make available directly to our participants, and others are available through bookstores and other sources.

3. What we offer is consistent with the most effective methods yet discovered for resolving emotional and behavioral problems. As scientific knowledge advances, our teachings will be modified accordingly. Individuals with religious beliefs are likely to find our program as compatible with their beliefs as other scientifically derived knowledge and applications.

4. The length of time an individual will derive help from our services is variable. For many sincere participants there will come a time when attending our groups, or participating in our other services, is more in conflict with the pursuit of their life goals than enhancing them. Although these participants will always be welcome back if they want to come, this conflict signals that the time for graduation has arrived.

One of the most enduring satisfactions in life is helping others. The individuals who have nurtured SMART Recovery® thus far have reported intense satisfaction at witnessing the positive changes our participants have experienced, and at witnessing the influence we are having on professional addictive behavior treatment. We offer to others, whether graduates of our efforts or not, the opportunity to join us in experiencing that satisfaction.

http://www.smartrecovery.org/intro/index.htm

APPENDIX 10.6. Moderation Management

Nine Steps Toward Moderation and Positive Lifestyle Changes

1. Attend meetings or on-line groups and learn about the program of Moderation Management.
2. Abstain from alcoholic beverages for 30 days and complete steps three through six during this time.
3. Examine how drinking has affected your life.
4. Write down your life priorities.
5. Take a look at how much, how often, and under what circumstances you had been drinking.
6. Learn the MM guidelines and limits for moderate drinking.
7. Set moderate drinking limits and start weekly "small steps" toward balance and moderation in other areas of your life.
8. Review your progress and update your goals.
9. Continue to make positive lifestyle changes and attend meetings whenever you need ongoing support or would like to help newcomers.

Source: http://www.moderation.org/readings.shtml#9steps; Moderation Management Network, Inc. 22 West 27th Street, 5th Floor, New York, NY 10001.

APPENDIX 10.7. The Twelve Steps of Nicotine Anonymous

1. We admitted we were powerless over nicotine—that our lives had become unmanageable.
2. Came to believe that a Power greater than ourselves could restore us to sanity.
3. Made a decision to turn our will and our lives over to the care of God as we understood Him.
4. Made a searching and fearless moral inventory of ourselves.
5. Admitted to God, to ourselves, and to another human being the exact nature of our wrongs.
6. Were entirely ready to have God remove all these defects of character.
7. Humbly asked Him to remove our shortcomings.
8. Made a list of all persons we had harmed, and became willing to make amends to them all.
9. Made direct amends to such people wherever possible, except when to do so would injure them or others.
10. Continued to take personal inventory and when we were wrong promptly admitted it.
11. Sought through prayer and meditation to improve our conscious contact with God as we understood Him, praying only for knowledge of His will for us and the power to carry that out.
12. Having had a spiritual awakening as the result of these steps, we tried to carry this message to nicotine users and to practice these principles in all our affairs.

References

Abbott, A. A. (1994). A feminist approach to substance abuse treatment and service delivery. In M. M. Olson (Ed.), *Women's health and social work: Feminist perspectives* (pp. 67–83). New York: Haworth Press.

Agency for Healthcare Research and Quality Technical Reviews and Summaries. (2008, May 18). *Treating tobacco use and dependence: 2008 Update. Executive Summary, Health Services/Technology Assessment Text (HSTAT)*. Retrieved January 18, 2009, from http://www.ncbi.nlm.nih.gov/books/bv.fcgi?rid=hstat2.section.28189

Al-Anon Family Group Headquarters. (2007). *Who are the members of Al-Anon and Alateen?* Virginia Beach, VA: Author.

Alcoholics Anonymous World Services. (1997). *Alcoholics Anonymous 1996 membership survey.* New York: Author.

Alcoholics Anonymous World Services. (2001). *AA for the black and African American alcoholic* [Brochure]. New York: Author.

Alcoholics Anonymous World Services. (2008). *Alcoholics Anonymous 2007 membership survey.* New York: Author. Retrieved January 1, 2009, from http://www.aa.org/lang/en/catalog.cfm?origpage=75&product=65

American Psychiatric Association. (1980). *Diagnostic and statistical manual of mental disorders* (3rd ed.). Washington, DC: Author.

American Society for Addiction Medicine. (2005). *Public policy statement on the relationship between treatment and self help: A joint statement of the American Society of Addiction Medicine, the American Academy of Addiction Psychiatry, and the American Psychiatric Association.* Retrieved January 1, 2009, from http://www.asam.org/1TREATMENT%20AND%20SELF-HELP%20-%20JOINT%2012-971.pdf

Anderson, R. E., Carter, I. E., & Lowe, G. R. (1999). *Human behavior in the social environment: A social systems approach* (5th ed.). New York: Aldine de Gruyter.

Association for the Advancement of Social Work with Groups (AASWG). (2006). *Standards for social work practice with groups.* Alexandria, VA: Author. Retrieved January 1, 2009, from http://www.aaswg.org/

Beckman, L. J. (1993). Alcoholics Anonymous and gender issues. In B. S. McCrady & W. R. Miller (Eds.), *Research on alcoholics anonymous: Opportunities and alternatives* (pp. 233–248). New Brunswick, NJ: Rutgers Center of Alcohol Studies.

Bepko, C., & Krestan, J. (1985). *The responsibility trap: A blueprint for treating the alcoholic family.* New York: Free Press.

Blume, S. B. (1998). Alcoholism in women. *Harvard Mental Health Letter, 14*(9), 5–7.

Brown, A. E., Whitney, S. N., Schneider, M. A., & Vega, C. P. (2006). Alcohol recovery and spirituality: Strangers, friends, or partners. *Southern Medical Journal, 99,* 654–657.

Buddie, A. M. (2004). Alternatives to Twelve-Step programs. *Journal of Forensic Psychology Practice, 4*(3), 61–70.

Buelow, G. D., & Buelow, S. A. (1998). *Psychotherapy in chemical dependence treatment: A practical and integrative approach.* Pacific Grove, CA: Brooks/Cole.

Burman, S., & Allen-Meares, P. (1991). Criteria for selecting practice theories: Working with alcoholic women. *Families in Society, 72,* 387–393.

Center for Substance Abuse Treatment. (1994). *Practical approaches in the treatment of women who abuse alcohol and other drugs.* Rockville, MD: U.S. Department of Health and Human Services, Public Health Service.

Center for Substance Abuse Treatment. (1998). *Substance abuse among older adults* (Treatment Improvement Protocol [TIP] Series 26, DHHS Publication No. (SMA) 98–3179). Rockville, MD: Substance Abuse and Mental Health Services Administration.

Center for Substance Abuse Treatment. (2001). Introduction to *substance abuse treatment for lesbian, gay, bisexual, and transgender individuals* (DHHS Publication No. (SMA) 01–3498). Rockville, MD: Substance Abuse and Mental Health Services Administration

Center for Substance Abuse Treatment. (2005). *Substance abuse treatment: Group therapy* (Treatment Improvement Protocol [TIP] Series 41, DHHS Publication No. [SMA] 05–3991). Rockville, MD: Substance Abuse and Mental Health Services Administration.

Center for Substance Abuse Treatment. (2006). *Substance abuse: Clinical issues in intensive outpatient treatment* (Treatment Improvement Protocol [TIP] Series 47, DHHS Publication No. [SMA] 06–4182). Rockville, MD: Substance Abuse and Mental Health Services Administration.

Christakis, N. A., & Fowler, J. H. (2008). The collective dynamics of smoking in a large social network. *New England Journal of Medicine, 358,* 2249–2258.

Collins, B. G. (1993). Reconstruing codependency using self-in-relation theory: A feminist perspective. *Social Work, 38,* 470–476.

Corrigan, E. M. (1983). Alcoholic women in treatment: A summary of findings. In D. Cook, C. Fewell, & J. Riolo (Eds.), *Social work treatment of alcohol problems* (pp. 109–118). New Brunswick, NJ: Rutgers Center of Alcohol Studies.

Crnkovic, A. E., & DelCampos, R. L. (1998). A systems approach to the treatment of chemical addiction. *Contemporary Family Therapy, 20*(1), 25–36.

DeCarlo, A., & Hockman, E. (2003). RAP therapy: A group work intervention method for urban adolescents. *Social Work with Groups, 26*(3), 45–59.

Delgado, M. (2007). *Social work practice with Latinos: A cultural assets paradigm.* New York: Oxford University Press.

Delgado, M., & de Saxe Zerden, L. (2007). Latino cultural assets and substance abuse services: Opportunity knocks. *Journal of Ethnic & Cultural Diversity in Social Work, 16*(3–4), 135–142.

Duffy, K. (2007). Knitting through recovery one stitch at a time: Knitting as an experiential teaching method for affect management in group therapy. *Journal of Groups in Addiction & Recovery, 2*(1), 67–83.

Emrick, C. D. (1994). Alcoholics anonymous and other 12-step groups. In M. Galanter & H. D. Kleber (Eds.), *The American Psychiatric Press textbook of substance abuse treatment* (pp. 351–358). Washington, DC: American Psychiatric Press.

Emrick, C. D., Tonigan, J. S., Montgomery, H., & Little, L. (1993). Alcoholics Anonymous: What is currently known? In B. S. McCrady & W. R. Miller (Eds.), *Research on Alcoholics Anonymous: Opportunities and alternatives* (pp. 41–76). New Brunswick, NJ: Rutgers Center of Alcohol Studies.

Félix-Ortiz, M., Salazar, M. R., González, J. R., Sorensen, J. L., & Plock, D. (2000). A qualitative evaluation of an assisted self-help group for drug-addicted clients in a structured outpatient treatment setting. *Community Mental Health Journal, 36,* 339–350.

Flores, P. J. (1988). *Group psychotherapy with addicted populations.* New York: Haworth Press.

Galanter, M., Egelko, S., & Edwards, H. (1993). Rational Recovery: Alternative to AA for addiction? *American Journal of Drug and Alcohol Abuse, 19,* 499–510.

Galinsky, M. J., & Schopler, J. H. (1994). Negative experiences in support groups. *Social Work in Health Care, 20*(1), 77–95.

Glaser, F. B. (1993). Matchless? Alcoholics Anonymous and the matching hypothesis. In B. S. McCrady & W. R. Miller (Eds.), *Research on Alcoholics Anonymous: Opportunities and alternatives* (pp. 379–396). New Brunswick, NJ: Rutgers Center of Alcohol Studies.

Glicken, D. (2005). *Improving the effectiveness of the helping professions: An evidence-based approach to practice.* Thousand Oaks, CA: Sage Publications.

Golden, S. J., Khantzian, E. J., & McAuliffe, W. E. (1994). Group therapy. In M. Galanter & H. D. Kleber (Eds.), *The American Psychiatric Press textbook of substance abuse treatment* (pp. 303–314). Washington, DC: American Psychiatric Press.

Greenfield, S. F. (2002). Perspectives—Women and alcohol use disorders. *Harvard Review of Psychiatry, 10*(2), 76–85.

Gutierrez, L. M. (1990). Working with women of color: An empowerment perspective. *Social Work, 35,* 149–153.

Gutierrez, L. M., & Ortega, R. (1991). Developing methods to empower Latinos: The importance of groups. *Social Work with Groups, 14*(2), 23–43.

Gutiérrez, L., Yeakley, A., & Ortega, R. (2000). Educating students for social work with Latinos: Issues for the new millennium. *Journal of Social Work Education, 36,* 541–557.

Hester, R. K. (1994). Outcome research: Alcoholism. In M. Galanter & H. D. Kleber (Eds.), *The American Psychiatric Press textbook of substance abuse treatment* (pp. 35–43). Washington, DC: American Psychiatric Press.

Hoffman, A., & Slade, J. (1993). Following the pioneers: Addressing tobacco in chemical dependency treatment. *Journal of Substance Abuse Treatment, 10,* 153–160.

Humphreys, K. (1997). Clinicians' referral and matching of substance abuse patients to self-help groups after treatment. *Psychiatric Services, 48,* 1445–1449.

Humphreys, K. (2003). A research-based analysis of the Moderation Management controversy. *Psychiatric Services, 54,* 621–622.

Humphreys, K., & Moos, R. H. (1996). Reduced substance-abuse-related healthcare costs among voluntary participants in alcoholics anonymous. *Psychiatric Services, 47,* 709–713.

Kelly, J. F., & Myers, M. G. (2007). Adolescents' participation in Alcoholics Anonymous and Narcotics Anonymous: Review, implications and future directions. *Journal of Psychoactive Drugs, 39*(3), 259–269.

Kirst-Ashman, K. K., & Hull, G. H. (2009). *Understanding generalist practice* (5th ed.). Belmont, CA: Thomson.

Kishline, A. (1994). *Moderate drinking: The moderation management guide for people who want to reduce their drinking.* New York: Crown Trade.

Kosberg, J. I. (2002). Heterosexual males: A group forgotten by the profession of social work. *Journal of Sociology & Social Welfare, 29*(3), 51–70.

Kosok, A. (2006). The *Moderation Management* programme in 2004: What type of drinker seeks controlled drinking? *International Journal of Drug Policy, 17,* 295–303.

Krentzman, A. R. (2007). The evidence base for the effectiveness of Alcoholics Anonymous: Implications for social work practice. *Journal of Social Work Practice in the Addictions, 7*(4), 27–48.

Liechtenstein, E. (1999). Nicotine Anonymous: Community resource and research implications. *Psychology of Addictive Behaviors, 13*(1), 60–68.

Little, J. (2006). Harm reduction therapy groups: Engaging drinkers and drug users in a process of change. *Journal of Groups in Addiction & Recovery, 1*(1), 69–93.

Lyter, L. L. (1993). *Alcohol abstinent adolescents: How some kids "just say no!"* Unpublished doctoral dissertation, Rutgers, the State University of New Jersey, New Brunswick.

Lyter, L. L., & Lyter, S. C. (2003). Why some youth don't use alcohol: Protective factors and implications for parenting skills. *Journal of Social Work Practice in the Addictions, 3*(2), 3–23.

Makela, K. (1996). *Alcoholics Anonymous as a mutual-help movement: A study in eight societies.* Madison: University of Wisconsin Press.

McCrady, B. S., & Raytek, H. (1993). Women and substance abuse: Treatment modalities and outcomes. In E. S. Lisansky Gomberg, & T. D. Nirenberg (Eds.), *Women and substance abuse* (pp. 314–338). Norwood, NJ: Ablex.

McKay, M. M., Gonzales, J. J., Stone, S., Ryland, D, & Kohner, K. (1995). Multi family therapy groups: A responsive intervention model for inner-city families. *Social Work with Groups, 18*(4), 41–56.

Memmott, J. L. (2003). Social work practice with the elderly substance abuser. *Journal of Social Work Practice in the Addictions, 3*(2), 85–103.

Mermelstein, R., Cohen, S., Lichtenstein, E., Baer, J. S., & Kamarck, T. (1986). Social support and smoking cessation and maintenance. *Journal of Consulting and Clinical Psychology, 54,* 447–453.

Miller, W. R., & Rollnick, S. (2002). *Motivational interviewing: Preparing people to change* (2nd ed.). New York: Guilford Press.

Moderation Management. (2008). *What is Moderation Management?* Retrieved January 1, 2009, from http://www.moderation.org/whatisMM.shtml

Moos, R. H., & Moos, B. S. (2005). Paths of entry into Alcoholics Anonymous: Consequences for participation and remission. *Alcoholism: Clinical and Experimental Research, 29,* 1858–1868.

National Association of Social Workers. (2001). *Standards for cultural competence in social work practice.* Washington, DC: Author.

National Association of Social Workers. (2005). *Standards for social work practice with clients with substance use disorders.* Washington, DC: Author.

National Association of Social Workers. (2008). *Code of ethics of the National Association of Social Workers.* Washington, DC: Author.

National Institute on Drug Abuse (NIDA). (2006). *NIDA info facts: Cigarettes and other tobacco products.* Washington, D.C.: National Institutes of Health, U.S. Department of Health and Human Services. Retrieved January 1, 2009, from http://www.drugabuse.gov/Infofacts/Tobacco.html

Nicotine Anonymous World Services. (2008). *Nicotine Anonymous: The book.* San Francisco: Author.

O'Donnell, S. M. (1994). The care of dependent African-American children in Chicago: The struggle between black self-help and professionalism. *Journal of Social History, 27,* 763–776.

Office of Applied Studies. (2001). *Summary of findings from the 2000 National Household Survey on Drug Abuse* (NHSDA Series H–13, DHHS Publication No. [SMA] 01-3549). Retrieved August 22, 2008, from http://oas.samhsa.gov/NHSDA/2kNHSDA/2kNHSDA.htm

O'Neill, J. V. (1999, July). Substance abuse: The common thread. *NASW News,* p. 3.

Orford, J., Templeton, L., Velleman, R., & Copello, A. (2005). Family members of relatives with alcohol, drug and gambling problems: A set of standardized questionnaires for assessing stress, coping and strain. *Addiction, 100,* 1611–1624.

Ouimette, P. C., Moos, R. H., & Finney, J. W. (1998, September). Influence of outpatient treatment and 12-step group involvement on one-year substance abuse treatment outcomes. *Journal of Studies on Alcohol, 59,* 513–522.

Pandina, R. J. (Ed.). (1978). *Coping with adolescent substance use.* Rockville, MD: NIDA.

Peele, S. (2007). *Addiction-proof your child: A realistic approach to preventing drug, alcohol, and other dependencies.* New York: Three Rivers Press.

Powell, T. J. (1990). *Working with self-help.* Silver Spring, MD: NASW Press.

Prochaska, J. O. (1991). Assessing how people change. *Cancer, 67,* 805–807.

Prochaska, J. O. (1997, October 31). *Processes of change in addictive behaviors.* Colloquium presented as part of the Cooper Colloquium Series, Center of Alcohol Studies, Rutgers, the State University of New Jersey, Piscataway, NJ.

Prochaska, J. O., Norcross, J. C., & DiClemente, C. C. (1994). *Changing for good.* New York: William Morrow.

Sanders, J. M. (2006). Women and the twelve steps of Alcoholics Anonymous: A gendered narrative. *Alcoholism Treatment Quarterly, 24*(3), 3–29.

Schmidt, E. A., Carns, A., & Chandler, C. (2001). Assessing the efficacy of rational recovery in the treatment of alcohol/drug dependency. *Alcoholism Treatment Quarterly, 19*(1), 97–106.

Schuckit, M. A. (1999). Goals of treatment. In M. Galanter & H. D. Kleber (Eds.), *The American Psychiatric Press textbook of substance abuse treatment* (2nd ed., pp. 89–96). Washington, DC: American Psychiatric Press.

Sharma, M., & Atri, A. (2006). Editorial. Substance abuse in African Americans: In search of a culturally competent research agenda. *Journal of Alcohol and Drug Education, 50*(3), 3–7.

Shute, N. (1997, September 8). What AA won't tell you. *US News & World Report,* pp. 55–65.

SMART Recovery. (2008). [Web site] Retrieved January 17, 2009, from http://www.smartrecovery.org

Sorocco, K. H., & Ferrell, S. W. (2006). Alcohol use among older adults. *Journal of General Psychology, 133,* 453–467.

Stocker, S. (1998). Men and women in drug abuse treatment relapse at different rates and for different reasons. *NIDA Notes, 13*(4). Retrieved August 11, 2008, from http://www.drugabuse.gov/NIDA_Notes/NNVol13N4/Relapse.html

Stofle, G. S., & Harrington, S. (2002). Treating addictions on the Internet: Can it be done? *Journal of Social Work Practice in the Addictions, 2*(2), 85–92.

Substance Abuse and Mental Health Services Administration, Office of Applied Studies. (2006). *Treatment Episode Data Set (TEDS). Highlights—2006. National admissions to substance abuse treatment services* (DASIS Series: S-40, DHHS Publication No. [SMA] 08–4313). Rockville, MD: Author.

Substance Abuse and Mental Health Services Administration, Office of Applied Studies. (2007a, November 8). *The DASIS report: Older adults in substance abuse treatment: 2005.* Rockville, MD: Author.

Substance Abuse and Mental Health Services Administration, Office of Applied Studies. (2007b, August 2). *The NSDUH report: Gender differences in alcohol use and alcohol dependence or abuse: 2004 and 2005.* Rockville, MD: Author.

Substance Abuse and Mental Health Services Administration, Office of Applied Studies. (2007c). *Results from the 2006 National Survey on Drug Use and Health: National findings.* (NSDUH Series H-32, DHHS Publication No. SMA 07–4293). Rockville, MD: Author.

Substance Abuse and Mental Health Services Administration, Office of Applied Studies. (2008, January 24). *The NSDUH report: Nicotine dependence: 2006.* Rockville, MD: Author.

Tighe, E., & Saxe, L. (2006). Community-based substance abuse reduction and the gap between treatment need and treatment utilization: Analysis of data from the "Fighting Back" general population survey. *Journal of Drug Issues, 36*(2), 295–312.

Trimpey, J. (2009a). *Frequently asked questions.* Retrieved October 2, 2009, from http://www.rational.org/index.php?id=33

Trimpey, J. (2009b). *Quick start on rational recovery.* Retrieved October 2, 2009, from http://rational.org/index.php?id=115

Trimpey, J. (2009c). *Rational recovery and professional issues.* Retrieved October 2, 2009, from http://www.rational.org/index.php?id=52

Trimpey, J., (2009d). *Zero tolerance in the family.* Retrieved October 2, 2009, from http://www.rational.org/index.php?id=66

U.S. Census Bureau. (2001). *Overview of race and Hispanic origin.* Retrieved August 22, 2008, from http://www.census.gov/prod/2001pubs/c2kbr01–1.pdf

U.S. Department of Health and Human Services. (2004). *The health consequences of smoking: A report of the surgeon general.* Atlanta: U.S. Department of Health and Human Services, Centers for Disease Control and Prevention, National Center for Chronic Disease Prevention and Health Promotion, Office on Smoking and Health

Vaillant, G. E. (1995). *The natural history of alcoholism revisited.* Cambridge, MA: Harvard University Press.

Vannicelli, M. (1995). Group psychotherapy with substance abusers and family members. In A. M. Washton (Ed.), *Psychotherapy and substance abuse: A practitioner's handbook* (pp. 337–356). New York: Guilford Press.

Velasquez, M. M., Stephens, N. S., & Ingersoll, K. (2006). Motivational interviewing in groups. *Journal of Groups in Addiction & Recovery, 1*(1), 27–50.

Velicer, W. F., Prochaska, J. O., & Redding, C. A. (2006). Tailored communications for smoking cessation: Past successes and future directions. *Drug and Alcohol Review, 25,* 49–57.

Wallace, J. (2006). Theory of 12-step oriented treatment. In F. Rotgers, J. Morgenstern, & S. T. Walters (Eds.), *Treating substance abuse: Theory and technique* (pp. 9–30). New York: Guilford Press.

Washington, O. G. M., & Moxley, D. P. (2003). Group interventions with low-income African American women recovering from chemical dependency. *Health & Social Work, 28,* 146–156.

Wells, K., Klap, R., Koike, A., & Sherbourne, C. (2001). Ethnic disparities in unmet need for alcoholism, drug abuse, and mental health. *American Journal of Psychiatry, 158,* 2027–2032.

Witkiewitz, K. (2005). Defining relapse from a harm reduction perspective. *Journal of Evidence-Based Social Work, 2*(1–2), 191–206.

Wuthnow, R. (1996). *Sharing the journey.* New York: Free Press.

Zarski, J. J., Aponte, H. J., Bixenstine, C., & Cibik, P. (1992). Beyond home-based family intervention: A multi-family approach toward change. *Contemporary Family Therapy, 14*(1), 3–14.

Family Intervention Strategies

11

Steven M. Granich and Michael D. Paulus

Overview

The years of the new millennium have yielded an evolving body of knowledge and evidence-based practices addressing the treatment of families impacted by alcohol, tobacco, and other drugs (ATOD). This chapter emphasizes a family focus, grounded in a socially and culturally bound context, to understand ATOD misuse and its effects on families. Intervention strategies to address ATOD misuse are drawn from a range of theoretical orientations to help clinicians assess and address what goes on within the family and how recovery from ATOD misuse can be guided. This chapter also explores a number of general considerations associated with interventions with ATOD-misusing families, including notions about progression of addiction in the family; the necessity to assess, individualize, and address the complex interactions among family members; and the reduction of the risk of negative outcomes from an evidence-based framework.

In approaching interventions for ATOD misusers, it is essential to address their problems within the context of their larger social environment, specifically, the family. Family-focused clinicians seek to understand the ATOD misuser from an ecological perspective. This means understanding the subtle complexities, identifying the reciprocal relationships, and pinpointing the influences between the ATOD misuser and others within his or her environment. This ecological approach assists the family clinician in establishing the influences and interactions that may contribute to ATOD misuse patterns. This understanding of influences and interactions ultimately guides family interventions in a direction that addresses the relationships between the substance abuser and his or her environment. For example,

Alcoholics Anonymous, Al-Anon, and Alateen all incorporate some aspects of the ecological perspective. The focus of these support groups is on the reciprocal influence of people, places, and things on ATOD misuse, and the use of detachment to effectively change the interaction pattern between significant others, children, and the ATOD misuser. These approaches of support groups clearly emanate from viewing the problem in the context of the person within his or her larger social environment.

This chapter examines a number of intervention strategies that can be used by clinicians who work with substance abusers and their families. It begins by setting the context within which family work takes place. Specifics of family focus and the social and cultural contexts associated with interventions with families are established. The chapter then moves to a discussion of a number of preparatory treatment tasks. These tasks serve to clarify, for the clinician, the purpose of the intervention process with substance abusers and their families. This preparation is a crucial first step toward setting the therapeutic climate for an intervention to be successful. With the context for family work and the preparatory treatment tasks set, the chapter illustrates a number of interventions with families challenged by a member involved in substance abuse. This is done in a format that explores a specific area of family focus in terms of the impact of ATOD effects that may be experienced by families and introduces an intervention strategy to effect change.

The "Solution-Focused Genogram" provides a guide to exploration of family interaction styles and their implications for intervention. "Strengths-Oriented Family Therapy (SOFT) updates the use of the traditional strengths perspective by integrating family strengths with solution-focused interventions. "Ethnic-focused intervention" is presented to enhance a clearer understanding of the cultural implications of ATOD treatment within the family context. "Behavioral Marital Therapy (BMT)" looks at the specific negotiation skills used in establishing behavioral change agreements within families. A variation of BMT, "Behavioral Couples Therapy (BCT)," also is described. The use of the "Communication-Focused Genogram" is mentioned as a vehicle for improving communication among family members. An integrated examination of "family interactive patterns" is introduced to clinicians in an evidence-based approach guided by "Multisystemic Therapy (MST), Brief Strategic Family Therapy (BSFT)," and "Multidimensional Family Therapy (MDFT)." "Couples Relapse Prevention (RP)" illustrates a set of maintenance interventions as a follow-up to various family interventions. Finally, "Pressures to Change" and the "Community Reinforcement Approach" are reviewed as means of influencing incompatible activities and environmental contingencies when moving toward family recovery.

Evidence-based practice is very important within the context of working with families with ATOD problems. Support for evidence-based practice is very strong within the field of ATOD and families. Evidence-based practice relies on the best evidence available (Apsche, Bass, & Houston, 2007; Rishel, 2007). Patterson, Miller, Carnes, and Wilson (2004) stated, "More recently, significant clinical research has emerged to guide MFTs (Marriage and Family Therapists) in their clinical decisions" (p. 183). In fact, drug courts, which are at the forefront of evidence-based treatment involving family intervention, require that treatments be evidence based and have effective outcomes. All the interventions presented here reflect evidence-based and best practices.

Family treatment of substance abuse allows for certain advantages that may not be found in other types of interventions, primarily group and individual therapy. Family treatment allows for the whole family to receive the benefits of intervention (Kaufman & Yoshioka, 2005). Family therapy helps the whole family understand addiction and work on it from a systems perspective. The family organizes around the symptoms, and the role of the family therapist is to intervene in this system through various approaches that are based on evidence-based outcomes. Rubin (2008) makes it clear that evidence-based practice is the basis for effective practice. He states, "Evidence-based practice is a way to designate certain interventions as empirically supported under certain conditions" (p. 6). Evidence-based practice is effectively using findings from the field of family therapy research to guide family intervention with substance abusers.

Family Focus

As described in Goldenberg and Goldenberg (2008):

> A family is far more than a collection of individuals sharing a specific physical and psychological space. While families occur in a diversity of forms and complexities in today's rapidly changing society, and represent a multiplicity of cultural heritages, each may be considered a natural, sustained social system with properties all its own—one that has an evolved set of rules, is replete with assigned and ascribed roles for its members, has an organized power structure, has developed intricate overt and covert forms of communication, and has elaborated ways of negotiating and problem solving that permit various tasks to be performed effectively. The relationship between the members of this microculture is deep and multilayered and is based largely on a shared history, shared internalized perceptions

and assumptions about the world, and a shared sense of purpose. Within such a system individuals are tied to one another by powerful, durable, reciprocal, multigenerational emotional attachments and loyalties that may fluctuate in intensity over time but nevertheless persist over the lifetime of the family. (p. 1)

This description of family has been further complicated by the fundamental structural changes that families have undergone over the past generation. Contemporary families are characterized by diverse family forms and styles in ethnic groupings. Families are in various forms such as stepfamily, gay or lesbian family, divorced family, and single-parent family. This chapter addresses the subtle and complex ways that ATOD-related problems permeate the many facets of "family" as outlined earlier and incorporates intervention strategies that specifically work toward restoring the positive components of this "natural social system."

Clinical practice experience makes it evident that there are a number of characteristics that delineate substance-abusing families from other seriously dysfunctional families. Substance-abusing families have problems with communication, boundaries, power structure, organization, and parenting skills. Typically they are not adept at working with other systems in the community. Merikangas (1990), in a review of family studies, reported that the average risk for developing ATOD-related problems is seven times greater among first-degree relatives of ATOD misusers than the controls in the studies.

Clearly, ATOD misuse has many debilitating influences on the fundamental facets of family. These serve to create its own properties within family functioning, establishing altered interactional patterns, and contributing to inconsistent, unstable negotiating and problem-solving capacities. Interventions with families with ATOD problems require strategies that accommodate an understanding of the various impacts on these facets of family to guide the treatment processes.

Social Context

Social processes of ATOD misuse are broad and ubiquitous. These social processes include the ATOD abuser's effects on interactions with others in his or her larger social environment. Kelly, Day, and Striessguth (2000) detailed how exposure to alcohol in early development contributes to noticeable changes in social behavior. Perkins (2002) reported that by the time a student goes to college, the ability of parents to influence their child's drinking style diminishes substantially. Miller-Day (2002) found that teenagers prefer talking to "Mother" about risky topics like alcohol and tobacco use. However, in the sample involved in this study, fewer than half of the participants engaged with their parents in communication about ATOD misuse. This finding suggests that social interaction between parents and children may be affected by the parents' or the child's ATOD misuse interests. Although not a finding in the study, it could be hypothesized that decreased ATOD misuse might improve parent–child communication, or ongoing parent–child communication might contribute to decreased ATOD misuse. Productive work, when intervening with families with ATOD problems, will invariably begin with the establishment of a basic understanding of the meaning of these social influences on the family and their potential influence on and role in the intervention process.

Cultural Context

Families confronted with substance abuse problems come from diverse ethnic and cultural roots. As a result, ethnicity and culture become factors in differentiating intervention strategies with families with ATOD misuse problems. Kaufman and Yoshioka (2005) insisted that therapists recognize and appreciate the structures of families from different cultures. They believe that "a sensitive therapist pays attention, senses cultural nuances, and learns from clients" (p. 15).

Families from ethnic groups often hold differing views of rules, roles, structure, negotiating, and problem solving in their families. This, coupled with a shared sense of history that includes facing prejudice, discrimination, and limited access to privilege and resources, results in distinctions between family processes, especially those processes that speak to intervening with family ATOD misuse problems. An added complexity in dealing with the family's cultural context is the assumption that a given group's experiences with ATOD misuse problems are culturally homogeneous. Heath (1991) reported that developments in the field of ethnic and racial relations demand that intra-ethnic variations be taken into consideration when examining ATOD-related problems. Heath (1991) continued, stating such considerations should include

1. assessment of ethnic identification,
2. culture retention,
3. incorporation of mainstream culture, and
4. whether individuals are foreign born or native born. (p. 610)

Rothman (2008) sees culturally competent practice as engagement, trust, relationship building, assessment, need definition, contracting, intervention, evaluation, and termination. He stated, "effective practice involves the utilization of both practice and diversity frameworks, knowledge about the client's population, effective and accurate communication, the application of social work skills consonant with these, and the appropriate use of community resources and advocacy" (p. 48). These findings point to the necessity that interventions with families with ATOD misuse problems have cultural specificity and sensitivity incorporated into them.

Interventions with Families with ATOD Problems

Preparatory Discussion

In this section of the chapter, a number of interventions with families, who experience ATOD misuse, are presented within the context of the facets of family focus (Goldenberg & Goldenberg, 2008) described at the beginning of this chapter. A discussion of effects of ATOD misuse on specific aspects of family functioning will be followed by a corresponding intervention strategy that addresses the listed aspects of family functioning being affected. This integrative approach to interventions with families with ATOD misuse problems is guided by a conclusion of a survey of theoretical bases of family approaches by McCrady and Esptein who summarize that:

> Family models have evolved over the past 60 years into contemporary models that emphasize the multiple determinants of psychoactive substance abuse disorders, the multiple factors that maintain these disorders, and the complex interrelationships between the substance user and the familial and other interpersonal environments in which he/she exists. A rich body of empirical literature provides strong support for family-based models and for the effectiveness of treatments based on these models. Research knowledge is limited by its lack of attention to gender, cultural, racial, and sexual orientation issues among subjects, the lack of couples treatment research on drug users, and the lack of family treatment research on substance abusers. (1996, pp. 136–137)

The following section integrates and synthesizes a number of ATOD family intervention strategies in light of the scope of established limitations posed by the body of existing knowledge.

Successful Treatment Tasks with Families and Adolescents

Initiating family interventions directed at ATOD misuse by a family member requires a clear purpose for the intervention on the part of the family therapist. Such interventions can be successful with families and adolescents. Donohue and Azrin

(2001) and McCrady and Epstein (1996) described the treatment tasks essential for working with families and adolescents where there are ATOD issues. In working with ATOD families and adolescents, efforts are made to modify the boundaries, structures, hierarchies, and connections to other systems. To assist with this clarity of purpose process, McCrady and Epstein established a number of tasks required for family treatment to be successful. These tasks are similar to other family therapy approaches (Kaufman & Yoshioka, 2005). They include the following:

(1) *Engagement into therapy* requires identifying the family member(s) and the ATOD misuser who will be involved in the intervention. Of course, involvement is subject to willingness, availability, and perceived leverage. Engagement of only one family member still allows the therapist the opportunity to incorporate family-based approaches into the therapy process.

(2) *Assessment* is hinged on the ability to identify a number of important family intervention assessment foci: a) factors leading to use; b) the complex structure of interrelationships in the family which maintain use; and c) consequences of use. Also, assessment should examine patterns of interaction across all of the facets of family functioning.

(3) *Introduction of change procedure to affect ATOD use* includes knowledge of a selection of interventions that focus on initiating and maintaining abstinence. Particular attention needs to be made to move a family from pre-contemplation to the contemplation of change stage (Prochaska, Norcross, & DiClemente, 1994). McCrady and Epstein (1996) suggested that pharmacologic methods may be considered to facilitate achievement of this goal.

(4) *Modification, reinforcement, and maintenance of abstinence* focus on the change processes required of individual family members involved in the intervention and the therapist's flexibility to adapt and adjust to what works in impacting interactions of family members. This task emphasizes those family tasks which facilitate and support change.

(5) *Modification of family interaction* requires addressing patterns of family interaction that interfere with "effective family functioning" (McCrady & Epstein, p. 113).

McCrady and Epstein (1996) noted that although the tasks mentioned in the preceding paragraph are described in a sequential manner, consideration of threats to safety of family members would lead a therapist to be flexible in carrying out these tasks. By establishing a clear vision of the climate needed for this process to occur, this framework does provide essential guidance to those engaging in intervention with families troubled by ATOD misuse.

Intervention with families covers a wide gamut, from children and adolescents to young adults to older adults. The following examples illustrate modifications that address the range and unique intervention needs.

Donohue and Azrin (2001) developed an eight-step process of preparing adolescent substance abusers and their families for successful intervention involvement. They provide the following useful protocol (family behavioral therapy) for use with adolescents:

1. Describe problems that others (usually parents, judges, and teachers) have recently caused him or her (the substance using adolescent).
2. Provide empathy for the above elicited concerns.
3. Review benefits that other youth have reported as a result of participating in the program (e.g. reduced time in jail/probation, better treatment from parents).
4. Elicit potential benefits from the youth's perspective.
5. Ask the youth to identify what s/he is looking for in a therapist; tell him/her that his/her assigned therapist will stress these attributes (the therapist is later instructed to emphasize those attributes during therapy).
6. Provide snacks and soda for the youth's pleasure (The snacks and sodas are offered as reinforcement for the youth to assist in establishing commitment to the treatment program).
7. Elicit potential problems that may cause the youth to miss scheduled appointments (e.g. parents and youth have an argument immediately prior to the appointment time).
8. Engage the youth in an exercise to identify solutions to problems that may come up. (p. 206)

This process is repeated with the parents or guardians as well. Follow-up visits typically include reflection on positive comments and developments from the prior session. This process can serve to set the stage for successful engagement and linkage with the treatment process.

More is now known about the parts of the process of family intervention that seem most valuable to the consumers of these services. McCollum and Trepper (1995) asked a small group of women in drug treatment facilities what they had found most helpful to them during their couples therapy at the treatment facility. The women reported:

1. a therapist with an attitude of caring and non-judgementalness who would guide the couple,
2. a therapist that facilitated exploration of new realizations that would lead the couple to new frameworks within which they could understand their own and their partner's actions, and
3. a therapist that would assist in the initiation of new actions that would take the couple beyond the actions that caused trouble for them in the past. (p. 73)

Any intervention with families, couples, or significant others must be grounded in the principles listed above.

Substance Abuse and Effects on Families

Gainey, Haggerty, Fleming, and Catalano (2007) confirmed that ATOD misuse affects fulfillment of basic human needs, striking at the core of family security. To pay for their drug of choice, ATOD-misusing parents may use money needed for family food, clothing, and health care. Substance abuse severely affects the marriage and children in the family. In the vast majority of cases, the substance-dependent family member develops a primary relationship with his or her drug of choice, not his or her significant other(s). Stromwall et al. (2008) found a high occurring rate of co-occurring disorders among parents in the child welfare system. They found evidence that child neglect or maltreatment cases frequently involve substance abuse.

When substance abuse impairs the major parental role functioning to the extent that an adequate environment cannot be provided for children in the family, alternate care is needed. This is most often provided through a temporary or permanent home placement in the foster care system, serving to further erode the continuity of the family unit. Even when mandatory reunification plans are intact, the family will need months and years to re-establish a sense of security within the family system.

Without question, substance abuse has major effects on the family. Extensive problems in marriages and families have been well documented in the literature. Arguments, child and spouse abuse, and escalating crises that distress the family functioning and structure are common.

The problems and conflicts that may be experienced within these families can, in turn, bring about, support, and maintain the substance abuse. The alcohol and other drug use can serve as a way to cope with dysfunctional family patterns and relationships (Saatcioglu, Erim, & Cakmak, 2006). Saatcioglu et al. said, "alcohol is the central focus in many families involving an alcoholic individual, and most important family relationships revolve around this focus, and the stability of the family depends upon phenomena associated with alcohol" (p. 126).

Interventions with Families with Substance Abuse

Family Focus, Effects, and Associated Interventions

In this section, a selection of related characteristics of "family focus" from the description by Goldenberg and Goldenberg (2008) presented at the beginning of the chapter will be examined by an intervention strategy that a family therapist may use to address substance abuse problems in the family. A number of case examples, which illustrate specific strategies, will be included.

The following intervention strategies are presented: (1) Solution-Focused Genogram; (2) SOFT; (3) ethnic-focused intervention; (4) family interactive patterns from a Multidimensional approach, Multisystemic approach, and BSFT; (5) BMT; (6) RP; and (7) Community Reinforcement Approach.

Solution-Focused Genogram and SOFT

> A family is a natural social system, with properties all its own. The family is a collection of individuals sharing a specific physical and psychological space, with an evolved set of rules, replete with assigned and ascribed roles for its members. (Goldenberg & Goldenberg, 2008, p. 5)

ATOD Effects: With ATOD misuse in a family, it is not uncommon to see a number of individuals, within or associated with the family, experiencing ATOD-related events across generations. It can become apparent that some family members experience difficulties with ATOD misuse, whereas others have managed to avoid it. ATOD misuse can be seen to manifest itself in histories of violence, marital instability, impaired parent–child relationships, and cutoffs of family contact between members.

Intervention

Kuehl (1995) proposed the use of the Solution-Focused Genogram to intervene with ATOD misuse problems within families. A genogram is used to examine multigenerational influences on family systems. In this model Kuehl attempts to update the use of the genogram, integrating the wealth of information it represents with the intervention possibilities that flow from the basic tenets and techniques of solution-focused therapies (see Figure 11.1). The case of Tom and Alice (see Case

FIGURE 11.1: Solution-Focused Genogram

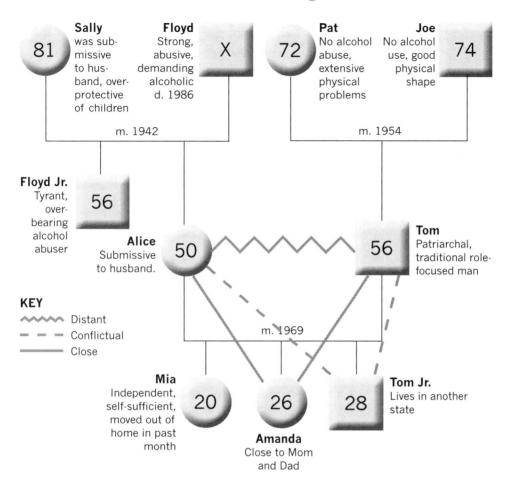

Example 11.1) illustrates the application of the Solution-Focused Genogram and related assessment and intervention strategies.

This intervention uses the information obtained from the genogram to pinpoint helpful responses that clients were not aware of previously and, from this, generates new responses that were previously not present. Genograms are very useful in understanding ATOD issues within the dynamics of the family. Conflict, cutoffs, loyalty issues, unbalanced systems, and other family dynamics can be discerned and then worked on in treatment. A genogram is a very effective diagnostic and assessment tool for ATOD families. The genogram can direct the practitioner to various levels of intervention within the family system such as working on boundaries, loyalties, cutoffs, emotional distance, and lack of differentiation. The

▼
▼
▼

CASE EXAMPLE 11.1. The Case of Tom and Alice

Tom and Alice have been married since 1969. Tom, a 56-year-old Polish American male, is a very traditional, patriarchal man who is focused on controlling Alice. Alice, 50 years old, is very submissive to her husband. Tom and Alice have been faithful to each other and have three children: Mia, age 20; Amanda, age 26; and Tom, Jr., age 28. Tom has a problem with drinking alcohol.

Tom and Alice participate in therapy sessions with a therapist familiar with multi-generational effects of addiction. The therapist discovers that Tom's mother and father, Pat and Joe did not abuse alcohol in their lives. However, Alice's family suffered from alcohol addiction. Her father, Floyd, was strong, abusive, and demanding and died from alcoholism in 1986. Her mother, Sally, was submissive to her husband, Floyd, and very overprotective of her children. Alice's brother, Floyd, Jr., was a tyrant, overbearing, and an alcohol abuser. After doing the genogram, the couple gained some insight into the multi-generational effects of alcohol abuse.

On the basis of the genogram, the therapist began to use presuppositional and scaling questions with the couple. In the session there was an opening of the vision of being a couple with Tom not drinking alcohol. The therapist asked Tom to look at the dynamics of his family. He had him question the cutoff from his oldest son. Also, the therapist asked for exceptions to family instances of addiction. It was asked who in the family had lived life without addiction.

In the next session the therapist used scaling questions to ascertain any improvement in the relationship with the couple. It was found that on a scale of one to 10 that the couple was operating at a five. Tom had not been drinking during the week. The therapist asked the miracle question of what life would be like if a miracle occurred and Tom was no longer drinking. There was an exploration of the spiritual background of the couple. The couple explored how multigenerational influences still continue to have power over them.

The counseling progressed for 10 more sessions over a course of six months using the genogram and reshaping the narrative of the family. Both Alice and Tom understood the multi-generational influences of their families and began to reshape their lives. Over time, Tom stopped drinking and was able to develop a more egalitarian relationship with his wife.

author proposes using the following intervention strategies in concert with geno-grams to initiate change.

Presuppositional and Scaling Questions. Originating from research done by O'Hanlon and Weiner-Davis (1989), presuppositional questions are designed to enhance client awareness of personal strengths and the inevitability of change in their lives. Such questions presuppose success; that is, "When things get better, . . . " and "What will be happening when you. . . . ?" Scaling questions are designed to break problems and solutions into smaller manageable parts, allowing for recognition of small changes in the intervention process. Such questions as "On a scale of 1 to 10 (where the scale parameters are defined), where do you rate?" or "How do you get from a 5 to a 7. . . . ?" begin to partialize client concerns.

Focus on Spiritual Influences in the Family System. (Frame, 2000) discussed the use of the spiritual genogram. This intonation of the solution-focused geno-gram "enables clients to make sense of their families' religious/spiritual heritage and to explore the ways in which their experiences impact present couple or family issues" (p. 211). This spiritual portion of the genogram is helpful in working with families with ATOD misuse by unraveling family concerns related to guilt, forgive-ness, and powerlessness, as well as family sources of hope, meaning, inner strength, and reconciling doubt, all issues that may be important in the recovery process.

Exceptions and Relative Family Influence. These questions, developed by White and Epston (1990), seek to find the family's ability not to let problems have absolute influence. In a genogram, identifying family members who have escaped substance abuse problems helps locate family exceptions in multigenerational influence. Such questions as "Who in your family has dealt successfully with alco-hol and other drug problems?" and "How do you think they did it?" help in the ini-tial conceptualization of solutions. Uncertainty as to the answers of these questions gives the client guidance on where to begin to look for solutions.

Between Session Investigations. Clients can be guided to talk with family members who have successfully addressed ATOD misuse problems and pro-cess these findings with the therapist. This process tends to increase awareness that positive multigenerational influences exist along with negative experiences. Kuehl (1995) related that this intervention strategy "may help clients decrease reactivity characteristic of emotional fusion, thus facilitating the process of dif-ferentiation" (p. 243).

"Back to Future Generation" Questions. Many clients from families with sub-stance abuse problems are often predominantly problem focused. This question-ing technique helps clients conceptualize changes they would like to see happen, and does so in a clear, concrete way, so as to guide the change effort from the

direction they are currently taking. Asking the client "What would you like to see different from the way things have gone in your family?" begins the process of initiating change.

Collapsing Intergenerational Time. These questioning strategies follow up on the "back to the future generations" question responses. Once clients have identified what they want to be different, they now are ready to identify what they are already doing to achieve these changes and how they will commit to sustaining these changes in the months to come. This strategy gives the therapist a focus on a time frame to work with, while the clients engage in the process of resolving the identified problems.

Externalizing the Problems across Generations. This strategy works to move the onus of the substance problem from inside the family, and reframing it as being outside the family. This has the effect of liberating the client to act independent of the problem (White & Epston, 1990). Kuehl (1995) suggested pointing to a specific problem depicted in the genogram and asking "How have you kept this problem from completely taking over you lives?" in an attempt to visually offset the problem.

Normalizing. This method from O'Hanlon and Weiner-Davis (1989) works as a method to depathologize family experiences by using the genogram to make sense out of the etiology of the ATOD problem and to help clients disengage from the uncertain understandings they have had about themselves and their families.

Ethical Consideration of Therapist and Family. Peluso (2006) detailed the use of the "Ethical Genogram" in how social workers operate in a critical evaluative way. However, these same principles may be of benefit in the assessment of family functioning. Exploration of the family priorities of beneficence, non-malfeasance, justice, autonomy, and fidelity in the genogram process not only establishes structural family connections, but also may delineate the ethical glue, or lack thereof, that may cement these connections.

Counter Documents. Kuehl succinctly addresses the benefits of this intervention strategy:

> By graphically representing the documented change, clients can not only take home an image of their progress at the end of therapy but can also help construct the image along the way, adding a sense of personal investment that can increase the document's meaningfulness. (1995, p. 244)

Combining the genogram with solution-focused and narrative interventions allows the therapist to focus the change effort from a framework that clearly operates from the client's frame of reference and understanding.

SOFT

A specific treatment program for adolescent substance abusers has been tested by researchers. It draws on a traditional social work focus, the strengths perspective, as a unique feature. D. C. Smith and Hall (2008) developed SOFT, a treatment approach that draws on three unique features:

- A pretreatment family motivational session called the Strengths Oriented Referral for Teens (SORT) which prepares a referral for treatment.
- A foundation in solution focused language and treatment techniques
- A formal strengths and resources assessment in the early stages of treatment. (p. 185)

The SOFT program follows a number of treatment stages. Beginning with an "initial strengths assessment," which looks at initiating treatment, areas of strength in the adolescent are identified. This gives the client and the family members a place to start that is positive and allows the treatment work to build from strength, rather than a deficit. This seems to provide the family something to add to in the treatment process.

The process of this treatment moves on to completing "immediate concerns checklists" that allows the family to prioritize concerns for what needs to be addressed first and what can be put aside for another time. "Solution Plans" are created to include the client and family members in the process of guiding the activities of treatment. Finally, earlier goals are revised and changed as understanding of the situation unfolds.

The treatment includes the use of a structured "multi-family group" configuration, which addresses specific topical foci in the group setting. Follow-up to the family responses to the group topics are reviewed and skill practice for families is facilitated.

The main underpinning of this approach comes from a strengths-based focus and integration of the many of the six core values of social work (especially social justice, worth and dignity of a person, and the importance of human relationships) (NASW, 2008).

Research findings have found that six months after engagement in this treatment program, participants had a significantly lower substance use frequency and substance related problems. The authors correctly conclude that "SOFT is a promising new family-based treatment for adolescents with substance abuse problems that is consistent with social work values" (D. C. Smith & Hall, 2008, p. 188).

The case of Sam (see Case Example 11.2) reflects the strengths-oriented approach in working with families with substance abuse issues. This theoretical approach takes into account the strengths of the client and family, rather than solely the problems, and works from that basis. The strengths-oriented approach has a solution-focused basis, seeing positives as the basis for movement in treatment.

Ethnic-Focused Intervention

Families from ethnic groups often hold differing views of rules, roles, structure, negotiating, and problem solving in their family. This coupled with a shared sense of history that includes facing prejudice, discrimination and limited access to privilege results in distinctions between family processes." (Goldenberg & Goldenberg, 2008, p. 5)

Stanton and Heath (1995) reported that patterns of ATOD misuse in ethnic families can be exacerbated by frequent acculturation problems and parent–child cultural disparity. McGoldrick, Giordano, and Garcia-Preto (2005) emphasized the importance of culture in the understanding family dynamics. To fully comprehend the effects of ATOD use, one must consider the wisdom of Heath (1991) who wisely pointed out that ethnicity does not have to do with forms but with relationships. He continued, saying,

> We must acknowledge the dynamism that is intrinsic to any population is at least as significant a factor beyond the group itself. The composition of the ethnic group is in constant flux as individuals are born, age, marry or divorce, change jobs, become ill or well, and die. This is the case even in those rare instances where social boundaries are relatively closed and few people pass from one such group to another. But social boundaries tend to be remarkably permeable, and the mobility of individuals between ethnic groups is a widespread phenomenon, recognized in everyone's experience and not just a vague theoretic possibility. (Heath, 1991, p. 624)

When closely examining the effects of ATOD misuse in ethnic families, the preceding perspective advanced by Heath must be taken into consideration when choosing an intervention.

Intervention

Cheung (1991) noted specific areas of attention that should be explored when implementing an intervention with an ethnic family with ATOD misuse problems.

CASE EXAMPLE 11.2. The Case of Sam

Sam is a 15-year-old Native American male whose father is in the military. He has a history of alcohol and cocaine use. His father, a single parent, is very demanding. The social worker has been trained in strengths-oriented treatment. The father is a drill sergeant and sees very few strengths in his son. The father feels that his son should obey and respect him as an Indian elder.

The social worker did a strengths assessment and identified numerous strengths such as the son playing basketball, passing all courses in school, wanting to stop drinking and using cocaine, and wanting to love his father. The father acknowledges that his son has some strengths.

An immediate concerns checklist was formulated with the son and father. Both father and son wanted Sam to stop using drugs, improve his grades, continue to play basketball, and improve father son communication and trust. Son and father came up with a solutions plan to address these issues.

As the sessions progressed, the father began to see the strengths that the son had. The father recognized that he needed to see his son as a growing young man with weaknesses and strengths. He began to have greater faith in his son's ability to seek responsible choices and, in turn, Sam's respect for his father began to increase. It is anticipated that the positive aspects of their relationship will continue to grow, accompanied by positive changes in both father and son.

Assessment of Ethnic Identification. The stronger a person's ethnic identity, the stronger his or her commitment will be to the ethnic group and the more ethnic cultural values and behaviors will be retained. From this cultural identification will come a clearer understanding of the meaning of the use of ATOD and the meaning of treatment for the problem(s).

Culture Retention. It is pointed out by Cheung (1991) that the retention of ethnic culture by an ethnic person is not a static quality. He stated that:

> the amount of ethnic culture retained varies with a number of factors. It is likely to be negatively associated with the length of time an immigrant has been in the host country, and positively associated with the number of opportunities to practice the culture. (p. 591)

Incorporation of Mainstream Culture. ATOD misuse, when cultural incorporation occurs, can begin to gradually resemble that of mainstream culture. For those who possess little ability to incorporate, the cultural shock of being caught between conflicting sets of cultural values may result in many adjustment problems to the mainstream society, many of which may center on ATOD misuse.

As previously noted, Cheung (1991) addressed the relevance of these considerations with the concept of cultural consensus. According to Cheung, degree of acculturation varies with degree of mainstream assimilation and amalgamation. Given the complications of ethnicity in interventions with ATOD misuse problems, therapists are challenged to make adaptation to ethnic realities in their practice with ethnic families. This requires attention to both individual and systemic concerns; resources and strategies must be revised on the basis of the contributions and character of the ethnic reality (Devore & Schlesinger, 1999).

Multicultural Competence. Beatty (2007) stated that there is little difference in overall drug use based on race–ethnicity. However, there are important ethnic differences such as various ethnic groups using more of one drug than another. Lassitier and Chung (2006) saw cultural competence as important in dealing with substance-dependent clients. This requirement of cultural competence among social workers is delineated in the NASW *Code of Ethics* (2008) and operationalized in the *Standards for Cultural Competence in Social Work Practice* (NASW, 2001).

Delgado and de Saxe Zerden (2007) saw understanding the Latino culture as an asset in working with Hispanics in a culturally competent way. The use of Pentecostal churches in Latino communities can aid in the recovery of substance abusers. In the case of Pablo (see Case Example 11.3), which follows, the therapist uses culturally competent practice with a Latino family. Awareness of cultural factors such as machismo, the role of women in Hispanic culture, folk medicine, and BCT helps the Asian American social worker move Pablo toward recovery.

The use of cultural competence techniques in the case assists the social worker to change families who have a different worldview. When there is an addiction problem within an ATOD family, using treatment techniques is often not enough. Having a cultural perspective can often effect the change that is necessary. The Case of Pablo illustrates this.

Social workers are committed to being culturally competent in their code of ethics (NASW, 2008). Standard 1.05, Cultural Competence and Social Diversity, states that the social worker should have knowledge of other cultures, provide culturally sensitive services, and continue to have education in the area of understanding race, ethnicity, national origin, color, sex, sexual orientation, age, marital status, religion, and mental or physical disability. Rothman (2008) stated, "Diversity competence is necessary if these vulnerable members of society are to be provided with responsible, caring, culturally congruent service; thus, attaining cultural competence is a necessary commitment to effective social work practice" (p 13).

A diversity perspective is important in working with families in which there is alcohol and other drug use. Substance dependency puts enormous stress on the family structure; being sensitive to cultural issues works on cultural strengths, which can aid recovery. For example, in working with Hispanic families, use of folk practices can be helpful in the healing process. With Native Americans, spiritual practices can be useful in the recovery of the family and the person who is dependent on substances.

BMT

"A family has elaborate ways of negotiating and problem solving that permit various tasks to be performed effectively" (Goldenberg & Goldenberg, 2008, p. 1).

BMT is an evidence-based treatment for couples, based on communication, negotiation, and the establishment of contracts between members of the couple (Nelson & Sullivan, 2007). Communication is an important aspect of working with families with ATOD problems. Examining the genogram from a communication perspective can assist a therapist in working on communication. It can help the family and the worker focus on understanding communication patterns between the couple and the multigenerational influences that are present. It is important to identify the potential origination source of maladaptive communication skills that the couple can examine, evaluate, and adjust to their current circumstances. The couple needs to gain understanding of where their current communication style came from together with insight into how it needs to be adapted to fit their current relationship.

Intervention

O'Farrell (1993) described an aspect of BMT that specifically addresses the negotiation of behavioral change agreements. This intervention relies heavily on the development of shared rewarding activities (SRAs) and positive specific requests (PSRs) to effect the negotiating and problem-solving skills of ATOD misuse-affected couples.

SRAs are characterized by the listing of possible homework activities, which would involve the individual, spouse, or other family members at home or away from home. These SRA lists from both partners are then compared and one or two selected for activation. The planning of the enactment of a selected SRA is

CASE EXAMPLE 11.3. The Case of Pablo

Pablo is a 48-year-old Hispanic male who is seeing a social worker with his wife. The social worker is Asian American and speaks some Spanish. From a cultural competence perspective the social worker realizes that he must be sensitive to the Hispanic culture and has an understanding of the Hispanic culture including respect, dignity, machismo, and the close-knit religious families. Both Pablo and his wife, Rosana, speak some English. Pablo is employed at a factory in a nearby town as a manager. He and his wife, Rosana, age 46, have three children who live near the married couple. The couple has been married for 20 years, and they have been financially stable. Recently, Pablo's drinking has gotten worse. He goes to the bars on a regular basis and spends less time with his wife. His wife suspects that he is seeing other women.

Pablo is a very traditional Hispanic male and believes that he can do what he wants and that his wife needs to listen to him. He has hit her several times earlier in the marriage. Rosana is fed up with her husband but is financially dependent on him. She feels that it is her obligation to stay in the marriage. The social worker is dealing with the cultural aspects of this problem in that Rosana feels that she should be passive but is frustrated by being so. The social worker talks with Rosana privately about being a Hispanic woman. It is explained that Rosana can use her role as the female and as being very respected to influence her husband to stop drinking. The social worker emphasized the use of patience and Rosana's husband's respect for Rosana.

accomplished in a group, with possible pitfalls described, and the couple goes off to take part in the chosen SRA with the agreement to avoid discussing problems or conflicts during the SRA.

Use of PSRs is a way in which each partner learns to state his or her desires in the form of positive (what you want, not what you don't want) and specific (what, where, and when) requests—not demands, but requests—that show possibility for negotiation and compromise (O'Farrell, 1993).

This process has the effect of eliminating the "insertion of misleading premises" (O'Farrell, 1993) into the couple's interaction through the use of specific negotiating and compromising practice, where one partner agrees to do one thing requested by the other. Agreements and decision making are also reviewed. O'Farrell points out:

The social worker engages the family and ascertains that he does not need a translator because of the level of English understanding of the couple. He identifies the problems with the couple as being marital discord and the drinking problem of the husband. Pablo believes in folk medicine and has been going to a healer to help him with his alcohol problem. The social worker complements Pablo for eliciting the help of a healer for his problems with alcohol. Also Pablo has talked with his priest who has encouraged him to go to an Alcoholics Anonymous (AA) group. In the counseling session the social worker supports Pablo going to AA.

Within the context of the Hispanic culture the social worker used behavioral couples therapy in order to deal with this problem. He started Sharing Reward Activities with the couple and a Recovery Contract with Pablo. By teaching communication skills the partners were better able to relate to each other. Toward the end of therapy the social worker facilitated a continuing recovery plan.

Treatment was successful with the couple. Using a spiritual healer and the AA meetings were very helpful for Pablo. The social worker used the role of Pablo as the father in the house to encourage responsible behavior. Also, the social worker, within a cultural context, used the strength of the family to encourage Pablo to stop using alcohol. The couple also agreed to further marital therapy to deal with other issues around the marriage and to reinforce gains made with the recovery contract. The couple will be referred to a Hispanic counseling center for continuing marital therapy.

to increase the perception that each spouse freely chooses to do his or her part of the agreement, each spouse chooses which request he or she desires to fulfill from the partner's PSR list. Thus each spouse volunteers to make changes needed to improve the marital relationship. (p. 189)

Fals-Stewart and colleagues (2005) saw a variation of BMT, BCT, as having the strongest empirical support for treating substance use with couples. McCollum and colleagues (2003) also found use for this BMT approach for substance abusing women. Fals-Stewart and colleagues identify the following as methods of BCT:

- Therapist works to use intimate partner as a support system for recovery.
- Partners develop a daily Recovery Contract.

- Partners agree to engage in a daily Sobriety Trust Discussion which involves discussion of intention not to use drugs or alcohol.
- Partners record the performance of significant other on calendar, and this is discussed in session.
- Standard couple-based behavioral assignments are developed to enhance quality of relationship.
- Couple commits to using a continuing Recovery Contract.

O'Farrell (2006) discussed a recovery contract and detailed elements of the contract:

1. Daily trust discussion with partner responsibilities
2. Focusing on the present and future in the discussions, not bringing up the past
3. Ensuring attendance at self-help group including 12-step groups for both partners
4. Weekly drug screens for partner in recovery.

The Case of Tom and Allen (see Case Example 11.4) serves as an example of the ways couples can negotiate and solve problems. BMT is the practical application of behavioral, problem-solving, and negotiation techniques by the practitioner. The therapist uses a genogram to understand the multigenerational patterns of communication with Tom and Allen, as well as family member substance abuse patterns. The genogram helped the couple to gain insight into why there were historical problems with communication. BCT is the application of behavioral theory to working with a couple. The therapist in the case example used SRAs as a way to join the couple together. Also, there was the use of a recovery contract to help the couples follow their selected plan.

Family Interactive Patterns

"Families typically display stable, collaborative, purposeful, and recurring patterns of interactive sequences" (Goldenberg & Goldenberg, 2008, pp. 7–8).

As reported in Rotunda, Scherer, and Imm (1995), a consistent finding in the body of knowledge is that families who experience substance abuse problems among its members are more negative and conflict prone than non-ATOD-misusing families. As more and more talking occurs during periods of intoxication, the disinhibiting effects of substance abuse tend to influence the communication in the

Case Example 11.4. The Case of Tom and Allen

Tom (56 years old) and Allen (50 years old) have been living together for 30 years. Their adult children are independent and living in other parts of the state. They both felt like they had done well in their lives with their jobs and raising their children. The children were adopted by the couple. When the youngest child moved out of Tom and Allen's home, Tom began to drink more heavily on the weekends. This escalated to the point where Tom would drink to intoxication and then fall asleep most weekend days, leaving Allen feeling lonely and depressed. After a confrontation by Allen and their oldest daughter, Amanda, Tom agreed to attend a family therapy session to discuss the changes that were taking place in his behavior and the effects this was having on Allen.

The family therapist first took a developmental history of Allen and Tom in reference to their gay-identity development. Both Allen and Tom in school had problems with other students when they were developing their gay identities. Both struggled with dating other men until they found their permanent relationship with each other. They both achieved a sense of self acceptance in their relationship with each other. The therapist found that both Allen's and Tom's families were accepting of Tom and Allen being gay. Problems with identity did not seem to be an issue with this gay couple.

In addition, the therapist used a communication-focused genogram to explain the multi-generational effects of problems with communication. Both Allen's and Tom's fathers had problems negotiating and problem solving with their wives. This resulted in the multi-generational transmission of problematic negotiating and communication patterns between Allen and Tom.

In the session, Allen communicated his loneliness and building anger at Tom regarding his weekend binge drinking. Tom related he just wanted to relax on the weekends. He stated he felt like he had earned the right to "kick back" at this time in his life. Allen was concerned about his increased drinking and was feeling left out of their life together as Tom escaped into intoxication. He did not agree with Tom that Tom was "kicking back" at this time.

(continued)

CASE EXAMPLE 11.4. *(continued)*

Although this couple was able to communicate their emotions and needs readily to each other, this communication was not translating into effective problem solving and negotiation skill for either Allen or Tom. They began their first two sessions working on shared activities and problems solving skills. It was determined that Tom and Allen needed to develop a set of shared rewarding activities (SRAs). They were given a homework assignment to each list ten activities they felt they would both like to engage in on the weekends, with the specific instruction not to share their lists until the next session.

At the next session the lists of SRAs were shared. It was revealed that Tom and Allen had procrastinated in doing their lists until the weekend and had, in fact, shared their lists with each other during the weekend. Their lists included three areas where there was shared interest: (1) visiting the children, (2) square dancing, and (3) gardening (to include activities around the house, i.e., maintenance and repairs). With the identification of these shared rewarding activities, planning began (with a calendar in hand, for when they would engage in these activities). The couple agreed to avoid discussion of Tom's weekend binge drinking problem during these SRAs and agreed to attempt to "enjoy being with each other" during the activity. Subsequent sessions reinforced this planning process and helped to develop Tom and Allen's skills at making positive specific requests (PSRs) of each other. Allen became more adept at telling Tom what he wanted (more time with Tom), when he wanted it (weekend days). The couple practiced making requests of each other that would be open for negotiation and compromise. Tom was able to get his time to "kick back" in exchange for a night of square dancing. Both Tom and Allen felt that they were freely choosing to engage in theses SRAs.

At a later session a recovery contract was discussed. They discussed their partner responsibilities, ensuring that both partners went to Twelve Step meetings, and making sure that Tom took weekly alcohol screens. They came up with a weekly schedule for each partner to do caring things for the other such as rubbing the partner's back, sharing mutual chores, and not bringing up past problems. As these requests and negotiations took place, Tom's drinking decreased and their relationship adapted to fit their new status of being a gay couple with no children living in the home now.

direction of negative affect, criticism, and disagreement. Rotunda et al. point out that this penchant for conflict creates a potential "therapeutic atmosphere tainted with overt anger, hidden resentments, shame and hopelessness" (p. 97).

Intervention

To influence these family interactive patterns, researchers and practitioners have developed approaches to deal with systemic and negative communication patterns with families. Fischer, Pidcock, and Fletcher-Stephens (2007) see MST, BSFT, and MDFT as supporting change throughout a system with substance dependency and misuse problems. MST was developed in the late 1970s and had success initially with violent and chronic juvenile offenders. BSFT improves family interactions. MDFT is a family-based drug abuse treatment for teenage substance abusers.

MST

Huey, Henggeler, Brondino, and Pickrel (2000) stated that MST is designed to improve family cohesion and to enhance skill and resource development to monitor and discipline children. MST therapists open lines of communication, reduce conflict between family members, and encourage improved quality time between parents and children. These therapists use systemic strengths and devise appropriate interventions. MST engages adolescents in prosocial behavior and finds ways in the community to monitor the adolescent's behavior.

Swenson, Henggeler, Taylor, and Addison (2005) discussed the details of the multisystemic approach. It is rooted in systems theory and the social–ecological approach and reflects an understanding of the adolescent in a system of extended family, peers, neighbors, schools, and other community influences. They elaborated on the intervention necessary to be successful with MST:

- MST believes that the therapist must engage the client and the family in the ecology of the community. MST therapists work hard in the community engaging the family. They persist with families that are resistant.
- MST relies on the ecological actors (families, peers, and other community members) to support the substance-abusing adolescent in recovery. Therapists work with and assess different aspects of the system that impinge on the behavior of the teenager.
- MST is home based, time limited, and delivered in the environment, with the child, family members, and therapists being on call 24 hours a day, seven days a week.

- MST is a team approach with strict guidelines for supervision to determine goals.
- MST is quality control oriented, with every effort made to maintain the fidelity of the program with reviews conducted consistently on a weekly basis.

BSFT

Fischer and colleagues (2007) described BSFT as a structural family systems approach that works on improving family interactions. BSFT is problem focused and attempts to change repetitive patterns of family interaction. The BSFT approach includes developing a therapeutic alliance, identifying family strengths and problem relations, developing a problem-focused strategy, implementing changes, and reinforcing strengths of the family. Strategies of change include changing alliances, shifting interpersonal boundaries, conflict resolution skills, and providing parenting guidance.

MDFT

Liddle et al. (2001) explained that MDFT derives from research on adolescent and family development. Treatment occurs in stages of relationship building, building social competence, developing antidrug use attitudes and behavior, building a nondeviant network, working on developmental tasks, enhancing parenting styles, and finally generalizing accomplishments.

MDFT has developed treatment protocols for implementation of this treatment method (Liddle, 2002). Four modules include working with adolescent, parent, family interaction, and extrafamilial systems. Interventions normally last for three months. There are three stages to intervention, with the first stage being building trust with the family and adolescent. Current crisis such as conflict in home, arrests, and legal charges can mobilize positive forces for change. In MDFT, interventions are geared toward creating positive expectations where there is a feeling that life can change. There is a need for visiting the school and the neighborhood to obtain an ecological perspective on the family and to intervene in systems that affect the family.

Liddle (2002) discussed the second stage of MDFT in which the therapist mobilizes various systems to counter pessimism. The therapist works with the system to establish concrete alternatives to drug use and drug-using lifestyle. In the third stage, change is solidified for the family. The relationship among MST–BSFT–MDFT is illustrated in the case of John (see Case Example 11.5).

MST is rooted in a social systems perspective taking into account family members, community, and other agencies to solve the youth's problem. MST therapists work on communication issues, family conflict, and the time spent with parents and children. BSFT therapists work on changing repetitive patterns of behavior. MDFT therapists, like MST therapists, work on individual, family, and extra-family systems issues. In the case example of John, the therapist worked with both John, who had a co-occurring disorder, and his mother, who had a problem with alcohol. The intervention with John involved working with the church, probation officer, and school system. In MST, the therapist engages the client, the family, and the community, relying on all participants to help the youth into recovery.

RP

"A family has an organized power structure, evolved a set of rules, and is replete with assigned and ascribed roles for its members" (Goldenberg & Goldenberg, 2008, p. 1).

The family environments associated with substance abuse and dependency are often characterized by extensive marital conflict and parent–child conflict. Families with active substance-abusing parents have been observed as being more disengaged or functioning more independently of each other, effectively undermining and challenging roles and rules in the family (Reich, Earls, & Powell, 1988; Steinglass, Tislenko, & Rice, 1985). These rules and role functions may tend to incorporate substance abuse factors into their definitions within the family. In the spousal subsystem, decreased functioning in the substance-dependent spouse may contribute to overfunctioning and -compensating in role functioning by the non-substance-dependent spouse. Role boundaries apparent during sobriety may break down as a result of confused spousal rule setting and blurred role functioning, leading to heightened potential for relapse.

In the parent–child subsystem, parental substance dependency has been suggested to influence childhood role development (Black, Bucky, & Wilder-Padilla, 1986; Hunt, 1989). The effects of the substance dependence may promote the development of distance, disengagement, and scapegoating in families.

Intervention

Existing research suggests that spouse or significant other involvement can be most effective as sobriety begins. A comprehensive intervention strategy has been developed to address the high relapse rates and lack of participation in family treatment. O'Farrell (1993) outlined the RP sessions as a maintenance intervention after BMT. The RP sessions consist of a succession of negotiable time-limited sessions that focus on three primary goals:

Maintenance of Changes Achieved in BMT Group. This first goal entails the completion of a continuing recovery plan. This plan establishes the connection of

▼
▼
▼

CASE EXAMPLE 11.5. The Case of John

John presented as a 14-year-old African American male who had a serious drug problem with marijuana and behavior problems in school including truancy and constant suspensions. He was diagnosed with co-occurring disorders of oppositional defiant behavior and attention deficit/hyperactivity disorder (ADHD). John was referred by probation because he had a history of burglaries in the community. John stated that he was motivated for treatment.

John lives with his mother in a small house in a lower SES neighborhood. His mother works daily and is not at home to supervise her son. Mother has a problem with drinking alcohol. An MST therapist went to the home to assess the situation. Mother was referred to an outpatient treatment program in the community where she could get some help. The MST therapist also referred mother to an Alcoholics Anonymous (AA) meeting where she could get additional help. She attended AA daily and made progress toward her sobriety. Her progress in treatment had an impact on John's recovery. The therapist also worked with the probation officer and the school system. The school system was very cooperative and a coach was involved in the life of the young man. In addition, there was a neighbor that took John to church every Sunday. His MST therapist did an assessment of the situation. It was found to be a strength that John wanted to perform better in school and stop using marijuana.

John continued smoking marijuana based on drug screens from the probation office. The two therapists assign to this family visited two times

the interventions and behavior changes addressed in the BMT group that will persist in the RP sessions.

Use of Skills Learned in BMT Group. This second goal attempts to address two recovery debilitating issues: (1) unresolved marital issues and (2) emerging problems in later recovery.

Unresolved marital issues often revolve around problems in what O'Farrell (1993) termed difficulties in role adjustment. As sobriety develops, roles that were lost in the family are now redefined. To address this issue, communication and negotiation skills are enacted. This is done by the therapist initiating discussion between the couple on the role adjustment issue. Structured discussion requires a week to help the mother and son work out conflicts over chores, management of behavior, John not leaving the house after hours, and taking his medication for improved attention in school.

Treatment for this young man lasted for four months. The two therapists working with this family were on call 24 hours a day, seven days a week. The therapists met with the treatment team on a weekly basis, receiving help from a supervisor. During the course of treatment the young man reduced his use of marijuana and began to consistently take his medication for ADHD. Both therapists worked on decreasing conflict between the mother and son. They also worked with the school on making this young man accountable for his behavior. Work was done with the teachers to encourage him to do well in his classes. In addition, the therapists worked with the young man to gain more self-control so that he could work in the classroom on a consistent basis. They also educated him on the importance of taking his medication. John was supposed to be taking Adderall and eventually he took it consistently. John was informed that he was taking Adderall, the expected results from the medication, and the possible side effects. He and his family were asked what their expectations of the medication were. In the end MST was successful with this young man. Along the course of treatment the Global Assessment of Individual needs (GAIN) instrument was used to assess his progress in treatment. (The GAIN is an instrument that measures progress in treatment in the area of substance abuse and mental health.)

spouses to speak one at a time without interruption, while using communication skills (listening and speaking) learned in BMT. Negotiation and compromise skills are established to deal with the unresolved marital issues.

Emerging problems in later recovery many times revolve around issues of sex and intimacy (O'Farrell, 1990). As couples become more willing to address a problem that may have had long-standing presence in their relationship, therapists will need to be responsive to this readiness. RP sessions may include dating sessions as described by O'Farrell (1990) as "a procedure involving each partner alternately being responsible for setting and arranging social 'dates' in conjunction with sexual sessions . . . devoted to verbal and physical communication about sexual likes and dislikes, non-demand pleasuring, and sexual experimentation" (p. 312). These dating and sexual sessions begin the process of rebuilding the couple's sexual relationship.

Relapse Prevention Planning. This final goal of the RP sessions entails the identification of high-risk triggers for relapse and the formulation of a relapse prevention plan that involves rehearsing responses to triggers and discussing ways of minimizing duration and negative consequences of ATOD misuse should it occur.

Fals-Stewart et al. (2005) described relapse prevention planning as the last stage of BMT. With the advent of brief therapy, the duration of relapse prevention sessions become negotiable. Once the partners complete the couple's therapy, they work on the continuing recovery plan consisting of

- a written continuing recovery plan
- continuation of daily sobriety trust discussion
- contingency plans for a potential relapse
- negotiation of posttreatment relapse prevention sessions, with tapering off of sessions over time.

O'Farrell (2006) described the contingency plan for relapse consisting of

- identifying high-risk situations
- making plan to minimize relapse
- not arguing with the person who is intoxicated or under the influence
- getting help or leaving if the client develops fear of getting hurt.

Pressures to Change and Community Reinforcement Approach

Social influence is the impact of environment, where the environment includes the interaction of physical setting, social setting, and the interpersonal behavior of others. Social influences to use do not occur in isolation from other influence; social influences can be direct as seen in role modeling, imitation, and reinforcement of behavior, and social influences may be indirect where use may be influenced by the values, attitudes and behaviors of others. (Goldenberg & Goldenberg, 2008, p. 7)

Often, in the family situation where substance abuse affects the home, we see a reduction in regular participation in social functions and activities outside the home by family members. Accompanying this reduction in social interactions may be a decrease in family interaction and a decline in considerations regarding personal appearance and changes in self-image.

Intervention

Barber and Gilbertson (1997) recommended the pressures-to-change approach in which incompatible activities and environmental contingencies are arranged hierarchically by significant others to bring increasing pressure on drinkers to reduce their drinking or seek treatment. This process of pressure to change uses environmental contingencies such as family, job, church, and other forces in the environment to bring pressure on the substance-dependent person to begin the process of change. This process begins with the administration of assessment tools to the significant others to address the drinker's use pattern and extent of problems caused by the drinker's substance use. With this strategy, adapted versions of the Short Version of the Michigan Alcohol Screening Test (SMAST) (Selzer, Vinokur, & van Rooijen, 1975), the Drinker's Partner Distress scale (DPD) (Crisp & Barber, 1995), and a daily drinking diary are used. The pressures-to-change approach, developed by Barber, Gilbertson, and Crisp (1995), trains significant others on how to use five levels of pressure on the substance abuser to encourage him or her to seek help or moderate his or her use. Barber et al. have arranged these levels in ascending order, with the highest level of pressure used only when all else has failed. These authors recommend that this model be applied over a four- to six-week period.

The levels in this approach proceed as follows:

Level One: Feedback and Education—Intervention at this level focuses on feedback to the client based on the perceptions of their significant others on the various assessment items. This is coupled with three treatment objectives as outlined by the authors:

1) helping clients cope by being more in control of their own reactions.
2) encouraging reduction in substance use
3) enticing treatment participation. (p. 72)

During this level of treatment, the aspect of incremental pressure is introduced to the client with an overview of what is to be covered in future sessions.

Level Two: Incompatible Activities—During this level, the focus begins to ascertain a functional analysis of the substance abuser's behaviors. A simple use diary is initiated with the following foci:

1) situations in which alcohol and other drugs are consumed,
2) whether intoxication is achieved,
3) problems that substance abuse creates, and
4) client responses to substance-induced behavior. (p. 74)

This level of intervention teaches the substance abuser by focusing on some of the perceived benefits of their use and begins to provide cues and consequences of using too much.

> *Level Three: Responding*—During this level, client responses to use are examined. Triggers and reinforcers to use are identified, and contingencies are planned for and practiced.

> *Level Four: Contracting*—This level asserts pressure on the substance abuser to commit to abstinence or moderation at what have come to be identified by this intervention process as "high-risk times." A view of reasonable contract construction and how to address contingencies, if the contract is broken, characterize this level.

> *Level Five: Confrontation*—This level consists of providing feedback about the effects of the substance abuse on those people close to him or her. Effective confrontation can take the following forms:

> 1) a written declaration of the significant other's love for the substance abuser,
> 2) feedback about the ways in which the substance abuser's behavior diminishes their relationship, and
> 3) a simple, unambiguous plea for the substance abuser to change or seek help. (p. 76)

This intervention strategy is meant to be enacted until the client decides to change or seek treatment. The case of Tiffany and David (see Case Example 11.6) serves as an example of the influence and power of the social environment. It illustrates how the substance abuser's behavior diminishes his relationship with his wife. It also helps David recognize the negative impact of his drinking. It supports David's strengths, such as giving up his use of methadone and heroin.

Intervention: Community reinforcement theory is an evidence-based practice that is very helpful to the social work practitioner in working with families in which interaction with the social environment has been impaired. This theory draws on an ecological viewpoint seeing the family in relation to the community. The point of intersection between person and the environment is the basis of this family ATOD intervention.

J. E. Smith and Myers (2004) have pioneered an approach called Community Reinforcement and Family Treatment. In this practice model, the therapist works with families to identify behaviors in their substance-abusing family members.

CASE EXAMPLE 11.6. The Case of Tiffany and David

Tiffany (27 years old) has been married to David (33 years old) for four years. Tiffany has lived with David's polysubstance abuse throughout their courtship and marriage. Tiffany has a history of sexual abuse before the marriage and has difficulty being intimate with David. At times she is very distant from David and has a past history of enabling her husband's behavior. She has been abused physically by David in the past. Currently, David is not abusing Tiffany. David has a past history of being on metha-done; he has successfully abstained from methadone and heroin for four years now. His primary problem now is drinking. They have four children both from previous marriages. Recently, David was arrested for his sec-ond DWI and was mandated for evaluation for alcohol treatment by the local magistrate. During their marriage Tiffany and David have argued frequently about David's drinking and Tiffany has experienced many nega-tive consequences of David's misuse of alcohol. Tiffany uses the defense mechanism of avoidance to deal with David. Although Tiffany wishes to remain with David, she wants to learn to take care of herself in this rela-tionship and encourage David to get help for his alcohol misuse problem.

The session began with Tiffany completing a checklist of ways in which David's drinking has affected her life in a negative way. She identi-fied (1) being embarrassed in public, (2) physical and verbal abuse, and (3) misuse of family financial resources as the three most significant effects. David also completed an assessment interview and the findings of both interviews were explored and discussed with the couple.

David became quite solemn at that point in the session as Tiffany shared her feedback with him. Discussion at this point in the session focused on clarifying for the couple that David's drinking is his behavior and that he must take ownership of this behavior. It was emphasized that Tiffany cannot be blamed or held responsible for his drinking. David quietly responded that he did understand this. Tiffany told David "I love you and want to stay with you but I can't keep living like this . . . it is too much for me." David sat silently, but his hands were trembling. Finally David said, "This has all gotten to be too much for me too." He acknowl-edged that he needed to do something about his drinking and commit-ted to entering treatment. Tiffany told David, "I am going to have to

(continued)

CASE EXAMPLE 11.6. *(continued)*

change too. I want to learn how to support you and take care of myself, too. I want us both to get better. But there are many things going on that have to stop."

At this time in the session we explored the process of how people change. David and Tiffany asked many questions. They both agreed, "We now can't ignore that this is a problem in our marriage anymore." They both made a commitment to begin to address the problem and to each examine what is their own responsibility to change in this situation. David made a verbal commitment to initiate a period of abstinence to be able to examine the different triggers and situations that put him at high risk to misuse alcohol. Tiffany expressed her interest in learning different ways to respond to David that will not reinforce his drinking. She stated she was determined to support his efforts to change. She wanted to diminish any role she may play in reinforcing his ATOD misuse and to increase any influence which may help to foster his abstinence.

Subsequently, the family members examine how they could work to reinforce or apply consequences for behaviors in a way that may move the substance abusing family member to commit to engage in treatment. Different sequences of behaviors are practiced in this model, which may lead members to identifying dangerous situations that they may find themselves in with their substance abusing family member. Also, the model focuses on opportunities for positive reinforcements to apply when the substance abusing family member has not been using alcohol or drugs. J. E. Smith and Myers have found this approach to be effective in moving substance abusing family members to engage in treatment 68 percent of the time.

Conclusions

The interventions described in this chapter represent some promising approaches currently available to those who intervene with families with substance abuse problems. All represent evidence-based practice strategies. The approaches presented here have been subjected to sound research, unless otherwise noted. This chapter has addressed the problems of substance abusers within the context of their larger social environment—their family. It has emphasized that by focusing interventions on the influences and interactions within the family, using social and cultural foci, contributing factors to substance abuse patterns can be identified and addressed. This chapter has set the context within which family work takes place. The interventions presented have incorporated a broad spectrum of theoretical orientations that approach the family as a whole and encourage recovery among all family members.

Clinicians who wish to take on the challenging job of addressing the substance abuse in family systems do have a substantial body of knowledge to guide and direct them. Preparation of the clinician for this demanding endeavor is seemingly as crucial as is the application of the models and intervention strategies discussed in this chapter. Becoming ready to enact intervention strategies by setting a paradigm that works for the individual family therapist will require integration and synthesis of concepts from a number of different theoretical orientations, while simultaneously applying and testing intervention strategies that fit the families' characteristics, situations, and needs. This level of adaptability, flexibility, and sophistication on the part of the clinician will undoubtedly lead to the attainment of desired outcomes and effective treatment of substance abuse problems in the families they serve.

A number of implications for the development of interventions with families are indicated. First, the training and preparation of those who work with families with substance abuse problems must begin with the crucial first step of learning how to set the therapeutic climate for an intervention to be successful. The specific preparations reviewed in this chapter are the foundation for the application of all interventions. Second, although most interventions presented include the involvement of other family members in the treatment activity, family therapists may need to be prepared to work with substance abusers who are not willing or able to include other family members in their treatment.

Using the strategies presented in this chapter, a family therapist can facilitate greater understanding in the substance abuser of the subtle complexities and reciprocal relationships that have affected the substance abuser and others in his or her environment. This may be the best initial avenue for intervention with some clients. However, this understanding may also encourage future intervention with the involvement of other family members. More study and exploration of the unforeseen hidden challenges inherent in this treatment area are always beneficial. The therapist used spiritual aspects to encourage hope for the couple.

References

Apsche, J. A., Bass, C. K., & Houston, M. A. (2007). Family MDT: vs. treatment as usual in a community setting. *International Journal of Behavioral and Consultation Therapy, 3*(1), 145–153.

Barber, J. G., & Gilbertson, R. (1997). Unilateral interventions for women living with heavy drinkers. *Social Work, 42,* 69–78.

Barber, J. G., Gilbertson, R., & Crisp, B. R. (1995). Promoting controlled drinking. *Families in Society, 76,* 248–253.

Beatty, L. (2007). Introduction. *Journal of Ethnicity in Substance Abuse, 6*(2), 11–13.

Black, C., Bucky, S. F., & Wilder-Padilla, S. (1986). The interpersonal and emotional consequences of being an adult child of an alcoholic. *International Journal of the Addictions, 21,* 213–231.

Cheung, Y. W. (1991). Ethnicity and alcohol/drug use revisited: A framework for future research. *International Journal of the Addictions, 25,* 581–605.

Crisp, B. R., & Barber, J. G. (1995). The Drinkers Partner Distress scale: An instrument for measuring the distress caused by drinkers to their partners. *International Journal of the Addictions, 30,* 1009–1017.

Delgado, M., & de Saxe Zerden, L. S. (2007). Latino cultural assets and substance abuse services: Opportunity knocks. *Journal of Ethnic and Cultural Diversity in Social Work, 16*(3–4), 135–142.

Devore, W., & Schlesinger, E. G. (1999). *Ethnic sensitive social work practice* (5th ed.). Needham Heights, MA: Allyn & Bacon.

Donohue, B., & Azrin, N. (2001). Family behavior therapy. In E. F. Wagner & H. B. Waldron (Eds.), *Innovations in adolescent substance abuse innovations* (pp. 205–227). London: Pergamon Press.

Fals-Stewart, W., O'Farrell, T. J., Birchler, G. R., Cordova, J., & Kelley, M. L. (2005). Behavioral couples therapy for alcoholism and drug abuse: Where we've been, where we are, and where we're going. *Journal of Cognitive Psychotherapy: An International Quarterly, 19*(3), 229–246.

Fischer, J. L., Pidcock, B. W., & Fletcher-Stephens, B. J. (2007). Family response to adolescence, youth and alcohol. *Alcoholism Treatment Quarterly, 25*(1–2), 27–41.

Frame, M. W. (2000). The spiritual genogram in family therapy. *Journal of Marital & Family Therapy, 26*(2), 211–216.

Gainey, R. R., Haggerty, K. P., Fleming, C. B., & Catalano, R. F. (2007). Teaching parenting skills in a methadone treatment setting [Research Note]. *Social Work Research, 31,* 185–190.

Goldenberg, I., & Goldenberg, H. (2008). *Family therapy: An overview* (7th ed.). Pacific Grove, CA: Brooks/Cole.

Heath, D. B. (1991). Uses and misuses of the concept of ethnicity in alcohol studies: An essay in deconstruction. *International Journal of the Addictions, 25,* 607–628.

Huey, S. J., Henggeler, S. W., Brondino, M. J., & Pickrel, S. G. (2000). Mechanisms of change in multisystemic therapy: Reducing delinquent behavior through therapist adherence and improved family and peer functioning. *Journal of Consulting and Clinical Psychology, 68*(3), 441–467.

Hunt, P. (1989). Adult children of alcoholic parents: A three-group study (Doctoral dissertation, Boston University, 1989). *Dissertation Abstracts International, 50,* 1110B.

Kaufman, E., & Yoshioka, M. (2005). *Substance abuse treatment and family therapy: A treatment improvement protocol.* Washington, DC: U.S. Department of Health and Human Services.

Kelly, S. J., Day, N., & Streissguth, A. P. (2000). Effects of prenatal alcohol exposure on social behavior in humans and other species. *Neurotoxicology and Teratology, 22*(2), 143–149.

Kuehl, B. P. (1995). The solution-oriented genogram: A collaborative approach. *Journal of Marital and Family Therapy, 21,* 239–250.

Lassitier, P., & Chung, C. Y. (2006). Perceived multicultural competency of certified substance abuse counselors. *Journal of Addictions and Offender Counseling, 26,* 73–83.

Liddle, H. A. (2002). *Multidimensional family for adolescent substance abusers* (Vol. 5, DHHS Publication No. 02–3660). Rockville, MD: Center for Substance Abuse Treatment, Substance Abuse and Mental Health Services Administration.

Liddle, H. A., Dakof, G. A., Parker, K., Diamond, G. S., Barrett, K., & Tejada, M. (2001). Multidimensional family therapy for adolescent drug abuse: Results of a randomized clinical trial. *American Journal of Drug and Alcohol Abuse, 27,* 651–688.

McCollum, E. E., Lewis, R. A., Nelson, R. A., Trepper, T. S., & Wetchier, J. (2003). Couple treatment for drug abusing women: Effects on drug use and need for treatment. *Journal of Couple & Relationship Therapy, 2*(4), 1–18.

McCollum, E. E., & Trepper, T. S. (1995). Little by little, pulling me through—Women's perceptions of successful drug treatment: A qualitative inquiry. *Journal of Family Psychotherapy, 6,* 63–82.

McCrady, B. S., & Epstein, E. E. (1996). Theoretical bases of family approaches to substance abuse treatment. In F. Rotgers, D. S. Keller, & J. Morgenstern (Eds.), *Treating substance abuse* (pp. 117–143). New York: Guilford Press.

McGoldrick, M., Giordano, J., & Garcia-Preto, N. (2005). *Ethnicity and family therapy.* New York: Guilford Press.

Merikangas, K. R. (1990). The genetic epidemiology of alcoholism. *Psychological Medicine, 20,* 11–22.

Miller-Day, M. A. (2002). Parent–adolescent communication about alcohol, tobacco, and other drug use. *Journal of Adolescent Research, 17,* 604–616.

National Association of Social Workers. (2001). *Standards for cultural competence in social work practice.* Washington, DC: Author.

National Association of Social Workers. (2008). *Code of ethics of the National Association of Social Workers.* Washington, DC: Author.

Nelson, T. S. & Sullivan, N. J. (2007). Couples therapy and addiction. *Journal of Couples & Relationship Therapy, 6*(1–2), 45–56.

O'Farrell, T. J. (1990). Sexual functioning of male alcoholics. In R. L. Collins, K. E. Leonard, B. A. Miller, & J. S. Searles (Eds.), *Alcohol and the family* (pp. 244–271). New York: Guilford Press.

O'Farrell, T. J. (1993). A behavioral marital therapy couples group program for alcoholics and their spouses. In T. J. O'Farrell (Ed.), *Treating alcohol problems: Marital and family interventions* (pp. 170–209). New York: Guilford Press.

O'Farrell, T. J. (2006, December 1). *Behavioral couples therapy for alcoholism and substance abuse.* Presentation at the 31st Annual SECAD Conference, National Association of Addiction Treatment Providers, Atlanta.

O'Hanlon, W. H., & Weiner-Davis, M. (1989). *In search of solutions.* New York: W. W. Norton.

Patterson, J. E., Miller, R. B., Carnes, S., & Wilson, S. (2004). Evidence-based practice for marriage and family therapists. *Journal of Marital and Family Therapy, 30*(2), 183–195.

Peluso, P. R. (2006). Expanding the use of the ethical genogram: Incorporating the ethical principles to help clarify counselors ethical decision-making styles. *Family Journal, 14*(2), 158–163.

Perkins, H. W. (2002). Social norms and the preventions of alcohol misuse in collegiate contexts. *Journal of Studies on Alcohol, 14*(Suppl.), 164–172.

Prochaska, J. O., Norcross, J. C., & DiClemente, C. C. (1994). *Changing for good.* New York: William Morrow.

Reich, W., Earls, T., & Powell, J. (1988). A comparison of the home and social environments of children of alcoholic and non-alcoholic parents. *British Journal of Addictions, 83,* 831–839.

Rishel, C. W. (2007). Evidence-based prevention in mental health: What is it and how do we get there? *American Journal of Orthopsychiatry, 77,* 153–164.

Rothman, J. C. (2008). *Cultural competence in process and practice.* Boston: Pearson.

Rotunda, R. J., Scherer, D. G., & Imm, P. S. (1995). Family systems and alcohol misuse: Research on the effects of alcoholism on family functioning and effective family interventions. *Professional Psychology: Research and Practice, 26,* 94–104.

Rubin, A. (2008). *Practitioner's guide to using research for evidence-based practice.* Hoboken, NJ: John Wiley & Sons.

Saatcioglu, O., Erim, R., & Cakmak, D. (2006). Role of family in alcohol and substance abuse. *Psychiatry and Clinical Neurosciences, 60,* 125–132.

Selzer, M. L., Vinokur, A., & van Rooijen, L. (1975). A self-administered Short Michigan Alcoholism Screening Test (SMAST). *Journal of Studies on Alcohol, 36,* 117–126.

Smith, D. C., & Hall, J. A. (2008). Strengths-oriented family therapy for adolescents with substance abuse problems [Practice Update]. *Social Work, 53,* 185–188.

Smith, J. E., & Myers, R. J. (2004). *Motivating substance abusers to enter treatment: Working with family members.* New York: Guilford Press.

Stanton, M. D., & Heath, A. W. (1995). Family treatment of alcohol and drug abuse. In R. H. Mikesell, D. Lusterman, & S. H. McDaniel (Eds.), *Integrating family therapy* (pp. 271–283). Washington, DC: American Psychological Association.

Steinglass, P., Tislenko, L., & Reiss, D. (1985). Stability/instability in the alcoholic: Marriage: The interrelationships between course of alcoholism, family process and marital outcome. *Family Process, 24,* 365–376.

Stromwall, L. K., Larson, N. C., Nieri, T., Holley, L. C. , Topping, D., Castillo, J., & Ashford, J. B. (2008). Parents with co-occurring mental health and substance abuse conditions involved in child protection services: Clinical profile and treatment needs. *Child Welfare, 87,* 95–113.

Swenson, C. S., Henggeler, S. W., Taylor, I. S., & Addison, O. W. (2005). *Multisystemic therapy and neighborhood partnerships.* New York: Guilford Press.

White, M., & Epston, D. (1990). *Narrative means to therapeutic ends.* New York: W. W. Norton.

12

The Important Role
of Prevention

David I. Siegel

Introduction: Importance of Prevention

In this book so far, we have emphasized the importance of practice intervention to address substance misuse and abuse. However, for a social problem that involves dependence (complicating treatment); relates to crime and violence; and has tremendous impact on individuals, family, neighborhoods, and society, the importance of prevention is undeniable.

Imagine, for example, "when Hispanic immigrant parents with limited English proficiency arrive in the United States they are faced with the daunting task of raising children in an unfamiliar and foreign culture" (Tapia et al., 2006, p. 147). Numerous obstacles, such as cultural incompatibilities between the receiving culture and culture of origin, social isolation, and marginalization from sources of support, potentially place their children at risk for drug abuse and other antisocial behaviors. In Latin America, the family is often prioritized above the individual. Values such as respect for adults, conformity, and a sense of duty to parents are regarded as important aspects of parent–child relationships in Latin American countries. After arriving in the United States, there may be an inverted family hierarchy because parents must rely on their adolescent children, who learn English in school, to help with everyday transactions, for example, with banking and groceries. Differential acculturation may seem problematic as parents see Americanized behaviors as disrespectful to the family; adolescents may perceive parents' behavior as overcontrolling and may withdraw, or may rebel further.

▼
▼
▼

Coatsworth, Pantin, and Szapocznik (2002) indicated that

> parents' lack of familiarity and knowledge about the common value orientations that guide daily activities in their new host culture serves to isolate them from the important developmental contexts of their children's social environment. For example, Hispanic immigrant parents are generally not aware of the responsibility that American culture places on parents to monitor behavior and school performance. (p. 118)

If not corrected, this lack of parental awareness may translate into unsupervised adolescent activities and increase the likelihood of problem behaviors, particularly substance abuse. What will happen to these children if not for excellent prevention programs such as Familias Unidas (Prado et al., 2008)? To address this issue, the prevention program and its practitioners must demonstrate cultural competence. According to Kirst-Ashman (2008), *cultural competence* is "the set of knowledge and skills that a social worker must develop in order to be effective with multicultural clients" (p. 37). This example shows the importance of prevention programs and their components which will be emphasized in this chapter.

Systems Conception

The levels of prevention can be considered from a socioecological perspective. Heflinger and Christens (2006), following Bronfenbrenner's (1979) lead, indicated that problems involve several levels of analysis.

> Ontogenetic factors entail familiar focus on the individual. Bronfenbrenner's nested approach, however, shows that the individual is always impacted by influences at other levels and that the larger systems impact the individual level. The microsystemic factors are family and peer groups, and the interaction between these immediate influences. Mesosystemic factors are local neighborhood or community, social institutions, culture and the interactions among them. Macrosystemic components are the furthest removed influences that operate at a societal or global scale. (Heflinger & Christens, 2006, p. 381)

History, Morality, and Disease: The Influence of Macrosystem Factors

Prevention models reflect the philosophies and attitudes of the time and the predominant theories of causation. In this regard the history of alcoholism and the temperance movement is quite instructive.

The debate between those who believed alcoholism was a "disease" and those who believed it was a "social" or "moral" problem is quite evident in the history of attitudes and treatment and the Women's Christian Temperance movement. Before the 19th century there was not a disease concept, and drinking was considered one's own responsibility. During the 19th century, "Benjamin Rush was one of the first physicians to document patients' descriptions of their experiences of being addicted to alcohol" (Roiblatt & Dinis, 2004, p. 654). He and Thomas Trotter in Great Britain described alcoholism as a disease "in which the alcoholic suffered gradual and progressive addiction leading to loss of control over the consumption of alcohol" (Bride & Nackerud, 2002, pp. 127–128).

As a result of the Washingtonian movement (of doctors) and others in the medical community promoting the disease model, a range of self-help homes and inebriate asylums were developed with reformed drunkards, doctors, and social philanthropists joining forces to treat alcoholism (Bride & Nackerud, 2002; Roiblatt & Dinis, 2004). However, the disease concept was not the primary perspective of the day and most citizens considered drinking to be a moral problem. This was in accord with the basic conception of social problems in those times and the early role of the friendly visitors of the Charity Organization Societies who provided moral counseling to assuage poverty (see, for example, Trattner, 1999).

Roiblatt and Dinis (2004) indicated that alcohol, just like crime and violence, was viewed primarily as an individual moral decision. Alcohol was an easy target to explain a variety of social ills in a burgeoning industrial and more urban society. It was variously attributed to explain poverty, crime, pauperism, misery, degeneracy, tuberculosis, gambling, rioting, debauchery, Sabbath breaking, rowdyism, ignorance, cancer, syphilis, inconstancy, and insanity. Reform movements, which focused on issues such as slavery and women's suffrage, also focused on the elimination of alcohol and led to the formation of the Women's Christian Temperance movement and, later, the Anti Saloon League. At the same time that empirical support for the disease concept began to build, the temperance movement reached the height of its influence and was committed to a moral interpretation of poverty in which alcoholics were considered weak-willed. Most of the prominent social workers of the day, including Jane Addams, were supporters of the temperance movement and considered alcoholism to be a cause of poverty.

Paradoxically, Bride and Nackeride (2002) indicated the temperance movement eventually co-opted the disease concept, "claiming that alcohol in any form would lead to habitual drunkenness in anyone who drank, thereby justifying the goal of national prohibition" (p. 128). Thus, the conflict between disease and morality in views of alcohol are deeply rooted in our history. In the early twentieth century morality and disease concepts led to prohibition as prevention.

Macrosystem Changes

Now in the 21st century, changes in the macrosystem have affected every other system. The economy has changed with nations affecting one another. Alcohol and other drugs have become big business, with international cartels and corporations controlling production and distribution. Substances are strongly related to crime, economic strata, and characteristics of the neighborhood. Models of causation have changed to include cognitive behavioral perspectives, the influence of genes and neurotransmitters, and learning theory. Risk and resilience have been defined and include factors in the individual, family, peers, and neighborhood. Models of treatment have changed to include the process of change model, motivational interviewing, and cognitive and behavioral interventions. All these changes, in turn, have influenced models and practices of prevention.

Worldwide Economic Issues

Production and trafficking in drugs have become part of worldwide economic issues and competition among nations. This affects not only the relationship between the United States and other nations, but also the supply of various drugs in this country. For example, there is a debate on whether Afghanistan profits exponentially from the opium trade, and how these profits help fund the Taliban ("Letters: Is Afghanistan a Narco-state?" 2008; U.S. Reports Gains," 2008). There is an ongoing history of cocaine smuggling between Andean (South American) countries and the United States covering 30 years ("Waving, not Drowning," 2008). U.S. Speaker of the House Nancy Pelosi (D-CA) has tried to kill the U.S. Colombia Free Trade Agreement because of inaction on paramilitary (drug smuggling) groups (Huang, Kosterman, Catalano, Hawkins, & Abbott, 2008), President Alvaro Uribe has tried to reduce violence, and the latest smuggling tactic is homemade submarines ("Uribe Calls Pelosi's Bluff," 2008). In Mexico, the war between varying drug cartels has led to horrible violence, abuse, and murder ("The Long War," 2008). As a result, the U.S. Congress has variously proposed initiatives to help fund enforcement efforts in these countries, sometimes with human rights improvements as a condition (Graham-Silverman, 2008; "Mexico: Antidrug Aid's Strings Intact," 2008). Lately the larger Melanesian countries of Papua New Guinea, Fiji, the Solomon Islands, and Vanatua have become hotbeds of drug smuggling. Pacific islands are used as transit points between source countries, for example, East Asia, for ice and heroin; South America, for cocaine; and markets in the United States, Canada, Australia, and New Zealand (Windybank, 2008).

Advertising Policy

An area where economic interest has an effect on the relative balance between societal responsibility and individual freedom is that of advertising policy. There has been an extensive history of debate between the U.S. Congress, the alcohol (beer, wine, and distilled spirits) industry, the Bureau of Alcohol Tobacco and Firearms, other public agencies (Federal Communications Commission [FCC], the Federal Trade Commission [FTC]), and public health and advocacy groups regarding alcohol advertising policies in the United States from the 1980s to the present (Giesbrecht et al., 2004). Issues have included the effect of advertising on adults and young people, both in the short term and in the long term. Specific issues related to advertising include whether it is deliberately focused on young people, the exposure of young people to advertising related to sports, restriction of alcohol advertising during prime time, broadcast limitations on advertising of spirits, the question of warning labels regarding drinking effects and drunk driving, whether wine companies can claim positive benefits of drinking red wine, airing of counteradvertising (education, media campaigns against binge drinking on campus), targeting of young healthy drinkers by health promotion activities, and strengthening codes to eliminate sexism and glamorization of high-risk behaviors. A recent issue is that restrictions on alcohol advertising are vulnerable to challenge under international trade agreements (Gould, 2005). Again, the promotion of drinking creates economic gains for many; there is the question of social control versus individual responsibility and consideration of protection for, and rights of, young people.

For example, there is particular concern about advertising aimed toward young people, who combine low tolerance for alcohol with high motivation to experiment and for whom drinking is correlated with many social issues, including drunk driving, crashes, noisy parties, property damage, unwanted pregnancies, and sexually transmitted diseases (Giesbrecht et al., 2004; U.S. Department of Health and Human Services, 1997). Alcohol advertising that appeals to young people is considered potentially harmful by a number of groups and government bodies. Despite concerns raised, public health advocates suggest that the intent of some advertising is deliberately focused on young people (for example, Garfield, Chung, & Rathouz, 2003; Jackson, Hastings, Wheeler, Eadie, & Mackintosh, 2000). Studies have been mixed regarding the effects of alcohol policies on young people. However, it seems while advertising has small, if any, impact on sales in the short term, positive response to alcohol commercials has substantial impact as an educator to long-term drinking and drinking problems (Casswell, 1995; Giesbrecht et al., 2004). A study in New Zealand found that positive responses to beer advertisements were associated with frequency of current drinking and expectation of future drinking among children (Wyllie, Zhang, & Casswell, 1998).

The issue of broadcast advertising of spirits has been debated as far back as 1993. There has been a clear issue of jurisdiction as to whether it be the purview of the FTC, the FCC, or needed an act of Congress for regulation. Consideration of proposed legislation to regulate alcohol advertising leaves congressional representatives in a difficult position in which a "no" vote would appear to favor alcohol abuse and a "yes" vote would restrict free speech. Public health advocates indicate that the alcohol industry influences legislation with massive contributions of money.

For many years, jurisdictional concerns were allayed when the major broadcast networks signed statements upholding a voluntary ban on liquor advertising, leaving cable networks as the only option remaining to advertisers of distilled spirits (Giesbracht et al., 2004). Lately, however, this ban has been violated in an increasingly nonregulatory environment. It seems beer and spirits lobbyists are not always aligned, as beer interests feel spirits advertising could cause a public reaction to alcohol advertising in general. There is the question of equivalency versus perception that spirits are more harmful than beer. Thus, the question of alcohol advertising remains a product of our political and regulatory process, economic issues, and corporate lobbying.

Direct-to-consumer (DTC) advertising of prescription drugs has also been the subject of controversy. Although the use of prescription medication has a very different function than that of alcohol, there are still the questions of the influence of economics, social control versus freedom, and cultural differences between nations. According to Diehl, Mueller, and Terlutter (2008), "whereas advertising for non-prescription pharmaceuticals has been directed to consumers for decades, direct-to-consumer (DTC) advertising for prescription drugs is a relatively recent phenomenon" (p. 100). DTC advertising is currently allowed in the United States and New Zealand but is banned throughout Europe and the rest of the world. Yuan (2008), in referencing Young, indicated that in 1997,

> the Food and Drug Administration opened the gates for DTC advertising of prescription drugs on broadcast media by allowing pharmaceutical companies to provide less detailed information about risks associated with drug products in television and radio commercials than is required of print advertisements. (Yuan, 2008, p. 30)

The pharmaceutical industry, many doctors, and pharmacists indicate consumer directed advertising is a helpful source of information, increases patient communication with their doctors, and informs patients about new drugs and treatments. However, doctors, pharmacists, and opponents express concern about the quality of information contained in pharmaceutical advertising, and the consumers' ability to comprehend it (Diehl et al., 2008; Naik et al., 2007). Although medical consumerism and participation in health decision making is assumed, some patients may be eager to talk to their doctors about specific drugs, whereas others may be hesitant. A great concern is whether this becomes a battle of brand names rather than a search for the best drugs for the situation. It also has been argued that the nature of advertising is to depict a product's benefits, and to conceal all risks or possible side effects. Although advertisers are required to provide information regarding risks and side effects, "many consumers may have difficulty comprehending such complex information" (Diehl et al., pp. 104–105). A survey of consumers by Steyer (1999) revealed 61 percent noted that the ads caused confusion about risks and benefits. It seems likely that the differing approaches to prescription advertising between countries relate to cultural differences as well the profits to be made in a capitalistic system. Naik and colleagues (2007) indicated that "pharmaceutical companies spent an estimated 4.2 billion on direct to consumer advertising in 2005" (p. 1). There is also the question of harmful combinations of prescriptions which will be addressed later.

Prevention Programs: Microsystems

Because alcohol and other drugs may be dependence producing, have side effects, and relate to crime and violence, it would seem that society should emphasize an orientation to prevention of their use. Much progress has been made in the creation of evidence-based prevention programs, though there are methodological issues in developing evidence and more research is needed.

Adolescents and School-Based Prevention

In the United States, adolescence has been a prime target for drug prevention efforts. Botvin and Griffin (2007) indicated that "in the USA and other countries, the initial stages of substance abuse typically include experimentation with alcohol and tobacco during the early and middle years of adolescence" (p. 608). Positive messages about use in the media may contribute to adolescent use. At this stage, youths become more involved in social situations including experimentation with drugs with same age or older peers. "Some adolescents may smoke, drink or use drugs to fit in with peers or conform to peer pressure" (p. 608). Substance use may be one of many behaviors and roles adolescents use to establish personal identity and separation from parents.

Rates of substance use and abuse tend to peak in late adolescence and early adulthood. Johnston, O'Malley, Bachman, and Schulenberg (2006), in their respected "monitoring the future" survey, indicated that in 2005 more than half (58 percent) of those about to graduate high school report having been drunk once in their life, about a quarter (23 percent) were current tobacco smokers, and about 1 in 3 had used marijuana in the last year. About half (50.4 percent) of high school seniors reported using any illicit drug in their lifetime. Although illegal, experimentation with alcohol and other drugs during adolescence has been found to be statistically normative (MacMaster, Holleran, & Chaffin, 2005). Substance abuse constitutes a potential risk for a host of other problems; however, most youths who experiment with alcohol and other drugs in their lifetime do not develop a substance abuse problem. Unfortunately, a subset will become regular uses of substances and some will progress to experimentation and regular use of more serious drugs.

School-based drug prevention programs are especially popular, as schools have the ability to reach large numbers of school age children, and programs developed during school hours are relatively easy to implement (Soole, Mazerolle, & Rombouts, 2008). Following criticism of drug prevention programs in the early 1990s, and, in the wake of findings pointing to the relatively unabated usage rates of alcohol, tobacco, and other drugs, the effectiveness of substance abuse prevention programs has been seriously questioned (Gorman, Conde, & Huber, 2007; Skiba, Monroe, & Wodarski, 2004). For example, Project DARE (Drug Abuse Resistance Education), which was used in 50 percent of school districts nationwide, typically reported positive effects in reducing drug use. However, a meta-analysis found the impact of DARE's core curriculum was slight and not statistically significant. Although DARE's positive effect on knowledge, attitudes, and skills was encouraging, these aspects could not be linked to reductions in drug use (Durlak, 1997; Skiba et al., 2004). As a result,

> federal agencies in the United States such as the Department of Education and Substance Abuse and Mental Health Service Administration (SAMHSA) began to emphasize the importance of research in determining the funding of interventions. One manifestation of this in the area of school based drug prevention has been a proliferation of government-sponsored publications and websites that list intervention programs that are said to have been shown to be effective in one or more experimental or quasi-experimental studies. (Gorman et al., 2007, p. 585)

The term "evidence based" became a call for evaluation research of drug prevention.

Methodological Issues

This concern was effective in motivating a proliferation of models of prevention of adolescent substance use and abuse in school, and/or in combination with other systems, as well as in "evidence-based evaluation of programs." For example, Soole and colleagues (2008) identified 149 programs evaluating school-based drug programs that included an illicit drug use outcome measure. Gradually, various models and principles of effective programs have been teased out. However, given the nature of the problem and the different contexts in which it arises, certain methodological issues keep arising. According to Gorman, Conde, and Huber (2007), questions have been asked about the criteria used to judge program effectiveness, the consistency by which these criteria have been applied by expert panels, and whether the results from evaluations of selected programs actually meet these criteria. Reports that have evaluated data analysis and presentation findings indicate that the designation of effectiveness often is based on isolated statistically significant findings rather than the preponderance of available evidence. Gorman and colleagues also suggest assumptions about effectiveness are often the outcome of questionable data analysis practices, such as multiple subgroup analysis, post hoc sample refinement, and use of one tailed significance tests.

Soole and colleagues (2008), in their review of school-based programs that influence illicit drug use, found only 37.7 percent of treatment comparison contrasts scored 5 (the highest rating) for rigor, which included randomized experimental design groups (groups comparable at pre-intervention), 26.25 percent scored 3 to 4.5, where a score of 4 indicates use of a randomized experimental design (noticeable difference between groups at pre-intervention) and a score of 3 involved a matched comparison quasi-experimental design (groups comparable at pre-intervention). The remaining 36 percent used comparisons of less rigor: 2 = matched comparison quasi-experimental design (noticeable difference between groups at pre-intervention), 1 = nonequivalent comparison quasi-experimental design (groups comparable at pre intervention), and 0 = no equivalent comparison quasi-experimental design (noticeable differences between groups at pre-intervention). The problem of attrition of subjects in substance abuse studies and its effect on sample size was the primary reason for exclusion from the review. Another methodology problem is that programs that are effective in one sociocultural context may not be effective in another. For example, Project Northland, a comprehensive multilevel, multiyear project seemed quite effective in northwest Minnesota, though not nearly as much so in inner-city urban Chicago (Komro et al., 2008; Perry et al., 2002).

The term "evidence" in evidence-based prevention is valid to the degree that there is rigor in the research design, the data analysis is appropriate, control groups are really controls, and the degree of generalization of findings is appropriate to the sample. A means of monitoring studies is through meta-analysis, in which the researchers evaluate the rigor of component studies. Soole and colleagues (2008) defined *meta-analysis* as "a range of systematic, qualitative methods used to synthesize research findings from multiple studies investigating similar outcome variables" (p. 269). If there are similar findings in many studies relating to similar methodologies and outcomes, methods of prevention in different populations are supported.

Risk and Protective Factors

On the basis of the discouraging 1990s' reviews of prevention strategies and the inadequacy of simplistic views of substance abuse causation, researchers began realizing there were many variables in play in causing substance abuse (Corrigan, Loneck, Videka, & Brown, 2007). These came to be known as *risk factors* and were defined by Coie, Watt, West, Hawkins, Asarnow, and Markman (1993) as "variables associated with a high probability of onset, greater severity, and longer duration of major mental health problems" (p. 1013). There also seemed to be variables that kept children from experimenting with and abusing substances, which became known as protective factors. Coie and colleagues defined these as "conditions that improve people's resistance to risk factors and disorder" (p. 1013). Typical domains for typologies of risk include community, family, school, peer, and individual. One conceptualization is included in Table 12.1. These conceptions are supported by systems theories that emphasize the interaction of the inner world of an individual with that of the environment of peers and community surrounding him or her (Corrigan et al., 2007). Corrigan and colleagues indicate other theories used to support this systemic thinking were social influence models (see, for example, Atkinson, Richard & Carlson, 2001; Kelder & Perry, 1993) and social learning theories (see, for example, Bukstein, 1995; Clayton et al., 1995).

A comprehensive analysis of the theories underlying risk and protective factors for substance abuse are beyond the scope of this chapter, however, a few will be mentioned. Tarter, Sambrano and Dunn (2002) used developmental theory to identify different phenotypes or specific biobehavioral characteristics that are associated with the risk of substance abuse at each stage of development. Phenotypes are the product of many genes interacting with numerous factors in the environment.

TABLE 12.1: Risk and Protective Factors, Communities That Care Youth Survey

Risk Factors	Protective Factors
Community	
Low neighborhood attachment	Opportunity for prosocial community involvement
Community disorganization	Rewards for prosocial community involvement
High transitions and mobility	
Laws and norms favorable to drug use	
Perceived availability of drugs	
Extreme economic deprivation	
School	
Academic failure	Opportunity for prosocial school involvement
Low commitment to school	Rewards for prosocial school involvement
Family	
Poor family management	Opportunities for prosocial family involvement
High family conflict	Rewards for prosocial family involvement
Family history of antisocial behavior	Family attachment
Parental attitudes favorable to drug use	
Parental attitudes favorable to anti-social behavior	
Individual/Peer	
Rebelliousness	Religiosity
Early initiation of antisocial behavior	Belief in the moral order
Attitudes favorable to drug use	Social skills
Attitudes favorable to antisocial behavior	Prosocial peer attachment
Peer drug use	Resilient temperament
Peer antisocial behavior	Sociability
Peer rewards for antisocial behavior	
Sensation seeking	
Impulsiveness	
Peer rejection	

Source: Arthur, M. W., Hawkins, J. D., Aollard, J. A., Catalano, R. F., & Baglioni, A. J. (2002). Measuring risk and protective factors for substance abuse, delinquency, and other adolescent problem behaviors: The Communities that Care Youth Survey. *Evaluation Review, 26,* 575–601. Copyright © 2002 by Sage Publications. Adapted by permission of Sage Publications.

▼
▼
▼

For example, the phenotype at the neonatal, infancy phase related to later substance abuse is difficult temperament, at infancy or early childhood it is insecure attachment, in childhood it is externalizing behavior, and in adolescence it is substance abuse. Four factors related to these phenotypes and developmental pathways were chosen for further study in prevention projects with four age groups—3–5, 6–8, 9–11, and 12–14—funded by CSAP studies. The factors were social competence, school bonding and achievement, self regulation and parental involvement. These were found to be protective factors in reducing the risk of substance use and misuse.

Another developmental theory, which has gained much empirical support, is the Social Development Model (SDM), which is based on social control theory, social learning theory, and differential association theory (Corrigan et al., 2007; Herrenkohl et al., 2000; Huang et al., 2001). SDM stages are based on social or external stimuli. Corrigan and colleagues indicated that,

> different socializing units are more salient at different points in a child's life. . . . The family unit exerts the most influence in socializing preschool children. As they move into elementary school, teachers and peers begin to have an impact on a child's socialization. In middle school, the peer group plays an ever increasing part, and in high school, a more complex mixture of both individual people and society as a whole, in the form of role expectations and mores, interact in the socializing process. (p. 22)

With a consistent socializing process, bonding occurs with the socializing unit. However, involvement must precede bonding and involvement consists of four constructs.

1. Perceived opportunity for involvement in activities and interactions with others.
2. The degree of interaction and involvement is important. Attendance does not automatically lead to performance.
3. A child must possess, or be taught, the skills needed to participate in involvement and interactions.
4. Behavior must be reinforced with a meaningful reward to be maintained.

(Corrigan et al., 2007, p. 23)

According to SDM theory, risk factors are those that block the opportunity for involvement and interaction, while protective factors are those that enhance these processes (see Table 12.1).

Models and Principles

With knowledge of applicable developmental theories and understanding of risk and protective factors, one can review types of prevention programs and principles of prevention that have proved, through a preponderance of literature, to have various degrees of effectiveness in preventing licit and illicit substance abuse. Because of methodological issues, such as those mentioned earlier, findings are sometimes inconsistent. It seems that research focused on information dissemination interventions (with or without fear appeals as to what will happen to you if you use drugs) do not change tobacco, alcohol, or other drug abuse behavior or intentions to use substances in the future. This also seemed true when self esteem building or better decision making were added (Botvin & Botvin, 1992; Botvin & Griffin, 2007; Skiba, Monroe, & Wodarski, 2004). Botvin and Grifffin indicated that contemporary approaches derived from psychosocial theories and focused on risk and protective factors that promote the initiation or avoidance of drug use in the early stages of substance abuse have been more effective (see, for example, Hawkins, Catalano, & Miller, 1992).

Resistance-Skills Training

Contemporary prevention programs focus on teaching drug-refusal skills (resistance-skills training), correcting normative expectations regarding the prevalence of substance use, and enhancing general social and personal competence skills. Social influences may come from peers, parents, or older siblings (for example, through modeling and other messages), or mass media (for example, through high status role models). Prevention programs that focus on social resistance-skills training teach students how to identify social situations in which they are likely to experience peer pressure to smoke, drink, or use drugs and how to avoid these high risk situations. "Students are taught what to say (i.e., the specific content of a refusal message) and how to say it in the most effective way" (Botvin & Griffin, 2007, p. 610). Examples of well-known early resistance-skills training programs that showed at least short-term effectiveness in reducing smoking, marijuana, and alcohol use include Adolescent Learning Experiences in Resistance Training (Project ALERT) (Ellickson, Bell, & McGuigan, 1993; Ellickson, McCaffrey, Ghosh-Dastidar, & Longshire, 2003), Self Management and Resistance Training (Project SMART) (Graham et al., 1990), and the Midwest Prevention Project (Rohrbach, Hodgson, Booker, & Montgomery, 1994). Botvin and Griffin's review found significant effects in reducing the initiation of smoking, alcohol, and marijuana use and that these effects are evident for up to three years in reduction of cigarette smoking. Many of these programs include material to combat the perception that substance abuse is widespread among peers and adults. This normative component needs more evidence-based exploration.

Soole, Mazzerole, and Rombouts' (2008) review distinguished between the resistance training (what to say and how) and social influence (increase awareness of social influence to smoke, drink, and use drugs; increase knowledge of immediate negative consequence). Using the resistance-skills training portion of this approach, they found significant results in the more rigorous studies in initiation of drug abuse. Girls benefited more than boys, with an indicated immediate preventive result in reducing marijuana initiation rates among baseline non-users. They did not find evidence of the effectiveness of the social influence component, which includes the DARE family of substance abuse prevention programs. It should be emphasized that their review focused on illicit drugs, rather than alcohol or tobacco smoking.

Competence Enhancement

Another important program type or component is competence enhancement, also called Life-Skills Training (LST). Young people without the skills and abilities to achieve developmental goals such as peer approval and positive self-image may be more likely to engage in substance abuse. Those with poor social and personal competence skills may be more vulnerable to social, environmental, and motivational forces that promote substance abuse. Thus, "competence enhancement prevention approaches teach generic social and personal skills such as decision-making skills, interpersonal communication skills, assertiveness, and skills for anxiety and anger management" (Botvin & Griffin, 2007, p. 611). Previous meta-analytic studies have found that prevention programs that combine social resistance skills and competency enhancement approaches are among the most effective (see, for example, Tobler & Stratton, 1997). In the review by Soole et al. (2008), in regard to competency enhancement, focusing on illicit drugs, the more rigorous studies, as well as less rigorous studies, found mixed results. In the former, two-thirds had nonsignificant results, whereas one-third found reductions or slower growth in illicit drug use as a result of prevention programs. In the less rigorous studies, half found significant reductions in marijuana use.

The prevention model called LST has been one of the most researched, and one of the most controversial programs. LST emphasizes the teaching of generic, personal and social skills, norm setting, and drug resistance skills (Mackillop, Ryabchenko, & Lisman, 2006). It increases adolescent knowledge about substance use, correcting cognitive misperceptions that contribute to substance use, and provides coping skills to reduce the need or likelihood of using drugs to manage stress and anxiety. Through a series of studies by Botvin and colleagues, mentioned in an article by Botvin, Griffin, Paul, and McCauley (2003), the LST approach was found to be effective in preventing cigarette smoking (Botvin & Eng, 1982: Botvin, Resnick, & Baker, 1983); alcohol use (Botvin, Schinke, et al., 1995); marijuana use (Botvin, Baker, et al., 1995; Botvin et al., 1990) and polydrug use (Botvin, Baker, et al., 1995; Botvin et al., 1997). The results of a large scale randomized trial found that prevention effects were evident more than six years later (Botvin et al., 2000).

Recent studies involving LST have had mixed results. Seal (2006) studied a total of 170 Thai students in grades 7 through 12 who were randomly selected.

> Post test results indicated that the LST program used with the intervention group had a positive impact on the group's knowledge level, attitudes, life skills, and frequency of tobacco and drug use. In addition, the students in the intervention group had significantly higher mean test scores for health consequences knowledge ($p < 0.01$). Furthermore, the results revealed that the mean scores for the life skills, such as refusal, decision making and problem solving, of the students in the intervention group were significantly higher at post test than those of the control group. The students in the intervention group were less likely to use tobacco and drugs at post-test compared with those in the control group. (pp. 165–166)

Smith et al. (2004) evaluated LST and I-LST (Infused-Life Skills Training) in a rural setting. They indicated that "most often the LST curriculum is taught by one or two teachers within the framework of a single course" (p. 55). However, during infused LST training a matrix of LST principles was mapped onto the curricular content areas of the participating teachers in their usual subject areas. "For example, a normative belief clarification lesson might be infused into a math lesson by graphing the percentage of U.S. students that do not use marijuana" (p. 56).

Nine small, rural districts were randomly assigned to LST, I-LST, or control conditions in grade 7. At the end of the first year of programming the treatment demonstrated no significant impact on the boys. However, for the girls, the LST program and I-LST program significantly reduced alcohol use, binge drinking, and marijuana use, and the former also reduced inhalant use. By the end of year two, the boys remained unaffected by the program and all effects were lost for LST girls and for I-LST girls; the only effect remaining was lower use of cigarettes compared

▼
▼
▼

with the control group girls. The authors indicated that because parental permission was needed, the highest risk students may not have participated in the study. The study could not account for school effects.

Because LST is a prevention program, a reanalysis was done excluding time 1 users (from time one above). Although there was still no effect on boys, the effects on girls at the end of the second year indicated a positive LST effect on smoking and a positive I-LST effect on smoking, drunkenness, and marijuana use. Different gender effects were consistence with earlier studies (Blake, Amaro, Scwartz, & Flinchbaugh, 2001). Were differences, compared with previous studies, attributable to this being a rural area, a bias in sampling, school effects, the problems of self-reporting, or in the program itself? Most of the studies of LST were done by the same research group. Therefore, it seems more large-scale randomized studies of this promising program, using rigorous research designs, are needed to show its effects with different populations.

Characteristics of Effective Programs

Through accumulation of research findings, characteristics of effective programs have been developed by SAMHSA (2003). As cited by MacMaster and colleagues (2005), these include

1. Program content addressing life skills or knowledge and skills related to substances (noting that substance related content alone is inadequate).
2. Opportunities to practice/use new knowledge.
3. Community building beyond individual-level change.
4. Structured curricula with clear and easy directions.
5. Consistent messages sent through multiple channels.
6. Emphasis on relationship as a precursor to the delivery of program content.
7. Utilization of naturally occurring social networks and parental and social system involvement wherever possible.
8. Emphasis on integrating programs into clients' real lives.
9. Strength focus and assets rather than deficit modeling.
10. Continuity through high fidelity to the program, dosage adequacy and consistency. (p. 97)

As indicated previously, MacMaster et al. (2005) support the notion that instead of information provision, recent research supports the efficacy of a combination of life skills and resistance training interventions. Other principles mentioned above, and the risk and resilience factors previously discussed, need further investigation.

Peer Influence

Several studies have tried to increase the effects on drug use of positive peer influence. Soole et al. (2008) found that peer involvement in the delivery of a program seemed to strengthen the positive effect of the program, although these findings did not reach statistical significance. In contrast, Valente et al. (2007) found that peer leaders have been used extensively in tobacco and substance abuse prevention programs and that previous studies and meta-analyses had shown "peer led programs have been more effective in reducing substance abuse than programs lacking a peer component" (p. 1805). In their 2007 study, students were asked to nominate their classmates who would make good leaders. "Peer leaders were taught how to facilitate group discussion, how to manage group interaction, and were encouraged to embrace anti-substance use norms" (p. 1807). Five hundred forty-one students in 75 classes from 14 alternative high schools were divided into three groups: (1) Towards No Drug Abuse, (TND), which includes motivation skills and decision making; (2) TND network, which in addition to the program TND, encourages small group discussions in groups created from naturally occurring friendships and led by a student leader; and (3) the control group.

Although receiving TND was not associated with changes in substance use, receiving TND network (with peer leaders) was associated with decreased marijuana and cocaine use and decreased composite use (different drugs) compared with the control group. However, if a student received the network (peer-led curriculum) and had friends in the class who reported using substances, he or she was likely to increase his or her substance-abusing behaviors over the one-year interval. Thus, the network curriculum appeared to achieve its goal of increasing peer influence, however, peer influence in the context of an alternative high school was potentially negative for adolescents with drug-using friends. It seems peer influence can have positive or negative effects and the characteristics of the sample should be considered in whether or not to use it.

Family Factors in the Microsystem

Within the microsystem, addressing family factors in prevention is also crucial. Several key programs are presented as examples.

Strengthening Families Program for Parents and Youth (10–14)

In accord with the model of risk and protective factors presented earlier, working with the family in adolescent substance abuse prevention seems appropriate.

▼
▼
▼

The Strengthening Families Program for Parents and Youth 10–14 (SFP 10–14) is a program that is on the list of model programs of SAMHSA (2008). As described by Molgaard, Spoth, & Redmond (2000), it is a seven-week curriculum designed to bring parents together with their 10- to 14-year-old children, with the goal of reducing substance abuse and other problem behaviors in youth. The SFP 10–14 consists of seven sessions plus four booster sessions. Parents and youths attend separate skill-building sessions for the first hour and spend the second hour together in supervised family activities. In the family sessions that follow, youths and parents practice problem solving as a family for situations when rules are broken (see Table 12.2).

TABLE 12.2: Session Topics, Strengthening Families Program

Primary Sessions	Booster Sessions
Parent	
Using Love and Limits	Handling Stress
Making House Rules	Communicating When You Don't Agree
Encouraging Good Behavior	Reviewing Love and Limit Skills
Using Consequences	Reviewing How to Help with Peer Pressure
Building Bridges	
Protecting Against Substance Abuse	
Getting Help for Special Family Needs	
Youth	
Having Goals and Dreams	Handling Conflict
Appreciating Parents	Making Good Friends
Dealing With Stress	Getting the Message Across
Following Rules	Practicing Our Skills
Handling Peer Pressure I	
Handling Peer Pressure II	
Reaching Out to Others	
Family	
Supporting Goals and Dreams	Understanding Each Other
Appreciating Family Members	Listening to Each Other
Using Family Meetings	Understanding Family Roles
Understanding Family Values	Using Family Strengths
Building Family Communication	
Reaching Goals	
Putting It All Together and Graduation	

Source: Adapted from Molgaard, V. K., Spoth, R. L., & Redmond, C. (2000). Competency training: The Strengthening Families Program: For Parents and Youth 10–14 (OJJDP Juvenile Justice Bulletin 182208, p. 5). Washington, DC: U.S. Department of Justice, Office of Juvenile Justice and Delinquency Prevention.

Iowa Strengthening Families Groups

Molgaard et al. (2000), using a total of 162 families in 21 Iowa Strengthening Families (ISFP) groups at 11 different schools, in a longitudinal controlled study, demonstrated positive results for both parents and youths. Comparisons between the intervention and control groups showed significantly improved parenting behaviors. These behaviors were associated with general child management and parent–child affectivity. Significant intervention control differences were found in substance abuse, conduct problems, school-related problem behaviors, peer resistance, and affiliation with antisocial peers. At 1½ years follow-up, "there was a 60-percent reduction in the first time use of alcohol without parental permission in the intervention group" (p. 5). At four years postbaseline, as compared with youths in the control group, those in the ISFP group showed delayed initiation of alcohol, tobacco, and marijuana use and lower frequency of alcohol and tobacco use, as well as lower levels of overt and covert aggressive behaviors and hostility in interactions with parents (Spoth, Redmond, & Shin, 2000, 2001).

LST Combined with the SFP

A recent trend in the literature is to combine LST with the SFP. Spoth, Randall, Shin, and Redmond (2005) studied seventh graders enrolled in 36 rural schools in 22 contiguous counties in a midwestern state. "Schools were randomly assigned to the classroom-based LST + SFP 10-14, (received both approaches), the LST only, or a minimal contact control condition entailing leaflets on teen development" (p. 373). Students were administered the Substance Abuse Initiation Index (SII) consisting of three items: (1) Have you ever had a drink of alcohol? (2) Have you ever smoked a cigarette? and (3) Have you ever smoked marijuana (grass, pot) or hashish (hash)? Increased scores over time on the SII for the LST + SFP 10-14 condition were significantly lower than those for both the control group and the LST-only group. Furthermore, at the 2.5 years past baseline data collection point, the difference in the SII scores between the LST + SFP 10-14 and control groups approached significance $[t(1, 4049) = 1.57, p = .06]$. A significant difference in rate between the LST-only condition and the control group was not found for this variable.

There were no statistically significant intervention effects found for regular alcohol use, although the LST + SFP 10-14 group increased at a slower rate than the control group $[t(1, 65) = 1.35, p < .10]$. Mean score for weekly drunkenness for the LST + SFP 10-14 condition was found to be statistically different from the control condition at the follow-up assessment 2.5 years past baseline $[t(1, 65) = 1.87, p = .03]$. The LST alone adjusted mean score was also lower than that for controls

[$t(1, 65) = 1.44$, $p = .08$]. The observed rate of growth in weekly drunkenness was lower than in the control conditions for both intervention conditions [$t(1, 65) = 1.51$, $p = .07$] for LST only; [$t(1, 65) = 1.38$, $p = .09$] for LST + SFP 10-14. Although these findings are promising, Gorman et al. (2007) have pointed to the fragility of the SFP and LST combined findings, suggesting that further large-scale randomized surveys are necessary.

Mentoring and Family Strengthening Initiative

Wang, Matthew, Bellamy, and James (2005) reported on data from the 2002–2003 Mentoring and Family Strengthening Initiative funded by CSAP of SAMHSA. Ethnic minority adolescents ($N = 790$) ages 11 to 16 were included in seven project sites nationwide. Beginning from an ecological system perspective on human development, a conceptual model was developed. This model specified "a series of links among family protective factors, associated with an adolescent's self control, school connectedness, and engagement in substance use behavior" (p. 532). Following Kumpfer, Alvarado, and Woodside (2003), "it was hypothesized that a high level of family protective factors would be associated with a high level of self control and school connectiveness" (p. 531). Structural equation modeling was used to test the most effective model and pathways for explaining problem behaviors. Measures were developed for social support, family involvement, family supervision, self control, school connectedness, and substance abuse. Figure 12.1 shows the hypothesized pathways between variables and standardized path coefficients.

All three exogenous variables (family involvement, social support, and family supervision) showed a positive relationship with the self-control latent variable. However, only family involvement was significant. Self-control and social support were significantly related to school connectiveness and decreased school substance abuse. The most supported pathway to decreased substance abuse was family involvement→self control→school connectedness→substance abuse. Wang et al. (2005) indicated that "the theory appears to suggest that family protective factors effect children's substance use through cognitive behavioral changes, implying there is no direct link between family protective factors and substance abuse" (p. 540).

Cultural Competence and Family Intervention

Culture is an important aspect of the mesosystem. According to Kirst-Ashman (2008) it is

> a way of life including widespread values and behavior. It involves the sum total of life patterns passed on from generation to generation within a

Figure 12.1. SEM Model of Substance Use Pathways for Minority Adolescents (N = 790)

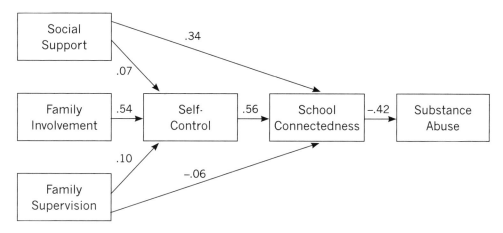

Note: SEM = structural equation model. The numbers are standardized path coefficients.
Source: Wang, M. Q., Matthew, R., Bellamy, N., & James, S. (2005). A structural model of the substance use pathways among minority youth. *American Journal of Health and Behavior, 29,* 531–541. Adapted with permission of the American Academy of Health Behavior.

group of people and includes institutions, language, religious ideals, habits of thinking, artistic expressions, and patterns of social and interpersonal relationships. Aspects of culture are often related to people's ethnic, racial and spiritual heritage. (p. 36)

Culture affects people's ways of thinking about and attitudes toward drugs. Cultural competence, defined earlier as "the set of knowledge and skills that a social worker must develop in order to be effective with multi-cultural clients" (Kirst-Ashman, 2008, p. 37), is a crucial component of effective substance abuse prevention programs. Substance abuse prevention often plays a major role in family interventions. Families are an important source of cultural beliefs, practices, and heritage, although sometimes different rates of acculturation in the United States between parents and adolescents can lead to problem behaviors. Therefore, managing this transaction between factors in the family and culture that affect substance use is crucial to prevention programs.

Familias Unidas with Hispanic Adolescents

In the beginning of this chapter, the difficulty of Hispanic immigrant parents with limited English proficiency arriving in the United States, and their daunting task of raising children in an unfamiliar and foreign culture, was developed. The numerous obstacles that place their children at risk of substance abuse such as cultural incompatibility between the receiving culture and culture of origin, social isolation, and marginalization were also mentioned. To address this issue, cultural competence is demonstrated by Familias Unidas with Hispanic adolescents. It has also completed some of the best work in conceptualizing the relationship between family-centered intervention and adolescent problem behaviors, particularly substance abuse (Coatsworth, Pantin, & Szapocznik, 2002; Prado et al., 2008; Tapia et al., 2006).

Familias Unidas maintains a strong family focus and is a multiple-level intervention that operates with and between various systems in the family's relationship to the social environment. This is important because of parents' expectations for respect and conformity among their children, their need to monitor adolescent behavior, and potential differences in acculturation between parents and adolescents. Using ecodevelopmental theory (Tapia et al., 2006), the exosystem refers to experiences that directly involve the parent, but not the adolescent. These may have an indirect influence on adolescent behavior (for example, family work stress). The mesosystem is composed of interactions between or among important members of different contexts in which the adolescent participates directly. For example, increasing parental involvement in the adolescent's school world protects adolescents against school disinterest and dropout and, consequently, against substance abuse and other problem behaviors. The innermost layer is the microsystem in which the child is a direct participant (for example, family, peers, school).

Coatsworth et al.'s (2002) model for prevention shows intervention goals and activities for each system level. In the exosystem, goals involve building a parental support network with subgoals of building social support, changing parental beliefs and attitudes, and building parenting skills. Activities involve group participatory learning or discussion and parent role plays. In the mesosystem, goals in the parental school realm include expanding parental beliefs about importance of involvement and increasing parental involvement in school. Activities are parent–teacher–counselor meetings. In the parent–peer realm, goals are to increase parental involvement and monitoring of peers and building relationships with peer's parents. Activities are supervised peer activities.

In the microsystem, realms of family, school, and peers are included. In the family, goals are to build family cohesion, structure, and beliefs, to have appropriate use of parental control strategies, strengthen the parent–adolescent bond, and build parental efficacy. Activities are home visits focusing on cohesion, structure, beliefs, and conflict. In the school, goals are to improve achievement and school community building. Activities include adolescent activity groups and tutoring.

For peers, goals are enhanced social competence and positive peer relationships, while activities include adolescent activity groups and supervised peer activities. The desired effects on individual adolescent development are to promote social competence, self-regulation and control, prosocial behavior, academic achievement, school bonding, and preventing substance use and problem behaviors.

Familias Unidas + PATH

In a randomized control study of 266 eighth-grade Hispanic adolescents (Prado, Pantin, & Briones, 2007), Familias Unidas + PATH (a parent–preadolescent training for HIV prevention) were superior to two control conditions in preventing and reducing cigarette use, reducing illegal drug use, and reducing sexual behavior. The findings affirmed the importance of family functioning in the prevention of substance abuse. Positive parenting and parent–adolescent communication were associated with significant difference favoring the Familias Unidas + PATH group in slowing the growth trajectory of smoking. Positive parenting was associated with significant difference favoring the Familias Unidas + PATH group in slowing the growth trajectory of illicit drug use.

Mexican American Female Adolescents

In a study by Valdez, Mikow, and Cepeda (2006), the role of family was investigated in a cross-sectional study of 150 Mexican American gang-affiliated female adolescents. The authors indicated that "substance abuse is often part of a constellation of behaviors that are precursors to more serious problems as young adults" (p. 32). It seems the substance abuse gender gap has been closing, resulting in female adolescents becoming more involved in risk taking and other deleterious behaviors. Valdez et al. indicated that "the Hispanic concept of family is rooted in loyalty, emotional closeness and interdependence that functions not only in the immediate family, but extends to kinship networks" (p. 34). They follow Alva and Jones (1994) in identifying personal stress as having a negative impact on adolescent identity formation, school performance, and prosocial behavior. In this sample of economically disadvantaged Mexican American gang-affiliated female adolescents involved in a cluster of problematic behaviors, including violence, delinquency, sex, teenage pregnancy, school dropout, and drug use, findings indicated that positive family relationships, and, in particular, the mother–daughter relationship, are protective factors for alcohol and tobacco use. "In the last year from the time of interview, alcohol and tobacco use decreased as the socio-emotional support of the mother increased" (p. 44). Findings regarding illicit drug-use indicated that as the number of family acculturation stress events increased, the use of marijuana, cocaine, and benzodiazepines increased in the last year. In contrast, as the number of the family's problem solving and behavioral strategies for managing difficult situations increased, marijuana, cocaine, and benzodiazephine use decreased.

African American High School Students

A study of "Substance Use and Academic Performance among African American High School Students" by Williams et al. (2007) supported the influence of family factors. In the sample of African youths attending an urban high school in middle America, the results indicated that marijuana use, parental substance use norms, and family financial concerns were all associated with students' academic intentions. "Grade point average was associated with both marijuana abuse and parental substance abuse norms" (p. 151). The findings were also consistent with earlier studies showing that African American students consistently had lower rates of marijuana and alcohol abuse (Johnston, O'Malley, & Backman, 2000). These findings support previous findings that among African American families, parental norms regarding drinking and parenting styles are significant predictors of adolescent problem behaviors (Peterson, Hawkins, Abbott, & Catalano, 1995).

Other Cultural Issues

Keepin' it REAL

Keepin' it REAL is a school-based adolescent substance intervention program that was designed to test the effectiveness of culturally grounded prevention messages and the importance of their match to the ethnicity of program participants. The intervention was developed within a narrative and performance framework to enhance cultural identification, to promote personal anti-drug norms and behaviors and to develop decision making and resistance skills. (Kulis & Marsiglia, 2004, p. 3)

It focuses on five key elements of adolescent life—communication competence, narrative knowledge, motivating norms, social learning, and learned resistance skills. "All components teach cognitive skills, appropriate behaviors, and communication competencies for successful use of four 'REAL' resistance strategies: refuse, explain, avoid and leave" (Kulis & Marsiglia, 2004, p. 4). An important component of keepin' it REAL was to develop different strategies from the specific values of a targeted cultural group. Two culturally grounded versions were created: a Latino version, primarily reflecting Mexican American and Mexican values; and the non-Latino version, grounded in European and African American values (African Americans were less than 5 percent of the sample). A third multicultural version was created by taking half the lessons from the Latino version and half the lessons from the non-Latino version. Self-report data were obtained from 3,402 Mexican-heritage students at baseline and 14 months after completing the curriculum. They were enrolled in 35 Phoenix, Arizona, middle schools.

Although all groups reported increases in substance abuse, compared with control group students, students in the Latino version reported smaller increases in overall substance abuse and recent marijuana use as well as stronger intentions to refuse substance offers, greater confidence in their ability to do so, and smaller estimates of peer substance abuse. Students in the multicultural version reported significantly less alcohol, marijuana and overall substance use. There were no significant program effects for students in the non-Latino version (Kulis & Marsiglia, 2004).

The findings supported the matching of culturally grounded programs to ethnic groups. However, because the differences between the Latino group and the multicultural group were not significant, the question remains whether strict cultural matching is needed or just incorporating cultural elements in the program. Further reporting, with operational specificity, will be helpful to this initiative, and it should be indicated that no version decreased substance abuse, but rather slowed its growth.

Theories of Cultural-Level Influence

There are many theories of cultural-level influence on substance use and misuse (Johnson, 2007). These influences involve many different dimensions of culture. Hofstede (2001) suggested that masculine versus feminine orientations identify the degree of assertiveness in a society. Triandis (1995) indicated in individualistic cultures, people are independent actors who emphasize personal interests. In contrast, people in collectivist cultures emphasize their membership and duties to well defined groups. Gudykunst and Kim (1997) indicated that cultures high in uncertainty avoidance typically value consensus and have more formal rules and less tolerance for deviant people and groups. Schwartz (1992) proposed a set of 10 universal value dimensions: power, achievement, hedonism, stimulation, self-direction, universalism, tolerance, benevolence, tradition, and security.

▼
▼
▼

Triandis (1996) has described cultural tightness as being the degree to which norms are strictly enforced and violations are punished, and cultural complexity as the varying number of elements that constitute or define any given cultural group. Siegel (2001) has shown how varying cultures have varying time perspectives, often related to their environs of origin, conceptions of space, relationship to the economy, history, and experience of oppression.

An ongoing issue for the field is how these various cultural dimensions relate to substance use and therefore how to incorporate their principles in prevention programs. Triandis (1995) suggested that substance misuse may be lower in collectivist cultures where people have stronger emotional bonds to each other. Sue (1987) interpreted lower alcohol rates among Asians to be a consequence of collectivist social values. This also may be related to a different physiological response to alcohol among Asians [see chapter 4 for more detailed information]. More anxiety-prone and stressful cultures may have higher rates of substance abuse. This author believes the experience of oppression affects one's experience of time and place and perhaps should be dealt with directly in prevention programs. Phase-based prevention may not work in cultures with a circular or open conception of time and space, such as Native Americans or some Asian or African cultures (Siegel, 2001). Therefore, the cultural arena deserves more attention as sources of principles of prevention.

Neighborhood and Community Focus

As part of the mesosystem and a source of risk and protective factors, it would seem that the neighborhood would be an important factor in prevention programs. In the model mapped by Arthur and colleagues (2002) (see Table 12.1), the neighborhood could be the source of risk factors such as low neighborhood attachment and community disorganization. Protective factors would include prosocial community involvement coupled with rewards for prosocial community involvement. In a discussion of the relative influence of neighborhood, family, and youths on adolescent drug abuse, Wright, Bobashev, and Folsom (2007) used the 1999 National Household Survey on Substance Abuse, which includes approximately 25,000 youths ages 12 to 17. They concluded 6 percent of the variance in whether kids use drugs was due to the neighborhood, compared with 79 percent as function of the youths only and 15 percent due to the household. However, others believe conceptions of the neighborhood in substance abuse studies have been quite limited, focusing on drug- and crime-related issues, and do not include complete understanding of neighborhood ties, functions, and institutions (Siegel, Green, Abbott, & Mogul, 2007).

The Role of Coalitions

Flewelling et al. (2005) indicated that "despite the popularity and perceived potential effectiveness of community-based coalitions in helping to prevent and reduce adolescent substance abuse, empirical evidence supporting this approach is sparse" (p. 333). Collins, Johnson, and Becker (2007) indicate the literature on coalitions, in general, has produced mixed findings in terms of their effectiveness.

Kentucky Incentives for Prevention

Collins and colleagues (2007) report on 20 coalitions that received the Kentucky Incentives for Prevention program (KIP) to implement comprehensive youth substance abuse prevention strategies aimed at reducing the use of alcohol, tobacco, and other drugs among 12- to 17-year-olds. Of the 19 coalitions that developed and implemented comprehensive coalitions between 1999 and 2002, 12 served a single county, six encompassed multiple counties, and one targeted youth in selected public schools within a large urban school district.

"Intervention activities of community coalitions receiving KIP funding included coalition development, comprehensive planning, implementation of school-based prevention interventions, and participation in training/technical guidance" (Collins et al., 2007, p. 987). Coalition activities fell into several broad categories such as formalizing, energizing, and notifying.

> Comprehensive planning activities were grouped into several types as well. These included: a) needs and resource assessment; b) development of goals and measurable objectives; c) planning and implementation of evidenced prevention interventions; d) development of intervention and evaluation plans; e) resource development and allocation; and f) development of sustainability plans for science based interventions. (p. 987)

Each coalition implemented one to four scientific–based interventions. They included universal school-based preventions, universal family-based prevention activities by one community, and universal environmental interventions by seven coalitions. One hundred ten pairs of schools were studied. In the eighth grade, 63 KIP schools were matched with 38 non-KIP schools. In the 10th grade, 47 KIP schools were match with 27 non-KIP schools. Short-term results (using eighth-grade data) showed no significant decreases in prevalence of substance abuse outcomes and, in fact, a significant small increase in one substance (inhalants). Sustained results (using 10th-grade data) showed significant, though small, decreases

▼
▼
▼

in three of six substance abuse outcomes: past month prevalence of cigarette use, alcohol use, and binge drinking. The short-term effects showed significant KIP effects in the desired direction on four of nine positive risk factors: school days skipped, neighborhood adults' attitudes favorable to drug use, perceived low risk of being caught for drug use, and perceived availability of drugs. In the sustained results only two of the positive risk and protective factors—friends' use of drugs, and perceived availability of drugs—were significantly related to KIP. This study indicates coalitions have potential in prevention, although the effects were not dramatic. Although community coalitions were used, only one neighborhood factor was studied, and this was directly related to drug attitudes.

Kids in Cooperation with Kids

Rollin, Rubin, and Wright (2000) used a consortium model to implement a community-based prevention consortium model called Kids in Cooperation with Kids (Project KIKK). Along with Project KIKK, the consortium consisted of the Boys and Girls Club; Department of Adult Education at Florida State University; Mothers in Crisis; Richards High School Share Service Clinic; Tallahasse Boys Choir; Tallahasse Police Department; Tallahasse Housing Foundation; Tallahasse Community College; Terrell House; Family Involvement and Community Development Team; and the Orange Avenue Tenants' Association. The Boys and Girls Club acted as the figurehead of the consortium and the mediator among all affiliated organizations. The authors indicated one of the problems of consortiums, "even in a cooperative situation, organizational leaders may have a tendency of defending their unique method of assisting individuals in the community. This may cause the leaders to put the needs of their particular organization before the needs of the youth and families" (p. 36). The KIKK curriculum is composed of nine units highly associated with the promotion of drug refusal skills and health-promotion activities. For evaluation, as of this writing, the following tools were used, the Smart Moves Drug Knowledge questionnaire (Boys and Girls Club, Inc., 1990); Social Skills Rating System-Student form, Students Attitudes About Conflict Revised, Piers-Harris Self-Concept Scale, which is a self-report of self-esteem for children; and the KIKK Questionnaire, which measures attitudes related to substance abuse, teenage pregnancy prevention, school attitudes, aggressive behavior, and stress reduction. As of yet, there was no formal procedure that follows up on drug consumption of participants that have successfully completed the program. There also seems to be a lack of motivation from youth to fully participate in the evaluation process. It would seem one expert evaluation team should be assigned to this task.

Neighborhood Components of Prevention

The neighborhood component of prevention appears broader than the idea of Community Coalitions and Consortiums or the testing of neighborhood attitudes about substances or violence. Vimpani (2005) indicated that "homeostasis can be threatened in middle childhood by dysfunctional crime-prone neighborhoods where low levels of collective supervision of young people is provided, increasing the likelihood of criminal behavior including substance misuse" (p. 114). Saleebey (2004), writing on the "power of place," indicated that "attention to the more immediate physical and social environment of our lives may give us an additional focus for understanding individuals and families and their behaviors and well being" (p. 9). Place attachment and the accompanying development of personal identity may be affected by fears concerning the environment, traffic, and crime (Spencer & Wooley, 2000). Community violence can have a strong influence on one's sense of belongingness and security (Errante, 1997; Spencer & Wooley, 2000).

Poverty itself may interfere with parental role models (Wilson, 1991). Steptoe and Feldman (2001) indicated that people in lower socioeconomic areas report more problems with the neighborhoods in which they live. They showed a positive relationship between a scale of neighborhood problems (litter in the street, smells and fumes, fear of walking around after dark, problems with dogs, noise from traffic or other homes, lack of entertainment, traffic and road safety, lack of places to shop, vandalism, disturbance by neighbors or youngsters, lack of social capital, poor health, and individual deprivation level. The scale was also related to psychological stress and inability to carry out the tasks of daily living.

From another perspective (Putnam, 1993; Sampson, 2004), neighborhoods are sources of social capital or the networks, norms, and trust that facilitate coordination and cooperation for mutual benefit. Neighborhoods bereft of social capital are less able to realize common values and maintain the social controls that foster safety. Wilson (1991) indicated that social capital is most effective when producing collective resources for social control. It is the characteristics of the network that may produce social bonding or social control.

Siegel, Green, Abbott, and Mogul (2007), in their study of leavers and returners to welfare, showed that the neighborhood conditions of those who returned to welfare were significantly different from the conditions of the neighborhoods of those who had left welfare and not returned, especially in use and sale of drugs and presence of guns. An alarming 71 percent of returners indicated the use or sale of drugs in the neighborhood, compared with a still high 51 percent of leavers, whereas 42 percent of returners reported the sale of guns in the neighborhood compared with 27 percent of leavers. Sixty-four percent of leavers and 61 percent of returners indicated the presence of unsupervised teenagers in the neighborhood. For returners particularly, the combination of availability of drugs, unsupervised teens in the neighborhood, and availability of guns in the neighborhood seemed potent. For both groups, there were strong relationships between neighborhood conditions and quality of life.

According to Fellin (2001), some of the issues important in mapping a neighborhood's strengths include the following: the number and types of places people gather for fun and good works; the number and locations of people who have skills that are being underused; the existence and location of businesses that play positive roles in the community; the numbers, types, and locations of community volunteers; the number and type of civic groups, clubs, and neighborhood organizations; and the number and types of people who are willing to exchange services with each other. Therefore, preventing substance use and misuse could surely involve building neighborhoods through development of neighborhood organizations for social ties and social relationships, economic development programs, and programs such as community policing.

Harm Reduction and Prevention

MacMaster and colleagues (2005) discussed how the process of change model has become an increasingly used perspective in substance abuse treatment. It suggests five stages that individuals must cycle through: precontemplation, contemplation, preparation, action, and maintenance (Prochaska, DiClemente, & Norcross, 1992). This model suggests that individuals, including adolescents, may not all be at the action stages and so some nonabstinence-based perspectives such as the harm reduction model may be important to substance misuse and abuse prevention. As summarized by MacMaster et al., the following five assumptions are common to harm reduction discussions.

1. Substance use has and will be part of our world: accepting this reality leads to a focus on reducing drug-related harm rather than reducing drug use itself.
2. Abstinence from substances is clearly effective at reducing substance related harm; however, it is only one of many possible objectives of services to substance users.
3. Substance use inherently causes harm, however, many of the most harmful consequences of substance use (HIV/AIDS, Hepatitis-C, overdoses,

automobile accidents) can be effectively eliminated without complete abstinence.

4. Services to substance users must be provided in a relevant "user friendly" manner if they are to be effective in helping people to minimize their substance-related harm.

5. Substance use must be understood from a broad perspective and not solely as an individual act; accepting this idea moves interventions away from the use of coercion of individuals and criminal justice solutions and towards a public health/social work perspective. (p. 98)

Alcohol Skills Training Program

It is beyond the scope of this chapter to review the large body of literature and theory supporting either abstinence, harm reduction, or some combination of the two as legitimate goals for substance abuse service (see, for example, Rotgers, Morgenstein, & Walters, 2007). MacMaster and colleagues (2005) suggested that progression through the stages of change model can continue for individuals who access nonabstinence-based treatment. Therefore, for purposes of broadening the framework for prevention-based services, MacMaster et al. reviewed studies showing that harm reduction strategies have decreased problems associated with alcohol use for college-aged drinkers. For example, they indicate the Alcohol Skills Training Program (ASTP), a six-week program for young adult drinkers, uses a cognitive–behavioral approach to the prevention of alcohol problems by stressing the moderate use of, or abstinence from, dependence-producing substances. The ASTP program, and its offshoot, the Brief Alcohol Screening and Intervention for College Students (BASICS), provides skill-based training around setting drinking limits, monitoring one's own drinking, rehearsing drink refusal, and practicing other useful behaviors through role play (Dimeff, Baer, Kivlahan, & Marlatt, 1998; Fromme, Marlatt, Baer, & Kivlahan, 1994). It is a nonconfrontational harm-reduction approach to help students reduce their alcohol consumption and decrease the behavioral and health risks associated with heavy drinking.

Participants in the BASICS program at the University of Washington reduced the amount of alcohol consumed each time they drank to a larger extent than a control group of other high-risk drinkers. Findings for program participants also showed that their alcohol- related problems (fighting, vandalism, driving under the influence [DUI], having blackouts, missing classes, and having unprotected sex) were also reduced to a larger extent when compared to a control group (Marlatt et al., 1998).

Motivational Interviewing

In another example of harm reduction, Monti et al. (1999) studied 18- and 19-year-old individuals with either a positive blood alcohol concentration or a report of alcohol use prior to trauma, who were admitted to a hospital emergency room. The 94 participants were assigned either to a control group of standard care or the experimental group (consisting of standard care plus motivational interviewing focused on empathy and developing goals to reduce alcohol-related harm). Results indicated that adolescents who were exposed to a harm reduction method (now called brief motivational interviewing) were significantly less likely to drink and drive and were significantly less likely to have alcohol-related injuries or problems than those adolescents in the standard care group.

Syringe Exchange

Of all interventions under the harm reduction rubric, syringe exchange has had the most notoriety. It has been deployed with increasing regularity within this country despite bans on federal funding. Syringe exchange attempts to remove the agent through which HIV/AIDS is spread (the shared syringe), without necessarily eliminating the drug use itself. There is increasing evidence this is effective at facilitating changes for injection drug users who are not seeking abstinence, in decreasing HIV rates, decreasing the sharing of injection equipment, increasing the prevalence of disinfection of equipment, and sometimes in serving as conduits for abstinence-based drug treatment programs (see, for example, Bluenthal, Kral, Errington, & Edlin, 1998; Des Jarlais et al., 1996; Hagan et al., 1993; Heimer, 1998).

College Student Prevention

Larimer, Kilmer, and Lee (2005) indicated that use of illicit drugs, as well as alcohol, is a large problem for college-age students. Over half of all college students and young adults have tried an illicit drug at least once in their lifetime. Substance abuse may provide students with the opportunity to facilitate the transition to college (for example, facilitating interpersonal relations or feelings of maturity, or helping to cope with new demands and expectations). Larimer et al. indicated that "often viewed as a rite of passage, drug experimentation is seen as normative by many students" (p. 432). Many will cease or reduce use once they leave college and take on full-time adult roles. West and Graham (2005) indicated that attention to the rates of substance abuse and misuse by college students is driven in part by the frequency and severity of negative consequences students incur while under the influence, including increased risk for being sick, injured in accidents, and victims of sexual assaults and other crimes. Larimer et al. indicated that while substance abuse prevention programs abound on college campuses, very few programs have been systematically evaluated using strong research designs.

Fund for Improvement of Post Secondary Education

The Fund for Improvement of Post Secondary Education (FIPSE) mentioned funding two studies related to improvement in the past 10 years. The first (Miller, Toscova, Miller, & Sanchez, 2001) used a multicomponent, campus-wide intervention to target five levels of intervention simultaneously (individual, small group, organization, community, and policy). Intervention components included extensive print media focusing on risk perception regarding alcohol and other drug use, DUI, and riding with impaired drivers; videotapes designed to encourage students to enroll in courses focusing on alcohol and other drug prevention; several campus-wide events such as alcohol and other drug awareness weeks; and distribution of referral information and availability of individual "drinker checkups." Results indicated that, in comparison with a control campus where drinking and drug use increased over time, use rates for several classes of illicit drugs and some high-risk drinking behaviors stabilized or underwent a modest decrease on the intervention campus. There were several limitations to the research design including lack of comparability between control and intervention campuses and difficulty in attributing differences in outcome to any particular intervention component.

In the second FIPSE study mentioned earlier, McCambridge and Strang (2004) used a cluster randomization design to evaluate a 60-minute motivational intervention regarding alcohol, tobacco, and other drug use with students recruited from ten further education colleges (similar to vocational or technical schools or community colleges in the United States) in London. Findings indicated that participants in the motivational intervention ($n - 105$) significantly reduced their marijuana, other drug, tobacco, and alcohol use at three-month follow-up relative to control participants. Findings were encouraging, although Larimer et al. (2005) indicated that again "the cluster randomization procedure failed to create equivalent groups at baseline on many variables of potential relevance to outcomes" (p. 437).

The National Advisory Council of the National Institute on Alcohol Abuse and Alcoholism (NIAAA), based on an extensive review of the literature including 24 commissioned papers (NIAAA, 2002a, 2002b), established a task force comprising researchers, college presidents, and students to develop prevention approaches and future research needs to address college drinking. Three tier 1 strategies (those found to have evidence of effectiveness with college populations) were recommended, although they differ mostly in degree of emphasis and time commitment: (1) combining cognitive behavioral skills with norms clarification and motivational enhancement interventions, (2) offering brief motivational enhancement interventions, and (3) challenging alcohol expectancies. The first two strategies typically combine individual feedback about alcohol use, expectations about alcohol, normative comparisons (how much do people use), risks, and consequences of use with specific therapeutic strategies (such as directive use of reflective listening techniques and a nonjudgmental therapeutic stance) to increase motivation to change behavior. The latter strategy relates to expected positive social, sexual, and mood-enhancing effects. These components are similar to many recommended for adolescent substance abusers. Again, methodological limitations need to be addressed to gain greater research rigor in further studies.

Web-based Personalized Feedback (WPF), Web-based Education (WE)

Recent research suggests that computer programs and the Web may be effective in providing normative feedback to students (see, for example, Walters, Miller, & Chiauzzi, 2005). Doumas and Haustveit (2008) addressed the gap in the literature evaluating personalized feedback, particularly Web-based, in regard to the intercollegiate athlete. The Web is now very popular for college students; whereas college students may be skeptical about discussing their drinking with a health practitioner, they are interested in how their drinking compares with the drinking of their peers. Intercollegiate athletes were recruited from the athletic department at an NCAA Division 1 University in the Northwest. Students were randomly assigned to either a WPF intervention (WPF) or a WE group. There was a final sample of 52 athletes with 28 (54 percent) in the WPF condition and 24 (46 percent) in the WE condition.

> Participants in the WPF condition completed a 15-minute web-based program designed to reduce high risk drinking by providing personalized feedback and normative data regarding drinking and the alcohol-related risks. The on-line assessment collects basic demographic information and information on alcohol consumption, drinking behavior, and alcohol related consequences. Personalized graphed feedback is provided immediately in the following domains: a pie chart depicting levels of drinking

in relation to national peer norms, a summary of the number of days the participant consumed alcohol and number of drinks consumed in the past year, approximate financial cost of drinking in the past year, calories associated with drinking, how quickly the body processes alcohol, risk status for negative consequences associated with drinking and risk status for problematic drinking based on the participant's *Alcohol Use Disorders Identification Test* (AUDIT) score. (p. 218)

For weekly drinking, peak alcohol consumption, and frequency of drinking to intoxication, high-risk student athletes in the WPF group reported they had reduced their drinking significantly more than those in the WE control group. Changes in beliefs about typical student drinking were positively related to reported reductions in weekly drinking, peak consumption, and drinking to intoxication from baseline to three-month assessment for the WPF group only. Findings provide initial support for the use of Web-based feedback programs in intercollegiate athletics, although this study was hampered by the small sample size.

HeadOn: Substance Abuse Prevention

Marsch, Bickel, and Badger (2006) developed a computer-based substance abuse prevention program for middle aged-adolescents called HeadOn: Substance Abuse Prevention for Grades 6–8.

Computer-based modules in the HeadOn program address: 1) various classes of drugs and their immediate and long term physiological and behavioral effects, 2) the risks of experimentation with drugs, 3) the potential consequences of drug use, 4) a cost–benefit reasoning strategy that youth can use to effectively responding to drug offers, 5) drug refusal skill training, 6) risks of misusing prescription drugs, 7) how to effectively understand and resist advertisements for licit drugs, 8) misconceptions many youth have in which they tend to overestimate the percentage of their peers who use drugs, 9) social skills training (e.g. effective communication skills), and 10) self management skills training. All modules are integrated via a cab driver narrator who takes the program user to various neighborhoods where they can access various program modules. (p. 73)

Participants in Marsch et al.'s (2006) study were students in four middle schools in the state of Vermont. Participants in two schools received training using a more traditional LST program. Students in the two other schools received the HeadOn computer-based training. In all, 272 adolescents participated, of which 113 completed the HeadOn computer-based intervention and 159 received the LST intervention. Differences were difficult to assess because the HeadOn group at baseline reported higher levels of substance use than did the LST group. The HeadOn group, however, generally achieved comparable or close to comparable outcomes on all outcome measures compared to the LST group. These outcomes included reduction in alcohol and cigarette use. The HeadOn group showed significantly greater reduction in those who thought a greater number of their peers used cigarettes, alcohol, and marijuana. Compared with baseline, participants in the HeadOn group showed marked decreases in their positive attitudes toward drugs. Although, again, this study was hampered by baseline differences between the two sample groups (HeadOn students had higher levels of use and risky behavior), it shows the potential for computer and Web-based cost-effective prevention programs.

Prevention among Older Adults

Prevention among older adults, particularly in regard to alcohol use and misuse, deserves special attention because of specific biopsychosocial dynamics, longer drinking histories, and varying effects of alcohol on older people. Although prevalence rates vary across studies, it seems clear that rates of alcohol abuse and dependence are lower in samples of older adults than younger ones. In the Blow et al. (2000) sample of 8,578 men and women ages 55 to 97 (mean age: 68.8) screened in primary care settings, 10.57 percent of men and 3.4 percent of women engaged in at-risk drinking (nine or more drinks per week for women, 12 or more drinks for men). Barrick and Connors (2002) indicated that even the best estimates are low because of "inadequacy of diagnostic criteria, fewer opportunities to observe adverse consequences in older adults, geographical location and cultural differences and a misinterpretation of abuse symptoms" (p. 585). These rates can be expected to increase because of broader acceptance of alcohol consumption among baby boomers born after World War II and greater acceptance of women's drinking.

Barrick and Connors (2002) indicated that a major distinguishing characteristic of older problem drinkers is whether they are in the late or early onset categories. Late onset drinkers are defined as older adults whose problems with drinking began in their 60s or following retirement. Late-onset drinking is associated with coping with a broad array of age-related changes and stressors (for example, retirement, changes in the marital relationship), as well as a better prognosis following treatment. Early-onset drinkers report a greater family history of alcohol abuse and more comorbid psychiatric disorders.

Wilson et al. (2007) indicated that "older adults may experience unfavorable health effects from alcohol consumption, even at relatively low levels, because of age-related physiological changes and because alcohol interacts detrimentally with common medical conditions, medications, and diminishing functional status" (p. 445). Epstein, Fischer-Elber, and Al-Otaiba (2007) indicated that "due to differences in metabolism, women of all ages compared to men are at higher risk for negative physical, medical, social, and psychological consequences associated with at risk and higher levels of alcohol consumption" (p. 33). Epstein et al. also indicated that

> aging women face new sets of antecedents related to challenges in the middle and older adult phases of life such as menopause, retirement, "empty nest," limited mobility and illness. As women age, they are subject to an even greater physiological susceptibility to alcohol's effect, as well as to a risk of synergistic effects of alcohol in combination with prescription drugs. On the other hand, there is mixed research indicating that older women may benefit from the buffering effects of low levels of alcohol on hormonal declines associated with menopause, perhaps serving as a protective factor against Coronary Heart Disease and osteoporosis. However with heavy drinking, these benefits are either reversed or eclipsed. In addition, any alcohol consumption increases the risk for breast cancer. (pp. 31–32)

In a sample of 92 older and 83 younger adults, Satre and Knight (2001) examined age and sex differences in expectancies and alcohol consumption. Older adults reported significantly lower mean expectancy levels for drinking alcohol than did the younger sample on sociability, courage, reduced negative affect, cognitive–behavioral impairment, and risk taking. When comparing drinkers with abstainers, abstainers scored significantly higher on measures of negative expectancies, including cognitive and behavioral impairment, negative self-concept, and risk taking. However, drinkers also scored higher on two positive expectancy subscales, courage, and enhanced sexuality. One significant difference was by gender, with men expecting more positive effects than women.

Satre and Knight (2001) indicated four possible explanations of lower levels of both positive and negative expectancies among older adults: (1) With the relatively lower quantities of alcohol consumed by the older sample, dramatic positive effects are unlikely, while negative effects are of minimal concern; (2) it is possible the items on the scale did not adequately capture older adults' concerns about alcohol (for example, falling, interactions with medications, long-term impact on health); (3) expectancies about alcohol are different in the initiation phase than once a pattern of drinking has been established. The cognitive component (of expectancies) may recede from consciousness, and the response of drinking may automatically follow antecedent stimuli. "The explicit evaluation of consequences may have ceased" (p. 80); and (4) there is a greater stigma associated with drinking expectations in older adults who won't admit as readily to drinking. Because working with expectations is an important component of alcohol abuse prevention and treatment, scales should be designed to gauge not only differences is use among the older adults, but also their expectations for alcohol, so that both factors can be addressed.

Prescription Drugs and Over-the-Counter Medication

Another large substance issue for older adults involves psychoactive prescription drugs and over-the-counter medications. According to the consensus panel for the treatment improvement protocol series (SAMHSA, 1998), a large share of prescriptions for older adults are for psychoactive, mood-changing drugs that carry the potential for misuse, abuse, or dependency. The drugs most used and misused include shorter-acting anxiolytic benzodiazepines such as alprazolam (Xanax) and lorazepam (Ativan). Benzodiazepine hypnotics used widely include triazolam (Halcion) and temazepam (Restoril). The drug-taking patterns of psychoactive prescription drug users can be described as a continuum that ranges from appropriate use for medical or psychiatric indications through misuse by the patient or the prescribing health care practitioner to persistent abuse and dependence (SAMHSA, 1998). Older adults are less likely to use psychoactive medications nontherapeutically, so problems with drugs generally fall into the misuse category and are unintentional. For example, they may misunderstand directions for appropriate use. This can progress into abuse if an older adult continues to use a medication nontherapeutically for the desirable effects it provides.

Unfortunately, both long- and short-acting benzodiazepines tend to result in psychological dependence, even when these medications are taken at therapeutic doses for as short as two months. Withdrawal symptoms are experienced by 40 percent to 80 percent of people who discontinue benzodiazepines after four to six months of regular use (SAMHSA, 1998).

The aging process, with its physiological changes, accumulating physical health problems, and other psychosocial stressors, makes prescription drug use more likely and more risky. Drug-drug and drug-alcohol interactions are of increased importance in older adults for several reasons. Older adults take more prescription drugs, so the potential for interactions is increased. An interaction is likely to be more problematic in older adults because of slowed metabolic and clearance mechanisms. The aging body is more susceptible to adverse interactions, thus the risk for drug interaction is increased for those for whom an adverse reaction would be most dangerous. Also, as with alcohol, an elderly person's expectations for prescription drugs and their interactions may relate to age-specific behaviors such as falls, long-term health effects, and relationship to chronic diseases.

Identification and Screening

According the literature (SAMHSA, 1998; Sorocco & Ferrell, 2006), the key to prevention for misuse and abuse of alcohol and other drugs for older adults is identification and screening. The majority of older adults see physicians regularly, so this provides an opportunity; but many older adults do not self-identify these issues, so physicians need to be updated on screening methods. Home health care providers also have unparalleled opportunities for screening. SAMHSA indicates the identification of substance abuse among older adults should not be the purview of health care workers alone, multitiered case finding methods in the community are crucial. This includes friends and family; staff of senior centers, including drivers and volunteers; leisure clubs; health fairs; congregate meal sites; Meals on Wheels; and senior day care programs. Barriers to screening may include ageist assumptions about behavior, bias against recognizing older people as having alcohol or other drug problems and complications caused by other problems with similar symptoms. Warning signs can easily be confused with, or masked by, other conditions.

There are effective, validated instruments available for screening older adults that may not be known to providers. The topic of screening can be introduced in a number of ways:

1. Self-administered and self-scored mass screenings can be part of a larger presentation at an American Association of Retired Persons or leisure club meeting on the topic of alcohol's effects on older adults.
2. Recently developed self-scored computerized screening tests can be used.
3. Visiting nurses and home health aides can integrate a brief screen into the list of health questions normally posed to patients.
4. Although it is preferable to use standardized screening questionnaires, friendly visitors, Meals-On-Wheels volunteers, caretakers, and health providers can also interject screening questions into their normal conversations with older adults.

Therefore, it seems training regarding screening is needed for multiple systems of people who regularly come into contact with older adults.

Screening Instruments for Older Adults

CAGE

Sorocco and Ferrell (2006) cite SAMHSA's consensus panel 26 (1998) which recommended both the CAGE (Cut down, Annoyed, Guilty, Eye opener) questionnaire (Ewing, 1984) and the Michigan Alcohol Screening Test-Geriatric version (MAST-G) (Blow et al., 1992) as useful instruments for this population. (The CAGE is described in greater detail in chapter 8.)

MAST-G and AUDIT

MAST-G is unique in that it was specifically developed for use with older adults. An advantage is that it includes the elder-specific consequences of drinking. Sorocco and Ferrell (2006) indicated "an example is item # 20: Have you ever increased your drinking after a loss in your life" (p. 458)? Because it is a 24 item test, which is too long for some settings, the Short Michigan Alcoholism Screening Test-Geriatric is also available. The Alcohol Use Disorders Identification Test (AUDIT) (Babor, de la Fuenta, Saunders, & Grant, 1992) is a 10-item test with significant support for use with younger populations. Sorocco and Ferrell indicated that because there has been strong cross-cultural research validating the AUDIT for use with various ethnic groups, the AUDIT is recommended for the screening of ethnic minority older adults (SAMHSA, 1998). Beause only a modest level of agreement has been found among these measures, it is helpful to use multiple measures. (See chapter 8 for greater detail about both the MAST and the AUDIT.)

Once an assessment is made, the health care provider reports his or her findings to the patient (Kaempf, O'Donnell, & Oslin, 1999), the caregivers, and significant others. The discussion should be empathic. Sorocco and Ferrell (2006) indicated that

> The care provider should first express his or her concern when a drinking problem has been identified. It is important for the caregiver to be specific about drinking problems and the health risks associated with drinking (or other substances). After stating this concern, the patient should be advised on an appropriate course of action. In cases of alcohol dependency, older adults should be advised to stop drinking and to provide a history of failed attempts to cut down, of any contraindicated medical condition, and of any medications they are currently taking that may lead to adverse reactions with alcohol. Such patients should be referred for additional evaluation and treatment. When making a referral, the patient should be involved in the referral decision and the discussion of treatment. If there is no evidence

of alcohol dependence, older adults who drink above the recommended level should be provided with educational materials and, at least, advised to cut down on their drinking. Care providers should provide specific limits, and ask the patient to set specific drinking goals. (p. 459)

Discussion of treatment is beyond the scope of this chapter. It should be mentioned that brief interventions are often effective with older adults. SAMHSA indicates nine suggested steps for conducting an elder-specific brief intervention: (1) individual feedback on screening measure outcomes; (2) discussion of types of drinkers and the patient's unique pattern; (3) possible reasons for drinking; (4) consequences of heavy drinking; (5) reasons to cut down or quit drinking; (6) sensible drinking limits and strategies for cutting down; (7) devising a drinking agreement; (8) discussing how to cope with risky situations; and (9) summary of session.

FRAMES Model

The FRAMES (Feedback, Responsibility, Advice, Menu, Empathy, and Self-efficacy) model developed by Miller and Rollnick (2002) provides useful feedback to the older adult from individual screening outcomes, places the responsibility to change drinking behavior on the client, and offers him or her specific drinking recommendations (advice) as well as a menu of options regarding ways to change drinking behaviors. Family interventions, motivational counseling, motivational counseling combined with naltrexone (medical treatment), and cognitive behavioral interventions have all been reported as effective in longer term treatment (Sorocco & Ferrel, 2006).

Summary

Much recent evidence-based research has occurred regarding development of substance abuse prevention programs since the disappointing findings reported in the 1990s. This has been accompanied by the development of many promising programs, models, and principles. This effort and expenditure seems justified by the dependence-producing nature of substances; effects on individuals, families, and neighborhoods; and relationships to crime and violence. However, the rigor of the numerous prevention studies varies greatly. The terms "scientific" or "evidence based," when applied to a program, are meant to inspire trust, and, therefore, should not be used lightly. This terminology carries with it some responsibility for the validity of the design of evaluation research. Therefore, programs must be justified by large-scale controlled studies in which control groups really are controls, matching the characteristics of experimental groups.

▼
▼
▼

The neighborhood component of prevention is often ignored in the studies of prevention programs or is covered by a question or two regarding neighborhood attitudes toward drugs and crime. Neighborhood factors may be more difficult to control than school or family factors. However, the power of place (Saleebey, 2004); the effect of neighborhoods on place attachment and personal identity (Spencer & Wooley, 2000); the need for neighborhood support, social capital, and bonding (Putnam, 1993, Sampson, 2004); the negative effects of lack of teenage supervision (Siegel et al., 2007; Wilson, 1991); and the neighborhood as a source of drug deals and crime (Siegel et al., 2007; Vimpani, 2005) support the position that improvements in the neighborhood are important components of prevention. Furthermore, poverty in the neighborhood has numerous effects (Steptoe & Feldman, 2001; Wilson, 1991). Neighborhood programs such as clubs, recreation centers, services, as well as neighborhood economic and social development programs, are important components of prevention.

Drugs are also related to distribution by international cartels and to the economic viability of nations, and they are marketed and advertised by corporate interests who may target the young or most vulnerable populations. Therefore, prevention becomes even more important and includes prosocial advertising policy and agreements between nations. Drug prevention from a systemic perspective involves interventions in all of the micro, meso, and macro systems.

Although the developed "evidence-based" prevention programs are hopeful, research should involve large-scale controlled studies, so that the research methodology justifies the desire for evidence, control, and experimental groups that are equivalent and findings that are not unduly influenced by school, place, or missing data effects (participants drop out of the study). Continuing efforts toward prevention are in accord with professional values of social justice and beneficence, the foundation of social work.

References

Alva, S. A., & Jones, M. (1994). Psychosocial adjustment and self reported patterns of alcohol use among Hispanic adolescents. *Journal of Early Adolescence, 14,* 432–448.

Arthur, M. W., Hawkins, J. D., Aollard, J. A., Catalano, R. F., & Baglioni, A. J. (2002). Measuring risk and protective factors for substance abuse, delinquency, and other adolescent problem behaviors: The communities that care youth survey. *Evaluation Review, 26,* 575–601.

Atkinson, J. S., Richard, A. J., & Carlson, J. W. (2001). The influence of peer, family and school relationships in substance use among participants in a youth jobs program. *Journal of Child and Adolescent Substance Abuse, 11*(1), 45–54.

Babor, T. F., de la Fuenta, J. R., Saunders, J., & Grant, M. (1992). *AUDIT: The Alcohol Use Disorders Identification Test; Guidelines for its use in primary health care.* Geneva: World Health Organization.

Barrick, C., & Connors, G. J. (2002). Relapse prevention and maintaining abstinence in older adults with alcohol-use disorders. *Drugs & Aging, 19,* 583–594.

Blake, S. M., Amaro, H., Schwartz, P. M., & Flinchbaugh, L. J. (2001). A review of Substance abuse prevention intervention for young adolescent girls. *Journal of Early Adolescence, 21,* 294–324.

Blow, F. C., Brower, K. J., Schulenberg, J. E., Demo-Dananberg, L. M., Young, J. P., & Beresford, T. P. (1992). The Michigan Alcoholism Screening Test Geriatric Version (MAST-G): A new elderly specific screening instrument. *Alcoholism: Clinical and Experimental Research, 16,* 372.

Blow, F. C., Walton, M. A., Barry, K. L., Coyne, J. C., Mudd, S. A., & Copeland, L. A. (2000). The relationship between alcohol problems and health functioning of older adults in primary care settings. *Journal of the American Geriatric Society, 48,* 769–774.

Bluenthal, R., Kral, A., Erringer, E., & Edlin, B. (1998). Use of illegal syringe exchange and injection-related risk behaviors among street-recruited injection drug users in Oakland, CA, 1992–1995. *Journal of AIDS, 18,* 515.

Botvin, G. J., Baker, E., Dusenbury, L. D., Botvin, E. M., & Diaz, T. (1995). Long-term follow-up results of a randomized drug abuse prevention trial in a white middle-class population. *JAMA, 273,* 1106–1112.

Botvin, G. J., Baker, E., Dusenbury, L. D., Tortu, S., & Botvin, E. M. (1990). Preventing adolescent drug abuse through a multimodal cognitive–behavioral approach: Results of a three year study. *Journal of Counseling & Clinical Psychology, 58,* 437–447.

Botvin, G. J., & Botvin, E. M. (1992). School-based and community-based prevention approaches. In J. Lowinson, P. Ruiz, & R. Millman (Eds.), *Comprehensive textbook of substance abuse* (pp. 910–927). Baltimore: Williams & Wilkins.

Botvin, G. J., & Eng, A. (1982). The efficacy of a multi-component approach to the prevention of cigarette smoking. *Preventive Medicine, 11,* 199–211.

Botvin, G. J., Epstein, J. A., Baker, E., Diaz, T., Ifill-Williams, M., Miller, N., & Cardwell, J. (1997). School-based drug abuse prevention with inner-city minority youth. *Journal of Child and Adolescent Substance Abuse, 6,* 5–19.

Botvin, G. J., & Griffin, K. W. (2007). School-based progammes to prevent alcohol, tobacco and other drug use. *International Review of Psychiatry, 19,* 607–615.

Botvin, G. J., Griffin, K. W., Diaz, T., Scheir, L. M., Williams, C., & Epstein, J. A. (2000). Preventing illicit drug use in adolescents: Long-term follow up data from a randomized control trial of a school population. *Addictive Behaviors, 25,* 769–774.

Botvin, G. J., Griffin, K. W., Paul, E., & McCauley, A. P. (2003). Preventing tobacco and alcohol use among elementary school students through life skills training. *Journal of Child & Adolescent Substance Abuse, 12,* 1–17.

Botvin, G. J., Resnick, N., & Baker, E. (1983). The effects of scheduling format and booster sessions on a broad spectrum psychosocial approach to smoking prevention. *Journal of Behavioral Medicine, 6,* 359–379.

Botvin, G. J., Schinke, S. P, Epstein, J. A., Diaz, T., & Botvin, E. M. (1995). Effectiveness of culturally-focused and generic skills training approaches to alcohol and drug abuse prevention among minority adolescents: Two year follow-up results. *Psychology of Addictive Behaviors, 9,* 183–194.

Boys & Girls Club, Inc. (1990). Smart Moves Questionnaire. Tallahassee, FL: Author.

Bride, B. E., & Nackerud, L. (2002). The disease model of alcoholism: A Kunian perspective. *Journal of Sociology and Social Welfare, 29*(2), 125–141.

Bronfenbrenner, U. (1979). *The ecology of human development.* Cambridge, MA: Harvard University Press.

Bukstein, O. G. (1995). *Adolescent substance abuse: Assessment, prevention, and treatment.* Oxford, England: John Wiley & Sons.

Casswell, S. (1995). Public discourse on alcohol: Implications for public policy. In H. D. Holder & G. Edwards (Eds.), *Alcohol and public policy, evidence and issues* (pp. 190–211). Oxford, England: Oxford University Press.

Clayton, R. R., Leukfield, C. G., Dohohew, L., Bardow, M., & Harrington, N. G. (1995). Risk and protective factors: A brief review. *Drugs and Society, 8*(3–4), 7–14.

Coatsworth, J. D., Pantin, H., & Szapocznik, J. (2002). Familias Unidas: A family-centered ecodevelopmental intervention to reduce risk for problem behavior among Hispanic adolescents. *Clinical Child and Family Psychology Review, 5*(2), 113–132.

Coie, J. D, Watt, N. F., West, S. G., Hawkins, J. D., Asarnow, J. R., & Markman, H. J. (1993). The science of prevention: A conceptual framework and some directions for a national research program. *American Psychologist, 48,* 1013–1022.

Collins, D., Johnson, K., & Becker, B. J. (2007). A meta-analysis of direct and mediating effects of community coalitions that implemented science-based substance abuse prevention interventions. *Substance Use & Misuse, 42,* 985–1007.

Corrigan, M. J., Loneck, B., Videka, L., & Brown, M. C. (2007). Moving the risk and protective factor framework toward individualized assessment in adolescent substance abuse prevention. *Journal of Child & Adolescent Substance Abuse, 16*(3), 17–33.

Des Jarlais, D., Marmor, M., Paone, D. Titus, S., Shi, Q., Perils, T., et al. (1996). HIV incidence among injection drug users in New York City syringe exchange programs. *Lancet, 348,* 987–991.

Diehl, S., Mueller, B., & Terlutter, R. (2008). Consumer response towards non-prescription drug advertising in the US and Germany. *International Journal of Advertising, 27*(1), 99–131.

Dimeff, L., Baer, J., Kivlahan, D., & Marlatt, G. (1998). *Brief alcohol screening and intervention for college students: A harm reduction approach.* New York: Guilford Press.

Doumas, D. M., & Haustveit, T. (2008). Reducing heavy drinking in intercollegiate athletes: Evaluation of a Web-based personalized feedback program. *Sport Psychologist, 22,* 212–228.

Durlak, J. A. (1997). *Successful prevention programs for children and adolescents.* New York: Plenum Press.

Ellickson, P. L., Bell, R. M., & McGuigan, K. (1993). Preventing adolescent drug use: Long-term results of a junior high school program. *American Journal of Public Health, 83,* 856–861.

Ellickson, P. L., McCaffrey, D. F., Ghosh-Dastidar, B., & Longshire, D. L. (2003). New inroads in preventing adolescent drug use: Results from a large-scale trial of Project ALERT in middle schools. *American Journal of Public Health, 93,* 1830–1836.

Epstein, E. E., Fischer-Elber, K., & Al-Otaiba, Z. (2007). Women, aging and alcohol use disorders. *Journal of Women and Aging, 19*(1–2), 31–48.

Errante, A. (1997). Close to home: Comparative perspectives on childhood and community violence. *American Journal of Education, 105,* 355–400.

Ewing, J. A. (1984). Detecting alcoholism: The CAGE questionnaire. *JAMA, 252,* 1905–1907.

Fellin, P. (2001). *The community and the social worker* (3rd ed.). Itasca, IL: F. E. Peacock.

Flewelling, R. L., Austin, D., Hale, K., LaPlante, M., Liebig, M., Piasecki, L., & Uerz, L. (2005). Implementing research-based substance abuse prevention in communities: Effects of a coalition-based prevention initiative in Vermont. *Journal of Community Psychology, 33,* 333–353.

Fromme, K., Marlatt, G., Baer, J., & Kivlahan, D. (1994). The alcohol skills training program: A group intervention for young adult drinkers. *Journal of Substance Abuse Treatment, 11,* 143–154.

Garfield, C. F., Chung, P. J., & Rathouz, P. J. (2003). Alcohol advertising in magazines and adolescent readership. *JAMA, 289,* 2424–2429.

Giesbrecht, N., Johnson, S., Anglin, L., Greenfield, T., & Kavanagh, L. (2004). Alcohol advertising policies in the United States: National promotion and control initiatives. *Contemporary Drug Problems, 31,* 673–710.

Gorman, D. M., Conde, E., & Huber, J. C. (2007). The creation of evidence in "evidence-based" drug prevention: A critique of the Strengthening Families Program Plus Life Skills Training evaluation. *Drug and Alcohol Review, 26,* 585–593.

Gould, E. (2005). Treaties and alcohol advertising policy. *Journal of Public Health Policy, 26,* 359–376.

Graham, J. W., Johnson, C. A., Hansen, W. B., Flay, B. R., & Gee, M. (1990). Drug use prevention programs, gender and ethnicity: Evaluation of three seventh grade SMART cohorts. *Preventive Medicine, 19,* 305–313.

Graham-Silverman, A. (2008). House votes to fund media initiative, help countries fight drug trafficking. *CQ Weekly, 66*(24), 1628.

Gudykunst, W. B., & Kim, Y. Y. (1997). *Communicating with strangers* (3rd ed.). Boston: McGraw-Hill.

Hagan, H., Des Jarlais, D., Purchase, D., Friedman, S., Reid, T., & Bell, T. (1993). An interview study of participants in the Tacoma, Washington, syringe exchange. *Addiction, 88,* 1691–1697.

Hawkins, J. D., Catalano, R. F., & Miller, J. Y. (1992). Risk and protective factors for alcohol and other drug problems in adolescence and early childhood: Implications for substance abuse prevention. *Psychological Bulletin, 112,* 64–105.

Heflinger, C. A., & Christens, B. (2006). Rural behavioral health services for children and adolescents: An ecological and community psychology analysis. *Journal of Community Psychology, 34,* 379–400.

Heimer, R. (1998). Can syringe exchange serve as a conduit to substance abuse treatment? *Journal of Substance Abuse Treatment, 15,* 183–191.

Herrenkohl, T. I., Maguin, E., Hill, K. G., Hawkins, J. D., & Abbott, R. D. (2000). Developmental risk factors for youth violence. *Journal of Adolescent Health, 26,* 176–186.

Hofstede, G. (2001). *Culture's consequences* (2nd ed.). Thousand Oaks, CA: Sage Publications.

Huang, B., Kosterman, R., Catalano, R. F., Hawkins, J. D., & Abbott, R. D. (2001). Model mediation in the etiology of violent behavior in adolescence: A test of the social development model. *Criminology, 39*(1), 75–107.

In columbia, war against rebels easing. (2008, June 30). *USA Today,* p. 5A.

Jackson, M. C., Hastings, G., Wheeler, C., Eadie, D., & Mackintosh, A. M. (2000). Marketing alcohol to young people: Implications for industry, regulation and research policy. *Addiction, 95*(Suppl. 4), S597–S608.

Johnson, T.P. (2007). Cultural-level influence on substance use and misuse. *Substance Use & Misuse, 42,* 305–316.

Johnston, L. D., O'Malley, P. M., & Bachman, J. G. (2000, December 14). *Ecstasy use rises sharply among teens in 2000: Use of many other drugs steady, but significant declines reported for some* [National Press Release]. Retrieved December 28, 2001, from http://www.monitoringthefuture.org

Johnston, L. D., O'Malley, P. M., Bachman, J. G., & Schulenberg, J. E. (2006). *Monitoring the future national results on adolescent drug use: Overview of key findings, 2005* (NIH Publication No. 06-5882). Bethesda, MD: National Institute on Drug Abuse.

Kaempf, G., O'Donnell, C., & Oslin, D. W. (1999). The BRENDA Model: A psychosocial addiction model to identify and treat alcohol disorders in elders. *Geriatric Nursing, 20,* 302–304.

Kelder, S. H., & Perry, C. L. (1993). Prevention substance abuse. In D.S. Glenwick & L.A. Jensen (Eds.), *Promoting health and mental health in children, youth, and families* (pp. 75–97). New York: Springer.

Kirst-Ashman, K. K. (2008). *Human behavior, communities, organizations, and groups in the macro social environment.* Belmont, CA: Brooks/Cole.

Komro, K. A., Perry, C. L., Veblen-Mortenson, S., Farbakhsh, K., Toomey, T. L., Stigler, M. H., et al. (2008). Outcomes from a randomized controlled trial of a multi-component alcohol use prevention intervention for urban youth: Project Northland Chicago. *Addiction, 103,* 606–618.

Kulis, S., & Marsiglia, F. F. (2004). *Keeping it real with adolescents of Mexican descent: Developing and testing evidence–based, substance use prevention* (ASA proceedings-34589). Paper presented at the American Sociological Association Annual Meeting, San Francisco.

Kumpfer, K. L., Alvarado, R., & Woodside, H. O. (2003). Family–based interventions for substance use and misuse prevention. *Substance Use Misuse, 38,* 1759–1787.

Larimer, M. E., Kilmer, J. R., & Lee, C. M. (2005). College student drug prevention: A review of individually-oriented prevention strategies. *Journal of Drug Issues, 35,* 431–455.

Letters: Is Afghanistan a narco-state? (2008, August 10). *New York Times Magazine,* p. 6.

The long war of Genaro Garcia Luna. (2008, July 13). *New York Times Magazine,* p. 32.

Mackillop, J., Ryabcenko, K. A., & Lisman, S. A. (2006). Life skills training outcomes and potential mechanisms in a community implementation: A preliminary investigation. *Substance Use & Misuse, 41,* 1921–1935.

MacMaster, S., Holleran, L., & Chaffin, K. (2005). Empirical and theoretical support for the inclusion of non-abstinence-based perspectives in prevention services for substance using adolescents. *Journal of Evidence-Based Social Work, 2*(1–2), 91–111.

Marlatt, G. A., Baer, J. S., Kivlahan, D. R., Dimeff, L. A., Larimer, M. E., Quigley, L. A., et al. (1998). Screening and brief intervention for high-risk college student drinkers: Results from a two year follow-up assessment. *Journal of Consulting and Clinical Psychology, 66,* 604–615.

Marsch, L. A., Bickel, W. K., & Badger, G. J. (2006). Applying computer technology to substance abuse prevention science: results of a preliminary examination. *Journal of Child & Adolescent Substance Abuse, 16*(2), 69–94.

McCambridge, J., & Strang, J. (2004). The efficacy of single-session motivational interviewing in reducing drug consumption and perception of drug-related risk and harm among young people: Results from a multi-site cluster randomized trial. *Addiction, 99,* 39–52.

Mexico: Antidrug aid's strings intact. (2008, June 11). *New York Times,* p. 10.

Miller, W. R., & Rollnick, S. (2002). *Motivational interviewing: Preparing people for change* (2nd ed.). New York: Guilford Press.

Miller, W. R., Toscova, R. T., Miller, J. H., & Sanchez, V. (2001). A theory-based motivational approach for reducing alcohol/drug problems in college. *Health Education and Behavior, 27,* 744–759.

Molgaard, V. K., Spoth, R. L., & Redmond, C. (2000). *Competency training: The Strengthening Families program: For parents and youth 10–14* (OJJDP Juvenile Justice Bulletin 182208). Retrieved January 3, 2009, from http://www.ncjrs.gov/html/ojjdp/2000-8-1/contents.html

Monti, P. M., Spirito, A., Myers, M., Colby, S. M., Barnett, N. P., Rohsenow, D. J., Woolard, R., & Lewnader, W. (1999). Brief intervention for harm reduction with alcohol-positive older adolescents in a hospital emergency department. *Journal of Consulting and Clinical Psychology, 67,* 989–994.

Naik, R. K., Borrego, M. E., Gupchup, G. V., Dodd, M., & Sather, M. R. (2007). Pharmacy student's knowledge, attitudes, and evaluation of direct-to-consumer advertising. *American Journal of Pharmaceutical Education, 71*(5), 1–10.

National Institute on Alcohol Abuse and Alcoholism. (2002a). *A call to action: Changing the culture of drinking at U.S. colleges* (NIH Publication No. 02-5010). Bethesda, MD: Author.

National Institute on Alcohol Abuse and Alcoholism. (2002b). *Journal of Studies on Alcohol—College drinking, what it is, and what to do about it: A review of the state of the science* (Suppl. 14). Piscataway, NJ: Rutgers Center of Alcohol Studies.

Perry, C. L., Williams, C. L., Veblen-Mortensen, S., Stigler, M., Munson, K. A., Farbakhsh, K., Jones, R. M., & Forster, J. L. (2002). Project Northland: Long-term outcomes of community action to reduce adolescent alcohol use. *Health Education Research, 17*(1), 117–132.

Peterson, P. I., Hawkins, J. D., Abbott, R. D., & Catalano, R. F. (1995). Disentangling the effects of parental drinking, family management, and parental alcohol norms on current drinking by black and white adolescents. In G. M. Boyd, J. Howard, & R. A. Zucker (Eds.), *Alcohol problems among adolescents: Current directions in prevention research* (pp. 33–59). Hillsdale, NJ: Lawrence Erlbaum.

Prado, G., Pantin, H., & Briones, R. (2007). A randomized controlled trial of a parent centered intervention in preventing substance abuse and HIV risk behavior in Hispanic adolescents. *Journal of Consulting and Clinical Psychology, 75,* 914–926.

Prado, G., Szapocnik, J., Maldonado-Molina, M., Schwartz, S. J., & Pantin, H. (2008). Drug use, abuse, prevalence, etiology, prevention and treatment in Hispanic adolescents: A cultural perspective. *Journal of Drug Issues, 38*(1), 5–36.

Prochaska, J. O., DiClemente, C. C., & Norcross, J. G. (1992). In search of how people change: Applications to addictive behavior. *American Psychologist, 47,* 1102–1114.

Putnam, R. (1993). The prosperous community. *Current, 356,* 4–9.

Rohrbach, L. A., Hodgson, C. S., Booker, B. I., & Montgomery, S. B. (1994). Parental perception of drug abuse prevention: Results from the Midwestern Prevention Project. *Journal of Research on Adolescences, 4,* 295–317.

Roiblatt, R., & Dinis, M. (2004). The lost link: Social work in early 20th century alcohol policy. *Social Service Review, 78,* 652–674.

Rollin, S. A., Rubin, R. I., & Wright, J. C. (2000). The evolution of a community-based drug prevention program for youth. *Journal of Alcohol and Drug Education, 45*(3), 33–46.

Rotgers, F., Morgenstern, J., & Walters, S. T. (2007). *Treating substance abuse.* New York: Guilford Press.

Saleebey, D. (2004). "The power of place": Another look at the environment. *Families in Society, 85*(1), 7–16.

Sampson, R. J. (2004). Network and neighborhoods: The implications of connectivity for thinking about crime in the modern city. In H. McCarthy, P. Miller, & P. Skidmore (Eds.), *Network logic: Who governs in an interconnected world?* (pp. 157–166). London: Demos.

Satre, D. D., & Knight, B. G. (2001). Alcohol expectancies and their relationship to alcohol use: Age and sex differences. *Aging & Mental Health, 5*(1), 73–83.

Schwartz, S. (1992). Universals in the content and structure of values: Theoretical advances and empirical tests in 20 countries. In M. P. Zanna (Ed.), *Advances in experimental social psychology* (Vol 25, pp. 1–65). San Diego: Academic Press.

Seal, N. (2006). Preventing tobacco and drug use among Thai high school students through life skills training. *Nursing & Health Science, 8*(3), 164–168.

Siegel, D. I. (2001). Time and social work: Multicultural variables. *New Global Development: Journal of International and Comparative Social Welfare, 17*(2), 73–85.

Siegel, D. I., Green, J., Abbott, A., & Mogul, M. (2007). Welfare leavers and returners: Correlates of quality of life. *Journal of Human Behavior in the Social Environment, 15*(1), 69–97.

Skiba, D., Monroe, J., & Wodarski, J. S. (2004). Adolescent substance use: Reviewing the effectiveness of prevention strategies. *Social Work, 49,* 343–353.

Smith, E. A., Swisher, J. D., Vicary, J. R., Bechtel, L. J., Minner, D., Henry, K. L., & Palmer, R. (2004). Evaluation of life skills training and infused-life skills training in a rural setting: Outcomes at two years. *Drug Education, 48*(1), 51–70.

Soole, D, Mazerolle, L., & Rombouts, S. (2008). School-based drug prevention programs: A review of what works. *Australian and New Zealand Journal of* Criminology, *41*(2), 259–286.

Sorocco, K. H., & Ferrell, S.W. (2006). Alcohol use among older adults. *Journal of General Psychology, 133,* 453–467.

Spencer, C., & Wooley, H. (2000). Children and the city: A summary of recent environmental psychology research. *Child Care Health and Development, 26*(3), 181–198.

Spoth, R., Randall, K. G., Shin, C., & Redmond, C. (2005). Randomized study of combined universal family and school preventive interventions: Patterns of long term effects on initiation, regular use, and weekly drunkenness. *Psychology of Addictive Behaviors, 19,* 372–381.

Spoth, R., Redmond, C., & Shin, C. (2000). Modeling factors influencing enrollment in family-focused preventive intervention research. *Prevention Science, 1,* 213–225.

Spoth, R., Redmond, C., & Shin, C. (2001). Randomized trial of brief family interventions for general population: Adolescent substance abuse outcomes four years following baseline. *Journal of Consulting and Clinical Psychology, 69,* 627–642.

Steptoe, A., & Feldman, P. J. (2001). Neighborhood problems as sources of chronic stress: Development of a measure of neighborhood problems, and associations with socioeconomic status and health. *Annual Behavioral Medicine, 23*(3), 177–185.

Steyer, T. (1999, June 20). Do drug ads educate or mislead consumers? *St. Lewis Post-Dispatch,* p. A-9.

Substance Abuse and Mental Health Services Administration (SAMHSA). (1998). *Substance abuse among older adults: Treatment improvement protocol* (TIP; Series #26). Rockville, MD: U.S. Department of Health and Human Services.

Substance Abuse and Mental Health Administration (SAMSHA). (2003). Science-based prevention *programs and principles: Effectives substance abuse and mental health Programs for every community* (USDHHS Publication No. SMA 03-3764). Washington, DC: U.S. Government Printing Office.

Substance Abuse and Mental Health Administration (SAMSHA). (2008). *SAMHSA model programs: Strengthening Families Programs for Parents and Youth 10–14.* Retrieved January 10, 2009, from http://www.nrepp.samhsaa.gov/programfulldetails.asp?Program-ID=212

Sue, D. (1987). Use and abuse of alcohol by Asian Americans. *Journal of Psychoactive Drugs, 19,* 57–76.

Tapia, M. I., Schwartz, S. J., Prado, G., Lopez, B., & Pantin, H. (2006). Parent-centered intervention: A practical approach for preventing drug abuse in Hispanic adolescents. *Research on Social Work Practice, 16,* 146–165.

Tarter, R. E., Sambrano, S., & Dunn, M. G. (2002). Predictor variables by developmental stages: A center for substance abuse prevention multisite study. *Psychology of Addictive Behavior, 16*(43), S3–S10.

Tobler, N. S., & Stratton, H. H. (1997). Effectiveness of school-based drug prevention programs: A meta-analysis of the research. *Journal of Primary Prevention, 18,* 71–128.

Trattner, W. (1999). *From poor law to welfare state.* New York: Free Press.

Triandis, H. C. (1995). *Individualism-collectivism.* Boulder, CO: Westview Press.

Triandis, H. C. (1996). The psychological measurement of cultural syndromes. *American Psychologist, 51,* 407–417.

Uribe calls Pelosi's bluff. (2009, May 14). *Wall Street Journal–Eastern Edition,* p. 20.

U.S. Department of Health and Human Services. (1997). *Alcohol and health, Ninth Special report to the U.S. Congress.* Washington, DC: Author.

U.S. reports gains against Taliban fighers. (2008, June 3). *New York Times Magazine,* p. 13.

Valdez, A., Mikow, J., & Cepeda, A. (2006). The role of stress, family coping, ethnic identity and mother–daughter relationships on substance use among gang-affiliated Hispanic females. *Journal of Social Work Practice in the Addiction, 6*(4), 31–54.

Valente, T. W., Ritt-Olson, A., Stacy, A., Unger, J. B., Okamoto, J., & Sussman, S. (2007). Peer acceleration: Effects of a social network tailored substance abuse prevention program among high-risk adolescents. *Addiction, 102,* 1804–1815.

Vimpani, G. (2005). Getting the mix right: Family, community and social policy interventions to improve outcomes for young people at risk of substance abuse. *Drug and Alcohol Review, 24,* 111–129.

Walters, S., Miller, E., & Chiauzzi, E. (2005). Wired for wellness: E-interventions for addressing college drinking. *Journal of Substance Abuse Treatment, 29,* 139–145.

Wang, M. Q., Matthew, R., Bellamy, N., & James, S. (2005). A structural model of the substance use pathways among minority youth. *American Journal of Health and Behavior, 29,* 531–541.

Waving, not drowning. (2008, May 3). *Economist, 387*(8578), 48.

West, S. L., Graham, C. W. (2005). A survey of substance abuse prevention efforts at Virginia's colleges and universities. *Journal of American College Health, 54*(3), 185–191.

Williams, J. H., Davis, L. E., Johnson, S. D., Williams, T. R., Saunders, J. A., & Nebbitt, V. E. (2007). Substance use and academic performance among African American high school students. *Social Work Research, 31,* 151–161.

Wilson, S. R., Fink, A., Verghese, S., Beck, J. C., Nguyen, K., & Lavori, P. (2007). Adding an alcohol-related risk score to an existing categorical risk classification for older adults: Sensitivity to group differences. *Journal of the American Geriatric Society, 55,* 445–450.

Wilson, W. J. (1991). Studying inner city dislocations: The challenge of public policy research. *American Sociological Review, 56,* 1-4.

Windybank, S. (2008). The illegal pacific, part 1: Organized crime. *Policy, 24*(1), 32–38.

Wright, D. A., Bobashev, G., & Folsom, R. (2007). Understanding the relative influence of neighborhood, family and youth on adolescent drug use. *Substance Use & Misuse, 42,* 2159–2171.

Wyllie, A., Zhang, J. F., & Casswell, S. (1998). Responses to televised alcohol advertisements associated with drinking behavior of 10–17-year-olds. *Addiction, 93,* 361–371.

Yuan, S. (2008). Public responses to direct-to-consumer advertising of prescription drugs. *Journal of Advertising Research, 48*(1), 30–41.

Epilogue

Where Do We Go From Here?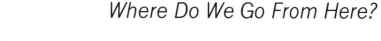
Confronting Upcoming ATOD Challenges

Ann A. Abbott

Clients exhibiting problems resulting from ATOD use, abuse, or misuse, or problems such as co-occurring disorders (mental health issues compounded by ATOD issues) make up a significant portion of social workers' caseloads. The challenges of working with these clients are monumental; the supports remain limited. The systems or ecological perspective advanced by the social work profession has served the profession well in its mission of helping many ATOD clients move toward a more satisfying, less problem-ridden state. The profession's commitment to seeking evidence-based practice has been enhanced by social work's contribution to rigorous research guided by the social work value base and ethical standards. However, the question remains: Can more be accomplished in our quest for best practices?

Changing Demographics

In examining current demographics related to ATOD use, we find some positive gains and some emerging concerns. It is important to note that, on the one hand, the news is improving in relation to some aspects of teenage drug use. "Smoking, drinking, and the misuse of stimulants ... have continued on downward trends that have been evident in the past decade"; on the other hand, "other substance use trends are flattening or showing signs of increase" (Yan, 2009b, p. 7; also see www.moni toringthefuture.org). Despite downward trends for alcohol use, Yan noted that "28 percent of 12th graders admitted being drunk in the prior 30 days" (p. 7). Again, in referencing Monitoring the Future data, he expressed concern about peak levels of misuse of prescription drugs, in particular, opioids such as OxyContin and Vicodin.

It is cause for concern that, in analyzing data from autopsies performed in 2007 by the Florida Medical Examiners Commission, the "rate of deaths caused by prescription drugs was three times the rate of deaths caused by all illicit drugs combined. Law enforcement officials said that the shift toward prescription-drug abuse, which began ... about eight years ago, showed no sign of letting up ... " (Cave, 2008, p. A10).

Another concern involves findings of the 2007 National Survey on Drug Use and Health, which reports major increases in the use of illegal drugs among the 50-plus age group. For example, the illicit drug use (marijuana, cocaine, and hallucinogens) of baby boomers, ages 50 to 54, increased from 3.4 percent in 2002 to 5.7 percent in 2007. Even greater increases were noted for those ages 55 to 59 whose illicit drug use increased from 1.9 percent in 2002 to 4.1 percent in 2007. This is in contrast to the illicit drug use among those ages 12 to 17 which declined more than 2 percent during the same time period (Jacobs, 2008). What Jacobs noted was that patterns of use tend to follow demographic groups; increasing age does not necessarily mean one is going to change one's lifelong ATOD usage patterns.

Of equal concern is the growing number of older women who are being admitted for substance abuse treatment for the use of hard-core drugs.

> Data from the Substance Abuse and Mental Health Services Administration revealed that the total number of admissions to treatment services from 1996 to 2005 (the last year for which detailed data are available) stayed about the same among people under 40, but jumped 52 percent among those 40 and older. Of the 40 and older group, the rise in admissions among men was 44 percent. Among women, it was 82 percent. (Blow, 2008, p. A27)

> Of even greater concern is the prediction that

> these trends could grow stronger. A 2006 report by the National Institute on Drug Abuse (NIDA) focused on drug use among baby boomers, all of whom were 41–59 years old in 2005. It concluded that "the large size of this cohort, coupled with greater lifetime rates of drug use than previous generations, might result in unprecedented high numbers of older drug users in the next 15 to 20 years." (Blow, 2008, p. A27)

What is true today may not be the case tomorrow. We must look not only at age, but also at specific substances used, client characteristics and behaviors based on use, and best practices for treatment.

Emerging Trends

Marijuana

Some major emerging trends are in the works. The illegal status of marijuana is being challenged on a number of fronts; however, in reality, reported use of marijuana is higher in the United States than it is in many other industrialized and emerging nations. Over 42 percent of the U.S. population has admitted ever using marijuana. This can be compared with the Netherlands (19.8 percent), France (19.0 percent), South Africa (8.4 percent), Mexico (7.8 percent), and Japan (1.5 percent) (Hayashi, 2009)

In the decade prior to 2007, in New York City alone, "400,000 people were apprehended for marijuana misdemeanors . . . almost 10 times the number arrested in the previous decade" (Peele, 2009, p. A11). But change is in the air. A number of states have voted to allow the use of marijuana for medical purposes. Will more follow? And is this one major step toward legalizing all marijuana use? (See Bowden, 2009.)

Crime? Punishment? or Treatment?

Recently, New York legislators voted to reduce the number of laws requiring mandatory prison terms for some low-level nonviolent drug felonies. Such action will cut the prison population by thousands. For many in the prison population, "three decades have shown that the core issue is often addiction 'a treatable illness', with far lower recidivism for those who get treatment instead of prison" (Virtanen, 2009, p. A3). Is this the start of a national trend toward greater recognition of the impact of good treatment on addressing the power of substances on individuals' behavior? Will social workers be prepared to enter the debate?

Nicotine

On June 11, 2009, the U.S. Senate (79–17) passed a major bill designed to tighten regulation over cigarettes (Wilson, 2009b). It gives "the government unprecedented power over the making and marketing of tobacco products" (McCullough, 2009, p. A1). The U.S. House of Representatives passed a nearly identical bill in April 2009, and approved the Senate version (307–97) on June 12, 2009. The law, signed by President Barack H. Obama on June 22, 2009, titled the Family Smoking Prevention and Tobacco Control Act, will allow the Federal Drug Administration (FDA) to set standards controlling the nicotine and other chemical content in cigarettes. It "stops short of empowering the FDA to outlaw smoking or ban tobacco" (Wilson, 2009b, p. A1).

It will take several years for the actual implementation of what many consider to be a monumental shift in addressing the harmful efforts of tobacco products.

In addition to limiting nicotine content, it will give the FDA power to ban most tobacco flavorings as well as tighten regulations on the advertising and marketing of tobacco products. (Although tobacco is used by approximately one out of five Americans, it is "one of the least-regulated consumer products. Pet food and cosmetics are more heavily controlled" [Layton, 2009, p. A2].)

The Congressional Budget Office (CBO) predicts this new piece of legislation will "reduce teen smoking by 11 percent and adult smoking by 2 percent over the next decade" (Wilson, 2009b, p. A1). Some individuals worry that, rather than reduce consumption of tobacco products, the law will drive increased development of illegal markets to counter the effects on new legislation on legal products.

This new law did not happen in isolation. Over the years, especially since the surgeon general's first report on smoking in 1964, actions have been developed to counter smoking and its deadly effects (Wilson, 2009a, p. A4). Despite elation on the part of many, there are those who see this law with jaundiced eyes. Some are concerned that new marketing regulations will make it more difficult for tobacco companies "to market smokeless alternatives to cigarettes that are far less lethal because they contain fewer carcinogens than cigarettes and don't enter the lungs. And while reducing the tar or nicotine content of an individual cigarette might make it safer, it will also induce some people to smoke more to achieve the same fix" ("Washington's Marlboro Men," 2009, p. A12).

Others worry about the ban on flavored tobacco products. The banning of menthol, the most popular cigarette flavor, was deferred to additional studies. "Menthol brands account for less than 30% of the U.S. market but are favored by 75% of black smokers. Black public health officials understandably have opposed the exemptions. But black lawyers apparently believe that banning an unhealthy product used by a disproportionate number of black voters is the greater evil" ("Washington's Marlboro Men," 2009, p. A12).

What we do know is that public views on smoking and tobacco products have changed significantly during recent years. During the past decade major changes have occurred that directly affect smoking. A number of countries, states, and municipalities have banned smoking in public places, including restaurants and worksites. One city council in California banned smoking in one's own home if it is located in an apartment complex (Sobel, 2009). Ontario, Canada, has banned smoking in cars with children under age 16 present. The American Medical Association has recently unveiled a program designed to publicly shame the film industry for showing smoking in their movies. They are urging that movies depicting smoking be rated for viewing by adults only (Barnes, 2009).

Seventy percent of smokers indicate that they want to quit. "Former addicts say heroin can be easier to quit than cigarettes" (Sobel, 2009, p. D3). Even North Carolina, the nation's largest grower of tobacco, has voted to prohibit smoking in bars and restaurants (Brown, 2009).

Some states are increasing cigarette taxes with the hope that it will increase revenue, but realize that typically a 10 percent increase in price results in a 3 percent to 5 percent reduction in use (Dewan, 2009). Typically an increase in cigarette tax has little impact on smokers' behavior, other than driving them to find places for cheaper purchases (Tamari, 2009).

Some contend that an increase in cigarette tax is discriminatory, aimed at the working class and poor. Others continue to believe it will reduce use, and, in turn, decrease the presence of secondhand and thirdhand smoke, which is almost as dangerous a health hazard as firsthand smoke (Rabin, 2009).

Social workers and others working in the field of substance-related disorders need to keep abreast of new developments in the area. They will need to know the issues and related changes as well as modify treatment to accommodate new developments.

Harm Reduction

Other newer initiatives aimed at reducing the harm generated by drug use include supervised injection sites for heroin, cocaine, or speed such as those established in Vancouver, British Columbia. They reframed drug use as primarily a public health issue, not a criminal one (Beiser, 2008). "If you accept the notion that people aren't going to stop abusing drugs it makes sense to try to minimize the damage they inflict on themselves and the rest of us while they're at it. Harm reduction is less about compassion than it is about enlightened self-interest" (p. 62). They have even experimented with giving users prescription heroin with the intent of minimizing crime associated with maintaining a habit.

Other trials conducted by Dutch and Canadian researchers have found that heroin-assisted treatment plus methadone under medical supervision has been more effective than methadone alone in improving long-term outcomes for heroin addicts (Yan, 2009a).

Another newer approach to treatment includes the use of handheld devices such as a PalmPilot to help users kick the heroin habit. Each time the user gets the urge to use, he or she engages the PalmPilot for immediate guidance and reinforcement (Arehart-Treichel, 2009). Given our society's reliance on mobile phones and other electronic devices, it would seem logical that such treatments are soon to be tested. Additional examples include electronic devices that measure blood alcohol levels, blocking activation of car ignitions ("How to Stop Drunk Drivers," 2006); and Web-based self-assessment instruments designed to identify current alcohol problems or predict future ones (Beck, 2009).

Other Promising Interventions

Drug courts are continuing to emerge as useful vehicles for directing ATOD users to treatment rather than traditional prison sentences (Shea, 2009). Acupuncture is another treatment that is beginning to be recognized as a viable alternative or supplement to more traditional treatment (Brook, 2009).

Advertising

One area of concern that is just beginning to be addressed with vigor is that of pharmaceutical advertising. The focus on current advertising supports the idea that a pill can cure all ills—sleeplessness, depression, anxiety, to name a few. Dartmouth Medial School (Singer, 2009) is urging federal regulators to clearly spell out the risks and benefits in all advertising, similar to the detail given on food labels, for example, number of grams of fat, calories, or carbohydrates. Rather than advertising that drug "X" guarantees a good night's sleep, indicate how much less time it typically takes to fall asleep when using the drug, how long does one typically sleep when taking the drug (compared with not taking it), and the various possible side effects, such as dizziness, drowsiness, dry mouth, unpleasant taste in mouth, nausea, upset stomach, and habit-forming potential.

In a similar vein, when a drug used to facilitate wakefulness in people who experience a sleep disorder at the other end of the spectrum, such as narcolepsy, is used by healthy individuals, will the idea that it will make them more alert and improve their cognitive abilities contribute to long-term dependence or abuse? Research has shown that the drug increases dopamine levels in the brain and, thus, may have potential for abuse (Rubin, 2009).

Dietary supplements are advertised to cure a variety of concerns, including sexual performance and weight loss. Stories abound of individuals who took "love potions" or performance enhancers only to discover that the supplement caused major problems, including life-threatening ones, when taken in combinations with prescribed medications. A recent article in the *Journal of the American Medical Association* indicated that one out of 50 older adults is currently taking fatal combinations of prescribed and over-the-counter medications or supplements (Gebel, 2009b). Dietary supplements can be equally devastating (Gebel, 2009a). This illustrates another area that calls for truth in advertising, especially the related risks of dangerous drug combinations.

Macro-Level Issues

Data released in late May 2009 revealed that spending by the federal government related to smoking, alcohol, and illegal drugs reached $468 billion in 2005. Most of that money was spent on treating the health care costs related to diseases primarily resulting from substance use or for incarceration. Just over 2 percent was devoted to prevention, treatment, and research (Eckholm, 2009). Our federal, state, and local governments spend $44.1 billion annually enforcing prohibitions or seven times as much as we spend on treatment. Only 14 percent of incarcerated prisoners with drug problems receive treatment for them (Kristof, 2009). The important message here is that social workers must keep abreast of usage trends, allocation of resources, and opportunities to effect reallocation of funds. Improving treatment is essential, but resources must be available to cover not only the cost of treatment, but also research related to assessing the effectiveness of various interventions, as well as continued engagement in prevention efforts. Thus, social workers must be prepared to participate in advocacy. Some may use politically active strategies; others will rely on the value of the pen and carefully constructed research.

In addition, macro-level initiatives frequently focus on the impact of drugs entering U.S. borders from such places as Afghanistan and Pakistan (Peters, 2009), Columbia (Regalado, 2009), Mexico (Gamerman, 2009), and Peru (Romero, 2009). Social workers are not trained to patrol or block action at the borders. However, if better informed, they will be prepared to enter the debate about the pros and cons of legalization on drugs (Fields, 2009; also see Duke, 2009, and Walters, 2009a, 2009b). Some, including the new White House Drug Czar, Gil Kerlikowske, think that the war on drugs, as we know it, is lost; so do others such as Leonard Pitts (2009). Perhaps legalization would allow us to have more resources and, thus, be more effective in reducing the impact of drugs on our fellow citizens, our clients, their families, and society in general. It "would underscore a shift favoring treatment over incarceration" (Fields, p. A3). The primary question is whether increased revenue gained by legalization would be adequate to sufficiently increase treatment options and prevention efforts directed at reducing substance abuse, dependence, and misuse. Whereas Drug Czar Kerlikowske supports the former, others such as Walters (2009a, 2009b) strongly believe that increased availability would lead to increased use.

Prevention Efforts

As we have already learned, prevention efforts are effective and, in many instances, less costly than long-term treatment or interdiction. One prevention action includes the continued development of lower carcinogen, smokeless tobacco (Helliker, 2009). Children are being primed to effectively ask their parents to quit smoking, and are producing positive results (Painter, 2009). Efforts on NIAAA's Web site to encourage people to rethink their drinking habits have been shown to have helped people recognize problems earlier and perhaps take action earlier in changing their behavior (Beck, 2009).

The problems generated by ATOD may seem overwhelming, but as noted in chapter 7, the process of change begins with one small step. By better preparing more social workers to enter the field of ATOD, by continuing to develop new approaches to treatment, by conducting research designed to measure the effectiveness of various treatment protocols, by advocating for increased support for ATOD services, by supporting the integration of mental health and ATOD services, by entering the debate about best avenues for approaching the problem (legalization versus modification of current practices), by keeping up to date on new developments in the field, and by endorsing prevention practices, we are taking significant steps in a positive direction. It is the intent of this book to prepare readers for stepping into the field of ATOD: to prepare them not only to be more informed practitioners, but also to be more attuned to current challenges and better prepared to strive for increased effectiveness in the field. This is just the beginning of the journey. With continued training, knowledge, and stamina, the journey should prove to be a successful, life-changing endeavor, personally and professionally for all one meets along the way.

References

Arehart-Treichel, J. (2009, February 8). Could an addiction fighting tool be in the palm of your hand? *Psychiatric News*, p. 16.

Barnes, B. (2009, May 28). Cigarettes in popular films are target of health groups. *New York Times*, p. C2.

Beck, M. (2009, March 10). To your health: New Web site helps predict alcohol problems. *Wall Street Journal*, D1.

Beiser, V. (2008). First, reduce harm. *Miller-McCune, 1*(6), 61–71.

Blow, C. M. (2008, June 14). Why is mom in rehab? *New York Times*, A27.

Bowden, M. (2009, April 19). Marijuana should be legal, and left alone. *Philadelphia Inquirer*, pp. C1, C6.

Brook, D. (2009, April 13). Helping inmates break free. *Philadelphia Inquirer*, pp. E1–E2.

Brown, R. (2009, May 20). North Carolina approves ban on smoking. *New York Times*, p. A16.

Cave, D. (2008, June 14). Legal drugs kill far more than illegal, Florida says. *New York Times*, p. A10.

Dewan, S. (2009, March 21). States look at tobacco to balance budget. *New York Times,* p. A8.

Duke, S. B. (2009, April 25–26). Decriminalizing the possession and use of marijuana would raise billions in taxes and eliminate much of the profits that fuel bloodshed and violence in Mexico. *Wall Street Journal,* pp. W1–W2.

Eckholm, E. (2009, May 28). Governments' drug-abuse costs hit $468 billion, study says. *New York Times,* p. A15.

Fields, G. (2009, May 14). White House czar call for end to "war on drugs." *Wall Street Journal,* p. A3.

Gamerman, E. (2009, April 10). The antidrug campaign tries a new message. *Wall Street Journal,* p. W12.

Gebel, E. (2009a, June 1). Hydroxycut hazard. *Philadelphia Inquirer,* pp. E1–E2.

Gebel, E. (2009b, January 19). A supplement of trouble. *Philadelphia Inquirer,* pp. D1–D2.

Hayashi, Y. (2009, March 4). In drug-leery Japan, arrests for marijuana are on the rise. *Wall Street Journal,* p. A12.

Helliker, K. (2009, April 13). With tobacco-patent suit, Star Scientific presses for clout. *Wall Street Journal,* p. B3.

How to stop drunk drivers. (2006, February 1). *Parade Magazine,* p. 6.

Jacobs, T. (2008). Monkey see, monkey brew. *Miller-McCune, 1*(6), 18–19.

Kristof, N. D. (2009, June 14). Drugs won the war. *New York Times,* p. 10.

Layton, L. (2009, June 13). Tobacco bill sent to Obama. *Philadelphia Inquirer,* p. A2.

McCullough, M. (2009, June 12). Senate: Let FDA regulate tobacco. *Philadelphia Inquirer,* pp. A1, A10.

Painter, K. (2009, March 16). Getting dad, mom to quit. *USA Today,* p. 5D.

Peele, S. (2009, February 5). Arrest Michael Phelps! *Wall Street Journal,* pp. A11.

Peters, G. (2009, May 19). Take the war to the drug lords. *New York Times,* p. A23.

Pitts, L. (2009, April 2). "War on drugs" seems lost. *Philadelphia Inquirer,* p. A15.

Rabin, R. C. (2009, April 9). Smoke affects high rates of New York nonsmokers, study finds. *New York Times,* p. A21.

Regalado, A. (2009, April 16). Colombia captures alleged drug lord wanted in the U.S. *Wall Street Journal,* p. A6.

Romero, S. (2009, March 18). Cocaine trade helps rebels reignite war in Peru. *New York Times,* pp. A1, A10.

Rubin, R. (2009, March 18). A warning on off-label use of sleep-disorder drug. *USA Today,* p. 6D.

Shea, K. B. (2009, May 19). A health addiction to helping others. *Philadelphia Inquirer,* p. B2.

Singer, N. (2009, February 26). A push to spell out a drug's risks and benefits. *New York Times,* p. B3.

Sobel, R. K. (2009, January 19). Our president-elect and his lethal puffing. *Philadelphia Inquirer,* pp. D1, D3.

Tamari, J. (2009, March 5). Cigarette paradox: Raise taxes cut revenue. *Philadelphia Inquirer,* pp. A1, A12.

Virtanen, M. (2009, March 28). N.Y. to soften its harsh drug laws. *Philadelphia Inquirer,* p. A3.

Walters, J. P. (2009a, March 6). Drug legalization isn't the answer. *Wall Street Journal,* p. A15.

Walters, J. P. (2009b, April 25–26). Progress in Colombia provides clear evidence that the war on drugs is winnable, while history repeatedly shows that relaxed restrictions lead to more abuse and addiction. *Wall Street Journal,* pp. W1–W2.

Washington's Marlboro men [Editorial]. (2009, June 13–14). *Wall Street Journal,,* p. A12.

Wilson, D. (2009a, June 12). Regulating tobacco industry is a recent concept. *New York Times,* p. A4.

Wilson, D. (2009b, June 12). Senate approves tight regulation over cigarettes. *New York Times,* pp. A1, A4.

Yan, J. (2009a, February 8). Heroin-assisted treatment helps some patients. *Psychiatric News,* p. 16.

Yan, J. (2009b, January 16). News is mostly good on teen drug use. *Psychiatric News,* p. 7.

About the Authors

Ann A. Abbott, PhD, LCSW, professor and chair/director, Department of Graduate Social Work, West Chester University, served as editor for this second edition, having previously served as editor of the first edition, which grew out of a faculty development grant from the U.S. Department of Health and Human Services—Public Health Service, Substance Abuse and Mental Health Services Administration (DHHS-PHS-SAMHSA). Prior to her current position, Dr. Abbott was an associate dean and faculty member at Rutgers University, School of Social Work for 20 years. In addition to substance abuse issues, her interests include social work values and ethics, professional socialization, social worker safety, supervision, and risk management. Dr. Abbott is a past national president of NASW. Currently she serves on several social work editorial boards and on the board of the Eastern Evaluation Research Society.

Laura Blankertz, PhD, has served as director of Research at Matrix Research Institute and Horizon House, a large psychiatric rehabilitation agency, and the University of Pennsylvania /Matrix Research Institute Research and Training Center on Employment for Individuals with Severe Mental Illness. She has served as principal investigator for federally funded multisite grants for dually diagnosed homeless individuals and employment for individuals with severe mental illness. Her current interests are evidence-based practices for individuals with severe mental illness and substance abuse and supported employment for individuals with substance abuse. She has published extensively in the areas of psychiatric rehabilitation, co-occurring disorders, and employment for individuals with disabilities. She is past president and current board member of the Eastern Evaluation Research Society.

Raymond Bolden, Jr., DSW, ACSW, executive director, the Salem County Inter Agency Council of Human Services (New Jersey), is responsible for the administration and operation of a multiservice organization serving three counties and providing a variety of services for community residents. In addition to his 30 years in the field, he is an adjunct assistant professor, Department of Graduate Social Work, West Chester University of Pennsylvania, teaching courses in social policy, Human Behavior in the Social Environment, and Social Work and Chemical Dependency.

Steven M. Granich, PhD, LCSW, assistant professor of social work at Lock Haven University of Pennsylvania, has extensive experience in social work and family therapy working with families and adolescent substance abusers. He is a licensed clinical social worker, licensed marriage and family therapist, and certified supervisor for addiction counselors. Dr. Granich has worked with drug courts for seven years and has been a speaker at three National Drug Court Conferences, including one presentation in Seattle, Washington on Engaging Families in Drug Court.

Langdon Holloway, PhD, LCSW (NY), LCADC (NJ), has worked extensively in addictions and co-occurring disorders. She has presented training programs for county councils on substance abuse. She was director of Partial Care and Dual Focus Programs, Clinic for Mental Health, Paterson, New Jersey. Her research is on adolescence, divorce, and alcohol use. She has served as the chairperson of the ATOD Committee, NASW-NJ. Most recently, she served as visiting instructor, Department of Graduate Social Work, West Chester University of Pennsylvania.

Lloyd L. Lyter, PhD, LSW, is professor of social work, Central PA Program and director, Institute for Social Work Research, Education, & Consultation, Marywood University. He has over 25 years of clinical and administrative experience in social work, mental health, and chemical dependence programs. He serves on the review boards of professional journals and publishes and presents regularly at state, regional, national, and international conferences in his areas of interest and expertise, chemical dependence, psychopathology, and ethics.

Sharon C. Lyter, PhD, LCSW (PA), is a social work educator with experience serving as a field director with Rutgers University, assistant professor and program director at Bloomsburg University (PA), and now associate professor at Kutztown University's (PA) combined BSW/MSW program. Her research interests include field education, impaired social workers, supervision and use of constructive criticism, social worker safety, cultural competence, and parenting issues related to addictions.

Gwenelle S. O'Neal, DSW, LSW, is associate professor of social work, Department of Graduate Social Work, West Chester University of Pennsylvania, where she teaches courses in Human Behavior in the Social Environment and Community Practice. Her areas of interest include multicultural literature, and universal design for learning techniques to enhance student engagement; techniques for services in communities; and program assessment and development. Dr. O'Neal has worked (professionally or as a volunteer) in various organizations—educational, mental health (including work with co-occurring disorders), and communities in Georgia, New York, New Jersey, and Pennsylvania.

Michael D. Paulus, PhD, MSW, is associate professor of social work, Lock Haven University. His areas of teaching include human behavior in the social environment and social work practice. He has practiced more than 18 years in chemical dependency treatment settings.

David I. Siegel, DSW, LSW, is professor of social work and chair of the Curriculum Committee, Department of Graduate Social Work, West Chester University of Pennsylvania. As principal investigator of a Temporary Assistance for Needy Families project, he has conducted research and published several articles on many aspects of employment and quality of life of past and present welfare recipients, including the issue of drugs in the neighborhood. In addition, he teaches an elective in Social Work and Chemical Dependency. His first job in social work was working with low-income individuals with substance-related problems at Bellevue Hospital in New York City.

Author Index

Liese, B. S., 158, 304, 307, 308
Linehan, M. M., 316, 317
Linhorst, D. M., 23, 83, 322
Lisman, S. A., 459
Litt, M. D., 90–91
Little, J., 341
Little, L., 355
Livermore, G., 3, 80
Lobel, M., 157
Loew, G. R., 331
Loewenberg, F. M., 63, 64
Logli, P. A., 85
Loneck, B., 454
Longabaugh, R., 290, 294, 310
Longshire, D. L., 457
Lowinson, J. H., 124, 125
Lubin, B., 279
Luborsky, L., 255
Luciano, M., 129
Luczak, S. E., 121
Lumry, A. E., 254
Lyons, P., 288
Lyter, L. L., 334, 374, 375
Lyter, S. C., 334, 375

MacAndrew, C., 254, 268
MacKenzie, D. L., 287
Mackillop, J., 459
Mackintosh, A. M., 449
MacMaster, S., 452, 460, 474, 475
Magruder-Habib, K., 250
Mahan, S., 85, 86
Mahlum, A., 220
Mailick, M., 263
Makela, K., 346, 351, 381, 382
Malouf, J. L., 70
Mancini, M. A., 23, 83, 93, 322
Manning, M., 212
Manuel, J. K., 49
Marcellus, L., 85
Marinelli, P. W., 161
Markman, H. J., 454
Markoff, L. S., 195
Marlatt, G. A., 23, 73, 93, 95, 210, 221,
     222, 223, 231, 236, 261, 311, 312, 365,
     475
Marsch, L. A., 479
Marsden, M. E., 289

Marsiglia, F. F., 468, 469
Martin, N. G., 129
Mattaini, M. A., 23
Matthew, R., 464, 465
Matthews, M., Jr., 88
Matzger, H., 288–289
Maxwell, J. C., 132
May, P. A., 12
Mayfield, D. G., 247, 252
Mays, V. M., 199, 291
Mazerolle, L., 452, 458
McAdoo, E. G., 254
McAuliffe, W. E., 335
McCaffrey, D. F., 457
McCambridge, J., 477
McCauley, A. P., 459
McCollum, E. E., 412, 425
McCrady, B. S., 46, 304, 379, 380, 410, 411
McCullough, M., 497
McDowell, D., 129, 132
McGoldrick, M., 420
McGrady, G. A., 151
McGue, M., 281
McGuigan, K., 457
McKay, M. M., 344
McKeel, A. J., 320
McKinley, J. C., 254, 268
McLellan, A. T., 255, 261, 268
McLeod, G., 247
McMain, S., 315
McMillin, C. S., 43
McPherson, D., 34
Meier, B. R., 299
Memmott, J. L., 375
Merikangas, K. R., 408
Mermelstein, R., 368
Merriam-Webster, Inc., 154
Merton, R. K., 54
Merz, J. F., 249
Meyer, C., 32
Mezzich, A., 256
Middleton, P., 7
Mikow, J., 467
Miles, D., 195
Milkman, H. B., 315
Mill, J. S., 93
Miller, B. A., 195, 251
Miller, C. A., 256

Subject Index

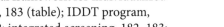